CompTIA®

CASP+®

Study Guide

Exam CAS-004

Fourth Edition

CompTIA®
CASP+®
Study Guide
Exam CAS-004
Fourth Edition

Nadean H. Tanner

Jeff T. Parker

SYBEX®
A Wiley Brand

Acknowledgments

My first three books were dedicated to Kenneth, Shelby, and Gavin: thank you for your love and support and all your electronical advice.

To Kelly Talbot, my editor, thank you for your kind patience and making things easy when you could, which wasn't often.

To Chris Crayton, my technical editor, you were right—most of the time. As a woman in IT for 20+ years, I know there are still man-made disasters.

And to Ophelia. . .because I can, so I did.

About the Authors

Nadean H. Tanner is the senior manager of consulting at Mandiant, working most recently on building real-world cyber range engagements to practice threat hunting and incident response. She has been in IT for more than 20 years and specifically in cybersecurity for more than a decade. She holds more than 30 industry certifications including CompTIA CASP+, Security+, and (ISC)^2 CISSP.

Tanner has trained and consulted for Fortune 500 companies and the U.S. Department of Defense in cybersecurity, forensics, analysis, red/blue teaming, vulnerability management, and security awareness.

She is the author of the *Cybersecurity Blue Team Toolkit*, published by Wiley in 2019, and *CASP+ Practice Tests: Exam CAS-004*, published by Sybex in 2020. She also was the technical editor for the *CompTIA Security+ Study Guide: Exam SY0-601* and *CompTIA PenTest+ Study Guide: Exam PT0-002* written by Mike Chapple and David Seidl.

In her spare time, Tanner enjoys speaking at technical conferences such as Black Hat, Wild West Hacking Fest, and OWASP events.

Jeff T. Parker is an information security professional with more than 20 years' experience in cybersecurity consulting and IT risk management. Jeff started in information security while working as a software engineer for HP in Boston, Massachusetts. Jeff then took the role of a global IT risk manager for Deutsche Post to enjoy Prague in the Czech Republic with his family for several years. There he developed and oversaw the implementation of a new IT risk management strategy. Today, Jeff most enjoys time with his two children in Nova Scotia. Currently, Jeff is developing custom e-learning courses in security awareness for Mariner Innovations.

Jeff maintains several certifications, including CISSP, CEH, and CompTIA's CySA+ and ITT+. He also coauthored the book *Wireshark for Security Professionals: Using Wireshark and the Metasploit Framework* (Wiley, 2017) with Jessey Bullock. Jeff also has written Wiley practice exam books for the CompTIA certifications CySA+ and the A+ (2018 and 2019, respectively).

About the Technical Editor

Chris Crayton is a technical consultant, trainer, author, and industry-leading technical editor. He has worked as a computer technology and networking instructor, information security director, network administrator, network engineer, and PC specialist. Chris has authored several print and online books on PC repair, CompTIA A+, CompTIA Security+, and Microsoft Windows. He has also served as technical editor and content contributor on numerous technical titles for several of the leading publishing companies. He holds numerous industry certifications, has been recognized with many professional and teaching awards, and has served as a state-level SkillsUSA final competition judge.

Contents at a Glance

Contents

Table of Exercises

Introduction

The CASP+ certification was developed by the Computer Technology Industry Association (CompTIA) to provide an industry-wide means of certifying the competency of security professionals who have a minimum of 10 years' general hands-on IT experience with at least 5 years' hands-on IT security experience. The security professional's job is to protect the confidentiality, integrity, and availability of an organization's valuable information assets. As such, these individuals need to have the ability to apply critical thinking and judgment.

According to CompTIA, the CASP+ certification is a vendor-neutral credential. CASP+ validates advanced-level security skills and knowledge internationally. There is no prerequisite, but CASP+ certification is intended to follow CompTIA Network+, Security+, CySA+, Cloud+, and PenTest+ or equivalent certifications/experience and has a technical, "hands-on" focus at the enterprise level.

Many certification books present material for you to memorize before the exam, but this book goes a step further in that it offers best practices, tips, and hands-on exercises that help those in the field of security better protect critical assets, build defense in depth, and accurately assess risk.

If you're preparing to take the CASP+ exam, it is a good idea to find out as much information as possible about computer security practices and techniques. Because this test is designed for those with years of experience, you will be better prepared by having the most hands-on experience possible; this study guide was written with this in mind. We have included hands-on exercises, real-world scenarios, and review questions at the end of each chapter to give you some idea as to what the exam is like. You should be able to answer at least 90 percent of the test questions in this book correctly before attempting the exam; if you're unable to do so, reread the problematic chapters and try the questions again. Your score should improve.

Before You Begin the CompTIA CASP+ Certification Exam

Before you begin studying for the exam, it's good for you to know that the CASP+ certification is offered by CompTIA (an industry association responsible for many certifications) and is granted to those who obtain a passing score on a single exam. Before you begin studying for the exam, learn all you can about the certification.

A list of the CASP+ CAS-004 exam objectives is presented in this introduction. See the section "The CASP+ Exam Objective Map."

Obtaining CASP+ certification demonstrates that you can help your organization design and maintain system and network security services to secure the organization's assets. By obtaining CASP+ certification, you show that you have the technical knowledge and skills required to conceptualize, design, and engineer secure solutions across complex enterprise environments.

Who Should Read This Book

The *CompTIA CASP+ Study Guide: Exam CAS-004, Fourth Edition*, is designed to give you insight into the working world of IT security, and it describes the types of tasks and activities that a security professional with 5–10 years of experience carries out. Organized classes and study groups are the ideal structures for obtaining and practicing with the recommended equipment.

 College classes, training classes, and boot camps are recommended ways to gain proficiency with the tools and techniques discussed in the book. However, nothing delivers hands-on learning like experiencing your own attempts, successes, and mistakes—on a home lab. More on home labs later.

What You Will Learn

This *CompTIA CASP+ Study Guide* covers all you need to know to pass the CASP+ exam. The exam is based on exam objectives, and this study guide is based on the current iteration of the CASP+ exam, version CAS-004.

Per the CASP+ CompTIA objectives for exam version CAS-004, the four domains include the following:

- Domain 1.0 Security Architecture
- Domain 2.0 Security Operations
- Domain 3.0 Security Engineering and Cryptography
- Domain 4.0 Governance, Risk, and Compliance

Each of these four domains further divide into objectives. For example, the fourth domain, "Governance, Risk, and Compliance," is covered across three objectives:

4.1 Given a set of requirements, apply the appropriate risk strategies.

4.2 Explain the importance of managing and mitigating vendor risk.

4.3 Explain compliance frameworks and legal considerations, and their organizational impact.

4.4 Explain the importance of business continuity and disaster recovery concepts.

These objectives read like a job task, but they are more akin to a named subset of knowledge. Many subobjectives and topics are found under each objective. These are listed hierarchically, ranging from 20 to 50 topics per objective. Yes, that's a lot of topics when you add it all up. In short, there is a lot of material to cover. Next, we address how the book tackles it all.

How This Book Is Organized

Remember how we just explained the CASP+ exam is based on domains and objectives? Your goal for exam preparation is essentially to cover all of those subobjectives and topics. That was our goal, too, in writing this study guide, so that's how we structured this book—around the same exam objectives, specifically calling out every subobjective and topic. If a topic or phrase from the exam objectives list isn't specifically called out, the concepts and understanding behind that topic or phrase are discussed thoroughly in the relevant chapters.

Nonetheless, CompTIA didn't structure the exam objectives to make for good reading or an easy flow. It would be simple to tell you that each chapter correlates exactly to two or three objectives. Instead, the book is laid out to create a balance between a relevant flow of information for learning and relatable coverage of the exam objectives. This book structure then serves to be most helpful for identifying and filling any knowledge gaps that you might have in a certain area and, in turn, best prepare you for the exam.

Extra Bits

Beyond what the exam requires, there is of course some "added value" in the form of tips, notes, stories, and URLs where you can go for additional information online. This is typical for the Sybex study guide format. The extra bits are obviously set apart from the study guide text, and they can be enjoyed as you wish. In most cases, URLs will point to a recent news event related to the topic at hand, a link to the cited regulation, or the site where a tool can be downloaded. If a particular concept interests you, you are encouraged to follow up with that article or URL. What you will learn in this study guide is exactly what you need to know to prepare for the CASP+ certification exam. What you will learn from those tips, notes, and URLs is additional context in which the topic at hand may be better understood. Next, we discuss what you should already have in order to be successful when learning from this book.

Requirements: Practice and Experience

To be most successful in reading and learning from this book, you will need to bring something to the table yourself, that is, your experience.

Experience

You're preparing to take one of CompTIA's most advanced certification exams. CompTIA's website associates the CASP+ exam with the SANS Institute GIAC Certified Enterprise Defender (GCED) exam, as only these two exams focus on "cybersecurity practitioner skills" at an advanced level. In comparison, the Certified Information Systems Security Professional (CISSP) and Certified Information Security Manager (CISM) exams focus on cybersecurity management skills.

The CASP+ exam covers a very wide range of information security topics. Understandably, the range is as wide as the range of information security job disciplines. As each of us grows from a junior level to the higher-level, technical lead roles, the time we spend working in one specialty area overshadows our exposure to other specialties. For example, three senior security practitioners working as an Active Directory engineer, a malware reverse engineer, and a network administrator might be highly skilled in their respective jobs yet have only a simple understanding of each other's roles. The exam topics include specific techniques and technologies that would be familiar to people who have held lead roles in the corresponding area of information security. Someone with experience in one or more technical areas has a great advantage, and that experience will benefit the candidate studying from this book and taking the CASP+ exam.

Last, CompTIA's recommended level of experience is a minimum of 10 years of general hands-on IT experience, including at least five years of hands-on technical security experience. If you have the five years, it is very likely that you have had at least minimal exposure to or understanding of most topics covered, enough for you to benefit from reading this book.

Practice

Given that the certification's title includes the word *practitioner*, you are expected to have, or be capable of building, a home lab for yourself. This does not mean that you need a 42U rack full of servers and network hardware in the basement (though it might bring up a lot of excitement at home). A home lab can be as simple as having one or two virtualized machines (VMs) running on your laptop or desktop with adequate CPU and RAM. This can be done using VirtualBox or VMware Workstation Player, both of which are free. There are many prebuilt VMs available online, designed specifically for security practice. A home lab can be started at little to no cost and be running within 15 minutes. No excuses.

Dedicating some routine time on a home lab will advance your skills and experience as well as demonstrate your passion for the subject. Current and future managers will love it! Seriously, though, when you make time to build, tweak, break, and rebuild systems in your home lab, not only do you readily advance your skills and learn new technologies, but you do so without the consequences of bringing down production.

The final reason for building up a home lab is that it gives you an immediate environment on which to try some of the tools and techniques mentioned in this CASP+ study guide. As with the experience mentioned earlier, your success on the exam is affected by how much you have learned from reading versus how much you understand from doing. The best of success to you on the exam and in your career.

 Like all exams, the CASP+ certification from CompTIA is updated periodically and may eventually be retired or replaced. At some point after CompTIA is no longer offering this exam, the old editions of our books and online tools will be retired. If you have purchased this book after the exam was retired, or are attempting to register in the Sybex online learning environment after the exam was retired, please know that we make no guarantees that this exam's online Sybex tools will be available once the exam is no longer available.

How to Use This Book

Here is how the book is structured, chapter by chapter:

Chapter 1, "Risk Management"   This chapter covers risk management, in particular the security risks surrounding business and industry. The chapter also discusses risk mitigation strategies and controls, including making risk determinations based on a variety of metrics, strategy recommendations based on risk appetite, and business continuity planning.

Chapter 2, "Configure and Implement Endpoint Security Controls"   This chapter starts with security controls for host devices. Topics include host hardening, external I/O restrictions, secure operating systems, and several variants of endpoint security software. To wrap up the wide umbrella of network security concepts and architectures, this chapter covers network access control, security zones, and network-enabled devices. Finally, the secure configuration and baselining of network devices are discussed.

Chapter 3, "Security Operations Scenarios"   This chapter concentrates on managing threats that require resources such as time, money, and intelligence. This chapter also includes threat management including active hunting for a breach as well as how to proactively protect an organization from compromise.

Chapter 4, "Security Ops: Vulnerability Assessments and Operational Risk"   This chapter covers security controls around software vulnerabilities, specific application issues, and operating system vulnerabilities. The chapter also covers material related to incident response and incident recovery. Finally, a large section of the chapter is dedicated to policies and procedures related to security, privacy, and contracts.

Chapter 5, "Compliance and Vendor Risk"   This chapter focuses on managing and mitigating vendor risk as well as compliance frameworks and legal considerations and their organizational impact. Emphasis is on integrating diverse industries, many different data considerations, and geographic and legal considerations. It also covers the different regulations, accreditations, and standards that affect cybersecurity.

Chapter 6, "Cryptography and PKI"   This chapter covers cryptographic techniques, implementations of both hardware and protocols, and various cryptographic applications.

Chapter 7, "Incident Response and Forensics"   This chapter covers research: best practices, research methods, threat intelligence, and the global security community. Additionally, there is related coverage of incident recovery and how severity is determined. This chapter also discusses the research requirements related to contracts. Last, post-incident response, lessons learned, and reporting are also covered.

Chapter 8, "Security Architecture"   This chapter covers material related to how business and technology meet in the enterprise environment. In particular, the chapter addresses technical integration of hosts, storage, networks, and applications in an enterprise architecture. Also, this chapter includes coverage of the interaction between business units and their security goals.

Chapter 9, "Secure Cloud and Virtualization"   This chapter concentrates on cloud and virtualization technologies. It includes cloud service models, cloud security services, the security-related pros and cons of virtualization, and data security considerations. There is also heavy coverage of several physical and virtual network devices as they relate to security.

Chapter 10, "Mobility and Emerging Technologies"   This chapter focuses on mobility and integration with enterprise security, including analysis and impact, implementing security controls, and determining the correct solution for an environment. Coverage of cost-benefit analysis and evaluation of a proposed solution as to its performance, latency, scalability, capability, usability, and maintainability while taking availability metrics into account are discussed.

Appendix: Answers to Review Questions   Here you'll find the answers to the review questions that appear at the end of each chapter.

Tips for Taking the CASP+ Exam

The CASP+ exam is a standard pass/fail exam with a maximum of 90 questions. You will have 165 minutes (2 hours, 45 minutes) to finish. There will be multiple-choice and performance-based questions (PBQs).

   If you're not familiar with PBQs but you have the recommended real-world experience, then there is little to worry about. For many candidates, PBQs are a comfortable opportunity to demonstrate experience. Unlike a multiple-choice question, the PBQ is a simulation of a scenario. The scenario is one you would likely encounter in the real world. The "catch" on PBQs versus multiple-choice questions is the time you spend on them. Unlike a multiple-choice question where you might spend a few seconds or a minute reading, the PBQ might involve more reading and then the time to apply or simulate the action asked of you. Luckily, the PBQs tend to occur early on in the test, and you will likely have only three to five PBQs for the entire exam (but no guarantees here). Just gauge your time carefully as you progress through the exam.

Here are our tips for taking the CASP+ exam:

- If you are taking the exam at a testing facility, bring two forms of ID with you. One must be a photo ID, such as a driver's license. The other can be a major credit card or a passport. Both forms must include a signature.

- Arrive early at the exam center. This gives you a chance to relax and, if it helps, to review any study materials you brought. Some people prefer to bring nothing, and some might want a final review of exam-related information.

- When you are ready to enter the testing room, everything must go into an available locker. No material is allowed in the testing area.

- Read the questions carefully. Again, *carefully*. Don't be tempted to jump to an early conclusion. Know what each question is asking.

- Don't leave any unanswered questions. If you must, select your "best guess" and mark the question for later review.

- Questions will include extra information that doesn't apply to the actual problem (just as in the real world).

- You have the option of going through the exam several times to review before you submit it, or marking questions for later review. Some people mark about 10 to 20 questions and then go back to them after they have completed all of the other questions.

- Use all of your time to review, and change your answers only if you misread the question. Don't rush through it.

- Again, breathe deeply and read *carefully*.

For the latest pricing on the exams and updates to the registration procedures, visit CompTIA's website at `www.comptia.org`.

Interactive Online Learning Environment and TestBank

Studying the material in this book is an important part of preparing for the exam, but we provide additional tools to help you prepare. The online TestBank will help you understand the types of questions that will appear on the certification exam.

The sample tests in the TestBank include all the questions in each chapter as well as the questions from the assessment test. In addition, there are two practice exams. You can use these tests to evaluate your understanding and identify areas that may require additional study.

The flashcards in the TestBank will push the limits of what you should know for the certification exam. There are 100 questions, which are provided in digital format. Each flashcard has one question and one correct answer.

The online glossary is a searchable list of key terms introduced in this exam guide that you should know for the exam.

To start using these to study for the exam, go to www.wiley.com/go/sybextestprep and register your book to receive your unique PIN; once you have the PIN, return to www.wiley.com/go/sybextestprep, find your book, and follow the register or login link to register a new account or add this book to an existing account.

CompTIA CASP+ Study Guide Exam Objectives

This table provides the extent, by percentage, that each domain is represented on the actual examination.

Domain	% of Examination
1.0 Security Architecture	29%
2.0 Security Operations	30%
3.0 Security Engineering and Cryptography	26%
4.0 Governance, Risk, and Compliance	15%
Total	100%

The CASP+ Exam Objective Map

This table is where you can find the objectives covered in this book.

Objective	Chapter
Domain 1.0 Security Architecture	
1.1 Given a scenario, analyze the security requirements and objectives to ensure an appropriate, secure network architecture or a new or existing network.	8

Objective	Chapter
3.4 Explain how cloud technologies adoption impacts organizational security.	9
3.5 Given a business requirement, implement the appropriate PKI solution.	6
3.6 Given a business requirement, implement cryptographic protocols and algorithms.	6
3.7 Given a scenario, troubleshoot issues with cryptographic implementations.	6
Domain 4.0 Governance, Risk, and Compliance	
4.1 Given a set of requirements, apply the appropriate risk strategies.	1
4.2 Explain the importance of managing and mitigating vendor risk.	5
4.3 Explain compliance frameworks and legal considerations and their organizational impact.	5
4.4 Explain the importance of business continuity and disaster recovery concepts.	1

Reader Support for This Book

John Wiley & Sons provides the following for its readers.

Companion Download Files

As you work through the examples in this book, the project files you need are all available for download from www.wiley.com/go/sybextestprep.

How to Contact the Publisher

If you believe you've found a mistake in this book, please bring it to our attention. At John Wiley & Sons, we understand how important it is to provide our customers with accurate content, but even with our best efforts an error may occur.

In order to submit your possible errata, please email it to our Customer Service Team at wileysupport@wiley.com with the subject line "Possible Book Errata Submission."

Assessment Test

1. Alice is an administrator who works in the finance department. She has clicked a link in an email that has executed unwanted actions in a web application she is using. What type of attack is this?

    A. XXS

    B. CSRF

    C. SQLi

    D. Buffer overflow

2. You are exploring the best option for your organization to move from a physical data center to virtual machines hosted on bare-metal servers. Which of the following is the BEST option for that move?

    A. Type 1 hypervisor

    B. Type 2 hypervisor

    C. iPaaS

    D. IaaS

3. You are looking for a replacement for POP3. Which of the following protocols offers advantages over POP3 for mobile users?

    A. HTTPS

    B. NTP

    C. IMAP

    D. SMTP

4. DNSSEC provides authority and data integrity. DNSSEC will not protect against which of the following?

    A. Spoofing

    B. Kiting/tasting

    C. Verification

    D. Masquerade

5. You have built an access control list for a router that is subject to PCI DSS. The ACL you have built contains four commands that deny HTTP, POP3, FTP, and Telnet. No traffic is coming through the router. What is the most likely reason?

    A. Traffic is dropped because of the "deny TCP any HTTP" statement.

    B. Traffic is dropped because of the "deny TCP any FTP" statement.

    C. Traffic is accepted but not forwarded to the proper location.

    D. There are no permit statements in the ACL.

6. You are evaluating the security policy of a large enterprise. There are many elements and points of enforcement, including email and remote access systems. XML is the natural choice as the basis for the common security policy language. What language standard should be implemented with XML for a fine-grained, attribute-based access control?

   A. OASIS

   B. SAMLv2

   C. SOAP

   D. XACML

7. Using Microsoft Network Monitor, you have captured traffic on TCP port 23. Your security policy states that port 23 is not to be used. What client-server protocol is probably running over this port?

   A. SNMP

   B. Telnet

   C. PuTTY

   D. FTP

8. TCP is connection oriented, while UDP is connectionless. Which of these is NOT a valid header in a UDP packet?

   A. Source port

   B. Destination port

   C. Length

   D. Sequence number

9. You are having difficulties reaching tech support for a specific web application that has crashed. You have to find the agreement between your company and the provider. What is the document that requires a provider to maintain a certain level of support?

   A. NDA

   B. SLA

   C. MOU

   D. MTTR

10. Which of the following would be considered a detective and administrative control?

   A. Fences and gates

   B. IDS and honeypots

   C. IPS and antivirus

   D. Audit logs

11. You have interviewed several candidates for a position that is open in your security department. Human resources will need to conduct a background check before offering a position to your final candidate. Why is a background check necessary?

    A. Helps provide the right person for the right job

    B. Is a single point of failure

    C. Reinforces a separation of duties

    D. Improves performance

12. You have finished conducting an audit to verify the protection mechanisms you have placed on information systems. What is this type of audit called?

    A. Information security audit

    B. Operational audit

    C. Forensic audit

    D. Procedure audit

13. You have been instructed to remove all data from a hard drive with the caveat that you want to reuse the drive. Which of the following would be the BEST option?

    A. Put the hard drive in the microwave for two minutes

    B. Empty the recycle bin

    C. Degauss the drive

    D. Perform a seven-pass bit-level drive wipe

14. You want to form a legal partnership with another organization. Which of these is the BEST description of a partnership?

    A. A business that legally has no separate existence from the owner

    B. A business where the owners are not personally liable for the company's debts

    C. A form of business operation that declares the business is a separate legal entity from the board of directors

    D. A legal form of business between two or more individuals who share management and profits

15. The manufacturer of a motherboard advertises the presence of a TPM chip. What is TPM used for?

    A. Speed

    B. Encryption

    C. Hyperthreading

    D. Authentication

16. Your company is conducting new web business with companies with home offices in the EU. Under the rules of GDPR, visitors to the website may exercise their EU data rights that include which of the following?

   A. Not be informed of a breach

   B. To have their presence on a site erased

   C. To not be taxed on purchases

   D. Receive a healthy discount

17. As you are building a business continuity plan, you are investigating cybersecurity threats for your manufacturing organization. Cyberthreats to your business would not include _____.

   A. Ransomware

   B. DDoS

   C. Intellectual property theft

   D. Resource management

18. You have both mycompany.com and www.mycompany.com pointing to the same application hosted by the same server. What type of DNS record is this found in?

   A. Authentication

   B. SOA

   C. CNAME

   D. AWS

19. You are conducting a risk analysis for your company, specifically looking at quantitative data. Which of these would NOT be considered quantitative?

   A. Volume

   B. Temperature

   C. Pressure

   D. Reputation

20. You have investigated a breach into your network. You found lower-level credentials used to access files and functions reserved for higher-privilege credentials. What is this called?

   A. Phishing

   B. Dumpster diving

   C. Privilege escalation

   D. Pass-the-hash

21. Who in your organization is responsible for setting goals and directing risk analysis?

   A. Board of directors

   B. CIO

   C. Senior management

   D. Human resources

22. Your training manager is copying MP4 security awareness videos to mobile devices from their laptop. What is this called?

A. Uploading

B. Downloading

C. Blueloading

D. Sideloading

23. You work for a publicly traded company. While evaluating your organization's information classification, some information can be given the lowest-level classification. The lowest level of public-sector information classification is which of the following?

A. Secret

B. FOUO

C. Public

D. Unclassified

24. You have calculated the single loss expectancy of a mission-critical asset by multiplying the asset value by the exposure factor. What else could your team review if you were interested in qualitative costs?

A. Cost of repair

B. Value of lost data

C. Lost productivity

D. Public relations

25. The users on your network should have only the access needed to do their jobs. What is this security control called?

A. Single point of failure

B. Least privilege

C. Separate of duties

D. Mandatory vacations

26. You need an IDS but have no security budget. What IDS tool listed is open source?

A. Nexpose

B. Nessus

C. Snort

D. PuTTY

27. Windows supports remote access protocols through the GUI. Remote access allows you to connect to a remote host in a different location over a network or over the Internet. What tool is native in Windows that provides this access?

A. TeamViewer

B. Remote Desktop Connection

C. Terminal Desktop Server

D. Wireshark

28. You have an end user who has called the help desk because they visited a website that instructed them to reset their DNS. What is the command you use at the Windows command line to accomplish this?

A. netstat

B. tracert

C. ipconfig /renew

D. ipconfig /flushdns

29. To prepare for appropriate preventative measures, you have downloaded a tool that will allow you to check weak credentials on your network. Which of the tools listed will perform a simple dictionary attack on NTLM passwords?

A. L0phtCrack

B. Wireshark

C. Maltego

D. Social-Engineer Toolkit

30. You are a privileged user launching Nmap. You use the default nmap scan: #nmap target. What is the default option?

A. -sS

B. -A

C. -O

D. -SYN

Answers to Assessment Test

1. B. A cross-site request forgery (CSRF) is an attack that forces an end user to execute actions in a web application that they are currently authenticating. As an administrator, CSRF can compromise an entire web application.

2. A. A Type 1 hypervisor is a hypervisor installed on a bare-metal server, meaning that the hypervisor is its own operating system. Type 1 hypervisors usually perform better due to the direct access to physical hardware.

3. C. Internet Message Access Protocol (IMAP) can be used as a replacement for POP3. It can be beneficial for mobile users because of folder management, remote mail, and the ability to sign in from multiple mobile devices. SMTP is used to send mail; IMAP and POP3 are used to receive mail.

4. B. DNSSEC does not protect against DNS kiting or tasting. DNS kiting, or tasting, is a practice where someone registers, cancels, and registers the domain again, all within a grace period. Income can be earned from the site because the site is functional, but you don't have to pay to register the site.

5. D. There must be a permit statement on an access control list (ACL). Otherwise, all deny statements will add to the implicit deny all, and nothing is permitted.

6. D. Extensible Access Control Markup Language (XACML) has architecture and a processing model that helps evaluate access requests according to rules placed in policies.

7. B. Telnet is a protocol used to establish a connection to TCP port 23. It is blocked because there is no built-in security and should be avoided because of eavesdropping. Usernames and passwords are sent in the clear.

8. D. User Datagram Protocol (UDP) is connectionless, so there will not be a sequence number.

9. B. A service level agreement (SLA) will be the agreement between parties that lists the level of support that your company will receive from the provider.

10. D. Audit logs would be a detective control function and an administrative control type.

11. A. A background should be conducted on any candidate that you are bringing into your organization. Credentials need to be validated, and positions and experience verified. This way you have the right person in the right position.

12. A. An information security audit is performed to ensure that the protections you have placed on information systems are working as expected.

13. D. If you want to use the drive again after removing all data, then perform a seven-pass drive wipe at the bit level. Degaussing will ruin the drive and make it inoperable. Emptying the recycle bin or microwaving the drive will not actually remove any data.

14. D. A partnership is a type of business where two or more individuals share potential profits as well as risk.

15. B. A Trusted Platform Module (TPM) chip is technology designed to provide hardware-based encryption.

16. B. The General Data Protection Regulation (GDPR) is a legal framework that sets guidelines for the collection and processing of personal information (PI) for all people who live in the European Union (EU).

17. D. Resource management is not a threat to a manufacturing organization.

18. C. Canonical name (CNAME) records are used to alias one name to another.

19. D. Quantitative data can be expressed as numbers. If you can measure it, it is a quantity.

20. C. Security mechanisms should prevent unauthorized access and usage of data and functions. These preventive measures are circumvented by attackers finding new vulnerabilities and security gaps.

21. C. Senior management is responsible for setting goals, initiating analysis, and making sure the proper people and resources are assigned and available during risk analysis.

22. D. Sideloading is a term that refers to transferring a file between two local devices without using the Internet. A file can be transferred using Wi-Fi, Bluetooth, or USB. Sideloading can also describe installing applications on Android devices that do not reside in the Google Play store.

23. C. Public classification means that it can be released and freely distributed. FOUO means For Official Use Only. Secret and Unclassified are governmental information classifications.

24. D. Public relations would be a qualitative control because it does not seek a numerical or mathematical statistic. Qualitative is subjective and deals with words and meaning.

25. B. The principle of least privilege is the practice of limiting the access rights of users to the minimum to get their job done. This reduces the risk of attackers gaining access to systems and compromising critical systems.

26. C. Snort is an open-source, free, and lightweight network intrusion detection system (IDS) for both Windows and Linux that detects any new threats to a network.

27. B. Remote Desktop Connection (RDC) will allow a user to authenticate and have access to all programs, files, and network resources on a system.

28. D. The command-line interface (CLI) command to flush and reset the cached contents of DNS is `ipconfig /flushdns`.

29. A. These are four great hacking tools that are free and available on the Internet. Remember to use your powers for good.

30. A. The default option for privileged users is `-sS`. This is a TCP SYN scan. Nmap will send a SYN packet, as if you were going to open a real connection, and you wait for a response. If you get a SYN/ACK back, the port is open. An RST means the port is closed.

Chapter

1

Risk Management

THE FOLLOWING COMPTIA CASP+ EXAM OBJECTIVES ARE COVERED IN THIS CHAPTER:

✓ **4.1 Given a set of requirements, apply the appropriate risk strategies**

- **Risk assessment**
  - Likelihood
  - Impact
  - Qualitative vs. quantitative
  - Exposure factor
  - Asset value
  - Total cost of ownership (TCO)
  - Return on investment (ROI)
  - Mean time to recovery (MTTR)
  - Mean time between failure (MTBF)
  - Annualized loss expectancy (ALE)
  - Annualized rate of occurrence (ARO)
  - Single loss expectancy (SLE)
  - Gap analysis
- **Risk handling techniques**
  - Transfer
  - Accept
  - Avoid
  - Mitigate
- **Risk types**
  - Inherent
  - Residual
  - Exceptions

- Training and awareness for users
- Auditing requirements and frequency

✓ **4.4 Explain the Importance of Business Continuity and Disaster Recovery Concepts**

- **Business impact analysis**
    - Recovery point objective
    - Recovery time objective
    - Recovery service level
    - Mission essential functions
- **Privacy impact assessment**
- **Disaster recovery plan (DRP)/business continuity plan (BCP)**
    - Cold site
    - Warm site
    - Hot site
    - Mobile site
- **Incident response plan**
    - Roles/responsibilities
    - After-action reports
- **Testing plans**
    - Checklist
    - Walk-through
    - Tabletop exercises
    - Full interruption test
    - Parallel test/simulation test

This chapter discusses risk. As a CASP+, you should be able to interpret business and industry influences and explain associated security risks. From a computing standpoint, risk is all around you. Everywhere you turn, there are risks; they begin the minute you first turn on a computer and grow exponentially the moment the network card becomes active.

Even in the nontechnical sense, there is risk: Who do you let in the facility? Are visitors escorted? Do you allow employees to connect personal devices such as tablet computers, smartphones, and so forth to company networks? There is even risk when deciding what approach to use for email. You may use an in-house email server or outsource email and use a cloud-based solution, such as Gmail or Outlook.com. Here again, you will find that there is the potential for risk in each choice. These are just the tip of the iceberg. This chapter discusses what CompTIA expects you to know for the exam related to risk.

Risk Terminology

Before discussing risk management, it is important to make sure that some basic terms are defined. All industries share basic vocabulary and semantics. IT security is no different, and within the topic of risk, there are some terms that you will see again and again. Let's begin by reviewing these terms:

Asset An *asset* is an item of value to an institution, such as data, hardware, software, or physical property. An asset is an item or collection of items that has a quantitative (numeric) or qualitative (subjective) value to a company.

Risk *Risk* is the probability or likelihood of the occurrence or realization of a threat.

Vulnerability A *vulnerability* can be described as a weakness in hardware, software, or components that may be exploited in order for a threat to destroy, damage, or compromise an asset.

Threat A *threat* is any agent, condition, or circumstance that could potentially cause harm, loss, damage, or compromise to an IT asset or data asset. The likelihood of the threat is the probability of occurrence or the odds that the event will actually occur.

Motivation   *Motivation* is the driving force behind the activity. As an example, hackers can be motivated by many different reasons. Some common reasons include prestige, money, fame, and challenge.

Risk Source   The *source* of a risk can be either internal or external. Internal risk can be anything from a disgruntled employee to a failed hard drive. External risk includes natural disasters such as floods and person-made events such as strikes and protests. As an example, the risk source might be that the lock on a server cabinet is broken, whereas the threat is that someone can now steal the server hard drive.

From the standpoint of IT security, the following are some common examples of threats:

Natural Disaster   *Natural disasters* are events over which we have no control, such as bad weather (hurricanes, snowstorms, tornadoes), fires, floods, earthquakes, and tsunamis, but could also include global events like pandemics.

Malicious Code   *Malicious code* includes all forms of damaging programs, such as viruses, worms, Trojans, keyloggers, and so forth. This software is distinguishable in that it is developed to damage, alter, expose, or destroy a system or data. For example, viruses are executable programs that can replicate and attach to and infect other executable objects. Some viruses also perform destructive or discreet activities (payload) after replication and infection are accomplished.

Breach of Physical Security   A *breach of physical security* can be instigated by a trusted insider or an untrusted outsider. Intruders, vandals, and thieves remove sensitive information, destroy data, or physically damage or remove hardware such as hard drives and mobile devices.

Hacker Attack   *Hacker attacks* generally result in stolen, lost, damaged, or modified data. Loss or damage to an organization's data can be a critical threat if there are no backups or external archiving of the data as part of the organization's data recovery and business continuity plan. Also, if the compromised data is of a confidential nature, this can also be a critical threat to the organization, depending on the potential damage that can arise from this compromise.

Distributed Denial of Service   A *distributed denial-of-service (DDoS)* attack on a network or web-based system is designed to bring down the network or prevent access to a particular device by flooding it with useless traffic. DDoS attacks can be launched in several ways. What was done manually with simple tools before is now automated and coordinated, on a massive scale with multiple systems.

The attack might leverage networked devices, such as the famous Mirai malware-driven botnet that used multiple systems simultaneously. Or, an attacker may also use more advanced DDoS tools such as Tribal Flood Network, Shaft, or Low Orbit Ion Cannon.

Currently, most DDoS attacks are launched via botnets. Regardless of the technique, the result is that the targeted system has a reduced or limited ability to communicate.

Cyberterrorism   *Cyberterrorism* is when attackers use computers, Internet communications, and other cyber tools to penetrate and disrupt critical national infrastructures such as water, electric, and gas plants; oil and gasoline refineries; nuclear power plants; waste management plants; and so on.

This list is by no means all-inclusive.

The Risk Assessment Process

All companies have only a limited amount of funds, and those funds must be spent wisely. This means spending money in areas that need the most protection. The purpose of the *risk assessment* is to identify weaknesses and gaps in the deployment of controls and to identify more accurately what areas require the highest level of protection. It evaluates risks in terms of the likelihood and the magnitude of an impact, to determine a response strategy, and to monitor progress in reducing the threat. The risk assessment will also identify a baseline for the organization's current level of information security. This baseline will form the foundation for how the organization needs to increase or enhance its current level of security based on the criticality or exposure to risk that is identified during the risk assessment.

There are several important aspects of the risk assessment process:

- Asset identification
- Information classification
- The actual risk assessment
- Risk analysis options for risk appetite and deterrence
- Implementing controls

The following sections discuss each step of the process and provide an overview of the risk assessment process.

Asset Identification

Information and systems must have value to determine their worth. Asset identification is the process of identifying all of the organization's assets. A good inventory management system can help greatly in identifying assets. Just keep in mind that assets can be both tangible and intangible. The following assets commonly are examined:

- Tangible
  - Documentation
  - Data

- Hardware
- Software
- Intangible
  - Reputation (goodwill)
  - Services

 **Real World Scenario**

Does Reputation Have a Value?

Although we typically think of assets as something tangible, an asset can also be intangible. Reputation is one good example. As businesses have grown larger and the Internet has increased the ability for news stories to move quickly around the world, companies must work harder at protecting their reputations. The experiences of global organizations such as BP and Johnson & Johnson demonstrate how protecting corporate reputations means moving beyond compliance to manage the corporate image. Should customers decide that a company has poor practices or has failed to provide effective security controls, billions of dollars could be lost.

Once all assets are identified, the individuals assessing them must ask more than just what the asset originally cost. They must also start to consider the return on investment (ROI) of any potential control that may be used. Other key considerations are as follows:

- What did the asset cost to acquire or create?
- What is the liability if the asset is compromised?
- What is the production cost if the asset is made unavailable?
- What is the value of the asset to competitors and foreign governments?
- How critical is the asset, and how would its loss affect the company?

 Placing a value on an asset is never easy. Asset valuation is a difficult task, and it requires a lot of expertise and work to do it properly. In real life, the process is typically carried out by a team of professionals who have a background in such tasks and have access to specialized software and tools.

Asset identification and valuation can be made easier if an information classification program has been put in place. Information can be classified into levels of *confidentiality*, *integrity*, and *availability* based on the specific organization or industry. This is known as the *CIA security triad*. We will examine this topic next.

Information Classification

Information classification strengthens the organization in many ways. Labeling information secret or strictly confidential helps employees see the value of the information and give it a higher standard of care. Information classification also specifies how employees are to handle specific information. For example, company policy might state, "All sensitive documents must be removed from the employee's desk when leaving work. We support a clean desk policy."

Two widely used information classification systems have been adopted. Each is focused on a different portion of the CIA security triad. These two approaches are as follows:

Government Classification System   This system focuses on confidentiality.

Commercial Classification System   This system focuses on integrity.

The governmental information classification system is divided into the categories Unclassified, Confidential, Secret, and Top Secret, as you can see in Table 1.1.

TABLE 1.1   Governmental information classification

Classification	Description
Top Secret	Its disclosure would cause grave damage to national security. This information requires the highest level of control.
Secret	Its disclosure would be expected to cause serious damage to national security and may divulge significant scientific, technological, operational, and logistical as well as many other developments.
Confidential	Its disclosure could cause damage to national security and should be safeguarded against.
Unclassified	Information is not sensitive and need not be protected unless For Official Use Only (FOUO) is appended to the classification. Unclassified information would not normally cause damage, but over time Unclassified FOUO information could be compiled to deduce information of a higher classification.

The commercial information classification system is focused not just on confidentiality but also on the integrity of information; therefore, it is categorized as public, sensitive, private, and confidential, as shown in Table 1.2.

TABLE 1.2   Commercial information classification

Classification	Description
Confidential	This is the most sensitive rating. This is the information that keeps a company competitive. Not only is this information for internal use only, but its release or alteration could seriously affect or damage a corporation.
Private	This category of restricted information is considered personal in nature and might include medical records or human resource information.
Sensitive	This information requires controls to prevent its release to unauthorized parties. Damage could result from its loss of confidentiality or its loss of integrity.
Public	This is similar to unclassified information in that its disclosure or release would cause no damage to the corporation.

Depending on the industry in which the business operates and its specific needs, one of these options will typically fit better than the others. Regardless of the classification system chosen, security professionals play a key role in categorizing information and helping to determine classification guidelines. Once an organization starts the classification process, it's forced to ask what would happen if specific information was released and how its release would damage or affect the organization.

Risk Assessment

With an organization's assets inventoried, valued, and classified, the next step can begin. This step, the actual risk assessment itself, is where potential risks and threats are identified. These activities are typically carried out by a risk assessment team, and the likelihood of the threat is determined. The team is tasked by top management with identifying threats and examining the impact of the identified threats.

This process can be based on real dollar amounts or on nondollar values. When nondollar values are used, the team typically determines the minimum required security controls based on an aggregate score. One common approach is to determine the aggregate by combining the identified vulnerabilities as they apply to confidentiality, integrity, and availability of the asset. Before we look at qualitative and quantitative risk assessment, let's briefly review some facts about the team that will be carrying out this project.

The Risk Management Team

The *risk management team* is responsible for identifying and analyzing risks. Its members should consist of managers and employees from across the company. After the purpose and membership of the team are established, the team can begin developing and implementing a risk management program.

This team should be led by someone high enough up in the corporate structure to communicate easily with senior management and obtain the funding that will be needed for the risk assessment process to be a success. A successful outcome can be measured in many different ways. A success may mean that the team is able to decrease insurance costs, reduce attacks against the company's website, or verify compliance with privacy laws.

With a team in place and funding secured, the team will next turn its attention to gathering data and identifying threats. The first people to ask about threats should always be the asset owners; they know what the business is facing and where the threats may come from. IT will help map those business threats into IT-related concerns. The following additional sources may be used:

- Actuarial tables and insurance records
- Audit reports
- Business owners and senior managers
- Facility records
- Legal counsel
- Human resources
- Government records
- Network administrators
- Operations
- Security administrators

 A threat is any circumstance or event that has the potential to impact an asset negatively by means of unauthorized access, destruction, disclosure, or modification.

Quantitative and Qualitative Risk Assessment

Now that the team has been established and has started to assemble data, a decision has to be made as to what type of risk analysis will be performed. The two techniques for doing this are as follows:

Quantitative Risk Assessment   This method assigns a cost (monetary value) to the elements of risk assessment and the assets and threats of a risk analysis.

Qualitative Risk Assessment   This method ranks threats by nonmonetary value and is based on scenario, intuition, and experience.

Quantitative Risk Assessment

Thus far, we have discussed building a risk management team that has the support of senior management, identifying tangible and nontangible assets, and starting to identify potential threats. The impact of these threats must be measured in some way. One approach is to assess the threat in dollar terms. The team is simply asking the question, "What would this cost?"

A threat may not result in a loss. For a loss to occur, the threat must be coupled with a vulnerability. The vulnerability could be the penetrability of a hollow-core server room door. Or, maybe it's the lack of a hardened backup facility elsewhere. It might even be the lack of video surveillance in the reception area. The resulting loss could be any of the following:

- Financial loss
- Danger or injury to staff, clients, or customers
- Breach of confidence or violation of law
- Exposure of confidential information
- Theft of equipment, hardware, or software

To start the calculation of loss, you would need to quantify all elements of the process, including the value of the asset, the impact, and the threat frequency. Here are the steps for doing this:

1. Determine the asset value (AV) for each information asset.
2. Identify threats to the asset.
3. Determine the exposure factor (EF) for each information asset in relation to each threat.
4. Calculate the single loss expectancy (SLE).
5. Calculate the annualized rate of occurrence (ARO).
6. Calculate the annualized loss expectancy (ALE).

 Calculation of loss is a time-consuming process because it must be done for all assets.

The two most widely used *quantitative risk assessment* formulas are as follows:

$$SLE = AV \times EF$$

and

$$ALE = ARO \times SLE$$

The strength of a quantitative risk assessment is that it assigns dollar values. Dollar values are easy to understand. If someone says that a potential threat coupled with a vulnerability could result in a $1 million loss, this value is easy for management to work with and conceptualize. The primary disadvantage of quantitative risk assessment is that because it is dollar-based, the team must attempt to compute a dollar value for all elements. This is time-consuming, and some qualitative measures must be applied to quantitative elements. Because this is such a huge task, quantitative assessments are usually performed with the help of automated software tools. These tools can help with trend analysis and to look for patterns over time. Trend analysis examines historical loss data to determine patterns in loss frequency or loss severity. As an example, hurricanes along the Atlantic coast are becoming more destructive. In fact, three of the top five most costly Atlantic hurricanes in U.S. history occurred in 2017.

`en.wikipedia.org/wiki/List_of_costliest_Atlantic_hurricanes`

Let's look at a simple example of quantitative risk assessment in action. In Exercise 1.1, you will calculate the ALE for a file server.

EXERCISE 1.1

Calculating Annualized Loss Expectancy

As a security practitioner for a medium-sized firm, you have been asked to determine the ALE for a file server. Your organization has installed a file server with data valued at $25,000. The organization uses the file server to allow remote offices to upload their daily records to be processed the following morning. Currently, this server is not fully patched and does not have an antivirus program installed. Your research indicates that there is a 95 percent chance that the new file server will become infected within one year. If such an infection were to occur, you estimate that 75 percent of the data value could be lost. Without antivirus, there's a good chance that recovering the missing files and restoring the server could require up to four hours and divert the support team from other duties. An approved vendor has offered to sell a site license for the needed software for $175.

1. **Examine the exposure factor.** This has been calculated at 75 percent. Remember that the exposure factor identifies the percentage of the asset value that will be affected by the successful execution of the threat.

2. **Determine the SLE.** The formula is as follows:

   $$SLE = AV \times EF$$

   Since we know the asset value is $25,000 and the exposure factor is 75 percent, the resulting SLE will be $18,750.

3. **Evaluate the ARO.** The ARO is a value that represents the estimated frequency with which a given threat is expected to occur. This is defined as the number of times that this event is expected to happen in one year. Your research indicates that there is a 95 percent chance that an infection will occur in one year.

4. **Calculate the ALE.** The ALE is an annual expected financial loss to an organization's IT asset because of a particular threat occurring within one year.

   $$ALE = ARO \times SLE$$

   or

   $$\$18,750 \times 0.95 = \$17,812.50$$

With an annualized loss expectancy so high, it makes sense for the company to purchase antivirus software. Without antivirus software to mitigate the risk, the ALE is a significant portion of the cost of the file server.

In the real world, risk calculations rely heavily on probability and expectancy. Software products, actuary tables, industry information, and the history of prior events can help, but some events are hard to calculate. Storms or other natural phenomena are not easy to assign to patterns. Such events can be considered stochastic. A *stochastic event* is based on random behavior because the occurrence of individual events cannot be predicted, yet measuring the distribution of all observations usually follows a predictable pattern.

Quantitative risk management faces challenges when estimating risk, so you must rely on some elements of the qualitative approach.

Qualitative Risk Assessment

The second method by which the risk assessment can be completed is by qualitative means. *Qualitative risk assessment* is scenario-based and does not attempt to assign dollar values to the components of the risk analysis. Part of this process requires the team to perform extreme scenario planning and look at worst-case scenarios. As an example, what if a hurricane hit your surfboard manufacturing facility on Galveston Island? How bad could it be? It's like playing a game of "what if?"

A qualitative assessment ranks the potential of a threat and sensitivity of assets by grade or scale such as low, medium, or high. You can see an example of this in National Institute of Standards and Technology (NIST) SP 800-53 (nvd.nist.gov/800-53). This document assigns the potential impact on confidentiality, integrity, and availability (CIA) using the values low, moderate, and high. You will want the support of a team of individuals to help you assess potential risks, and you should incorporate stakeholder input into impact-level decisions on the controls needed to protect the CIA of identified assets. Since a rating of low, medium, or high is subjective, each category must be defined. Examples are as follows:

Low   Minor inconvenience; can be tolerated for a short period of time but will not result in financial loss

Medium   Can result in damage to an organization, cost a moderate amount of money to repair, and result in negative publicity

High   Will result in a loss of goodwill between the company and client or employee; may result in a large legal action or fine or cause the company to lose significant revenue or earnings

Although a qualitative assessment generally requires much less time than a quantitative one, a qualitative assessment does not provide cost values. Table 1.3 shows an example of a scored result of a qualitative review. One common approach is specified in Federal Information Processing Standard (FIPS) publication 199 (csrc.nist.gov/publications/detail/fips/199/final). It defines the process of determining the aggregate score by first measuring impact on CIA and ranking risk as high, medium, or low. Because cost values are absent, this method lacks the rigor that accounting teams and management typically prefer.

TABLE 1.3   Sample qualitative aggregate score findings

Asset	Loss of confidentiality	Loss of integrity	Loss of availability
PII	High	High	Medium
Web server	Medium	Medium	Low
PR material	Low	Low	Low
HR employee records	High	High	Medium

Some examples of qualitative assessment techniques are as follows:

ISAM   The *INFOSEC Assessment Methodology (ISAM)* provides nongovernment organizations with the ability to complete a qualitative assessment that ranks assets as critical, high, medium, or low and to determine the impact based on CIA.

Delphi Technique   The *Delphi Technique* is a group assessment process that allows individuals to contribute anonymous opinions and is often used to forecast the likelihood and outcomes of different types of events.

Facilitated Risk Assessment Process   The *Facilitated Risk Assessment Process (FRAP)* is a subjective process that obtains results by asking a series of questions. It is designed to be completed in a matter of hours, making it a quick process to perform.

Two other assessment techniques used to study failures include failure modes and effects analysis (FMEA) and failure mode, effects, and criticality analysis (FMECA). FMEA is used for the analysis of potential failures within a system. FMECA is similar, but it includes a criticality analysis.

Risk Assessment Options

With the quantitative or qualitative risk assessment complete, the next step is to make a risk determination and decide which security controls should be applied.

The first step is to examine the amount of loss and the total impact that was calculated earlier. Risk ranking is one approach. An aggregate score can be used to examine the impact of the loss of confidentiality, integrity, or availability. A risk-ranking matrix looks at the severity and frequency of each consequence. For example, severity might be ranked on a scale of 1 to 4, and frequency is ranked by the occurrence assigned to each impact, where 4 is the highest and 1 is the lowest. Figure 1.1 shows an example of a risk-ranking matrix and one method for determining a risk score.

FIGURE 1.1   Risk-ranking matrix

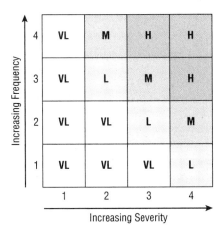

The outcome of this process is the ranking of priorities and data that can be used to determine how to deal with the risk. How you deal with risk will depend on the organization's *risk appetite*; that is, the total amount of risk the company is willing to accept. When speaking to individual risks, risk tolerance describes the amount of risk the organization is willing to accept. There are four possible alternatives for handling the potential risks:

Avoid   To *avoid* the risk means to eliminate the risk, to withdraw from the practice, or to not become involved. This may be a viable option; there may also be an opportunity cost associated with avoiding the activity.

Accept   To *accept* the risk means that it is understood and has been evaluated. Senior management has made the decision that the benefits of moving forward outweigh the risk. If those in charge have not been provided with good data on risk or have made invalid assumptions, poor choices may be made. This can give rise to disasters with global impact (BP, Fukushima, Chernobyl, Challenger, and so on).

Transfer   To *transfer* the risk is to deflect it to a third party. For example, insurance is obtained. Instead of managing the risk directly, the organization incurs an ongoing continual cost from that third party.

Mitigate   To *mitigate* the risk means that a control is used to reduce the risk. For example, installing a firewall is one method by which risk can be mitigated.

Just keep in mind that you can never eliminate all risk. There will always be some remaining residual risk. *Residual risk* is the risk that remains after your organization has taken proper precautions and implemented appropriate controls. There is also *inherent risk*, defined as the risk of carrying out a specific activity. As an example, an inherent risk of riding a motorcycle is that you might get hit by a car.

A particular risk may be intentionally left unmitigated or controlled in a manner that would normally be unacceptable. That risk would be an exemption to the typical risk management process. Risk exception recognizes the areas where you are not compliant in regard to laws, policies, or regulations. Resources are at risk for exposure to malicious activity and/or for penalties issued due to noncompliance. Exemptions are handled on a case-by-case basis, and as the name implies, they are strictly against the norm. An organization is expected to have prepared for such an occurrence through an exemption policy. The policy would dictate what management levels are required to approve the exemption, how it's documented, and how it will be monitored.

Finally, *risk deterrence* is having some process, policy, or system in place that discourages others from exploiting a vulnerability that, if exploited, would realize the risk. For example, what if, despite all of the mitigating controls in place, a server of top-secret military plans is accessible from the Internet? A risk deterrent is the law in place that, when enforced, would put an attacker in prison for exploiting the server.

Regardless of what you decide, you should incorporate stakeholder input into your decisions on how to deal with the identified risk. With so many risks to consider, the best place to start is with those that have a high-risk score. These items have the potential to cause great harm to the organization and should be addressed first. There are sometimes *risk exceptions*, such as when loss of life is a factor.

 One easy way to remember these for the CASP+ exam is to think of AATM (avoid, accept, transfer, mitigate). Though not a cash machine, it may help you pass the exam.

Implementing Controls

Once a decision has been made on how to handle identified risk, it is time to execute risk mitigation planning, strategies, and controls. The document used to drive the process forward is the *risk assessment report*. This report contains all of the findings, information, assessments, and recommendations for the organization. The final assessment report becomes the instrument for management to make sound business decisions pertaining to what controls should be implemented.

This will require that you have designed some type of information classification system. These systems are usually based on either confidentiality or integrity. Regardless of the classification systems you use, you must classify and categorize data types into levels of CIA based on the organization/industry. As an example, the DoD might be more interested in the confidentiality of information, whereas a cloud service provider might be more interested in availability. The risk team will want to determine the minimum required security controls based on aggregate score. Without an asset valuation, it is difficult to understand a control's return on investment (ROI) or cost-benefit analysis, pertaining to the investment in security countermeasures. Controls can be physical, technical, or operational.

Physical Controls   Examples include locks, fences, CCTV, lights, gates, and guards.

Technical Controls   You will want to implement technical controls based on CIA requirements and the policies of the organization. Examples of such controls include encryption, VPNs, security protocols (IPsec, SSL, TLS, and so on), VLANs, firewalls, and IDSs.

Operational Controls   Examples include hiring practices, security awareness training, employment practices, termination practices, business continuity, and disaster testing and training.

Controls can also serve many purposes, such as prevention, deterrence, correction, mitigation, and so on. Once the proper control has been designed, it must be put in place. As an example, a fence is a physical control that can be used to deter or even delay an attacker. The purpose of implementing controls is to address the identified risks, threats, and vulnerabilities. To implement controls, a budget must be established. Although much of the risk assessment process has been performed by the team, now it's time for management to prioritize, create a budget, and have a tactical and strategic plan for implementing the recommendations presented in the final report. To determine what controls to put in place, you must consider the *total cost of ownership (TCO)*. The TCO can help determine the total cost of an asset or countermeasure. It includes purchase price, maintenance fees, updates, insurance, and the like. All costs are included. The risk assessment team must try to find a solution that provides the greatest risk reduction while maintaining the lowest annual cost.

These recommendations may have an impact on the entire organization and may take months, if not years, to implement fully. For the business to benefit from the technical recommendations and controls in place, it is necessary to translate technical risks into business terms. The recommendations must be structured and prioritized in the context that suits the business. This prioritization of tactical and strategic recommendations will enable the organization to make sound business decisions with the defined goals and objectives of the risk and vulnerability assessment.

Once controls are implemented, there is still more work to be done, as employees must be trained. IT security must work with management to implement ongoing security awareness and security training. Implementing organizational change requires an education and security awareness training plan for all employees or authorized users of the organization's IT systems, resources, and data. Mitigating risk requires all employees and users within the organization to abide by the security awareness training.

Policies Used to Manage Employees

A CASP+ must support the development of policies used to manage employees. Most employees want to do the right thing, are honest, and seek to excel in their jobs, but there must still be a structure of control. This control begins before an employee is onboarded (hired) and continues until their employment is offboarded (terminated).

Employee controls help protect the organization and build good security. Understand how each of the controls in the following sections is used and its primary attributes.

Pre-Employment Policies

Before an employee is hired, controls should be applied regarding how the potential employee is interviewed, what information is collected about the individual, and what is checked.

Many organizations start the pre-employment process with a background check. A *background check* is used to verify that the employee has a clean background and that any negative history is uncovered before employment. Although a background check is a good start, let's not forget education. *Education verification* is the act of verifying someone's educational background. With the rise of degree mills, it is easier than ever for individuals to fake their educational backgrounds, and the only way a company can know for sure is if the potential employee's credentials are verified.

Once employees are hired, an array of other policies will help manage their access to sensitive information and their levels of control. This is our next topic.

Employment Policies

For most new employees, a new job starts with initial training. This initial training provides employees with information on how to handle certain situations and what types of activities are and are not allowed. Employees don't know proper policies and procedures if they are not informed and trained. It is at this point that many employees will be asked to sign an acceptable use policy (AUP). The AUP defines what employees, contractors, and third parties are authorized to do on the organization's IT infrastructure and its assets. AUPs are common for access to IT resources, systems, applications, Internet, email, company phone systems (landlines), and company-issued or company-paid smartphones and other handheld devices. Employees are also given employee handbooks. Employees should sign an acknowledging receipt of all this information stating that they agree to follow the rules and regulations specified.

A nondisclosure agreement (NDA) is another important and legally enforceable document. An NDA is a contract that establishes confidentiality between two parties—the owner of the information and the recipient of that information.

 AUPs typically outline what is and what is not acceptable behavior and the consequences of prohibited activities.

The handbook should detail the employee code of conduct, acceptable use of company assets, and employee responsibilities to the company. It should address the following issues:

- Security practices, policies, and procedures
- Paid holiday and vacation policy

- Work schedule and overtime policy
- Moonlighting and outside employment
- Employee evaluations
- Disaster response and emergency procedures
- Disciplinary procedures for noncompliance

Companies use a variety of controls to limit what an employee does and what level of access the employee holds. Although these practices may not be applicable for every business, they are common techniques used to limit the damage that could be caused by an unethical employee. In many ways, it's about least privilege. The *principle of least privilege* means that just because an employee is cleared to access a particular file, document, or physical location, this doesn't mean that they should be able to do so. Employees are given just enough access to allow them to conduct their normal duties, and nothing more. Common employee controls include the following:

Mandatory Vacations   Uncovers misuse and gives the organization a time to audit the employee while they are not at work. The mandatory vacation is most commonly found in financial firms or applied to job roles where money is handled.

Job Rotation   Rotates employees to new areas of assignment. This not only helps ensure backup if an employee is not available, but job rotation also can reduce fraud or misuse by providing the company with a means of rotating people to prevent an individual from having too much control over an area.

Dual Control   Requires employees to work together to complete critical actions, thereby forcing employees who are planning anything illegal to collude with others. A common example is that of a combination or code for a safe. Two employees are required to open it successfully. Closely related to dual control is the *m* of *n* concept. This simply means that an activity, such as cryptographic recovery, is divided up among several individuals so that no one person acting alone can perform the entire key recovery process.

Separation of Duties   Limits what one employee can do. For example, one employee may be able to write a check, but another must approve it.

Least Privilege   Restricts the employee's access to only what is needed to do the job and nothing more. Closely related to the concept of least privilege is need to know.

 NOTE   IT security must support the development of HR policies that address such issues as separation of duties, job rotation, mandatory vacation, and least privilege.

Even if someone has met all of the requirements to be employed by a company and has been initially trained, this does not mean they are trained forever. Anytime a new process or technology is introduced in an organization, employees should be trained in its proper operation. Security training also needs to be repeated on an annual basis. The short-term benefit of training and awareness for users is that it helps clarify acceptable behavior. As for the long term, training helps reinforce the danger from hackers and cybercrime. Raising the awareness of employees makes a potential attacker's job harder. Awareness training can consist of lunch schedules, learning programs, multiday events, or even degree programs. Common training methods include the following:

- Apprenticeship programs
- Classroom training
- Continuing education programs
- Degree programs
- In-house training
- On-the-job training
- Vendor training

 A successful employee awareness program will tailor the message to fit the audience. Nontechnical employees will need a different message than technical employees.

End of Employment and Termination Procedures

According to the Bureau of Labor Statistics, the average person will have seven different jobs in their lifetime. For a company, this means that employees will come and go. They may leave for another job, move to another area, or even retire.

This means that our final topic in this area is termination. Human resources must have approved, effective procedures in place for the termination of employees, and HR must interface with IT security to make sure that access is terminated at the time of the employee's departure. IT security must partner with HR, legal, management, and other entities to make these systems work and to maintain compliance.

These security procedures should include processes for voluntary and involuntary separation. HR should work with security to ensure that the employee has returned all equipment that has been in their possession, such as access tokens, keys, ID cards, company credit cards, and mobile devices. If termination is involuntary, there needs to be a defined process on how to address or handle the situation properly. Issues such as employee escort, exit interviews, review of nondisclosure agreements (NDAs), and suspension of network access must all be covered in the applicable policy.

NOTE   Terminating an employee's access at the proper time is critical. Department heads must report termination to HR in a timely manner, and this information must be acted on. In 2009, Fannie Mae fired a contract programmer at noon, yet did not terminate their access until midnight. In those 12 hours, it is believed the former contractor loaded a logic bomb into the company's network designed to knock out 4,000 servers. You can read more at www.wired.com/threatlevel/2009/01/fannie.

What procedure does your company follow when employees are terminated? Exercise 1.2 reviews a company's need to have a defined procedure to handle departure.

EXERCISE 1.2

Reviewing the Employee Termination Process

The CASP+ knows well the risks inherent in granting an unauthorized person access to sensitive areas or systems. When that person is someone who just recently lost access, there might be an added risk of malicious attack or theft of data.

1. How is the IT security department made aware of the termination? Is it a manual or automated process?

2. Is employee access terminated at the time of departure?

3. Is an exit interview performed?

4. Are exiting employees asked to return keys, laptops, smartphones, and other physical property?

5. Is the former employee reminded of any NDAs or other documents such as noncompete agreements they may have signed?

6. What are the obligations of the receiving party? What level of protection must they apply to the information they have received?

7. What time period applies to the NDA? Most NDAs don't last forever and have a time period applied, such as 1 year, 5 years, or 10 years.

8. Based on the previous questions, would you recommend changes to your company's termination procedures? Are there ways to work with HR to improve the process?

Cost-Benefit Analysis

Cost-benefit analysis is a technique used to determine whether a planned action is or is not acceptable. One common way to determine the cost-benefit analysis is to calculate the *return on investment (ROI)*. ROI is determined by dividing net profit by total assets.

For ROI to be accurately calculated, it's critical to maintain proper *asset management*. Asset management is defined in the context of maintaining control over your inventory, which must be identified, managed, and continually monitored to derive a reliable return on investment.

For projects that require some future evaluation, a payback analysis may be conducted. The payback analysis determines how much time will lapse before accrued benefits will overtake accrued and continuing costs.

Cost-benefit analysis consists of three steps: calculate costs, calculate benefits, and compare the results. A cost-benefit analysis will typically ask the following kinds of questions:

- Is the solution to the problem viable?

- Do the benefits of the plan of action outweigh the costs?

- Is the application or program beneficial to the organization?

Where the cost-benefit analysis requires quantification and proof of cost-effectiveness, analysis includes intangible benefits that can be hard to quantify. One area that is often overlooked when evaluating these items is the total cost of ownership (TCO). TCO is the purchase price of an asset plus the cost of operation. As an example, you may buy a NextGen firewall for $10,000. But that's not TCO. You must also consider the costs of environmental modifications, compatibility with other countermeasures, maintenance costs, testing costs, support contracts, and so on. If you combine all those items, you arrive at the TCO.

Continuous Monitoring

You can think of monitoring as a type of change management. Anytime a change is made to systems or the operating environment, a reassessment should be performed to see how the change affects a potential risk.

Continuous monitoring allows organizations to evaluate the operating effectiveness of controls on or near a real-time basis. Because continuous monitoring occurs immediately or closely after events in which the key controls are used, it enables the enterprise to detect control failures quickly and find ways to make improvements quickly. NIST SP 800-37 (`csrc .nist.gov/publications/detail/sp/800-37/rev-2/final`) describes continuous monitoring as an effective, organization-wide program that should include the following:

- Configuration management

- Control processes

- Security impact analyses

- Assessment of selected security

- Security status reporting

- Active involvement of asset owners

SP 800-37 also states that the continuous monitoring should address these functions:

- Reporting progress
- Addressing vulnerabilities
- Describing how the information system owner intends to address those vulnerabilities

During the lifetime of an asset, changes will occur. People come and go, equipment changes are made, configurations change, and processes are revised. These changes will affect the organization's security posture. The result has to be assessed to determine whether these changes have altered the desired security state in a negative way.

As new assets are identified or change value and as risks are reassessed and monitored, the *risk management life cycle* is revealed. Risks are continuously reviewed, reassessed, and responded to throughout the life cycle. How exactly each life-cycle step is labeled or structured depends on the risk management framework adopted by the organization.

Throughout the risk management life cycle, the organization is entering and updating data into its *risk register*. The risk register is involved at nearly every step of the risk management process. The risk register should contain each risk as it is identified, assessed, owned by someone, responded to, and ultimately reassessed and monitored.

Enterprise Security Architecture Frameworks and Governance

Enterprise Security Architecture (ESA) frameworks describe the processes used to plan, allocate, and control information security resources. ESA frameworks are used for IT governance and include people, processes, and technologies. Here are two examples of ESA frameworks:

Enterprise Architecture (EA)   Used by the federal government to ensure that business strategy and IT investments are aligned

Sherwood Applied Business Security Architecture (SABSA)   Another perspective on strategy based on an architectural viewpoint

Regardless of the architecture used, the goal is to measure performance and ensure that companies are receiving the best return on their security investment. ESA frameworks typically include strategy, action plans, and provisions for monitoring as well as defined metrics such as these:

- Strategic alignment
- Effective risk management
- Value delivery

- Resource management
- Performance measurement
- Process assurance integration

The chosen ESA framework must balance technical and procedural solutions to support the long-term needs of the business and deliver substantial long-term efficiency and effectiveness. Some of the most popular risk management frameworks (RMFs) include the FISMA risk management framework, COSO Enterprise Risk Management Framework, and ISO 31000 for Risk Management.

Training and Awareness for Users

The role of training cannot be emphasized enough. Most employees want to do the right thing and genuinely want to see the organization thrive. However, it is the responsibility of the company to provide training. It is also important to remember that employees don't know proper policies and procedures unless they are informed as to what they are.

Just consider something as basic as emergency response. Without proper training, some employees may be tempted to simply stop what they are doing and run for the door; this may even be OK, but what's the approved response? Does each employee know what to do? Do employees know how to respond in the face of a cyberattack, disaster, weather emergency, or any other situation? Training helps assure that employees know how to respond to potential security risks and incidents.

Consider adopting the "prudent person rule" to ensure that training incorporates the procedures followed by other firms in the same industry, such as those used by banks, hospitals, credit card handlers, or others.

Training does offer a good return as it increases effectiveness and efficiency. When new security processes or technologies are introduced, employees should be trained in them. Training increases morale and helps employees strive to do a better job.

Building a Security Awareness Program

As a security administrator, you know all about the importance of good security practices. Now imagine that you have been asked to develop a security awareness program. With this in mind, where would you start, and what would you do to help ensure that the program is a success?

The first thing that you should do is to make a list of items that can help raise awareness of good security practices. The following list includes some of the questions you should consider asking:

1. Does the program have the support of senior management?

2. Do you have existing policies and procedures that dictate good security practices?

3. Can you get all employees involved and make sure that they hear the message at least once a year?

4. Can you get help from security representatives in each area of the company to assist in the awareness program and address security incidents?

5. Can you implement annual self-assessment surveys?

An awareness program cannot be conducted in a vacuum. It takes time to change people's practices and attitudes. Consider the current security culture before expecting radical change overnight.

 Timing is of critical importance when dealing with training. Security training needs to be performed when employees are hired, including AUP training and policy sign-off, and then followed up with annual reinforcement. As a CASP+, you will need to engage the HR department. In some organizations, the training task is assigned solely to HR, which has no idea how to conduct security training and may not even recognize the importance of it.

Best Practices for Risk Assessments

If you are tasked with taking part in a risk assessment, a key concern will be to define its goals and objectives. One good place to start is the mission statement. The *mission statement* typically defines a company's primary goal.

There are many techniques to consider when conducting a risk and vulnerability assessment. These best practices or approaches vary depending on the scope of the assessment and what the team is trying to protect. To secure and protect assets properly, significant amounts of time, money, and resources are required. Only then can the proper level of security be designed and implemented properly. When preparing and conducting a risk assessment, consider the following best practices or approaches:

- Create a risk assessment policy.
- Inventory and maintain a database of IT infrastructure components and IT assets.

- Define risk assessment goals and objectives in line with the organizational business drivers.

- Identify a consistent risk assessment methodology and approach for your organization.

- Conduct an asset valuation or asset criticality valuation as per a standard definition for the organization.

- Limit the scope of the risk assessment by identifying and categorizing IT infrastructure components and assets as critical, major, and minor.

- Understand and evaluate the risks, threats, and vulnerabilities to those categorized IT infrastructure components and assets.

- Define a consistent standard or yardstick of measurement for securing the organization's critical, major, and minor IT infrastructure.

- Create a business continuity plan to help ensure that critical processes and activities can continue in case of a disaster or emergency.

- Perform the risk and vulnerability assessment as per the defined standard.

Implementing these risk assessment best practices is not easy. It requires careful analysis and decision-making unique to the organization's business drivers and priorities as an organization. Table 1.4 shows an example summary of annualized loss expectancies. The proposed "cost," or single loss expectancy, is fairly low when considering that most services can be replaced nearly free of charge by cloud providers.

TABLE 1.4   Annualized loss expectancy (ALE) of DMZ assets

Asset	Threat	SLE	ARO	ALE	Countermeasure
Web server	DoS	$300	1	$300	Redundant web servers
Email server	Open relay	$0	.01	$0	Closing relay
DNS server	Cache poisoning	$100	.25	$25	DNSSEC
Firewall	Enumeration	$500	.2	$100	Hardening
Database	SQL injection	$10,000	2	$20,000	Web application firewall and input validation

You can see that the result of the risk assessment process is to determine which items to address first. You must keep in mind that all companies have limited assets and that not every single vulnerability can be addressed. The best way to start is to determine which items would cause the most damage or which represent the greatest threat to the organization. In most situations, this will mean that the ALE will be examined. As an example, in Table 1.4, it's noted that a SQL injection attack has an ALE of $20,000. It would be of utmost importance to start by examining this threat and assessing what would be the cost of implementing a countermeasure.

Finally, you will want to keep in mind that the risk assessment process is not a one-time event. As items change, or on a periodic basis, the risk assessment process must be repeated.

Business Continuity Planning and Disaster Recovery

In general terms, *business continuity planning (BCP)* is the formation of a plan for what to do should the business suffer an interruption. This plan is often based on the results of a *business impact analysis (BIA)*. A BIA is a formal process designed to identify mission-essential functions in an organization and facilitate the identification of the critical systems that support those functions that must be continued during an emergency.

A disaster is any event that has the potential to disrupt an organization's business. The occurrence of a disaster triggers the activation of the organization's *disaster recovery plan (DRP)*.

Organizations must conduct site risk assessments for each of their facilities and create a DRP that, combined with a BIA, identifies and prioritizes the risks posed to the facility by an internal or external disaster. These assessments are considered to be a subset of business continuity planning. Business continuity planning includes the strategy to resume a business whether it has been interrupted by a minor event or a major disaster.

Two key concepts in business continuity planning are the *recovery point objective (RPO)* and the *recovery time objective (RTO)*. To understand these terms, first imagine that a business has experienced a significant interruption to its operations. Let's say that the business's operations normally involve processing payment transactions. Established business continuity planning states that a set duration of time is allowed to pass before the amount of transaction data lost during an interruption exceeds the tolerable amount. For example, imagine an inline rolling storage of two hours of transaction data. In the event of an outage, any portion up to two hours could then be processed after full operations are restored. That set duration of time is the RPO.

The RTO is more concrete. Now recall that it takes 30 minutes to recover from the disruption. It takes 30 minutes to get all servers booted up and tap into the server that's holding the two hours' worth of backlogged data. The RTO is the amount of actual time (duration) since the beginning of the interruption that is deemed tolerable before the interruption is considered intolerable to the business

Another element of the rebuilding process that helps control costs is the *recovery service level (RSL)*. The RSL is a percentage measurement (0–100 percent) of how much computing power is needed. This is based on a percentage of the production system that you will need during an emergency.

As stated earlier, an interruption could be anything ranging from a minor power hiccup to a total building collapse. In terms of a short power hiccup, let's use the example of a storage array failure. To recover from that failure, the storage engineer requires 12 hours on average to replace the hardware involved and rebuild the data from backups. The *mean time to recovery (MTTR)* is then 12 hours. The MTTR describes the length of time between an interruption and the recovery from that interruption.

Now let's say that the power hiccups cause subsequent disk failures, which occur on average every month. Another important business continuity concept is the *mean time between failure (MTBF)*. In this case, MTBF is around 30 or 31 days.

Let's say our data center suffered a great outage and we need to implement our disaster recovery plan. Our DR planning includes readying an offsite location to become our new data center. What kind of offsite infrastructure is prepared depends on two big factors:

- How quickly should our new infrastructure help us recover?
- Does the need for our offsite infrastructure justify its expense?

The answers to those two questions will decide which of the following sites we prepare:

Cold Site   We have a place filled with our to-be infrastructure. Equipment is effectively only available to set up. At least partial setup and configuration are assumed not yet done. This *cold site* is the cheapest and will require the most time to have running. Likely initial steps involve opening boxes.

Warm Site   We have a place with equipment set up and configured, ready to turn on. In fact, our *warm site* is probably running but still requires considerable effort to resume operations. Likely initial steps involve restoring backups.

Hot Site   We have a place with equipment set up and running as a copy of our recently lost data center. Effort to resume operations should be minimal for a *hot site*. Likely initial steps involve assuring minimal data loss since the disaster event.

Mobile Site   A *mobile site* is what it sounds like: a site that can be moved or mobilized to a new location. Picture a truck trailer filled with equipment to mirror your data center.

Reviewing the Effectiveness of Existing Security Controls

It would be nice to think that all of our defensive security controls will work as designed. This is usually not the case. Consider for a moment the Maginot Line. This physical defensive structure was designed by the French before World War II as a line of concrete fortifications, tank obstacles, artillery casements, and machine gun posts to hold back the

Germans in case of an attack. However, the Maginot Line did not work as planned. At the start of the war, the Germans simply drove around it and attacked from behind the line.

This same concept can be applied to network security controls. Although we may believe that they have a high level of effectiveness, this may or may not be true. Security controls must be tested and evaluated to ensure their effectiveness. Firewalls and edge security devices do work well at stopping external attacks, but what happens when an attacker is internal and behind these edge controls? Some of the methods used to review the effectiveness of existing security controls are as follows:

Gap Analysis   A *gap analysis* involves an examination of an area or environment designed to report the difference between "where we are" and "where we want to be." The analysis of that gap provides an objective viewpoint that helps form the steps necessary to close that gap.

Audits   An *information security audit* is typically a review of a company's technical, physical, and administrative controls. There are many kinds of audits with multiple objectives; the most common types with which the CASP+ will likely be involved deal with security controls. Auditors usually follow one or more of these audit standards:

- Control Objectives for Information and Related Technology (COBIT) guidelines that are developed and maintained by ISACA (formerly known as the Information Systems Audit and Control Association)
- FISMA, which specifies the minimum-security compliance standards for government systems, including the military
- Financial Accounting Standards Board (FASB)
- Generally Accepted Accounting Principles (GAAP)
- American Institute of Certified Public Accountants (AICPA)
- Statements on Accounting Standards (SAS)
- Public Company Accounting Oversight Board (PCAOB), issuer of audit standards

Vulnerability Assessments   *Vulnerability assessment* tools and scanners provide information on vulnerabilities within a targeted application or system or an entire network. Vulnerabilities are often graded on a scale of high, medium, or low. Vulnerability assessment tools usually provide advice on how to fix or manage the security risks that they have discovered. Externally administered vulnerability assessment services are available and are usually implemented by means of a stand-alone hardware device or by means of an installed software agent.

Although these tools work well, they are not perfect in that they offer only a snapshot in time of what problems have been identified. There is also the issue that vulnerability assessment scanners typically don't fix problems. They identify problems and then only some of the problems. Finally, any given tool can produce false positives or false negatives or may not even identify specific problems. Examples of well-known vulnerability assessment tools include Nikto, Nessus, Wireshark, Metasploit, Nmap, Retina, LanGuard, OpenVAS, and SAINT.

Ethical Hacking   *Ethical hacking* is the process of looking at a network in the same way as an attacker would. The ethical hacker is attempting to determine what the attacker can access and obtain, what an attacker can do with that information, and whether anyone would notice what the attacker is doing. Ethical hacking requires the testing team to work with management to assess the value of its assets, what is most critical, and how much protection is in place to protect these assets.

 Ethical hackers are also known for penetration testing, or they may even be described as being part of a team such as red or tiger.

Conducting Lessons Learned and After-Action Reviews

After a contract has been signed or a service level agreement (SLA) has been established, an organization should conduct one or more lessons learned or after-action reviews to determine the effectiveness of the agreement process and to identify any necessary improvements to existing policies, processes, and other organizational practices. An SLA is a written contract that specifies the levels of service that will be provided by the vendor and what the customer can do if the vendor fails to meet the SLA terms. SLAs commonly cover the issues of response time.

The purpose of a lessons learned, or after-action review, is to provide insights and recommendations for when these processes are repeated. These activities can occur throughout many different types of projects, including the software development life cycle (SDLC) and incident response. The lessons learned process should be conducted after a sufficient time has elapsed after the signing of a contract. Here are some of the items that should be reviewed during the lessons learned process:

- Policies and procedures
- Technology, configuration, or system enhancements
- Personnel resources, including response team resources
- Communication procedures
- Training
- The security measures put in place
- Whether enough information was available to complete the agreement properly

- How well the partner provided its required service
- Whether the procedures outlined in the response plan were adequate and worked as intended
- Whether significant problems were encountered during the RFP process

Any relevant lessons learned should be included in the revised agreement process for reference, and the updated documents should be communicated to all of the relevant personnel.

Creation, Collection, and Analysis of Metrics

Businesses rely on monitoring and reporting to gauge how business is going and to decide what to change, fix, or improve. Before you can monitor something, you first need to know what to monitor. Most of the time, this is obvious. If you're driving your car, you're monitoring your speed and fuel usage. But what about sales, operations, or financials? Someone first has to create what to monitor, and then they can move on to collect and analyze the data.

Metrics

When monitoring something like your car's speed or your network switch's utilization, you need a snapshot value to measure. That measured value is the metric. Your car is going 65 miles per hour, and your switch is humming along at 35 percent utilization. Both numbers are *metrics*.

Metric creation and collection are not difficult. The difficulty lies in understanding the value behind the metric. Back to the car analogy, what if a driver wanted to know the number of tire revolutions instead of the car's speed? You could argue that both would tell the driver how "fast" they're driving, relatively speaking, that is, until you understand that differences in tire size make measuring tire revolutions an unreliable metric. The same thoughtfulness has to be applied for creating and collecting IT and security metrics.

Once valid metrics are created and understood, you can also create *key performance indicators (KPIs)* and *key risk indicators (KRIs)*. KPIs and KRIs are a special kind of measurement that also includes a goal. If a metric answers the question "What are we doing?" then a KPI answers the question "How are we doing?" and a KRI then addresses the question "How careful must we be?"

Key performance indicators can help an organization better measure important metrics such as scalability, availability, and reliability. For example, KPIs related to uptime provide insight into *availability*. Similarly, KPIs related to how often a failure occurs and its impact will help provide insight on *reliability*. Lastly, when it comes to *scalability*, an important KPI may indicate the growth of infrastructure. Knowing the growth in demand for services can then help the growth KPI illustrate scalability.

Trend Data

Analyzing collected metrics doesn't have to originate from within the organization. A CASP+ must analyze and interpret trend data to anticipate cyber defense aids. Luckily, many good sources of information are available to help in this process. One example is the FBI's Internet Crime Complaint Center (IC3) (`www.ic3.gov`). Each year, reports provide an overall review of cybercrime for the preceding year.

Analyzing Security Solutions to Ensure They Meet Business Needs

The CASP+ may be responsible for analyzing security solutions to ensure that they meet business needs. The CASP+ should examine the areas of performance, maintainability, and availability and their related areas, as described here:

Performance   Performance is the accomplishment of a given task measured against preset known standards of accuracy, completeness, cost, and speed.

Uptime Agreements   *Uptime agreements (UAs)* are one of the most well-known types of SLAs. UAs detail the agreed-on amount of uptime. For example, they can be used for network services such as a WAN link or equipment like servers.

Time Service Factor   The *time service factor (TSF)* is the percentage of help-desk or response calls answered within a given time.

Abandon Rate   The *abandon rate (AR)* is the number of callers who hang up while waiting for a service representative to answer.

First Call Resolution   The *first call resolution (FCR)* is the number of resolutions that are made on the first call and do not require the user to call back to the help desk to follow up or seek additional measures for resolution.

Latency   *Latency* can be described as delay. Latency can be examined to determine how long it takes an application to respond or even the amount of delay in a WAN network. Different applications can support varying amounts of latency. Some programs, such as FTP, can easily handle latency, while others, such as VoIP, do not handle latency well. The CASP+ must research specific applications to determine the acceptable amount of latency.

Scalability   *Scalability* is the ability of a program, application, or network to continue to function as scale, volume, or throughput is changed. The CASP+ should examine current security needs and assess future growth to ensure that any selected solutions can meet long-term needs.

Capability   *Capability* is the ability to meet or achieve a specific goal.

Usability   The International Organization for Standardization (ISO) defines *usability* as "the extent to which a product can be used by specified users to achieve specified goals."

Security Requirements   Organizations may require security in place, but the controls put in place to maintain that security must be usable. In other words, implementing security requirements that render a business process moot is unusable. The difference between *usability* and *security requirements* is that security requirements meet the criteria of usability to viable and effective. To meet both needs, a *trade-off analysis* may be required to find out whether both requirements are satisfied. Trade-off analysis can identify problems that demand finding a balance between different factors, such as the time and cost.

Recoverability   *Recoverability* is yet another important characteristic in that it defines the capability to restore systems to the exact point in time at which the failure occurred.

Maintainability   Yet another important characteristic of any proposed security solution is its *maintainability*. As an example of maintainability, the U.S. space shuttle was originally designed for a projected life span of 100 launches, or 10 years of operational life. The shuttle was retired in 2011 after about 30 years of service. Our point is that although your chosen solutions may not last two or three times the original design life, it is important that they be maintainable through the expected time of use.

Availability   *Availability* refers to the functional state of a system and, in the networking world, is often simplified to uptime. Some terms that you should understand are mean time between failure (MTBF) and mean time to recovery (MTTR). MTBF is the total operating time divided by the number of failures; MTTR refers to the amount of time it takes to restore a system if and when a failure occurs.

Testing Plans

What's that phrase? An ounce of prevention is worth a pound of cure? In other words, a little prevention goes a long way. *Testing plans* are the first step in prevention. A testing plan provides a planned approach to practice procedures such as those drafted for disaster recovery. The following are a variety of testing plans:

Walk-Through   The team will "walk through" and analyze the steps of disaster recovery. No actual recovery infrastructure setup is done as in a parallel test. The *walk-through test* is a straightforward exercise where you manually perform the steps without causing any real disruption.

Checklist   Perhaps the easiest form of testing is simply reading through the *checklist* of procedures and steps toward disaster recovery. Any glaring gaps or concerns are analyzed further.

Tabletop Exercise The goal of a *tabletop exercise* is to raise situational awareness in the context of information security. It is also designed to foster discussion of incident response in brief, practical discussion periods. For management, tabletop exercises provide a great opportunity to demonstrate scenarios that are most likely to occur for the incident response group.

Parallel Tests and Simulation Tests To simulate a disaster recovery by running through all the steps alongside the disaster recovery systems and processes, you should conduct a *parallel test*. The *simulation test* is going through all motions, but production systems are still running.

Full Interruption Test As you might suspect, a *full interruption test* is the true test of confidence in disaster recovery planning. Production systems are temporarily taken offline once disaster recovery systems are set up and ready to assume the place of the shutdown systems.

Internal and External Audits

An *internal audit* is one conducted to improve an entity's operations. Medium-sized and large-sized operations usually have an internal auditing department to monitor the operations of the organization regarding the improvement of effectiveness, control, governance processes, and risk management. The department accomplishes this by providing recommendations and suggestions on the basis of the assessment of data and business transactions. The main purpose of an internal audit is to provide an independent opinion and consultancy to senior management and those charged with governance (governing bodies). Internal audits are mostly performed by an employee of the organization; however, some organizations hire the services of an audit firm for an internal audit.

An *external audit* indicates an audit of the organization by an independent audit firm, which is not controlled by the organization that it is auditing. An external audit is performed because of statutory requirements in order to express an opinion on whether the security controls, processes, and documentation are in accordance with acceptable standards and regulatory requirements in all material aspects. For an external audit, the auditor is required not to have any prior association with the organization; that is, an external auditor must be independent in their work.

Auditing requirements and frequency can be determined by a few factors, such as corporate policy. But perhaps the most common factor is regulatory compliance. A regulation might require an organization to audit annually or semi-annually.

Using Judgment to Solve Difficult Problems

Sometimes, you have to use judgment to solve difficult problems that do not have a best solution. This is where your years of experience come in handy! Ever wonder why some car mechanics are so good at diagnosing and repairing problems? That's because they have mastered the process of using judgment and experience to work through problems. There is no one right way to work through problems, since each person must find a method that works best for them. We will show you one approach here. Try it and see if it works for you.

Define the Problem   You've been told there is a problem. Obtain a specific description of the problem. What are the symptoms?

Gather the Facts   Ask yourself (or another CASP+) these questions when something fails or is not working properly:

- Did it ever work?

- What changed?

- Was a new piece of hardware or software added, such as a firewall or intrusion detection system?

- When did this first happen?

- Does anyone else have the same problem?

Brainstorm   You are at the point where it's easy to change the first thing to come to mind. However, the best course of action is to think about all the possibilities for why something doesn't work or why something is behaving in a certain way.

Implement   This is where you make a step-by-step list of the possibilities for testing. Test each possibility to see if it corrects the problem. Be careful to change one thing at a time to avoid creating any new problems. If the step-by-step procedure fails to fix the problem, then return to the beginning of the process and start over.

Evaluate   Think back to what you have done, and then document causes and solutions to the problem. Share your newfound knowledge with friends and co-workers.

Summary

A CASP+ must understand threats to the business, potential risks, and ways to mitigate risks. Risk is something that you must deal with every day on a personal and business level. Policy is one way to deal with risk. On the people side of the business, policy should dictate what employees can and cannot do. Even when risk is identified and has been associated with a vulnerability, a potential cost must still be determined. This cost can be derived via quantitative or qualitative methods. Each offers advantages and disadvantages and helps provide the tools to determine whether a threat should be accepted, avoided, mitigated, or transferred. You will want to know basic risk formulas and how to perform calculations for items such as SLE and ALE should you be asked to do so for the exam. Finally, a CASP+ must also understand the importance of proper planning and testing of business continuity planning and disaster recovery. Without BCP and DR, a business simply waits for the next disaster.

Exam Essentials

Be able to describe specific risk assessment techniques.   Two basic techniques can be used to perform risk analysis: qualitative and quantitative. Qualitative risk assessment is more subjective, not monetary-based, and uses descriptors such as critical, high, medium, and low. Quantitative risk assessment assigns and uses monetary values against known risks.

Know how to make a risk determination assessment.   Risk and vulnerability assessments provide the necessary information about an organization's IT infrastructure and its assets' current level of security so that the assessor can provide recommendations for increasing or enhancing that level of security. Understand that conducting a risk assessment is difficult and prone to error. Once the risk is identified and assessed, realize that analyzing the results is often problematic in itself.

Know how and when to apply security controls.   Controls may or may not be applied. All companies have only limited funds to implement controls, and the cost of the control should not exceed the value of the asset. Performing a quantitative or qualitative risk assessment can help make the case for whether a control should be applied.

Know the various ways to address risk.   Threats coupled with vulnerabilities can lead to a loss. To prevent or deal with the potential risk, several approaches can be used, which include accept, avoid, mitigate, and transfer.

Know the importance of business continuity and disaster recovery concepts.   Businesses cannot survive a disaster without proper planning. Business continuity and disaster recovery plans must be in place, reviewed and practiced periodically, and updated on a schedule. Be sure you understand business impact analysis (BIA), privacy impact assessments, disaster recovery planning (DRP), business continuity planning (BCP), incident response, and testing plans.

Be able to apply the appropriate risk strategies and types of risk assessments.   Risk assessments are a formalized approach to risk prioritization that lets an organization conduct reviews in a structured manner. Risk assessments follow two different analysis methodologies: quantitative risk assessments that use numeric data in the analysis, resulting in assessments that allow the very straightforward prioritization of risks, and qualitative risk assessments that use subjective data for the assessment of risks that are difficult to quantify.

Understand risk mitigation, strategy, and best practices.   Risk mitigation is the process of applying controls to reduce the probability or impact of a risk. Risk management is the most common risk management strategy, and the vast majority of the work of security professionals revolves around mitigating risks through the design, implementation, and management of security controls. Many of these controls involve engineering trade-offs between functionality, performance, and security.

Review Questions

You can find the answers in Appendix.

1. Which of the following is not an advantage of quantitative risk assessments?
   - **A.** Examination of real threats
   - **B.** Fast results
   - **C.** Subjective opinions
   - **D.** Dollar values

2. Which of the following is the formula for SLE?
   - **A.** SLE = AV × EF
   - **B.** SLE = AV / EF
   - **C.** SLE = ARO × EF
   - **D.** SLE = ARO × AV

3. Which of the following is not an advantage of qualitative risk assessments?
   - **A.** Speed
   - **B.** Use of numeric dollar values
   - **C.** Based on CIA
   - **D.** Performed by a team

4. Which of the following is the formula for ALE?
   - **A.** ALE = AV × ARO
   - **B.** ALE = ARO × SLE
   - **C.** ALE = SLE / ARO
   - **D.** ALE = AV / ARO

5. Which of the following is the approach for dealing with risk that incurs an ongoing continual cost from a third party?
   - **A.** Accept
   - **B.** Avoid
   - **C.** Mitigate
   - **D.** Transfer

6. Implementation of a firewall best maps to which of the following?
   - **A.** Accept
   - **B.** Avoid
   - **C.** Mitigate
   - **D.** Transfer

7. After determining the exposure factor, which is the next step of the quantitative risk assessment process?

   A. Determine the SLE.

   B. Determine the ARO.

   C. Determine the ALE.

   D. Determine the AV.

8. When problem solving, which of the following steps or guidance involves making a step-by-step list of the possibilities for testing?

   A. Implement

   B. Gather the facts

   C. Brainstorm

   D. Evaluate

9. Which of the following most helps employees know how to respond to potential security risks and incidents?

   A. Brainstorm

   B. Separation of duties

   C. Security awareness training

   D. Mandatory vacation

10. A(n) _____ can be described as a weakness in hardware, software, or components that may be exploited in order for a threat to destroy, damage, or compromise an asset.

   A. Vulnerability

   B. Threat

   C. Exposure

   D. Risk

11. A(n) _____ is any agent, condition, or circumstance that could potentially cause harm to, loss of, or damage to an IT asset or data asset, or compromise it.

   A. Vulnerability

   B. Risk

   C. Threat

   D. Exposure

12. Which of the following is not an acceptable audit standard for an auditor to follow?

   A. COBIT

   B. GAAP

   C. FISMA

   D. OpenVAS

13. Which of the following helps describe reporting the difference between "where we are" and "where we want to be"?

   A. Lessons learned report

   B. After-action report

   C. Audit

   D. Gap analysis

14. Nikto, Nessus, Retina, LanGuard, and SAINT are useful for what kind of activity?

   A. Exploitation

   B. Threat assessment

   C. Control auditing

   D. Vulnerability scanning

15. As one of the most well-known types of SLAs, which of the following details the agreed-on amount of uptime?

   A. RTO

   B. UA

   C. FCR

   D. TSF

16. The concept that users should have only the access needed is known as which of the following?

   A. Audited control

   B. Defense in depth

   C. Deny all

   D. Least privilege

17. Which of the following types of testing is best described as manually performing the recovery steps without causing any real disruption?

   A. Full interruption test

   B. Checklist

   C. Walk-through test

   D. Simulation test

18. What type of disaster recovery site is the cheapest to maintain?

   A. Mobile site

   B. Cold site

   C. Warm site

   D. Hot site

19. Which of the following terms is described as the length of time between an interruption and the recovery from that interruption?

    A. MTTR

    B. RPO

    C. MTBF

    D. Availability

20. Which of the following describes the scenario where two employees are required to open a safe, each of them with its combination or code?

    A. Dual control

    B. Separation of duties

    C. Job rotation

    D. Least privilege

Chapter

2

Configure and Implement Endpoint Security Controls

THE FOLLOWING COMPTIA CASP+ EXAM OBJECTIVES ARE COVERED IN THIS CHAPTER:

✓ **3.2 Given a scenario, configure and implement endpoint security controls.**

- **Hardening techniques**
    - Removing unneeded services
    - Disabling unused accounts
    - Images/templates
    - Remove end-of-life devices
    - Remove end-of-support devices
    - Local drive encryption
    - Enable no execute (NX)/execute never (XN) bit
    - Disabling central processing unit (CPU) virtualization support
    - Secure encrypted enclaves/memory encryption
    - Shell restrictions
    - Address space layout randomization (ASLR)
- **Processes**
    - Patching
        - Firmware
        - Application
    - Logging
    - Monitoring

- **Mandatory access control**
  - Security-Enhanced Linux (SELinux)/Security-Enhanced Android (SEAndroid)
  - Kernel vs. middleware
- **Trustworthy computing**
  - Trusted Platform Module (TPM)
  - Secure Boot
  - Unified Extensible Firmware Interface (UEFI)/basic input/output system (BIOS) protection
  - Attestation services
  - Hardware security module (HSM)
  - Measured boot
  - Self-encrypting drives (SEDs)
  - Compensating controls
  - Antivirus
  - Application controls
  - Host-based intrusion detection system (HIDS)/ Host-based intrusion prevention system (HIPS)
  - Host-based firewall
  - Endpoint detection and response (EDR)
  - Redundant hardware
  - Self-healing hardware
  - User and entity behavior analytics (UEBA)

Did you ever think about how many layers are in an onion? As you peel back one layer, there seems to be another after another. A comprehensive security solution should be designed the same way, that is, as a series of layers. This is often called *defense in depth*. This chapter discusses comprehensive security solutions including hardening techniques, using trusted operating systems, and implementing compensating controls. The defense-in-depth approach looks at more than just basic security concepts. This methodology is the sum of the methods, techniques, tools, people, and controls used to protect critical assets and information.

Hardening Techniques

Hardening techniques include a variety of steps carried out to remove unwanted services and features for the purpose of making it harder for an attacker to access a computer successfully by reducing the attack surface. Because it's easy to overlook something in the hardening process, companies should adopt a standard methodology to harden computers and devices. Different OSs such as macOS, Linux, and Windows will require different security baselines. Some administrators refer to a *golden image* as a master image that can be used to clone and deploy other devices consistently. System cloning is an effective method of establishing a baseline configuration for your organization. It requires effort and expertise to establish and maintain images for deployment. Also, hardening techniques for workstations will be different from hardening techniques for servers.

Although this may seem like a simple concept, good security practices start with physical security. If an attacker can physically access a system, it becomes a trivial task to take control of it. Systems should be physically secured. Training users to turn off systems when not in use is a basic control, along with the implementation of password-protected screensavers and automatic logoffs.

Physical equipment and software have life cycles and will not last forever. When physical equipment reaches its final stages of use in an organization, plans should be made around end of life (EOL), and that equipment should be removed from the network. Software has a similar cycle, and once it has reached the end of support by the manufacturer, plans should be in place for a replacement.

Hosts should be hardened so that they are secure before the OS even fully boots. Several items can be used as boot loader protections, including the following:

Secure Boot   This is a security standard developed by members of the PC industry to help make sure your PC boots using only software that is trusted by the device manufacturer. Secure Boot uses self-signed 2048-bit RSA keys in X.509 certificate format and is enabled in the UEFI/BIOS.

Measured Launch   This method works with Trusted Platform Module (TPM) and the Secure Boot process to determine if an OS is allowed to load and what portions can execute. With Secure Boot, PCs with UEFI firmware and a Trusted Platform Module (TPM) can be configured to load only trusted operating system boot loaders. With Measured Boot or Measured Launch, the PC's firmware logs the boot process, and Windows can send it to a trusted server that will objectively assess the PC's health.

IMA   Integrity Measurement Architecture (IMA) was developed by IBM to verify the integrity and trust of Linux OSs.

BIOS/UEFI   *Unified Extensible Firmware Interface (UEFI)* first became a requirement back on Windows 8. UEFI is a replacement or add-on to BIOS that is similar to an OS that runs before your final OS starts up. It was designed to block rootkits and other malware that could take control of BIOS-based systems.

Securing the network equipment and host computers represents the multilayer security approach that is sometimes called defense in depth. Here are some of the general areas that you should examine when hardening host systems:

Using Application Approved List and Application Block/Deny List   An application approved list can be defined as a list of entities that are granted access. An application block/deny list is just the opposite; it lists what cannot be accessed. As an example, you might place YouTube on an application block/deny list so that employees cannot access that website. Think of an *application approved list* as implicit "allow none" unless added to the list and an *application block/deny list* as implicit "allow all" unless added to the list.

If you have heard of whitelisting and blacklisting, those were the terms that were formerly used to describe application approved list and application block/deny list.

Implementing Security/Group Policy   Microsoft created Group Policy with the introduction of Windows 2000. You can think of group policies as groupings of user configuration settings and computer configuration settings that can be linked to objects in Active Directory (AD). These are applied to users and computers. Group Policy allows the security administrator to maintain a consistent security configuration across hundreds of computers. When setting up security options in Group Policy, the initial security settings relate specifically to the Account Policies and Local Policies nodes. Account policies contain a password policy, account lockout policy, and Kerberos policy. Local policies apply to audit policies, user rights, and security options.

Attestation Services   Attestation means that you are validating something as true. *Attestation services* can be designed as hardware-based, software-based, or hybrid. The Trusted Platform Module (TPM) is a specialized form of hardware security module that creates and stores cryptographic keys. TPM enables tamper-resistant full-disk encryption for a local hard drive.

NX/XN Bit Use   *NX (No-eXecute)* is a bit in CPUs that greatly enhances the security of that CPU as it operates. The purpose of NX is to segregate memory areas used for processor instruction and data storage. This feature used to be found only on CPUs with the Harvard architecture (with storage and instruction memory areas separated). Now, thanks to growing concerns for security, processors of the von Neumann architecture (shared storage and instruction memories) are also adopting the NX bit feature.

Today, given various processor manufacturers, these are different terms for essentially the same bit. Obviously, when a CPU manufacturer brands a No-eXecute bit as their own, they can promote its unique security features. Be aware that Intel markets its technology as the *XD* (execute disable) bit, while AMD brands its technology as *EVP* (enhanced virus protection). Finally, for CPUs built on the ARM architecture, the feature is called *XN* (execute never).

Another approach to protecting data is using secure and encrypted enclaves. A secure enclave allows an application to run securely at the hardware level. All data is encrypted in memory and is decrypted only while at the hardware level. The data is secure even if the OS or root user is compromised.

Address Space Layout Randomization Use

Address space layout randomization (ASLR) is a technique designed to protect against buffer overflow attacks, initially implemented in 2003. Presently, all major operating systems—server, desktop, and mobile—incorporate ASLR.

How does ASLR work? In a buffer overflow attack, an attacker needs to know the location in the code where a given function accepts input. The attacker will feed just the right amount of garbage to that code location, including a malicious payload. Ideally, the attacker also includes an instruction to go to another point in the code, and the malicious payload and instruction will run with the privileges of the application.

To say that making a buffer overflow work "properly" is difficult is an understatement. Rarely does an attacker have the actual source code to know the precise location in the code where the targeted function accepts input. Even if the location is available, buffer overflow development requires a large number of "hit-and-miss" trials. However, overflow attacks do happen, and worse, they are repeatable, given that the code location doesn't change.

How does ASLR protect against this? ASLR randomizes the location of different portions of the code. Therefore, even if an attacker managed to make a buffer overflow work once, it may never work again on the same code.

The challenge to software developers is that their code must be compiled to support ASLR from the start. Many years ago this posed a difficult hurdle, but ASLR support is now the default.

Even so, the implementation of ASLR is not infallible with regard to application compatibility. In late November 2017, it was suspected that Microsoft's ASLR was broken in Windows versions 8 through 10. Microsoft explained that the problem was a configuration issue when working with applications that don't opt in to ASLR. More can be learned about mandatory ASLR here:

```
blogs.technet.microsoft.com/srd/2017/11/21/clarifying-the-behavior
-of-mandatory-aslr
```

Hardware Security Module and Trusted Platform Module

A wide variety of products are available to encrypt data in existing disk and media drive products. *Data-at-rest encryption* options include software encryption, such as encrypted file system (EFS) and VeraCrypt.

There are two well-known hardware encryption options to better protect data. Those hardware encryption options are the *Hardware Security Module (HSM)* and the *Trusted Platform Module (TPM)*.

An HSM is a type of secure cryptoprocessor used for managing cryptographic keys. While connected to an HSM, a system can make keys, sign objects, and validate signatures.

A TPM is a specialized chip that can be installed on the motherboard of a computer, and it is used for hardware authentication. The TPM authenticates the computer in question rather than the user. It uses the boot sequence of the computer to determine the trusted status of a platform. The TPM places the cryptographic processes at the hardware level. If someone removes the drives and attempts to boot the hard drive from another computer, the hard drive will fail and deny all access. This provides a greater level of security than a software encryption option that may have been used to encrypt only a few folders on the hard drive. TPM was designed as an inexpensive way to report securely on the environment that booted and to identify the system.

Both HSM and TPM work well for hard drives and fixed storage devices, but portable devices must also be protected against damage, unauthorized access, and exposure. One good approach is to require all employees who use portable devices, USB thumb drives, handheld devices, or any removable storage media devices to be held responsible for their safekeeping and proper security. This starts with policy and extends to user training. For example, policy might be configured to require laptop and tablet computer users to connect to the corporate intranet at least once a week to receive the latest software patches and security updates. Policy can also be established that requires the use of encryption on portable devices. Depending on the company and the level of security needed, the security professional might also restrict the use of personal devices at work and block the ability of these devices to be plugged into company equipment.

Another option for drive encryption is a self-encrypting drive (SED). A SED is a hard disk drive (HDD) or solid-state drive (SSD) designed to automatically encrypt and decrypt drive data without the need for user input or disk encryption software. When the SED is powered on in the host system, data being written to and read from the drive is being encrypted and decrypted instantly; no other steps or software are needed to encrypt and decrypt the drive's data.

As you have learned so far, security professionals need to know about many common types of security tools, techniques, and procedures, as well as when and how to use them. Hardening techniques focus on reducing the attack surface of an endpoint system by disabling unnecessary or unwanted services and changing security options from defaults to more secure settings that match the device's risk profile and security needs.

Patching and updating systems also help. Having a fully patched system image is part of a hardening process. System configuration standards, naming standards, hardening scripts, programs, and procedures help to ensure that systems are correctly inventoried and protected. Drive encryption keeps data secure if drives are stolen or lost. At the end of their life cycle, when devices are retired or fail, sanitization procedures are used to ensure that remnant data doesn't leak. Wiping drives and physical destruction are both common options.

Other controls and techniques can include the following:

Using a Standard Operating Environment   A standard operating system is a standard build of a host system. The idea is that a standard build is used throughout the organization. One advantage is the reduction in the total cost of ownership (TCO). However, the real advantage is that the configuration is consistent. This standardized image is easier to test where there is a uniform environment when updates are required and when security patches are needed.

The most recent security patches should be tested and then installed on host systems as soon as possible. The only exception is when applying them immediately would interfere with business requirements.

Keep in mind the five Ps of security and performance: Proper Planning Prevents Poor Performance and security issues.

Fixing Known Vulnerabilities   Building a secure baseline is a good start to host security, but one big area of concern is fixing known vulnerabilities. To stay on top of this process, you should periodically run vulnerability assessment tools. Vulnerability assessment tools such as Nessus, SAINT, and Retina are designed to run on a weekly or monthly basis to look for known vulnerabilities and problems. Identifying these problems and patching them in an expedient manner helps to reduce overall risk of attack.

Exercise 2.1 shows you how to run a security scanner to identify vulnerabilities.

Running a Security Scanner to Identify Vulnerabilities

1. Download N-Stalker at www.nstalker.com/products/editions/free.

2. Install the program on a Microsoft system.

3. Start the program, and enter the IP address of a computer you would like to scan.

4. Complete the scan and save the results.

5. Review the results.

Notice that the results are classified as red, yellow, or green. Red items are high-risk issues that demand immediate remediation. Yellow items are medium risk, and green items are low risk.

Hardening and Removing Unnecessary Services   Another important component of securing systems is the process of hardening the system. The most direct way of beginning this process is by removing unwanted services. Think of it as a variation of the principle of least privilege. This process involves removing unnecessary applications, disabling unneeded services, closing unnecessary ports, and setting restrictive permissions on files. This process reduces the attack surface, and it is intended to make the system more resistant to attack. Although you should apply the process to all systems for which you are responsible, you must handle each OS uniquely and take different steps to secure it.

If you are tasked with hardening a Linux system, you should consider Bastille Linux. This tool automates the hardening process on a Linux system. You can find the tool at sourceforge.net/projects/bastille-linux.

Applying Command Shell Restrictions   Restricting the user's access to the command prompt is another way to tighten security. Many commands that a user can run from the command prompt can weaken security or allow a malicious individual to escalate privilege on a host system. Consider the default configuration of a Windows Server 2019 computer: Telnet, TFTP, and a host of other command-line executables are turned off by default. This is a basic example of command-line restrictions. In another example, say that you have a kiosk in the lobby of your business where customers can learn more about your products and services and even fill out a job application. Additional capability should be disabled to implement the principle of least privilege. Although it is important to provide users with what they need to do the job or task at hand, it's good security practice to disable access to nonessential programs. In some situations, this may include command shell restrictions. Allowing a user to run commands from the command line can offer a hacker an avenue for attack. Command-line access should be restricted unless needed.

Exercise 2.2 shows you how to bypass command shell restrictions.

EXERCISE 2.2

Bypassing Command Shell Restrictions

This exercise demonstrates one technique that a malicious user or attacker might use to bypass command shell restrictions. This technique makes use of StickyKeys.

1. Press the Shift key five times on a Windows computer, and display the Sticky Keys option.

2. Close the program.

3. Locate the Sticky Keys application at `c:\windows\system32\sethc.exe`.

4. Save `cmd.exe` as **sethc.exe**, and replace the original program. (Windows will prompt for administrator permissions to carry out this exercise.)

5. Press the Shift key five times on a Windows computer, and now `cmd.exe` opens instead of Sticky Keys.

Notice that even with restrictions in place, this allows a malicious user to access a command prompt.

Using Warning Banners   *Warning banners* are brief messages that inform users of specific policies and procedures regarding the use of applications and services. A warning banner can be a splash screen, pop-up, or message box that informs the user of specific rules. Warning banners are crucial in that they inform the user about specific behavior or activities that may or may not be allowed. As the warning banner states the result of specific behavior, any excuses are removed from the user so that a violation can be logged. Warning banners should contain what is considered proper usage, expectations of privacy, and penalties for noncompliance.

 Security professionals should consult their legal department when deciding what services or applications to display with a banner. Legal, HR, and management should consider the needs of the company and their users carefully before selecting particular verbiage.

Using Restricted Interfaces   A *restricted interface* is a profile that dictates what programs, menus, applications, commands, or functions are available within an environment. This technique allows a security administrator to control the user's environment and dictate the objects to which they have access. The environment is considered a restricted interface because the user can use it only to interface with the operating system, installed applications, and resources. In modern operating systems, an individual profile can follow the user to any mobile device under the administrator's control.

Configuring Dedicated Interfaces   A *dedicated interface* is a port that is devoted to specific traffic. As an example, many companies place their wireless LAN on a dedicated interface and keep it separate from other internal network traffic.

Using Out-of-Band Management   *Out-of-band management* is the concept of employing a dedicated management channel, separate from the network channel or cabling used by servers.

Configuring a Management Interface   A *management interface* is designed to be used as a way to manage a computer or server that may be powered off or otherwise unresponsive. A management interface makes use of a network connection to the hardware rather than to an operating system or login shell. Management interfaces often use an out-of-band NIC.

Managing a Data Interface   A *data interface* is used with databases to generate process templates. *Process templates* are reusable collections of activity types. They allow system integrators and others who work with different clients to manipulate similar types of data.

Scripting and Replication   One of the great things about PowerShell is its ability to script basic window commands of SQL server objects easily. You can also use it to script replication objects. This can be used as part of a disaster recovery plan so that you always have a script available to re-create replications.

Scripting and replication are also an approach for automating patch management.

Trusted Operating Systems

A *trusted operating system (trusted OS)* can be defined as one that has implemented sufficient controls to support multilevel security. Multilevel security provides the OS with the ability to process and handle information at different security levels. At the very least, this granularity may mean that you can process data as a user or as root or administrator. Trusted OSs must be tested to demonstrate evidence of correctness to meet specific standards. These standards require the trusted OS to have undergone testing and validation. Testing offers the OS vendor a way to promote the features of the system. Testing allows the buyer to verify the system and to check that the OS performs in the manner the vendor claims.

Trusted operating systems extend beyond software and have to take into consideration the hardware on which they reside. This is the purpose of the trusted computer base. The *trusted computer base (TCB)* is the sum of all of the protection mechanisms within a computer, and it is responsible for enforcing the security policy. This includes hardware, software, controls, and processes.

The following documents are some of the guidelines used to validate a trusted OS:

Trusted Computer System Evaluation Criteria (TCSEC)   One of the original trusted OS testing standards was the *Trusted Computer System Evaluation Criteria (TCSEC)*. TCSEC, also known as the *Orange Book*, was developed to evaluate stand-alone systems. It actually has been deprecated and has long ago been replaced by the Common Criteria, but it deserves mention as it was one of the first trusted OS testing standards. Its basis of measurement is confidentiality. It was designed to rate systems and place them into one of four categories:

> **A: Verified Protection**   An A-rated system is the highest security division.
>
> **B: Mandatory Security**   A B-rated system has mandatory protection of the TCB.
>
> **C: Discretionary Protection**   A C-rated system provides discretionary protection of the TCB.
>
> **D: Minimal Protection**   A D-rated system fails to meet any of the standards of A, B, or C, and basically it has no security controls.

Information Technology Security Evaluation Criteria   *Information Technology Security Evaluation Criteria (ITSEC)* was another early standard developed in the 1980s and first published in May 1990. It was designed to meet the needs of the European market. ITSEC examines the confidentiality, integrity, and availability of an entire system. It was unique in that it was the first standard to unify markets and bring all of Europe under one set of guidelines. The evaluation is actually divided into two parts: one part evaluates functionality, and the other part evaluates assurance. There are 10 functionality (F) classes and 7 assurance (E) classes. Assurance classes rate the effectiveness and correctness of a system.

Common Criteria   The International Organization for Standardization (ISO) created Common Criteria (ISO 15408) to be a global standard that built on TCSEC, ITSEC, and others. Common Criteria essentially replaced ITSEC. Common Criteria examined different areas of the trusted OS, including physical and logical controls, startup and recovery, reference mediation, and privileged states. Common Criteria categorizes assurance into one of eight increasingly strict levels of assurance. These are referred to as *evaluation assurance levels (EALs)*. EALs provide a specific level of confidence in the security functions of the system being analyzed. The seven levels of assurance are as follows:

> **EAL 1:** Functionality tested
>
> **EAL 2:** Structurally tested
>
> **EAL 3:** Methodically checked and tested

EAL 4: Methodically designed, tested, and reviewed

EAL 5: Semi-formally designed and tested

EAL 6: Semi-formally verified, designed, and tested

EAL 7: Formally verified, designed, and tested

 Since the rollout of the Common Criteria EAL, several operating system vendors have certified their OSs at EAL Level 3 and EAL Level 4. In fact, it's now common to see an OS certification level at an "augmented" status, meaning that the OS achieved a level between two EALs. In that case, the EAL certification is denoted with a + symbol.

Regardless of how it is tested or which specific set of criteria is used, a trusted OS includes the following basic attributes:

Hardware Protection   A trusted OS must be designed from the ground up. Secure hardware is the beginning.

Long-Term Protected Storage   A trusted OS must have the ability to offer protected storage that lasts across power cycles and other events.

Isolation   A trusted OS must be able to isolate programs. It must be able to keep program A from accessing information from program B.

Separation of User Processes from Supervisor Processes   User and supervisor functions must be separated.

The TCB is responsible for confidentiality and integrity. It is the only portion of a system that operates at a high level of trust. This level of trust is where the security kernel resides. The security kernel handles all user and application requests for access to system resources. A small security kernel is easy to verify, test, and validate as secure.

So, while the trusted OS is built on the TCB, both of these concepts are based on theory. Much of the work on these models started in the early 1970s. During this period, the U.S. government funded a series of papers focused on computer security. These papers form the basic building blocks for trusted computing security models. *Security models* determine how security will be implemented, what subjects can access the system, and to what objects they will have access. Simply stated, they are a way to formalize the design of a trusted OS. Security models build on controls designed to enforce integrity and confidentiality.

Mandatory access control (MAC) has been used by the government for many years. All files controlled by the MAC policies are based on different categorized security levels including classified, secret, or top secret. MAC allows for the system to run at the same or lower levels. Overriding MAC requires authorization from senior management.

Examples of trusted OSs include SELinux, SEAndroid, and Trusted Solaris. *SELinux (Security-Enhanced Linux)*, available now for just over 20 years, started as a collaborative effort between the National Security Agency (NSA) and Red Hat, and it continues to be improved. SELinux brings MAC to the Linux kernel, allowing for much stricter access control. For the CASP+ exam, remember this point as a way to distinguish *kernel* from *middleware*.

Middleware is a type of computer software that provides services to software applications beyond those available from the operating system. It can be described as "software glue." Middleware makes it easier for software developers to implement communication and input/output, so they can focus on the specific purposes of their applications. While core kernel functionality can be provided only by the operating system itself, some functionality previously provided by separately sold middleware is now integrated in operating systems.

The Android operating system uses the Linux kernel at its core and also provides an application framework that developers incorporate into their applications. In addition, Android provides a middleware layer, including libraries that provide services such as data storage, screen display, multimedia, and web browsing. Because the middleware libraries are compiled to machine language, services execute quickly. Middleware libraries also implement device-specific functions, so applications and the application framework need not concern themselves with variations between various Android devices.

SEAndroid brings the same MAC benefit to the Android kernel. Android uses the concept of *application sandboxing*, or isolating and restricting its applications in their own respective memory and drive space. Starting with version 4.3, Android took on SELinux to extend that isolation even further. Between versions 4.3 and 5.0, Android partially enforced the restriction to a subset of domains. In Android speak, a *domain* is akin to a running process. With Android kernel 5.0 and later, Android fully enforces SELinux in the kernel.

Trusted Solaris also provides MAC as well as features like read-only protection for host or guest environments that Solaris dubs "immutable zones." The immunity provided is applied via a zone configuration property file that is used to set any exemptions to the file system. Those exemptions allow writes to be permitted. At the time of this writing, the property file is set to one of five possible settings, ranging from "strict" (absolutely no writes) to "none" (full read-write access), with intermediate variants of access to the /etc and /var directories.

Compensating Controls

Security is hardly a new concern for most organizations. In many companies, security is relegated to the technology agenda and gets only marginal attention and budget consideration. In today's economy, many computer security officers (CSOs) are being asked to provide better security than was provided yesterday with more modest budgets. For companies to survive in today's world, a paradigm shift is needed—the real threat is no longer a stranger lurking outside the company's main gate. Over the last decade, information-related crime and cyberattacks have become the crime of choice for a growing cadre of criminals.

Effective security requires the CASP+ to work with others throughout the organization to integrate the needs of the company into holistic security solutions using compensating controls. Given a scenario, a CASP+ should be able to facilitate collaboration across diverse business units to achieve the related security goals. A comprehensive security solution is essential to the enterprise's continuity of business operations and maintaining the confidentiality and integrity of data. The integration of enterprise tools is needed to protect information and systems from unauthorized access, use, disclosure, disruption, modification, or destruction and sometimes requires thinking outside the box.

Antivirus   This is a no-brainer, right? This no such thing as a 100 percent trusted network, and endpoints are vulnerable to the connected network. Give your endpoint some added protection of *antivirus* unless, for some specialized reason, it would cause interruptions.

Application Controls   If changes to the application allow for reducing risk while business needs remain satisfied, then why not make use of *application controls* that further harden the system? Application control includes completeness and validity checks, identification, authentication, authorization, input controls, and forensic controls, among others. An example of an application control is the validity check, which reviews the data entered into a data entry screen to ensure that it meets a set of predetermined range criteria.

Host-Based Intrusion Detection System (HIDS)/Host-Based Intrusion Prevention System (HIPS)   HIDSs and HIPSs can be useful as detective and preventative controls. They provide more information for your security operations center (SOC) personnel. If incident handling, HIDSs and HIPSs might also be helpful in containing the incident by letting you know if other hosts were affected.

Host-Based Firewall   This is another endpoint layer of defense where we are reminded that no network is to be trusted 100 percent. The *host-based firewall* may not help stop a host from launching an incident, but it can help mitigate the host being another victim.

Endpoint Detection and Response (EDR)   EDR is a relatively new term, but in the age of advanced persistent threats (APTs), your endpoints will benefit from *endpoint detection and response*. EDR is far more comprehensive and capable than a HIDS/HIPS. An EDR solution offers multiple capabilities and tools. EDR software is used to help companies identify and remediate threats related to network-connected endpoints. These tools inform security professionals of vulnerable or infected endpoints and guide them through the remediation process. After incidents have been resolved, EDR tools help teams investigate issues and the vulnerable components that allowed an endpoint to become compromised. Here are some examples:

- MVISION Endpoint Security
- VMware Carbon Black EDR
- Palo Alto Networks Traps
- Microsoft Defender for Endpoint

Redundant Hardware   Consider the scenario where you know the mean time between failures (MTBF) of a particular technology is unacceptable. It could be because that business need is particularly critical and cannot be serviced easily. But one way to reduce downtime is to inject some high availability (HA) in there, utilizing *redundant hardware*. Where there is one, make it two. With *redundant hardware*, the MTBF hasn't changed, but the risk of a failure causing an outage is much lower.

Self-Healing Hardware   Another new term and concept, *self-healing hardware* is pretty self-explanatory. In the event of a failure or security incident, your hardware detects, responds to, and fixes the failure's impact. Personally, I find this concept a bit baffling, but CompTIA would like to make sure you're aware of it. You should understand that self-healing is not limited to hardware. Consider the scenario where a system responds to a software issue by rolling back the change to resume a known-good state.

Self-Encrypting Drives   Similar to the autonomous *self-healing hardware*, a self-encrypting drive will initiate encryption of newly written data.

User and Entity Behavior Analytics (UEBA)   This is a fascinating expansion of the older field of user analytics where only employee behavior is monitored. *User and entity behavior analytics* includes becoming more in tune with both employees and the entity. This technology helps mitigate a variety of risks by detecting odd behavior, such as detecting an unauthorized user or a Trojaned device.

Thank You: Compensating vs. Mitigating Controls

Just a sidebar. If you are screaming at me "Jeff, these are mitigating controls, not compensating controls," yes, you're right. Thank you, scholarly security professional. For the record, the term *compensating controls* is straight from CompTIA's Exam Objectives, and that's why it's used here. But yes, a mitigating control is one that reduces the threat from happening and is considered a permanent one, while a compensating control implies temporary use because the normally desired control is unavailable.

Summary

A CASP+ must understand the need to harden and secure endpoint devices. Securing the environment must include the endpoint, not ignore the last line of defense. Various technologies and techniques were discussed, including *how* the endpoint is left more secure. Be familiar with all the listed compensating and mitigating controls, and understand how each control may or may not reduce a particular risk.

The CASP+ should understand how trusted operating systems can provide a far smaller attack surface, providing security from the kernel outward. Lastly, the CASP+ should be able to name and explain the purpose of various hardware and software-based controls.

Exam Essentials

Understand how specific endpoints face different risks.   Consider scenarios where risks may affect endpoints differently. What sort of hardening or controls would apply? Controls may or may not be applied for a variety of reasons.

Know why and when to apply hardening techniques.   Consider scenarios where certain hardening techniques would or would not be effective.

Know that techniques are not exclusive or one-size-fits-all.   Of course, as you read through techniques or technologies discussed in the chapter, think about how you can (and perhaps should) apply multiple controls to maximize risk mitigation.

Understand how a compensating control might mitigate a risk.   The exam might throw a risk at you and then offer several compensating controls. Will you be able to spot which control will have the best (or least) effect on that risk? Be familiar with compensating controls such as antivirus, application controls, HIDSs/HIPSs, host-based firewalls, endpoint detection and response (EDR), redundant hardware, self-healing hardware, and user and entity behavior analytics (UEBA).

Review Questions

You can find the answers in Appendix.

1. What term describes removing unwanted services and features for the purpose of making it more difficult for an attacker to attack a computer successfully?

   A. Locking down

   B. Reducing the attack surface

   C. Hardening

   D. Mitigating risk

2. Which of the following areas are included as part of the Trusted Computer Base?

   A. Hardware

   B. Hardware and firmware

   C. Processes and controls

   D. All of the above

3. The Hardware Security Module (HSM) and the Trusted Platform Module (TPM) provide what hardening technique?

   A. Hard drive encryption

   B. Trusted user authentication

   C. Portable drive encryption

   D. Protection against buffer overflow

4. Which trusted OS started as a collaborative effort between the NSA and Red Hat?

   A. SEAndroid

   B. SELinux

   C. Trusted Solaris

   D. TrustedARM

5. Which of the following will have the least effect in reducing the threat of personal portable drives being used in the organization?

   A. Policy

   B. User training

   C. Host-based HSM and TPM

   D. Prohibiting personal portable drives in the organization

6. Which is not a trusted operating system?

   A. SEAndroid

   B. SELinux

   C. Trusted Solaris

   D. TrustedARM

7. What cryptoprocessor is used to manage cryptographic keys?

  A. Trusted Platform Module (TPM)

  B. Hardware Security Module (HSM)

  C. Self-encrypting drive (SED)

  D. Unified Extensible Firmware Interface (UEFI)

8. What is the primary purpose of attestation services?

  A. Authenticating processes

  B. Attesting false positives

  C. Validating something as true

  D. Isolating a process from attack

9. Which of the following is NOT a basic attribute of a trusted OS?

  A. Long-term protected storage

  B. Separation of user processes from supervisor processes

  C. Isolation

  D. Air gap

10. What is a primary benefit of using a standard build or standard operating systems throughout the organization?

  A. Reduced cost of ownership

  B. Patch management diversity

  C. Increased logging

  D. Smaller network footprint

11. Which of the following is used with databases to generate process templates?

  A. Management interface

  B. Dedicated interface

  C. Data interface

  D. Restricted interface

12. What standard replaced the Trusted Computer System Evaluation Criteria (TCSEC), developed to evaluate stand-alone systems?

  A. Rainbow tables

  B. Red teaming

  C. Orange U-hardening

  D. Common Criteria

13. What compensating control is a form of high availability (HA)?

  A. Endpoint detection and response (EDR)

  B. Host-based firewall

  C. Host-based intrusion detection system (HIDS)

  D. Redundant hardware

14. How many evaluation assurance levels (EALs) are referenced in the Common Criteria?

   A. Five

   B. Six

   C. Seven

   D. Eight

15. What term describes a hard drive that automatically initiates encryption of newly written data?

   A. Self-healing drive

   B. TBD encryption

   C. Self-encrypting drive

   D. TPM-based encryption

16. What hardening technique was designed to block rootkits and other malware that could take control of BIOS-based systems and was first required in Windows 8?

   A. BIOS/UEFI

   B. NS/XN

   C. ASLR

   D. SEDs

17. What is the purpose of the NX (No-eXecute) bit?

   A. Monitor for buffer overflow attempts

   B. Perform hardware encryption during processing

   C. Segregate the processor's memory areas

   D. Allow the BIOS to be protected

18. What technology helps mitigate a variety of risks by detecting odd behavior, such as detecting an unauthorized user or a Trojaned device?

   A. SED

   B. TPM

   C. UEBA

   D. UA

19. How does ASLR protect against buffer overflow attacks?

   A. Relocating the process in memory

   B. Encrypting executable code

   C. Randomizing portions of the code

   D. Encrypting code while in memory during processing

20. What is the term that describes the isolation and restriction of applications in their own respective memory and drive space in the trusted OS SEAndroid?

   A. Security enhanced applications

   B. Out-of-band applications

   C. Application sandboxing

   D. Application isolation

Chapter

3

Security Operations Scenarios

THE FOLLOWING COMPTIA CASP+ EXAM OBJECTIVES ARE COVERED IN THIS CHAPTER:

✓ **Given a scenario, perform threat management activities.**

- **Intelligence types**
  - Tactical
    - Commodity malware
  - Strategic
    - Targeted attacks
  - Operational
    - Threat hunting
    - Threat emulation
- **Actor types**
  - Advanced persistent threat (APT)/nation-state
  - Insider threat
  - Competitor
  - Hacktivist
  - Script kiddie
  - Organized crime
- **Threat actor properties**
  - Resource
    - Time
    - Money
  - Supply chain access
  - Create vulnerabilities
  - Capabilities/sophistication
  - Identifying techniques

- Intelligence collection methods
  - Intelligence feeds
  - Deep web
  - Proprietary
  - Open-source intelligence (OSINT)
  - Human intelligence (HUMINT)
- Frameworks
  - MITRE Adversarial Tactics, Techniques and Common Knowledge (ATT&CK)
    - ATT&CK for industrial control system (ICS)
  - Diamond Model of Intrusion Analysis
  - Cyber Kill Chain

✓ **Given a scenario, analyze indicators of compromise and formulate an appropriate response.**

- Indicators of compromise
  - Packet capture (PCAP)
  - Logs
    - Network logs
    - Vulnerability logs
    - Operating system logs
    - Access logs
    - NetFlow logs
  - Notifications
    - FIM alerts
    - SIEM alerts
    - DLP alerts
    - IDS/IPS alerts
    - Antivirus alerts
  - Notification severity/priorities
  - Unusual process activity

- **Response**

  - Firewall rules
  - IPS/IDS rules
  - ACL rules
  - Signature rules
  - Behavior rules
  - DLP rules
  - Scripts/regular expressions

The CASP+ exam does enjoy scenario questions. Regarding threat actors and mitigation strategies in security operations, this chapter discusses all the topics you can expect to see in those scenario-formatted questions. Additional scenario topics are covered in subsequent chapters in this book. However, this chapter covers those topics revolving around security operations. You should then identify and analyze the vulnerabilities left open to those threats. And lastly in this chapter, you will understand the risk of those vulnerabilities being exploited and how to respond to them.

Threat Management

For the CASP+ exam you'll be expected to be familiar with the types of intelligence and how each factors into threat management. Not unlike with conventional warfare, cyber intelligence is important for knowing what threatens you, identifying your weaknesses before your threat does, managing all risk, and being ready to respond to whatever attacks first. This includes understanding the concepts of threat hunting and threat emulation.

Types of Intelligence

The types of intelligence can be categorized in three ways. They vary in how their value relates to the threats.

Operational   *Operational* intelligence strives to keep business going as planned. You are looking to identify the trends and systemic risks that threaten on an ongoing basis. Operational intelligence includes actively threat hunting for the malicious in your environment and working toward understanding those threats the best you can, before they create an incident, as well as using threat emulation to take new information about attacks and convert it into usable signatures. This gives an organization the ability to block those threats before they have an opportunity to do damage within an enterprise ecosystem.

Tactical   *Tactical* intelligence represents the "here and now" of needed information. You are looking to understand a specific discovery, perhaps a threat found in the course of incident response. For example, the security operations center (SOC) may have identified a common piece of commodity malware in your environment. Commodity malware is publicly available code that can be purchased but is not customized and used by many threat actors. If this type of threat is found within the organization, a high degree of tactical intelligence will help quickly identify and navigate the response to it.

Strategic   *Strategic* threat intelligence asks questions while looking further out. Who will be the threat the organization will soon face or can expect to face? What sort of *targeted attacks* can your industry or the organization come to expect? For example, an industrial espionage attack may target your organization because of specific value or product.

Threat Hunting

The concept of *threat hunting* means to search for and identify security threats and problems that have yet to be discovered in the environment. The act of threat hunting usually involves going well beyond the typical security technologies and safeguards. The potential reward is preferable to some undiscovered malware. The prize to be sought would be the capable insider threat or shadow IT which, until discovered, had been "flying under the radar." Other potential discoveries can be bad configurations or outdated processes.

Remember that threat hunting is proactive, unlike most security appliances and technologies. Too often, security devices respond to a threat based on a matching signature. Threat hunting, on the other hand, is a practice or exercise that requires perseverance and creativity. Since human threats, especially ones already established on the inside, will be careful not to reveal their motives or reason, hunt teaming requires patience and vigilance to flush out the threats.

Threat Emulation

The value in carefully analyzing a threat is more than just research. When you can imitate how a threat works and interacts with the vulnerability, you understand more how to mitigate the risk of that threat. *Threat emulation* is the approach and activity of better understanding a threat for the sake of ultimately minimizing it.

Actor Types

To understand how and why various threats affect your operations, it's first necessary to cover the types of *threat actors* that threaten your operations. The FBI characterizes threat actors into three broad categories: organized crime, state-sponsored attacker, and cyberterrorist. Of these three groups, the FBI describes *organized crime* as the group we see most heavily involved in cybercrime today. A large portion of this activity originates from Eastern Europe and Russia. Originating from Russia or former Soviet states has been some of the most notorious malware that has targeted global consumers, banks, and retailers over the past few years: LoJax, Bad Rabbit, and NotPetya, to name just a few. Many of these organized crime groups have more than ample resources and skills to be a global threat. They have the sophistication, time, and money to leverage vulnerabilities to create new threats and new exploits (zero-day).

In 2021, Colonial Pipeline, an American oil pipeline system that originates in Houston, Texas, and carries gasoline and jet fuel mainly to the southeastern United States, suffered a ransomware cyberattack that impacted computerized equipment managing the pipeline. Also in 2021, work stopped at several U.S. meat processing plants after the world's largest meat producer was hit with a major cyberattack.

With all the confusion about the names of threat actors, the same might be said for the good guys. One term to describe an individual who tests the security of a network, application, or system is *ethical hacker*. An *ethical hacker* is an individual who performs authorized security tests and other vulnerability assessment activities to help organizations secure their infrastructures. Hackers are typically divided into different categories, which can include the following:

Authorized These individuals perform ethical hacking to help secure companies and organizations. They work within the boundaries of the law and with the permission of the organization.

Unauthorized These individuals are criminal attackers and may be driven by greed, revenge, or the challenge of breaking into a company.

Semi-authorized These individuals typically follow the law but sometimes venture over to the darker side of unauthorized hacking. You could think of them as Luke Skywalker from *Star Wars*. They cannot decide if they will join the Force or go with the Dark Side.

If you've heard of white-hat, black-hat, and gray-hat hackers, those terms correlate to authorized, unauthorized, and semi-authorized hackers.

Criminal hacking has changed over the years, as has the source of emerging threats. Most of the hacking culture today grew out of the phone phreaking activities of the 1960s. These individuals hacked telecommunication and PBX systems to explore their capabilities and make free phone calls. Their activities included physical theft, stolen calling cards, access to telecommunication services, and the reprogramming of telecommunications equipment.

One early phreaker was John Draper, aka Captain Crunch. He is given credit for finding that a toy whistle inside of a box of Cap'n Crunch cereal had the same frequency, 2600 Hz, as the trunking signal of AT&T. This toy whistle could be used to place free long-distance phone calls.

One of the early phone hacking magazines is *2600*. It's still available at www.2600.com.

One example of cybercrime is the attacks conducted by Albert Gonzales. In 2007, he was accused of stealing more than 170 million credit card numbers; this was the largest credit card security breach at that time. You can read more about this at www.nytimes.com/2010/11/14/magazine/14Hacker-t.html.

A wide range of threat actors exists. Some are individuals, while others are part of larger organizations. Each has its own goals and approaches. Some of the most common types of threat actors include the following:

Nation-State Hackers and Cyberterrorists   These individuals have some form of backing from a country or state and are typically focused on gathering intelligence, stealing data, and possessing advanced technology and knowledge that another nation or country may have. Several examples of alleged nation-state hacking are GhostNet, Stuxnet, and Shady RAT.

It is common for well-financed nation-state groups to place *advanced persistent threats (APTs)* in a compromised system. The APT serves to maintain accessibility to the "pwned" machine. Because APT malware can be advanced, the threat may stay even if the system administrators attempt to contain and eradicate it.

This category includes those individuals or groups of individuals seeking to engage in recruitment for the purpose of attacking and/or compromising critical infrastructures and industrial control systems (ICSs), such as nuclear power plants, power generation stations, and water treatment plants.

Disgruntled Employees   Disgruntled employees pose an *insider threat* as individuals who are upset with their current or former employers. These individuals may or may not have advanced hacking skills, but they do have access to and knowledge of the target that an outsider may not have. Proper human resource processes and good operational controls can go a long way toward preventing problems.

The insider threat is especially dangerous, since the insider already holds considerable trust with the organization. The insider knows internal policies, is familiar with the organizational structure, has awareness of business processes, and, most of all, has network access as a trusted employee.

Organized Crime   Today, a large portion of hacking activity is driven by monetary needs, and this type of threat continues to grow as the rewards get larger. These attackers are typically organized crime groups targeting banks, financial institutions, companies, and end users. Their goal is usually to obtain credit card numbers, personal information, steal identities, and perform other activities related to stealing money.

Further, given the strong drive for financial gain, the organized and well-funded hacker will persevere, no matter the time involved. Resources such as time and money are not in short supply!

Competitors   Don't forget that any company's intellectual property (IP) is regarded as the prime target for the competition.

Script Kiddies   This derogatory term is used to describe people who use hacking techniques but have limited skills. Often such attackers rely almost entirely on automated tools they download from the Internet. These attackers often have little knowledge of how their attacks actually work, and they are simply seeking out convenient targets of opportunity.

Hacktivists   These are individuals who hack for a cause. Groups such as Anonymous and LulzSec have been closely identified with this movement. Figure 3.1 shows the LulzSec Twitter page.

FIGURE 3.1   LulzSec

Resources   If I ask what sets bad actors apart from each other, the first answer is likely their skill set. Yes, having capability and perseverance is a big discriminator. Let's not forget how important things such as *time* and *money* are.

Most bad actors are doing their day jobs in addition to poking and probing at vulnerabilities. But what about those nation-state hackers and the for-hire or criminal hackers? Threatening your environment *is* their day job. When their reward, in all respects, is successfully ruining your day, you know they are highly motivated to do so.

Supply Chain Access   Often the easier way to hurt an organization is not to hit them directly. Instead, a hacker may focus on *supply chain access*, opting to cripple or disrupt a different organization on which the target relies. This affects the company's reputation more than their own infrastructure. There is little in the way of technical controls for mitigating supply chain attacks. Mitigations could include the following:

- Knowing suppliers and looking upstream as well as downstream
- Conducting a risk assessment
- Utilizing third-party testing
- Regularly scanning and patching all vulnerable systems
- Using strong passwords
- Ensuring your staff has set up multifactor authentication everywhere possible

 Supply chain access is one of the many new terms for this CASP+ exam. Fortunately, you are already aware of many examples, such as Stuxnet, the Target data breach (2013), British Airways (2018), SolarWinds (2020), and Microsoft Exchange Server (February 2021). All of these occurred because of reliance on a service or product outside the company's immediate control. They are supply chain attacks. You can read more about a few of them at www.secureworldexpo.com/industry-news/10-official-u.s.-quotes-on-solarwinds-and-microsoft-exchange-attacks.

Intelligence Collection Methods

How is data collected? Where does it come from? When it comes to collecting intelligence regarding threat management, a range of tools and techniques exist, but they generally can be divided into two broad categories: open-source intelligence (OSINT) and human intelligence (HUMINT), which is related to social engineering.

Open-Source Intelligence

The *open-source intelligence (OSINT)* method allows required information to be delivered as highly relevant research results that can easily be validated and transformed into high-quality intelligence. The idea behind gathering OSINT originated in the military, but it was found to be of great value in the civilian domain as well. OSINT is broadly defined as using established intelligence tradecraft on open sources of information. Open sources range from foreign language translation to exploitation/analysis of multiple, independent, publicly available sources of information. OSINT sources include commercial, scientific, and technical databases; symposium proceedings; published strategies and doctrine; think-tank publications; patent information; and other open-source documents available to the general public. A variety of exploitation techniques are practiced in OSINT, including monitoring social media and gathering contact information from sites such as WHOIS, search engines, and other records.

It's important to note that information being readily available does not make that information free to use as we wish. Information accessibility has value and perhaps a cost associated with producing it. Information created by commercial research or effort can label that information as *proprietary* and protected. In threat research it is important to respect the difference between available and free to reuse. For example, threat intelligence research firms publish intelligence feeds to disseminate their findings. These *intelligence feeds* are highly valuable partly because of the vast effort behind making them.

Social Media

Social media provides a treasure trove of open-source information for attackers. Visiting the personal social pages for an employee will yield their likes, passions, political leanings, and maybe even their thoughts about their employers. The opportunity for a social engineer to exploit the social media sites of a potential target is not just theory, as we all know from current events at the time of this writing.

Deep Web

The Deep Web has become popularized and mysterious to people who haven't gone there and woefully under-indexed for those who try. (That was a joke.) The *Deep Web* is a part of the Internet that is not indexed or searchable by conventional search engines. It can be treated as another source of information. However, like with many sources, enjoy it with a bit of skepticism. The Deep Web is different from the Dark Web, even though the words get used interchangeably. The Dark Web is also not indexed, but users of the Dark Web focus on anonymity and have access to illegal activities and information. It is in these illegal markets where you can purchase *commodity malware*.

WHOIS

If an attacker wants to learn more about the organization's technical contact or registration information about their domain, the site that provides both is WHOIS.

Routing Tables

Unlike social media rich with personal information, or record-keeping sites like WHOIS, open-source intelligence can also be more obscure but still empirical and highly valuable. Routing tables are found on any device aware of the network outside of the subnet, which can be any system, router, or layer 3 switch. The routing table is the set of "rules" or paths between routes. Obviously, this is valuable to anyone looking to learn about what network subnets or spaces a system has been or could be talking to.

DNS Records

Another publicly available repository of information about some of the organization's infrastructure is its *DNS records*. Through DNS records, an attacker can learn much about a company's domain, subdomains, and the blocks of IP addresses or services used by that system. Mitigation can include the following:

- Auditing DNS zones
- Keeping DNS servers patched and current
- Hiding the BIND version
- Restricting zone transfers
- Disabling DNS recursion to prevent DNS poisoning attacks
- Using isolated DNS servers
- Using a DDOS mitigation provider
- Using two-factor authentication

Human Intelligence and Social Engineering

No technology can build or betray confidentiality and trust like human interaction. If you agree with that, consider speaking with a trained professional. But seriously, humans do thrive on interaction and relationships. This can be for good or bad. For our purposes, we're talking about human interaction used for the sake of gathering information.

It's commonly said that the second-oldest profession is spying. *Human intelligence (HUMINT)* is the personal side of spying or collecting intelligence. While OSINT might involve dumpster diving and scouring social media, HUMINT involves building a genuine rapport and leveraging it for information or access.

HUMINT can be considered a portion of social engineering. Social engineering encompasses a spectrum of methods and devices, such as email, texts, and phone calls.

Speaking personally, social engineering is part of my job. More specifically, when a client asks my employer to perform social engineering, I am sent off for an onsite engagement. Phishing and other online social engineering gets done between myself and others.

My onsite work does not include breaking in after hours with specialized tools. I respect professionals who have that skill and practice. One of the penetration testers on my team is skillful at lock picking, but for now, such tools are outside our rules of engagement. We must stick to social engineering. Plus, unlike a door-opening tool, real people give you access and point you right where you need to be.

Instead, I gain access only by interacting with an employee. Naturally, that insider is not aware of my goal. In social engineering, the engagement is based on deceit, and time is needed to build a rapport. I do get in, but people do take more time than tools. And perhaps most importantly, I am ever careful to not put someone in a position of being embarrassed or being left feeling more vulnerable afterward. The goal is security awareness and team education. In almost every case, I am not forced to reveal the identity or insider who allowed me in.

Frameworks

This section discusses the frameworks promoted today regarding threat management and how attacks happen. You should familiarize yourself with the frameworks and related standard nomenclature.

MITRE Adversarial Tactics, Techniques and Common Knowledge

The MITRE Adversarial Tactics, Techniques and Common Knowledge (ATT&CK) framework is what happens when you take the brains of a well-schooled, methodical attacker and spray them on a highly organized matrix. Not a delicate picture, but neither is the ATT&CK matrix.

MITRE is the not-for-profit research organization that brought you the Common Vulnerabilities and Exposures (CVE), the leader in ranking and categorizing vulnerabilities. MITRE's *ATT&CK framework* by its full name is Adversarial Tactics, Techniques and Common Knowledge. So, yes, this means taking the brains of an attacker and categorizing them into methods and flow.

The MITRE ATT&CK Matrix for Enterprise is organized to identify top-level tactics that include hundreds of techniques that attackers use. In examining the ATT&CK Matrix, you are probably *identifying techniques* that seem to relate to only one operating system. Meanwhile, the overall structure and the majority of tactics and techniques can apply to any platform. The ATT&CK Matrix for Enterprise accommodates all OSs, but MITRE does have matrices specific to Windows, Linux, macOS, and mobile systems.

Let's take a quick look at the top-level tactics from the ATT&CK framework. Later, with other frameworks, you can compare and contrast the length and flow. The tactics from the MITRE ATT&CK Matrix for Enterprise include the following:

- Reconnaissance
- Resource development
- Initial access
- Execution
- Persistence
- Privilege escalation
- Defense evasion
- Credential access
- Discovery
- Lateral movement
- Collection

- Command and control
- Exfiltration
- Impact

 If you're not yet familiar with an ATT&CK matrix, it is highly recommended that you explore the structure and layout in some detail. A great resource is attack.mitre.org. It provides a high-level look at the overall layout. You can examine how it flows progressively through the steps of an attack. And you can browse each of the tactics to see the various techniques an attacker uses so that you fully appreciate how an attacker mindset gets documented into a linear flow.

ATT&CK for Industrial Control Systems

There is an ATT&CK matrix tailored for industrial control systems (ICSs). Recall that ICS refers to operational technology systems that monitor and control industrial operations, such as wastewater and other utilities, manufacturing, and so on. This also applies to supervisory control and data acquisition (SCADA) systems.

There is something important to understand here about ATT&CK for ICS. The ICS matrix does not seek to replace the more generic "IT" version of ATT&CK. Obviously, industry control systems also include the enterprise IT, so a replacement would just result in 90 percent duplication. The ATT&CK for ICS spotlights the attack techniques and tactics particular to the industry control components.

The MITRE ATT&CK for ICS tactics include the following:

- Collection
- Command and control
- Discovery
- Evasion
- Execution
- Impact
- Impair process control
- Inhibit response function
- Initial access
- Lateral movement
- Persistence

There is some overlap but even at the highest level you notice the shifted focus. Dig into the techniques, and you'll see how ATT&CK for ICS is quite different from IT systems. A good resource for exploring this is collaborate.mitre.org/attackics/index.php/Main_Page.

Cyber Kill Chain

The Cyber Kill Chain is similar to MITRE's ATT&CK framework, since both describe how an attacker goes about compromising a system or network. A noticeable difference is that the *Cyber Kill Chain* is shorter and more concise. Another difference is the ATT&CK framework is fixed in terms of naming those top-level tactics. The Cyber Kill Chain can be found in a few different iterations. Lockheed Martin started it, evolving it from a military model. Now Gartner has its version, which is not too different but Gartner claims it as its own. For the CASP+ exam, it's best if you remember the terms of the Lockheed Martin model. The Cyber Kill Chain tactics follow these steps:

1. Reconnaissance
2. Weaponization
3. Delivery
4. Exploitation
5. Installation
6. Command & control (C2)
7. Actions on objectives

To learn more about the Cyber Kill Chain, see `lockheedmartin.com/en-us/capabilities/cyber/cyber-kill-chain.html`.

Diamond Model of Intrusion Analysis

An altogether different concept is the Diamond Model of Intrusion Analysis, which is presented as a simple diamond shape. Each corner of the diamond is labeled like this:

- Left corner: Infrastructure
- Top corner: Adversary
- Right corner: Capability
- Bottom corner: Victim

Far from the linear progression of steps of the other two models, the *Diamond Model of Intrusion Analysis* aims to help threat intelligence analysts organize large amounts of data. Every incident connects these labels to insight and knowledge as well as exposes knowledge gaps. Using this model, an intelligence analyst can show with precision how an adversary uses their capability within an infrastructure against the victim.

The CASP+ exam does not require that you have experience using the model, or even know how to work with it. However, it's a good idea to know at least how to label it. I suggest you watch a 10-minute YouTube video called *Diamond Model of Intrusion Analysis: An Overview* (`youtube.com/watch?v=3PoQLOJr5WI`).

Indicators of Compromise

Indicators of compromise (IoCs) are evidence that a security incident occurred and more investigation is needed to reveal the consequences. IoCs can be subtle or blatantly obvious. Using a house as an analogy, an IoC might be as subtle as fingerprints on the window or as obvious as broken glass on the floor. In the security space, IoCs can come from a variety of sources. They range from log entries, alerts and notifications, or detecting activity or traffic that seems out of the ordinary. In any event, IoCs can become foreshadowing for the incident response team.

Reading the Logs

Logs are the greatest source of IoCs. As great as logs are, they are a double-edged sword. The more you log, the more detailed information you're gathering, at your disposal, ready for your review. And the more you log, the more there is to review. Logs provide evidence that will prove useful in any forensic audit after a security breach. Some compliance requirements will state how long logs must be kept.

Intelligent log management goes a long way toward watching for indicators of compromise. Let's review the types of logs proving to be a good source for IoCs.

Network Logs   Network devices are the eyes and ears of the network. Network switches and routers can monitor for abnormal traffic, odd levels of traffic, unusual sources or destinations, triggered rules, and signatures. Use this capability to watch the perimeter as well as interior networks. When the time comes to investigate indicators of compromise, your *network logs* can provide breadcrumbs to follow.

Vulnerability Logs   Identifying and assessing vulnerabilities is a key part of risk management. After scanning a system for vulnerabilities, keep those logs as your baseline. Those *vulnerability logs* are a valuable resource when trying to understand or validate an indicator of compromise.

Operating System Logs   OS logs are your one-stop shop to tons of information related to the host system, the server's interfaces, OS errors, and failures. As with other logs, you get out of *operating system logs* only as much as you allow the operating system to record.

Windows Event Viewer Application, Security, and System logs can be critical in a forensic investigation. Windows Event logs are stored locally in `%SystemRoot%\System32\Winevt\Logs\`.

Most Linux log files are stored in a plain ASCII text file and are in the `/var/log` directory and subdirectory. Logs are generated by the Linux system daemon log, syslogd, or rsyslogd.

Access Logs   Want to know who signed in to what, when, and from where? *Access logs* can answer all those questions. Depending on whether sufficient logging is done, an access log can either confirm suspicions or instill doubt.

NetFlow Logs   In case you're not familiar with network monitoring protocol NetFlow, Cisco created it to assist in collecting statistics on IP traffic as it traverses the network. There are a variety of commercial tools to gather and make pretty graphs from what NetFlow monitors. Those *NetFlow logs* might be a gold mine to you when reviewed in conjunction with network device logs.

NetFlow collects packets via a router interface. They are then provided to a NetFlow collector. A NetFlow application can then analyze the data, which is useful for incident investigations for intrusion analysis. An alternative to NetFlow is sFlow (sampled flow), which is also used for network monitoring. sFlow samples packets and provides analysis to identify unauthorized network activity and investigate DDoS attacks.

Intrusion Detection and Prevention

Intrusion detection has come a long way since the concept was created in the 1980s. Early intrusion detection and prevention systems (IDPSs) were clearly divided into two broad types: network intrusion detection systems (NIDSs) and host-based intrusion detection systems (HIDSs). These can be further divided into categories based on the internal engine or approach to detecting anomalies and *unusual process activity*. They typically include the following:

- *Signature*: Seeks to match based on known *signature rules*

- *Anomaly*: Examines traffic and looks for activity that is abnormal, based on *behavior rules*

- *Protocol*: Examines data and compares it to a database of known protocols and their activity

The IT security industry has grown to require more from these devices. This is how intrusion prevention systems (IPSs) were born. The IPS was designed to move beyond IDSs and provide the capability to enforce computer security policies, acceptable use policies, or standard security practices. Today, this technology has continued to evolve into what is known as *intrusion detection and prevention (IDP)*. IDPs can record information related to observed events, generate *notifications*, generate *IDS/IPS alerts*, and create reports. Many IDPs can also respond to a detected threat by attempting to prevent it from succeeding. They use several response techniques, which involve the IDPs stopping the attack itself, changing the security environment through alteration of a firewall setting, or changing the attack's content.

Many IDPs exist, and some are community based and therefore free. Snort is one of the most popular and has been around for several years now. A more recent addition to the community is Suricata. It is offered by the Open Information Security Foundation

(OISF) with funding from the U.S. Department of Homeland Security (DHS) and the U.S. Navy's Space and Warfare Command (SPAWAR) as well as the Open Information Security Foundation (OISF) Consortium. More information about Suricata is available at suricata-ids.org.

Threat intelligence sources may also provide IoCs. These are the telltale signs that an attack has taken place and may include file signatures, log patterns, and other evidence left behind by attackers. IoC may also be found in file and code repositories that offer threat intelligence information.

Exercise 3.1 will demonstrate how to perform a basic *packet capture* with WinDump and how this technology can be used to monitor and detect anomalies as well as look for indicators of compromise.

EXERCISE 3.1

Using WinDump to Sniff Traffic

One easy way to sniff traffic is with WinDump.

1. Download and install WinDump to a Windows computer from www.winpcap.org/windump.

2. Open WinDump from the Administrative Command Prompt.

3. Open a second command prompt and ping 4.2.2.2.

4. Press Ctrl+C to stop WinDump, and scroll up to review the captured packets.

A good source of additional information on IDP is NIST 800-94, a guideline to intrusion detection and prevention systems. It can be found at csrc.nist.gov/publications/detail/sp/800-94/final.

Notifications and Responses to IoCs

When we first recognize an indicator of compromise and our minds ask 100 questions at once, the panicked reaction is to respond. We want to respond immediately. The superior approach is to avoid panic and dig deeper for more information to make a more informed response. Tools that are monitoring and digesting information from our network can alert us when human hands are needed.

FIM Alerts   Would you know if the master price list was changed? Imagine the scenario where the master price list is updated every Monday morning. However, on Thursday, your service responsible for file integrity monitoring alerts you that a change was made by someone not in the appropriate department.

File integrity monitoring (FIM) will monitor for changes in the file. *FIM alerts* can tell you practically in real time, permitting you to immediately investigate. This wouldn't include end-user files, which we can safely expect to change constantly.

Antivirus Alerts   On end devices, commonly on an end-user workstation or production server, the antivirus software is working quietly in the background. However, when it does float an antivirus alert to the workstation user, it is an immediate indicator of compromise warranting further research.

IPS/IDS Rules and Alerts   Alerts from intrusion detection systems and intrusion prevention systems prove a significant indicator of suspect activity on the network. IDS or IPS alerts come when activity might get triggered when the activity matches the signature.

Depending how the organization manages alerts, the notification may feed into a security information and event management (SIEM) system. *SIEM alerts* provide security analysts a more centralized view compared to receiving alerts directly from individual systems.

Scripts/Regular Expressions   In earlier years, intrusion detection and antivirus systems had a processing technique using *regular expressions* (regex) and *scripts* to identify a match between a known signature and what was seen on the wire. Regex or regular expression matching was the default approach, but regex matching does take considerable overhead in memory. With the speed and volume of traffic today, regex matching is not quite fast enough, and other methods have met the need.

DLP Rules and Alerts   Detecting and blocking data exfiltration requires the use of security event management solutions that can closely monitor outbound data transmissions. *Data loss prevention (DLP)* requires the analysis of egress network traffic for anomalies and the use of better outbound firewall controls that perform *deep packet inspection.* Deep packet inspection normally occurs by a device at a network boundary, for example by a web application firewall at the trusted network's perimeter. To select where such a device should be placed in any organization, it's important to have a data flow diagram, depicting where and how data flows throughout the network. On this device, DLP rules establish what and how data flows will trigger *DLP alerts.* A DLP alert warns the security analyst or administrator of the likelihood of data being exfiltrated out of the network.

More notification types and rules to trigger are discussed in the following section through other situations. However, here we can already understand how valuable an alert or notification is to kick off our training in reviewing IoCs and possibly moving onto incident response.

Response

Firewalls can be hardware, software, or a combination of both. They are usually located at the demarcation line between trusted and untrusted network elements. Firewalls play a critical role in the separation of important assets. Figure 3.2 shows an example of the placement of a typical firewall.

FIGURE 3.2   Firewall placement and design

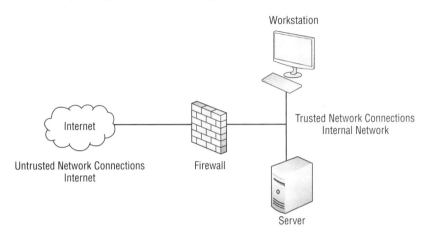

Firewall rules determine what type of traffic is inspected, what is allowed to pass, and what is blocked. The most basic way to configure firewall rules is by means of an *access control list (ACL)*. An ACL is used for packet filtering and for selecting the types of traffic to be analyzed, forwarded, or influenced in some way by the firewall or device. ACLs are a basic example of *data flow enforcement*. Simple firewalls, and more specifically ACL configuration, may block traffic based on the source and destination address. However, more advanced configurations may deny traffic based on interface, port, protocol, thresholds, and various other criteria. Before implementing ACLs, be sure to perform secure configuration and baselining of networking and security components. Rules placed in an ACL can be used for more than just allowing or blocking traffic. For example, rules may also log activity for later inspection or to record an alarm. Table 3.1 shows an example rule set.

TABLE 3.1   Basic rule set

Rule number	Action	Protocol	Port	Direction	Comment
Rule 20	Allow	DNS	53 UDP	Outbound	None
Rule 50	Allow	HTTP, HTTPS	80, 443	Outbound	None
Rule 100	Allow	SMTP	25	Inbound	To mail server
Rule 101	Allow	SMTP	25	Outbound	From mail server
Rule 255	Deny	ALL	—	Bidirectional	None

ACLs work from the top down, and by default there is an implicit deny all clause at the end of every ACL. Anything that is not explicitly permitted is denied. It is important to note that this implicit deny is there even if it is not present when you're viewing the ACL.

For the CASP+ exam, you will need to have a basic understanding of ACLs and their format. The command syntax format of a standard ACL in a Cisco IOS environment is as follows:

```
access-list access-list-number {permit|deny}
{host|source source-wildcard|any}
```

There are also extended ACLs. These rules have the ability to look more closely at the traffic and inspect for more items, such as the following:

- Protocol
- Port numbers
- Differentiated services code point (DSCP) value
- Precedence value
- State of the synchronize sequence number (SYN) bit

The command syntax formats of extended IP, ICMP, TCP, and UDP ACLs are shown here:

IP traffic
```
access-list access-list-number
 [dynamic dynamic-name [timeout minutes]]
 {deny|permit} protocol source source-wildcard
 destination destination-wildcard [precedence precedence]
 [tos tos] [log|log-input] [time-range time-range-name]
```

ICMP traffic
```
access-list access-list-number
 [dynamic dynamic-name [timeout minutes]]
 { deny|permit } icmp source source-wildcard
 destination destination-wildcard
 [icmp-type [icmp-code] |icmp-message]
 [precedence precedence] [tos tos] [log|log-input]
 [time-range time-range-name]
```

TCP traffic
```
access-list access-list-number
 [dynamic dynamic-name [timeout minutes]]
 { deny|permit } tcp source source-wildcard [operator [port]]
 destination destination-wildcard [operator [port]]
 [established] [precedence precedence] [tos tos]
 [log|log-input] [time-range time-range-name]
```

UDP traffic

```
access-list access-list-number
 [dynamic dynamic-name [timeout minutes]]
 { deny|permit } udp source source-wildcard [operator [port]]
 destination destination-wildcard [operator [port]]
 [precedence precedence] [tos tos] [log|log-input]
 [time-range time-range-name]
```

Let's review how basic rules work. Figure 3.3 shows a basic network configuration with two segments of the network separated by a router and a common connection to the Internet.

FIGURE 3.3   Basic network with firewall

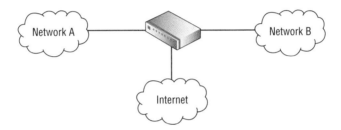

In our first example, assume that the decision has been made to block all Telnet traffic. Telnet sends information via clear text, and it is not considered a secure protocol.

```
hostname R1
!
interface ethernet0
ip access-group 102 in
!
access-list 102 deny tcp any any eq 23
access-list 102 permit ip any any
```

In this configuration, all TCP traffic bound for port 23 is blocked by the firewall. All other traffic is permitted.

For this example, Telnet to ports other than TCP/23 would still be allowed. If you want to block Telnet to any TCP port, you need other controls. It is also good to know that standard ACLs are often used to restrict Telnet, or ideally SSH access to a device such as a router, by limiting that access to specific IP addresses. Extended ACLs are used for many more tasks. Also note that the previous example is for demonstration purposes only. As stated earlier, it is generally considered best practice to permit only that which is required and deny everything else, following the principle of least privilege.

> If it has been a while since you have configured or analyzed ACLs, you may want to consider downloading one of the many router simulators that are available. These are great practice tools, and they may be helpful if you're asked an ACL question on the exam. Although the examples provided here are very straightforward, those on the exam may not be. Incidentally, access control is definitely a topic that every CASP+ should master.

Exercise 3.2 shows you how to review a basic ACL.

EXERCISE 3.2

Reviewing and Assessing ACLs

You have been asked to examine an ACL that was developed to allow permissible traffic that is part of a valid session to communicate with either a Telnet or a web server. Upon reviewing the ACL, can you spot any problems with the newly created extended IP access list 101?

```
permit tcp host 4.2.2.2 eq telnet host 192.168.123.1 eq 11006
 deny tcp any host WebServer eq https
 deny ip any any
```

Can you identify any problems with this configuration? Notice that the second line should be an `allow` and not a deny. As written, the `deny` statement would block HTTPS traffic and not allow it.

Here is another ACL whose functionality you've been asked to comment on:

```
interface ethernet0
 deny ip any any
 deny tcp 10.10.10.128 0.0.0.63 any eq smtp
 deny tcp any eq 23 int ethernet 0
 permit tcp any any
 access-group 110 out
```

Can you see any issues with this ACL? The primary problem here is that the deny `ip any any` line will prevent the additional lines below it from processing, so the `permit tcp any any` line is irrelevant in this case. Remove the initial deny statement, and the ACL will function as expected. Once the ACL reaches a matching rule, such as deny `all IP`, the two entries below it will not be acted upon.

Host-based firewalls are devices that run directly on a network host or device. A host-based firewall is deployed for the purpose of protecting the device on which it's installed from an attack. A host-based firewall usually has predefined rules to protect the host against specific attack patterns.

Some host-based firewalls can also prevent malicious software from attacking other devices on a network. Adding a host-based firewall builds on the concept of defense in depth.

Host-based firewalls work by inspecting and controlling inbound and outbound traffic from the host on which the firewall is placed. Although there are many kinds of firewalls, only a host-based firewall is designed to reside on the end host and to protect it from an attack. Like all firewalls, a host-based firewall works by inspecting traffic as it passes through the interface. It works in much the same way as do border guards and customs agents. The host layer adds to other devices on the network and perimeter.

As people and products pass over the border of one country and go to another, they are inspected. All firewalls work by using predefined rule sets. Higher-level and application-layer firewalls can make determinations on traffic based on behavior as well. Firewalls and other network inspection devices add to defense in depth by adding another layer of control.

Summary

Threat management is a full-time job. Managing threats requires resources such as time, money, and intelligence. It requires a firm grasp of the actors involved, including their sophistication and techniques. And threat management should involve actively hunting and proactively mitigating against those threats.

Luckily, there are resources for the good guys, such as intelligence feeds, tools, and frameworks to help you. The CASP+ exam candidate should understand the properties and methods of various threat actors. Candidates should recognize the frameworks available and the concepts within. Lastly, the CASP+ candidate must be able to recognize indicators of compromise, know where to find more, and appreciate how to respond with the appropriate tools and rules.

Exam Essentials

Know the various ways someone can gather information.   Getting open-source information from online and offline resources makes for a massive list of sources. Understand where to look for the type of information you want. Understand how HUMINT differs from OSINT.

Be able to name specific indicators of compromise.   Understand what an indicator of compromise is. Know where to search for more information and the significance of what you find.

Know what kinds of actors threaten you.   Bad actor types come with all manner of financial backing, skills, and available resources.

Know how and when to apply ACLs.   Access control lists are a valuable commodity when it comes to network access control. Learn how to read, write, and understand them.

Review Questions

You can find the answers in Appendix.

1. What term describes the search for an insider threat or shadow IT, which, until discovered, had been "flying under the radar?"

   A. Threat hunting

   B. Threat emulation

   C. Intelligence

   D. Targeted attacks

2. LoJax, Bad Rabbit, and NotPetya are three examples of what?

   A. Zero-day threats

   B. Malware

   C. APTs

   D. Competitors

3. You discover log entries that raise suspicion that a security incident might have occurred. You decide more investigation is needed. What describes what you found?

   A. Vulnerabilities

   B. ACLs

   C. Threat intelligence types

   D. Indicators of compromise

4. What is a key strength the disgruntled employee has over an outsider?

   A. Trust

   B. Time

   C. Money

   D. Signature

5. Your manager asks if you've noticed any abnormal volumes of network traffic or other network issues. What logs might help you answer those concerns?

   A. FIM logs

   B. NetFlow logs

   C. Firewall logs

   D. Access logs

6. Which of the following alerts warns the security analyst or administrator of the likelihood that data was exfiltrated out of the network?

   A. IoC

   B. FIM

   C. DLP

   D. ICE

7. What intrusion detection processing technique is common for identifying a positive match but struggles to keep up with today's traffic speeds and volumes?

    A. SIEM

    B. Regular expressions

    C. Signature-based

    D. Anomaly or behavior

8. Which of the following can block traffic based on the source and destination address?

    A. The Deep Web

    B. Script kiddie

    C. ICS

    D. ACL

9. In the following example of an access control list, which of the following answers is true?

```
hostname R1
!
Interface ethernet0
Ip access-group 102 in
!
access-list 102 deny tcp any any eq 23
access-list 102 permit ip any any
```

    A. TCP traffic bound for port 102 is permitted.

    B. TCP traffic bound for port 23 is blocked.

    C. TCP traffic bound for port 102 is blocked.

    D. TCP traffic bound for port 23 is permitted.

10. You got an alert that unusual changes were made to files in a customer directory. What type of alert was this?

    A. DLP

    B. IDS

    C. FIM

    D. IPS

11. Which of the following is not a label for the conceptual Diamond Model of Intrusion Analysis?

    A. Capability

    B. Attacks

    C. Victim

    D. Infrastructure

12. For the purpose of better understanding a company, an employee is tasked with browsing social media, listening to recorded speeches, and reading patents. What type of intelligence gathering is this employee performing?

- **A.** HUMINT
- **B.** APT
- **C.** OSINT
- **D.** ATT&CK

13. A determined security analyst discovered some evidence on a system that warranted more investigation. Ultimately, the analyst identified that advanced malware was resident and difficult to remove. The security analyst recommended the system be rebuilt from scratch. What is it the analyst had discovered?

- **A.** IoC
- **B.** ACL
- **C.** DLP
- **D.** APT

14. What intelligence collection method is described as the personal side of spying or collecting intelligence?

- **A.** Lessons learned report
- **B.** Deep Web
- **C.** HUMINT
- **D.** OSINT

15. If you needed to find out an organization's technical contact or registration information about their domain, what OSINT resource might be helpful?

- **A.** DNS records
- **B.** Deep Web
- **C.** TRA
- **D.** WHOIS

16. Whether following the Cyber Kill Chain or the ATT&CK framework, which of the following tactics would occur first?

- **A.** Reconnaissance
- **B.** Command and control
- **C.** Exfiltration
- **D.** Discovery

17. In the ATT&CK framework, which of the following tactics occurs last?

- **A.** Initial access
- **B.** Persistence
- **C.** Discovery
- **D.** Defense evasion

18. For the purpose of gaining access to a competitor's property, you are tasked with befriending the competitor's employees, using social media, conversations, and empathy to build personal trust. What type of intelligence gathering are you performing?

A. HUMINT

B. APT

C. OSINT

D. ATT&CK

19. Which dangerous category of bad actors describes those seeking to compromise critical infrastructures such as nuclear power plants, power generation stations, and water treatment plants?

A. Script kiddie

B. Organized crime

C. Insider threat

D. Nation-state

20. A few months after the legal firm Dewey, Cheatem, and Howe outsourced their accounts receivable department, the law firm suffered from hacked bank accounts. They are growing suspicious of an attack. Which of the following terms describes what likely happened?

A. Denial-of-service attack

B. SYN flood attack

C. Disgruntled employee

D. Supply chain attack

Chapter

4

Security Ops: Vulnerability Assessments and Operational Risk

THE FOLLOWING COMPTIA CASP+ EXAM OBJECTIVES ARE COVERED IN THIS CHAPTER:

✓ **2.3 Given a scenario, perform vulnerability management activities.**

- **Vulnerability scans**

    - Credentialed vs. non-credentialed

    - Agent-based/server-based

    - Criticality ranking

    - Active vs. passive

- **Security Content Automation Protocol (SCAP)**

    - Extensible Configuration Checklist Description Format (XCCDF)

    - Open Vulnerability and Assessment Language (OVAL)

    - Common Platform Enumeration (CPE)

    - Common Vulnerabilities and Exposures (CVE)

    - Common Vulnerability Scoring System (CVSS)

    - Common Configuration Enumeration (CCE)

    - Asset Reporting Format (ARF)

- **Self-assessment vs. third-party vendor assessment**

- **Patch management**

- **Information sources**

    - Advisories

    - Bulletins

- Vendor websites
- Information Sharing and Analysis Centers (ISACs)
- News reports

✓ **2.4 Given a scenario, use the appropriate vulnerability assessment and penetration testing methods and tools.**

- **Methods**
  - Static analysis
  - Dynamic analysis
  - Side-channel analysis
  - Reverse engineering
    - Software
    - Hardware
  - Wireless vulnerability scan
  - Software composition analysis
  - Fuzz testing
  - Pivoting
  - Post-exploitation
  - Persistence
- **Tools**
  - SCAP scanner
  - Network traffic analyzer
  - Vulnerability scanner
  - Protocol analyzer
  - Port scanner
  - HTTP interceptor
  - Exploit framework
  - Password cracker
- **Dependency management**
- **Requirements**

- Scope of work
- Rules of engagement
- Invasive vs. non-invasive
- Asset inventory
- Permissions and access
- Corporate policy considerations
- Facility considerations
- Physical security considerations
- Rescan for corrections/changes

✓ **2.5 Given a scenario, analyze vulnerabilities and recommend risk mitigations.**

- **Vulnerabilities**
    - Race conditions
    - Overflows
        - Buffer
        - Integer
    - Broken authentication
    - Unsecure references
    - Poor exception handling
    - Security misconfiguration
    - Improper headers
    - Information disclosure
    - Certificate errors
    - Weak cryptography implementations
    - Weak ciphers
    - Weak cipher suite implementations
    - Software composition analysis
    - Use of vulnerable frameworks and software modules
    - Use of unsafe functions

- Third-party libraries
  - Dependencies
  - Code injections/malicious changes
  - End of support/end of life
  - Regression issues
- **Inherently vulnerable system/application**
  - Client-side processing vs. server-side processing
  - JSON/representational state transfer (REST)
  - Browser extensions
    - Flash
    - ActiveX
  - Hypertext Markup Language 5 (HTML5)
  - Asynchronous JavaScript and XML (AJAX)
  - Simple Object Access Protocol (SOAP)
  - Machine code vs. bytecode or interpreted vs. emulated
- **Attacks**
  - Directory traversal
  - Cross-site scripting (XSS)
  - Cross-site request forgery (CSRF)
  - Injection
    - XML
    - LDAP
    - Structured Query Language (SQL)
    - Command
    - Process
  - Sandbox escape
  - Virtual machine (VM) hopping
  - VM escape
  - Border Gateway Protocol (BGP)/route hijacking

- Interception attacks
- Denial-of-service (DoS)/DDoS
- Authentication bypass
- Social engineering
- VLAN hopping

✓ **2.6 Given a scenario, use processes to reduce risk.**

- **Proactive and detection**
  - Hunts
  - Developing countermeasures
  - Deceptive technologies
    - Honeynet
    - Honeypot
    - Decoy files
    - Simulators
    - Dynamic network configurations
- **Security data analytics**
  - Processing pipelines
    - Data
    - Stream
  - Indexing and search
  - Log collection and curation
  - Database activity monitoring
- **Preventive**
  - Antivirus
  - Immutable systems
  - Hardening
  - Sandbox detonation
- **Application control**
  - License technologies
  - Allow list vs. block list

- Time of check vs. time of use
- Atomic execution
- **Security automation**
  - Cron/scheduled tasks
  - Bash
  - PowerShell
  - Python
- **Physical security**
  - Review of lighting
  - Review of visitor logs
  - Camera reviews
  - Open spaces vs. confined spaces

This chapter discusses vulnerability management and operational risk. As a CASP+, you should be able to manage vulnerabilities, identify business and industry information sources, and explain associated security risks.

The Center for Internet Security (CIS) is a community-driven nonprofit globally recognized for their controls and guidelines that proactively safeguard an enterprise. The critical security controls documentation lists continuous vulnerability management as a high priority. You must have an asset inventory list, know what software you have on those assets, know who has access, and understand the inherent vulnerabilities and risk that result from that combination (www.cisecurity.org).

Technical and nontechnical risk is all around you. Everywhere you turn, there are risks; they begin the minute you first turn on a computer and grow exponentially the moment the network card becomes active. A security professional is always asking hypothetical questions such as "Who do you let in the facility? Are visitors escorted? Do you allow employees to plug personal devices such as smartphones into company-issued computers and laptops?" There is potential for vulnerabilities and threats in every physical and digital choice you make. This chapter discusses these items and includes what CompTIA expects you to know for the exam related to vulnerability management, operational risk, and where to find the latest information to stay up to date.

Terminology

Before discussing vulnerabilities and risk management, it is important to make sure that some basic terms are defined. You may be challenged to identify the risk, threat, and vulnerability in a specific situation. All industries share basic terms and semantics. IT security is no different, and within the topic of risk, there are some terms that you will see again and again. Let's define them here:

Asset   An *asset* is an item of value to an institution, such as data, hardware, software, or physical property. An asset is an item or collection of items that has a quantitative or qualitative value to a company. Some organizations consider employees assets.

Risk   *Risk* is the probability or likelihood of the occurrence or realization of a threat.

Vulnerability   A *vulnerability* can be described as a weakness in hardware, software, or a component that may be exploited in order for a threat to destroy, damage, or compromise an asset.

Threat   A *threat* is any agent, condition, or circumstance that could cause harm, loss, damage, or compromise to an IT asset or data asset. The likelihood of the threat is the probability of occurrence or the odds that the event will actually occur.

Motivation   *Motivation* is the driving force behind the activity. For example, attackers can be motivated by many different reasons. Some common reasons include prestige, money, fame, and challenge.

Risk Source   The *source* of a risk can be internal or external. Internal risk can be anything from a disgruntled employee to a failed hard drive. External risk includes natural disasters such as floods and human-made events such as strikes and protests. As an example, the risk source might be that the lock on a server cabinet is broken, whereas the threat is that someone can now steal the server hard drive.

From the standpoint of IT security, a *threat* is any situation that affects the confidentiality, integrity, or availability of an IT asset (data, system, software, or hardware). Here are some common examples of threats:

Natural Disaster   *Natural disasters* are events over which we have no control, such as bad weather (hurricanes, snowstorms, tornadoes), fires, floods, earthquakes, and tsunamis.

Malicious Code   *Malicious code* includes all forms of damaging programs, such as viruses, worms, Trojans, keyloggers, and so forth. This software is distinguishable in that it is developed to damage, alter, expose, or destroy a system or data. For example, viruses are executable programs that replicate and attach to and infect other executable objects. Some viruses also perform destructive or discreet activities (payload) after replication and infection is accomplished.

Breach of Physical Security   A *breach of physical security* can be instigated by a trusted insider or an untrusted outsider. Intruders, vandals, and thieves remove sensitive information, destroy data, or physically damage or remove hardware such as hard drives and laptops.

Hacker Attack   *Hacker attacks* generally result in stolen, lost, damaged, or modified data. Loss or damage to an organization's data can be a critical threat if there are no backups or external archiving of the data as part of the organization's data recovery and business continuity plan. Also, if the compromised data is of a confidential nature, this can also be a critical threat to the organization, depending on the potential damage that can arise from this compromise.

Vulnerability Management

A *vulnerability* is a weakness in a system design, in the implementation of an operational procedure, or in how software or code was developed (for example, coding errors, backdoors not removed in production, or vulnerabilities in code). Vulnerabilities may be eliminated or reduced by the correct implementation of safeguards and compensating countermeasures.

You must know your environment better than an attacker and use that attacker's mindset in key controls to develop your security program. Enterprise organizations have many options in the tools used to troubleshoot networks, identify assets, and regularly assess for vulnerabilities. It is a cyclic endeavor, as shown in Figure 4.1.

FIGURE 4.1   The vulnerability management life cycle

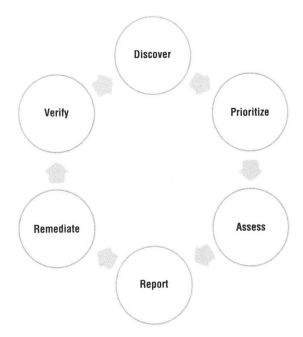

Vulnerability time is the time between when the vulnerability is discovered and when it is patched. The vulnerability window is when an IT asset is most vulnerable. This window has become increasing important because it can be much larger than it was in the past. The cycle of creating malware based on known vulnerabilities keeps getting shorter.

Some organizations outsource vulnerability management tasks or use vulnerability management as a service (VMaaS). When you have reduced dependencies on internal resources, you can better prioritize the human resources to other areas of security. The outsourced third party should be able to provide actionable intelligence and increased visibility, and provide a proactive approach to patching and remediation. It can also be a great way to assist in complying with regulations, such as SOX, that require vulnerability scanning for financial organization.

You cannot protect what you don't know you have. In the discovery phase of this cycle, you will determine what assets are on your network communicating to other devices. There are many ways to configure scanning tools. For example, a scanning tool can send a packet to a TCP port and wait for the SYN-ACK response, or it can send a UDP packet and wait for the reset response if the port is closed. Once the scanning tool knows the asset is alive on the network, you can configure the scan to then try to discover the operating system of that endpoint by using credentials.

Credentialed/uncredentialed scans are often called authorized/unauthorized scans. An *uncredentialed scan* typically uses ICMP and pings an asset from the outside to see if it responds. It is a great way to understand what your network looks like to an outsider who is scanning your environment to look for a way in.

A *credentialed scan* is more intense, uses more resources, and gives you critical insight into an asset, specifically vulnerabilities you may need to mitigate. We use service account credentials during a scan to sign in to an asset. With authorization, we are able to look deeper into the asset from the inside. A credentialed scan can give you information such as patch level of operating system and what software and software version is loaded on a machine and how it is configured. It takes exponentially longer to run an in-depth credentialed scan. Specific operating systems and network service applications leave different types of data in their TCP, UDP, and ICMP packets. This data is analyzed to give you an OS fingerprint.

OS fingerprinting is used by defenders to determine which vulnerabilities might be present and prioritize when and how to mitigate them. It is used by attackers to find vulnerabilities and try to exploit them. Fingerprinting can be active or passive. An *active vulnerability scan* determines a target OS by sending packets to the system and examining the response. Most active fingerprinting is done with variations of the tool Nmap, which can be downloaded at nmap.org.

Active vulnerability scan and passive vulnerability scan are specific Objective 2.3 terms on the CASP+ exam. You may hear others in the industry call this active and passive fingerprinting or footprinting.

Passive vulnerability scanning is a better way of avoiding detection from IDSs, IPSs, or firewalls. Passive fingerprinting uses a collected sample of packets from a host called a *packet capture* or a .pcap file. Passive scanning makes a guess about a target operating system and is less accurate than an active fingerprint. Passive scanning is mitigated by making sure that network interface cards (NICs) are not operating in promiscuous mode. The true advantage of passive vulnerability scanning is that it allows you to look for vulnerabilities without interfering with host systems. It also allows you to perform continuous scanning. One of the issues with active vulnerability scanning is that some testing routines can cause host systems to hang or crash. A popular tool to use for passive fingerprinting is Ettercap. Ettercap is a suite of tools used for host analysis, sniffing live connections, and content filtering, and can be found at ettercap-project.org.

A popular tool that is used to create a .pcap file is Wireshark. Wireshark is a tool that every network or security administrator should know. It is an open-source tool used for capturing network traffic and analyzing packets at an extremely granular level. Packet capturing can tell you about transmit time, source, destination, and protocol type. This can be critical information for evaluating events that are happening or troubleshooting devices across your network. It can also help a security analyst determine whether network traffic is a malicious attack, what type of attack, the IP addresses that were targeted, and where the attack originated. As a result, you will be able to create rules on a firewall to block the IP addresses where the malicious traffic originated.

When you don't have time to wait for a credentialed scan launched directly from the server hosting the scanning software timed to run on a schedule, but you need to analyze the same information from an asset in real time, an alternative to *server-based* scanning is using *agent-based scanning*. With agent-based scanning, a small piece of software is installed on the endpoint and is programmed to check in at certain timed intervals, from every 30 minutes to every 24 hours.

> *Server-based* and *agent-based vulnerability scan* are CASP+ objective terms.

When you use an agent on a host, credentialed scans are not necessary. One benefit of agent-based scanning is that the risk of service account credentials being exposed and used maliciously for lateral movement and privilege escalation is minimized. An agent will automatically collect data from the endpoint and share updated information. Another benefit of using agent-based scanning is that, with more of the workforce working from home, this type of methodology gives remote employees who rarely join the corporate network the ability to have their assets evaluated for vulnerabilities.

Once you're able to map out the assets, hosts, nodes, and intermediary devices on your network, then you're able to move to the next step of vulnerability management, which is prioritization.

Not all devices are created equal. A *domain* is a group of computers and other devices on a network that are accessed and administered with a common set of rules. A Windows domain controller (DC) is a Microsoft server that responds to login authentication requests within a network. In an enterprise environment, if a DC fails, your help desk will explode with calls because of the inability of users to log into the domain. However, if you have a marketing department with a small file server that it backs up to once a month and this machine fails, then it might warrant a phone call or two. After you know what machines exist on your network, you must prioritize which assets are mission critical.

Once you have identified which assets have a heartbeat and you know which assets would cause chaos through failure or compromise, the next step is to determine the assets' vulnerabilities. This is usually accomplished by analyzing the operating system, ports that are open, services running on those ports, and the versions of applications you have installed on those assets.

Now you're ready to build a report. Some reports will bubble up to upper management and require information such as trending analysis and vulnerability remediation plans. The decisions that upper management make based on these reports could be budgetary or based on head count. The more technical reports usually trickle down to the asset owner and contain what needs to be fixed on that device.

With the report in hand, you now have a list of vulnerabilities in your environment and on what devices they reside. Some software with advanced capabilities can generate instructions on how to remediate those vulnerabilities. Most of these technical reports will give you a qualitative severity rating for vulnerabilities based on the *Common Vulnerability Scoring System (CVSS)*. The National Institute of Standards and Technology (NIST) maintains the National Vulnerability Database (NVD). In this database, located at nvd.nist.gov, you can see a historical quantitative analysis of every reported vulnerability based on scope, access vector, complexity, and authentication, as well as the impact on confidentiality, integrity, and availability. Basically, this means every vulnerability will have a criticality ranking of 0 to 10, with 0 being tolerable and 10 being critical, as shown in Figure 4.2.

FIGURE 4.2   Qualitative severity rating scale of CVSS 3.1

RATING	CVSS SCORE
NONE	0.0
LOW	0.1 – 3.9
MEDIUM	4.0 – 6.9
HIGH	7.0 – 8.9
CRITICAL	9.0 – 10.0

Two catalogs of known vulnerabilities that you must know are the Common Vulnerabilities and Exposures (CVE), which is a list of publicly known vulnerabilities containing an ID number, description, and reference, and Common Vulnerability Scoring System (CVSS), which provides a score from 0 to 10 that indicates the criticality ranking of all known vulnerabilities.

When dealing with risk, software is one area with which the security professional must be very concerned. Vulnerabilities in various kinds of software are commonplace, as shown in the following examples:

Firmware   *Firmware* is software that is usually stored in ROM and loaded during system power-up. As firmware is embedded, it can be used to hide malicious code such as firmware rootkits.

Operating System   Operating system software is loaded on workstations, servers, laptops, tablets, and smartphones. Unpatched OSs can be a huge risk, especially for servers and Internet-connected systems.

Configuration Files   These files consist of the configuration files and configuration setups for devices. Configuration files can be altered to run unauthorized programs or batch files.

Application Software   This software is made up of the application or executable file that is run on a laptop, workstation, or smartphone. Unpatched applications are among the biggest targets of attackers today. In earlier years, desktop applications such as

Adobe Reader and Microsoft Office were the target of exploits. Today, applications intended for mobile devices are popular targets.

In Exercise 4.1, you will learn how vulnerabilities are identified and tracked.

Tracking Vulnerabilities in Software

Software vulnerabilities are tracked by the U.S. Computer Emergency Readiness Team (US-CERT) in a publicly accessible database referred to as the National Vulnerability Database (NVD). Once a vulnerability is discovered, it's given a number and added to the database. Each vulnerability or exposure included on the Common Vulnerabilities and Exposures (CVE) list has one common, standardized CVE name.

It is important to understand how CVEs are structured.

1. Go to nvd.nist.gov/search.

2. Go to Search in the menu and click the Vulnerabilities-CVE button.

3. In the Keyword Search text box, enter **Windows**.

4. Identify the vulnerabilities associated with Windows OS that are listed chronologically.

5. Now search for the specific operating system your asset is using. For example, **Windows 11**. How many vulnerabilities have been posted this year? How many of those have a critical CVSS severity rating?

Security Content Automation Protocol

Security Content Automation Protocol (SCAP) is a methodology of using vulnerability management standards in combination with policy, measurement, and compliance for standardization and automation.

There are two types of SCAP products. They are content producers and content consumers. Content producers are tools that generate SCAP source data. Content consumers are products that take existing SCAP content, process it, and produce relevant SCAP results. A *SCAP scanner* is used to apply an industry security standard to organizations that don't currently have one or to those that have weak implementations of security standards. SCAP allows security administrators to scan computers, software, and other devices based on a predetermined security baseline in order to determine how the configuration and software patches that are implemented compare to the baseline standard. The National Vulnerability Database (NVD) is the U.S. government content repository for SCAP.

While searching and investigating Windows vulnerabilities in Exercise 4.1, one of the options while querying the NVD is to look for US-CERT technical alerts and vulnerability notes as well as *OVAL Queries*. OVAL is an acronym for Open Vulnerability and Assessment

Language. OVAL is a community-driven effort to standardize assessing and reporting to provide results that are reproducible. OVAL was originally sponsored by the U. S. Department of Homeland Security and is now maintained by CIS. Details can be found at `oval.cisecurity.org`.

OVAL is an open language to check for configuration issues, programs, and patches that exist on an asset. It is not a vulnerability scanner. OVAL is capable of sharing the technical details of how to find a vulnerability in a system, and because of the public community-driven content, many vendors, researchers, and other security professionals are able to collaborate to develop XML-based definitions that help identify issues on an asset.

The OVAL Interpreter is a free command-line tool you can download from `source-forge.net` to collect system information and evaluate and generate an OVAL definition. It was created to use OVAL files and schemas and execute content on an endpoint. OVAL definitions provide a way choose what endpoint information should be evaluated, suggest what values should be found, and produce a report of what was observed versus what was expected.

Another specification language sponsored by NIST and used for security benchmarking is the Extensible Configuration Checklist Description Format (XCCDF). *XCCDF*, like OVAL, is used for standardization but is specifically used for checklists and benchmarks or other configuration specifications. By using these types of standards, you create a safer environment based on good security practices. XCCDF is also XML based and supports the exchange of information, document generation, and automated compliance testing.

Another standardization in the SCAP toolbox is the use of Common Platform Enumeration (CPE). *CPE* is a method of generally identifying classes of hardware and software in an enterprise. A CPE can identify whether hardware or software has been installed, but is not as granular as version or serial number. For example, if the CPE of a hardware device is identified in your environment as a Cisco ASA firewall appliance, then it could activate a vulnerability management tool to check the device for known general vulnerabilities and then prompt a configuration management tool to verify it follows your organization's policies regarding firewalls.

Similar to the CVE list shown in Exercise 4.1, there is a list for Common Configuration Enumeration (CCE). The *CCE* list (`ncp.nist.gov/cce/index`) assigns individual identifiers for system configurations so that data can be indexed across multiple tools, which improves any workflow. There are CCE Identifiers in the NIST Security Configuration Guides, CIS Benchmarks, and the Defense Information Systems Agency Security Technical Implementation Guides (DISASTIGS). As you see in Figure 4.3, for the CCE for Red Hat Linux, each CCE has an ID number, description, parameter, technical mechanism, and reference. The CCE identifiers associated with configuration controls act as a translator between machine-readable executables and human-readable guidance documents.

In keeping with the conversation around standardization of IT security best practices, the Asset Reporting Format (ARF) is used as a model for the consistent use of data in reports and correlation. *ARF* is vendor neutral, extremely flexible, and can be used for any kind of asset, not just IT devices. To learn more about ARF, see `csrc.nist.gov/projects/security-content-automation-protocol/specifications/arf`.

FIGURE 4.3 CCE-80785-9 for Red Hat Enterprise Linux 8

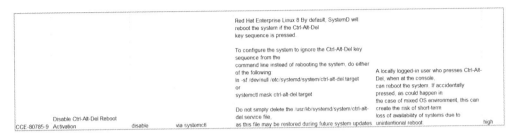

Self-Assessment vs. Third-Party Vendor Assessment

With an organization's assets inventoried, valued, and classified, the next step can begin. This step, *risk assessment*, is where potential risks and threats are identified. These activities are typically carried out by a risk assessment team, and the goal is to determine the likelihood of the threat. The team is tasked by upper management with identifying all threats and examining the impact of those threats.

There are several types of risk assessments, but the basic steps are the same, guiding you to make the right decision. The process begins by identifying the right task force of employees to lead the assessment and evaluate the results. After reviewing existing security policies, including those around vulnerability management and the maintenance of a database of IT assets, this team should prepare a list of potential threats based on experience and expertise. When the impact and likelihood of each threat has been evaluated, the next step is planning the proper controls and actions to be taken in case the worst happens.

An internal self-assessment of policies, procedures, guidelines, standards, tooling, people, and processes may be acceptable for organizations with very low risk. A *risk management team* is responsible for identifying and analyzing all risks. Its members should consist of managers and employees from across the company.

After the purpose of the team is established, the team can be assigned responsibility for developing and implementing a risk management program. This team should be led by someone high enough up the corporate structure to communicate easily with senior management and obtain the funding that will be needed for the risk assessment process to be a success. A successful outcome can be measured in many different ways. A success may mean that the team is able to decrease insurance costs, reduce attacks against the company's website, or verify compliance with privacy laws.

With a team in place and funding secured, the team will next turn its attention to gathering data and identifying threats. The first people to ask about threats should always be the asset owners because they know what the business is facing and where the threats come from. IT will help map those business threats into IT-related concerns. The following additional sources may be used:

- Actuarial tables and insurance records
- Audit reports

- Business owners and senior managers

- Facility records

- Legal counsel

- Human resources

- Government records

- Network administrators

- Operations

- Security administrators

- Industry advisories and bulletins

- Vendor websites

- Information sharing and analysis centers (ISACs)

Risk isn't just the result of natural events—it can also be tied to people. Depending on the business model and where a company does business, many people may visit the facility, including employees, contractors, customers, sales reps, and so forth. The risk that an individual may cause some form of incident is real. This risk may be the result of accidental situations or of actions that are deliberate. The source of the risk may be insiders or outsiders. Although we tend to trust those with whom we work, a large percentage of attacks are launched by insiders. Insiders possess the means and opportunity to launch an attack, whereas outsiders may have only motive. Therefore, insiders are in a much better place to launch an attack. The following are areas of concern when assessing both insider and outsider risk:

Abuse of Resources   This exposure can include any use of a resource that is not authorized by policy and procedure, and it may include items such as reading unprotected files, violating copyright, playing time-consuming computer games, using computer accounts for unauthorized activities such as outside work (moonlighting), sending spam email, and distributing other items for personal profit or illegal purposes.

Access and Theft of Sensitive Information   This exposure is linked directly to the loss of confidentiality. Information has value, and the loss of sensitive information can be extremely expensive. Theft of intellectual property has devastating consequences for businesses.

Alteration of Equipment Settings or Information   If an employee can access a system or change a setting, access controls can be bypassed and potentially altered.

Disclosure of Information   This category of exposure covers all threats that involve the deliberate or accidental disclosure of sensitive information. The privacy of information is affected because information is exposed without authorization.

Embezzlement   This is the risk of fraudulent appropriation of money or services from an organization. Various types of controls should be implemented to prevent this type of exposure.

Physical Destruction This threat can come from insiders or outsiders. Destruction of physical assets can cost organizations huge sums of money.

Theft Theft of company assets can range from mildly annoying to extremely damaging. Your CEO's laptop might be stolen from an airport. In this case, is the real loss the laptop, or is it the plans for next year's new product release?

Unauthorized Entry The control of who enters a facility, when they enter, and what they have access to is critical to the security of an organization.

Higher levels of risk assessment should be done by a third-party organization. A *third-party assessment* is done by a neutral party and analyzes the many risks to your organization, including the risk introduced from other third-party relationships including vendors, contractors, service providers, or suppliers. The risks that threaten those parties threaten your enterprise as well. Every introduction of a new third party expands the possibility of threats.

Some suppliers are hesitant to expose their level of risk, but it is critical that you seek the proper level of assessment to minimize the adverse effect on your organization. An organization that you are planning to work with could share their data with a subcontractor. You will want to know how and where that data is being used or stored, who has access to it, and whether it's encrypted and with which algorithm.

Third-party assessments are usually conducted against an industry framework like National Institute of Standards and Technology (NIST) or International Organization for Standardization (ISO). The NIST framework is usually used by federal, state, and local governments and enterprises doing business with those governments. ISO is typically used by private and public corporations and other market-driven companies. Some assessments are rooted in compliance with a federal standard such as the Health Insurance Portability and Accountability Act (HIPAA) or an industry standard such as Payment Card Industry Data Security Standard (PCI-DSS).

Organizations should also go through a source strategy to determine what tasks should be completed by internal employees or external third parties. Outsourcing is one common approach. *Outsourcing* can be defined as an arrangement in which one company provides services for another company that may or may not have been provided in house. Outsourcing has become a much bigger issue in the emerging global economy, and it is something security professionals need to review closely. There will always be concerns when ensuring that third-party providers have the requisite levels of information security.

Outsourcing has become much more common in the IT field throughout the course of the last decade or so. In some cases, the entire information management function of a company is outsourced, including planning and business analysis as well as the installation, management, and servicing of the network and workstations. The following services are commonly outsourced:

- Application/web hosting
- Check processing
- Computer help desk
- Credit card processing

- Data entry
- Payroll and check processing

Crucial to the outsourcing decision is determining whether a task is part of the organization's core competency or proficiency that defines the organization. Security should play a large role in making the decision to outsource because some tasks take on a much greater risk if performed by someone outside the organization. Any decision should pass a thorough business process review.

Patch Management

Patch management is a vital area of systems management. As your security model matures, it becomes necessary to develop a strategy for managing patches and upgrades to systems and software. Most software patches are necessary to fix existing problems with software that are discovered after the initial release. A great many of these are security focused. Other patches might have to do with some type of specific addition or enhancement to the functionality of software. In Figure 4.4, you see an example of the patch management life cycle.

FIGURE 4.4   The patch management life cycle

On March 14, 2017, Microsoft issued a critical security bulletin for the MS17-010. This vulnerability, nicknamed EternalBlue, was an exploit written by the National Security Agency (NSA) that was leaked to the general public by the Shadow Brokers hacker group exactly one month later. EternalBlue exploits a Microsoft Server Message Block (SMB) vulnerability, and, in short, the NSA warned Microsoft about the theft of the exploit, allowing the company to prepare a patch. Too many people did not install the patch, and in May of the same year, the WannaCry ransomware virus used the EternalBlue exploit to infect these vulnerable systems. More emergency patches were released by Microsoft. Again, many people did not patch, and in June, the NotPetya malware, which also uses EternalBlue, swamped the globe, focusing on Ukraine in June 2017.

If organizations had been paying attention in March 2017, they would have been fine. If they had paid attention in April 2017, they would have learned how to circumvent the exploit. In May and then again in June, patches could have been run and the problem averted. The exploit is still a problem today and has morphed into many variations, targeting the cryptocurrency industry with malware called WannaMine. *Cryptojacking* is a term to define the process where malware silently infects a victim's computer and then uses that machine's resources to run very complex decryption routines that create currency. Monero is a legitimate cryptocurrency that can be added to a digital wallet and spent, like Bitcoin and Ethereum. It sounds fairly harmless, but thinking back to the CIA triad, with cryptojacking malware you are losing your CPU and RAM resources to the mining malware, and it can easily spread across your network. If you think of the volumes of processing power and bandwidth it will consume in your organization, you definitely don't want this infection. Your systems will be generating cryptocurrency for the bad guys.

The lesson learned is that we must keep our systems up to date. In a patch management program, you will have to include operating system patches and updates for Microsoft, Apple, and Linux as well as third-party applications such as Chrome, Firefox, Java, and Adobe. You may have other software or firmware on your network. If you have a system with software, you must have a security policy outlining when to patch it. If you take the risk of not patching, you will leave your systems vulnerable to an attack that is preventable.

The patch management life cycle will start with an audit where you scan your environment for needed patches. After you know which patches are needed, and before you roll out those updates to the entire organization, best practice is to test those patches on a nonproduction system. If you do not, you risk breaking something with what should have fixed it. If you are able to identify issues before a global production rollout, your operations should not be impacted. Once you know what patches are missing and which patches are viable, install them on the vulnerable systems. Most of the time, this is done with Windows Update. Most enterprise-sized organizations use some type of patch management software solution.

Focusing on your most vulnerable systems like those running Windows operating systems, as well as highly vulnerable third-party programs like Adobe and Java, is one of patch management's key concepts. Starting with your riskiest yet mission-critical devices allows you to allocate time and resources where they will be best utilized and will provide the most risk mitigation.

Depending on the size of your organization, how many people you have on your cybersecurity team, the hours they can devote to patch management, and how many systems need to be kept up to date, you may want to utilize third-party patch management software. For Microsoft patching specifically, Microsoft includes a tool called Windows Server Update Services (WSUS) with all Windows Server operating systems. There are many tools available that are web-based, desktop management software. This software can remotely manage and schedule updates for Windows, Mac, and Linux, both in local area networks and across wide area networks. In addition to patch management, software installation, and service pack management, you can also use it to standardize desktops. You can use it to keep your images current and synchronized by applying the same wallpapers, shortcuts, printer settings, and much more.

The time between the discovery of a vulnerability and the action an IT administrator should take to protect the environment from that vulnerability should be as short as possible, especially on assets that are mission critical. That philosophy can possibly cause issues where rapid patch management causes a problem with change management and quality assurance testing. It will be a balance evaluating the risk of an unpatched system with the possibility of breaking that system in the process of fixing it. Creating a patch management program where you document your strategy for establishing, documenting, and maintaining the changes is vital to IT security.

Information Sources

As a security professional, you must perform ongoing research to keep up with current threats and changes to the industry. Many resources are available to help you in your research. A few are listed here and serve as only a small sampling of what's available to you. They are divided up into trends and tools.

You may remember your first computer or when, years ago, you may have told someone that if they would just run an antivirus program, they were safe from most online threats. This was a common perception before the year 2000. Today, antivirus programs are a small part of the protection needed to defend against digital threats. It is important to note that some operating systems are much more susceptible to viruses than others, with nearly 90 percent of ransomware targeting Microsoft Windows operating systems while ransomware targeting macOSs are in the single digits.

Other protective measures a security professional can evaluate for their environment is the deployment of immutable systems. Immutable infrastructure refers to those servers that cannot be changed or modified. To make changes, you have to redeploy the entire server or virtual machine and decommission the old. Some benefits would be the consistency and reliability of those assets, but it requires dedicated resources. Every update or security patch requires a redeployment.

A CASP+ must perform vulnerability research and stay abreast of current security trends. Such research can help identify weaknesses and alert administrators before a network is attacked. Research can also help in identifying and correcting potential security problems before they become worse.

There are many places to get cybersecurity information today, from websites, blogs, conferences, government advisories, and bulletins to major media outlets. By staying current in our career field, you strengthen your professional skill set. Knowing what is currently happening in the professional landscape of cybersecurity and connecting with the best resources for timely information make you an asset to your organization and our industry.

Advisories   Advisory documents can be shared by governmental agencies or vendors. Advisory organizations share information so that security professionals can understand

the threats and risks to their organization and make informed decisions. (See `www`
`.cisecurity.org/resources/?type=advisory`.)

Bulletins   Bulletins are periodic documents released to summarize vulnerabilities, risks,
and threats to cybersecurity. Patch information can be a part of the bulletin. One of the
best resource organizations to subscribe to that leads the effort in cybersecurity and
communication is the Cybersecurity and Infrastructure Security Agency. (See `us-cert`
`.cisa.gov`.)

Vendor Website   Most vendors supply their customers with updates and patches
through their products and/or software. Some vendors release their updates to improve
performance, enhance features, or fix problems.

Information Sharing and Analysis Centers (ISACs)   According to the Information
Technology – Information Sharing and Analysis Center (IT-ISAC) website, "The IT-
ISAC mission is to grow a diverse community of companies that leverage information
technology and have in common a commitment to cyber-security; to serve as a force
multiplier that enables collaboration and sharing of relevant, actionable cyber threat
information and effective security policies and practices for the benefit of all." (See `www`
`.it-isac.org`.)

News Reports   There are many sources for cybersecurity news online. One of the best
ways to stay informed is to subscribe to these news sources. The following are several
websites that you can bookmark, subscribe to RSS feeds, and read about cyberattacks,
hacking awareness, and increasing digital defense:

`www.thehackernews.com`

`www.threatpost.com`

`www.darkreading.com`

`www.wired.com`

`www.cnet.com`

`www.kb.cert.org/vuls`

`www.securiteam.com`

`www.securitytracker.com`

`www.securityfocus.com`

`www.hackerwatch.org`

`hackerstorm.co.uk`

`hak5.org`

`securityweekly.com`

`www.exploit-db.com`

As you keep up with the latest information regarding security best practices, processes for
hardening systems in an enterprise should be evaluated on a regular basis. Many standard

recommendations and checklists ensure that servers are configured to protect them against most cyberattacks. These steps include user, network, NTP, service configuration, update installation, as well turning on logging and monitoring. While configuring how updates are installed, a best practice is to use sandboxes to evaluate effectiveness and security in new software. Sandboxes are extremely effective at catching zero-day attacks because you are watching the behavior on systems rather than looking for a signature. This is called *sandbox detonation*. However, adversaries are evolving their methods. As we saw in the SolarWinds attack by the UNC2452 group, the malware had been written to be dormant for 14 days after installation and evaded detection by many organizations except FireEye/Mandiant.

To read more briefs about the SolarWinds UNC2452 group, visit `www.mandiant.com/ solarwinds-break-resource-center`.

Tools

Knowing where to get information is important, but you must also know where to obtain security tools safely. You should know better than to download any tool from just any site. Having the chance to verify a binary's integrity by hash value (for example, MD5, SHA1, or SHA256) should boost your confidence in the binary. For example, if you want to download a tool like Wireshark, look for their published hash for the file to ensure it has not been tampered with. Reputable software will have a hash readily available in a variety of algorithms and look something like this:

```
wireshark-3.6.0.tar.xz: 39687684 bytes
SHA256(wireshark-3.6.0.tar.xz)
=9cc8f7fc5bb1d66fbdfdf95cde6e1c98633c303f9af9b33ae9f1fcf022fedf06
RIPEMD160(wireshark-3.6.0.tar.xz)=1ecec1acd1c10be69654afac3f4f2d0acaf42a3c
SHA1(wireshark-3.6.0.tar.xz)=98248f0e6c19408fbb796398f998cf90d7ed9ca6
```

For the purpose of the CASP+ exam, these tools have been arranged into a logical order. Security assessments usually follow a well-defined methodology. The focus here is to step you through the process and briefly discuss some of the tools that can be used at each step. It is also important to note that some enterprise-grade tools can serve multiple functions. The tools are divided into the following categories:

- SCAP scanner
- Network traffic analyzer
- Vulnerability scanner
- Protocol analyzer
- Port scanner
- HTTP interceptor
- Exploit framework
- Password cracker

Some of these tools have already been introduced in this chapter, and the rest will be discussed in the sections to come.

Another great list can be found at `sectools.org`. The SecTools site lists the 125 top-rated network security tools, subdivided into categories. Anyone in the security field would be well advised to go over the list and investigate tools with which they are unfamiliar, because these tools can be used maliciously just as easily as they can be used for good.

Don't let the age of the SecTools list fool you. SecTools was last updated in 2011, and this is apparent since they still call the live pentesting Linux distribution "BackTrack." (It's been Kali since 2013.) Nonetheless, even though many tools have been released since 2011, most of us would still agree that this tool list remains an excellent foundation. Any security practitioner should at least be familiar with all of them and well versed in how to use some of them. This site is a great place to find tools that you don't know about or have not used. The following are the top 12 tools listed when we last visited:

1. *Wireshark*: A highly rated packet sniffer and network analysis tool.

2. *Metasploit*: An all-in-one security assessment tool available in free and paid versions.

3. *Nessus*: A well-known vulnerability assessment tool that can scan Windows, Linux, and Unix computers. A free version is offered for home use, and there's a commercial version as well.

4. *Aircrack-ng*: Designed for cracking 802.11 wireless WEP and WPA/WPA2-PSK encryption. The latest version of Aircrack-ng (version1.6) can see WPA3.

5. *Snort*: One of the best-known IDS tools on the market.

6. *Cain & Abel*: A Windows-based tool that can perform numerous activities, such as enumeration, ARP poisoning, password cracking, and wireless analysis.

7. *Kali*: A bootable live CD that has a variety of security tools.

8. *Netcat*: A command-line tool that runs in Linux and Windows. It has many uses, such as a remote listener, port scanning, and banner grabbing, and it can also be used to transfer files. Alternatives include socat and cryptcat, which is the cryptographic alternative.

9. *TCP Dump*: A command-line packet analysis tool that runs on Linux; there is also a Windows version called WinDump.

10. *John the Ripper*: A command-line password-cracking tool that will run on both Linux and Windows computers.

11. *Hping*: A packet-crafting tool that can be used for scanning and other security activities.

12. *Kismet*: A Linux-based wireless security tool that lets you capture broadcast and non-broadcast SSIDs.

Footprinting Tools

The first step of any assessment is footprinting. *Footprinting* is determining how much information is exposed to outsiders and what its potential damage is. We like to think of footprinting as old-fashioned detective work. It's all about putting together the pieces of information that you've collected. Footprinting is typically divided into two categories: active and passive reconnaissance.

Active Reconnaissance   Interacting with the target in some type of active way, such as calling the targeted company and asking for a tour

Passive Reconnaissance   Interacting with the target in a passive way, such as reviewing the targeted company's website or looking at its job postings

A good place to start your passive reconnaissance is at the target's website. It's surprising how much information some companies leak on their sites and how attackers could use the information. Email addresses could be used for phishing, employee names could be used for social engineering, or organization locations could be used to plan physical attacks. Companies must consider the security implications of what they make public on their websites, although it's always about finding a balance. Companies also post a wealth of information in job postings, such as the types of technologies used. Although the security assessment team may not spend weeks performing footprinting activities, they may spend a few hours or a day.

To get an idea of the types of information that you can find on a business website, take a moment to review Exercise 4.2.

EXERCISE 4.2

Performing Passive Reconnaissance on Your Company, School, or Another Organization

Spend 20 minutes footprinting your own organization to see what kind of information is publicly available.

1. Go to your company's website and look for contact names, email addresses, and phone numbers.

2. Using a WHOIS tool such as `whois.domaintools.com`, perform a WHOIS query on your company and see who is listed as the contact person. Is it a generic name or a real person's information?

3. Do a search of company job listings, and look for information about what technologies are used. Do the job request lists specify Microsoft, Apple, or Cisco technologies or products?

4. Go to `www.sec.gov` and do a search for a financial listing of your company. Are any records present? Do they list company earnings and income?

5. Go to `toolbar.netcraft.com/site_report?url=undefined#last_reboot`, and do a search on what your company website is running. Are the server version and type listed? Are they correct?

It's not just the company's website that's going to be examined during the footprinting phase. The security assessment team will most likely use Google's built-in functionality for advanced search queries. Google commands such as `intitle` instruct Google to search for a term within the title of a document, whereas others, like `filetype`, allow individuals to search only within the text of a particular type of file.

WHOIS records are another area that will be examined. Next, take a look at the IANA, ARIN, and RIPE databases. You can manually step through this process or use one of the many websites created for this purpose, such as `www.dnsstuff.com`. Many organizations take the time to remove employee names from WHOIS records, but others leave this information for an attacker to harvest. A favorite tool for DNS reconnaissance and research is `dnsdumpster.com`.

There are some other sites a penetration testing team may visit while footprinting:

Job Search Sites   These sites can be used to discover the types of equipment an organization uses.

Financial Records   Publicly traded companies can be searched at Hoovers/Dun and Bradstreet (`www.dnb.com`) and the Security Exchange Commission (`www.sec.gov`). Such records include names and addresses of officers, board members, and senior executives; financial data; and information about acquired or divested industries.

Old Websites   The Internet Archive website hosts the Wayback Machine (`wayback.archive.org`). It's a catalog of more than 40 billion web pages from as far back as 1996.

Social Media   Social media can include a large number of technologies such as Internet forums, weblogs, social blogs, microblogs, wikis, podcasts, and social networks. One of the big issues with social media is privacy and the amount of information that can be gathered through these sites. During a penetration test, social networking sites such as LinkedIn, Facebook, Instagram, and Twitter should also be reviewed. These are the same services that an attacker would examine to see what kind of information is posted.

Please Rob Me   This is a proof-of-concept website set up to aggregate information from various social network sites to determine whether someone is home or away so that their house could be robbed.

We Know What You Are Doing   This is a website set up to mine Facebook data to find things such as who is high on drugs and who wants to be fired.

Robin Sage   This is a fake Facebook profile that was used to trick individuals such as the chief of staff for a U.S. congressman, several senior executives at defense contractors, and others into connecting with the fake profile.

Catfishing   This means pretending to be someone or setting up a fake profile on a social network site. Believing a profile belongs to someone you care about (or have other strong feelings for/against) is a strong lure for a response that can be used against you. Unfortunately, this happens too often in adolescent bullying.

Another key consideration is metadata embedded into documents or PDFs, or even EXIF data in photos. This has become a serious risk, and tools like Fingerprinting Organizations with Collected Archives (FOCA) can show hidden metadata with sensitive information like internal shares, usernames, software versions, and so on. Take a moment to review the blog post at securityonline.info/foca.

Port Scanners

A *port scanner* is a tool that is used to scan TCP and UDP ports and report their status. Port scanners make use of protocols such as TCP, UDP, and ICMP.

Port scanning allows the individual running the probe to determine what services are running on the targeted computer. Ports are tied to and used by both connection-oriented TCP and connectionless UDP. Although applications can be made to operate on nonstandard ports, the established port numbers serve as the de facto standard. There are 65,536 ports, divided into well-known ports (0–1,024), registered ports (1,024–49,151), and dynamic ports (49,152–65,535).

 Just a refresher note: connection-oriented TCP uses a process called the *three-way handshake* to exchange information. The sender initiates a connection to the server with the SYN (synchronize) flag. The server replies with both the SYN and ACK (acknowledge) flags. The original sender responds with a single ACK flag. If all steps are completed correctly, then a TCP connection is established. A common exploit of this process is a SYN flood. A SYN flood is a type of distributed denial of service (DDoS) attack that exploits the three-way handshake to gobble up resources and render it unresponsive, flooding it with SYNs and not waiting for the ACKs.

Common port scanning techniques include the following:

TCP Full Connect Scan   Attempts to complete all three steps of the TCP handshake.

TCP SYN Scan   Half-open scan developed to be not as easily detectable as the "noisier" scans described later in this chapter. Today, this type of scan is just as likely to be detected. Open ports reply with a SYN/ACK, and closed ports respond with an RST/ACK.

TCP FIN Scan   Sends a FIN packet to the target port. Closed ports should send back an RST.

TCP NULL Scan   Sends a packet with no flags set. Closed ports should return an RST.

TCP ACK Scan   Attempts to determine rule sets or identify whether stateless inspection is being used. If an ICMP destination unreachable message is returned (Type 3 Code 13), then the port is considered to be filtered.

TCP XMAS Scan   Toggled on the FIN, URG, and PSH flags. Closed ports should return an RST. This scan is arguably the noisiest, raising alarms even in a mediocre SIEM on the first XMAS packet.

 Port scanning is not illegal in the United States, but it is always a best practice to get permission first.

The most popular port scanning tool is Nmap. It runs on Linux and Windows, and it is also available as both a command-line and GUI-based application. Nmap can perform many scan types. Of the many port scanning tools available, Nmap is one of the best known, and you should focus on it for the exam. You can download Nmap at `nmap.org/download .html`. Some basic Nmap port scanning switches are shown here:

TCP Connect scan: `Nmap -sT`

TCP SYN scan: `Nmap -sS`

UDP scan: `Nmap -sU`

OS fingerprint: `Nmap -O` (which has an option to limit the scan, `-T`, or to make it more aggressive in its timing, `-T5`)

Network Enumeration

Network enumeration is the next step in the penetration testing process. Enumeration can be described as the process of gathering information from networked devices. The following information can be obtained from enumeration:

- Device information
- Active Directory information
- Open shares
- Router information
- Device status

Here are some of the tools that can be used as a network enumerator:

The OS's Command Line   Entering `C:\>net use \\target\ipc$ "" /u:""` allows a user to attempt to exploit a Windows computer running NetBIOS by connecting to a null session.

Simple Network Management Protocol Queries   If *Simple Network Management Protocol (SNMP)* version 1 or version 2 is present on a computer, tools to query the device, such as snmpwalk, snmputil, or even SolarWinds IP Network Browser, can be used to access information such as user accounts, interfaces, and running applications. Since SNMP is used for monitoring and performance management, consider using SNMPv3 for any large deployment because of the extra layer of security protocols such as Transport Layer Security (TLS).

OS Fingerprinting Tools   These tools can be used to determine the version of operating system running. Popular OS fingerprinting tools include Nmap, P0f, and Xprobe2.

Built-in Tools   A variety of tools are built into operating systems that can be used for enumeration; examples include `ipconfig`, `traceroute`, `ping`, `netstat`, and `nbtstat`. Each of these tools can be executed from the command line.

Packet Sniffers and Protocol Analyzers

Most people lump these tools together, but there is a minor distinction. A packet sniffer technically only captures a packet. A protocol analyzer can both capture and analyze a packet. Wireshark is a tool that does both sniffing and packet analysis. You can download Wireshark at `www.wireshark.org/download.html`. The download page will have the proper version for your computer's architecture and version operating system. A new version typically comes out every other month.

The CASP+ exam will expect you to understand not only packet sniffers like Wireshark but also common protocols such as IPv4 and IPv6. Spend some time reviewing these protocols. There are many differences between IPv4 and IPv6, the most obvious being the capacity of address space. Another difference is that IPv6 has IPsec built in, whereas it is only an add-on to IPv4.

These types of tools function by placing the host system's network card into *promiscuous mode*. A network card in promiscuous mode can receive all of the data that it can see, not just packets addressed to it. They operate at the Data Link layer of the Open Systems Interconnection (OSI) model but show the packet details captured from different network media, breaking down the OSI model into the data link, network, transport, and application layers. Sniffers can capture everything on the wire and record it for later review. They allow the user to see all of the data that is contained in the packet, even information that some may want to keep private. Many older protocols such as FTP and Telnet send usernames and passwords via clear text. Anyone with a sniffer can intercept this data and easily reuse it.

If a sniffer is connected to a hub, *passive sniffing* can be performed. When sniffing is performed on a switched network, it is known as *active sniffing* because switches segment traffic and know to which particular port to send traffic and block it from all of the rest. Switches pose a hurdle to anyone wanting to sniff traffic for legitimate or illegitimate reasons.

Because switches segment traffic, it is no longer possible to monitor all of the traffic by attaching a promiscuous-mode device to a single port. To get around this limitation, switch manufacturers have developed solutions known as port mirroring, switch mirroring, or, on Cisco switches, *switched port analyzers (SPANs)*. Spanning a port allows the user to see not just traffic destined for their specific ports but all of the traffic being forwarded by the switch. This feature enables the switch to be configured so that when data is forwarded to any port on the switch, it is also forwarded to the SPAN port. This functionality is a great feature when using a sniffer and also for devices such as IDSs like Snort.

Vulnerable Web Applications

A great way to learn is to explore and exploit prebuilt applications that are designed to be deliberately exploitable. Some are available as virtual machines, and some are fully contained environments with both toolsets and VMs included. The vast majority are free, so there's little reason not to have some ready, if not running.

Some vulnerable web applications follow a "theme," such as a store or casino, while other full environments are just given colorful names.

The following is a list of a few vulnerable web applications or VMs:

BadStore: `www.vulnhub.com/entry/badstore-123,41`

WebSecurity Dojo, a learning environment of multiple VMs: `sourceforge.net/projects/websecuritydojo`

Metasploitable 2: `information.rapid7.com/download-metasploitable-2017.html`

DVWA: `github.com/ethicalhack3r/DVWA`

Microsoft Windows

A CASP+ should have a good working knowledge not only of security-related tools but also of common operating systems such as Microsoft Windows 8x, Windows 10, Windows Server 2008, Windows Server 2012, and Windows Server 2016. You can currently download a 180-day free trial of Windows Server 2019 or Windows Server in the cloud at `www.microsoft.com/en-us/windows-server/trial`.

The most current version of Windows Server can be evaluated here: `www.microsoft.com/en-us/evalcenter/evaluate-windows-server-2022`.

If you must use Windows 11, you can download it here: `www.microsoft.com/software-download/windows11`.

Linux

Linux systems are used in most large organizations. A CASP+ should have a good basic understanding of these systems and how they are configured and secured. One way to pick up some skills is to check out the Fedora Linux Security Lab, a live operating system, at `labs.fedoraproject.org/en/security`.

Virtualization Tools

Virtualization has become a widely accepted means of increasing infrastructure without having to buy more physical hardware. A CASP+ should understand basic virtualization products such as VMware Player, QEMU, and VirtualBox. You can download a copy of VMware Player at `www.vmware.com/products/workstation-player.html`, QEMU at `www.qemu.org`, and VirtualBox at `www.virtualbox.org/wiki/Downloads`.

Visualization Tools

Not to be confused with virtualization, *data visualization* is the presentation of data in a pictorial or graphical format. Data visualization lets decision-makers see the analytics presented visually so that they can grasp difficult concepts or identify new patterns. With interactive visualization, you can take a concept a step further by using the technology to drill down into charts and graphs for more detail, interactively changing what data you see and how it's processed. Some of the most popular data visualization tools are Tableau, Qlikview, Fusion-Charts, Highcharts, Datawrapper, Plotly, and Sisense.

Vulnerability Assessment Tools

Vulnerability scanners are used to scan internal or external computers for vulnerabilities. Some vulnerability assessment tools are open source, while others are commercial and may require annual subscription or license fees. These tools can be grouped into three broad categories:

Source Code Scanners   *Source code scanners* can be used to assist in code reviews. If you have access to the code during the development of a software product, these tools offer the ability to find common problems and issues. RATS and Flawfinder are two such tools. Source code scanners can detect problems such as buffer overflows, race conditions, privilege escalation, and tainted input. While they are helpful, these tools can produce a large number of false positives. The tools are good at finding specific functions that don't perform proper bounds checking. Some functions in the C language don't check buffer size, such as `scanf()`, `strcpy()`, `bcopy()`, `vsprintf()`, and `gets()`.

CASP+ candidates should know vulnerable C language functions—you may be asked to identify them for the exam.

Application Scanners   There are situations where you may not have access to the code. For example, suppose that you just bought Microsoft's latest web server product; Microsoft most likely will not give you access to its code. This is the type of situation in which application scanners are useful. *Application scanners* can test completed applications rather than source code. They look for vulnerabilities and other issues that can happen at runtime. Application scanners can also do input and bounds testing.

System Scanners   The final category of scanners is *system scanners*. Why just examine a single application when there are tools available to probe an entire network and all the systems connected to it? A system scanner can be run against a single address or a range of addresses. The primary advantage of system-level scanners is that they can probe entire local or remote systems or networks for a variety of vulnerabilities. Nessus, SAINT, and Retina are all examples of system scanners.

When using a vulnerability scanner, you will need to decide which approach works best. For example, you might run the tool from outside a network to see what an attacker can access, from inside the network without usernames and passwords to specific systems, or from inside the network with a credentialed scan using usernames and passwords. Each approach will yield different results. Running outside the network security perimeter offers the advantage of seeing the network as an outsider would. Just keep in mind that this tells the user nothing about user rights or even what needs to be patched or updated. Many vulnerability-scanning tools are available. A few are listed here:

Open Vulnerability Assessment System   *Open Vulnerability Assessment System (Open-VAS)* is a vulnerability assessment framework designed for vulnerability scanning. Open-VAS provides a daily update of current vulnerabilities.

Nessus   This is a well-established vulnerability scanner that can scan an array of systems such as Unix, Linux, and Windows computers.

SAINT   SAINT is a commercial vulnerability scanning and identification tool.

GFI LanGuard   This is a full-service scanner that reports information such as the service pack level of each machine, missing security patches, open shares, open ports, and missing service packs and patches on the computer.

Retina   This is a commercial product from BeyondTrust (formerly eEye Digital Security). This application provides extensive vulnerability scanning and identification across network platforms and devices.

Today, software such as Nessus, Retina, and OpenVAS is used by many companies for the purpose of periodic vulnerability assessment. If you would like to demo Nessus, find it at `www.tenable.com/products/nessus/nessus-professional`. OpenVAS can be downloaded at `www.openvas.org/download.html`. Another popular vulnerability scanner is eEye Retina. It offers support for NIST's Security Content Automation Protocol (SCAP), which makes it a solid contender for the government sector.

HTTP Interceptors

HTTP interceptors are programs that can be used to assess and analyze web traffic. All clear text information that is passed between the client browser and web application can be examined. Thus, if the application were to transmit the password in the clear without encryption, you could easily see it. Interceptors work by proxying traffic between the web client and the web server. They intercept every request issued to the application and every response received for both HTTP and HTTPS. An intercepting proxy is tremendously useful when it allows a common user to "look under the hood" and start to understand better how the application is passing data, such as, for example:

- Is the password encrypted?
- Are input parameters checked?

- Is data being accepted from the client with validation?
- Is client-side processing used?
- Does the cookie hold session information?
- Is the cookie HTTP or HTTPs?

These are just a few of the questions that an interceptor can help you answer. Some examples of HTTP interceptors are Burp Suite, WebScarab, and Paros Proxy.

Burp Suite (`portswigger.net/burp`) is a Java-based web penetration testing graphical tool developed by PortSwigger Web Security. It has become an industry-standard suite of tools used by security professionals. There are three versions: the community edition that can be downloaded freely and the professional and enterprise versions that have a trial period. Burp Suite helps you identify vulnerabilities and verify attack vectors that are affecting your web applications. In its simplest form, Burp Suite can be used as a proxy server, scanner, and intruder.

Burp Suite captures and analyzes each request to and from the target web application. This allows the interception, inspection, and possible modification of the raw traffic. Penetration testers can pause, manipulate, and replay individual HTTP requests to analyze potential parameters or injection points. Intruders can perform automated attacks on web applications. The tool can configure an algorithm that makes malicious HTTP requests as well as test for things like SQL injection and cross-site scripting (CSS). Certain injection points can be specified for manual as well as automated fuzzing attacks to discover potentially unintended application behaviors, crashes, and error messages. Fuzzing is a technique that allows you to test software by putting invalid or unexpected data into the computer program and monitoring the behavior.

Password-Cracking Tools

Password cracking is the process of retrieving and attempting to decrypt encrypted passwords that have been stored in or transmitted by a computer system. Password-cracking tools can be used to test the strength of your passwords in one of three basic ways: dictionary, hybrid, and brute-force.

Dictionary Password Cracking   *Dictionary password cracking* pulls words from dictionaries or word lists to attempt to discover a user's password. A dictionary attack uses a predefined dictionary to look for a match between the encrypted password and the encrypted dictionary word. Many times, dictionary password audits will recover a user's password in a very short period of time. If passwords are well-known dictionary-based words, dictionary tools will crack them quickly.

Hybrid Password Cracking   *Hybrid password cracking* uses a dictionary or a word list and then prepends or appends characters and numbers to dictionary words in an attempt to crack the user's password. For example, the password trustme might be tested as 123trustme, trustm3, emtsurt, tru3tme, and so on. These various approaches increase the odds of successfully recovering an ordinary word that has had a little variation added in.

Brute-Force Password Cracking   Brute-force attacks use random numbers and characters to crack a user's password. *Brute-force password cracking* can attempt every combination of letters, numbers, and characters. A brute-force audit on an encrypted password may require minutes, hours, days, months, or even many years, depending on the complexity and length of the password. Reducing the time requires faster CPUs or the use of distributed computing.

Historically, these three approaches were the primary methods used to crack encrypted passwords. Some passwords were considered secure because it would just require too much time to crack them. This time factor was what made these passwords seem secure. This theory no longer completely holds true with the use of a password-cracking technique known as a *rainbow table*. The rainbow table technique was developed by Philippe Oechslin, and it makes use of a time/memory trade-off technique. It works by computing all possible passwords in advance. Once this time-consuming process is complete, the passwords and their corresponding encrypted values are stored in a file called the *rainbow table*. An encrypted password can be quickly compared to the values stored in the table and cracked within a few seconds unless the password has been salted.

Passwords should never be stored in clear text. Password salting is a technique used to protect passwords should the database they are being stored in gets compromised. Passwords get an added secret string of 32 characters or more and then hashed, making it nearly impossible to reverse engineer.

Listed here are some examples of password-cracking programs:

John the Ripper   A Windows and Linux password-cracking program, John the Ripper cracks most common passwords, including Kerberos, AFS, and Windows LM hashes.

L0phtCrack   A Windows password-cracking program that has been around since 1997, L0phtCrack can extract hashes from the local machine or a remote machine and can sniff passwords from the local network.

Cain & Abel   Cain & Abel (or simply Cain) is a multipurpose password-cracking tool that can perform a variety of tasks, including Windows enumeration, sniffing, and password cracking. Cain uses dictionary, brute-force, and rainbow-table methods.

Ophcrack   Ophcrack is a password-cracking tool that implements rainbow tables. It has several tables that can be downloaded, or you can search the Web for others.

Password-cracking techniques continue to advance. One example is the use of GPUs for password cracking. You can get an Amazon cloud of GPUs, load your rainbow tables, and crack passwords very quickly. There are also some non–rainbow-table password collection initiatives like crackstation.net. This site is just a collection, but it's big, and since people are adding passwords, it is building a library of passwords that people are likely to use.

SSH and Telnet Utilities

CASP+ candidates should understand basic transfer technologies and know which are secure and which are not. For example, Telnet is not secure, whereas SSH offers encryption. PuTTY is an example of an SSH client. You can download PuTTY, a free SSHv2 client, at `www`
`.chiark.greenend.org.uk/~sgtatham/putty`.

Threat Modeling Tools

One good example of this type of tool is Microsoft's Security Development Lifecycle (SDL) Threat Modeling Tool. It's easy to use and provides guidance in the risk management process. You can learn more about the SDL Threat Modeling Tool at `docs.microsoft.com/`
`en-us/azure/security/develop/threat-modeling-tool`.

Computer Forensic Tools

Helix is a well-known incident response, computer forensics, and e-discovery tool. The initial release (2009R1) was free, but its successor, Helix3, is available for a 30-day evaluation only. You can download Helix at `www.e-fense.com/h3-enterprise.php`. There are many other forensic tools. Some well-known commercial tools include EnCase Forensic and AccessData's Forensic Toolkit (FTK).

Assessments

A *security assessment* refers to a systematic examination of an organization's network, policies, and security controls. Security assessments are used to determine the adequacy of security measures, identify security deficiencies, and provide data from which to predict the effectiveness of potential security measures. A security assessment can follow different approaches and techniques.

Security Audit

A *security audit* is an independent review and examination of an IT system used to determine the adequacy of the controls. A security audit also looks at the existing policy and how it maps to operational procedures.

Vulnerability Assessment

A *vulnerability assessment* typically makes use of automated tools such as Nessus, SAINT, and Retina. These tools can examine systems, applications, and devices and assess their controls and report on their levels of security. Vulnerability assessment tools are typically run weekly or monthly to find systems that may not be secured or that are missing critical patches and software updates.

Penetration Testing

Penetration testing is designed to look at the network in an adversarial fashion. Penetration testing can be used to answer questions such as what type of information an attacker could see if they targeted the company and what the attacker could do with the information. Penetration testing is focused on finding low-hanging fruit and seeing what a computer criminal could accomplish on the network. Penetration testing is discussed in more detail in the "Penetration Testing" section later in this chapter.

Security Testing

A CASP+ concentrates on security testing. This allows you to find any bugs before a software application is released to the public. Security testing is a subtype of software testing that involves identifying risks, threats, and vulnerabilities in the code of an application. Testers assess various elements of security such as the confidentiality, integrity, continuity, vulnerability, and authenticity of the web application.

A web application is a client-side and server-side software application that the client interacts with through a web browser. Common web applications include email, online sales, auctions, games, social media, collaboration tools, and much more. Web application testing is a software practice that ensures quality by testing that a web application is working as intended with functionality, usability, and compatibility testing.

Secure coding refers to the practice of building software with a high level of security and quality. Building secure software requires that you do the following:

- Understand common software weaknesses that lead to security vulnerabilities.

- Follow secure coding standards and practices.

- Perform in-depth code reviews.

The problem that many companies face is that programmers are not typically security professionals and are driven by different factors. Many times, there is a rush to develop code and get it released to market. There is also the fact that the programmer is usually most concerned with getting the application to function. Secure coding requires programmers to consider the concerns of security professionals and address all security requirements specified for the software in development while adhering to prescribed coding standards.

A code analyzer is a Java application compatible with C, C++, Java, assembly, HTML, Perl, Ruby, SQL, Go, and user-defined software source metrics. Code analyzers calculate metrics across multiple source trees as one project. Code analyzers have a nice tree view of the project and offer flexible reporting capabilities.

Fuzz Testing

Analyzing code can be done one of several ways. The first method, using a *fuzzer*, involves intentionally injecting a variety of input into the code to produce an unexpected or unwanted result, such as a crash. The input will come fast and furious, in large volumes of data (dubbed "fuzz"), with the goal that the application will reveal its weaknesses.

It works by automatically feeding a program multiple input iterations that are specially constructed to trigger an internal error indicative of a bug and potentially crash it. Such program errors and crashes are indicative of the existence of a security vulnerability, which can later be researched and fixed. The great advantage of fuzz testing is that the test design is extremely simple and free of preconceptions about system behavior. Some examples of fuzzing tools include the following:

SPIKE   This is a collection of many fuzzers from Immunity.

SPIKEFile   This is another file format fuzzer for attacking ELF (Linux) binaries from iDefense.

WFuzzer   This is a fuzzer for web app vulnerabilities.

Mangle   This is a fuzzer for generating odd HTML tags. It will also autolaunch a browser.

Tag Brute Forcer   This is used for fuzzing ActiveX applications.

IP Stack Integrity & Stability Checker   The IP Stack Integrity & Stability Checker (ISIC) is designed to test the stability of an IP stack and its component stacks such as TCP, UDP, and ICMP. ISIC generates loads of pseudorandom packets of the target protocol to test its response.

Static and Dynamic Analysis

Another approach to security testing is to use *static code analysis*. This is often called SAST. With this method, the software is neither run nor executed; rather, it is reviewed statically. As you can imagine, if an application has millions of lines of code, a static code review is impossible. Therefore, you must rely on static code analysis tools. The code to be reviewed is fed input into the static code analysis tool. With this type of testing, the feedback is fast and accurate. You will know exactly where the vulnerability is and the cause, and SAST makes it easier to remediate.

Finally, there is *dynamic code analysis* (DAST). The difference between dynamic and static code analysis is that while a static review does not execute the application, during dynamic code analysis, the application is run, and you can observe how the code behaves. The advantage of using dynamic testing is that it allows you to analyze execution logic and live data. Because the software is running, you can check for attacks like SQL injection and cross-site scripting.

As part of good security code hygiene, it is advisable to both methods. One is not better than the other. Both tests are necessary to find what the other does not.

Reverse Engineering

Reverse engineering offers great insight into how something works. Remember that reverse engineering involves taking hardware or software apart or analyzing it in a form that reveals how and why the subject performs the way it does. As a penetration tester, you might use reverse engineering tools to go beyond what vulnerability testing shows. Reverse engineering a client's in-house developed application can reveal potential weaknesses and issues before their competitor discovers the same.

Side-Channel vs. Covert Channel Analysis

A channel is a path for confidential or sensitive data. The goal is to keep this data confidential. *Side-channel analysis* will attempt to identify information in programs that expose confidential information and find security flaws that would otherwise be hard for a software developer to find. A side channel exists and leaks information through characteristics in operation. Some cryptography is vulnerable because the operation of the algorithm varies depending on the key being used. You're not using the key itself, but an attacker could gain information from observing the timing to reassemble parts of the key. A *covert channel* is hidden, intentionally designed to conceal the leakage of confidential or sensitive data. Whether intentional or not, analysis of both is important before code is released to the public.

Wireless Scanning

Wireless networks play a larger role in business today than they ever have before. After all, they are easy to set up, easy to use, and free from cables. A wireless assessment, also known as wireless site survey, examines an organization's wireless network. It addresses issues such as whether encryption is being used and, if so, what type and whether it can be cracked. Wireless testing also examines the potential for DoS attacks, Address Resolution Protocol (ARP) poisoning, and on-path (formerly known as man-in-the-middle, or MitM) attacks.

Wireless isn't just Wi-Fi and 802.11b/g/n/ac/ax. Wireless can include Bluetooth or even more esoteric protocols like Zigbee, such as in wireless HVAC systems. There is also radio frequency identification (RFID), which is used in everything from tags in clothing at big-box chain stores to employee badges for building access control.

802.11 wireless connectivity is something commonly reviewed during a penetration test. Wireless networks have become popular because of their low cost and convenience. Who wants to run 1,000 feet of cable? Wireless networks were originally protected with *Wired Equivalent Privacy (WEP)*. WEP encrypts data with the RC4 encryption algorithm. The key was limited to 40 or 104 bits. This provides a limited level of encryption, which is relatively easy to compromise. These weaknesses led to the development of a short-term fix known as *Wi-Fi Protected Access (WPA)*. WPA was much more secure because it used Temporal Key Integrity Protocol (TKIP). In 2004, the IEEE approved the next upgrade to wireless security, which was *WPA2*. It is officially known as 802.11i. This wireless security standard makes use of the Advanced Encryption Standard (AES). WPA2 supports key sizes of up to 256 bits. In 2018, the Wi-Fi Alliance announced WPA3. WPA3 is much better at circumventing replay attacks. WPA3 comes in three modes: Personal SAE, Enterprise ENT, and Enhanced Open. WPA3 uses Simultaneous Authentication of Equals (SAE) as a secure key exchange protocol, leading to stronger defense against password guessing. WPA3 Enterprise adds a 192-bit cryptographic tooling to ensure protection.

A variety of tools can be used during wireless assessments. A few of these tools are listed here:

SolarWinds Network Performance Monitor   SolarWinds delivers central visibility and control through a single pane of glass. SolarWinds allows the correlation of configuration, virtual, server, and application information to diagnose network performance issues.

ManageEngine NetFlow Analyzer   NetFlow Analyzer is a traffic analytics tool to provide real-time clarity into network performance. This solution collects, inspects, and reports what and who is using the network bandwidth.

Kismet   This is a Linux-based 802.11 wireless sniffer that can monitor and sniff raw packets from wireless networks. Kismet can detect standard and hidden network names and can analyze nonbeaconing hidden networks.

NetStumbler   This is a Windows-based GUI tool that uses a wireless scanner. NetStumbler operates by sending out a steady stream of broadcast packets on all channels.

LinkFerret   LinkFerret is a Windows-based application designed to sniff 802.11 network traffic.

Wireshark   This is a packet capture and analysis utility available for both Linux and Windows platforms. It is most often used for wired networks, but it can capture wireless data if provided with the correct drivers.

Software Composition Analysis

The software written today is a conglomeration of open-source libraries and third-party components with an occasional original building block to hold things together. The benefits of using this type of model can be improved value and speed to production, but it is important to evaluate quality. Component analysis is identifying those areas of code that you did not write and performing risk analysis. According to the Open Web Application Security Project, this is called *security component analysis* (SCA). Some common risk factors for combining different types of code include age, function, type, and known vulnerabilities.

Pivoting

Pivoting is a technique to route the traffic from a hacked computer toward other networks that are not accessible by a hacker machine. This could be carried out by Metasploit, Netcat, or other utilities meant to channel communication. The hacker breaks into the first network and then uses it as a jumping-off point from which to exploit internal machines on another network. This is called *pivoting* because the hacker is using the first network as a pivot to gain access to the second network.

Penetration Testing

Penetration testing follows a standard methodology that is similar to what an attacker would use. The big difference is that the penetration test is done without malice and with the permission of the targeted company. Before the penetration test is started, the client and the penetration test team meet to discuss the goals of the test. It might be designed to examine what someone outside or inside, with or without access, could access and exploit. Once this initial meeting has occurred, the team develops a contract for the client to review; once everyone agrees to the scope and rules of engagement and the contract is signed, the penetration test can begin.

Within the scope and rules of engagement will be information about start and end dates, times, assets, and IP lists to touch and not to touch. You can find many documents including rules of engagements and sample debriefs at `sans.org`. Other considerations to be factored into these agreements could be corporate policies regarding testing, facility locations, and staffing, as well as physical security. Organizations that have compliance requirements for penetration testing have these tests repeated annually. Ideally, the vulnerability reports generated in previous years will be corrected, and the changes make the organization safer.

The most critical step to complete before beginning a penetration test is to obtain written permission. You should also have a company point of contact (POC), and a letter authorizing the test should be kept with the team. This can be especially valuable when doing the testing onsite and the security folks bust open the door with armed guards.

The penetration test typically follows these steps:

Footprinting   The purpose of this step is to examine what kinds of information are available about the target company.

Scanning   This step includes port scanning and OS fingerprinting. Tools such as Nmap and Zenmap are commonly used port scanners. Results help determine what vulnerabilities might be exploited for access.

One good way to learn what web services are running on a computer system is to telnet to open ports and look for any banners that are returned, a technique that is known as *banner grabbing*. For example, you'd type www.mysite.com 80. You can also use Nmap and Netcat.

Gaining Access   This step is the point at which the penetration testing team attempts to gain access to the target's network. Methods may include social engineering, exploiting weak passwords, Trojan horses, and keyloggers.

Post Exploitation   Now that you have access, the goal is to use techniques that escalate privilege. After gaining access, the penetration test team must become system, root, or administrator to obtain full control. Techniques used to accomplish this task may include buffer overflow, SQL injection, or XSS.

Privilege Escalation   Once an attacker has access, they will attempt to refer to the process of an attacker elevating their privilege on a system from a low-level user to administrator or root. Privilege escalation occurs when code runs with higher privileges than those of the user who executed it. Privilege escalation techniques include the following:

> **Vertical Privilege Escalation**   A lower-privilege user or application accesses functions or content reserved for higher-privilege users or applications.

> **Horizontal Privilege Escalation**   A normal user accesses functions or content reserved for another normal user.

Applications and operating systems seek to prevent these types of attacks in various ways. One is by building in rings of protection. The *rings-of-protection model* provides the operating system with various levels at which to execute code or restrict access to it. It provides much greater granularity than a system that just operates in user and privileged modes. As you move toward the outer bounds of the model, you have less privilege. As you move to the inner bounds, you have more privilege.

Persistence   Systems may be patched, vulnerabilities found, or the security breach may be noticed. This step is when the penetration test team seeks to maintain their access. This may be accomplished by creating accounts, planting backdoors, or creating an encrypted tunnel.

Covering/Clearing Tracks   Once the objectives of the test are accomplished, the team will remove any items that have been placed on the network, restore systems, and remove any remaining code.

Determining Recommendations   This is the point in the process when the team starts to do a final review of their findings. Through meetings and reviews, the team begins to determine its recommendations.

Writing a Report and Presenting Findings   The final step is to create the report. The report lists the vulnerabilities and risks that have been discovered. The report also lists recommendations regarding administrative, technical, and physical controls that should be implemented to secure the organization's critical assets better.

Keeping the Client Informed

While you're performing a penetration test, one critical task is to keep the client informed. Throughout the process, the client should be kept aware of the team's findings so that there are no surprises in the report.

Assessment Types

There are several different approaches to penetration testing. Depending on the situation and what your employer or client is seeking, the assessment may proceed in one of several ways. These include the following:

No Knowledge Testing   With this type of test, there is very little or no knowledge of the target network or its systems. This testing simulates an outsider attack, as outsiders usually don't know much about the network or systems that they are probing. The penetration test team must gather all types of information about the target before starting the test. The team typically verifies that the IP address range is correct before attempting to penetrate the network and beginning to profile its strengths and weaknesses. The company's personnel should not know that they are being tested. This provides the additional advantage of determining how effectively personnel are adhering to monitoring, detection, and response policies, as well as the policies' effectiveness.

Full Knowledge Testing   A test with full knowledge takes the opposite approach of a test with no knowledge testing. This assessment is one in which the penetration test team has full knowledge of the network, systems, and infrastructure. This information allows the penetration test to follow a more structured approach.

One good way to learn more about the process of penetration testing is to take some time to review the *Open Source Security Testing Methodology Manual (OSSTMM)*. OSSTMM is a framework for security assessments that details required activities and timing. It can be found at www
.isecom.org/OSSTMM.3.pdf.

Tabletop Exercise   The goal of a *tabletop exercise* is to raise situational awareness in the context of information security. It is also designed to foster discussion on incident response in brief, practical discussion periods. For management, tabletop exercises provide a great opportunity to demonstrate to the incident response group the scenarios that are most likely to occur.

Internal and External Audits   An *internal audit* is one conducted to improve an entity's operations. Medium-sized and large-sized operations usually have an internal auditing department to monitor the operations of the organization regarding the improvement of effectiveness, control, governance processes, and risk management. The department accomplishes this by providing recommendations and suggestions on the basis of the assessment of data and business transactions. The main purpose of an internal audit is to provide an independent opinion and consultancy to senior management and those charged with governance (governing bodies). Internal audits are mostly performed by an employee of the organization; however, some organizations hire the services of an audit firm for an internal audit.

An *external audit* indicates an audit of the organization by an independent audit firm that is not controlled by the organization that it is auditing. An external audit is performed because of statutory requirements in order to express an opinion on whether the security controls, processes, and documentation are in accordance with acceptable standards and regulatory requirements in all material aspects. For an external audit, the auditor is required not to have any prior association with the organization; that is, an external auditor must be independent in their work.

Vulnerability Assessment Areas

Not all security assessments are the same; for each individual assessment, different areas may be reviewed. Sometimes, a security assessment may not focus on the network, firewalls, insiders, or even outsiders. After all, code is the common component that allows applications and software to meet our needs. Even in a well-deployed and secured network, a weak application can expose a company's critical assets to an attacker. A security code review is an examination of an application that is designed to identify and assess threats to an organization. Common areas of assessment are discussed in the following sections.

Denial-of-Service

DoS testing looks at a company's ability to withstand a potential DoS attack. Some organizations may also do this to examine how the network operates under a heavy load or high utilization. Goals for this category of test typically include assessing the impact of a DoS attack, determining the performance of the network, and measuring the impact of the devices that are being attacked.

A DoS attack is an attack on availability. It is intended to prevent access to legitimate users of a system, website, or network causing loss of revenue, impacting customer trust, and forcing an enterprise to spend time, effort, and money to remediate. Most DoS attacks are accomplished by flooding a target with ICMP traffic or sending traffic like an overflow type attack that makes it crash. A distributed denial of service (DDoS) has the same ill intent but is orchestrated from many sources. DDos can impact business for days to months as an organization attempts to recover.

Telephony

Testing voice systems involves more than just traditional phone systems. Telephony testing includes an examination of voice over IP (VoIP), fax, PBX, and all voice lines. There are still computers hooked up to modems for items such as vendor access to specialized systems (for example, HVAC) as well as emergency backup remote access for networking staff. Each area can be critical to a company. For example, if a company's PBX is hacked, it can be subject to tool fraud, loss of revenue, and even loss of confidential information.

Application and Security Code Testing

Application exploits are a broad category of attack vectors that computer criminals use to target applications. There are many ways in which an attacker can target applications. Regardless of the path taken, if successful, the attacker can do harm to your business or organization. The resulting damage may range from minor impact to putting your company out of business. Depending on how the application has been designed, an application exploit may be easy to find or extremely difficult to pinpoint. With so much to consider, there needs to be a starting point. As such, OWASP lists the top 10 application security risks in 2021 as follows:

1. Broken access control
2. Cryptographic failure
3. Injection
4. Insecure design
5. Security misconfiguration
6. Vulnerable and outdated components
7. Identification and authentication failure
8. Software and data integrity failure
9. Security logging and monitoring failure
10. Server-side request forgery (SSRF)

A security code review assumes that you have all of the sources available for the application that is being examined. There are times when you may not have the code or when items such as external libraries or components are not accessible. In situations where you don't have the code, unknown environment testing techniques may be used as well as tools such as Rough Auditing Tool for Security (RATS) and Flawfinder.

Regression Testing

Regression testing is used after a change is made to verify that the inputs and outputs are still correct. This is important from a security standpoint, as poor input validation is one of the most common security flaws exploited during an application attack.

Regardless of the situation, areas of concern include items such as initial data supplied by the user. Any values supplied by a user must be checked to see if they are valid. All inputs, processed data, values being stored or processed, and output data must be examined.

Social Engineering

Social engineering or "hacking the human" is deceiving someone into giving out information or access to information that they should not have. If you are asked to perform a social engineering test as part of a security assessment, there are some common areas to review. These areas include help desk, onsite employees, and contractors. As an attack vector, social engineering is potentially one of the most dangerous attacks because it does not directly target technology. Having good firewalls, intrusion detection systems (IDSs), and perimeter security means little if an attacker using a social engineering technique can call up the help desk using VoIP (vishing) and ask for a password. Social engineering is dangerous because the attacks target people. Social engineering can be person-to-person or computer-based.

Social media provides a treasure trove of information for attackers. Visiting the personal social pages for an employee will yield their likes, passions, political leanings, and maybe even thoughts about their employers. The opportunity for a social engineer to exploit the social media sites of a potential target is not just theory, as we all know from current events at the time of this writing.

Physical Testing

Physical testing involves the examination of a company's physical controls. This can include locks, gates, fences, guards, authentication, and physical asset control. A portion of any good penetration test is to attempt physical entry. A security consultant will try to bypass doors and climb fences, take pictures of internal and external lighting, avoid signing into any visitor logbook, and determine if the cameras are actively monitoring a space or only recording it for a possible review.

Other possible components of physical penetration testing are to look for network jacks in public areas of the business and to try to gain access to any sensitive areas, like a server room or executive boardroom. Some penetration testers will dumpster dive, looking through trash to see what is openly thrown away.

Vulnerabilities

Often in cybersecurity, senior management aspires to reduce their vulnerability management score to zero for the entire enterprise. They want sysadmins to patch everything and engineers to place compensating controls in every location as well as tasking DevSecOps to upgrade all of the software. This is not a sustainable model of protection in an ecosystem where the only constant is change. An evolving digital landscape forces cybersecurity professionals to prioritize vulnerabilities that affect mission-critical assets while balancing time and resources.

One of the best ways to accomplish this is to administratively identify assets that are most important to the business, complete a tactical vulnerability assessment, and strategically examine the vulnerabilities on those assets. Some vulnerabilities are hard for an attacker to reach and difficult to perpetrate as well as having little impact on the business. These should have a low priority as opposed to some of those listed next, which could bring an organization to a complete standstill.

Buffer Overflow

A *buffer overflow* occurs when the amount of data written into a buffer exceeds the limit of the buffer. This can allow a malicious user to do just about anything. Buffers have a finite amount of space allocated for any one task. For example, if you have allocated a 32-character buffer and then attempt to stuff 64 characters into it, you're going to have a problem.

A buffer is a temporary data storage area. The buffer should have a defined length that the program creates. Continuing with our earlier example, a program should be written to check that you are not trying to stuff 64 characters into a 32-character buffer. Although this seems straightforward, this type of error checking does not always occur.

A buffer overflow can lead to all types of security breaches because values will be accepted by applications no matter what the format. Most of the time, this may not be a problem. However, it may cause the program to crash, or if crafted correctly by an attacker, the information may be interpreted as instructions and executed. If this happens, almost anything is possible, including opening a shell command to execute customized code. Whereas an integer overflow resets the pointer or overflows to zero, a buffer overflow allows an attacker to run their code on the victim's machine. Attackers seeking to launch a buffer overflow typically follow these steps:

1. Find the presence and location of a buffer.

2. Write more data into the buffer than it can handle.

3. Overwrite the return address of a function.

4. Change the execution flow to the attacker's code.

An attacker who completes these steps can run applications at the same level of access as the vulnerable process. Then the attacker might create a backdoor or use a tool such as Cryptcat or Netcat to redirect input/output. Once this is accomplished, the attacker can then redirect the shell for command-line access.

Integer Overflow

Integer overflow occurs when a program or application attempts to store in a variable a number that is larger than that variable's type can handle. Consider the situation where an allocated buffer can hold a value up to 65,535. If someone can exceed this value and tries to store a value in an unsigned integer type that is larger than the maximum value, only the modulus remains—for example, $65,535 + 1 = 0$. Because the maximum size has been exceeded, the value essentially wraps around to 0. The result can cause some unusual behavior if the resulting value is used in a computation.

An example of this problem can be seen in many classic video games, such as Pac-Man. Pac-Man used an 8-bit counter, so that if a player was good enough to complete 255 levels, the game would crash; the counter used to draw out each game level overflowed to zero. Classic video games are far removed from the complex applications we use today, but the concept remains the same.

 Readers wanting to learn more about buffer overflows should check out "Smashing the Stack for Fun and Profit" at insecure.org/stf/smash-stack.html.

Memory Leaks

Memory leaks are the result of an application not freeing up memory that it has allocated, used, and no longer needs. Memory leaks are a common programming error in some standard libraries. The problem occurs when an application cannot properly deallocate memory that was previously allocated. Although the leak may initially be small, over time programs that leak more and more memory can display symptoms ranging from decreasing performance to running out of memory and locking up or crashing. Memory leaks are more likely in some programming languages than in others. As an example, in the C programming language, you used the `malloc` function call to allocate a piece of memory, but you might forget to call `free` corresponding to the `malloc` function to release the memory. If this process is repeated hundreds of times, a huge amount of memory may be lost.

Memory leaks are found in common programming languages such as C/C++ and C#. Although C has the ability to allocate and deallocate memory dynamically, it also means that C/C++ applications are some of the most common in which to find memory-handling problems. In C#, some common memory leaks include not removing event listeners that keep objects alive and keeping database connections open when they are no longer needed.

Race Conditions (TOC/TOU)

Race conditions are a form of attack that typically targets timing. The objective is to exploit the delay between the *time of check (TOC)* and the *time of use (TOU)*. These attacks are sometimes called *asynchronous attacks*. This is because the attacker is racing to make a change to the object after it has been stored but before the system uses it.

A race condition is considered one of the most difficult application issues to detect during application security testing. Race conditions are best identified early in the process, during the code review. Race conditions can also be difficult to exploit because the attacker may have to attempt to exploit the race condition many times before succeeding.

Race conditions can prevent protective systems from functioning properly or deny the availability of resources to their rightful users. As an example, items are written to a database faster than another application can process the data. Erroneous data is written, and an error situation occurs.

Programmers can eliminate race conditions if their code processes exclusive-lock resources in a given sequence and unlocks the resources in the reverse order.

Resource Exhaustion

Resource exhaustion is a *denial-of-service (DoS)* technique that occurs when the resources necessary to perform an action are completely consumed. This prevents required actions from taking place. The impact of resource exhaustion is the disruption of normal operations and communications. Many times, it is easier for an attacker to accomplish this than to gain access to a system or application. Listed here are some classic DoS tools. Keep in mind that these are listed here to demonstrate how these types of tools have been used over the years. Most of these attacks are no longer effective today, and for newer resource exhaustion attacks, load balancers are typically used to provide a centralized defense.

Smurf   Exploits the Internet Control Message Protocol (ICMP) by sending a spoofed ping packet addressed to the broadcast address with the victim's address listed as the source.

SYN Flood   Disrupts Transmission Control Protocol (TCP) connections by sending a large number of fake packets with the SYN flag set. This large number of half-open TCP connections fills the buffer on the victim's system and results in resource exhaustion.

Ping of Death   An oversized packet is illegal but possible when fragmentation is used. When the fragments are reassembled at the other end into a complete packet, it causes a buffer overflow on older systems.

Teardrop   Sends packets that are malformed, with the fragmentation offset value tweaked so that the receiving packets overlap. The victim does not know how to process these overlapping fragments, and they crash or lock up the receiving system, thereby causing a denial of service.

Land   Sends a packet with the same source and destination port and IP address as in a TCP SYN packet. As the system does not know how to handle such traffic, the CPU usage is pushed up to 100 percent, and all existing resources are consumed.

Trinoo   Floods the victim with unwanted traffic. In the late 1990s, Trinoo was easy for an attacker to use and was very powerful in that it could flood a target system and consume all available bandwidth.

    Flood guards can be used to protect a network from classic downstream DoS attacks, VoIP server and SIP attacks, and more modern DoS threats such as Low Orbit Ion Cannon (LOIC).

Data Remnants

Data remnants consist of data that remains on the media after formatting or wiping the drive. The security concern is, regardless of the formatting method or extent of data wiping efforts, that residual digital data remains. There are data recovery companies whose revenues count on taking whatever steps are necessary to find those data remnants. The only way to ensure that there are no data remnants is through the physical destruction of the media.

Use of Third-Party Libraries

An application issue that plagues a surprisingly large number of companies is the use of *third-party libraries*. The attraction of using something already created is clear: money and time saved. However, there is a big security risk as well.

When developers at a company can find code that fits their needs and is already working, then why would they "reinvent the wheel?" They can plug in a third-party library to accomplish the required tasks. The problem is that the third-party library is an unknown, untested product when compared with the policies and safe coding practices of the in-house developers.

Code Reuse

Code reuse is, as the name implies, the use of a single piece of code several times, whether it's within an application or reused as an application evolves from one version to the next.

Similar to using a third-party library, reusing code saves time and money. Why would a developer succumb to rewriting the same block of code (and possibly introducing errors) when the application can instead be directed to a single block of code to be used repeatedly when needed?

When practiced with security in mind, code reuse is certainly a positive practice—for example, when a subroutine is required for several aspects of an application. The subroutine was developed securely, so there is little or no added risk. However, if one application's code, however modular it is, were repurposed for the next version or for another application, then this practice might skip the evaluation steps required and introduce new risks.

Cryptographic Vulnerabilities

Cryptography includes methods such as symmetric encryption, asymmetric encryption, hashing, certificates, and digital signatures. Each provides specific attributes and solutions. These cryptographic service goals include privacy, authentication, integrity, and nonrepudiation. In cryptography, there is a formula that was created in the 19th century called Kerckhoffs' principle. Auguste Kerckhoffs was a Dutch cryptographer, and he stated that "a cryptographic system should be secure even if everything about the system, except the key, is public knowledge."

Attacks on cryptographic systems are nothing new. The formal name for this activity is *cryptanalysis*, which is the study of analyzing cryptography and attempting to determine the key value of a cryptographic system. Depending on the strength of the key that is targeted by the attacker, success may mean that someone could gain access to confidential information or pretend to be an authenticated party to a communication.

Nonrepudiation and attestation are key advantages of certificates on any platform, but they do have their weaknesses. Different entities can use certificates. *Issuance to entities* identifies to whom the CA issues certificates. A certificate might be issued to a user, a system, or an application. The CA not only issues the certificate, but it also vouches for the authenticity of entities. An organization may decide to have itself act as a CA, which is less trustworthy because it has not been vetted through an official certificate authority. Anyone can generate a self-signed certificate.

If you decide to use a third party to issue a certificate, there is a cost. These organizations are generally for-profit and will charge fees for you to maintain your certificate. Some organizations may choose to use wildcard certificates to cut costs. A *wildcard certificate* allows the purchaser to secure an unlimited number of subdomain certificates on a domain name. The advantage is that you buy and maintain only one certificate. The drawback is that you are using just one certificate and private key on multiple websites and private servers. If just one of these servers or websites is compromised, all of the others under the wildcard certificate will be exposed.

If a private key is exposed or another situation arises where a certificate must be revoked, PKI has a way to deal with such situations, that is, when a CRL is used. These lists can be checked via the *Online Certificate Status Protocol (OCSP)*, an Internet protocol used for obtaining the revocation status of an X.509 digital certificate.

There are many other ways an attacker can target a system, such as a brute-force attack. A brute-force attack tries all possible solutions, but it can be time-consuming and use quite a bit of CPU power. However, if your organization is using a weak cipher or encryption/decryption algorithm that uses a key of insufficient length, the encryption could be broken. The larger the key size, the stronger the cipher.

Broken Authentication

Authentication is another key goal of cryptography. First, *authentication* is associated with digital signatures. Authentication provides a way to ensure that a message is from whom we believe it's from. In its basic form, authentication is used to determine identity.

When implementing a cryptographic system, there has to be consideration of strength versus performance versus feasibility to implement versus interoperability. Stronger systems typically require more process power and longer encryption/decryption times. The strength of a cryptosystem relies on the strength of an algorithm and the complexity of the key generation process. The strength of the encryption mechanism also rests on the size and complexity of the key. If the cryptosystem uses a weak key generation process, then the entire process is weak. The key size goes a long way in determining the strength of the cryptosystem.

There is a real need for strong cryptographic controls. For example, this is the reason for the creation of secure directory services. This solution makes use of Secure Sockets Layer (SSL). LDAP over SSL (LDAPS) provides for secure communications between the LDAP servers and client systems by means of encrypted SSL connections. To use this service, SSL has to be present on both the client and server and be able to be configured to make use of certificates.

Security Misconfiguration

Investigating computer crime is complex. There may be either an insider threat or an outsider threat. Many times, incidents are just accidents and could be caused by nonmalicious threats or misconfigurations. Other incidents are deliberate and may be dealt with in a number of ways.

Security misconfiguration ranks number five on the list of OWASP top 10 web application security risks. Applications are found missing appropriate hardening or improperly configured permissions. Also, an issue with many software deployments is that the version being used is out of date or known vulnerabilities are not patched or mitigated. Pervasive are the unnecessary features that are enabled and installed, ports open that don't need to be, and default accounts and passwords still enabled.

Inherently Vulnerable System/ Application

Applications are written in a programming language. Programming languages can be low level (so that the system easily understands the language) or high level (so that they are easily understood by humans but must be translated for the system). What all programs have in common is that they were developed in code and written by humans. There are generally three ways in which security of the application can be addressed: by design, by default, and by deployment.

Security by design means that the security measures are built in and that security code reviews must be carried out to uncover potential security problems during the early stages of the development process. The longer the delay in this process, the greater the cost to fix the problem. *Security by default* means that security is set to a secure or restrictive setting by default. As an example, OpenBSD is installed at the most secure setting, that is, security by default. See `www.openbsd.org/security.html` for more information. *Security by deployment* means that security is added in when the product or application is deployed. Research has shown that every bug removed during a review saves nine hours in testing, debugging, and fixing of the code. As a result, it is much cheaper to add in early on than later. Reviews make the application more robust and more resistant to malicious attackers. A security code review helps new programmers identify common security problems and best practices.

Another issue is functionality. Users constantly ask for software that has greater functionality. Macros are an example of this. A macro is just a set of instructions designed to make some tasks easier. This same functionality is used, however, by the macro virus. The *macro virus* takes advantage of the power offered by word processors, spreadsheets, or other applications. This exploitation is inherent in the product, and all users are susceptible to it unless they choose to disable all macros and do without the functionality. Feature requests drive software development and hinder security because complexity is the enemy of security.

 Application security is of vital importance. As such, a CASP+ should understand that security must be checked at every step of the development process.

Client-Side Processing vs. Server-Side Processing

Before coding can begin, developers must decide what programming language they will use and where processes will be performed. Processes can be handled at the client end or the server. These are issues centered around the debate of *client-side processing* versus *server-side processing*. We will review this debate in the following sections. There are a number of issues and technologies to consider, including the following:

- JSON/REST
- Browser extensions
- Asynchronous JavaScript and XML (Ajax)
- JavaScript/applets
- Flash
- HTML5
- SOAP
- Web Services Security
- Buffer overflow
- Memory leaks
- Integer overflow
- Race conditions (TOC/TOU)
- Resource exhaustion
- Data remnants
- Use of third-party libraries
- Code reuse

Some of these considerations were discussed earlier in the "Vulnerabilities" section of this chapter. The rest will be discussed in the following sections.

JSON/REST

JavaScript Object Notation (JSON) is a lightweight, human-readable programming format that is a natural fit with JavaScript applications. It's an alternative to XML, and it is primarily used to transmit data between a server and a web application. One potential security issue is that JSON can be used to execute JavaScript. *Representational State Transfer (REST)* is used in mobile applications and mashup tools as a type of simple stateless architecture that generally runs over HTTP. It is considered easier to use than other technologies, such as SOAP. Its advantages include ease of use and modification and that it helps organize complex datasets.

Browser Extensions

A *browser extension* is a computer program that is used to enhance the functionality of a web browser. Browser extensions started off by performing basic tasks and now are increasingly used to significantly extend the functionality of client-side components. Browser extensions run within the browser, across multiple client platforms, and they provide the capability of a stand-alone application. Extensions are generally downloaded for the specific browser that you are using because not all are universal. Also, extensions may slow down browsing or potentially introduce security flaws. Some examples of extensions are as follows:

- TinyURL generator

- Print pages to PDF

- Heartbleed Notifier, which tells you if a site is vulnerable to the Heartbleed SSL security bug

Adobe Flash and Microsoft ActiveX are no longer supported or recommended browser extensions. Adobe Flash runs inside the same process and memory as the web browser, and frequent bugs in that software give hackers lots of opportunities to gain access to memory. When they do that, they can cause the browser to jump to a specific memory address and take control of the machine. ActiveX shared programs functionality and controlled small programs called *add-ons* used on the Internet. This technology was dropped with Internet Explorer 10 and Microsoft Edge was designed so that no ActiveX was needed. Signed ActiveX controls gave users a sense of security, when in reality, it was being used by attackers to install malware and spyware from infected websites.

Ajax

Asynchronous JavaScript and XML (Ajax) is used for developing web applications and combines XHTML, CSS, standards-based presentation, and JavaScript. Ajax allows content on web pages to update immediately when a user performs an action. Ajax, like other programming languages, can have security issues, primarily susceptibility to injection attacks. One design approach is to develop the application in Ajax so that it responds only to requests that were sent as expected. All malformed requests should be silently ignored, thereby reducing the possibility for security problems.

JavaScript/Applets

JavaScript is an object-oriented scripting language. It is an implementation of the ECMAScript language, and it is widely used in web pages and applications. It is useful for functions that interact with the Document Object Model (DOM) of the web page.

Somewhat related to JavaScript are Java applets. A *Java applet* is a snippet of code that is delivered to users in the form of bytecode, which acts similar to an assembler. These small amounts of code, which are typically one or two bytes, allow the programmer to deliver small specific instructions to be executed. Their advantage is speed and the fact that applets can be executed on many different platforms. When a Java-enabled browser encounters an applet, it fetches the bytecode and passes it to the browser, which then executes the code. Figure 4.5 shows how bytecode works.

FIGURE 4.5 How bytecode works

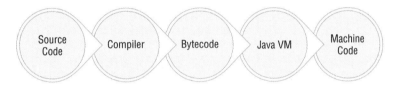

Bytecode is different from machine code. Bytecode is the code that gets created by compiling source code, and machine code is a set of instructions in machine language that can be understood and executed by a machine, namely, the CPU.

From a security standpoint, JavaScript is a concern because it can run locally in a user's browser. Although this means that it can respond to a user's actions quickly, it also means that JavaScript is vulnerable to XSS and CSRF. XSS can be dangerous. Consider the situation in which an attacker can launch an XSS attack while victims are connected to their bank's website. This could allow the attacker to access the banking application with the privileges of the victim. The result might be the disclosure of secret information or transferring of large amounts of money without the victim's authorization. CSRF is used in much the same way— the attacker uses JavaScript to trick the victim's browser into taking actions that the user didn't intend (such as transferring money at a bank website).

Commercial websites are not the only things that are vulnerable to CSRF. Security researchers have identified similar vulnerabilities in some Linksys home routers. See www.csoonline.com/article/3191254/security/flaws-let-attackers-hijack-multiple-linksys-router-models.html.

CASP+ test candidates should note that JavaScript is vulnerable to both XSS and CSRF.

Flash

Flash was designed to create interactive websites. One of its primary advantages is that it can be used with many different operating systems and devices. However, some vendors, such as Apple, do not fully support Flash. And according to CNN Tech, Flash has suffered from numerous problems over the years (money.cnn.com/2013/10/08/technology/security/adobe-security). These security problems include the following:

- In 2009, a vulnerability in Adobe Reader let hackers open backdoors into people's computers.

- In 2010, attackers created malicious PDF attachments to hack into several companies, including Adobe, Google, and Rackspace.

- In 2011, another bug gave hackers remote access to people's computers using Adobe Flash Player.

- In 2012, cyberhackers gained access to Adobe's security verification system by tapping into its internal servers.

Fortunately, today it's rare to find websites still relying on Flash. At the time of this writing, it's now used on less than 5 percent of total sites and declining. Adobe discontinued patches and support on December 31, 2020, and blocked Flash content from running in Flash Player. Beginning January 12, 2021, Adobe strongly recommends all users immediately uninstall Flash Player to help protect their systems.

ActiveX was also deprecated as of August 2020. ActiveX was a software framework created by Microsoft that allowed websites to embed multimedia files or software updates. As with anything IT related, what could be used for good was alternatively used by malicious websites. The functionality that ActiveX provided was reduced by HTML5 capabilities.

HTML5

The HTML5 markup language is designed to be backward compatible with previous versions of HTML. HTML5 has support for features and input types, as well as validation for forms, which didn't exist until HTML5. HTML5 was officially adopted in 2014, and since then it has seen a few improvements and revisions. For example, it has been extended to XHTML5 (SML-serialized HTML5). However, for the foreseeable future, HTML5 remains the latest content presentation language for the Web and the de facto cross-platform language for mobile applications because it includes features for lower-powered devices.

The Open Web Application Security Project (OWASP) has a great cheat sheet for implementing HTML5 securely. For example, this cheat sheet references ways that a DOM-based XSS vulnerability can be avoided if you configure pages to interpret exchange messages as data, never as the code itself. If you would like more information about configuring web messaging, web sockets, or geolocation, you can find the reference here:

cheatsheetseries.owasp.org/cheatsheets/HTML5_Security_Cheat_Sheet.
html#introduction.

SOAP

Simple Object Access Protocol (SOAP) is designed to exchange XML-based information in
computer networks. SOAP provides a basic messaging format. The message is a one-way
transmission between SOAP nodes. Messages consist of three parts: an envelope, a set of
processing rules, and a set of procedure calls and responses. The advantage of SOAP is that
it is built on open technologies, and it will work on a wide variety of platforms. However,
because SOAP can pass messages via HTML, there is the possibility that an attacker could
intercept these messages and alter or sniff the contents.

Built using XML, SOAP is a specification for exchanging information
associated with web services. SOAP can be exploited for attacks such as
buffer overflows so that various parameters can be exploited.

Web Services Security

Web Services Security (WS-Security, WSS) is a security technology developed by OASIS that
was designed as an extension to SOAP. One major issue with SOAP, just as with other applications, is poor input validation and sanitization of data. WS-Security was designed to take
input in the form of SOAP messages over protocols such as HTTPS. SOAP works with several formats, such as Security Assertion Markup Language (SAML), Kerberos, and X.509
certificates. SOAP can provide confidentiality, integrity, and nonrepudiation.

A CASP+ candidate needs to know that SOAP was developed by OASIS.

Attacks

One of the most important things you can do as an enterprise defender is to understand your
attack surface. To put the proper controls in place, organizations typically gather lists of
external-facing assets, web applications, databases, storage in the cloud, and VPN services.
Once you have a solid understanding of these, then you can begin the process of targeted
attack testing and assessment. The reason for targeted attack testing is to measure the effectiveness of currently used controls. You can use penetration testing or tabletop testing to
identify gaps in technical controls, create a response, and measure remediation, measuring
the risk and possibilities of these attacks of being successful in your network.

Cross-Site Scripting

Cross-site scripting (XSS) attacks are an application issue caused by an injection problem.
XSS occurs when malicious scripts are injected into otherwise trusted websites. The

malicious script is then passed to the end user's browser, which has no way to know that the script is malicious, since it has been passed from a trusted site. Once executed on the end user's computer, the malicious script can access any cookies, session tokens, or other sensitive information retained by their browser and used with that site. XSS attacks allow the attacker to gain a high level of control over the user's system and communicate directly with the site to which the user is connected.

XSS attacks occur when invalid input data is included in dynamic content that is sent to a user's web browser for rendering, as in the following examples:

```
index.php?name=guest<script>alert('attacked')</script>
```

or

```
index.php?name=<script>window.onload = function()
{var link=document.getElements⇒ByTagName("a");link[0].
href="http://not-real-xssattackexamples.com";}</script>
```

XSS can occur anywhere a web application uses input from a user in the output it generates, without validating or encoding it. Attackers can inject malicious JavaScript, VBScript, ActiveX, Flash, or HTML into headers for execution on the user's computer. The Common Weakness Enumeration list, specifically CWE-644, deals with an application that incorrectly interprets HTTP headers used in a web browser, resulting in an attacker using XSS against a user.

The CASP+ exam may feature one or more simulations where you will need to recognize scripts or commands; they will appear as </script> in the question.

> CASP+ candidates must be familiar with many well-known attacks such as XSS, CSRF, and directory traversal. One example is shown here (a non-functional template example):
>
> ```
> http://ip_address/scripts/%2e%2e%2f%2e%2e%2f/winnt/system32/
> cmd.exe?/c+dir
> ```
>
> Note the %2e%2e%2f%2e%2e%2f in the middle of the URL. Those are encoded Unicode characters. Each %2e%2e%2f is encoded Unicode, which, when decoded, represents ../. By having this string twice, a person browsing to that link would see the browser traverse back up two levels and then down to the Windows working directory in order to execute the command window.
>
> Again, this link is only a nonfunctional template, and it's clearly not intended for building your own actual directory traversal attack.

Cross-Site Request Forgery

Closely related to XSS is the *cross-site request forgery (CSRF) attack*. A CSRF attack tricks a user's browser into sending a forged HTTP request, including the user's session cookie and authentication information, to a vulnerable web application. CSRF allows an attacker to force the user's browser to generate requests so that the vulnerable application thinks that the legitimate request is from the victim.

One way to validate a user is using a Completely Automated Public Turing test to tell Computers and Humans Apart (CAPTCHA). CAPTCHA is a security measure where there is a challenge and response to authenticate the user. There are two parts to CAPTCHA, a random sequence of letters and numbers that are distorted but still human readable. The user has to type the letters into a text box to verify they are not a bot.

Both XSS and CSRF flaws are quite widespread. A good source for more information is the *Open Web Application Security Project (OWASP)* at www.owasp.org.

Injections

Many database products such as Microsoft SQL Server, MySQL, and Oracle allow sophisticated access queries to be made. If the database and the underlying OS do not have the proper security controls in place, the attacker can create queries against the database that disclose unauthorized information. This type of attack is generally known as *SQL injection*. A SQL injection attack is carried out when the attacker uses a series of malicious SQL queries to manipulate the SQL database directly. SQL injection attacks can be launched from the address bar of a website, from within application fields, or through queries and searches. Once the SQL injection is launched, the malformed input may cause the database to become unstable or leak information. Attackers use logic such as a single quote (') to test the database for vulnerabilities. Responses such as the one shown in the following code snippet give the attacker the feedback needed to know that the database is vulnerable to attack:

```
Microsoft OLE DB Provider for ODBC Drivers error '80040e14'
[Microsoft][ODBC SQL Server Driver][SQL Server]Syntax error converting
the nvarchar value 'sa_login' to a column of data type int.
/index.asp, line 5
```

Although knowing the syntax and response used for a database attack is not required exam knowledge, you should be able to recognize SQL probing where an attacker uses the single quote (') symbol.

Although the issues that cause SQL injection have been known for many years, they continue to be a common attack vector. Incidents of voter information theft in the run-up to the 2016 U.S. presidential election were made possible by SQL injection. One such case was documented to have occurred at the Illinois State Board of Election. The attack vector was indeed a SQL injection attack. Some of the symptoms that raised alarms were that "processor usage had spiked to 100 percent with no explanation" and evidence of automated SQL queries was determined from the analysis of server logs. To help seal this vulnerability, several new procedures and controls were put in place. See the following article:

https://abc7chicago.com/politics/how-the-russians-penetrated-illinois-election-computers/3778816

Preventing these types of input problems requires true *defense in depth*. This starts by filtering traffic before it ever enters the network. One approach is to use a *web application firewall (WAF)*, the next advancement in firewall design. WAFs analyze web traffic and can be used to filter out SQL injection attacks, malware, XSS, and CSRF. WAFs require a high degree of application awareness as they have the ability to analyze web traffic and look for items such as malicious XML injection constructs and SQL injection commands.

Another item that can be used to help defend against SQL injection attacks is a *database activity monitor (DAM)*. DAM systems have emerged because companies face many more threats such as SQL injection than in the past. There is also a much greater need for compliance so that companies can track what activity occurs within databases. Laws and regulations such as HIPAA and PCI DSS have increased this demand. DAMs basically monitor the database and analyze the type of activity that is occurring. You can think of DAM as being similar to *Security Information and Event Management (SIEM)*, except that SIEM systems like Splunk correlate and analyze events from multiple sources, whereas DAMs focus specifically on database access and activity.

Not only do you have to protect against SQL and XML injection, *LDAP injection* is another vulnerability if proper controls are not in place. In LDAP injection, queries are constructed from untrusted input without prior validation or sanitization. LDAP uses queries constructed from metacharacters such as brackets or quote symbols. These control the meaning of the query, which affects the type and number of objects retrieved from the directory. If an attacker can create an input command that processes these control characters, they can alter the query and change the intended behavior.

In Figure 4.6, watch how an attacker changing this LDAP search query finds a node with a given username and password by adding asterisks in strategic locations; it can change the query, and it always evaluates as true, in which case authentication has been bypassed.

FIGURE 4.6 LDAP injection

Original LDAP Query:

find("(&(cn=" + username +")(userPassword=" + pass +"))")

Malicious LDAP Query:

find("(&(cn=*)(cn=*))(|(cn=*)(userPassword=" + pass +"))")

Sandbox Escape

Application sandboxing is the process of writing files to a sandbox or temporary storage area instead of their normal location. Sandboxing is used to limit the ability of code to execute malicious actions on a user's computer. If you launch an application in the sandbox, it won't be able to edit the Registry or even make changes to other files on the user's hard drive.

What if there was an exploit that allowed malicious code to be executed from a sandbox outside an isolated environment, forcing code to be run or achieve a function?

In September 2020, Google awarded $20,000 USD as a bug bounty for two researchers who found a *sandbox escape* vulnerability in the Chrome web browser. The vulnerability, CVE-2020-6573, was described as high severity. In this specific case, combining multiple vulnerabilities caused remote code execution and launched arbitrary code in the browser's rendering process. In a sandbox escape vulnerability, an attacker can execute malicious code from a sandbox outside of an environment, forcing the device to run the code within it.

Improper Error Handling

A big part of security is building good controls to check all input data (input validation), processed data, and output data. Yet, even when this is done correctly, you must still deal with potential errors. Sometimes this is where application developers get into trouble because they provide the user with too much information. As an example, if we go to a web page that handles authentication and enter the wrong password, does the application respond with "wrong password" or the more ambiguous error "wrong username/password," which makes it a little harder for an intruder? Here are a couple of examples of this type of problem. First, there is the httpd.conf file:

```
<location /server-status>
SetHandler server-status
</Location>
```

This configuration file allows anyone to view the server status page, which contains detailed information about the current use of the web server. Another example is the php .ini file found on many web servers. When used, this file provides verbose error messages:

```
display_error = on
log_errors = on
Error_log = syslog
ignore_repeated_errors = Off
```

The limits of an application must always be tested to see what responses are returned and what error messages are displayed.

Geotagging

Geolocation and location-based services are another concern for the CASP+. This technology includes the ability to geotag the location of photographs. Most smartphone and tablet users turn this feature on when they activate a device, yet they never realize that this information is used in every photograph they take. Most people don't realize that *geotagging* is active on their smartphones, either because it is enabled by default and not exposed to the user as an option or because they were asked to enable it and then promptly forgot about it. As a result, individuals often share too much information, right down to their exact location.

The security concern is that hackers or others may have the ability to track the location of specific individuals. If you think this sounds a little creepy, it is! There is an application known as Creepy (`www.geocreepy.com`) that allows users to track individuals using the photos they have posted online. Creepy gathers geolocation-related information from social networking sites and presents the results using Google Maps.

Many applications also make use of this technology to identify a user's exact location. The idea is that that you can identify a user by their location for service or revenue. Examples include coupons from nearby coffee shops and restaurants.

Interception/Hijacking

Interception is defined by Merriam Webster as "the action or fact of preventing someone or something from continuing to a destination." There are many ways an attacker can intercept our information, and they can be difficult to detect. Interception can be perpetrated against our data in motion or our data at rest.

Message interception attacks exploit a weakness in a network. If you can intercept a message, think packet sniffing or key logging, you can get valuable information.

Session hijacking is a combination of interception and injection. It allows an attacker to avoid password protection by taking over an existing connection once authentication is complete.

BGP is used to exchange routing information but is considered antiquated and does not force encryption to be used. Border Gateway Protocol (BGP) hijacking, sometimes called *prefix hijacking* or *IP hijacking*, happens when an attacker redirects web traffic away from its intended destination. It instead sends incoming requests to IP addresses under the attacker's own control. It is easy for cybercriminals to impersonate the victim's IP address and impersonate the victim for phishing and spamming.

Although email has many great features and provides a level of communication previously not possible, it's not without problems. Now, before we beat it up too much, you must keep in mind that email was designed in a different era. Decades ago, security was not as much of a driving issue as usability. By default, email sends information via clear text, so it is susceptible to eavesdropping and interception. Email can be easily spoofed so that the true identity of the sender may be masked. Email is also a major conduit for spam, phishing, and viruses. Spam is unsolicited bulk mail.

Clickjacking

Clickjacking, or UI redressing, is described in Wikipedia as "a malicious technique of tricking web users into revealing confidential information or taking control of their computer while clicking on seemingly innocuous web pages." This attack works by controlling what the user sees when visiting a web page. Attackers construct a page in such a way that they control what links or buttons a user can see. Victims click on a visible link, yet in reality they are selecting another link that is not visible to them. This is made possible in the way the attacker designed the web page. In essence, the attacker constructed a page where what the user sees and clicks does not reflect what action the click actually performs.

Clickjacking targets state management. State management refers to the management of the state of one or more user interface controls, such as buttons, icons, or choice options in a graphical user interface. If an attacker can obscure the items chosen by the victim, the user has no way of seeing if a button is in the enabled state or if valid choices have been made. In many cases, a security professional may have no control over development of an application and be left with finding ways to defend against the vulnerability. To defend against the Flash-based vulnerabilities, set the Always Deny option in the Global Privacy Settings of your Flash Player plug-in. Other defenses include disabling plug-ins and using tools such as NoScript (`noscript.net/`).

Session Management

Session management attacks occur when an attacker breaks into the web application's session management mechanism to bypass the authentication controls and spoof the valid user. Two session management techniques are typically used:

- Session token prediction
- Session token sniffing and tampering

Session token prediction attacks occur when the tokens follow a predictable pattern or increment numerically. If an attacker can make a large number of requests, it may be easier to determine the pattern used by the web application.

In some situations, the token may not be encrypted or might even be using weak encoding such as hex-encoding or Base64. The attacker might also attempt to simply sniff a valid token with tools such as Wireshark or Burp Proxy.

If HTTP cookies are being used and the security flag is not set, the attacker can attempt to replay the cookie to gain unauthorized access. Other session management issues include the following:

Session IDs Placed in the URL   Some sites encode the session ID and place it in the URL for the page.

Time-Out Exploitation   If a victim uses a public computer and just closes the browser, the website may not log the user out, thus allowing an attacker to reopen the site and gain full access.

Firesheep is a good example of a modern session-hijacking tool that is easy to use and also demonstrates the vulnerabilities of poor session management. Now there is code that implements Firesheep as a browser-based tool. Code for this browser extension can be downloaded from `github.com/codebutler/firesheep`.

Input Validation

Input validation is the process of validating data received from the client. This flaw occurs when client input is not validated before being processed by the web application. Web application controls should be used to check that the input is valid. This becomes important because in many automated systems, the output of one system is the input of another. In such situations, data should be checked to validate the information from both the sending and receiving applications. For example, if you enter a negative quantity in a field that requires a positive value, will the web application actually accept it? It shouldn't!

VM Escape

Finally, there are security disadvantages in that you are now running multiple systems on one physical machine. Should this machine fail, you lose multiple systems. Viruses, worms, and malware also have the potential to migrate from one virtual machine to another. This is usually referred to as VM hopping or escape. *VM hopping* is when an attacker tries to gain control of other virtual machines on the same hypervisor.

VM escape simply means that the attacker is able to run malware or code on a virtual machine, which allows an operating system running within it to break out and interact directly with the hypervisor. This term is described in more detail here: `www.research-gate.net/publication/255791810_virtual_machine_escapes`. VM escape can be a serious problem when a single platform is hosting multiple VMs for many companies or VMs of various security levels.

Securing virtual servers requires the same focus on defense in depth that would be applied to securing physical systems.

VLAN Hopping

A potential attack against VLANs is VLAN hopping. *VLAN hopping* can be defined as an attack in which the attacker tries to send data to hosts that belong to other VLANs. This is accomplished by tagging the data with a different VLAN ID tag and labeling the data as belonging to a different VLAN than where it belongs. A VLAN tag is simply an extra field placed into the Ethernet frame. As an example, the 802.1Q tag uses a 32-bit field placed in between the source MAC and the Ether type field in the header. This attack can be launched in one of two ways: switch spoofing or double tagging.

Switch spoofing occurs when the attacker creates a trunk link between the switch and the attacker. This allows the attacker to communicate with hosts in all VLANs configured on that switch, and traffic for multiple VLANs is then accessible to the attacker. The second technique, double tagging, occurs when the attacker prepends two VLAN tags to packets that are in transit. The header is stripped off, and a second, false header is added. The spoofed VLAN header indicates that the data frame is destined for a host on a second, target VLAN. This technique allows the attacking host to bypass layer 3 security measures that are used to isolate hosts logically from one another.

Proactive Detection

You will never win a game of chess by only playing defense. To be successful at defending an organization, you will have to build out the offense. At a certain point in an organization's security maturity, you will have to start thinking about your adversaries and their attack methodology and build out teams that handle incident response, manage penetration testing, handle hunt teaming, and consume threat intelligence with the goal of being proactively defending your organization.

Incident Response

By the nature of the term, you know *incident response* to be a reactive, responsive effort. But what about *incident detection*? We know that later today hackers might attack our systems. We know that next week we might discover a newly compromised system. Why wait to react when we can be proactive and discover potential incidents ourselves before the bad guys have a chance to do any damage?

Hunt teaming is the name given to the in-house activity of seeking out those vulnerabilities before we have to react to an incident that has occurred. This is accomplished in several different ways. You and your team might perform log analysis on entire systems or other individual devices. This is more easily done if a SIEM is already in place that presents a centralized view of security and event information.

Analysis must be done on more than just the security logs. Many companies that use all of the same devices, logs, and monitoring are still breached. Beyond the objective analysis of logs, you must perform heuristics and behavioral analysis. Oftentimes as security professionals, we find that we have a better gut feeling and can adopt a more practical approach than those serving in other roles.

Countermeasures

Proper analysis and brainstorming will get a cybersecurity team started in the right direction. When implementing countermeasures to make changes to an existing vulnerability, please note we are not calling it a solution. A solution implies the problem has been corrected. A *countermeasure* is an action taken to negate or counteract a danger or threat. The same problem can occur in the future. But if the original countermeasure was successful, this problem will not happen again.

Using the impact/effort matrix, it will help to ask the right questions, such as how much effort is needed and what the anticipated impact is for future cybersecurity projects. In Figure 4.7, you see the Impact/Effort Matrix.

FIGURE 4.7   Impact/Effort Matrix

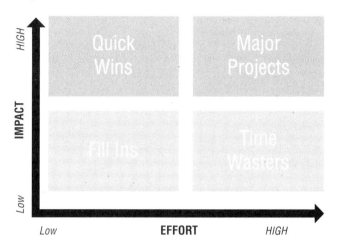

- **Quick wins:** Give the best return based on the effort.
- **Major projects:** Provide long-term returns but may be more complex to execute.
- **Fill ins:** Don't require a lot of effort but neither do they offer many benefits.
- **Time wasters:** Time-consuming activities with low impact that should be avoided.

Deceptive Technology

Deceptive technology is designed to lure attackers to a "sweet" location in the network where they think they are getting legitimate access to corporate data. In reality, they're being observed for their tactics and techniques.

These technologies include the following:

- **Honeynet:** A purposely semivulnerable network of machines to attract an attacker, set up as a decoy to divert attackers from the real network.
- **Honeypot:** A system set up with legitimate-looking data to bait attackers. These are used for research purposes to improve overall security.
- **Honeyfiles:** Decoy files on a server used as bait for attackers to access. These files could be named strategically to entice the attacker to open them. When opened, the file trips a silent alarm, notifying security that the decoy file was accessed.

As technology advances and attackers become more sophisticated, this type of deceptive technology is becoming a single layer in threat research. Automation and machine learning are becoming new ways to detect intruders. Deceptive technology is now capable of being integrated in security information and event management (SIEM), endpoint detection and response (EDR), and security orchestration, automation, and response (SOAR) software. Having these integrations helps ensure threat detection capabilities.

USB Key Drops

Physical honeypots like USB keys or other media can be used when other means of accessing an organization aren't possible. To perform a *USB drop key* attack, the thumb drive loaded with attack tools is aimed at common operating systems or software found in the target company. These drives are dropped in locations where they are likely to be found, sometimes with a label that indicates that the drive has interesting or important data on it. The goal of attacks like these is to have the drives or media found and then accessed on target computers. If the attack tools are successful, they phone home to a system allowing remote access through firewalls and other security barriers.

Simulation

Simulation is the action of pretending you're in a situation. In a computer model, it's usually for the purpose of studying. In recent years, cyber ranges and network *simulators* have become popular for hands-on experience for building a network, configuring ACLS, threat hunting, and more.

If it has been a while since you have configured or analyzed ACLs, you may want to consider downloading one of the many router simulators that are available. These are great practice tools, and they may be helpful if you're asked an ACL question on the exam.

Packet Tracer is Cisco's visual simulation tool that simulates dynamic network topologies comprised of Cisco routers, switches, firewalls, and more. Packet Tracer was originally designed as an educational aid for Cisco's Networking Academy but is an excellent simulator for anyone pursuing an entry-level Cisco certification, such as the CCENT or CCNA R&S.

There is absolutely no cost associated with using Cisco's Packet Tracer. It is completely free to download and use. The only requirement is that you create and log into Packet Tracer with a Cisco Networking Academy account, which is free to create.

Security Data Analytics

Poor data analysis can lead to making a poor business decision and choosing the wrong business strategy. Bad business decisions can lead to unhappy customers. Bad decisions in cybersecurity can lead to a breach that will bankrupt a company. To avoid making the wrong decision based on bad data, companies apply a data pipeline for moving and storing data.

A data pipeline is software that enables the automated flow of information from one point to another. This software prevents many common problems such as bottlenecks, corruption of information, and duplicate entries. A data pipeline consists of a series of data processing steps. If the data is not currently loaded into the data platform, it is ingested at the beginning of the pipeline. Then there are a series of steps in which each step delivers an output that is the input to the next step. This continues until the pipeline is complete. In some cases, steps may be run in parallel.

Data pipelines consist of three key elements: source, processing, and destination. In some data pipelines, the destination may be called a sink. Data pipelines enable the flow of data from an application to a data warehouse, from a data lake to an analytics database, or into a payment processing system.

Streaming data pipelines is a data pipeline architecture that handles millions of events at scale, in real time. As a result, you can collect, analyze, and store huge amounts of information. This allows for analytics, filtering, and reporting in real time. In Figure 4.8, you see an example of a data pipeline.

FIGURE 4.8   Data pipeline

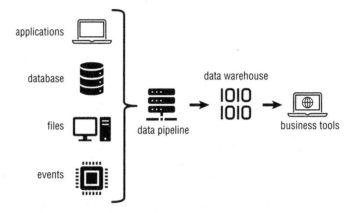

Benefits of using a data pipeline include making your organization more agile, economical, and transparent.

Application Control

Application control can be as granular as a tool in an operating system such as Windows Defender Application Control, which is made to protect computers against malware and other nefarious software. It enforces an explicit list of applications that are allowed to run on that PC. There are no hardware or firmware prerequisites, but it has to meet the minimum Windows version requirements to be executable.

Application control can be purchased and licensed by third-party software companies that enable you to allow or block certain applications throughout a network. There may be certain applications that are malicious and should be blocked, but they also could be genuine and authentic; for example, management has decided no one should be playing Solitaire at work.

A feature that falls under how applications are controlled is atomicity. Atomic execution is the ability of a database to dictate when a transaction is absolute. The database system decides either that a specific transaction must fully happen or that it does not happen at all. It will not be partially completed.

Atomicity is part of the ACID (atomicity, consistency, isolation, durability) model, which is used to guarantee the reliability and control of database transactions. It is essential that a database system that offers atomicity be able to do so even in a catastrophic power failure. The definition of atomic execution of a transaction depends on its implementation. For example, if you are ordering a pizza, the transaction has three parts. You have to choose the pizza, pay for it, and then enter your address to have it delivered. If any of these happen without the others, the pizzeria will have a confusing situation, such as a pizza paid for but no idea where to deliver it.

From a vendor standpoint, licensing applications is a way to ensure customers are in compliance with software license agreements that can protect from misuse or piracy. However, compliance with licensure for some vendors is based on monetary concerns. For example, some vulnerability products ration the number of assets that can be scanned for vulnerabilities, and if that number is exceeded, the customer is contacted to examine how they are using the product in their environment. Protecting intellectual property and defending against tampering for nefarious reasons would start with hardening the application and adding security controls into the application. For example, to prevent misuse of data, a vendor might add asymmetric and symmetric cryptography, or to prevent reverse engineering, a vendor could add signing and validating application binaries.

Allow and Block Lists

An allow list can be defined as a list of entities that are granted access. Block listing is just the opposite; it lists what cannot be accessed. For example, you may block list social media like Facebook and Instagram so that employees cannot visit those websites. Allow lists make more sense in an environment where an asset or service should not be public, and you can be more rigid about control.

Think of allow lists as an implicit "deny all" unless added to the list, while block listing is an implicit "allow all" unless added to the list. You rarely see these strategies implemented on the same technology at the same time.

Security Automation

The role of automation in cybersecurity operations, often referred to as SecOps, is to ease the heavy burden of cybersecurity by automating repetitive behaviors. Security automation tooling allows security teams to automate repetitive and time-consuming tasks with a goal of bettering the workflow and improving efficiency.

Automation allows you to prioritize threats and handle some cyberattacks automatically with courses of action that have been predetermined. This reduces human intervention and response time. Security automation is the machine-based execution of security actions with the power to programmatically detect, investigate, and remediate cyberthreats by identifying incoming threats, triaging, and prioritizing alerts as they emerge.

Automation can take a platform approach that is increasingly required to properly integrate DevOps with SecOps teams to better adapt to changes in how applications are deployed and managed. DevOps automates and monitors the process of software creation, ranging from integration, testing, and releasing to deploying and managing it. Choosing the correct platform configuration tool is a major challenge in implementation. The top competitors in the market include Chef, Ansible, and Puppet. Each of these tools has its strengths.

If your organization does not have a DevOps team to assist with the automation of security tasks, you could use Cron jobs, Bash, PowerShell, or Python for some of these tasks. All of these have their pros and cons that make them better for some tasks than others.

- Cron/scheduled tasks
  - Developed in 1975 by AT&T
  - Command-line utility
  - Job scheduler
  - Automates system maintenance and administration
  - Very suitable for low-level repetitive tasks
- Bash
  - Linux/Unix command language
  - Does not come preinstalled in Windows
  - Great for writing CLI scripts
  - Better startup time than Python
  - Poor debugging tools
- PowerShell
  - Microsoft Windows configuration management
  - General-purpose using cmdlets, file transfer, background jobs, pipelines
  - Continuous expansion with new cmdlets
- Python
  - Object-oriented programming (OOP)
  - Can be used for nearly any task, security or otherwise
  - Simple, easy to learn
  - Many libraries and documentation
  - Good debugging tools

Physical Security

Physical security cannot be forgotten, and often testing it is part of the penetration testing process of examining real-world vulnerabilities in the physical barriers that protect employees and sensitive information. Many organizations do a very good job of protecting their network and forget about the risk associated with theft of physical devices or the use of social engineering to convince a receptionist that you are from the cable company and need to be allowed into a server room.

Without strong physical security measures put in place, no CASP+ professional can say they have effective security controls in place. Not only is it important to put the proper security measures in place, such as the proper type of locks on the right type of doors, but these security measures must also be periodically reviewed as the business grows and expands to expose weak physical barriers.

Granular procedures should be in place for reviewing lighting, locking down areas, and examining visitor logs. There have been situations where an authorized visitor has unlocked a window so they would have easy access to a classified area for breaking into later. Security training for those taking care of highly secure areas is extremely important. Doors and windows as well electronic keys or badging could be leveraged for access. If the organization has fencing, gates, and security lighting, procedures should be in place to make sure that fencing gaps, gate controls, cameras, and lighting are working as intended. Accurate visitor logs and camera recordings should be stored properly according to procedures for future investigations, should a breach be detected in the future. These logs and camera recordings from sensitive areas could be even more important if a highly classified area is impacted.

Just as we have data classification, physical locations can be classified in a variety of ways. The National Counterintelligence and Security Center (NCSC) has specific technical specifications for construction and management of Sensitive Compartmented Information Facilities (SCIF). A SCIF is a secure room that guards against electronic surveillance and is used to deny unauthorized access. At this extreme of a confined space, every single opportunity for breach is examined with dedicated resources whose only role is to protect the people and data being housed, discussed, and stored at this location. At the other extreme, an open area will not have the same level of dedicated resources but should still be evaluated for any type of risk.

For more information on how to build, maintain, and review procedures and policies on SCIFs, you can visit www.dni.gov/files/Governance/IC-Tech-Specs-for-Const-and-Mgmt-of-SCIFs-v15.pdf.

Summary

This chapter focused on the importance of vulnerability and risk management. This is of critical importance to a security professional, since applications are a highly targeted area. Years ago, web servers were among the primary targets for attackers. Today, client-side systems are widely targeted. They are targeted in part because they are target rich. Vulnerable applications offer an attacker easy access to a system.

Although applications are important, that's only one area of concern. The network is also important. Networks must be able to withstand denial-of-service attacks, backdoor attacks, hijacking, password cracking, and so forth. Each takes advantage of inherent weaknesses in the network technologies. One of the best ways to defend against these threats and many others is to perform periodic testing. This testing can take the form of security audits, vulnerability scanning, and penetration testing. Each plays a role in helping to secure critical infrastructure and defending a network against attacks.

Exam Essentials

Know how software exploitation occurs.   Software exploitation involves using features or capabilities of a software product in an unplanned manner or one that was unanticipated by the software manufacturer. In many cases, the original feature enhanced the functionality of the product but, unfortunately, created a potential vulnerability.

Be able to describe specific application issues.   Some common application issues include XSS, CSRF, SQL injection, VM escape, interception attacks, and poor input validation.

Know the differences between vulnerability scanning and penetration testing.   Vulnerability scanning is typically performed with packaged programs such as SAINT, Nessus, or Retina. These programs can help identify vulnerable systems and applications that require patching. Penetration testing is usually performed in an adversarial manner, and questions raised include what attackers can see and what they can do with this knowledge. Penetration testing is similar to illegal attacks by computer criminals but done with the system owner's permission.

Be able to describe password cracking.   Password cracking is the process of retrieving and cracking passwords that have been stored in or transmitted by a computer system. Password-cracking tools can be used to test the strength of your passwords in one of several basic ways, including dictionary, hybrid, and brute-force attacks and rainbow tables.

Define penetration testing techniques.   Penetration testing can be performed with full knowledge of or very little information about the target network. Each technique offers advantages. Penetration testing may also be done with or without the knowledge of all insiders.

Be able to describe when code review should be used.   Before applications are deployed, they must be reviewed and tested. The type of test will vary depending on the situation. For example, if an organization builds the application in house, the code will most likely be available, and a full code review can be performed. In other situations, where a company buys an off-the-shelf application, the source code may not be available.

Be able to describe why social engineering attacks are hard to prevent.   Social engineering is hard to prevent as it does not target hardware or software; it targets people. Without proper training, employees may not know that certain security policies exist or how to react in specific situations. Training and awareness are the best defenses against social engineering attacks.

Review Questions

You can find the answers in Appendix.

1. Which of the following BEST defines risk in IT?

   A. You have a vulnerability with a known active threat.

   B. You have a threat with a known vulnerability.

   C. You have a risk with a known threat.

   D. You have a threat with a known exploit.

2. Charles is a systems manager. He is conducting a vulnerability assessment. Which of the following is not a requirement for him to know?

   A. Access controls

   B. Understanding of the systems to be evaluated

   C. Potential threats

   D. Passwords

3. Gavin has been assigned to hire a third party to do a security assessment of his automotive manufacturing plant. What type of testing will give him the most neutral review of his company's security profile?

   A. OSINT

   B. Vulnerability scanning

   C. No knowledge

   D. Blue hat

4. Olivia is the senior security analyst for a large online news organization. She was briefed by the incident response team that the organization has fallen victim to an XSS attack and malicious web scripting code had executed in a trusted web page. What does she do to prevent this from happening in the future?

   A. Make sure the web application can validate and sanitize input.

   B. Implement patch management immediately.

   C. Request an external penetration test.

   D. There is no way to prevent this from happening on a publicly facing web server.

5. Alonso, a security administrator, has been contacted by a senior human resources manager to investigate a possible situation. They suspect that malicious activities are being caused by internal personnel and need to know if it is intentional or unintentional. After investigating, you believe it is unintentional and the most likely cause is which of the following?

   A. Fraud

   B. Espionage

   C. Embezzlement

   D. Social engineering

6. MaryAnn works for an insurance company. The company has experienced a natural disaster and used a hot site for three months and now is going to return to the primary site. What processes should be restored first?

   A. Finance department

   B. External communication

   C. Mission critical

   D. Least business-critical

7. Paul has a mission-critical Windows server with the CVE-2021-24086 vulnerability in his network. It is the target of a distributed denial-of-service attack and has blue screened twice. Multiple systems are flooding the bandwidth of that system. Which information security goal is being impacted by this type of an attack?

   A. Availability

   B. Baselines

   C. Integrity

   D. Emergency response

8. Sergio works as a security analyst for a global manufacturer. His organization has had an incident in its production environment and needs to verify that chain of custody, due diligence, and proper processes have been followed. He has been told to verify the forensic bit stream. Of the options listed, which would be done first?

   A. Verify backups

   B. Create containment

   C. Compare hashes

   D. Prepare documentation

9. An IoT software startup company has hired Don to provide expertise on data security. Clients are very concerned about confidentiality. If confidentiality is stressed more than availability and integrity, which of the following scenarios is best suited for the client?

   A. Virtual servers in a highly available environment. The client will use redundant virtual storage and terminal services to access software.

   B. Virtual servers in a highly available environment. The client will use single virtual storage and terminal services to access software.

   C. The client is assigned virtual hosts running on shared hardware. Physical storage is partitioned with block cipher encryption.

   D. The client is assigned virtual hosts running shared hardware. Virtual storage is partitioned with streaming cipher encryption.

10. Pieter discovered a meterpreter shell running a keylogger on the CFO's laptop. What security tenet is the keylogger mostly likely to break?

   A. Availability

   B. Threats

   C. Integrity

   D. Confidentiality

11. Tiffany works for a healthcare facility for the elderly that has made the decision to begin outsourcing some IT systems. Which of the following statements is true?

A. All outsourcing frees your organization from any rules or requirements.

B. All compliance and regulatory requirements are passed on to the provider.

C. The IT systems are no longer configured, maintained, or evaluated by your organization.

D. The outsourcing organization is free from any rules or regulations.

12. Greg is a security researcher for a cybersecurity intelligence company. He is currently examining a third-party vendor his company would like to use. He has found a way to use SQLi to deface their web server due to a missing patch in the company's web application. What is the threat of doing business with this organization?

A. Web defacement

B. Unpatched applications

C. Hackers

D. Education awareness

13. Adriana is responsible for PCI-DSS compliance for her banking organization. The policy she is held to requires that she be able to remove information from a database. She cannot remove data due to technical restrictions. She is pursuing a compensating control to mitigate the risk. What is her best option?

A. Insurance

B. Encryption

C. Deletion

D. Exceptions

14. Marco is a consultant for a vulnerability assessment firm. He has been assigned a task to quantify risks associated with information technology when validating the abilities of new security controls and countermeasures. What is the best way to identify the risks?

A. Vulnerability management

B. Pentesting

C. Threat and risk assessment

D. Data reclassification

15. Many organizations prepare for highly technical attacks and forget about the simple low-tech means of gathering information. Dumpster diving can be used by penetration testers in gaining access to unauthorized information. Which of these would the proactive detection team suggest to reduce risk?

A. Data classification and printer restrictions of intellectual property

B. Purchasing shredders for the copy rooms

C. Creating policies and procedures for document shredding

D. Bringing on an intern to shred all printed documentation

16. A vendor of new software that is deployed across your corporate network has announced a critical update is needed for a specific vulnerability. Your CIO wants to know what the vulnerability time has been. When can you give them that information?

   A. After the patch is downloaded and installed in the affected system or device

   B. When the patch is released and available to the public

   C. When the patch is created by the vendor

   D. When the vulnerability is discovered

17. Due to time constraints and budget, Bradley's organization has opted to hire a third-party organization to start working on a very important vulnerability management project. Which of these are the benefits of outsourcing your vulnerability management program?

   A. Outsourcing is a valid option and not much concern since any and all damage is the responsibility of the third party.

   B. If the company has an acceptable security record, then it makes perfect sense to outsource anything.

   C. You should never outsource. It will lead to legal and compliance issues.

   D. Outsourcing vulnerability management can save time, increase visibility, prioritize remediation, and reduce dependency on internal resources.

18. What is the concern with using the C language commands `scanf()`, `strcpy()`, `bcopy()`, `vsprintf()`, and `gets()`?

   A. These commands are no longer supported in C.

   B. These commands don't check buffer size and lend themselves to buffer overflow attacks.

   C. These commands don't perform input validation and therefore lend themselves to injection attacks.

   D. There is no concern with using these commands.

19. As a security analyst, you are charged with running a vulnerability scan on the production network. While examining the scan results, you notice that various servers are missing patches. You decide to look for an automated process of installing patching on systems. Which of the following could automate this process?

   A. Security assessment

   B. Vulnerability management

   C. Vulnerability scanner

   D. Patch management system

20. Joe works for a retail organization. The corporate office is bombarded daily with hundreds of spam messages. He has implemented a CAPTCHA system on the corporate web server to prevent the SPAM messages. Which of the following other attacks will most likely be prevented?

   A. CSRF

   B. XSS

   C. Two-factor authentication

   D. XMLi

Chapter

5

Compliance and Vendor Risk

THE CASP+ EXAM TOPICS COVERED IN THIS CHAPTER INCLUDE:

✓ **4.2 Explain the importance of managing and mitigating vendor risk.**

- **Shared responsibility model (roles/responsibilities)**
  - Cloud service provider (CSP)
    - Geographic location
    - Infrastructure
    - Compute
    - Storage
    - Networking
    - Services
  - Client
    - Encryption
    - Operating systems
    - Applications
    - Data
- **Vendor lock-in and vendor lock-out**
- **Vendor viability**
  - Financial risk
  - Merger or acquisition risk
- **Meeting client requirements**
  - Legal
  - Change management
  - Staff turnover
  - Device and technical configurations

- **Support availability**
- **Geographical considerations**
- **Supply chain visibility**
- **Incident reporting requirements**
- **Source code escrows**
- **Ongoing vendor assessment tools**
- **Third-party dependencies**
    - Code
    - Hardware
    - Modules
- **Technical considerations**
    - Technical testing
    - Network segmentation
    - Transmission control
    - Shared credentials

✓ **4.3 Explain compliance frameworks and legal considerations and their organizational impact.**

- **Security concerns of integrating diverse industries**
- **Data considerations**
    - Data sovereignty
    - Data ownership
    - Data classifications
    - Data retention
    - Data types
        - Health
        - Financial
        - Intellectual property
        - Personally identifiable information (PII)
    - Data removal, destruction, and sanitization
- **Geographic considerations**

- Location of data
- Location of data subject
- Location of cloud provider

- **Third-party attestation of compliance**

- **Regulations, accreditations, and standards**
  - Payment Card Industry Data Security Standard (PCI DSS)
  - General Data Protection Regulation (GDPR)
  - International Organization for Standardization (ISO)
  - Capability Maturity Model Integration (CMMI)
  - National Institute of Standards and Technology (NIST)
  - Children's Online Privacy Protection Act (COPPA)
  - Common Criteria
  - Cloud Security Alliance (CSA) Security Trust Assurance and Risk (STAR)

- **Legal considerations**
  - Due diligence
  - Due care
  - Export controls
  - Legal holds
  - E-discovery

- **Contract and agreement types**
  - Service-level agreement (SLA)
  - Master service agreement (MSA)
  - Non-disclosure agreement (NDA)
  - Memorandum of understanding (MOU)
  - Interconnection security agreement (ISA)
  - Operational-level agreement
  - Privacy-level agreement

This chapter discusses securing shared cloud computing. Cloud computing has come a long way in the last 10 to 15 years, and it can be found everywhere today. Cloud computing is changing the concept of network boundaries.

In this chapter, we'll look at both the advantages and disadvantages of virtualization and cloud computing as well as the concerns that they raise for enterprise security. We will also discuss compliance frameworks and legal considerations that can impact your organization, such as contract and agreement types. These topics are the items that CompTIA expects you to know for the exam.

Shared Responsibility in Cloud Computing

One area that can have a huge impact on enterprise security is cloud computing—using a remote datacenter to manage access to applications and host data. *Cloud computing* can include virtual servers, services, or anything you consume over the Internet. It is a concept that seeks to redefine consumption and delivery models for IT services, but one of the biggest challenges of cloud computing is confusion over who has what responsibility. Many organizations have experienced an incident or event of some kind due to the confusion over shared responsibility in cloud computing.

There are many different ways to deploy in the cloud. In a cloud computing environment, the end user may not know the location or details of a specific technology; it is fully managed by the *cloud service provider (CSP)*. Cloud computing offers users the ability to increase capacity or add services as needed without investing in new datacenters, training new personnel, or maybe even licensing new software. This on-demand, or elastic, service can be added to upgraded, and provided at any time. Some of the largest CSPs are Amazon Web Services (AWS), Google Cloud Provider (GCP), Microsoft Azure, and IBM Cloud. Their services and costs vary, but as a whole, their options include storing, processing, and analyzing data; protecting data at rest and in motion; and offering a variety of developer tools to create applications in the cloud.

Although cloud computing offers many benefits, a security professional must keep in mind that if policy dictates, all in-house security requirements must be present in any elastic cloud-based solution. Security should be a factor with every component of integrating with the cloud.

Cloud Service/Infrastructure Models

Cloud computing architecture depends on the CSP and can include various models. *Public use services* are provided by an external provider. *Private use services* are implemented internally in a cloud design. A *hybrid architecture* offers a combination of public and private cloud services to accomplish an organization's goals.

A CSP has several cloud models that can be broken into several basic designs that include infrastructure as a service, monitoring as a service, software as a service, and platform as a service. Each design is described here:

Software as a Service   *Software as a service (SaaS)* is designed to provide a complete packaged solution. The software is rented out to the user. The service is usually provided through some type of front end or web portal. While the end user is free to use the service from anywhere, the company pays a per-use fee. As an example, www .salesforce.com offers this type of service.

Platform as a Service   *Platform as a service (PaaS)* provides a platform for your use. Services provided by this model include all phases of the software development life cycle (SDLC) and can use application programming interfaces (APIs), website portals, or gateway software. These solutions tend to be proprietary, which can cause problems if the customer moves away from the provider's platform. An example of PaaS is the G Suite; see gsuite.google.com.

Infrastructure as a Service   *Infrastructure as a service (IaaS)* describes a cloud solution where you are buying infrastructure. You purchase virtual power to execute your software as needed. This is much like running a virtual server on your own equipment, except that you are now running a virtual server on a virtual disk. This model is similar to a utility company model, as you pay for what you use. An example of this model is Amazon Web Services; see aws.amazon.com.

In Figure 5.1 you see how these different tiers build upon one another.

Cloud Computing Providers and Hosting Options

A wide range of companies provide cloud computing services. Some well-known examples include Amazon, Citrix, Dropbox, Google, IBM, iCloud, Microsoft, Rackspace, and VMware. These providers offer a range of services that include the following:

Public Clouds   Available to the general public. An example would be Google Drive.

Private Clouds   Operated for a single company or entity. An example would be a company's private cloud storage of travel expenses.

Hybrid Clouds   A combination of a public and private cloud. An example would be a company's cloud storage of projects with varied access for internal employees and vendors.

Community Clouds   Shared between several organizations. An example would be cloud storage for a group of schools.

Multitenancy   Used to host a single software application that hosts multiple customers. An example would be a collaborative workspace for several project contributors.

Single Tenancy   Hosts a single software application designed to support one customer. An example would be a specialized HR application for one organization.

FIGURE 5.1   Layers of cloud computing

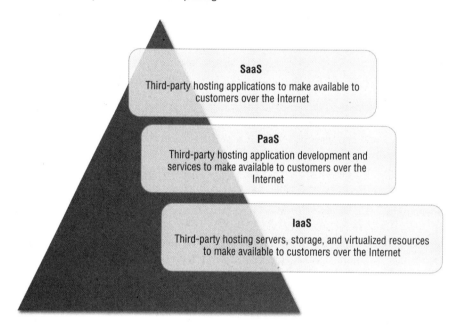

SaaS
Third-party hosting applications to make available to customers over the Internet

PaaS
Third-party hosting application development and services to make available to customers over the Internet

IaaS
Third-party hosting servers, storage, and virtualized resources to make available to customers over the Internet

Cloud computing is increasingly prevalent in almost every field. One prime example is cloud gaming, which is booming. You can read more about this at:

www.fortunebusinessinsights.com/blog/
top-10-cloud-gaming-companies-in-the-global-market-10605

In Exercise 5.1 you will examine the benefits of cloud computing.

EXERCISE 5.1

What Services Should Be Moved to the Cloud?

One of the first steps after identifying the benefits of cloud computing is to determine what services should or should not be moved to the cloud. Identify the parts of your organization's datacenter or application set that are not appropriate to move into the cloud.

1. What process would benefit most from the move?

2. Is the move cost effective?

3. What is the cost to provision the cloud service?

4. Does the cloud provider offer a trial period in which to evaluate the cloud services?

5. Is the cloud provider's business model suitable for this system?

6. Is the solution proprietary or open source?

7. Will the move offer the company a competitive advantage?

8. How does the company roll back if the cloud move doesn't go well?

9. What kind of disaster recovery can take place with the cloud configuration?

10. Can my company data be encrypted and isolated?

Based on your findings, what facts can you provide management about cloud-sourcing the data or application?

Although it is easy to see the benefits of a service, it's important not to overlook the costs. A CASP+ should be aware that most services require a startup fee. This is known as *provisioning*, which is nothing more than preparing and equipping a cloud service for new users. Some providers may also require minimum service length and even deprovisioning fees.

Benefits of Cloud Computing

On-demand, or elastic, cloud computing changes the way information and services are consumed and provided. Users can consume services at a rate that is set by their particular needs. Cloud computing offers several benefits, including the following:

Reduces Cost   Cloud technology saves procurement and maintenance of a company's own infrastructure and/or applications. Additionally, a cloud service is paid for as needed.

Increases Storage   Cloud providers have more storage capability that is elastic and has lower costs.

Provides a High Degree of Automation   Fewer employees are needed because local systems have been replaced with cloud-based solutions. The user does not need IT personnel to patch and update servers that have been outsourced to the cloud.

Offers Flexibility   Cloud computing offers much more flexibility than local-based solutions.

Provides More Mobility   One of the big marketing plugs is that users can access their data anywhere rather than having to remain at their desks.

Allows the Company's IT Department to Shift Focus   No hardware updates are required by the company—the cloud provider is now responsible. Companies are free to concentrate on innovation.

Anyone considering cloud-based services should make sure that they get a "try it, then buy it" clause. It's much the same as taking a new car for a test-drive before buying. You should never commit to a cloud-based service until you are sure that it functions the way you want it to. Some items to consider include an SLA, uptime guarantees, CPU, memory levels, bandwidth, cloud provider support time, and response time. Be sure to examine vendor viability, which is the capability of a vendor to survive in the marketplace and honor its contractual agreements. How financially secure is this organization? What are the odds that this cloud computing platform could be acquired while it is hosting your data?

 **Real World Scenario**

The Chain of Custody Evaporates in the Cloud

One concern with cloud computing is the way one company's data is separated from another company's data in the cloud. If the virtual slice next to yours is an illegal site or loaded with malware, what happens when the FBI seizes the data? More likely than not, they will seize the entire rack of servers. If they do so, your server would then be offline. When a company needs to figure out what happened in the event of a hack or compromise, cloud computing has the potential to be complicated and a tangled mess from a forensics and legal perspective. That is because the traditional methods and techniques don't apply. How will chain of custody be assured?

The benefits of cloud computing are many. One of the advantages of cloud computing is the ability to use someone else's storage. Another advantage is that when new resources are needed, the cloud can be leveraged, and the new resources may be implemented faster than if they were hosted locally at your company. With cloud computing, you pay as you go. Another benefit is the portability of the application. Users can access data from work, from home, or at client locations. There is also the ability of cloud computing to free up IT workers who may have been tied up performing updates, installing patches, or providing application support. The bottom line is that all of these reasons lead to reduced capital expense, which is what all companies are seeking.

When making decisions about selecting a cloud computing or software vendor, there are other considerations such as legal requirements, change management, employee churn, and configurations. Prior to looking at available vendors, it is best to define the organization's needs and what the application or platform would do for you. Many businesses have complex business processes and regulatory requirements. Key legal or compliance requirement questions for vendor assessment should include the following:

- Security
  - What type of encryption is being used?
  - How and where is information stored?
  - What measures are taken to prevent a data breach?
  - If you go out of business, what type of source code escrow or repository will you have access to?
- Infrastructure
  - Are there redundant backups in multiple locations?
  - What type of supply chain visibility do you have?
- Network
  - What type of systems are they using?
  - When are updates applied?
  - What type of tiered technical support do they offer?
  - Is support offered 24/7 or only during business hours?
- Data
  - Who controls the data in the event you no longer decide to use the vendor?
  - Who has access to the data?
  - What process is in place when an employee leaves the organization that your data is still safe?
  - Where is the data stored geographically?

- Incident management and disaster recovery services
  - What is the vendor's responsibility to notify you in the event of data breach or data loss?
  - Do they have a disaster recovery plan?
- Compliance requirements
  - What is done to protect confidential information?
  - Is data stored in compliance with regulations such as GDPR, HIPAA, PCI DSS, or SOX?

Security of On-Demand/Elastic Cloud Computing

Although cost and ease of use are two great benefits of cloud computing, there are significant security concerns when considering on-demand/elastic cloud computing. As a typical rule, the cloud service provider (CSP) is responsible for security of the cloud, while the client is responsible for security of their information while in the cloud. In Figure 5.2, you see the distribution of responsibility of security based on the layers of cloud computing mentioned earlier.

FIGURE 5.2   Distribution of security responsibility

On Premise	IaaS	PaaS	SaaS
Applications	Applications	Applications	Applications
Customer data	Customer data	Customer data	Customer data
Runtime	Runtime	Runtime	Runtime
Middleware	Middleware	Middleware	Middleware
Operating Systems	Operating Systems	Operating Systems	Operating Systems
Virtualization	Virtualization	Virtualization	Virtualization
Networking	Networking	Networking	Networking
Storage	Storage	Storage	Storage
Servers	Servers	Servers	Servers

■ Consumer responsibility   □ Provider responsibility

Cloud computing is a big change from the way IT services have been delivered and managed in the past. One of the advantages is the elasticity of the cloud, which provides the online illusion of an infinite supply of computing power. Cloud computing places assets outside the owner's security boundary. Historically, items inside the security perimeter were trusted, whereas items outside were not. With cloud computing, an organization is being forced to place their trust in the cloud provider. The cloud provider must develop sufficient controls to provide the same level of security that the organization would have had if the cloud were not used—or a greater level.

You must be aware of the security concerns of moving to a cloud-based service. The pressures are great to make these changes, but there is always a trade-off between security and usability.

Geographic Location

The cloud exists on hard drives on individual servers found in datacenters and server farms globally. CSPs might be based in one country and their servers anywhere else on the globe. Nothing is stored locally on a machine. Cloud data is accessible from any location from many devices, anytime you need it. Security is of utmost importance, so much so that some organizations have compliance requirements or company policy specifying that data be hosted in datacenters that their country has legal control over.

Infrastructure

The cloud shared responsibility and security model varies from vendor to vendor. The confusion about how a CSP operates, as well as terminology used to describe service offerings across a diverse landscape, can be difficult when implementing a secure infrastructure built of hardware, software, and APIs. Hardware and software components include servers, storage, networking, and virtualization, and accessing these can be done a multitude of ways including IaaS, SaaS, and PaaS, all described in more detail earlier in the chapter.

Compute

As a rule, the CSP is responsible for the security of the cloud, and the customer is responsible for security in the cloud. The CSP is responsible for the physical security of the cloud servers, global infrastructure, and the virtualization layer, and the customer, depending on the platform and model, is responsible for the rest, including networking controls, access management, and customer data.

In cloud computing, the generic term *compute* describes the concepts related to software computation including processing power, memory, networking, and storage. In the case of the AWS shared responsibility model, compute falls under the purview of the CSP.

Storage

Shared responsibility requires excellent communication and understanding between the customer and the provider, especially when it comes to data storage. Storage in the cloud is ultimately the responsibility of the customer across all cloud models. Best practices for secure cloud storage include confirming there are no publicly accessible storage areas, data is in a life-cycle management program and being kept for the right amount of time, and encryption with customer-managed keys and object versioning is being enforced.

Networking

Many people are using the cloud in some way and some may be unaware they are doing so, which can put them at risk. Cybersecurity professionals use the confidentiality/integrity/availability (CIA) triad in the implementation of security controls within a cloud network. To secure cloud services, the first step is to use the strongest encryption available. Another best practice is to review the user agreements and understand how the service protects your information. When signing up for a cloud provider, configure the privacy settings to limit how long the service keeps data and what kind of information is stored. Privacy settings should be reviewed periodically because the cloud may update agreements, leaving a gap in security controls. Guides like CIS Benchmarks or the AWS Well-Architected Framework can help build the networking framework for a secure implementation.

These are other questions that a security professional should ask when considering cloud-based solutions:

Does the data fall under regulatory requirements? Different countries have different requirements and controls placed on access. For example, organizations operating in the United States, Canada, or the European Union (EU) have many regulatory requirements. Examples of these include ISO 27002, Safe Harbor, Information Technology Infrastructure Library (ITIL), and Control Objectives for Information and Related Technology (COBIT). The CASP+ is responsible for ensuring that the cloud provider can meet these requirements and is willing to undergo certification, accreditation, and review as needed. The vendor's geographic location can be extremely important to compliance.

Who can access the data? Defense in depth is built on the concept that every security control is vulnerable. Cloud computing places much of the control in someone else's hands. One big area that is handed over to the cloud provider is access. Authentication and authorization are real concerns. Because the information or service now resides in the cloud, there is a much greater opportunity for access by outsiders. Insiders might pose an additional risk.

Insiders, or those with access, have the means and opportunity to launch an attack and lack only a motive. Anyone considering using the cloud needs to look at who is managing their data and what types of security controls are applied to individuals who may have logical or physical access.

 **Real World Scenario**

Read the Fine Print

For any cloud-based service that you are considering using, you will always want to read the fine print carefully. Dropbox revised its terms of service (TOS) to the following:

By submitting your stuff to the Services, you grant us (and those we work with to provide the Services) worldwide, non-exclusive, royalty-free, sublicensable rights to use, copy, distribute, prepare derivative works (such as translations or format conversions) of, perform, or publicly display that stuff to the extent reasonably necessary for the Service.

While the terms were changed after some users complained, the point remains that you should always pay close attention to what you are agreeing to for yourself or your company. TOS are a moving target!

To explain more about how terms of service can change over time, the following article provides examples from several companies:

`www.termsfeed.com/blog/update-notice-legal-agreements`

Does the cloud provider use a data classification system? A CASP+ should know how the cloud provider classifies data. Classification of data can run the gamut from a fully deployed classification system with multiple levels to a simple system that separates sensitive and unclassified data. Consumers of cloud services should ask whether encryption is used and how one customer's data is separated from another customer's data. Is encryption being used for data in transit or just for data at rest? Consumers of cloud services will also want to know what kind of encryption is being used.

Even Cloud-Based Email Needs Adequate Controls

Even basic services such as email require a thorough review before being moved to the cloud. Organizations are starting to move their email to cloud services hosted by Gmail, Yahoo email, and others, but there are issues to consider.

The increase in cloud email threats grew more than 60 percent in 2020 due to the rise in digital activity with new social engineering attacks, according to the Mimecast Threat Center.

What training does the cloud provider offer its employees? This is a rather important item in that people will always be the weakest link in security. Knowing how your provider trains their employees is an important item to review. Training helps employees know what the proper actions are and understand the security practices of the organization.

Staff turnover is very high in the technology industry. Training done well can reduce the likelihood of turnover while increasing the performance of an IT employee. Supervision can also be a major factor in staff leaving an organization. Training senior staff on how to lead teams more effectively and manage conflict is extremely beneficial.

What are the service level agreement (SLA) terms?   The SLA serves as a contracted level of guaranteed service between the cloud provider and the customer. An SLA is a contract that provides a certain level of protection. For a fee, the vendor agrees to repair, replace, or provide service within a contracted period of time. An SLA is usually based on what the customer specifies as the minimum level of services that will be provided.

Is there a right to audit?   This particular item is no small matter in that the cloud provider should agree in writing to the terms of audit. Where and how is your data stored? What controls are used? Do you have the right to perform a site visit or review records related to access control or storage?

Does the cloud provider have long-term viability?   Regardless of what service or application is being migrated to a cloud provider, you need to have confidence in the provider's long-term viability. There are costs not only to provision services but also for deprovisioning should the service no longer be available. If they were to go out of business, what would happen to your data? How long has the cloud provider been in business, and what is their track record? Will your data be returned if the company fails and, if so, in what format?

Could we experience vendor lock-in or lock-out?   Vendor lock-in can be difficult to plan for. *Vendor lock-in* happens when consumers become so integrated with a specific vendor or single cloud provider that they cannot easily move to another vendor without spending huge amounts of money, getting attorneys involved, or technical incompatibility; then the organization is at the mercy of the cloud provider. A related problem is *vendor lock-out*, when a consumer wants to leave a vendor but will have trouble transferring their data, services, and files. (In daily practice, you'll see that a lot of people use the terms *vendor lock-in* and *vendor lock-out* interchangeably.) The best way to avoid vendor lock-in and vendor lock-out is to understand the complex dependencies and commonalities of your technology stack as well as making apps portable, ensuring portability once migrated, and, as always, doing your due diligence.

⊕ Real World Scenario

What happens if your data disappears?

In 2021, Veritas Technologies, an enterprise data protection organization, released a report that highlights security issues with the adoption of the cloud. The research in the report finds that 57 percent of office workers have accidentally deleted files in the cloud and 29 percent would lie to cover up the mistake, 44 percent said no one noticed, and 17 percent said the data was not recoverable. The report can be found at www.veritas.com.

How will the cloud provider respond if there is a security breach?   Cloud-based services are an attractive target to computer criminals. If a security incident occurs, what support will you receive from the cloud provider? To reduce the amount of damage that these individuals can cause, cloud providers need to have incident response and handling policies in place. These policies should dictate how the organization handles various types of incidents. Cloud providers must have a computer security incident response team (CSIRT) that is tied into customer notification policies for law enforcement involvement.

What is the disaster recovery and business continuity plan (DR/BCP)?   Although you may not know the physical location of your services, they are physically located somewhere. All physical locations face threats, such as fire, storms, natural disasters, and loss of power. In the case of any of these events, the CASP+ will need to know how the cloud provider responds and what guarantee of continued services they are promising. There is also the issue of retired, replaced, or damaged equipment. Items such as hard drives need to be decommissioned properly. Should sensitive data be held on discarded hard drives, *data remanence* is a real issue. Data remanence is the remaining data, or remnants, that remain on the media after formatting or drive wiping. The only way to ensure there are no data remnants is through physical destruction of the media.

Cloud outages are not uncommon occurrences, and when they hit, they hit hard. In November 2021, Google Cloud, Snapchat, and Spotify experienced an outage for about an hour. More than 50,000 users reported the outage on downdetector.com. Many companies were affected, from Pokémon GO to Home Depot. In Figure 5.3, you see the Google Dashboard reporting the outage.

FIGURE 5.3   Google Cloud Status Dashboard

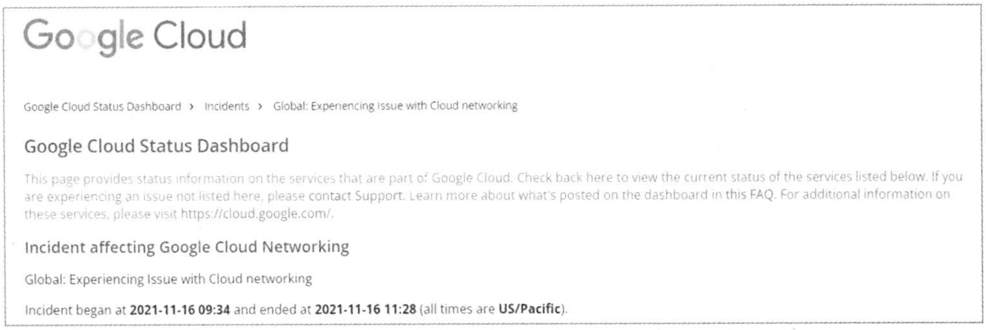

In Exercise 5.2, you will examine some common risks and issues associated with cloud computing as they would affect your organization.

EXERCISE 5.2

Identifying Risks and Issues with Cloud Computing

Before moving to any cloud-based service, a company needs to ensure that due diligence has been carried out. To help clarify some of the issues related to cloud computing, here is a list of questions about common risks and issues associated with cloud computing. What additional risks and issues may affect your organization specifically?

1. Is the data sensitive? Would loss or exposure of the data result in financial loss, fines, or penalties? How is it being encrypted?

2. What regulatory compliance requirements are met by storing information on the cloud-based service and transmitting such data between my company and the cloud? Where are these servers located?

3. How well can the company adjust to the loss of control of the data or application? If the solution is proprietary, how easy would it be to move to another provider or have multiple cloud providers?

4. What backup plan does the cloud provider have to protect customers in case of disasters?

5. What SLA does the cloud provider offer?

6. What type of vendor lock-in could we experience?

Based on your findings, what facts can you provide management about cloud-sourcing the data or application? Would you recommend the service?

More information will be covered regarding cloud and virtual environments in Chapter 9, "Secure Cloud and Virtualization."

Change Management

Change management is a formalized process that is implemented to control modifications made to systems and programs, whether in a cloud environment on premises. Change management provides a controlled process for change, and it is typically handled by a change review board. It also provides stakeholders with an opportunity to voice their concerns before changes are implemented. Before changes are made, the change management request should list specific items about the requested change. Items to record include change number, change type and description, change requestor name and time/date, change source, problem or reason for the change, and dates of the proposed change.

ISO 20000 defines change management as a needed process to "ensure all changes are assessed, approved, implemented and reviewed in a controlled manner." NIST 800-64 describes change management as a method to ensure that changes are approved, tested, reviewed, and implemented in a controlled way. Regardless of what guidelines or standards you follow, the change management process can be used to control change and to help ensure that security does not fall to a lower state. A typical change management process includes the following:

1. Change request
2. Change request approval
3. Planned review
4. A test of the change
5. Scheduled rollout of the change
6. Communication to those affected by the planned change
7. Implementation of the change
8. Documentation of all changes that occurred
9. Post-change review
10. Method to roll back the change if needed

Also, what is and is not covered by the policy should be specified. For example, some small changes, like an update to antivirus programs, may not be covered in the change control process, whereas larger institutional changes that have lasting effects on the company are included. The change control policy should also list how emergency changes are to occur, because a situation could arise in which changes must take place quickly without the normal reviews being completed before implementation. In such a situation, all of the steps should still be completed, but they may not be completed before implementation of the emergency change. Change management must be able to address any of the potential changes that can occur, including the following:

- Changes to policies, procedures, and standards
- Updates to requirements and new regulations
- Modified network, altered system settings, or fixes implemented
- Alterations to network configurations
- New networking devices or equipment
- Changes in company structure caused by acquisition, merger, or spinoff
- New computers, laptops, smartphones, or tablets installed
- New or updated applications
- Patches and updates installed
- New technologies integrated

Validation and Acceptance Testing

Before products are released, they must typically go through some type of validation and acceptance testing. The idea is to conduct tests to verify that the product or application meets the requirements laid out in the specification documents.

For some entities, validation is also performed. The U.S. federal government specifies this process as certification and accreditation. Federal agencies are required by law to have their IT systems and infrastructures certified and accredited. *Certification* is the process of validating that implemented systems are configured and operating as expected. If management agrees with the findings of the certification, the report is formally approved. When comparing products, all products must be validated with identical tests. The formal approval of the certification is the accreditation process and authorization to operate in a given environment.

 One important issue is to have a recovery plan to roll back a change if needed, because some changes can have unexpected results. Amazon has a guiding tenet in deploying AWS that says, "Avoid walking through one-way doors." It means stay away from options that are difficult to turn around from.

Testing and Evaluation

An important phase of cloud computing or any vendor/product acquisition is the testing and evaluation of systems. Before a system or service can be accepted, or deemed to reach a milestone in its development, that system must be evaluated against the expected criteria for that phase or project. If the system is tested against its specification requirements and passes, then its owners and users gain the assurance that the system will function as needed.

Testing spans cloud adoption, hardware, and software development, but the goal is to raise the assurance that the system will operate as expected. Further, testing may seek to verify that undesired aspects do not exist. For example, during the course of software development, an application might be evaluated for forbidden coding techniques.

Managing and Mitigating Risk

Companies must be aware of current and emerging threats and security trends to be able to adapt quickly. An example is the rise of advanced persistent threats (APTs). It is so important to remind users not to click unknown or suspicious links, even if they appear to be from someone they trust on a social networking site.

The need for proper controls is more critical when involving critical devices and technical configuration. Industrial control systems (ICSs) include Supervisory Control and Data Acquisition (SCADA), such as a system for managing a water or gas pipeline. When malware affects industrial control systems, it's conceivable that it could have disastrous consequences. If not causing imminent danger or widespread interruption to a community, ICS outages could at least produce costly results. Recall that the ICS malware Stuxnet targeted Iranian nuclear centrifuges. Their outage included permanent self-destruction of the industrial machinery.

A large number of emerging threats are driven by people out for financial gain, hacktivists, and nation-state hackers. Some believe that out of these three categories, the nation-state hackers are the most serious threat, both to corporations and to governments. To deal with emerging threats, companies should be prepared with a plan that lays out the key steps and resources to deploy immediately when a breach is detected.

Although many companies state financial issues as one of the items that are preventing better controls in dealing with security issues, the real question is when the company would prefer to spend the funds. Having a team come in after the security breach to fix the problem and figure out what occurred can be very costly. Implementing preventive controls before the event is more cost effective.

There is also the issue that money isn't always the solution. A big part of the solution in dealing with emerging threats is training and education. IT security policies need to be created, and employees must be educated on the value of the company's assets and how to protect them. At a minimum, the security awareness and training program should be documented in the enterprise-level policy and should include the following:

- Definition of security roles and responsibilities
- Development of program strategy and a program plan
- Implementation of the program plan
- Maintenance of the security awareness and training program

Geographical Considerations

Advances in technology now make it possible for device-tracking technologies to monitor assets and manage inventory to a much greater degree than ever before. As the Internet has grown, businesses have allowed customer access to data to, for example, track orders and find out where things are at any given time. Customer service expectations have also increased as consumers want to track packages in real time. Asset management is not just about tracking packages—it is also concerned with products being sold at retail, the tracking of patients in a hospital, and products in warehousing and distribution systems.

Geolocation technologies give individuals the ability to track the real-world location of an item. This technology includes the ability to geotag the location of photographs, but it can also be used by mobile applications to identify a user's exact location. The idea is that you can identify a user by their location for service or revenue. Examples include coupons from nearby coffee shops and restaurants. However, the security concern is that hackers or others potentially have the ability to track the location of specific individuals.

Geolocation technology can be useful in case of disasters or other emergencies. For example, many oil spill containment booms are now embedded with object tracking and containment technologies so that an oil spill can be tracked and contained to better prevent environmental damage.

Third-Party Dependencies

Rapid growth in *third-party dependencies* (including hardware, software, open-source libraries, code, modules, packages, and container images, etc.) has considerably changed the contemporary software development method. Most applications are developed on a blend of in-house and external code, and most computer hardware made of multiple components has a long list of suppliers.

Third-party hardware refers to the computing components that are developed outside of the original manufacturer. An organization may purchase hardware from Dell, but a specific hard drive could be made by Seagate or Kingston, and the video card could be made by NVIDIA or ZOTAC and the CPU made by AMD or Intel. These third-party components are supported by the company that made them, not Dell.

With the evolution of the Internet of Things (IoT) there are many hardware security issues with attackers concentrating on vulnerabilities on physical devices. Common hardware security issues include devices having default passwords, outdated firmware, and unprotected local access.

 In March 2021, at least 30 malicious Docker images (with a collective 20 million download volume) in Docker Hub were used to spread cryptomining malware accounting for cryptojacking operations worth $200,000. Cloud technology is largely reliant on containers, and Docker Hub is the default container registry for some environments. Attackers can use it to deploy miners on compromised cloud instances. More information about the attack can be found here: unit42.paloaltonetworks.com/malicious-cryptojacking-images.

Public open-source code repositories present a place for developers to use and share software libraries, packages, container images, and other works with many useful and well-developed features. The use of third-party dependencies does increase development efficiency and value, but the security risks of malicious code and vulnerabilities has created a backdoor for supply chain attacks.

Typosquatting and dependency confusion are two ways that attackers trick developers to download their malicious code. Typosquatting relies on the typos from the content supplied by threat actors. The malicious codes will be brought into the project and deployed to the production systems. Malicious packages conceal their contents by misspellings, commonly using a capital *I* in place of a lowercase *l*. In certain fonts, it is extremely difficult to tell the difference.

Dependency confusion happens when an attacker takes advantage of the default configuration of a package manager to force the download of a package they have tampered with by keeping the same name but with a higher version number.

Technical Considerations

As a CASP+, you must consider several technical security considerations. These include network segmentation, technical testing, transmission control, and shared credentials.

Testing is discussed throughout this chapter and this book, but let's take a look these other considerations.

Network segmentation is the practice of taking a large computer network and dividing it into several smaller, isolated subnetworks. Network segmentation using a screened subnet, also known as a DMZ, is a key part of compliance with PCI DSS. If a point-of-sale (POS) system is breached, cardholder data could still be secure because the database holding that information is in another subnet. If there was no network segmentation, the attacker could move around freely and steal the keys to the kingdom.

When looking at transmission control in the form of TCP/IP, information is broken up into packets, and the IP source generates a listing of the routes that packets must take to reach their intended destination. This listing may in turn be used by the recipient to send information back to the sender. At this time, threat actors can gain access to the source path and modify the options in the route for a data packet, which is called a *source route attack*. The attacker may also be able to read the data packets and gain access to confidential information or intellectual property. This security risk may be offset to some extent by dropping or forwarding any data packets that carry the source route option.

Other technical security considerations are shared and generic accounts or credentials. These accounts are often prohibited by security policies. While shared accounts can be useful, many organizations build delegation capabilities to allow multiple users to act in the same way or with the same rights to avoid shared account issues, like the inability to determine who was logged in to the shared account or what actions each user who shares the account took. All administrator or root account/credentials should not be shared with third-party vendors and should be monitored and audited on a schedule.

Security Concerns of Integrating Diverse Industries

Many substantial security risks arise when merging enterprises or hiring third-party organizations. These risks may be the result of a vendor relationship that starts somewhere along the organization's supply chain, or they may be the result of other business partnerships or conflicts within the merged entity.

A security professional can learn a great deal about an organization by reviewing the strategic plan and examining the company's policies and procedures. In the best-managed companies, high-level documents such as policies reflect management's view of the company. Policies should exist to cover most aspects of organizational control, since companies have legal and business requirements to have policies and procedures in place. One example of this is the Sarbanes-Oxley Act (SOX), a federal law that mandates financial record-keeping and reporting. This mandate places strict controls on companies and requires them to have policies and procedures in place. For those that are not compliant, there are fines and possible imprisonment of up to 20 years for those responsible. Policy should dictate who is responsible and what standards must be upheld to meet minimum corporate governance requirements.

Management is responsible for defining the structure of the organization and therefore must divide the company into smaller subgroups that control specific functions. Policies and procedures arc the controlling documents that dictate how activities occur in each of the general functional areas. A security professional should always look to see what documents are in place, with what frequency they are updated, and what activities they cover. You may find that companies don't have security policies in place. In some cases, it may be that technology has moved so fast that the company has not yet adapted. In other situations, it may be that the company just doesn't see the need for a policy or hasn't made policy development a priority.

As a security professional responsible for any type of acquisition or vendor agreement, you should keep in mind that documents such as policies and procedures are living documents that need to be reviewed periodically. Processes and procedures may have to change or be updated in light of policy, regulatory, environment, and business changes. Timing for this review will vary depending on the company and the business sector in which it operates. Although many companies review policies at least once a year, intervals can range from six months to five years. During the review, the following questions should be asked:

- Have procedures or processes changed?

- Is the policy relevant?

- Have the relevant laws changed?

- Does the change management process incorporate documentation change?

- Have industry best practices changed?

- Have periodic audit findings indicated a problem with documentation, such as policies and procedures?

When reviewing documentation, consider documents that address internal practices as well as the company's interactions with external entities, business partners, and contractors. A company may have contracts with vendors or suppliers for an array of products and services. During the review process of policies, procedures, and documentation, any of the following conditions may indicate potential problems:

- Negative audit findings

- Lack of documentation

- Out-of-date documentation

- Unsupported hardware changes or unauthorized purchases

- Employees who are unaware of or not knowledgeable about documentation

The CASP+ should support legal compliance and advocacy by partnering with HR, legal, management, and other entities to make sure that all stakeholders are involved. For items like employee concerns, HR should be involved. For items like compliance or Payment Card Industry Data Security Standard (PCI DSS), the legal department should be involved since these individuals will know the requirements under which the company must work.

Regulations, Accreditations, and Standards

Legislators and regulators around the world take an interest in cybersecurity due to the potential impact of cybersecurity shortcomings on individuals, government, and society. While the European Union (EU) has a broad-ranging data protection regulation, cybersecurity analysts in the United States are forced to deal with a patchwork of security regulations covering different industries and information categories.

Privacy and protection of sensitive information touch the organization in a way that no other items do. As a security professional, you may be asked to help build an effective privacy governance program or work with one that has already been developed. How such a program is managed will affect not only the customer's opinion of the firm but also the firm's financial status.

With mandates such as the Sarbanes-Oxley Act (SOX), the Health Insurance Portability and Accountability Act (HIPAA), and the Payment Card Industry Data Security Standard (PCI DSS), companies face a huge amount of regulation and monetary exposure should private policy violations occur and sensitive information be exposed. It's not just monetary losses a company could suffer if they fail to protect certain types of data; there is also the issue of lawsuits, bad publicity, and government investigations.

One of the reasons we see so many more laws governing sensitive information today than in the past is that the way information is stored, moved, and processed has changed. There was a time when credit card machines were manual. These mechanical devices required the operator to swipe the card and make a carbon copy duplicate of the card number and signature of the purchaser. Security rested in the physical protection of credit card information. People were sometimes told to tear up the credit card carbon copy so criminals could not steal the numbers.

Today credit card information is stored and processed electronically. Many of these electronic systems are connected to the Internet and make an attractive target for hackers. Just consider the process of paying for a meal with your credit card. From the point you hand your credit card to the server to the time the credit card bill arrives at your home, the data has passed many points at which a hacker can attempt to steal the information. Companies can be held liable if personal data is disclosed to an unauthorized person. The potential losses can be huge.

PCI DSS

The *Payment Card Industry Data Security Standard (PCI DSS)* provides detailed rules about the storage, processing, and transmission of credit and debit card information. PCI DSS is not a law but rather a contractual obligation that applies to credit card merchants and service providers worldwide.

If your organization accepts credit cards, debit cards, or any other type of electronic payment, you connect to a multifaceted and complicated structure of networks, banking, and credit card institutions. In this digital age when many attackers are looking to monetize their processes, fraud must be defended against, and every organization connecting to this structure must meet a minimum set of standards to protect this sensitive financial data. This is the PCI DSS. Companies that process and handle any amount of credit card information must implement specific controls including policies, procedures, network architecture, and software design to protect cardholder data. Failure to meet PCI DSS compliance mandates can suffer negative impact including fees, fines, and lost business.

Visa and MasterCard between 1988 and 1998 lost more than $750 million due to credit card fraud. PCI was established in 2004 with PCI DSS version 1.0 Security Architecture with a basic yet comprehensive list of security controls for merchants accepting credit cards. PCI DSS outlines best practices for companies handling payment card information and was developed collectively by American Express, Discover Financial Services, JDB International, MasterCard, and Visa. These best practices are used to improve security and outline the policies used to safeguard security systems that carry sensitive cardholder information. The most current version of PCI DSS is version 3.2.1, released May 31, 2018. PCI DSS standards are based on 12 requirements that involve network security and internal controls:

- Installing/maintaining a firewall configuration for networks and systems

- Avoiding using vendor-supplied defaults for passwords and other security procedures

- Protecting cardholder data during storage

- Using encryption during cardholder data transmissions in open and public networks

- Using and updating antivirus software

- Developing and maintaining secure network systems and applications

- Restricting user access to cardholder data

- Creating a unique ID for users who need to access cardholder data

- Restricting any physical access to cardholder information

- Tracking and monitoring all access to network systems and data

- Testing security processes and systems

- Maintaining information security policies

PCI DSS helps sellers to protect their vital cardholder data that contains *personally identifiable information* (PII). PII is any data that could potentially identify a specific individual. TechTarget defines PII as "any data about an individual that could potentially identify that person, such as a name, fingerprints or other biometric data, email address, street address, telephone number or social security number."

The PCI Security Standards Council (SSC) is now targeting a Q1 2022 publication date for PCI DSS v4.0. This timeline supports the inclusion of an additional request for comments (RFC) for the community to provide feedback on the PCI DSS v4.0 draft validation documents: www .pcisecuritystandards.org.

Protecting PII is essential for personal and data privacy as well as data and information security. Information that can uniquely identify someone as an individual, separate from everyone else, is PII and includes the following:

- Name
- Address
- Email
- Telephone number
- Date of birth
- Passport number
- Fingerprint
- Driver's license number
- Credit or debit card number
- Social Security number

Unfortunately, some companies have the preconceived notion that security controls will reduce the efficiency or speed of business processes. According to securitymagazine.com, the number of data breaches through September 30, 2021, has exceeded the total number of events in 2020 by 17 percent, with 1,291 breaches in 2021 compared to 1,108 breaches in 2020. These breaches affected millions of Americans. These companies did not have sufficient controls in place to protect personally identifiable information.

Your job as a security professional is to work with managers to help them see the importance of strong security controls. Good security practices are something that most managers or users do not instinctively know. They require education. A key component of the process is training and awareness for users. Part of the educational process is increasing the awareness of the costs involved if sensitive information is lost.

Here are some general privacy principles for PII:

- The PII data will be collected fairly and lawfully.
- The PII data will be used only for the purposes for which it was collected.
- The PII data will be kept secure while in storage and in transit.
- The PII data will be held only for a reasonable time.

Two areas of protection that a company's policy must address are protecting credit card data while it is at rest and while it is in transit. If your company deals with credit cards, PCI standards dictate that the stored cardholder data must be rendered unreadable or encrypted to protect customer privacy. To meet this requirement, your company must implement security controls that provide for encryption methods while the credit card data is being stored and while the credit card data moves across open, public networks. Companies that must comply with PCI standards state that documentation is one of the most tedious aspects of attaining and maintaining PCI compliance and is one area that typically needs more work.

A big component of providing the proper protection for PII is to make sure that there is a way to track privacy policy violations and measure their impact. One way to measure the impact is to verify that company policy has been based on a *privacy impact assessment (PIA)*. A PIA should determine the risks and effects of collecting, maintaining, and distributing PII in electronic-based systems. The PIA should be used to evaluate privacy risks and ensure that appropriate privacy controls exist. Existing controls should be examined to verify that accountability is present and that compliance is built in every time new projects or processes are scheduled to come online.

You can read more about PCI DSS and the best practices surrounding payment card information at `www.pcicomplianceguide.org/category/best-practices`.

GDPR

Sweeping data privacy laws like the *General Data Protection Regulation (GDPR)* implement strict security and privacy requirements for the personal information of European Union (EU) residents worldwide. GDPR significantly restricts how certain types of information may be stored and used by organizations and will be used to enforce these regulations with stiff fines and penalties. This 88-page regulation was put into effect on May 25, 2018. The GDPR will levy punitive penalties against those who breach its privacy and security standards, with fines reaching into the tens of millions of euros.

The GDPR defines an array of legal terms at length. Here are some of the most important ones:

- **Personal data:** Personal data is any information that relates to an individual who can be directly or indirectly identified (PII). Pseudonymous data can also fall under the definition if it's easy to ID someone from it.

- **Data processing:** Any action performed on data, whether automated or manual. The examples cited on `gdpr.eu` include collecting, recording, organizing, structuring, storing, using, and erasing.

- **Data subject:** The person whose data is processed. These are customers or site visitors.

- **Data controller:** The person who decides why and how personal data will be processed. If you're an owner or employee in your organization who handles data, this is you.

- **Data processor:** A third party that processes personal data on behalf of a data controller.

- **Data classification:** Identifying the types of data that an organization stores and processes and the sensitivity of that data, based on a set of rules. Data will fall into four categories:

- Public
- Internal Only
- Confidential
- Restricted

Here is a rundown of data subjects' privacy rights:

- The right to be informed
- The right of access
- The right to rectification
- The right to erasure
- The right to restrict processing
- The right to data portability
- The right to object
- Rights in relation to automated decision-making and profiling

With various countries imposing so many different requirements, organizations face a regulatory patchwork of inconsistent, unclear, and often contradictory demands. The implications for multinational companies are substantial: threats of regulatory action, disruptions to established business processes, and requirements to tighten controls for handling and processing information that crosses national boundaries. The overturning of the Safe Harbor agreement, governing how data is moved between EU countries and the United States, forced many companies to reexamine their own legal and policy frameworks for protecting personally identifiable data.

To address the challenges emerging from new and pending data privacy regulations, business and technology leaders need to work collectively with their compliance, legal, and technology teams to understand the impact regulations have on their businesses.

Data sovereignty is the concept that information that has been converted and stored in binary digital form is subject to the laws of the country in which it is located. With data theft and breaches dramatically on the rise, national governments around the globe are strengthening laws to protect their citizens' data, preserve national security, and, in some cases, protect local business interests.

Data sovereignty is different from data ownership. *Data ownership* is both the possession of the data and responsibility for the information. According to GDPR, data ownership refers to the explicit assignment of responsibility to every data element. A data owner can be a team or individual who has the right to access and edit the data and decide how it is used. Data ownership is important because it creates accountability. A data owner has a vested interest in the protection and integrity of their data and will create policies to ensure they are GDPR compliant. The data steward's role essentially is to support the user community. This individual is responsible for collecting, collating, and evaluating issues and problems with data. Typically, data stewards are assigned either based on subject areas or within line-of-business responsibilities. The main difference between a data owner and a data steward is that the latter is responsible for the quality of a defined dataset on day-to-day basis.

As regulations are drafted in a particular nation or region, even when they affect data and users around the globe, the question of *jurisdictions* is debated. Companies seek to minimize how a regulation affects their infrastructure and users. There is ongoing debate, but it seems that most data privacy regulation is tilted toward the user's benefit.

One side effect of GDPR is the resulting impact on cloud computing. Under GDPR, a company is considered the data controller and is responsible for keeping all the data safe, regardless of where that data is being stored. Key steps to take for geographical decisions regarding compliance in the cloud are strict privacy policies, terms of use, server location, security features, encryption, and legal guarantees for data protection.

ISO

The *International Organization for Standardization (ISO)* describes itself as "a network of the national standards institutes of 162 countries, one member per country, with a Central Secretariat in Geneva, Switzerland, that coordinates the system that forms a bridge between the public and private sectors."

An important ISO document for cybersecurity that is definitely worth reviewing is ISO 27002. This standard is considered a code of best practice for information security management. It grew out of ISO 17799 and British Standard 7799. ISO 27002 is considered a management guideline, not a technical document. You can learn more at `www.27000 .org/iso-27002.htm`. ISO 27002 provides best-practice recommendations on information security management for use by those responsible for leading, planning, implementing, or maintaining security. The ISO 27017 was created to include additional security controls for cloud computing.

The latest ISO 27002:2022 contains 93 controls; 11 are new, 24 have merged, and 58 are updated for guidance. The standard contains 14 control domains spread across four categories including organizational, physical, technological, and people. The 11 new controls are as follows:

- **Threat intelligence:** Understanding attackers and their methods in the context of your IT landscape

- **Information security for the use of cloud services:** Considering the introduction through operation to exit strategy regarding cloud initiatives

- **ICT readiness for business continuity:** Deriving the requirements for the IT landscape from the overall business processes and the ability to recover operational capabilities

- **Physical security monitoring:** Using alarm and monitoring systems to prevent unauthorized physical access

- **Configuration management:** Hardening and secure configuration of IT systems

- **Information deletion:** Compliance with external requirements, such as data protection deletion concepts

- **Data masking:** Using techniques that mask data, such as anonymization and pseudonymization, to bolster your data protection

- **Data leakage prevention:** Taking steps to help prevent sensitive data from being leaked
- **Monitoring activities:** Monitoring network security and application behavior to detect any network anomalies
- **Web filtering:** Helping prevent users from viewing specific URLs containing malicious code
- **Secure coding:** Using tools, commenting, tracking changes, and avoiding insecure programming methods to ensure secure coding

Another ISO document for cybersecurity professionals to be acquainted with is the ISO 15408, which was finalized after years of drafts and was initially published in 1997. It is currently in version 3.1, and it is more widely known as the Common Criteria. The purpose of the *Common Criteria* is to provide a common structure and language for expressing product and system IT security requirements. It's a way for vendors to describe what their products are capable of and for buyers to test such products to be sure they meet specific requirements. The Common Criteria provides assurance that the process of specification, implementation, and evaluation of a computer security product has been conducted in a rigorous and standard manner. As such, the Common Criteria can be used on a worldwide basis and is meaningful to a much larger audience.

CMMI

The *Capability Maturity Model Integration (CMMI)* was created by the Software Engineering Institute at Carnegie Mellon University as a method improvement tool for projects, divisions, or organizations. The DoD and U.S. government helped build the CMMI, which is a common requirement for DoD and U.S. government software development contracts. The CMMI is presently administered by the CMMI Institute, which was acquired by the ISACA in 2016. CMMI is a process and behavioral model that helps groups reorganize or restructure processes for improvement that decrease risk in software, product, and service development.

The CMMI model breaks down organizational maturity into five levels. While CMMI has its beginnings in software engineering, it has been generalized to incorporate other areas. There are three areas, all of which use the same five-level model:

- **Product and Service Development:** CMMI for Development (CMMI-DEV)
- **Service Establishment and Management:** CMMI for Services (CMMI-SVC)
- **Product and Service Acquisition:** CMMI for Acquisition (CMMI-ACQ)

For cybersecurity businesses that use CMMI, the aim is to raise the organization up to level 5, the "optimizing" maturity level. In Figure 5.4, you see the difference between the levels of CMMI from level 1 to level 5.

FIGURE 5.4 CMMI levels

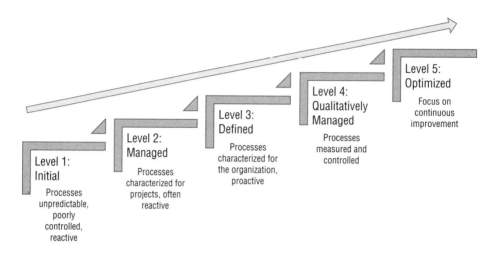

NIST

The *National Institute for Standards and Technology (NIST)* is responsible for developing cybersecurity standards across the U.S. federal government. The guidance and standard documents it produces often have wide applicability across the private sector and are commonly referred to by nongovernmental security analysts because they are available in the public domain.

In 2018, NIST released version 1.1 of a Cybersecurity Framework (CSF) (`www.nist.gov/cyberframework`), which provides a common language and systematic methodology for managing risk. The following are the five functions acting as the backbone in the core framework:

- **Identify:** Helps in developing an understanding of cybersecurity risks to people, systems, data, and assets

- **Protect:** Outlines the proper safeguards to make sure critical infrastructure is secure

- **Detect:** Defines how to identify a cybersecurity event

- **Respond:** Defines what action to take if a cybersecurity event occurs

- **Recover:** Identifies the plans necessary for resilience and restoration of services impaired due to a cybersecurity event

NIST also releases special publications for cybersecurity guidance such as the 800-100, which is the *Information Security Handbook: A Guide for Managers*, and 800-53, which is the *Security and Privacy Controls for Information Systems and Organizations*. NIST works closely with the Information Technology Laboratory (ITL) to promote the U.S. economy and public welfare by providing technical leadership for the nation's measurement and standards infrastructure. ITL develops tests, test methods, reference data, proof-of-concept implementations, and technical analyses to advance the development and productive use of information technology. ITL's responsibilities include the development of management, administrative, technical, and physical standards and guidelines for the cost-effective security and privacy of non-national, security-related information in federal information systems. This Special Publication 800 series reports on ITL's research, guidelines, and outreach efforts in information system security and its collaborative activities with industry, government, and academic organizations.

 The President's Executive Order (EO) on "Improving the Nation's Cybersecurity (14028)," issued on May 12, 2021, charges multiple agencies, including NIST, with enhancing cybersecurity through a variety of initiatives related to the security and integrity of the software supply chain.

COPPA

Children today spend more time online than ever before. From virtual school to online games, children spend hours on the Internet and deserve protection so that they may learn and play safely. The *Children's Online Privacy Protection Rule (COPPA)* was passed in the Congress of the United States in 1998. The rule summary from the Federal Trade Commission, which can be found at ftc.gov, states that COPPA imposes certain requirements on operators of websites or online services directed to children under 13 years of age, and on operators of other websites or online services that have actual knowledge that they are collecting personal information online from a child under 13 years of age.

Operators governed by COPPA must do the following:

- Post a clear and comprehensive online privacy policy describing their information practices for personal information collected online from children.

- Provide direct notice to parents and obtain verifiable parental consent, with limited exceptions, before collecting personal information online from children.

- Give parents the choice of consenting to the operator's collection and internal use of a child's information but prohibiting the operator from disclosing that information to third parties (unless disclosure is integral to the site or service, in which case, this must be made clear to parents).

- Provide parents access to their child's personal information to review and/or have the information deleted.

- Give parents the opportunity to prevent further use or online collection of a child's personal information.

- Maintain the confidentiality, security, and integrity of information they collect from children, including by taking reasonable steps to release such information only to parties capable of maintaining its confidentiality and security.

- Retain personal information collected online from a child for only as long as is necessary to fulfill the purpose for which it was collected and delete the information using reasonable measures to protect against its unauthorized access.

- Not condition a child's participation in an online activity on the child providing more information than is reasonably necessary to participate in that activity.

COPPA was implemented to protect children online, and fines for failing to comply with the law were recently increased to up to $43,280 per privacy violation per child. The FTC announced in September 2019 that Google and its subsidiary YouTube would pay a $170 million fine to settle the FTC's allegations that YouTube collected children's personal information without parental consent. YouTube collected information from children on pages specifically directed toward children, such as videos about children's toys and nursery rhymes.

CSA-STAR

The cybersecurity community offers many reference documents to help organizations come to a common understanding of the cloud and cloud security issues. The *Cloud Security Alliance (CSA)* is an industry organization focused on developing and promoting best practices in cloud security. It developed the Cloud Controls Matrix (CCM) as a reference document designed to help organizations understand the appropriate use of cloud security controls and map those controls to various regulatory standards. The CCM is a lengthy Excel spreadsheet, available for download from `cloudsecurityalliance.org`.

The Security, Trust, Assurance, and Risk (STAR) incorporates the fundamental principles of transparency, auditing, and coordination of standards outlined in the Cloud Controls Matrix (CCM). Publishing to the registry allows organizations to show customers their security and compliance posture, including the regulations, standards, and frameworks they follow. In Figure 5.5, you see the STAR levels outlined in the CCM.

FIGURE 5.5 CSA STAR levels

Levels of STAR

There are multiple levels of assurance for companies that submit to the STAR registry. Each level has a different set of requirements. You can also download the following information as a pdf here.

| **LEVEL ONE** | LEVEL TWO |

Level 1: Self-Assessment

At level one organizations can submit one or both of the security and privacy self-assessments. For the security assessment, organizations use the Cloud Controls Matrix to evaluate and document their security controls. The privacy assessment submissions are based on the GDPR Code of Conduct.

Who should pursue level one?

Organizations should pursue this level if they are...

- Operating in a low-risk environment
- Wanting to offer increased transparency around the security controls they have in place
- Looking for a cost-effective way to improve trust and transparency

HIPAA, SOX, and GLBA

You should also be familiar with several other compliance, regulatory frameworks, or standards that relate to privacy and the security of health, financial, PII, and other data, including HIPAA, SOX, and GLBA.

The *Health Insurance Portability and Accountability Act (HIPAA)* includes security and privacy rules that affect healthcare providers, health insurers, and health information clearinghouses in the United States. HIPAA was signed into law in 1996. It has two parts: Title I of the HIPAA protects health insurance coverage for workers and their families when they change or lose their jobs. Title II requires the U.S. Department of Health and Human Services (DHHS) to establish national standards for electronic healthcare transactions and national identifiers for providers, health plans, and employers.

Under HIPAA, the United States was required to publish a set of rules regarding privacy. The Privacy Rule dictates controls that organizations must put in place to protect personal information. The privacy rule defines three major purposes:

- "To protect and enhance the rights of consumers by providing them access to their health information and controlling the inappropriate use of that information."

- "To improve the quality of health care in the United States by restoring trust in the health care system among consumers, health care professionals, and the multitude of organizations and individuals committed to the delivery of care."

- "To improve the efficiency and effectiveness of health care delivery by creating a national framework for health privacy protection that builds on efforts by states, health systems, and individual organizations and individuals."

The *Sarbanes-Oxley (SOX) Act* applies to the financial records of U.S. publicly traded companies and requires that those companies have a strong degree of assurance around the IT systems that store and process those records. The SOX Act was signed into law in 2002. This act mandated a number of reforms to enhance corporate responsibility and financial disclosures and combat corporate and accounting fraud.

Sections 302 and 404 are the two sections that address IT infrastructures and information security.

- Section 302 requires the CEO and CFO to certify personally that the organization has the proper internal controls. It also mandates that the CEO and CFO report on the effectiveness of internal controls around financial reporting.

- Section 404 sets requirements on areas of the management's structure, control objectives, and control procedures. Staying compliant with Section 404 requires companies to establish an infrastructure that is designed to archive records and data and protect it from destruction, loss, unauthorized alteration, or other misuse. It requires that a set of comprehensive controls be put in place and holds CEOs and CFOs accountable.

Gramm-Leach-Bliley Act (GLBA) covers U.S. financial institutions, broadly defined. It requires that those institutions have a formal security program and designate an individual as having overall responsibility for that program. GLBA was signed into law in 1999 and resulted in the most sweeping overhaul of financial services regulation in the United States.

GLBA Title V addresses financial institution privacy with two subtitles. Subtitle A requires financial institutions to make certain disclosures about their privacy policies and to give individuals an opt-out capability. Subtitle B criminalizes *pretexting*, which can be described as the practice of obtaining personal information under false pretenses. In these situations, people misrepresent themselves to collect personal information.

Under GLBA, financial institutions are required to protect the confidentiality of individual privacy information. As specified in GLBA, financial institutions are required to develop, implement, and maintain a comprehensive information security program with appropriate administrative, technical, and physical safeguards. The controls specified in the information security program must include the following items:

- The assignment of a designated program manager for the organization's information security program
- A periodic risk and vulnerability assessment and audit
- A program of regular testing and monitoring
- The development of policies and procedures for control of sensitive information and PII

Remember that this is only a brief listing of security regulations. There are many other laws and obligations that apply to specific industries and data types. You should always consult your organization's legal counsel and subject matter experts when designing a compliance strategy for your organization. You'll need to understand the various national, territorial, and state laws that apply to your operations, and the advice of a well-versed attorney is crucial when interpreting and applying cybersecurity regulations to your specific business and technical environment.

Contract and Agreement Types

Organizations may deploy some standard agreements and practices to manage security risks. Commonly used agreements include the following:

- *Master service agreements (MSAs)* provide a top-level contract for the work that a vendor does with an organization over an extended period of time, setting the boundaries of the relationship to keep the workflow moving and resolve any disputes. It generally specifies payment terms, warranties, geographic location, and intellectual property ownership. The MSA typically includes detailed security and privacy constraints. Each time the organization enters into a new project with the vendor, they may then create a *statement of work* (SOW) that contains project-specific details and references the MSA.

- *Service level agreements (SLAs)* are critical contracts that specify the conditions of service that will be provided by the supplier and the remedies available to the customer if the vendor fails to abide by the SLA. SLAs commonly cover issues such as system availability, data durability, and response time. SLAs are usually written between a customer and external suppliers and should be reviewed by legal counsel. For critical security systems, customers should have a way to measure SLA performance data.

The SLA should specify the uptime, response time, and maximum outage time to which they are agreeing. An SLA can also be used as a type of contract with a hardware vendor that provides a certain level of protection. For a fee, the vendor agrees to repair or replace the equipment within the contracted time.

NOTE The SLA should specify items related to response time, time to recover, guaranteed space, and so on. Data recovery and storage are two items closely related to SLAs. Should systems fail and backups be needed, the storage and recovery of data will be key to keeping an organization running.

- A *memorandum of understanding (MOU)* documents aspects of the starting point relationship that define the purpose of the association. MOUs are an informal method that allows the parties to document their relationship to avoid future misunderstandings. MOUs are frequently used in cases where an internal service provider is offering a service to a client that is in a different business unit of the same company. Sometimes, an MOU may be used as a temporary device prior to an overall blanket contract or agreement. An MOU is different from an NDA. Whereas NDAs are used to maintain secrecy or confidentiality of information, the MOU goes much further: it outlines what each party is responsible for and what each party is to provide or perform.

  Choosing the right partner is extremely important and should be done with the utmost care. To be binding, the MOU must be signed by a representative from each organization who has the legal authority to sign. This is typically a member of senior management, someone from the legal department, or a board member. Such documents are typically secured since they are considered confidential. Confidentiality is required because the agreement may describe processes, activities, or even services provided that the signing parties would not want others to know about.

- *Privacy-level agreements (PLAs)* address privacy, which is one of the top concerns for cloud customers and regulators. Both cloud service providers (CSPs) and potential users struggle with the range of data protection legislation around the world. Inconsistencies between countries' legislations represent a significant hurdle in the broad adoption of cloud computing. Privacy compliance is a fundamental evaluation criterion when choosing a cloud service provider.

- *Business partnership agreements (BPAs)* exist when two companies agree to trade with each other in a collaborative partnership. For example, if two companies jointly develop and market manufactured goods, the BPA might identify each partner's obligations and the distribution of revenues. The BPA is a written agreement created by lawyers along with input from the partners and contains standard clauses related to security and cooperation.

- A *nondisclosure agreement (NDA)* is designed to protect confidential information. For example, before taking the CASP+ exam, you will be asked to sign an NDA stating that you will not reveal the test questions to others. Many companies require employees and contractors to sign NDAs at the time of employment or before gaining access to specific information.

NDAs are commonplace in the technology industry. Some employees have alleged that tech giants use them to discourage legally protected activities such as discussions of working conditions. See www.reuters .com/world/us/former-apple-worker-inspires-washington-state-measure-seeking-curb-ndas-2021-11-24.

In Exercise 5.3, you will review your company's NDA for areas and items it should contain.

EXERCISE 5.3

Reviewing Documents

Similar to reviewing security policies, a CASP+ might need to review business documents such as disclosure agreements or service agreements. You might be asked to review such a document by the company lawyer or a senior executive familiar with the conditions of the document, but you might not have the technical expertise to assess its feasibility.

1. Does your company have or make use of an NDA? If not, why not?

2. Is the existing or proposed NDA a one-way or a two-way NDA? A one-way NDA protects only the information of the company. Two-way NDAs are designed to protect the confidential information of both the client and the company.

3. Does the NDA clearly define confidential information?

4. Are controls put in place to protect confidential information?

5. What are the obligations of the receiving party? What level of protection must they apply to the information they have received?

6. What time period applies to the NDA? Most NDAs don't last forever and have a time period applied—such as one year, six years, or ten years.

Organizations need to select the agreement type(s) most appropriate for their specific circumstances. A CASP+ should also understand the following documents used to support security:

Business Impact Analysis   The *business impact analysis (BIA)* is a central part of the disaster recovery business continuity process. The BIA has three components: criticality prioritization, downtime estimates, and resource requirements. The BIA is used to identify costs linked to failures, such as loss of cash or replacement of equipment, cash flows, salaries, or other losses. The BIA can be quantitative or qualitative in design. Business impact analysis is explored further in Chapter 1, "Risk Management."

Interoperability Agreement   An *interoperability agreement (IA)* is a document that establishes and maintains requirements for organizations to be able to exchange data. As an example, United Airlines may share flight codes with Lufthansa Airlines, and as such both need access to a common dataset. These common datasets are typically specified through the use of protocols such as TCP/IP or standards such as XML or SQL.

Continuity of Operations   Just consider the natural and human-caused disasters that many of us have witnessed over the past several decades, coupled with increasingly stringent *regulatory requirements*. These events have led to a much greater need for business continuity. *Continuity of operations (COOP)* comprises all of the processes and procedures that organizations must put in place to ensure that businesses can continue to operate. The COOP document is needed because companies must have plans and procedures to continue operations in the event of a failure or catastrophe.

Interconnection Security Agreement   An *interconnection security agreement (ISA)* is a security document that details the requirements for establishing, maintaining, and operating an interconnection between systems or networks. The document specifies the requirements for connecting the systems and networks and details what security controls are to be used to protect the systems and sensitive data. An ISA typically details how specific systems and networks are connected and contains a drawing of the network topology.

Operating Level Agreement   An *operating level agreement (OLA)* works in conjunction with and supports the SLA process. The OLA defines the responsibilities of each partner's internal support group. So, whereas the SLA may promise no more than five minutes of downtime, the OLA defines what group and resources are used to meet the specified goal.

Uptime Agreement   An *uptime agreement (UA)* is one of the best-known types of SLA; it details the agreed amount of uptime. For example, UAs can be used for network services, such as a WAN link, or equipment, like servers. Common ratings for uptime include 99.999 percent (described in industry jargon as "five nines"), which is equal to about five minutes of downtime per year. If the UA was to specify 99.9999 percent ("six nines"), the downtime would drop to a maximum of around 30 seconds per year.

   One basic item that security professionals should review when dealing with business partners is the Statement of Auditing Standards 70 (SAS 70). The SAS 70 report verifies that the outsourcing or business partner has had its control objectives and activities examined by an independent accounting and auditing firm.

Third-Party Attestation of Compliance

It is critical to manage potential risk to your company and have the right safeguards in place. It is important to know that your vendors are managing and processing data according to your compliance needs. Many companies rely on third-party service providers to host or manage information, and these relationships challenge the regulatory, compliance, and data security requirements of the industry.

Outsourced providers must prove the proper and effective internal controls when accessing and processing data. Ensuring transparency in the compliance and control capabilities of third-party organizations demands the trust of your management team, board, and shareholders.

Third-party attestation services can help an organization deliver comfort and assurance to customers, shareholders, suppliers, regulators, and other stakeholders by creating reporting that delivers an objective opinion about your control environment and identifying weaknesses, issues, and risks to minimize disruptions to the business.

Using an information security framework like HITRUST CSF provides a way for organizations to comply with ISO and HIPAA. This framework is a set of 135 controls that meet the requirements and standards of several different compliance regulators and can complete a self-assessment internally or hire an assessor for an external engagement. These controls include third-party assurance, data classification, data retention, and rules for data removal, destruction, and sanitization.

In the HITRUST 9.5.0 Shared Responsibility Matrix, there are 13 control categories. In Control Reference 13.1, there are control specifications, regulatory factor types, and implementation instructions for data retention and sanitization.

> *Organizations will limit the retention of PII to only that which is deemed necessary and for as long as necessary to fulfill the organization's specific and legitimate purpose and/or required by law. Unless certain exceptions apply, PII must be deleted thereafter. Organizations will ensure that retention periods are appropriately followed and PII is disposed of in accordance with the defined retention periods.*
>
> *Regardless of the method of storage, organizations will destroy, erase, dispose, sanitize, and/or anonymize the PII in a manner which prevents PII from being lost, stolen, misused, or accessed without authorization once the PII is no longer needed for the stated purpose for which it was collected and/or at the end of the applicable legally required retention period.*

HIPAA is a federal act that regulates companies in healthcare and their affiliates by ensuring that they safeguard individuals' sensitive data and personal health information. HITRUST is a private organization that creates a framework to help companies achieve compliance standards created and enforced by HIPAA. An increasing number of health systems and hospitals are requiring their business associates to become HITRUST certified because the certification demonstrates that the organization has made a dedicated commitment to maintain the greatest level of protection for their customers' healthcare data.

Legal Considerations

When companies implement minimum levels of security for a legal defense, they may need to show that they have done what any reasonable and prudent organization would do in similar circumstances. This minimum level of security is known as a *standard of due care*. If this minimum level is not maintained, a company might be exposed to legal liability.

Such standards are increasingly important in the IT security field, because so much company data is kept in electronic databases. There are also large amounts of personally identifiable information (PII) kept electronically. This makes it imperative for companies to practice due care and due diligence.

Implementing best practices is not easy—different industries must provide different levels of compliance. One of the most important parts of an acquisition of a vendor or merger with a new company when it comes to security of integrating organizations is due care and due diligence. *Due care* in cybersecurity means taking acceptable and practical steps to defend your organization's reputational, financial, and legal best interests. *Due diligence* is the measure or exercise of care enacted by a prudent, rational individual or entity under certain circumstances. The act of performing due diligence results in legally defensible due care.

Due diligence tasks are time-consuming and complex. Incomplete investigation is one of the major causes of integration failure. Security concerns involve examining all of the elements of a company's operations with the objective of evaluating the condition of technology and assets to find any hidden risk or liability.

Some companies choose to implement more than the minimum level of required security. These efforts can be seen as best practices. *Best practices* seek to provide as much security as possible for information and information systems while balancing the issue of security versus usability. Any implemented control must not cost more than the asset it is protecting. Fiscal responsibility must be maintained.

The U.S. government maintains a complicated set of regulations that provide *export controls* to govern the export of goods—including technology, software, and technical data—to foreign countries and specified foreign entities and individuals. Cybersecurity products and services present a challenge because the exports may contain a mixture of different software, encryption functions, and controlled technical information.

As the importance of cybersecurity has grown from a national defense perspective, the U.S. government's interest in regulating the export of sensitive technology has grown. A growing number of enforcement actions involve selling software, encryption products, and other cybersecurity-related information abroad, such as an eight-year prison sentence for a resident who tries to obtain sensitive encryption, communications, and global positioning system equipment without a license.

The United States Commerce Department's Bureau of Industry and Security (BIS) released an interim final rule on October 20, 2021, establishing controls on the export, reexport, or transfer (in-country) of certain items that can be used for malicious cyber activities. This rule also created a new License Exception Authorized Cybersecurity Exports (ACE) and requested public comments on the projected impact of the proposed controls on U.S. industry and the cybersecurity community.

License Exception ACE would allow the export, reexport, and transfer (in-country) of "cybersecurity items" to most destinations, while maintaining a license requirement for exports to countries of national security or weapons of mass destruction concern. In addition, countries subject to a U.S. arms embargo involve a license.

 The U.S. government opposes the abuse of technology to harm human rights or conduct other nefarious cyber activities. These rules help guarantee that U.S. companies are not fueling authoritarian practices. U.S. exporters are encouraged to consult the U. S. State Department's Guidance on *Implementing the "Guiding Principles" for Transactions Linked to Foreign Government End Users for Products or Services with Surveillance Capabilities* to minimize the risk that their products or services are misused by others.

Often lawyers battle over the discovery of electronic data and how to get more data from adversaries in court. To accomplish this, a lawyer can issue a legal hold on electronic data. A *legal hold* could require that certain email messages be retained and intact until they are no longer required for *e-discovery* or litigation. Legal hold requirements apply both to the content of messages and to the metadata, which can offer evidence of transport and other important nonrepudiation evidence. A legal hold (also known as a *litigation hold*) is a notification sent from an organization's legal team to employees telling them not to delete electronically stored information (ESI) or discard paper documents that may be pertinent to a recent or pending legal case.

Having a legal hold process in place and using legal hold–specific tools is vital to show defensible and good faith efforts to preserve evidence. If documents are disposed of or emails are deleted after a litigation hold letter is issued, even without ill intent, a court can deem certain facts as established, prohibit the business from relying upon other documents to support a defense, or instruct a jury that an inference should be made that the missing documents would be harmful to the business. Considering these risks, a business should have a strategy in the event it receives a litigation hold letter.

Summary

This chapter focused on two broad areas:

- Managing and mitigating vendor risk
- Compliance frameworks and legal considerations and their organizational impact

The second part of this chapter focused on integrating diverse industries, many different data considerations, and geographic and legal considerations. It also covered the different regulations, accreditations, and standards that affect cybersecurity as well as covering what contract and agreement types protect your organization.

Exam Essentials

Be able to describe the process of performing ongoing research. Performing ongoing research means that the CASP+ must analyze industry trends and outline potential impact on an enterprise. This requires knowing best practices, understanding new technologies, knowing how to evaluate new security systems and services, and understanding documentation.

Be able to describe the correct regulation, accreditation, and standard for different organizations and controls. Many organizations have controls that make them unique, but they also have controls that unite them. A CASP+ must be able to identify an organization's vertical market and know which compliance and control would be used for that organization. HIPAA is for healthcare, and PCI DSS is for payment cards. ISO and NIST are for everyone.

Be able to analyze security contracts to ensure that they meet business needs. Although it may sometimes appear that there are many solutions to a problem, as a CASP+ you must ensure that proposed contracts meet the specific needs of your organization. This means that the agreement meets the required security, privacy, inner connectivity, and operational needs of the company.

Know the importance of managing and mitigating vendor risk. The shared responsibility model, including roles and responsibilities, is very important to cloud customers and providers. Understanding vendor agreements and the CIA triad implementation in storage, networking, and infrastructure becomes integral to vendor viability.

Know compliance frameworks and legal considerations and their organizational impact. Data consideration, third-party attestation, regulations, and standards are all very important to compliance and vendor risk. Legal and contractual agreement types, including privacy agreements, service level agreements, memorandums of understanding, and operational level agreements, are all fundamental for managing the needs of the organization.

Review Questions

You can find the answers in Appendix.

1. An external audit is a formal process involving an accredited third party. It can be expensive and time intensive. What is a key to a component having an external audit?

    A. An internal agent and a security framework

    B. An independent authority against a recognized standard

    C. A global internal assessment with gap analysis

    D. A validated outcome and scheduled future audits

2. Your organization decided to outsource systems that are not mission critical. You have been tasked to calculate the risk of outsourcing these systems because a recent key risk indicator review shows that core business functions are dependent on these outsourced systems. What is the best tool to use?

    A. Gap analysis

    B. Annual loss expectancy

    C. Total cost of ownership

    D. Business impact analysis

3. You need an agreement that lets your business implement a comprehensive risk allocation strategy and provides indemnification, the method that holds one party harmless against existing or future losses. What contract should you negotiate?

    A. Master service agreement

    B. Business impact agreement

    C. Interconnection security agreement

    D. Memorandum of understanding

4. You are a financial provider accessing a cloud-based server where your collaboration tool resides. What is the most important question you need to ask the vendor/host of this cloud-based server?

    A. Is this server PCI-DSS compliant?

    B. Is this server SCADA compliant?

    C. What is your SLA if the server goes down?

    D. What is the TCO of this software?

5. A data user reached out to the data steward to request permission to give access to sensitive information to a third-party marketing agency. The third-party vendor has been vetted by security to make sure they are trusted and viable. Who should be contacted next before access is granted?

    A. Data owner

    B. CEO

    C. Board of directors

    D. Marketing VP

6. Your organization's security policy specifies a length of time to keep data, after which the data must be destroyed to help mitigate the risk of that data being compromised. This type of policy helps reduce legal liability if the data becomes unrecoverable. What type of policy is this?

A. Data protection

B. Data remanence

C. Data retention

D. Data destruction

7. You are a service provider responsible for ensuring that an audit for PCI DSS occurs and that the correct documentation is completed by the relevant parties. This is part of the assessment you provide. What is this process called?

A. Service provider request

B. Attestation of compliance

C. Payment request

D. Security standards council

8. Your global software organization is required to conduct a BIA for any new company acquisition. Your organization has acquired a new software startup. Your organization and the startup outsource the LMS and CMS for education to noncompatible third parties. What are you most concerned about?

A. Data sovereignty

B. Encryption

C. Data migration

D. Disaster recovery

9. You must identify a person who will have the administrative control of and be accountable for a specific set of information and dataset. It could be the most senior person in a department. What is their role?

A. Cloud engineer

B. Data user

C. Data owner

D. Chief financial officer

10. You researched and conferred with your legal department as to what your data retention policy should be. Which of the following compliances places restrictions on data retention?

A. GLBA

B. HIPAA

C. SOX

D. All of the above

11. Your company holds large amounts of company data in electronic databases as well as personally identifiable information (PII) of customers and employees. What do you do to ensure that implemented controls provide the right amount of protection?

A. Best practices

B. Forensics

C. Due diligence

D. Auditing

12. Your HR recruiter, Jane, is having problems finding skilled applicants for a role that you have open for an IT security manager. Your division has discussed moving operation solutions to a third party that will manage and sustain processes. Which of the following deployment solutions is this most likely to be?

A. Cloud

B. Hosted

C. On-premises

D. Automated

13. Your financial company hires a third party to provide cloud-based processing that will have several different types of virtual hosts configured for different purposes, like multiple Linux Apache web server farms for different divisions. Which of the following best describes this service?

A. SaaS

B. PaaS

C. IaaS

D. AaaS

14. Alonzo is a security architect, and he has decided to build multiple virtual hosts with different security requirements. Numerous virtual hosts will be used for storage, while others will be used as databases. What should he do with these hosts?

A. Encrypt all hosts with AES

B. Store each host on a separate physical asset

C. Move these virtual hosts to the cloud for elasticity

D. Verify that each server has a valid certificate

15. Craig is a project manager with a software company. His organization needs to be able to use a third party's development tools to deploy specific cloud-based applications. Platform as a service (PaaS) is the choice that has been approved to launch these cloud services. Which of the following is not a true statement?

A. PaaS can use API to develop and deploy specific cloud-based services.

B. Cloud storage is a term used to describe the use of a third-party vendor's virtual file system as a document or repository.

C. You can purchase the resources you need from a cloud service provider on a pay-as-you-go basis.

D. With PaaS, you must buy and manage software licenses.

16. Asher has a newly formed IT team that is investigating cloud computing models. He would like to use a cloud computing model that is subscription based for general services, and the vendor oversees developing and managing as well as maintaining the pool of computer assets shared between various tenants across the network. The best choice for this situation would be which of the following?

A. Public

B. Private

C. Agnostic

D. Hybrid

17. Shanyn works for a governmental agency. Her organization has opted into a public cloud solution for all of the business customers' testing environments. Which one of these is not a disadvantage?

A. TCO can rise exponentially for large-scale use.

B. Not the best solution for security and availability for mission-critical data.

C. Low visibility and control of the environment and infrastructure, which might lead to compliance issues.

D. Reduced complexity and requirement of IT experts as the vendor manages the environment.

18. The objectives and key results (OKR) being measured by management for this quarter are to realize benefits of multitenancy cloud architecture. Which one of these results would not be applicable to a multitenancy cloud service?

A. Financial

B. Usage

C. Vulnerabilities

D. Onboarding

19. Yaniv is a cloud security consultant working with a large supply chain management firm that is advocating applying the highest level of protection across all cloud assets. His manager has suggested this is not what the priority should be. What would be a more strategic priority?

A. Determine what to protect through data discovery and classification.

B. Run an anti-malware software on all cloud instances daily.

C. Use vulnerability scanning software only on mission-critical servers.

D. Implement threat mitigation strategies on IoT devices.

20. While running IaaS environments, you retain the responsibility for the security of all operating systems, applications, and network traffic. Which of these would not be advantageous to deploy to protect this cloud environment?

A. Anti-malware should be installed.

B. Application whitelisting should be used.

C. Memory exploit prevention for single-purpose workloads.

D. Negotiate an SLA that spells out the details of the data the provider will share in case of an incident.

Chapter

6

Cryptography and PKI

THE FOLLOWING COMPTIA CASP+ EXAM OBJECTIVES ARE COVERED IN THIS CHAPTER:

✓ **1.7 Explain how cryptography and public key infrastructure (PKI) support security objectives and requirements.**

- Privacy and confidentiality requirements
- Integrity requirements
- Non-repudiation
- Compliance and policy requirements
- Common cryptography use cases
    - Data at rest
    - Data in transit
    - Data in process/data in use
    - Protection of web services
    - Embedded systems
    - Key escrow/management
    - Mobile security
    - Secure authentication
    - Smart card
- Common PKI use cases
    - Web services
    - Email
    - Code signing
    - Federation
    - Trust models
    - VPN
    - Enterprise and security automation/orchestration

✓ **3.5 Given a business requirement, implement the appropriate PKI solution.**

- PKI hierarchy
    - Certificate authority (CA)
    - Subordinate/Intermediate CA
    - Registration authority (RA)
- Certificate types
    - Wildcard certificate
    - Extended validation
    - Multidomain
    - General purpose
- Certificate usages/profiles/templates
    - Client authentication
    - Server authentication
    - Digital signatures
    - Code signing
- Extensions
    - Common name (CN)
    - Storage area network (SAN)
- Trusted providers
- Trust model
- Cross-certification
- Configure profiles
- Life-cycle management
- Public and private keys
- Digital signature
- Certificate pinning
- Certificate stapling
- Corporate signing requests (CSRs)

- Online Certificate Status Protocol (OCSP) vs. certificate revocation list (CRL)

- HTTP Strict Transport Security (HSTS)

✓ 3.6 Given a business requirement, implement the appropriate cryptographic protocols and algorithms.

- Hashing

    - Secure Hashing Algorithm (SHA)

    - Hash-based message authentication code (HMAC)

    - Message digest (MD)

    - RACE integrity primitives evaluation message digest (RIPEMD)

    - Poly1305

    - Symmetric algorithms

    - Modes of operation

        - Galois/Counter Mode (GCM)

        - Electronic codebook (ECB)

        - Cipher block chaining (CBC)

        - Counter (CTR)

        - Output feedback (OFB)

    - Stream and block

        - Advanced Encryption Standard (AES)

        - Triple digital encryption standard (3DES)

        - ChaCha

        - Salsa20

        - Asymmetric algorithms

    - Key agreement

        - Diffie-Hellman

        - Elliptic-curve Diffie-Hellman (ECDH)

    - Signing

        - Digital signature algorithm (DSA)

- Rivest, Shamir, and Adleman (RSA)
- Elliptic-curve digital signature algorithm (ECDSA)

- Protocols
  - Secure Sockets Layer (SSL)/Transport Layer Security (TLS)
  - Secure/Multipurpose Internet Mail Extensions (S/MIME)
  - Internet Protocol Security (IPsec)
  - Secure Shell (SSH)
  - EAP
- Elliptic curve cryptography
  - P256
  - P384
- Forward secrecy
- Authenticated encryption with associated data
- Key stretching
  - Password-based key derivation function 2 (PBKDF2)
  - Bcrypt

✓ **3.7 Given a scenario, troubleshoot issues with cryptographic implementations.**

- Implementation and configuration issues
  - Validity dates
  - Wrong certificate type
  - Revoked certificates
  - Incorrect name
  - Chain issues
    - Invalid root or intermediate CAs
    - Self-signed

- Weak signing algorithm
- Weak cipher suite
- Incorrect permissions
- Cipher mismatches
- Downgrade
- Keys
  - Mismatched
  - Improper key handling
  - Embedded keys
  - Rekeying
  - Exposed private keys
  - Crypto shredding
  - Cryptographic obfuscation
  - Key rotation
  - Compromised keys

This chapter discusses *cryptography*, which can be defined as the art of protecting information by transforming it into an unreadable format. Everywhere you turn you see cryptography. It is used to protect sensitive information, prove the identity of a claimant, and verify the integrity of an application or program. As a security professional for your company, which of the following would you consider more critical if you could choose only one?

- Provide a locking cable for every laptop user in the organization.
- Enforce full disk encryption for every mobile device.

Our choice would be full disk encryption. Typically, the data will be worth more than the cost of a replacement laptop. If the data is lost or exposed, you'll incur additional costs such as client notification and reputation loss.

As a security professional, you should have a basic understanding of cryptographic functions. This chapter will include cryptographic types, explaining symmetric and asymmetric encryption, hashing, digital signatures, and public key infrastructure. These concepts are important as we move on to more advanced topics and begin to look at cryptographic applications. Understanding them will help you prepare for the CompTIA exam and to implement cryptographic solutions to protect your company's assets better.

The History of Cryptography

Encryption is not a new concept. The desire to keep secrets is as old as civilization. There are basic ways in which encryption is used: for data at rest, data in motion, and data in process/data in use. Data at rest might be information on a laptop hard drive or in cloud storage. Data in motion might be data being processed by SQL, a URL requested via HTTP, or information traveling over a VPN at the local coffee shop bound for the corporate network. Data in process/data in use is exactly what it sounds like: data being processed, changed, updated, read, or modified in any way. In each of these cases, protection must be sufficient. The following list includes some examples of early cryptographic systems:

Scytale   This system functioned by wrapping a strip of papyrus or leather, on which a message was written, around a rod of fixed diameter. The recipient used a rod of the same diameter to read the message. Although such systems seem basic today, it worked well in the time of the Spartans. Even if someone was to intercept the message, it appeared as a jumble of meaningless letters.

Caesar's Cipher   Julius Caesar is known for an early form of encryption, the Caesar cipher, which was used to transmit messages sent between Caesar and his generals. The cipher worked by means of a simple substitution. Before a message was sent, the plain text was rotated forward by three characters (ROT3). Using Caesar's cipher to encrypt the word *cat* would result in *fdw*. Decrypting required moving back three characters.

Other Examples   Substitution ciphers replace one character for another. The best example of a substitution cipher is the Vigenère polyalphabetic cipher. Other historical systems include a running key cipher and the Vernam cipher. The running key cipher is another way to generate the keystream for use with the tabula recta. The Vernam is also known as the *onetime pad*.

Cryptographic Goals and Requirements

Cryptography includes methods such as symmetric encryption, asymmetric encryption, hashing, and digital signatures. Each provides specific attributes and solutions. These cryptographic services include the following goals:

Privacy   This is also called confidentiality. What is private (confidential) should stay private, whether at rest or in transit.

Authentication   There should be proof that the message is from the person or entity you believe it to be from.

Integrity   Information should remain unaltered at the point at which it was produced, while it is in transmission, and during storage.

Nonrepudiation   The sender of data is provided with proof of delivery, and the recipient is assured of the sender's identity.

An easy way to remember these items for the exam is to think of PAIN. This simple acronym (privacy, authentication, integrity, and nonrepudiation) should help you remember the basic cryptographic goals.

Consider how encryption can protect the *privacy* and confidentiality of information at rest or in transit. What if your CEO has been asked to travel to Asia for trade negotiations? Think about the CEO's laptop. If it is lost or compromised, how hard would it be for someone to remove unencrypted data? Strong encryption offers an easy way to protect that information should the equipment be lost, stolen, or accessed by unauthorized individuals. Applications such as CryptoForge and BitLocker offer the ability to encrypt a hard drive. PKWARE provides users with enterprise data security that persistently protects and manages data whenever it is used, shared, and stored, both inside and outside the organization. Sookasa transparently protects files across the Dropbox and Google Drive clouds as well as linked mobile devices while preserving the native user experience on the Windows, macOS, iOS, and Android operating systems.

Authentication is another key goal of cryptography. First, *authentication* is associated with digital signatures. Authentication provides a way to ensure that a message is from the person we believe it's from. In its basic form, authentication is used to determine identity. It is also part of the identification and authentication process.

Integrity is another cryptographic goal. Integrity is important while data is in transmission and in storage. *Integrity* means that information remains unaltered. Imagine the situation of needing to download a patch. Although the patch is available on the developer's site, you also have a copy on USB that was given to you by a colleague. Is the version on the USB the same as the one on the developer's website? Integrity verification programs that perform hashing such as MD5 or SHA can help you determine this. In this case specifically, the MD5 algorithm can be and is still used for integrity, but not confidentiality.

Nonrepudiation is assurance that an entity in a communication cannot deny authenticity. It is proof of the veracity of a claim. Nonrepudiation means that a sender of data receives proof of delivery and the recipient is assured of the sender's identity. Neither party should be able to deny having sent or received the data at a later date. This can be achieved with digital signatures. A *digital signature* provides authenticity, integrity, and nonrepudiation. In the days of face-to-face transactions, nonrepudiation was not as hard to prove. Today, the Internet makes many transactions faceless. We may never see the people we deal with; therefore, nonrepudiation becomes all the more critical. Nonrepudiation is achieved through digital signatures, digital certificates, and hash-based message authentication codes (HMACs).

When implementing a cryptographic system, there has to be consideration of strength versus performance versus feasibility to implement versus interoperability. Stronger systems typically require more process power and longer encryption/decryption times. Basically, you must consider how strong an encryption process should be. The strength of a cryptosystem relies on the strength of an algorithm and the complexity of the key generation process. The strength of the encryption mechanism also rests on the size and complexity of the key. If the cryptosystem uses a weak key generation process, then the entire process is weak. The key size goes a long way in determining the strength of the cryptosystem.

The designer of a cryptographic system must also understand the implications of cryptographic methods and design. As an example, Caesar might have thought his system of encryption was quite strong, but it would be seen as relativity insecure today. You need a sufficiently sized key to deter brute-force and other attacks. In the world of cryptography, key lengths are defined by the number of binary bits. So, for example, a 64-bit key has a keyspace of 2 to the power of 64, or 18,446,744,073,709,551,616.

Supporting Security Requirements

Knowing the basic goals discussed earlier can go a long way in helping you to understand that cryptography can be used as a tool to achieve confidentially, integrity, and availability (CIA). For example, let's consider the different types of requirements that might need to be met.

Compliance and Policy Requirements

One huge area of influence is compliance. *Compliance* can be defined as being in accordance with agreed-upon guidelines, specifications, legislation, or regulations. Auditors and audit findings play a huge role in maintaining compliance. Auditors typically report to the top of the organization and function by charter. *Control Objectives for Information and Related Technology (COBIT)* is one of the leading governance frameworks used by auditors to verify compliance. The U.S. federal government plays an active, large role in regulating the Internet, privacy, and corporate governance. This increased role is most visible in the upsurge in new laws and mandates that have been passed in the last 10 to 15 years.

Some of the major information security regulations facing organizations include the following:

- The *Health Insurance Portability and Accountability Act (HIPAA)* includes security and privacy rules that affect healthcare providers, health insurers, and health information clearinghouses in the United States.

- The *Payment Card Industry Data Security Standard (PCI DSS)* provides detailed rules about the storage, processing, and transmission of credit and debit card information. PCI DSS is not a law but rather a contractual obligation that applies to credit card merchants and service providers worldwide.

- The *Gramm-Leach-Bliley Act (GLBA)* covers U.S. financial institutions, broadly defined. It requires that those institutions have a formal security program and designate an individual as having overall responsibility for that program.

- The *Sarbanes-Oxley (SOX) Act* applies to the financial records of U.S. publicly traded companies and requires that those companies have a strong degree of assurance around the IT systems that store and process those records.

- The *General Data Protection Regulation (GDPR)* implements security and privacy requirements for the personal information of European Union residents worldwide.

- The *Family Educational Rights and Privacy Act (FERPA)* requires that U.S. educational institutions implement security and privacy controls for student educational records.

Privacy and Confidentiality Requirements

If you read about the major breaches in the last few years, most of them could have been avoided if the organization had subscribed to and executed controls. The Center for Internet Security (CIS) is a self-described forward-thinking, nonprofit entity dedicated to protecting private domains and public society from cyberthreats. The controls they publish are the global standard and are the recognized best practices for security. As our cyber worries evolve, so do these best practices.

The CISv8 controls have cross-compatibility or directly map to other cyber compliance and security standards like NIST 800-53, PCI DSS, and HIPAA. This translates to other organizations using these suggestions as regulations to aid in their respective compliance for privacy and confidentiality.

The NIST Cybersecurity Framework is another tool that organizations use to organize and strengthen their security posture using the CIS top controls as their baseline for several of their best practices. Let's look at these in more detail. Different nations have varying views of privacy, but most have some laws in place to protect the confidentiality of an individual's personally identifiable information (PII).

Integrity Requirements

In the United States, the banking and accounting failures of Lehman Brothers, Bear Stearns and AIG have long been analyzed and considered an example of how not to conduct business. Laws such as Sarbanes-Oxley, formed in the wake of the earlier Enron scandal, didn't adequately protect against such scandals from happening again.

While those laws might hold officers of publicly traded companies responsible and accountable for the accuracy of financial records, they could not protect against the deception and fraud demonstrated by Elizabeth Holmes, the founder and once-CEO of Theranos. Theranos, a blood-testing startup, was poised to become a major disruptor to the industry, but under Holmes, it instead became an example of how fleeting corporate integrity can be. Corporate integrity dictates that proper information security architecture be implemented.

Nonrepudiation

An important part of auditing and accounting is nonrepudiation. Nonrepudiation means that the person authenticated and authorized cannot deny the performance of an action. You do not want a situation where one person claims an action happened and another is in total opposition to the story. A traditional example of nonrepudiation is a signature you received in a document. In cybersecurity, nonrepudiation requires the creation of certain artifacts such as the following:

- An identity
- Authentication of that identity
- Evidence connecting that identity to an action

When you take a trip through an airport, you have to produce identification to authenticate you are who you say you are. Then you have to provide a ticket to an agent to access the boarding area. Your belongings are screened to make sure you're not bringing any malicious contraband with you into a secured area. When you board the plane, they scan your ticket to prove you gained access to the aircraft. Now the airline can track and audit if and when you traveled. This is fundamental access management. Now take the same concept and apply it to a networked environment.

With all these layers of access management, how often do we hear of people getting past security? What other layers of security are in place at an airport that you have not even considered? As a security professional, you become acutely aware of those layers of defense in depth. You always have to be thinking strategically and protectively and asking targeted questions. What if someone is impersonating another on my network? What if someone has too much access? What if someone does access the network but has brought ransomware along?

Diverse entities may very well be governed by different regulatory entities or regulations such as the Payment Card Industry Data Security Standard (PCI DSS) or Health Insurance Portability and Accountability Act (HIPAA). Other regulatory factors include export controls, such as use of encryption software. Companies dealing with controlled data types must meet the regulatory-imposed legal requirements, often related to storing, safeguarding, and reporting on that data.

Risks with Data

Data is the lifeblood of many organizations. Although the doctor's office of our childhood had a mountain of files, folders, and documents behind the receptionist's desk, today a computer holds the same information in a digital format. From the security professional's standpoint, there are several areas to consider: data at rest, data in transit, and data in process/data in use. Data at rest can be stored in hard drives, external physical storage, cloud storage, or even USB drives.

Data at Rest

A wide variety of products are available to encrypt data in existing disk and media drive products. *Data-at-rest encryption* options include software encryption, such as encrypted file system (EFS) and VeraCrypt.

Failure to protect data at rest properly can lead to attacks such as the following:

- *Pod slurping*, a technique for illicitly downloading or copying data from a computer. This is typically used for data exfiltration.
- USB malware, such as USB Switchblade and Hacksaw.
- Malware such as viruses, worms, Trojans, and keyloggers.

Protection of data at rest is not just for equipment during its useful life. It's also required at end of life. All equipment that reaches end of life should be properly disposed of. Proper disposal methods can include the following:

- Drive wiping
- Zeroization
- Degaussing
- Physical destruction

For the CASP+ exam, you will be expected to understand the importance of the proper disposal of data.

Data in Transit

Another concern is when data is in transit. Anytime data is being processed or moved from one location to another, it requires proper controls. The basic problem is that many protocols and applications send information via clear text. Services such as email, web, and FTP are not designed with security in mind and send information with few security controls and no encryption. Here are some examples of insecure protocols:

FTP   Clear text username and password

Telnet   Clear text username and password

HTTP   Clear text

SMTP   Username and password, along with all data passed in the clear

For data in transit that is not being protected by some form of encryption, there are many dangers including these:

- Eavesdropping
- Sniffing
- Hijacking
- Data alteration

High-value data requires protection. One approach is for the security professional to break the data into categories. For example, the organization may require all email users to use some form of encryption such as S/MIME, OpenPGP, or GPG. *Data-in-transit encryption* works to protect the confidentiality of data in transmission. Mobile users should be required to use *virtual private networks (VPNs)*. Individuals communicating with databases and web servers that hold sensitive information should use HTTPS, SSL, or TLS.

Data in Process/Data in Use

Data being sent over a network is data in motion. Data at rest is stored data that resides on hard drives, tapes, in the cloud, or on other storage media. Data in processing, or data in use, is data that is actively in use by a computer system. Data in use is data that is stored in the active memory of a computer system where it may be accessed by a process running on that system.

This type of data can be protected with technology such as smart cards. Smart cards are used in applications where security is of highest value such as credit cards, government identification cards, and e-documents like passports. They are often used with a personal identification number for multifactor authentication. When accessing, reading, or modifying data, smart cards can bring a stronger level of security.

Each of these data situations has risks that cryptography protects against. Data in motion may be susceptible to eavesdropping attacks, while data at rest is more susceptible to the theft of physical devices or misconfiguration in the cloud. Data in use may be accessed by unauthorized processes if the operating system does not implement process isolation.

Hashing

Hashing refers to a broad category of algorithms that are useful for their ability to provide integrity and authentication. Integrity ensures that the information remains unchanged and is in its true original form. Authentication provides the capability to ensure that messages were sent from those you believed sent them and that those messages are sent to their intended recipients.

Hashing is a method of translating a key into a code. It does this by assigning a random independent surrogate value that can still be identified as the original data. Hashing calculates a short, secret value from a dataset of any size but usually for an entire message. This value is recalculated independently on the receiving end and is compared to the submitted value to verify the sender's identity.

Hashing algorithms operate by taking a variable amount of data and compressing it into a fixed-length value referred to as a *hash value*. Hashing provides a fingerprint or message digest of the data. A well-designed hashing algorithm will not typically produce the same hash value or output for two different inputs. When this does occur, it is referred to as a *collision*.

Collisions can be a problem in the world of hashing. A *collision* occurs when two different files create the same hashed output. One way to deal with collisions is to increase the size of the hashing algorithm output, such as, for example, moving from SHA-256 to SHA-512 so that a larger hash is created. SHA-256 and SHA-512 are hash functions computed with eight 32-bit and 64-bit words. They only differ in the number of rounds. SHA-224 and SHA-384 are truncated versions of SHA-256 and SHA-512, computed with different initial values.

Hashing can be used to meet the goals of integrity and nonrepudiation, depending on how the algorithm is implemented. Hashing is one of the primary means used to perform change monitoring. As an example, you might use a program such as Tripwire, a well-known change monitoring program, to verify that the contents of a specific folder remain unchanged over time. One of the advantages of hashing is its ability to verify that information has remained unchanged, but it is also used in authentication systems and digital signatures. Figure 6.1 gives an overview of the hashing process.

FIGURE 6.1   Hashing process

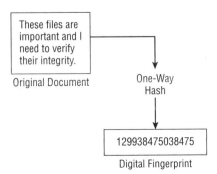

A *hash* is a one-way process and is not intended to be used to reproduce data. When a message or data file is hashed, the hashing algorithm examines every bit of the data while it is being processed. This means that if two files are close yet not exactly the same, their hashes will be different. For example, if we gave you a copy of a software program that had CASP+ exam study questions and you went to the Sybex website and downloaded the same software, hashing both files should result in the same value. Figure 6.2 shows an example of a cryptographic hash. It can be seen in the sha256sum column.

FIGURE 6.2   An example of a cryptographic hash on a software product

Download Kali Linux Images

We generate fresh Kali Linux image files every few months, which we make available for download. This page provides the links to **download Kali Linux** in its latest official release. For a release history, check our Kali Linux Releases page. Please note: You can find unofficial, untested weekly releases at http://cdimage.kali.org/kali-weekly/.

Image Name	Download	Size	Version	sha256sum
Kali Linux 64 Bit	HTTP | Torrent	2.8G	2018.2	56f677e2edfb2efcd0b08662ddde824e254c3d53567ebbbcdbbf5c03efd9bc0f
Kali Linux Light 64 Bit	HTTP | Torrent	865M	2018.2	554f020b0c89d5978928d31b8635a7eeddf0a3900abcacdbc39616f80d247f86
Kali Linux E17 64 Bit	HTTP | Torrent	2.6G	2018.2	be0a858c4a1862eb5d7b8875852e7d38ef852c335c3c23852a8b08807b4c3be8
Kali Linux Lxde 64 Bit	HTTP | Torrent	2.6G	2018.2	449ecca86b0f49a52f95a51acdde94745821020b7fc0bd2129628c56bc2d145d
Kali Linux Xfce 64 Bit	HTTP | Torrent	2.6G	2018.2	0e94035a0a56fccc49961b0da56b9243ed3da6a3f8d696884e6f0b936f74dbfb

If there were even a slight difference between the two files, the hashed values would be different. Comparing the hashes for the two files would indicate that the software we gave you had been altered. This same process is how programs such as Tripwire, MD5sum, and Windows System File Checker (sfc.exe) work. These kinds of programs can be used to monitor a file, a folder, or an entire hard drive for unauthorized changes. You also see this process used for functions such as code signing. *Code signing* is the process of digitally signing executables and scripts to confirm the software author. Code signing also guarantees that the code has not been altered or corrupted since it was signed by use of a hash. Listed here are some examples of hashing algorithms:

- Message Digest (MD)
- Secure Hash Algorithm (SHA)

- Message Authentication Code (MAC)
- Hashed Message Authentication Code (HMAC)
- RACE Integrity Primitives Evaluation Message Digest (RIPEMD)
- Poly1305

The following sections explore these hashing algorithms further.

Message Digest

The *MD algorithms* are a series of cryptographic algorithms that were developed by Ron Rivest. These have progressed throughout the years as technology has advanced. The first algorithm was MD2, which is considered outdated. One reason for its demise is that it was prone to collisions. MD4 was the next algorithm in the series. MD4 processes data in 512-bit blocks. Like MD2, MD4 was found to be subject to collisions and could potentially be vulnerable to forced collisions. These issues helped lead to the development of MD5, which processes a variable-size input and produces a fixed 128-bit output. A common implementation of MD5 is MD5sum. It's widely used to verify the integrity of a program or file. Consider the following example: if we received a copy of `snort.exe` from a friend, we could hash it and verify that the MD5sum matches what is found on the Sourcefire website:

```
C:\temp>md5sum snort.exe
d1bd4c6f099c4f0f26ea19e70f768d7f *snort.exe
```

Thus, a hash acts to prove the integrity of a file. Like MD4, MD5 processes the data in blocks of 512 bits. However, MD5 has also fallen from favor as it too has been shown to be vulnerable to collisions.

Secure Hash Algorithm

Secure Hash Algorithm (SHA) is similar to MD5. Some consider it a successor to MD5 because it produces a larger cryptographic hash. SHA outputs a 160-bit message digest. SHA-1 processes messages in 512-bit blocks and adds padding, if needed, to get the data to add up to the right number of bits. SHA-1 has only 111-bit effectiveness. SHA-1 is part of a family of SHA algorithms, including SHA-0, SHA-1, SHA-2, and SHA-3. SHA-0 is no longer considered secure, and SHA-1 is also now considered vulnerable to attacks. SHA-2 is the U.S. government's recommended replacement for the collision-vulnerable MD5. Some of the strongest versions currently available are SHA-256 and SHA-512. SHA-3 was released in 2012 and uses the Keccak algorithm.

Block cipher algorithms like AES and Triple DES in Electronic Code Book (ECB) and Cipher Block Chaining (CBC) mode require their input to be an exact multiple of the block size. If the plain text to be encrypted is not an exact multiple, you need to pad or extend the plain text before encrypting by adding a padding string. When decrypting, the receiving party needs to know how to remove the padding or extension.

Hash Algorithm of Variable Length

Hash algorithm of variable length (HAVAL) is another example of a one-way hashing algorithm that is similar to MD5. Unlike MD5, HAVAL is not tied to a fixed message-digest value. HAVAL-3-128 makes three passes and outputs a 128-bit fingerprint, and HAVAL-4-256 makes four passes and produces a fingerprint that is 256 bits in length. In late 2004, it was determined that HAVAL-3-128 yielded collisions.

Message Authentication Code

A *message authentication code (MAC)* is similar to a digital signature except that it uses symmetric encryption. MACs are created and verified with the same secret (symmetric) key. There are four types of MACs that you may come across in your career as a security professional: unconditionally secure, hash function based, stream cipher based, and block cipher based.

Hashed Message Authentication Code

Sometimes hashing by itself is not enough, and in such situations a *hashed message authentication code (HMAC)* may be needed. This functionality was added by including a shared secret key. Basically, HMAC functions by using a hashing algorithm such as MD5 or SHA-1 and then alters the initial state by adding a password. Even if someone can intercept and modify the data, it's of little use if that person does not possess the secret key. There is no easy way for the person to re-create the hashed value without it.

RACE Integrity Primitives Evaluation Message Digest

RACE integrity primitives evaluation message digest (RIPEMD) is in the Cryptocurrency Bitcoins standard. RIPEMD is based on the MD4 hash function and was published in four strengthened variants: RIPEMD-128, RIPEMD-160, RIPEMD-256, and RIPEMD-320.

The first RIPEMD-128 was not considered a good hash function because of major security problems, including the size of output was too small and easy to break. RIPEMD-160 is the next version; it increases the output length to 160 bit and increases the security level of the hash function. This function is designed to work as a replacement for 128-bit hash functions MD4, MD5, and RIPEMD-128 and is used as one of the alternatives to SHA-256 in Bitcoin.

Poly1305

The Poly1305 is a cryptographic message authentication code created by Daniel J. Bernstein. It is used to verify the data integrity and the authenticity of a message. Poly1305 takes a secret key and a message and produces an identifier that is difficult to create unless you know the secret key. This identifier is small and can be produced very quickly. This will authenticate a message and make sure it hasn't been altered.

The Poly1305 algorithm is defined in RFC 8439. More information can be found here: `https://datatracker.ietf.org/doc/html/rfc8439`.

Symmetric Algorithms

Symmetric encryption uses a single shared key for encryption and decryption. These are known as dual-use keys, as they can be used to lock and unlock data. Symmetric encryption is the oldest form of encryption. Historical systems such as scytale and Caesar's cipher are types of symmetric encryption. Symmetric encryption offers users privacy by keeping individuals who do not have the key from having access to the true contents of the message. Figure 6.3 shows the symmetric encryption process.

FIGURE 6.3 Symmetric encryption process

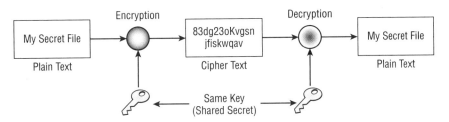

Notice how the plain text is encrypted with the single shared key and is then transmitted to the recipient of the message, who goes through the same process to decrypt the message. The dual use of keys is what makes this system so simple, but it also introduces weakness. Symmetric encryption is fast, and with a small key it can be used to encrypt bulk data quickly. It is also strong and difficult to break if the key is of sufficient size. However, symmetric encryption does have disadvantages.

The problem is key distribution. For symmetric encryption to be effective, there must be a secure method in place to transfer keys. In our modern world, there needs to be some type of out-of-band transmission. *Out-of-band transmission* means using a different means to transmit the key. As an example, if Bob wants to send Alice a secret message but is afraid that Mike can monitor their communication, how can he send the message? If the key is sent in clear text, Mike can intercept it. Bob could deliver the key in person, mail it, or even send a courier. All of these out-of-band methods are highly impractical in the world of e-commerce and electronic communications because they do not scale well.

Even if the problems of key exchange are overcome, there are still other concerns. Another problem is key management. If, for example, 10 people needed to communicate using symmetric encryption, the number of keys needed would be 45. As the number of people using symmetric encryption rises, so does the required number of keys. To determine the number of keys needed in symmetric encryption, the following formula is used:

$$n(n-1)/2$$

which simplifies to

$$n(n-1) \div 2 \left[or \, 10(10-1) \div 2 = 45 \, keys \right]$$

The third and final flaw with symmetric encryption is that it only provides confidentiality.

Some of the biggest challenges of key management across the enterprise can be made easier through security orchestration, automation, and response (SOAR). Public key infrastructure (PKI) isn't only about keeping keys stored securely. Through automation scripts and careful orchestration, the issuance and maintenance of keys can be done securely and with minimal risk of human error. PKI is discussed in more detail later in the "Public Key Infrastructure Hierarchy" section.

 For the CASP+ exam, you should understand the three primary issues involved with the use of symmetric encryption. These include concerns over key exchange and key management and the fact that symmetric encryption offers only confidentiality.

Although it is true that symmetric encryption is not perfect, it does offer some great features that make it an excellent choice for securing data and providing confidentiality. In the following sections, we will be discussing the following items (although not necessarily in this order):

- Modes of operation
  - Galois/counter mode (GCM)
  - Electronic codebook (ECB)
  - Cipher block chaining (CBC)
  - Counter (CTR)
  - Output feedback (OFB)
- Stream and block
  - Advanced Encryption Standard (AES)
  - Triple digital encryption standard (3DES)
  - ChaCha
  - Salsa20

But first, let's look at some of the specifics of symmetric encryption for a moment. Symmetric encryption is fast. It can encrypt and decrypt very quickly, and it is considered strong. Symmetric encryption is hard to break if a large key is used. Here are some well-known symmetric algorithms:

Data Encryption Standard The *Data Encryption Standard (DES)* was once the most common symmetric algorithm used. It has now been officially retired by the National Institute of Standards and Technology (NIST). Its short-term replacement was 3DES. Today, all versions of DES have been replaced by the Advanced Encryption Standard.

Advanced Encryption Standard The *Advanced Encryption Standard (AES)* is the symmetric algorithm chosen as a replacement for DES. It was adopted from the Rijndael algorithm, and it is used for sensitive and secret data. Its key sizes are 128-, 192-, and 256-bit.

Blowfish *Blowfish* is a general-purpose symmetric algorithm intended as a replacement for DES. Blowfish has a variable block size and up to a 448-bit key.

Carlisle Adams/Stafford Tavares *Carlisle Adams/Stafford Tavares (CAST)* is a 128- or 256-bit block cipher that was a candidate for AES.

International Data Encryption Algorithm The *International Data Encryption Algorithm (IDEA)* is a block cipher that uses a 128-bit key to encrypt 64-bit blocks of plain text. It is used by Pretty Good Privacy (PGP).

Rivest Cipher 4 *Rivest Cipher 4 (RC4)* is a stream-based cipher. Stream ciphers treat the data as a stream of bits.

Rivest Cipher 5 *Rivest Cipher 5 (RC5)* is a fast-block cipher. It is different from other symmetric algorithms in that it supports a variable block size, a variable key size, and a variable number of rounds. A *round* is a sequential repetition of a series of math functions. Allowable choices for the block size are 32, 64, and 128 bits. The key can range up to 2,040 bits.

Secure and Fast Encryption Routine *Secure and Fast Encryption Routine (SAFER)* is a block-based cipher that processes data in blocks of 64 and 128 bits.

Skipjack Promoted by the U.S. National Security Agency (NSA), *Skipjack* uses an 80-bit key and operates on 64-bit blocks of text. Skipjack faced opposition because the government would maintain a portion of the information required to reconstruct a Skipjack key so that legal authorities could decrypt communications between the affected parties when approved by a court.

Twofish *Twofish* is a block cipher that operates on 128-bit blocks of data and is capable of using cryptographic keys up to 256 bits in length.

Now let's look at some of the popular symmetric encryption standards in more depth.

Data Encryption Standard

DES was originally developed by IBM and then modified by NIST. The NSA endorsed the revised standard. It was published in 1977, and it was released by the American National Standards Institute (ANSI) in 1981.

DES is a symmetric encryption standard that is based on a 64-bit block that processes 64 bits of plain text at a time. DES outputs 64-bit blocks of cipher text. The DES key size is 56 bits, and DES has four primary modes of operation:

- Electronic codebook (ECB) mode
- Cipher block chaining (CBC) mode
- Output feedback (OFB) mode
- Cipher feedback (CFB) mode

All four modes use the 56-bit key, and though the standard lists the key as 64 bits, 8 bits are used for parity checking, so the true key size is actually 56 bits. *Parity checking* is a simple form of error detection. Each 64-bit, plaintext block is separated into two 32-bit blocks and then processed by the 56-bit key. The plain text is processed by the key through 16 rounds of transposition and substitution.

Examine closely any CASP+ exam question that mentions DES. Remember that although DES operates on 64-bit blocks, the effective key length is only 56 bits.

Electronic Codebook Mode

Electronic codebook (ECB) mode is the default mode of encryption used by DES, ECB, CBC, OFB, and CFB and also applies to 3DES. If the last block is not a full 64 bits, padding is added. ECB produces the greatest throughput, but it is also the easiest implementation of DES encryption to crack. If used with large amounts of data, it is easily broken because the same plain text encrypted with the same key always produces the same cipher text. This is why if you use ECB, you should do so only on small amounts of data.

When you're using ECB, keep in mind that a fixed key and a known repeating plaintext message will always produce the same cipher text.

Cipher Block Chaining Mode

When DES is operating in *cipher block chaining (CBC) mode*, it is somewhat similar to ECB except that CBC inserts some of the cipher text created from the previous block into the next one. This process is called *XORing*. It makes the cipher text more secure and less susceptible to cracking. CBC is aptly named because data from one block is used in the next, and the blocks are chained together. This chaining produces dependency, but it also results in more random cipher text.

Output Feedback Mode

Output feedback (OFB) mode is implemented as a stream cipher and uses plain text to feed back into the stream of cipher text. Transmission errors do not propagate throughout the encryption process. An initialization vector is used to create the seed value for the first encrypted block. DES XORs the plain text with a seed value to be applied with subsequent data.

Cipher Feedback Mode

Cipher feedback (CFB) mode can be implemented as a stream cipher and used to encrypt individual characters. CFB is similar to OFB in that previously generated cipher text is added to subsequent streams. Because the cipher text is streamed together, errors and corruption can propagate through the encryption process. This mode could be referring to DES, 3DES, or AES.

How secure is DES? Not as secure as it once was. Computing power has increased over the years, and that has decreased the time required to brute-force DES. In 1998, the Electronic Frontier Foundation was able to crack DES in about 23 hours, and that was more than 20 years ago. Today's computing power could brute-force DES in minutes.

Triple DES

Triple DES (3DES) was designed to be a stopgap solution. DES was initially certified for five years and was required to be recertified every five years. While easily passing these recertifications in the early years, DES began to encounter problems around the 1987 recertification. By 1993, NIST stated that DES was beginning to outlive its usefulness. It began looking for candidates to replace it. This new standard was to be referred to as the *Advanced Encryption Standard (AES)*.

AES was to be the long-term replacement, but something else was needed to fill the gap before AES was ready to be deployed. Therefore, to extend the usefulness of the DES encryption standard, 3DES was adopted. It can use two or three keys to encrypt data, depending on how it is implemented. It has an effective key length of 112 or 168 bits, and it performs 48 rounds of transpositions and substitutions. Although it is much more secure, it is as slow as one-third the speed of 56-bit DES.

Rijndael and the Advanced Encryption Standard

Rijndael is a block cipher adopted by NIST as the AES to replace DES. In 2002, NIST chose *Rijndael* to replace DES. Its name is derived from its two developers, Vincent Rijmen and

Joan Daemen. It is a fast, simple, robust encryption mechanism. Rijndael is also known to resist various types of attacks.

The Rijndael algorithm uses three layers of transformations to encrypt and decrypt blocks of message text:

- Linear mix transform

- Nonlinear transform

- Key addition transform

Rijndael uses a four-step, parallel series of rounds. Rijndael is an iterated block cipher that supports variable key and block lengths of 128, 192, or 256 bits:

- If both key and block size are 128 bits, there are 10 rounds.

- If both key and block size are 192 bits, there are 12 rounds.

- If both key and block size are 256 bits, there are 14 rounds.

Each of the following steps is performed during each round:

1. **Byte substitution**: Each byte is replaced by an s-box substitution.

2. **Shift row**: Bytes are arranged in a rectangle and shifted.

3. **Mix column**: Matrix multiplication is performed based on the arranged rectangle.

4. **Add round key**: Each byte of the state is combined with the round key.

On the last round, the fourth step is bypassed, and the first step is repeated.

ChaCha

ChaCha is a stream cipher developed by D.J. Bernstein in 2008. It is used as the core of the SHA-3 finalist, BLAKE. ChaCha20 consists of 20 rounds. ChaCha is used for improved mobile device browser performance while using the Internet. Engineers from Google needed a fast and secure stream cipher to add to TLS to provide a battery-friendly alternative to AES for mobile devices. ChaCha20-Poly1305 was included in Chrome 31 in November 2013, and Chrome for Android and iOS at the end of April 2014.

For more information, visit `https://cr.yp.to/chacha/chacha-20080128.pdf`.

Salsa20

Salsa20 is a stream cipher and was the precursor to ChaCha. Salsa can expand a 256-bit key into 264 randomly accessible streams of 264 randomly accessible 64-byte (512-bit) blocks.

International Data Encryption Algorithm

The *International Data Encryption Algorithm (IDEA)* is a 64-bit block cipher that uses a 128-bit key. It is different from others, as it avoids the use of s-boxes or lookup tables. Although IDEA is patented by a Swiss company, it is freely available for noncommercial use.

It is considered a secure encryption standard, and there have been no known attacks against it. Like DES, it operates in four distinct modes. At one time, it was thought that IDEA might replace DES, but patent royalties made that impractical.

Rivest Cipher Algorithms

The *RC cipher algorithm series* is part of a family of ciphers designed by Ron Rivest. Rivest ciphers include RC2, RC3, RC4, RC5, and RC6. RC2 is an older algorithm that maintains a variable key size, 64-bit block cipher that can be used as a substitute for DES. RC3 was broken as a cipher as it was being developed. So, RC3 was never actually used. RC4 was implemented as a stream cipher. The 40-bit version is what was originally available in WEP. It is most commonly found in the 128-bit key version. RC5 is a block cipher in which the number of rounds can range from 0 to 255, and the key can range from 0 bits to 2,048 bits in size. Finally, there is RC6. It features variable key size and rounds, and it added two features not found in RC5: integer multiplication and 4-bit working registers.

Counter Mode

Counter mode uses an arbitrary number that changes with each individual block of text encrypted. The counter is encrypted with the cipher, and the result is XOR'd into ciphertext. The lack of interdependency also means that the CTR mode is tolerant to a loss in blocks. The CTR mode is considered to be very secure and efficient for most purposes. Two ways it can be used are as follows:

- *Counter (CTR) mode* is similar to OFB since it turns a block mode into a stream cipher. Unlike OFB, CTR can be a mode of operation for either DES or AES.

- *Galois/Counter (GCM)* mode is unique to AES (AES-GCM). GCM is an authenticated encrypted mode (meaning it offers confidentiality and authentication) with a block size of 128 bits.

Asymmetric Encryption

Symmetric encryption does offer speed, but if you're looking for a cryptographic system that provides easy key exchange, you will have to consider asymmetric encryption. *Asymmetric encryption*, or *public key cryptography*, is different from symmetric encryption. It overcomes one of the big barriers of symmetric encryption: key distribution. Asymmetric encryption uses two unique keys, as shown in Figure 6.4. What one key does, the other key undoes.

Here's how asymmetric encryption works: Imagine that you want to send a co-worker a message. You use your co-worker's public key to encrypt the message. Your co-worker receives the message and uses a private key to decrypt it.

FIGURE 6.4 Asymmetric encryption

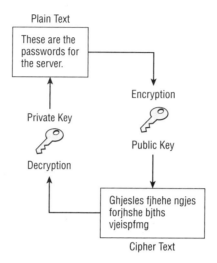

Public key cryptography is made possible by the use of one-way functions. A *one-way function*, or trapdoor, is a math operation that is easy to compute in one direction, yet it is almost impossible to compute in the other direction. Depending on the type of asymmetric encryption used, this difficulty is based on either the discrete logarithm problem or the factoring of a large number into its prime factors. Although the math behind the encryption process is not needed to pass the CASP+ exam, in algebra, *discrete logarithms* are group-theoretic analogs of ordinary logarithms. For example, if you are given two large prime numbers, it is easy to multiply them. However, if you are given only their product, it is difficult or impossible to find the factors with today's processing power. Asymmetric systems may also make use of a *zero-knowledge proof*. This concept allows you to prove your knowledge without revealing the fact to a third party.

If the message is encrypted with the public key, only the matching private key will decrypt it. The private key is kept secret, whereas the public key can be given to anyone. If the algorithm is properly designed, it should not be possible for someone to easily deduce the private key of a pair if that person has only the public key.

Consider the following example of asymmetric encryption: given the prime numbers 397 and 823, it is easy to multiply them together and get 326,731. However, if you are given the number 326,731, it's quite difficult to extract the two prime numbers, 397 and 823. Anyone who knows the trapdoor can perform the function in both directions, but if you are lacking the trapdoor, you can perform the function in only one direction. Trapdoor functions can be used in the forward direction for encryption and signature verification, whereas the inverse direction is used for decryption and signature generation.

The length of the cryptographic key is one of the most important security parameters that can be set. It's important to understand the capabilities of your encryption algorithm and choose a key length that provides an appropriate level of protection. This decision can be made by examining the difficulty of deciphering a given key length (measured in the amount of processing time required to defeat the cryptosystem) against how important the data is. The more critical your data, the stronger the key should be.

To help ensure your success on the CASP+ exam, Table 6.1 compares symmetric and asymmetric cryptographic systems.

TABLE 6.1   Attributes of symmetric and asymmetric encryption

Symmetric	Asymmetric
Confidentiality	Confidentiality, integrity, authentication, and nonrepudiation
One single shared key	Two keys: public and private
Requires an out-of-band exchange	Useful for in-band exchange
Not scalable; too many keys needed	Scalable; works for e-commerce
Small key size and fast	Larger key size required, and slower to process
Useful for bulk encryption	Best for small amounts of data, digital signatures, digital envelopes, and digital certificates

Diffie–Hellman

Dr. W. Diffie and Dr. M.E. Hellman released the first public key-exchange protocol in 1976. They developed it specifically for key exchange and not for data encryption or digital signatures. The *Diffie–Hellman protocol* was designed to allow two users to exchange a secret key over an insecure channel without any prior communication. The protocol functions with two system parameters: p and g. Both parameters are public and can be used by all of the system's users. Parameter p is a prime number, and parameter g, which is usually called a *generator*, is an integer less than p that has the following property: for every number n between 1 and $p - 1$ inclusive, there is a power k of g such that $g^k = n \bmod p$. Diffie–Hellman is used in conjunction with several authentication methods, including the Internet Key Exchange (IKE) component of IPsec.

$$g^k = n \bmod p$$

Diffie–Hellman was groundbreaking in its ability to allow two parties to exchange encryption keys securely, but it is not without its problems. It is vulnerable to on-path, formerly known as *man-in-the-middle (MitM)*, attacks because the key exchange process does not authenticate the participants. You should use digital signatures to alleviate this vulnerability.

Elliptic-curve Diffie–Hellman (ECDH) works nearly the same but adds algebraic curves to generate keys to be used by the parties. Both participating parties have to previously agree on a specific elliptic curve. ECDH is much faster than using the large numbers required in normal DH, and the ECDH discrete logarithm problem is harder to solve than the normal discrete logarithm problem. This means smaller keys can be used with ECDH.

RSA

The *RSA algorithm* is named after its inventors. Ron Rivest, Adi Shamir, and Len Adleman developed RSA in 1977. Although RSA, like other asymmetric algorithms, is slower than symmetric encryption systems, it offers secure key exchange and is considered very secure. RSA supports a key size up to 3,072 bits. The design of RSA is such that it has to use prime numbers whose product is much larger than 129 digits for security; 129-digit decimal numbers are factored using a number field sieve algorithm. RSA public and private keys are generated as follows:

1. Choose two large prime numbers, p and q, of equal length and compute $p \times q = n$, which is the public modulus.

2. Choose a random public key, e, so that e and $(p - 1)(q - 1)$ are relatively prime.

3. Compute $e \times d = 1 \bmod [(p - 1)(q - 1)]$, where d is the private key.

4. Thus, $d = e^{-1} \bmod [(p - 1)(q - 1)]$.

From these calculations, (d, n) is the private key, and (e, n) is the public key. The plain text, P, is encrypted to generate cipher text, C, as follows:

$$C = P^e \bmod n$$

and is decrypted to recover the plain text, P, as follows:

$$P = C^d \bmod n$$

RSA functions by breaking the plain text into equal-length blocks, with each block having fewer digits than n. Each block is encrypted and decrypted separately. Anyone attempting to crack RSA would be left with a tough challenge because of the difficulty of factoring a large integer into its two factors. Cracking an RSA key would require an extraordinary amount of computer processing power and time. The RSA algorithm has become the de facto standard for industrial-strength encryption, especially since the patent expired in 2000. It is built into many protocols, such as PGP; software products; and systems such as Mozilla Firefox, Google Chrome, and Microsoft Edge.

Elliptic Curve Cryptography

In 1985, two mathematicians, Neal Koblitz from the University of Washington and Victor Miller from IBM, independently proposed the application of *elliptic curve cryptography* (ECC) theory to develop secure cryptographic systems.

ECC can be found in smaller, less powerful devices such as smartphones and handheld devices. ECC is considered more secure than some of the other asymmetric algorithms because elliptic curve systems are harder to crack than those based on discrete log problems. Elliptic curves are usually defined over finite fields such as real and rational numbers, and they implement an analog to the discrete logarithm problem.

The strengths of various key lengths also vary greatly according to the cryptosystem you're using. For example, a 1,024-bit RSA key offers approximately the same degree of security as a 160-bit ECC key. ECC using a 256-bit key would require a 3,072-bit RSA key to achieve equivalent protection.

By increasing the bit key to 384, the security ECC would give is very strong. Longer keys are certainly more secure, but they also require more computational overhead. It's the classic trade-off of resources versus security constraints.

Any elliptic curve can be defined by the following equation:

$$y^2 = x^3 + ax + b$$

In this equation, x, y, a, and b are all real numbers. Each elliptic curve has a corresponding *elliptic curve group* made up of the points on the elliptic curve along with the point O, located at infinity. Two points within the same elliptic curve group (P and Q) can be added together with an elliptic curve addition algorithm. This operation is expressed as follows:

$$P + Q$$

This problem can be extended to involve multiplication by assuming that Q is a multiple of P, meaning the following:

$$Q = xP$$

Computer scientists and mathematicians believe that it is extremely hard to find x, even if P and Q are already known. This difficult problem, known as the elliptic curve discrete logarithm problem, forms the basis of elliptic curve cryptography.

ElGamal

ElGamal was released in 1985, and its security rests in part on the difficulty of solving discrete logarithm problems. It is an extension of the Diffie–Hellman key exchange. ElGamal consists of three discrete components: a key generator, an encryption algorithm, and a decryption algorithm. It can be used for digital signatures, key exchange, and encryption.

Hybrid Encryption and Electronic Data Exchange (EDI)

Sometimes mixing two things together makes good sense. Do you remember the commercial, "You got your chocolate in my peanut butter?" While you may not consider cryptography as tasty as chocolate, there is a real benefit to combining symmetric and asymmetric encryption. Symmetric encryption is fast, but key distribution is a problem. Asymmetric encryption offers easy key distribution, but it's not suited for large amounts of data. Combining the two into hybrid encryption uses the advantages of each and results in a truly powerful system. Public key cryptography is used as a key encapsulation scheme, and the private key cryptography is used as a data encapsulation scheme. Here is how the system works. If Bob wants to send a message to Alice, the following occurs:

1. Bob generates a random private key for a data encapsulation scheme. This session key is a symmetric key.

2. The data encapsulation happens when Bob encrypts the message using the symmetric key that was generated in step 1.

3. The key encapsulation happens when Bob encrypts the symmetric key using Alice's public key.

4. Bob sends both of these items, the encrypted message and the encrypted key, to Alice.

5. Alice uses her private key to decrypt the symmetric key and then uses the symmetric key to decrypt the message.

Almost all modern cryptographic systems make use of hybrid encryption. This method works well because it uses the strength of symmetric encryption and the key exchange capabilities of asymmetric encryption. Some good examples of hybrid cryptographic systems are IPsec, Secure Shell, Secure Electronic Transaction, Secure Sockets Layer, PGP, and Transport Layer Security. With hybrid systems, can we achieve perfect secrecy? This depends on items such as the algorithm, how the key is used, and how well keys are protected. The concept of *perfect forward secrecy (PFS)* refers to the goal of ensuring that the exposure of a single key will permit an attacker access only to data protected by a single key. To achieve PFS, the key used to protect transmission of data cannot be used to create any additional keys. Also, if the key being used to protect transmission of data is derived from some other keying material, that material cannot be used to create any additional keys.

For data in transit, *Electronic Data Interchange (EDI)* may be used. However, EDI is losing ground and being replaced with *Transaction Processing over XML (TPoX)*. EDI was designed specifically for security and to bridge the gap between dissimilar systems. EDI is used to exchange data in a format that both the sending and receiving systems can understand. ANSI X12 is the most common of the formats used. EDI offers real benefits for organizations, as it reduces paperwork and results in fewer errors because all information is transmitted electronically.

Although EDI eases communication, it must be implemented with the proper security controls. Luckily, EDI has controls that address the issue of security as well as lost or duplicate transactions and confidentiality. The following list includes some common EDI controls:

- Transmission controls to validate sender and receiver

- Manipulation controls to prevent unauthorized changes to data

- Authorization controls to authenticate communication partners

- Encryption controls to protect the confidentiality of information

EDI adds a new level of concern to organizations because documents are processed electronically. One major concern with EDI is authorization. This means that EDI processes should have an additional layer of application control.

Public Key Infrastructure Hierarchy

Public key infrastructure (PKI) allows two parties to communicate even if they were previously unknown to each other. PKI makes use of users, systems, and applications. It allows users that are previously unknown to each other to communicate over an insecure medium such as the Internet. The most common system of using PKI is that of a centralized certificate authority. Applications that make use of PKI commonly use X.509 certificates.

PKI facilitates e-commerce. Consider how different dealing with brick-and-mortar businesses is from transactions over the Internet. Dealing with brick-and-mortar businesses gives you plenty of opportunity to develop trust. After all, you can see who you are dealing with, talk to the employees, and get a good look at how they do business.

In the modern world of e-commerce, transactions are much less transparent. You may not be able to see with whom you are dealing, yet you might have full trust in them. PKI addresses these concerns and brings trust, integrity, and security to electronic transactions.

One nontechnical issue with key distribution is controlling access to keys. Any PKI system has to be carefully controlled to ensure that the wrong individuals don't get access to secret keys.

From a user's perspective, PKI may look seamless, yet in reality it is made up of many components. PKI consists of hardware, software, and policies that manage, create, store, and distribute keys and digital certificates. The basic components of PKI are as follows:

- The certificate authority (CA)

- The registration authority (RA)

- The certificate revocation list (CRL)

- Digital certificates

- A certificate distribution system

Certificate Authority

The *certificate authority (CA)* is like a passport office. The passport office is responsible for issuing passports, and passports are a standard for identification for anyone wanting to leave the country. Like passport offices, CAs vouch for your identity in a digital world. VeriSign, Thawte, and Entrust are some of the companies, or *trusted providers*, which perform CA services. The most commonly used model is the *hierarchical trust model*. Figure 6.5 shows an example of this model. In small organizations, a single trust model may be used. Its advantage is that it's not as complex and has less overhead than the hierarchical trust model.

FIGURE 6.5 Hierarchical trust model

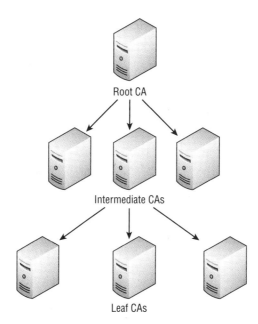

Root CA

Intermediate CAs

Leaf CAs

Although the companies mentioned are external CAs, some organizations may also decide to tackle these responsibilities by themselves. Regardless of who performs the services, the following steps are required:

1. The CA verifies the request for a certificate with the help of the registration authority.

2. The individual's identification is validated.

3. A certificate is created by the CA, which verifies that the person matches the public key that is being offered.

Certificate profiles can offer end devices the certificates to avoid having to manually install the certificates. The end device may be a client workstation or server in order to expedite *server authentication* or *client authentication*.

Subordinate and Intermediate Certificate Authorities

As the name implies, a *subordinate certification authority* is one step lower in the CA hierarchy. In terms of the hierarchy, the top-level CA is also called the root CA. The root CA is at the highest level, while a certificate authority that requests and authorizes certificates from the root CA is called the subordinate CA. While there is only one root CA in the hierarchy, there may be several subordinate CAs. Beneath the subordinate CA would be the certificate issued to services, users, or devices.

One more type of certificate authority is the *intermediate CA*. An intermediate CA is a subordinate CA that may have one or more subordinate CAs beneath it.

Cross-Certification

Let's use the example of an enterprise organization, where it may include multiple PKI solutions. This may be the case for scalability or efficiency reasons. With multiple PKI implementations, it can be beneficial for a CA of one PKI to trust the certificates from the second PKI. *Cross-certification* is used for CAs to trust the issued certificates across PKIs. In the real world, cross-certification is in effect an example of *federation*, chaining together multiple PKI implementations. Federation certainly helps with efficiency and ease of use, but the reliability of the trust is dependent on every chain, every PKI. Any compromise of one PKI solution could cause a domino effect of damage across multiple PKIs.

Registration Authority

If the CA is like a passport authority, the *registration authority (RA)* is like a middleman. Think of it as one of the rush services that you can use when you need to get your passport right away. The RA is positioned between the client and the CA. Although the RA cannot generate a certificate, it can accept requests, verify a person's identity, and pass along the information to the CA for certificate generation.

RAs play a key role when certificate services are expanded to cover large geographic areas. One central private or corporate CA can delegate its responsibilities to regional RAs; for example, there might be one RA in the United States, another in Canada, another in Europe, and another in India.

Digital Certificates

Digital certificates are critical to the PKI process. The digital certificate serves two roles. First, it ensures the integrity of the public key and makes sure that the key remains unchanged and in a valid state. Second, it validates that the public key is tied to the stated owner and that all associated information is true and correct. The information needed to accomplish these goals is added to the digital certificate.

Digital signatures play a vital role in proving your identity when performing electronic transactions.

Digital certificates are formatted to the X.509 standard. The most current version of X.509 is version 3. One of the main developments in version 3 was the addition of extensions. This version includes the flexibility to support other topologies such as *bridges* and *meshes*. It can operate as a web of trust, much like PGP. An X.509 certificate includes the following elements:

- Version
- Serial number
- Algorithm ID
- Issuer
- Validity
- Not before (a specified date)
- Not after (a specified date)
- Subject
- Subject public key information
- Public key algorithm
- Subject public key
- Issuer-unique identifier (optional)
- Subject-unique identifier (optional)
- Extensions (optional)

Different entities can use a certificate. *Issuance to entities* identifies to whom the CA issues certificates. The certificate might be issued to a user, a system, or an application. The CA not only issues the certificate, but it also vouches for the authenticity of entities. It is not mandatory that you use an external CA to issue certificates, but they are widely used. An organization may decide to have itself act as a CA. Regardless of whether a third party handles the duties or your company performs them, digital certificates will typically contain the following critical pieces of information:

- Identification information that includes username, serial number, and validity dates of the certificates.
- The public key of the certificate holder.
- The digital signature of the signature authority. This piece is critical since it validates the entire package.

If you decide to use a third party to issue a certificate, there is a cost. These organizations are generally for-profit and will charge fees for you to maintain your certificate in good standing.

Certificate Revocation List

Let's compare *Online Certificate Status Protocol (OCSP)* with the *certificate revocation list (CRL)*. Like passports, digital certificates do not stay valid for a lifetime. Certificates become invalid for many reasons, such as someone leaving the company, information changing, or a private key being compromised. For these reasons, the *certificate revocation list (CRL)* must be maintained.

The CRL is maintained by the CA, which signs the list to maintain its accuracy. Whenever problems are reported with digital certificates, the digital certificates are considered invalid and the CA has the serial number added to the CRL. Anyone requesting a digital certificate can check the CRL to verify the certificate's integrity. There are many reasons a certificate may become corrupted, including the following:

- The certificate expired.

- The DNS name or the IP address of the server changed.

- The server crashed and corrupted the certificate.

If the topic of OCSP and certificates interests you, be sure to check out Request for Comments (RFC) 6960. This RFC details CRL and OCSP.

Certificate Types

There is the option for a browser or device to verify that a certificate hasn't been revoked. That revocation checking as an option, though, is changed to a strict requirement in the case of one type of certificate, the *validation certificate*.

Some organizations may choose to use wildcard certificates to cut costs. A *wildcard certificate* allows the purchaser to secure an unlimited number of subdomain certificates on a domain name. The advantage is that you buy and maintain only one certificate. The drawback, however, is that you are using just one certificate and private key on multiple websites and private servers. If just one of these servers or websites is compromised, all of the others under the wildcard certificate will be exposed.

Wildcard certificates allow you to specify a wildcard character in the name. For example, a wildcard certificate for *.thesolutionfirm.com will allow you to use mail.thesolutionfirm.com, ftp.thesolution-firm.com, mail.china.thesolutionfirm.com, and so on.

A similarly beneficial option for secure multiple domains is the multidomain certificate. Unlike the wildcard, which secures multiple subdomains, the *multidomain certificate* will secure multiple websites. For example, a multidomain certificate could secure example.net, example.com, and example.org. The wildcard certificate could secure sub1.example.org, sub2.example.org, and sub3.example.org.

If a private key is exposed or another situation arises where a certificate must be rcvoked, PKI has a way to deal with such situations, that is, when a CRL is used. These lists can be checked via the *Online Certificate Status Protocol (OCSP)*, an Internet protocol used for obtaining the revocation status of an X.509 digital certificate. This process is much the same as maintaining a driver's license. Mike may have a driver's license, yet if he gets stopped by a police officer, the officer may still decide to run a check on Mike's license; he's checking on the status of Mike's license in the same way that the OCSP is used to check on the status of an X.509 certificate.

Certificate Distribution

Certificates can be distributed by a centralized service or by means of a public authority. The use of a CA is an example of centralized distribution: a trusted CA distributes a public key to another party. The certificate is signed by means of a digital signature of the CA to prove it is valid. The certificates can be passed from one CA to another by using a chain of trust. A chain of trust provides a trust relationship between entities. See Figure 6.6 for an example.

FIGURE 6.6 An example of a chain of trust

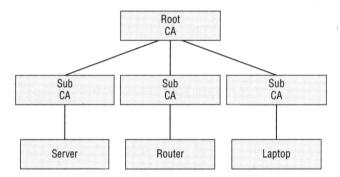

A second way to distribute keys is directly through a third party. This is called a *web of trust*. For example, if you email us with a question about the book, our return emails will include our public key. It's an easy way to distribute keys, but it does not offer the level of trust that would be obtained from a third-party CA such as VeriSign or Thawte. PGP and GPG are examples of systems that provide encryption and can use web-of-trust certificate distribution.

> **Tokens** PKI tokens provide secure storage for digital certificates and private keys. They allow public-key cryptography and digital signatures to be leveraged securely without the risk of leaking the private key information. PKI tokens are hardware devices that store digital certificates and private keys securely. When you need to encrypt, decrypt, or

sign something, the token does this internally in a secure chip, meaning that the keys are never at risk of being stolen.

Stapling   *Online Certificate Status Protocol (OCSP) stapling* or *certificate stapling* enhances performance of the website and privacy of the client. Prior to OCSP stapling, the OCSP request originates from a client to the CA server in order to validate an SSL certificate. OCSP stapling allows the certificate presenter to query the OCSP responder directly and then let them cache the response. This allows for a securely cached response, which is then delivered ("stapled") with a TLS/SSL handshake via the Certificate Status Request extension response. This helps to ensure that the browser gets the same response performance for the certificate status as it does for the website content.

OCSP stapling also addresses a privacy concern with OCSP that the certificate authority no longer receives the revocation requests directly from the client (browser). OCSP stapling further addresses the concerns about OCSP SSL negotiation delays by removing the need for a separate network connection to a certification authority's responder.

Pinning   *Certificate pinning* is the technique of telling your browser of choice that only certificates with a specific public key somewhere in the certificate chain are to be trusted. Current implementations are based on *trust on first use (TOFU)*, which means that your browser of choice will have to trust the connection the first time you use a site. This is because the pinning info is sent via an HTTP header by the web server. In the future, this can ideally be retrieved via DNSSEC-signed DNS records.

You pin the public key of a certificate. There are at least three certificates per site (site cert, intermediate cert, and root cert) that give you a few options on what to pin. Your site certificate will be replaced in the near future, commonly within three years, but it will most likely be replaced even before that due to reissues. You have no control over what intermediate certificate the CA will use on a reissue, so don't pin that. Certificate authorities have multiple root certs in trust stores, and you simply can't control which one they will use on reissues. You must rely on what you can control—your own public key in the certificate chain—so that is what you want to pin.

HTTP Public Key Pinning (HPKP) doesn't just let you provide a backup public key; it requires you to do so. This is useful when your private key gets compromised. Your backup key will then be used to generate a new certificate. The backup key should, of course, never be stored on the same infrastructure as your primary key, and it will never be used for anything else.

The Client's Role in PKI

Although the CA is responsible for a large portion of the work, in the world of PKI the client also has some duties. Clients are responsible for requesting digital certificates and for maintaining the security of their private key.

And even though certificates are issued, a client may still attempt to establish the connection insecurely. For example, if the user's browser were to initiate using HTTP instead of

HTTPS. One solution is to redirect the browser to switch to HTTPS. This is done by setting up a 301 redirect directive on the server.

However, a malicious user would be able to capture traffic leading up to the redirect. The optimal solution would be to utilize *HTTP Strict Transport Security (HSTS)*. When a web server directs the web browser to implement HSTS to only (strictly) utilize a secure connection starting with the browser, then this potential insecure capture is avoided.

Loss, compromise, or exposure of the private key would mean that communications are no longer secure. Protecting the private key is an important issue because for the attacker, it may be easier to target the key rather than to try to brute-force or crack the certificate service. Organizations should concern themselves with eight key management issues:

- Generation
- Distribution
- Installation
- Storage
- Recovery
- Change
- Control
- Disposal

Key recovery and control is an important issue that must be addressed. One basic recovery and control method is the *m* of *n* control method of access. This method is designed to ensure that no one person can have total control; it is closely related to dual control. If *n* administrators have the ability to perform a process, *m* of those administrators must authenticate for access to occur. *M* of *n* control should require physical presence for access.

Here is an example. Let's say that a typical *m* of *n* control method requires that four people have access to the archive server and that at least two of them must be present to accomplish access. In this situation, *m* = 2 and *n* = 4. This would ensure that no one person could compromise the security system or gain access.

 Real World Scenario

Trust in the World of PKI

Trust isn't a problem in small organizations, but the need to communicate within large organizations or with external clients and third parties requires developing a working trust model. Organizations typically follow one of several well-known trust models, such as single-authority trust, hierarchical trust, or web of trust.

Each model has its advantages and disadvantages, and as a CASP+ you may be asked to recommend a method to your organization. You should keep in mind that although a single authority model is simple, it's not well suited for large organizations; if it is managed by the company, cross-certification to other entities can be an issue. A hierarchical model is typically provided by a commercial entity. While this is more robust, there are associated ongoing fees.

Finally, there is the web of trust, the least complex of all models. It may work well for an individual or small group, but it has a low level of trust. Which model will you choose for your company?

Implementation of Cryptographic Solutions

Has this chapter got you thinking about all of the ways cryptography can be used and how valuable it is to a security professional? We hope that it has. The real question is, now that you're armed with some specific cryptographic solutions, how strong should the encryption be and where might you apply cryptographic solutions?

Encryption can be applied at the disk, block, file, record, and port:

Disk Encryption *Disk encryption* can use either hardware or software to encrypt an entire hard drive or volume. Such technology is incredibly important today. *Mobile security* is especially enhanced by encryption, considering how much sensitive information individuals have stored on mobile devices and tablets. Such items are easily lost or stolen. Common disk encryption products include BitLocker and AxCrypt.

Block Encryption *Block encryption* secures data in fixed-size groups of bits. An example of a block cipher that we have previously discussed is DES ECB. DES encrypts data in 64-bit blocks.

File Encryption You don't have to encrypt an entire hard drive or volume. In some situations, you may simply need to encrypt specific files. Examples of products that can be used for *file encryption* include AxCrypt and PGP.

Record Encryption Databases are a common area of attack. If you are storing sensitive information in a database, you may want to encrypt the entire database or just specific records. As an example of *record encryption*, in a medical facility you may want to protect records that hold Social Security numbers or other personal information, leaving only medical IDs and medical records open to the hospital staff.

Port Encryption Some services are just more secure than others. As an example of *port encryption*, Telnet, TCP port 23, sends data in the clear, whereas Secure Shell, port 22, uses encryption. Another example is HTTP, as port 80 is clear text, whereas HTTPS uses port 443.

These examples demonstrate that cryptography is one of the most valuable tools that a security professional can use, but the trade-offs between strength, performance, and usability must be considered. Each cryptographic solution has strengths and limitations. Organizations must perform a proper risk assessment to determine the level of threat and the amount of protection that each asset requires. That assessment will go a long way in determining the type of technology used. Is the data something that is useful for only the next few minutes, like orders to buy or sell stock? Is the information top-secret data on the next generation of fighter jets that have yet to start production? Where is the data being stored? How valuable is it to someone else? How long is it likely to remain valuable?

Even if the information does not require cryptographic solutions to provide privacy, you may still need controls that can help safeguard the information. One such technology is *digital rights management (DRM)*. DRM is an entire suite of technology designed to protect digital content. As an example, you may be reading a copy of this book on your tablet, yet that does not mean the publisher wants to provide free copies to 100 of your closest friends! That is the situation for which DRM is designed: it helps prevent copyright infringement online and thus helps the copyright holder maintain control of the information.

Next, you need to consider where to build in the protection. Cryptography can be used in many different situations to build a true defense in depth. If you think of cryptography in reference to the TCP/IP model, you can see where cryptographic solutions can be applied, from the application layer all the way down to the physical frame. Let's start at the top of the TCP/IP stack and work down through the layers, highlighting a few cryptographic solutions.

Application Layer Encryption

The following application layer protocols are just a few examples that can be used to add confidentiality, integrity, or nonrepudiation:

Secure Shell   *Secure Shell (SSH)* is an Internet application that provides secure remote access. It serves as a replacement for FTP, Telnet, and the Berkeley "r" utilities. SSH defaults to TCP port 22.

Secure Hypertext Transfer Protocol   *Secure Hypertext Transfer Protocol (S-HTTP)* is a superset of HTTP that was developed to provide secure communication with a web server. S-HTTP is a connectionless protocol designed to send individual messages securely.

 Hypertext Transfer Protocol Secure (HTTPS) is a secure extension of the Hypertext Transfer Protocol (HTTP). HTTPS runs over port 443 instead of port 80, which is used by the insecure HTTP.

Pretty Good Privacy   *Pretty Good Privacy (PGP)* was developed in 1991 by Phil Zimmermann to provide privacy and authentication. Over time, it evolved into open standards such as OpenPGP and GnuPGP. PGP builds a web of trust that is developed as users sign and issue their own keys. The goal of PGP was for it to become the "everyman's encryption." Popular programs such as HushMail, CounterMail, and K-9 Mail are based on PGP, providing end-to-end encryption.

GNU Privacy Guard   Does free sound good? If you are like many of us, the answer is yes, and that is where *GNU Privacy Guard (GPG)* comes into the equation. It is a licensed, free version of PGP. The idea was to provide a free version of PGP that everyone can use. Like PGP, GPG makes use of hybrid encryption and uses the best of both symmetric and asymmetric encryption. The symmetric portion is used for encryption and decryption, and the asymmetric portion is used for key exchange.

S/MIME   For those who prefer not to use PGP or GPG, there is another option for the security of email. That solution is *S/MIME (Secure/Multipurpose Internet Mail Extensions)*. S/MIME is a standard for public key encryption and signing of MIME data. S/MIME provides two basic services: digital signatures and message encryption. S/MIME is a popular solution for securing email, and it is built into most email software programs, such as Microsoft Outlook and Mozilla Thunderbird.

Secure Remote Access   A variety of applications can be used for *secure remote access*, such as SSH, Remote Desktop Protocol (RDP), and Virtual Network Computing (VNC). RDP is a proprietary protocol developed by Microsoft. It provides the remote user with a graphical interface to the remote computer. VNC is like RDP in that it allows graphic access to a remote computer. VNC makes use of the Remote Frame Buffer (RFB) protocol to control another computer remotely.

Remote technologies are a concept emphasized on the exam because so much of today's access is remote and many times it is over an open network such as the Internet.

Transport Layer Encryption

The transport layer of the TCP/IP stack can also be used to add cryptographic solutions to data communications. Some common examples follow:

Secure Sockets Layer   Netscape developed *Secure Sockets Layer (SSL)* for transmitting private documents over the Internet. SSL is application independent and cryptographically independent since the protocol itself is merely a framework for communicating certificates, encrypted keys, and data.

Transport Layer Security   The improved Transport Layer Security (TLS) is the successor protocol to SSL. It works in much the same way as the SSL, using encryption to protect the transfer of data and information. The two terms are often used interchangeably in the industry although SSL is still used.

Transport Layer Security (TLS) encrypts the communication between a host and a client. TLS consists of two layers: the Record Protocol and the TLS Handshake Protocol. Although TLS and SSL are functionally different, they provide the same services, and the terms are sometimes used interchangeably.

Wireless Transport Layer Security   *Wireless Transport Layer Security (WTLS)* encrypts the communication between a wireless host and a client. WTLS is a security protocol, and it is part of the Wireless Application Protocol (WAP) stack. WTLS was developed to address the problems, specifically the relatively low bandwidth and processing power, of mobile network devices. These issues will become increasingly important in the next few years as mobile banking is being widely used on smartphones.

    Transport layer encryption is not the same as transport encryption. The latter is associated with IPsec.

Internet Layer Controls

The *Internet layer* is home to IPsec, a well-known cryptographic solution. IPsec was developed to address the shortcomings of IPv4. It is an add-on for IPv4. IPsec can be used to encrypt just the data or the data and the header. With the depletion of IPv4 addresses, look for more attention to be paid to IPsec as it is built into IPv6. IPsec includes the following components:

Encapsulated Secure Payload (ESP)   *Encapsulated Secure Payload (ESP)* provides confidentiality by encrypting the data packet. The encrypted data is hidden, so its confidentiality is ensured.

Authentication Header (AH)   The *Authentication Header (AH)* provides integrity and authentication. The AH uses a hashing algorithm and symmetric key to calculate a message authentication code. This message authentication code is known as the *integrity check value (ICV)*. When the AH is received, an ICV is calculated and checked against the received value to verify integrity.

Security Association (SA)   For AH and ESP to work, some information must be exchanged to set up the secure session. This job is the responsibility of the *Security Association (SA)*. The SA is a one-way connection between the two parties. If both AH and ESP are used, a total of four connections are required. SAs use a symmetric key to encrypt communication. The Diffie–Hellman algorithm is used to generate this shared key.

Transport and Tunnel Mode   AH and ESP can work in one of two modes: transport mode or tunnel mode. *Transport mode* encrypts the data that is sent between peers. *Tunnel mode* encapsulates the entire packet and adds a new IP header. Tunnel mode is widely used with VPNs. The AH and the ESP can be used together or independently of each other.

Hardware Security Module (HSM)   Actually a physical control rather than an Internet layer control, but many organizations use *Hardware Security Modules (HSMs)* to store and retrieve escrowed keys securely. *Key escrow* or *key management* allows another trusted party to hold a copy of a key. They need to be managed at the same security level as the original key. HSM systems can be used to protect enterprise storage and data, and they can detect and prevent tampering by destroying the key material if unauthorized access is detected.

Additional Authentication Protocols

While the following protocols are not on this CASP+ exam revision, they are all worth mentioning as many of us will, or have, come across them in our careers.

Password Authentication Protocol (PAP)   We have included *Password Authentication Protocol (PAP)* here, but it should not be used. It is weak at best. PAP is not secure because the username and password are transmitted in clear text.

Challenge Handshake Authentication Protocol (CHAP)   *Challenge Handshake Authentication Protocol (CHAP)* is a more suitable option than PAP because it sends the client a random value that is used only once. Both the client and the server know the predefined secret password. The client uses the random value, nonce, and the secret password, and it calculates a one-way hash. The handshake process for CHAP is as follows:

1. The user sends a logon request from the client to the server.
2. The server sends a challenge back to the client.
3. The challenge is encrypted and then sent back to the server.
4. The server compares the value from the client and, if the information matches, grants authorization.

Extensible Authentication Protocol (EAP)   The *Extensible Authentication Protocol (EAP)* is an authentication framework that is commonly used for wireless networks. Many different implementations exist that use the EAP framework, including vendor-specific and open methods like EAP-TLS, LEAP, and EAP-TTLS. Each of these protocols implements EAP messages using that protocol's messaging standards. EAP is commonly used for wireless network authentication.

Authentication is a critical component and is used as a first line of defense to keep hackers off your network. Systems such as federated ID, AD, and single sign-on can be used to manage this process more securely.

Point-to-Point Tunneling Protocol (PPTP)   *Point-to-Point Tunneling Protocol (PPTP)* consists of two components: the transport that maintains the virtual connection and the encryption that ensures confidentiality. It can operate at a 40-bit or a 128-bit length.

Layer 2 Tunneling Protocol (L2TP)   *Layer 2 Tunneling Protocol (L2TP)* was created by Cisco and Microsoft to replace Layer 2 Forwarding (L2F) and PPTP. L2TP merged the capabilities of both L2F and PPTP into one tunneling protocol.

The Internet Assigned Number Authority (IANA) maintains a list of security protocols and their relationship to TCP/IP here:

`www.iana.org/assignments/service-names-port-numbers/`
`service-names-port-numbers.xhtml`

Cryptocurrency

Cryptocurrency is the medium of exchange similar to the U.S. dollar (USD) but designed for the purpose of exchanging digital information through a process made possible by certain principles of cryptography. Cryptocurrency uses cryptography to secure the digital transactions along with the ability to control the creation of new cryptocurrency coins. Cryptocurrency was first introduced as *Bitcoin* in 2009. Currently, there are hundreds of other known alternative cryptocurrencies, which are referred to as digital *altcoins*.

Cryptocurrency security is broken into two parts. The first part comes from the difficulty in finding the hash set intersection. This task is conducted by miners. The second and most common of the two cases is known as the 51 percent attack. Within this scenario, a miner has the power to mine more than 51 percent of the network. The miner can take control of the global blockchain ledger along with generating an alternative blockchain. At this point, the attacker is limited by the capabilities of their resources. The attack can also reverse the attacker's own transaction or even block other transactions.

The advantage of cryptocurrencies is that they are less susceptible to seizure by law enforcement or even the transaction holds placed on them from acquirers such as PayPal. Cryptocurrencies are all pseudo-anonymous, and some coins have added features to assist in creating true anonymity.

Digital Signatures

Digital signatures are a category of algorithms based on public key cryptography. They are used for verifying the authenticity and integrity of a message. To create a digital signature, the message is passed through a hashing algorithm. The resulting hashed value is then encrypted with the sender's private key. Upon receiving the message, the recipient decrypts the encrypted sum and then recalculates the expected message hash using the sender's public key. The values must match to prove the validity of the message and verify that it was sent by the party believed to have sent it. Digital signatures work because only that party has access to the private key. Let's break this process out step-by-step to help detail the operation:

1. Bob produces a message digest by passing a message through a hashing algorithm.

2. The message digest is then encrypted using Bob's private key.

3. The message is forwarded to the recipient, Alice.

4. Alice creates a message digest from the message with the same hashing algorithm that Bob used. Alice then decrypts Bob's signature digest by using Bob's public key.

5. Finally, Alice compares the two message digests: the one originally created by Bob and the other one that she created. If the two values match, Alice can rest assured that the message is unaltered.

Figure 6.7 illustrates the creation process. It shows how the hashing function ensures integrity and how the signing of the hash value provides authentication and nonrepudiation.

FIGURE 6.7   Digital signature creation

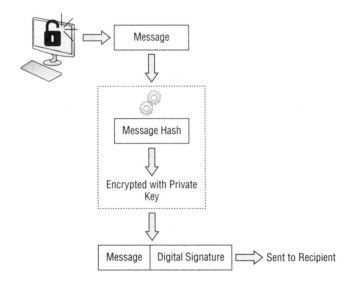

Message

Message Hash

Encrypted with Private Key

| Message | Digital Signature | ⟹ Sent to Recipient |

The digital signature is hashed with the sender's private key. This helps prove that only the sender could have completed the signing process.

To help ensure your success on the CASP+ exam, integrity verification methods are reviewed in Table 6.2.

TABLE 6.2   Integrity verification methods

Method	Description
Parity	Simple error detection code
Hashing	Integrity
Digital signature	Integrity, authentication, and nonrepudiation
Hashed MAC	Integrity and data origin authentication
CBC MAC	Integrity and data origin authentication
Checksum	Redundancy check, weak integrity

Digital signatures are typically used within the Digital Signature Standard. The Digital Signature Standard makes use of the Digital Signature Algorithm, and it also makes use of SHA-2 and public key encryption.

Recognizing Cryptographic Attacks

As long as there have been secrets, there have been people trying to uncover them. Attacks on cryptographic systems are nothing new. The formal name for this activity is *cryptanalysis*, which is the study of analyzing cryptography and attempting to determine the key value of a cryptographic system. Depending on which key is targeted by the attacker, it's possible that success may mean that someone could gain access to confidential information or pretend to be an authenticated party to a communication.

There are many ways an attacker can target a system for attack, such as a brute-force attack. A brute-force attack tries all possible solutions. One technique to make the attacker work longer and harder to perform a brute-force attack is *key stretching*. Key stretching refers to cryptographic techniques used to make a possibly weak cryptographic system, such as password generation, more secure. This technique hashes a password along with a random value known as a *salt*. This process can be repeated many times to produce a derived key. Typically, this might be a thousand or more iterations. This approach makes brute-force attacks time-consuming for an attacker. However, remember the previous discussion about the trade-off between strength, performance, and usability? Although it is more secure, the increased number of iterations will require more CPU power and time.

Password-based key derivation 2 (PBKDF2) is defined in RFC 2898. PBKDF2 is a specific key derivation function (KDF). A KDF is way to take a password and turn it into a symmetric key for cryptographic operations such as AES. AES can use any value as its input that meets certain length and entropy requirements. PBKDF2 can produce a hash of any length that meets those requirements for entropy.

PBKDF2 takes a password, a salt, an integer defining how many rounds of the hash function to undergo, and another integer describing the desired key length for the output. By increasing the number of rounds, you make the resulting output more computationally expensive. A use case of PBKDF2 is a means of hashing a password to avoid storing a plaintext password in a database.

The *Bcrypt* algorithm is based on the Blowfish cipher. Bcrypt helps in preventing the brute-force search attacks by increasing the number of rounds. The computation cost of the algorithm depends on parameterized rounds, so it can be increased as computers evolve. Just like PBKDF2, this method uses a salt to protect against rainbow table attacks.

Key stretching refers to cryptographic techniques used to make a brute-force attack slower and harder for the attacker to recover information such as passwords.

Many countries seek to control cryptographic algorithms and place controls on their use. These controls fall under the Wassenaar Arrangement on Export Controls for Conventional Arms and Dual-Use Goods and Technologies (see www.wassenaar.org). The goal of the agreement is to promote transparency in transfers of conventional arms and dual-use goods and technologies while also promoting greater responsibility in such transfers. The idea is to keep strong cryptography out of the hands of criminals and terrorists.

How Strong Is Your Password?

As a security administrator, you've no doubt heard many stories about how some people do very little to protect their passwords. Sometimes, people write their passwords down on sticky notes, place them under their keyboards, or even leave them on a scrap of paper taped to the monitor. As a security professional, you should not only help formulate good password policy but also help users understand why and how to protect passwords. One solution might be to offer password manager programs that can be used to secure passwords. Another approach is migration to biometric or token-based authentication systems.

For this scenario, you'll need to put yourself in the position of an attacker wanting to examine the strength of your password. From this perspective, you will test passwords with the following attributes:

- Create a password that is seven lowercase characters.

- Create a password that is seven uppercase and lowercase characters.

- Create a password that is 14 uppercase and lowercase characters and that includes at least one special character.

Submit each of the examples on the www.passwordmeter.com site, and test the strength. What are your conclusions?

Troubleshooting Cryptographic Implementations

There will be problems to troubleshoot. Guaranteed you've browsed to a website only to get the warning "Your connection is not private," offering you a Back to Safety button.

Sometimes the evidence points to one of the configuration problems, but in reality, the issue is much simpler. Keep in mind the troubleshooting acronym KISS, which stands for "keep it simple, stupid." For example, an incorrect certificate name error may just be caused by a browser cache or a bad browser plug-in. Try simple troubleshooting first, such as clearing the cache or testing in incognito mode, before immediately reconfiguring the corporate certificate authority.

Figure 6.8 is the warning screen expected when there is a certificate error.

FIGURE 6.8   "Your connection is not private" error

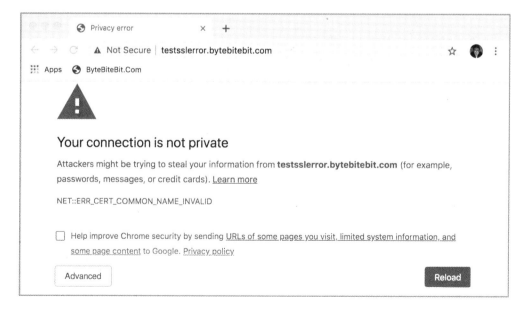

Let's start by recognizing some of the more common certificate issues.

Validity Dates   This is an easy one. Did the certificate expire? Was it post-dated like the rent check? Check the dates. If the valid dates of the certificate are outside the server's date and time, then the certificate is considered invalid. Of course, the real issue could be the server's date and time is wrongly set.

These are some basic ways to troubleshoot invalid SSL/TLS errors:

- Check the date on your computer. First you should check if the date and time on your computer is correct.
- Check for configuration errors.
- Check for domain mismatch.
- Get your certificate from a reliable CA.
- Check the certificate structure.
- Check for revocation.

Wrong Certificate Type   It goes beyond the CASP+ exam to differentiate between these validation levels of SSL certificates: domain validated (DV), organization validated (OV), and extended validation (EV).

However, if, for example, a single domain certificate were issued when a multido-main certificate was required, then this would fall under the blanket error category of "wrong type."

Revoked Certificates   Illegally purchased or wrongly issued certificates can and will be revoked eventually. The same can happen if the private key is compromised. A CRL is a list of CA certificates that have been revoked before expiration, and these certificates should never be trusted.

Incorrect Name   "NET::ERR_CERT_COMMON_NAME_INVALID" is the error that does actually happen too often when the certificate is for a different domain. If the name on the SSL certificate isn't the same as in the browser address bar, prepare for the browser to point that out to every visitor.

Even something as innocuous as leaving off the "www." when the certificate includes it can cause a *name mismatch* error.

Chain Issues   If the subordinate CA cannot reach the root CA, then the chain is broken. This issue may be fairly easy to spot, given the warnings, but may require online resources to troubleshoot. Free online services are the fastest way to test and validate the chain of trust.

Invalid Root or Intermediate CAs   If a certificate is installed without a valid chain of trust, the result is that the untrusted certificate's validity cannot be verified.

Self-Signed   If a certificate is installed without a valid chain of trust, the result is that the untrusted certificate's validity cannot be verified. In the case of a self-signed certificate, the chain of trust stops at the server.

Other issues will be more centered around the keys:

Embedded Keys   Some devices have the certificate embedded in the device. Maybe its processing power is limited, and maybe it's forced to rely on an outdated algorithm. These are issues to consider for embedded keys.

Rekeying   In PKI, rekeying is simply issuing a new certificate, but with all the old information as with the replaced certificate. This is not a renewal, which essentially extends the validity period of an old certificate (and the private key).

Exposed Private Keys and Improper Key Handling   Once the secret key is out, all confidentiality and integrity are compromised. It's safe to say that proper key handling is a critical element to maintaining a PKI implementation.

Crypto Shredding   *Crypto shredding* is intentionally deleting an encryption key. The consequence is effectively permanently encrypting the data. In practice, this can be useful when a client wants their data "erased" or inaccessible forever. This brings up the challenge of maintaining unique keys to enable every possible such request.

But the risk is, deleting the encryption key doesn't mean the encrypted data is not available. Encrypted data doesn't stay unencrypted when attacked with enough brute force.

Cryptographic Obfuscation   Unlike encryption that renders something entirely unreadable, *obfuscation* is the method of masking the data's value by mixing it or modifying it with nonsensical data. This scrambles the input into something too challenging to understand or recover. This is *not* the same as the poor practice of "security by obscurity." Obfuscation works best when the data is already fairly complex or not easily recovered. For instance, source code is unrecoverable with minimal obfuscation.

Key Rotation   Knowing when to rotate keys and certificates is based on their validity period. Interestingly enough, the maximum validity period has been contested and changed in recent years. In 2022, the maximum period is 825 days, but there is growing momentum to reduce it to 398 days.

In any case, key rotation must happen within those periods to maintain valid certificates and keys. And rotation can and should happen sooner if any compromise is detected.

Compromised Keys   The real danger of compromised keys is a malicious actor can now impersonate the intended source of the compromised certificate. The consequences of a malicious actor acting as the legitimate source can range from certified malware, decrypted communication, setting up on-path (formerly known as man-in-the-middle) attacks, forged traffic, and sniffing encrypted traffic. It's a bad thing.

Summary

This chapter focused on cryptography, a relatively deep component of the CASP+ content. While cryptography is on the CASP+ exam, it is also one of the most powerful tools of a security professional. It offers you the ability to protect sensitive information through the use of encryption. It can also offer you the ability to verify the integrity of patches, files, and important data. In addition, cryptography makes e-commerce possible. With cryptographic solutions such as PKI, you can trust that a third party is who they claim to be. These are but a few of the solutions cryptography offers.

As a security professional, you need to able to communicate with others about cryptographic solutions and services. You don't have to be able to write your own cryptographic algorithms. You do need to be able to offer solutions to real problems. There is not a week that goes by without a news report that lists stolen or lost media that contained personal information. As a security professional, you may be in a position to suggest that your company use full disk encryption (FDE) for all laptops. You may also have the opportunity to promote PGP as a standard to encrypt all email being used to discuss sensitive business matters. You may even be on a team preparing to roll out a new e-commerce site and be asked to offer your opinion on PKI. These are the types of solutions that security professionals offer every day.

Exam Essentials

Be able to describe which cryptographic solution is appropriate for a given situation.   Cryptographic solutions can be broadly divided into symmetric encryption, asymmetric encryption, hybrid encryption, and hashing. Each offers specific solutions such as privacy, authentication, integrity, and nonrepudiation.

Be able to describe the basic operation of PKI and understand advanced PKI concepts.   PKI allows two parties that are previously unknown to each other to communicate over an insecure public network. Such communications can then be used to exchange data securely and privately or for e-commerce. PKI systems make use of public and private keys. Keys are shared through a trusted certificate authority.

Know what terms such as *wildcard* mean when applied to PKI.

A wildcard certificate allows the purchaser to secure an unlimited number of subdomain certificates on a domain name. The advantage is that you buy and maintain only one certificate. The drawback, however, is that you are using just one certificate and private key on multiple websites and private servers.

Be able to describe transport encryption.   Transport encryption is one of the two modes in which IPsec can operate. When IPsec transport encryption is used, only the data portion or payload of each IP packet is encrypted. This leaves the IP header untouched and sent in the clear.

Be able to describe a digital signature.   A digital signature is a hash value that has been encrypted with the private key of the sender. It is used for authentication and integrity.

Be able to describe hashing.   Hashing refers to a broad category of algorithms that are useful for their ability to provide integrity and authentication. Hashing algorithms operate by taking a variable amount of data and compressing it into a fixed-length value referred to as a hash value.

Be able to describe code signing.   Code signing is the process of digitally signing executables and scripts to confirm the software author. Code signing also guarantees that the code has not been altered or corrupted since it was signed by use of a hash.

Know how nonrepudiation works.   Nonrepudiation is the ability to verify proof of identity. It is used to ensure that a sender of data is provided with proof of delivery and that the recipient is assured of the sender's identity.

Be able to define certificate authority hierarchy.   Understand the relationship between the root, subordinate, and intermediate CAs. Understand the importance of the chain of trust.

Be able to explain perfect forward secrecy.   Perfect forward secrecy is based on the concept that the exposure of a single key will permit an attacker access only to data protected by a single key.

Recognize and understand PKI implementation issues.   There are several configuration problems that can arise from poorly implemented PKI. Recognize the errors you might encounter and how to decipher them. Remember that troubleshooting begins with verifying the simple issues first.

Review Questions

You can find the answers in Appendix.

1. You have been asked by a member of senior management to explain the importance of encryption and define what symmetric encryption offers. Which of the following offers the best explanation?

   A. Nonrepudiation

   B. Confidentiality

   C. Hashing

   D. Privacy and authentication

2. As the security administrator for your organization, you must be aware of all types of hashing algorithms. Which fast-block algorithm was developed by Ron Rivest and offers a 128-bit output?

   A. Salsa20

   B. 3DES

   C. CHACHA

   D. RC5

3. A co-worker is concerned about the veracity of a claim because the sender of an email denies sending it. The co-worker wants a way to prove the authenticity of an email. Which would you recommend?

   A. Hashing

   B. Digital signature

   C. Symmetric encryption

   D. Asymmetric encryption

4. A junior administrator at a sister company called to report a possible exposed private key that is used for PKI transactions. The administrator would like to know the easiest way to check whether the lost key has been flagged by the system. What are you going to recommend to the administrator?

   A. Hashing

   B. Issuance to entities

   C. Adding to RA

   D. Wildcard verification

5. You've discovered that an expired certificate is being used repeatedly to gain logon privileges. To what list should the certificate have been added?

   A. Wildcard verification

   B. Expired key revocation list

   C. Online Certificate Status Department

   D. Certificate revocation list (CRL)

6. A junior administrator comes to you in a panic after seeing the cost for certificates. She would like to know if there is a way to get one certificate to cover all domains and subdomains for the organization. What solution can you offer?

   A. Wildcards

   B. Blanket certificates

   C. Distributed certificates

   D. No such solution exists

7. Which of the following is not an advantage of symmetric encryption?

   A. It's powerful.

   B. A small key works well for bulk encryption.

   C. It offers confidentiality.

   D. Key exchange is easy.

8. Most authentication systems make use of a one-way encryption process. Which of the following offers the best example of one-way encryption?

   A. Asymmetric encryption

   B. Symmetric encryption

   C. Hashing

   D. PKI

9. Which of the following algorithms would serve to prove the integrity of a file?

   A. RSA

   B. Diffie–Hellman

   C. SHA-256

   D. ECC

10. Which type of encryption offers the easiest key exchange and key management?

   A. Symmetric

   B. Asymmetric

   C. Hashing

   D. Digital signatures

11. SSL and TLS can best be categorized as which of the following?

   A. Symmetric encryption systems

   B. Asymmetric encryption systems

   C. Hashing systems

   D. Hybrid encryption systems

12. Which is the type of certificate to use for securing these example domains: `snakes.pets .com`, `budgies.pets.com`, and `chinchillas.pets.com`?

    A. Wildcard

    B. Multidomain

    C. Validation

    D. CRL

13. Which of the following is not a hashing algorithm?

    A. SHA-512

    B. ECDH

    C. Skipjack

    D. IDEA

14. A mobile user calls you from the road and informs you that he has been asked to travel to China on business. He wants suggestions for securing his hard drive. What do you recommend he use?

    A. S/MIME

    B. BitLocker

    C. Secure SMTP

    D. PKI

15. You were given a disk full of applications by a friend but are unsure about installing a couple of the applications on your company laptop. Is there an easy way to verify if the programs are original or if they have been tampered with?

    A. Verify with a hashing algorithm.

    B. Submit to a certificate authority.

    C. Scan with symmetric encryption.

    D. Check the programs against the CRL.

16. What is the correct term for when two different files are hashed and produce the same hashed output?

    A. Session key

    B. Digital signature

    C. Message digest

    D. Collision

17. You have been asked to suggest a simple trust system for distribution of encryption keys. Your client is a three-person company and wants a low-cost or free solution. Which of the following would you suggest?

    A. Single authority trust

    B. Hierarchical trust

    C. Spoke/hub trust

    D. Web of trust

18. Which of the following would properly describe a system that uses a symmetric key distributed by an asymmetric process?

    A. Digital signature

    B. Hybrid encryption

    C. HMAC

    D. Message digest

19. A CASP+ must understand the importance of encryption and cryptography. It is one of the key concepts used for the protection of data in transit, while being processed, or while at rest. With that in mind, 3DES ECB is an example of which of the following?

    A. Disk encryption

    B. Block encryption

    C. Port encryption

    D. Record encryption

20. Which of the following can be used to describe a physical security component that is used for cryptoprocessing and can be used to store digital keys securely?

    A. HSM

    B. TPM

    C. HMAC

    D. OCSP

Chapter

7

Incident Response and Forensics

THE CASP+ EXAM TOPICS COVERED IN THIS CHAPTER INCLUDE:

✓ **2.7 Given an incident, implement the appropriate response.**

- ▪ **Event classifications**
    - ▪ False positive
    - ▪ False negative
    - ▪ True positive
    - ▪ True negative
- ▪ **Triage event**
- ▪ **Pre-escalation tasks**
- ▪ **Incident response process**
    - ▪ Preparation
    - ▪ Detection
    - ▪ Analysis
    - ▪ Containment
    - ▪ Recovery
    - ▪ Lessons learned
- ▪ **Specific response playbooks/processes**
    - ▪ Scenarios
        - ▪ Ransomware
        - ▪ Data exfiltration
        - ▪ Social engineering
    - ▪ Non-automated response methods
    - ▪ Automated response methods
        - ▪ Runbooks
        - ▪ SOAR

- Communication plan

- Stakeholder management

✓ **2.8 Explain the importance of forensic concepts.**

- Legal vs. internal corporate purposes

- Forensic process

  - Identification

  - Evidence collection

    - Chain of custody

    - Order of volatility

      - Memory snapshots

      - Images

    - Cloning

  - Evidence preservation

    - Secure storage

    - Backups

  - Analysis

    - Forensics tools

  - Verification

  - Presentation

- Integrity preservation

  - Hashing

- Cryptanalysis

- Steganalysis

✓ **2.9 Given a scenario, use forensic analysis tools.**

- File carving tools

  - Foremost

  - Strings

- Binary analysis tools

  - Hex dump

  - Binwalk

- Ghidra
- GNU Project debugger (GDB)
- OllyDbg
- readelf
- objdump
- strace
- ldd
- file

Analysis tools

- ExifTool
- Nmap
- Aircrack-ng
- Volatility
- The Sleuth Kit
- Dynamically vs. statically linked

Imaging tools

- Forensic Toolkit (FTK) Imager
- dd

Hashing utilities

- sha256sum
- ssdeep

Live collection vs. post-mortem tools

- netstat
- ps
- vmstat
- ldd
- lsof
- netcat
- tcpdump
- conntrack
- Wireshark

In 2021, FireEye/Mandiant CEO Kevin Mandia testified before the United States Senate Intelligence Committee as the country was in the middle of responding to the SolarWinds supply chain attack. He said, "Speed is critical to the effective disruption or mitigation of an attack by an advanced threat actor." Many risk management solutions help with low-level security events, but having an experienced incident response and forensics team with expertise to quickly respond to an attack will increase success when dealing with a breach. This chapter discusses what a CASP+ should know about incident response and forensics.

The Incident Response Framework

The security maturity level of an organization directly influences the type of incident response they will have. A startup might have an untested incident response plan. It takes a high level of maturity to have a seasoned 24-hour security operations center (SOC) staffed with incident responders threat hunting for attackers in their network. Unless it's ransomware openly locking down assets, many organizations are told by third parties that they are compromised, and that is not a fast enough response in today's cyber realm. Things can and will go wrong quickly, and companies have to be prepared and looking. Unfortunately, not all networks or assets are 100 percent secure. Attackers' dwell time in a network is always changing, putting stress on analysts to detect and respond in real time. A CASP+ must be able to conduct incident response quickly and efficiently and implement documented recovery procedures as soon as an event becomes an incident.

Event Classifications

Incident response is both an art and a science. With education and experience, the art of incident response comes with understanding and intuition. The science of incident response comes with testing data. A huge mistake that incident responders can make is making assumptions and concluding that something is true when it is actually false, as well as concluding that something is false when it is really true. A *false positive* is when personnel determine something is true when it isn't. It is often called a false alarm. A *false negative* is saying something is false when it's accurate. In Figure 7.1, you see the relationship between reality and hypothetical decisions.

FIGURE 7.1   Relationship in hypothetical decision-making

Decision	Hypothesis True	Hypothesis False
Hypothesis Accepted	True Positive (Correct Outcome)	False Positive
Hypothesis Rejected	False Negative	True Negative (Correct Outcome)

In a criminal court, it is ideal to have a *true positive* or *true negative* decision, meaning the innocent are found innocent and the guilty are found guilty. It is not ideal but preferable to have a false negative, where a criminal is found innocent, rather than a false positive convicting someone who is innocent. However, entering the courthouse, it is preferable that a metal detector indicate metal is found (false positive) than fail to find a gun when it is actually present (false negative). In this situation, a false negative is a huge security risk.

Triage Events

In incident response, an event is something that is observed. It is unknown if it is malicious or not. Events happen hourly in most large organizations; however, many never progress into an actual incident. Events are changes that are captured in the environment. With tools configured properly, alerts can be generated to let the SOC team know that something happened. For example, an alert can be generated by a security information and event management (SIEM) tool providing real-time notification that an administrator changed their password. Administrators have a lot of control in an enterprise environment, so this is noteworthy, but not necessarily nefarious.

To be able to understand if this event is something to investigate further, it must be triaged. Triage happens when you enter an emergency room in a hospital. An emergency room nurse takes readings of temperature, blood pressure, oxygen levels, and other vital statistics. Those in life-or-death situations are rushed to immediate medical care. In cybersecurity, a *triage event* is the process of determining whether the event is an incident or a false positive. Having an efficient and thorough examination of events will reduce the time to respond and escalate valid events and alerts to the proper personnel for the next level of investigation. If the event is found to meet the criteria of an incident, it is sent to the next tier of incident handling.

An incident is an event with a confirmed negative consequence that could be, but is not limited to, a system breach. This breach could lead to outages, service degradation, data destruction, or data loss. For example, the SIEM tool alerted you that an administrator changed their password. You triage the event and find the machine that the administrator is signed into started sending large amounts of data to an unknown destination outside of the network. This type of situation definitely requires more investigation. It is not an incident until you know if the destination outside the network is a new cloud instance or a nefarious IP address. Once you know the IP address is malicious, the incident response playbook is put into action.

A crisis is an incident that escalates out of control. A crisis requires immediate attention because of the significant impact to the business, and it carries the threat of public disclosure.

An example of a crisis would be if the SIEM has alerted you that an administrator changed their password, the machine the administrator is logged into is a highly classified server holding many pieces of intellectual property, and HR has informed you that administrator is on leave from the organization. The exfiltration of large amounts of data is a confirmed malicious IP address, and your board of directors has been notified by the attacker group that the data is now being held for ransom. Your organization must pay millions in cryptocurrency in the next eight hours, or your mission-critical intellectual proprietary information will be published to the Internet. This type of situation is worthy of the label of a crisis, and unfortunately, this happens all the time.

Pre-Escalation Tasks

Different types of security incidents require different responses. Before any event can be acted on, there are *pre-escalation tasks* that should have taken place. Organizations must understand what types of attacks are likely to be used against their enterprise. For example, NIST lists many attack vectors to prepare for, such as compromised removable media like USB drives, spear phishing, web attacks, or theft/loss of equipment. The response to each of these is likely to be very different, and preparation for each will have a different response or playbook. For example, a user leaves their corporate cell phone in the back of a Lyft car. The user should know what department should be informed and within what time frame. The playbook that gets used will have a checklist of exactly what protective measures are in place for that device, such as an encrypted storage hard drive, what type of encryption is being used, and remote wipe capabilities. After the loss is verified, then instructions in that playbook detail how to perform the remote wipe on the device that is lost.

 Runbooks are often confused with playbooks, and some IT professionals use the terms interchangeably. While *runbooks* define individual processes, *playbooks* deal with overarching responses to larger issues or events and may incorporate multiple runbooks and personnel within them—think of a runbook as a chapter within a playbook. Runbooks are further discussed later in the "Response Playbooks and Processes" section.

The Incident Response Process

One of the most important aspects of a computer security incident response process is that the incident response plan has been prepared and tested before an incident ever occurs and the plan is imaginative enough to handle all types of situations. The plan should dictate how the organization handles various types of incidents, ideally containing them before they become crises. Most companies refer to the individuals that take part in these activities as members of the computer security incident response team (CSIRT).

The CASP+ exam will expect you to understand computer incident response and the importance of planning for adverse events before they occur. The Software Engineering Institute at Carnegie Mellon has a FAQ on CSIRT at resources.sei.cmu.edu/asset_files/ WhitePaper/2017_019_001_485654.pdf.

You have to design systems that facilitate incident response. The concept traces its roots back to the Morris worm. Because this worm knocked out more than 10 percent of the systems connected to the early Internet, the Defense Advanced Research Projects Agency (DARPA) approved the creation of a computer security incident response team (CSIRT). Having a CSIRT in place, along with the policies they need to function, can provide an organization with an effective and efficient means of dealing with a *data breach* or other unseen situation in a manner that can reduce the potential impact. Here are some common internal and external violations an incident response plan should address:

- Denial of service
- Ransomware
- Data exfiltration
- Social engineering
- Hardware theft
- Malicious software
- Data breach
- Terrorist attacks
- Unauthorized access
- Unauthorized software
- Physical intrusion
- Proper forensic response and investigation practices
- Website attacks
- Virus and worm attacks

The incident response plan needs to be able to determine which of these incidents occurred, and it must be designed to facilitate a response that considers the type of violation.

Adding threat intelligence to risk analysis will help to put these violations in the right order for your business vertical (specific industry or market niche). Many threat actors have a specific way of operating as well as identifiable verticals of attack. For example, the Iranian Advanced Persistent Threat Group 35 (APT35) targets the United States and Western Europe, specifically government personnel, energy, and telecommunications sectors. They use sophisticated social engineering techniques and spear phishing, harvest administrative credentials, and release malware like DRUBOT and BROKEYOLK. If your organization is aware of this Iranian threat group and you are in their crosshairs, your playbook might call for a sweep of the network looking for this malware and/or hashes of that malware to rule out this threat actor.

The incident response plan acts as a kind of playbook in that it details specific actions to be carried out. By having an incident response plan ready, the company can maintain or restore business continuity, defend against future attacks, or even sue attackers in civil court or file a criminal complaint against attackers. The goals of incident response are many, but the steps for reducing the damage from security incidents are well known and follow any one of a number of formats. Regardless of what method is used, these steps for the incident response process must be addressed:

Step 1: Preparation   The company must establish policies and procedures to address the potential of security incidents.

Step 2: Detection   This step is about the identification of events and incidents. Automated systems should be used to determine if an event occurred. The tools used for identification include intrusion detection systems (IDSs), intrusion protection systems (IPSs), firewalls, audits, logging, and observation. Today, many companies make use of a security information and event manager (SIEM) to find and identify anomalies. An SIEM is a computerized tool used for centralized storage and interpretation of logs and audit events.

Step 3: Analysis   This step is evaluating the nature of the incident, its specifics, and the potential threat it poses to the organization. There must be a means to verify that the event was real and not a false positive. Often, some of the same tools that are used for detection can also help with analysis.

Step 4: Containment   This step requires planning, training, and the plan execution. The incident response plan should dictate what action is required to be taken. The incident response team will need to have had the required level of training to handle the response properly. This team should also know how to contain the incident, mitigate the damage, and determine how to proceed. In addition to containing the incident (keeping the problem from getting any worse), the team must remove the problem so that the company can return to normal business processes.

Step 5: Recovery   This step involves restoring all affected systems to full functionality in as quick a timetable as safely possible. This can entail restoring data and files from backups, reestablishing the proper settings for systems, and more. This should also be done according to the incident response plan.

Step 6: Investigation and Closure   The team attempts to determine what happened, who did it, and how they did it. Once the investigation is complete, a report, either formal or informal, must be prepared. This report will be necessary to evaluate any needed changes to the incident response policies.

Step 7: Lessons Learned   At this final step, all of those involved review what happened and why. Most important, they determine what changes must be put in place to prevent future problems. Learning from what happened is the only way to prevent it from happening again. If you have worked in government, you are probably very familiar with the acronym for after-action report (AAR). These reports should contain what was successful as well as what can be improved upon in the future.

Response Playbooks and Processes

Different scenarios are going to require different processes and playbooks, but the fundamental template is the same. The way you prepare for and react to ransomware is going to be different from how you train and strategize for social engineering. Playbooks can be purchased from a number of vendors and should be shared across departments with a critical role in incident response, such as legal or human resources.

Playbooks have common components such as the initiating or triggering condition, the major steps according to policy and procedures, best practices, and the end goal or desired outcome. To build a playbook from the beginning, the first thing you must do is identify what the initiating event is and all possible actions that could happen in response to that condition. Afterward, you have to categorize all of those possible actions into what is required and build the playbook process order using the required steps. A good playbook will have the ideal end state as well as the regulatory laws the playbook takes care of. Figure 7.2 shows a template of a phishing playbook workflow.

FIGURE 7.2   Incident response playbook template

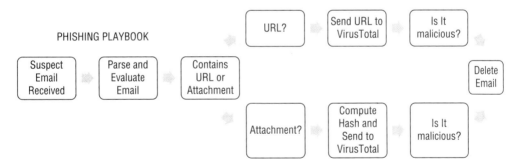

A good resource for anyone building a playbook would be the MITRE ATT&CK framework. This framework is a matrix of highly detailed, cross-referenced methods used by red teamers, threat hunters, and blue team defenders to classify the tactics, techniques, and procedures they use. Tactics describes the immediate technical objectives of the attacker; the technique is the method attackers use to achieve a tactic, and the procedures can be the tools or specific malware that the attacker has used. A good place to start with this framework is here: `attack.mitre.org`.

There are many playbooks online available for download. For ransomware, Rapid7 has an excellent whitepaper identifying the actions you take before ransomware hits to lower the risk, how ransomware attacks happen, and how to mitigate and lower the impact. You can find recommendations here: `www.rapid7.com/globalassets/_pdfs/whitepaper-guide/rapid7-insightidr-ransomware-playbook.pdf`. For other types of playbooks, an excellent resource can be found for many different types of malware, data breach, and virus outbreak scenarios here: `www.incidentresponse.com/playbooks`.

With incident response, a non-automated response method could be a human intervention. When speed is of the essence, an automated response method is an important element to have in place. A popular way to implement this is with a digital runbook. A *runbook* is a compilation of detailed routine procedures that a system administrator uses as a reference. When you are able to automate runbooks, you have less waiting and quicker turnaround times. Runbook automation enables you to translate operations and security knowledge into procedures that get run immediately should a situation meet certain criteria.

Even more advanced than an automated runbook is security orchestration, automation, and response (SOAR) tooling. Many security operations teams are too busy and struggle with noise (the volume of network traffic that makes it difficult to distinguish between legitimate data and security risks). Some teams lack the highly skilled talent needed to research advanced breaches. SOAR tools, if configured and customized properly, increase efficiency and consistency. SOAR allows companies to collect threat-related data from different sources and automate the responses to those threats. Some SOAR tools integrate disparate tools and can take control of the incident with prebuilt courses of action.

Communication Plan and Stakeholder Management

Even with a process in place, you need a team of relevant stakeholders to carry out the plan. The individuals on the team should have diverse skill sets. Members of the incident response team should come from the organization's various departments so they know their own areas and bring unique skills:

- Information security
- Legal counsel
- Network and system administrators
- Physical security
- Public and human relations

The team must include public relations and legal counsel when it becomes necessary to deal with potential media coverage and agree on the communication plan. When they are not given enough details, humans and media tend to speculate. When disclosing an incident to the public, only one designated person should be communicating information and only exactly what happened, how it affects customers, and what remediation steps are being taken. All questions from media or stockholders should be forwarded directly to that person.

Immediately after being notified of a security incident or breach, senior management will ask, "How bad is it?" Many factors go into answering that deceptively simple question, including the scope, impact, cost, downtime, and legal ramifications. *Scope* entails how far the incident goes, as in how many systems, subnets, or volumes of data have been affected. Naturally, the scope directly affects the impact. The *impact* is affected by the effort and time needed for recovery. These aren't questions to be answered easily or quickly. Only after full identification and containment can questions about recovery begin to be answered.

Then there's the issue of *cost*, both in monetary terms and in time required to address the problem. Monetary costs involve both team hours and hardware replacement. Time costs in terms of downtime are expensive as well.

Finally, what about the legal ramifications? The breach might have disclosed people's personal data, such as personal social media profiles. Perhaps worse, the breach could have regulatory consequences. Legal counsel must become involved in order to start the damage control.

Forensic specialists must know how to record evidence at the scene by taking photographs, documenting their activities in an investigator's notebook, interviewing suspects and witnesses, and knowing the proper procedures for collecting or seizing suspected systems or media. Doing the right thing is required to protect the chain of custody and legality of the evidence. Forensic procedures must document the complete journey of the evidence (from its beginning to the end) and be able to answer these questions:

- Who collected the evidence?
- How and where was it collected?
- Who took possession of the evidence?
- How was it stored, and was it secured while in storage?
- Who took it out of storage, and why was it removed?

This process, also known as *electronic discovery*, or *e-discovery*, deals with the review of electronic information for the purpose of recovery of evidence. The e-discovery process is all about how you find and extract documents and data stored in electronic format. The trend toward its use will only intensify in the future. Although most investigations may not go to court, computer forensic specialists must collect, review, and preserve structured data that may come from electronic records, contracts, and forms as well as a large amount of unstructured data like emails, chat sessions, and even electronic file fragments. During an investigation, formal records make up an essential part of the discovery process, but this is only half of the picture in today's electronic world. It is becoming increasingly common to ask for copies of selected email and other electronic communications for court cases and legal hearings. The data retention policy should specify how long information is stored. As an example, the IRS can ask for tax records as far back as seven years if you file a claim for a loss from securities or bad debt deductions. Therefore, most accountants advise businesses to keep tax records for seven years (`www.irs.gov/businesses/small-businesses-self-employed/how-long-should-i-keep-records`). Figure 7.3 lists common documents and how long that information should be retained.

FIGURE 7.3 Document retention

Employment Contracts — • Permanent

Tax Records — • 3 years, 7 years if claiming loss

Deeds — • 6 years

Medical Records — • 7 years

Trademarks — • Life of trademark +25 years

Copyright — • 120 years after author death

Patent deeds — • 25 years

By the nature of the term, you know incident response to be a reactive, responsive effort. But what about incident detection? We know that later today hackers could attack our systems. We know that next week we might discover a newly compromised system. Why wait to react when we can be proactive and discover potential incidents ourselves before the bad guys have a chance to do any damage?

Hunt teaming is the name given to the in-house activity of seeking out those vulnerabilities before we have to react to an incident that has occurred. This is accomplished in several different ways. You and your team might perform log analysis on entire systems or other individual devices. This is more easily done if a SIEM tool is already in place, which presents a centralized view of security and event information.

Analysis must be done on more than just the security logs. Many companies that use all of the same devices, logs, and monitoring are still breached regardless. Beyond the objective analysis of logs, you must perform heuristics and behavioral analysis. Oftentimes as security professionals, we find that we have a better gut feeling and can adopt a more practical approach than those serving in other roles.

There is significant overlap between incident detection and vulnerability management. Vulnerabilities exist, and it's up to us, as security professionals, to find them. Whether through hunt teaming, heuristic analysis, or waiting until our tools become aware of them, we will eventually discover the vulnerabilities. Vulnerabilities are found at the operating system, application, and firmware levels.

Operating system vulnerabilities are difficult to find, but there are security controls to help mitigate the risk of those vulnerabilities being exploited. Having a host-based firewall and/or intrusion detection system will defeat attacks originating in the network, while patch management helps curb exploits from local machines. Firmware vulnerabilities are more difficult to detect but are also very difficult to exploit, given that the attacker has no local access. These types of vulnerabilities are not applicable to a secured, enclosed device such as an encrypted enclave. Secured encrypted enclaves are separate hardware coprocessors that enhance a device's security.

The end goal of incident response is *minimization* of downtime. The problem needs to be fixed quickly so that normal operations can be resumed. It's critical that the process be carried out in such a way that the incident is documented in detail, and evidence is protected. No one plans on going to court, but it could occur. This means that *data handling* is of critical importance. From the point at which something occurs, the incident response team must determine if it's an event or an incident.

An *event* is a noticeable occurrence, whereas an *incident* means there has been a violation of policy or law. Many incident responders use an incident response plan (IRP) template supplied by NIST SP 800-53, which details exactly what information must be tracked. This template is often called the "spreadsheet of doom." An example and other useful documents can be found at www.cisa.gov/uscert/sites/default/files/c3vp/crr_resources_guides/CRR_Resource_Guide-IM.pdf.

Investigating computer crime is complex. There may be an insider threat or an outsider threat. Many times, incidents are just accidents and could be caused by nonmalicious threats or misconfigurations. Other incidents are deliberate and may be dealt with in a number of ways. This will typically be based on management's decision based on the following information:

- Criminal actions
- Civil lawsuits
- Job sanctions
- Termination
- Suspension

Missteps can render evidence useless and unusable in a court of law. This means that team members must be knowledgeable about the proper procedures and be trained on how to secure and isolate the scene to prevent contamination. This is the role of computer forensics, our next topic.

Incident response and *emergency response* are very similar; they both deal with unknown events that could cause harm or damage the organization. All organizations should plan for emergency events. The organization should appoint a team of information security professionals to help with the process. The team should also contain other technical and nontechnical members. For example, employees from both the HR and legal departments may also be on the team. One good place to start is the FEMA website. FEMA has a 10-page document that can be used to help businesses identify the goals and objectives for the emergency response plan. You can read more here: www.fema.gov/emergency-managers/national-preparedness/plan.

Forensic Concepts

The term *digital forensics* describes a structured, step-by-step process and analysis of data stored, processed, or retrieved on a computer system in a legal, approved way so that any evidence can be used in court as needed.

Although law enforcement has been practicing criminal forensics for many years, private companies are just starting to see the value of digital forensics. Digital forensics can be broken down into three broad categories:

Computer Forensics   The examination of physical media to obtain information for evidence

Software Analysis   The review of malware, viruses, and other dangerous software for analysis and potential identification of the author

Network Analysis   The analysis of network traffic and logs to identify the source and effect of the event

A corporation or organization might preserve, analyze, store, secure, and recover data for its own internal purposes, and it will employ various criteria for doing so. However, it is important to remember that the legal purposes of forensics always must be met, regardless of any other internal corporate needs.

Principles, Standards, and Practices

Because the collection of electronic information is such an important concern, the International Organization on Computer Evidence was created in 1995 to develop international principles for the procedures relating to evidence discovery. The goal was to develop standards and practices that would be recognized as legal among many countries and states. These principles are summarized as follows:

- When dealing with digital evidence, all of the generally accepted forensic and procedural principles must be applied.

- Upon seizing digital evidence, actions taken should not change the digital evidence.

- When it is necessary for a person to access original digital evidence, the person should be trained for that particular purpose.

- All activity relating to the seizure, access, storage, or transfer of digital evidence must be fully documented, preserved, and available for review.

- An individual is responsible for all actions taken with respect to digital evidence while the digital evidence is in their possession.

- Any agency that is responsible for seizing, accessing, storing, or transferring digital evidence is responsible for compliance with these principles.

Because electronic information can be changed so easily, a rigid methodology is to be followed, and the original is not used for analysis. Best practices in handling the media include the following:

- The original copy is secured and kept in an unchanged state.

- The original copy is hashed.

- The original copy is used to make two bit-level copies.

- The primary image is used as a library/control copy.
- The second copy is used as a working image and is analyzed.
- Both copies are hashed upon creation to ensure that they are exact copies.
- The original copy and the primary copy are secured in a controlled area.

 A bit-level copy captures all of the data on the copied media, including hidden data, residual data, file slack, and drive slack.

The Forensic Process

Once a forensic copy has been created, an analyst begins the process of moving from most volatile to least volatile information. Items such as volatile memory, RAM, system event logs, security logs, files, deleted files, and slack space are be examined. You will need to establish and review system, audit, and security logs. This process must be done correctly, because once the evidence is contaminated, it cannot be decontaminated; therefore, it is important to have a structured forensic process. The general steps of the forensic process are as follows:

Identify and Acquire   The information must be identified and retrieved. Once it is in the custody of the investigator, a copy is usually created. The standard practice dictates that a bit-level copy be made. A bit-level copy is an exact duplicate of the original data. This allows the investigator to examine the copy while leaving the original intact.

Preserve and Authenticate   Preservation is the act of maintaining the evidence in an unchanged state. This process requires that an investigator show that the data is unchanged and has not been tampered with. Authentication can be accomplished through the use of integrity checks and hashes such as MD5 and SHA. The argument has been made that MD5 is no longer reliable, and while that's true in terms of confidentiality, MD5 is still utilized industry-wide to confirm the integrity of software downloads. SHA-256 is the NIST recommended standard.

Analyze, Record, and Present   The investigator must be careful to examine the data and ensure that any activity is documented. The investigator will usually extract evidence by examining drive slack space, file slack space, hidden files, swap/page file data, Internet cache, and other locations such as the Recycle Bin. Specialized tools are available for this activity. All the activities of the investigator must be recorded to ensure that the information will be usable in court, if needed.

In the end, computer forensics is about the scientific examination and analysis of data held on storage media or in RAM. The results of such analysis are to discover what occurred, decide on potential sanctions against the perpetrator, and be prepared in case the evidence is required to be used in a court of law.

Electronic evidence is fragile, and there's only one chance to capture it correctly.

Security professionals should look carefully at the policies and procedures that define how forensic activities are to be carried out. Forensic analysis of compromised systems, smartphones, iPads, digital cameras, and USB thumb drives must be addressed. Any existing policy must specify how evidence is to be handled. The chain of custody helps protect the integrity preservation and reliability of the evidence by providing an evidence log that shows every access to evidence, from collection to appearance in court.

Digital forensics is an important role for business today. Responding to breaches and conducting e-discovery is important when defending an organization against criminal or civil allegations. Organizations must be able to organize and analyze essential data and make strategic decisions based on that information. It is important to have procedures in place for background investigations, compliance management, or investigations related to potential or threatened litigation. Some of these tasks can be taken care of by internal personnel, but some tasks will need the expertise of legal experts, whether internal or outsourced personnel.

 The primary goal of any incident response is the protection of the health and safety of people. In all emergency situations, the team that responds needs to practice triage, which is the process of determining which patient or incident should be treated first. The incident response process is similar in that you will need to determine which process or system you address first. There is also the fact that no matter how well your network is protected, eventually there will be an incident or emergency.

Here are some of the issues a CASP+ needs to know about:

Electronic Inventory and Asset Identification   Electronic inventory and asset identification deals with the concept of asset management. An asset can be defined as a tangible or nontangible item that has value. The level of security control used to protect an asset is determined by the type of asset and its value. In the forensic process, it is important to be able to identify the assets that have been compromised.

Data Recovery and Storage   Data recovery and storage are closely related to items such as RAID, database shadowing, and SLAs. Guidelines exist for such activities, but each company must create a strategy that maps to its specific backup, disaster recovery, and compliance needs.

Data Ownership   The data owner should have a voice in how information is protected. The data owner is the individual who has legal rights over a single piece or a dataset of elements.

Legal Holds   Legal holds are the activities that an organization can take to preserve and protect all forms of relevant information when it's reasonably anticipated that litigation will occur.

Chain of Custody   The concept of *chain of custody* is used to address the reliability and credibility of evidence. Chain of custody is all about the following questions: Who collected the evidence? Where was the evidence collected? How was the evidence stored? Why was it removed from storage? And who had possession of the evidence during this time? Chain of custody begins when evidence is seized and continues until the evidence is disposed of or returned to the owner.

Order of Volatility   If a form of system memory loses its contents when power is off, that form is considered *volatile*. When collecting from volatile memory, such as CPU cache or RAM, the incident handler must consider how volatile the memory is. The order of volatility deals with the order in which an incident or investigation would occur. The general rule when dealing with computer systems is always to move from most to least volatility. Taking memory snapshots as well as imaging hard drives should be an option for any forensic investigation.

The Internet Engineering Task Force (IETF) released a document titled Guidelines for Evidence Collection and Archiving. It is also known as RFC 3227. This document explains that the collection of evidence should start with the most volatile item and end with the least volatile item. So, according to the IETF, the Order of Volatility is as follows:

1. Registers, cache

2. Routing table, ARP cache, process table, kernel statistics, memory

3. Temporary file systems

4. Disk

5. Remote logging and monitoring data that is relevant to the system in question

6. Physical configuration, network topology

7. Archival media

Systems Designed to Facilitate Incident Response   Although this may seem counterintuitive to some, systems should be designed with incident response built in. Security professionals should be involved at each step of the software development life cycle (SDLC) process. Anytime new systems are designed or purchased, someone should be asking if the appropriate secure controls have been implemented. One approach as specified in the NIST documents consists of the following: implementation, monitoring, compliance, strategy, policy, and awareness.

The CASP+ exam will expect you to understand that security professionals should be involved at each step of the SDLC process. In practice, it is much more expensive to include security only at the end of the process.

Creating and backing up a forensic image will prevent loss of data. Loss of data could be damaging to any legal case you might have. There are many forensic tools that can be used for imaging. Using any of the freely available imaging solutions like Clonezilla (`clonezilla.org`) is an efficient way to create a fully configured and patched system image for distribution on your network as well as making backup forensic images. Clonezilla can be implemented from a server or a bootable device and gives users a variety of options based on their needs. One of the more flexible options of this solution can be deployed using a portable drive. This drive can contain prestaged images for onsite deployment as well as onsite forensic backup. Sometimes you will have a situation where a machine will not boot to the network, or it is against regulations to move an ailing asset and using a portable drive is ideal.

If you have an onsite technician lab, you can create an effective cloning system using a server machine, one or more technician machines, and a network switch to facilitate deployment to multiple systems at once. Cloning can be accomplished using software such as Clonezilla. There are two types of Clonezilla: Clonezilla Live and Clonezilla SE. Clonezilla SE is for an enterprise, where Clonezilla Live is for a single backup and restore. There are several methods to format a USB drive so that it is bootable. Rufus USB creator is lightweight, fast, and user friendly.

Once you have built a Clonezilla Live USB, you can boot your target machine with it. You may have to edit the BIOS/UEFI settings of the machine to be able to boot to USB. Set USB as the first priority when you edit the BIOS/UEFI. With Clonezilla Live, you are able to save a forensic image and restore that same image. In Clonezilla Live, two accounts are available. The first account is "user" with sudo privilege, and the password is "live." A sudo account will allow users to run programs with the security privileges of a superuser. The second account is an administration account "root" with no password. If you need root privilege, you can log in as user and run sudo -i to become root.

The master forensic image should be kept intact and hashed for verification. For redundancy in the case of litigation, two forensic images should be made and hashed. The first copy as well as the original should be locked in a secure area and never touched. The second one is for examination. Due diligence is used to create due care when it comes to the chain of custody for digital forensic evidence. It is important to take special care that all evidence is documented properly, verified, and examined only by those who have been trained specifically for it. It has been argued in federal court by nontechnical defense attorneys that writing on a CD-RW with a permanent marker was enough to change the data stored on the CD. To present this type of evidence and argue effectively that digital evidence has not been tampered with, procedures must be adhered to. Keeping up with the wide variety of data, electronic devices, and communication, as well as the evolving nature of information technology, can be difficult for law enforcement.

Most states have at least one digital forensics laboratory or department of digital forensics, and vendor-neutral certifications are offered through the Digital Forensics Certification Board (DFCB). Task forces including the Internet Crimes Against Children (ICAC) and the Joint Terrorism Task Force (JTTF) are comprised of officers with specialized training in search and seizure of digital evidence, cryptanalysis, and steganalysis.

Cryptography is the practice of transforming information in a way that it cannot be decoded without access to the decryption key. Cryptography consists of two main operations: encryption, which changes plaintext information into ciphertext using an encryption key, and decryption, which changes ciphertext back into plaintext using a decryption key. Cryptography has several important goals including confidentiality and integrity. We use encryption to protect sensitive information as well as to ensure that data is not maliciously or unintentionally altered. Another goal, authentication, refers to uses of encryption to validate identity, and nonrepudiation ensures that individuals can prove to a third party that a message came from its sender. Cryptography is discussed further in Chapter 6, "Cryptography and PKI."

Cryptanalysis is the act of obtaining plain text from cipher text without a cryptographic key. It is used by governments, the military, enterprises, and attackers to find weaknesses and crack cryptographic systems. The effort that someone has to do to reverse engineer cryptography is called the *work factor*. Techniques used to break cryptography include brute-force attacks, and tools that can be used include CrypTool, EverCrack, and CryptoBench.

Audio and video files have more storage than most images because the file size can be much larger. A video file of 500 MB is not uncommon, and changing of the file size allows for the embedding of data. Often, steganography tools will limit the capacity of the altered file. Finding or recovering steganographic data is known as *steganalysis*. Some common steganalysis techniques are listed here:

Stego-Only   Only the steganographic content is available for analysis.

Known-Stego   Both the original and the steganographic content are available for review.

Known-Message   The hidden message and the corresponding steganographic image are known.

To make steganalysis even harder, the person using steganography might not only hide the data, but they may also encrypt it. In these situations, recovery of the data can be quite difficult because you must not only find the data but also crack the encryption.

Forensic Analysis Tools

Incident response, with its several phases and objectives, has the incident handler use a variety of tools. While a handler might rely on a specialized tool for a specific task, oftentimes common command-line and networking tools support the incident handler in gathering information or confirming a suspicion. A few of these tool types, such as file carving, binary analysis, imaging, hashing, and live collection, are described here.

File Carving Tools

File carving is a process used in forensics to selectively pull structured data out of raw data from a disk drive. File carving is most often used to recover files from the unallocated space in a disk drive. Files are reconstructed by scanning the raw bytes and reassembling them. This is done by analyzing the header and footer of the file. File carving is often used by forensics experts in criminal cases for recovering any and all evidence.

Foremost

Foremost is a Linux-based data recovery forensic program. Foremost is free to the general public but was originally intended for law enforcement. It does not use the file system directly, but it copies and reads portions of the hard drive to the memory of the laptop or personal computer. Foremost is used mainly to recover images from hard drives and iPhones. If you decide to download the file, antivirus will sometimes detect it as malware.

Strings

Digital forensic text string search tools use match or indexing algorithms to search evidence. Scalpel is an open-source tool that performs file carving using *strings* to locate headers and footers in an image. The Boyer-Moore string-search algorithm has been the standard for string searching and is one of the options in Scalpel. This algorithm uses data collected to skip sections and run faster by looking for the tail end of a pattern rather than the beginning.

Binary Analysis Tools

Binary analysis, also known as binary code analysis, is threat assessment and vulnerability testing at the binary code level. It is very relevant to what we do as cybersecurity professionals as threat actors move up the Open Systems Interconnection (OSI) model. Many years ago, network-level attacks were the ones most prevalent. As the network became more impenetrable, attacks went to the application layers.

Binary analysis looks at the raw binaries that make up an application, which is very helpful when the source code is not available. An attempt is made to analyze and detect known security issues and create vulnerability reports that are actionable.

This section will look at a range of binary analysis tools. The discussion of one of them, dll, will actually take place later in the "Live Collection vs. Post-Mortem Tools" section.

Hex Dump

A *hex dump* is a hexadecimal view of computer data. Hexdump, the Linux utility, is a program that displays the contents of binary files in multiple outputs like hexadecimal, decimal, octal, or ASCII. It is very useful for viewing what is in a file at a byte level. There is also a `hexdump.exe` freeware Windows program that is a simplified version of the Linux utility to view file contents in hexadecimal code.

Binwalk

Binwalk is a fast, easy tool in Kali Linux that allows searching, analyzing, reverse engineering, and extracting firmware images. Binwalk uses the libmagic library, so it is compatible with Unix. It is one of the best tools for analyzing security vulnerabilities in firmware, specifically in the Internet of Things (IoT), where it improves the stability and security of devices and makes them resistant to attacks.

Ghidra

Ghidra is a reverse engineering tool created and maintained by the National Security Agency of the United States that was released at the RSA Conference in March 2019. Ghidra was designed to analyze malicious code and malware like viruses and ransomware by taking the compiled deployed software and decompiling it. This reverse engineering process is critical for taking nefarious software found in the wild and understanding how it works and who is responsible for it and protecting against it. Some analysts prefer the tool IDA-Pro by Hex-Rays, but it is only available for purchase.

GNU Project Debugger (GDB)

The *GNU Project debugger (GDB)* is a powerful tool for finding bugs and was one of the first programs to be written for the Free Software Foundation. It allows you to see what is going on inside a program when it crashes by tracking variables when problems occur and the reasons for errors. For example, if a core dump occurs, what was the statement or expression that happened immediately before the crash? It is the most popular debugger for Linux/Unix systems.

OllyDbg

Similar to GDB, *OllyDbg* is a freeware debugger but is specifically a 32-bit assembler level debugger. It too can be used to evaluate and debug malware and is easy to use on Windows. It can attach to running programs, debug multithread applications, decode calls to API, and assemble commands into the shortest binary form.

Objdump

Objdump is a command in Linux used to give information on object files. This is a handy command to use if you are a programmer trying to debug a program, but it is also used while compiling code. There are options that can be used with the command to control what information is displayed such as archive, private, or section headers.

Readelf

readelf is an architecture-independent command-line tool that displays information about 32-bit and 64-bit Executable and Linkable Format (ELF) format object files. ELF files are the standard file format for executable files, binaries, libraries, and core files. readelf is very similar to objdump but goes into more detail. The major difference between objdump and readelf is that readelf does not depend on the Binary File Descriptor Library (BFD), which is the library responsible for objdump.

Strace

Strace is a diagnostic and debugging tool for Linux. It is primarily used to monitor interactions between processes and the kernel, including systems calls and change of state. According to the strace man page, it is invaluable for solving problems with programs for which the source code is not readily available. Programmers use strace to isolate bugs, do sanity checks, and attempt to capture race conditions.

File

In Linux, this is where binary analysis begins. Before you start, you have to know what type of file you are dealing with. It could be a PDF, an image, a data file, a video file, or a plethora of different types of files. The `file` command will run three tests against a file including a file-system test based on the result of a stat system call, a magic test to see if the file has data in a particular format, and a language test to look for specific strings that can appear in the first few blocks of a file.

Analysis Tools

There are many tools that can be used for analysis and some virtual machines that are specifically designed and built for this purpose. If you are looking for a virtual machine with tooling for malware analysis, look at the REMnux distribution of Linux toolkit, which is excellent for reverse engineering. If you want a Windows distribution of a virtual machine to combine threat intelligence tools with hunt teaming, download a copy of the Threat Pursuit VM that has OpenCTI, Splunk, Maltego, MITRE Caldera, and RStudio already configured from Mandiant: `www.mandiant.com/resources/threatpursuit-vm-threat-intelligence-and-hunting-virtual-machine`.

ExifTool

ExifTool is a tool used for reading, writing, and editing meta information in many different formats for images, audio, video, and PDF documents. For example, if you run the command **>exiftool -h -nikon t/images/123.jpg**, you get all the information possible from the file including camera, model, date, time, ISO, size, quality, color, size, file number, owner name, serial number, lens size, etc. There is a Windows version as well as a macOS version available at `exiftool.org`.

Nmap

Nmap was originally built as a command-line tool you could execute through a shell or terminal window. The goal was to build a flexible and extremely powerful free open-source tool. Originally built on Linux for pure-hearted system administrators, it evolved and is available for Windows as well as in a graphical user interface (GUI) format, Zenmap. There are more than 100 command-line options in Nmap, but some of them were never fully documented by the author, Gordon Lyon.

In any size network but especially large, dynamic networks, it is vitally important to break down these complex networks and analyze traffic, facilitate issues, and fix connection problems. Network scanning is a process of finding assets that are alive or have a heartbeat and then gathering as much vital information about those assets as possible. Network scanning can be divided into four stages:

- Network mapping
- Open ports
- Services running
- Operating systems

Aircrack-ng

Aircrack-ng is a set of toolkits designed to assess security for wireless networks. It focuses on monitoring, attacking, testing, and cracking 802.11 wireless WEP and WPA/WPA2-PSK encryption. All the tools included are for the command line and come preinstalled in Kali-Linux. There are many tutorials on YouTube as well as step-by-step instructions on how to use Aircrack-ng to crack Wi-Fi networks; however, it is important that you understand that in situations where you do not own the Wi-Fi network or have permission to test the strength of its security, this could be considered illegal, and there have been cases of jail time given to neighbors "cracking" Wi-Fi networks.

 Can aircrack-ng work on WPA3? Not very well. . .the dragonfly handshake (also called *simultaneous authentication of equals*) is a mandatory part of WPA3. This handshake is resistant against offline dictionary attacks. In contrast, WPA2 networks that use a weak password are vulnerable to offline dictionary attacks. Since in practice many networks use weak passwords, resistance against this attack is a major improvement. In production, it's not often that you downgrade protocols, but you could see it with legacy or WPA3-incompatible devices, and in that type of situation, you could still attack with aircrack-ng.

Volatility

Volatile memory is computer memory that needs an electrical current to maintain stored data. When power is lost, data stored in volatile memory is lost, and this can include browsing history and chat conversations. Memory dumps are those files that contain a copy of all the volatile memory at a specific time, usually when the system crashes, which for Windows machines is affectionately called the "blue screen of death."

Volatility is an open-source memory forensics tool written in Python for incident response and malware analysis for both 32-bit and 64-bit systems. With Volatility, you can read memory/RAM captures, including the information copied to the operating system clipboard and command history. Other basic information can be retrieved using Volatility for RAM dump analysis, which includes date and time of captured images, running processes, open network sockets and connections, and memory addresses. Volatility is popular because there are plug-ins to gather even more information. Other tools that do this include SANS SIFT and Redline by FireEye.

The Sleuth Kit

The *Sleuth Kit* is a collection of command-line tools used to analyze disk images, search for files by keyword, and recover deleted files. It is used by many open-source and commercial Linux/Unix and Windows-based forensic tools, including Autopsy, which lends a graphical user interface (GUI) to the command-line utilities. Some commands include blkls, which displays data blocks inside a file system, which by default copies the contents of unallocated data blocks. There are many arguments you can add to blkls such as -e, which copies the entire file system; -s, which copies only the slack space of an image; and -a, which displays all allocated blocks.

Dynamically vs. Statically Linked

Static and dynamic links are two methodologies that can be used in analysis. *Static linking* is the process of copying all library modules used in a program into the final executable image so that the product is all-inclusive and independent. These files are usually quite large. *Dynamically linking* is binding those libraries in a shared approach; those files will be smaller.

During analysis, taking a computer program, which is a sequence of steps in a language that instructs the computer to perform certain tasks, requires reverse engineering. If all the code is in a single large file, the way you would analyze that software and the included libraries would be different than if you were combining external programs at runtime. The operating system performs dynamic linking, and if the library is moved, the program will no longer work.

Imaging Tools

Acquiring a forensic copy of a drive or device requires a tool that can create a complete copy of the device at a bit-for-bit level. The CASP+ candidate should consider a number of tools that can acquire disk images, including FTK and dd.

Forensic Toolkit Imager

Forensic Toolkit (FTK) Imager is a free tool for creating forensic images made by Access-Data. It can be used to locate deleted files and emails and look for test strings and other sensitive information. It supports raw-style format as well as SMART (ASR Data's format for their SMART forensic tool), E01 (Encase), and AFF (Advanced Forensics Format) formats commonly used for forensic tools.

Physical drives, logical drives, image files, and folders, as well as multi-CD/DVD volumes, are all supported by FTK Imager. In most cases, forensic capture is likely to come from a physical or logical drive.

In addition to drive imaging tools, forensic analysts are sometimes asked to capture live memory on a system. In addition to drive images, FTK imager can capture live memory from a system.

dd

dd is a free data forensic tool. It is included with every Linux and Unix distribution. dd can create perfect copies of any disk.

dd was originally developed to copy data from one device to another, from EBCDIC to ASCII. It is a powerful tool capable of a variety of other tasks.

dd can be used for backing up and restoring an entire hard drive partition; creating a virtual file system and backup images of CDs or DVDs, called ISO files; copying regions of raw device files, like backing up master boot records (MBRs); converting data formats like ASCII to EBCDIC; and converting lowercase to uppercase and vice versa, which make dd a handy supplement for running daily backups. From a forensic standpoint, the capability to create image files on different device types makes dd a valuable forensic tool. dd can also create image files on disks, CD-RW drives, and tapes.

dd and Unix systems together can create MD5 checksums for files as well as SHA-256 and SHA-512. dd provides a powerful, inexpensive tool that can verify that the image file has not been changed in any way. This is crucial, especially for evidence that might need to be used in court.

Even if a compromised system is not Unix-based, this is no reason not to use dd. Different variations of Linux distributions are available that boot off a disk and allow you to use dd to make your forensic copies.

 There are various Linux distributions available that boot from a disk and allow you to use dd to make forensic copies. Trinux is a powerful and flexible tool that makes dd a vital part of the incident handler's toolkit.

```
osdn.net/projects/sfnet_trinux/downloads/trinux-iso/0.890/
trinux-0.890.iso
```

Hashing Utilities

A *hash* is a defined mathematical procedure or function that converts a large amount of data into a fixed small string of data or integer. The output of a hash is known as a *hash value*, *hash code*, *hash sum*, *checksum*, *fingerprint*, or *message digest*. The following tools are utilities that are listed in the CASP+ exam objectives.

sha256sum

The program sha256sum was made to verify data integrity using the SHA-256 algorithm. These hashes can confirm authenticity as well. Comparing these hashes makes it possible to detect that a change in the file has happened or could cause errors. Most Linux distributions come with the sha256sum utility installed.

ssdeep

The ssdeep tool was created to compute context-triggered piecewise hashes (CTPH). This has also been called a *fuzzy hash*. The program can match signatures against a file of known signatures and report any matches. It can recursively look at a file of signatures and find any matches within that file as well as modified versions of a file, even when data has been deleted. Today ssdeep hashes are used for simple identification because of computational speed. It can be found inside the Kali Linux distribution.

Live Collection vs. Postmortem Tools

A *postmortem* is a written record of everything happening with an incident, including the incident's impact, the actions taken to mitigate and resolve it, the root cause, and the follow-up actions. To create an efficient and effective postmortem, the following tools will help collect the data needed to reduce repeat incidents.

nbtstat

As a security analyst, you will want to know what computer belongs to what IP address. For a security analyst working at a security operations center (SOC), this information is necessary when troubleshooting network issues. Sometimes you'll also want to see if there are devices on the network that don't belong there.

You could ping an IP address, but this tells you only if there is connectivity to the network device. You could also use the -a switch with the ping command to see if you get lucky and if it resolves the IP address to a name.

Besides using ping, another command-line utility that a security analyst can use to assist in finding the computer name associated with an IP address is the DOS command nbtstat, which is used to find NetBIOS computer names. The nbtstat command can also be invoked by opening a command prompt, choosing Start ➢ Run, and then entering **cmd** and clicking OK.

netstat

Netstat is an abbreviation for "network statistics." If a host is not listening on the correct port for a specific service, then no communication can occur. Take another step in your network path, and these ports may be listening, but this does not mean that a firewall is allowing the traffic to get to the device. To test that hypothesis, you can temporarily disable your host-based firewall causing the networking issue.

Netstat is a network utility tool that displays networking connections (incoming and outgoing), routing tables, and some other details such as protocol statistics. It will help you gauge the amount of network traffic and diagnose slow network speeds. Sounds simple, yes? From a cybersecurity standpoint, how quickly can you tell which ports are open for incoming connections? What ports are currently in use? What is the current state of connections that already exist?

The output from the `netstat` command is used to display the current state of all the connections on the device. This is an important part of configuration and troubleshooting. How do you know what is actually transpiring on the compromised system? Using the `netstat` command and the options –a for all and –n for addresses and ports, you will have a list of all active network conversations this machine is having.

When running `netstat` on your host, you may see both 0.0.0.0 and 127.0.0.1 in this list. A loopback address is accessible only from the machine you're running `netstat` on. The 0.0.0.0 is basically a "no particular address" placeholder. What you see after the 0.0.0.0 is called a *port*.

There are 65,536 windows and doors in your network ranging from 0 to 65,535. Ports can be TCP or UDP. Simply put, TCP means there is a connection made between the host and the destination. UDP doesn't worry about whether there is a connection made. Both TCP and UDP have 65,535 ports available to them. This was the highest number that could be represented by a 16-bit, or 2-byte, number. You may see this represented mathematically as $2^{16} - 1$.

The Internet Assigned Numbers Authority (IANA) maintains an official assignment of port numbers for specific uses. Sometimes this list becomes antiquated at the same time new technologies are becoming available. Some of the most common ones you might see are the "well-known" ports, which are 0–1023.

In Lab 7.1, you'll use the `netstat` command.

LAB 7.1

Using netstat

1. Open a command prompt or a terminal window.

2. At the command prompt, type **netstat –help**. Press Enter.

3. When the prompt is available, use **netstat –an –p TCP**. Press Enter.

4. Next type **netstat –sp TCP**. Press Enter.

If you see this machine is listening on port 135, this port is traditionally used for a service called epmap/`loc-srv`. That should tell you, among other things, that this is a Windows host. When a Windows host wants to connect to an RPC service on a remote machine, it checks for port 135.

The next port that you may notice is 443. Most IT professionals memorize this port early in their careers. Port 443 is Hypertext Transfer Protocol over TLS/SSL—better known as

HTTPS. HTTPS is the authentication of a website that is being accessed and protecting the confidentiality of the data being exchanged. Ports from 1023 all the way up to 49151 are "registered" ports. Above that, you have dynamic or private ports.

Netcat

Netcat, often abbreviated NC, is a Unix networking utility that allows users to establish network connections in order to read and write data from host to host. As a backend tool, Netcat has been dubbed the "Swiss Army knife for TCP/IP." It works using both TCP and UDP, but it can actually be used to create many more types of connections.

PS

In most Linux/Unix operating systems, the `ps` command, short for Process Status, will give you the currently running processes on a system in real time and is often used to kill or terminate those processes that are misbehaving. The outcome will be in four columns:

- PID: The unique process ID
- TTY: The type of terminal
- TIME: The time in minutes and seconds the process has been running
- CMD: The command that launched the process

There are many switches that can be used with `ps`. For example, if you wanted to show any process that is running as root, you would use the `ps -U root -u root` command. This will give you the same four columns as shown previously but only if they are running as root.

vmstat

The virtual memory statistics reporter, often referred to as the `vmstat` command-line tool, is a monitoring tool that collects and reports various system information and statistics about kernel threads in the run and wait queues, memory, paging, disks, interrupts, system calls, and CPU activity.

ldd

`ldd` is a Linux command-line utility that is used in case a user wants to know the shared library of an executable. There are many files starting with `lib*` in a Linux distribution. These files are libraries. To use `ldd`, run the command along with the executable as input. All shared library dependencies will be in the output.

lsof

In Linux, *lsof* stands for the "list of open files." This command gives you a list of all the files that are open by which process and shares details of all open files in the output. It can list common files, directories, shared libraries, regular and named pipes, Internet sockets, and many others. If you combine lsof with grep, it can be used for more advanced searching.

conntrack

In a Linux distribution, `conntrack` is connections tracker, allowing you to dump a list of all currently tracked connections and monitor connection tracking events, such as an event message for a newly established connection. This tool allows you to search, list, inspect, and maintain the connection tracking subsystem of the kernel.

memdump

`memdump` permits you to dump the contents of memory-resident pages that are specific to a particular process. The application dumps the physical memory contents, in raw form, to the standard output. Dumping the kernel memory is an option, but it can result in locking the system.

tcpdump

The most common packet analyzer in use today, `tcpdump` was created more than 30 years ago due to the necessity to capture and record network traffic as output. Within a few years, tcpdump was ported to work on several operating systems and platforms.

Wireshark

Wireshark is a tool that every network or security administrator should know. It is an open-source tool used for capturing network traffic and analyzing packets at an extremely granular level. Sometimes Wireshark is called a *network analyzer* or a *sniffer*. Packet capturing can tell you about transmit time, source, destination, and protocol type. This can be critical information for evaluating events that are happening or troubleshooting devices across your network. It can also help a security analyst determine whether network traffic is a malicious attack, what type of attack, the IP addresses that were targeted, and where the attack originated from. As a result, you will be able to create rules on a firewall to block the IP addresses where the malicious traffic originated.

Wireshark shows packet details captured from different network media, breaking down the Open Systems Interconnection (OSI) model into the data link, network, transport, and application layers. At the bottom of the workspace, you have an option to open the hexadecimal with corresponding ASCII values on the right.

Wireshark is a powerful tool and technically can be used for eavesdropping. When you plan to use this in a business environment, you will want to get written permission to use it and make sure your organization has a clearly defined security privacy policy that specifies the rights of individuals using the network. Stories abound of network administrators capturing usernames, passwords, email addresses, and other sensitive user data. Wireshark is legal to use, but it can become illegal if you attempt to monitor a network that you do not have explicit authorization to monitor.

Determining the resources that Wireshark needs depends on the size of the `.pcap` file you are examining. If you have a busy network, then the files will be large. Wireshark can run on Windows and Linux machines. You will need a supported network card for capturing data, such as an Ethernet card or a wireless adapter. To get the latest copy of Wireshark, visit www.wireshark.org. The download page will have the proper version for your computer's architecture and version operating system. A new version typically comes out every other month.

Summary

Incident response and forensics are an important part of the framework of security. This framework starts at a very high level in the organization, which is bound by legal and ethical concerns to provide a certain level of protection for critical assets and how an organization responds to a breach. Senior management plays a big role here—its members are the top tier of the company and are ultimately responsible. They are the individuals who must help define the policies and procedures that provide this framework for security. Policies are important in that they serve as a declaration of management's concern with protecting critical assets.

A CASP+ security professional should have knowledge of the tools needed for incident response as well as performing forensics with due care. Using the right tool at the right time decreases the amount of effort required to get a job done without causing damage to other equipment or businesses' bottom line. However, using the right tool the wrong way can be dangerous, causing harm to the enterprise.

Exam Essentials

Be able to explain an incident, event, and crisis.   Performing incident response, a CASP+ should be able to understand the triage and process of escalation between an event, the research to be done to call it an incident, and the tools necessary to explore the network for other indicators of compromise.

Be able to implement, follow, and create a playbook.   Responding quickly to an incident is of utmost importance. Creating and following a playbook that is written specifically for the event, whether it be ransomware, data exfiltration, or social engineering, is vital to the containment of a breach.

Be able to explain forensic concepts.   Be able to follow legal procedures and corporate policies as they pertain to the capture of forensic elements while following the proper processes of identification, collection, preservation, analysis, verification, and presentation.

Be able to choose the correct forensic analysis tool.   Given a scenario, choose the right file carving, binary analysis, imagine, or hashing utility for the collection of evidence.

Review Questions

You can find the answers in Appendix.

1. Your company has a fence around the perimeter of its datacenter. A light sensor is connected to the fence and trips an alarm whenever something impacts the fence or the sensor detects movement and automatically records it on video. The datacenter is located in an area with tumbleweeds that often impact the fence in the fall, causing alarm fatigue. In this scenario, what alert type is causing alarm fatigue?

    A. True positive

    B. True negative

    C. False positive

    D. False negative

2. During the lessons learned, your team is conducting an analysis of the incident playbook. What would *best* mitigate and manage the effects of an incident?

    A. Modifying the scenario the risk is based on

    B. Developing an agenda for recovery

    C. Choosing the members of the recovery team

    D. Implementing procedural controls

3. You work as a security analyst for a large banking organization that is about to disclose to the public that a substantial breach occurred. You are called into a meeting with the CISO and CEO to discuss how to ensure proper forensic action took place and that the incident response team responded appropriately. Which of these should you ensure happens after the incident?

    A. Avoid conflict of interest by hiring outside counsel.

    B. Create forensic images of all mission-critical servers.

    C. Perform a formal investigation yourself without law enforcement.

    D. Treat the incident as though a crime has been committed.

4. After an incident, it is important for you to create a lessons learned document. By conducting this critique, you evaluate the effectiveness of the response. With that after-incident mindset, what is the most important result you can derive from this document?

    A. Areas for improvement

    B. Magnitude of the problem

    C. Proper assessment of an incident

    D. Security assessment awareness

5. Your organization finished dealing with an incident that requires an after-action report (AAR). Your goal is to improve your organization's response to an event or a critical situation. Which of the following should *not* be included in the AAR?

   A. Analyze the event to determine what your strengths are and areas of improvement for your future response plan.

   B. Understand the entire event from multiple strategic, tactical, and operational viewpoints; compile a playbook for future training.

   C. Improve the communication of your organization's critical response, disaster recovery, and business continuity plans.

   D. Create network topology diagrams.

6. One of your end users contacted the security administrator because the cursor on his computer seems to be moving all by itself. If your company's focus is confidentiality, which of the following is the *best* action to take?

   A. Delay the intruder.

   B. Disconnect the intruder.

   C. Record the intruder.

   D. Monitor the intruder.

7. You are a security analyst working for a casino. You work with a security firm and have traced the origin of a ransomware attack to a connected fish tank in the casino lobby. The attack was stopped within seconds, and the threat was mitigated. What would have led to the quick discovery of the attack?

   A. Signatures

   B. Endpoint analysis

   C. SOAR

   D. Immunity learning

8. Your company's CISO hired an external security consultant to create playbooks for the organization's physical security. In the contract, the CISO noted a concern about unauthorized access to physical offices that would result in a digital compromise. What should the consultant include in this playbook?

   A. Procedures for how to automatically grant access to physical control systems and review logs.

   B. How to conduct internal audits of access logs and social media feeds.

   C. Installing CCTV on all entrances and exits to detect access.

   D. How to create the trigger event of gaining access to offices using social engineering techniques and then attempting to compromise the network.

9. Your new role within a security operations center is to support the development of policies and to implement standard IT security practices of incident response. You will be writing the procedures for how your incident team will manually respond to events. This would be considered which type of response?

   A. Least privilege

   B. Automated

   C. Nonautomated

   D. Forensic tasks

10. Your organization was breached, but you have been able to prove that sufficient due care and due diligence was taken. You have documented exactly when the workflow starts and what the response tasks should be. What is this document called?

   A. SOW

   B. NDA

   C. Runbook

   D. After-action report

11. You are working for the federal government as a vulnerability management supervisor. You are attempting to enable automated measurement and policy compliance to improve your security posture. What are you most likely to use?

   A. HTTPS

   B. SOAR

   C. STATE

   D. HIPAA

12. You are a project manager for an organization that just acquired another company. Your company uses mostly in-house tools for incident response, whereas the company you just acquired uses mostly outside vendors for incident response and contracts out for forensic work. Merging these two organizations needs to be quick, have an immediate return on investment (ROI), and retain the ability to customize systems. Each organization thinks their way is the best way. What do you do?

   A. Raise the issue with the CEO and board of directors to escalate the decision to outsource all services.

   B. Arrange a meeting between all department heads, project managers, and a representative from the board of directors to review requirements and calculate critical functions.

   C. Perform a cost-benefit analysis of in-house versus outsourcing and the ROI in-house.

   D. Calculate the time to deploy and support the new systems and compare the cost to outsourcing costs. Present the document to upper management for their final decision.

13. You had an incident and need to verify that chain of custody, due diligence, and identification processes were followed. You are told to verify the forensic bitstream. What will you do?

 A. Employ encryption

 B. Instigate containment

 C. Compare hashes

 D. Begin documentation

14. An attacker who compromised your network was caught and is being prosecuted. The logs from various pieces of equipment showing the attacker's actions are one of the key pieces of evidence. When the logs were examined, it was determined that the timestamps are inaccurate and off by years. What is likely to happen to the logs as related to the prosecution of the attacker?

 A. The defense attorney will likely be given an opportunity to correct the timestamps.

 B. The judge will likely enable a third party to correct the timestamps.

 C. The company will likely be given an opportunity to correct the timestamps, making them admissible in court.

 D. The logs will likely not be allowed in court because the timestamps are incorrect.

15. As a new director of security, you review your organization's security policy. The current policy states if a compromise is suspected or detected, you should immediately disconnect the system from the network, power it down, and physically secure the system. This mode worked well in the past. However, with malware authors reducing the footprint on a hard drive and storing as much as possible within RAM, which is cleared when the system is powered down, it is now widely recognized in forensics that it is best to do which of the following?

 A. Include volatile memory as part of the incident evidence collection, using tools that quickly analyze RAM.

 B. Power down because advanced persistent threats will still be evident on the hard drive.

 C. Pull the hard drive and RAM and then put them on dry ice indefinitely until they can be analyzed to store the digital evidence.

 D. Pull the plug and examine the network logs.

16. Your team is examining business continuity, incident detection, and response to determine its storage policy. One of the mitigating controls for this policy will be the hierarchy of evidence from most volatile to least volatile. For example, archival media is not volatile; the most volatile are registers, cache, and read-access memory. What is this called?

 A. Order of volatility

 B. IETF

 C. Guidelines of storage capacity

 D. RAID 0

17. After you are breached, one of the most difficult steps is to understand what actually occurred. Your technical team tells you which systems and data were violated, which vulnerabilities were used, and that the compromised systems are quarantined. What should your technical team do next?

   A. Report directly to the board of directors.

   B. Ensure there are no backdoors or logic bombs left behind by attackers.

   C. Place the CISO and CTO on administrative leave.

   D. Bring in a third party for a penetration test.

18. Your organization terminates an employee from the IT department. After the IT employee is escorted from the building, a complete forensic investigation on all systems that the IT employee had access to shows a logic bomb installed on a server. Only three IT staff members had access to that server, and the remaining IT employees did not have admin access; therefore, they could not have installed the logic bomb. Which of the following factors supports the evidence you have collected?

   A. Authorized people accessing evidence

   B. Improper storage of evidence

   C. Mislabeled evidence

   D. Alteration of digital evidence

19. Your organization wants to start digging deeper into malware analysis and needs software to spot vulnerabilities that can be exploited. You do not have the budget for IDA PRO this year, so an open-source tool is best. You also need to create your own plug-ins. Which of these tools meet that criteria?

   A. Hydra

   B. Immunity Debugger

   C. AngryIP

   D. Ghidra

20. Your breached organization is in the middle of an investigation, gathering evidence, performing forensics, and giving a presentation to upper management of all the proof gathered. What is the organization's next action after all the technical incident forensics are completed?

   A. Schedule a press conference.

   B. Notify the authorities.

   C. Notify all your vendors.

   D. File for cyber-insurance coverage.

Chapter

8

Security Architecture

THE CASP+ EXAM TOPICS COVERED IN THIS CHAPTER INCLUDE:

✓ **1.1 Given a scenario, analyze the security requirements and objectives to ensure an appropriate, secure network architecture for a new or existing network.**

- ▪ **Services**

  - ▪ Load balancer

  - ▪ Intrusion detection system (IDS)/network intrusion detection system (NIDS)/wireless intrusion detection system (WIDS)

  - ▪ Intrusion prevention system (IPS)/network intrusion prevention system (NIPS)/wireless intrusion prevention system (WIPS)

  - ▪ Web application firewall (WAF)

  - ▪ Network access control (NAC)

  - ▪ Virtual private network (VPN)

  - ▪ Domain Name System Security Extensions (DNSSEC)

  - ▪ Firewall/unified threat management (UTM)/next-generation firewall (NGFW)

  - ▪ Network address translation (NAT) gateway

  - ▪ Internet gateway

  - ▪ Forward/transparent proxy

  - ▪ Reverse proxy

  - ▪ Distributed denial-of-service (DDoS) protection

  - ▪ Routers

  - ▪ Mail security

  - ▪ Application programming interface (API) gateway/Extensible Markup Language (XML) gateway

  - ▪ Traffic mirroring

- Switched port analyzer (SPAN) ports
- Port mirroring
- Virtual private cloud (VPC)
- Network tap

- Sensors
  - Security information and event management (SIEM)
  - File integrity monitoring (FIM)
  - Simple Network Management Protocol (SNMP) traps
  - NetFlow
  - Data loss prevention (DLP)
  - Antivirus

- **Segmentation**
  - Microsegmentation
  - Local area network (LAN)/virtual local area network (VLAN)
  - Jump box
  - Screened subnet
  - Data zones
  - Staging environments
  - Guest environments
  - VPC/virtual network (VNET)
  - Availability zone
  - NAC lists
  - Policies/security groups
  - Regions
  - Access control lists (ACLs)
  - Peer-to-peer
  - Air gap

- **Deperimeterization/zero trust**
  - Cloud
  - Remote work
  - Mobile
  - Outsourcing and contracting
  - Wireless/radio frequency (RF) networks
- **Merging of networks from various organizations**
  - Peering
  - Cloud to on premises
  - Data sensitivity levels
  - Mergers and acquisitions
  - Cross-domain
  - Federation
  - Directory services
- **Software-defined networking (SDN)**
  - Open SDN
  - Hybrid SDN
  - SDN overlay

✓ **1.2 Given a scenario, analyze the organizational requirements to determine the proper infrastructure security design.**

- **Scalability**
  - Vertically
  - Horizontally
- **Resiliency**
  - High availability
  - Diversity/heterogeneity
  - Course of action orchestration
  - Distributed allocation
  - Redundancy
  - Replication
  - Clustering

- **Automation**
  - Autoscaling
  - Security Orchestration, Automation, and Response (SOAR)
  - Bootstrapping
- **Performance**
- **Containerization**
- **Virtualization**
- **Content delivery network**
- **Caching**

✓ **1.3 Given a scenario, integrate software applications securely into an enterprise architecture.**

- **Baseline and templates**
  - Secure design patterns/types of web technologies
    - Storage design patterns
  - Container APIs
  - Secure coding standards
  - Application vetting processes
  - API management
  - Middleware
- **Software assurance**
  - Sandboxing/development environment
  - Validating third-party libraries
  - Defined DevOps pipeline
  - Code signing
  - Interactive application security testing (IAST) vs. dynamic application security testing (DAST) vs. static application security testing (SAST)
- **Considerations of integrating enterprise applications**
  - Customer relationship management (CRM)
  - Enterprise resource planning (ERP)
  - Configuration management database (CMDB)

- Content management system (CMS)
- Integration enablers
  - Directory services
  - Domain name system (DNS)
  - Service-oriented architecture (SOA)
  - Enterprise service bus (ESB)
- **Integrating security into development life cycle**
  - Formal methods
  - Requirements
  - Fielding
  - Insertions and upgrades
  - Disposal and reuse
  - Testing
    - Regression
    - Unit testing
    - Integration testing
  - Development approaches
    - SecDevOps
    - Agile
    - Waterfall
    - Spiral
    - Versioning
    - Continuous integration/continuous delivery (CI/CD) pipelines
  - Best practices
    - Open Web Application Security Project (OWASP)
    - Proper Hypertext Transfer Protocol (HTTP) headers

✓ **1.4 Given a scenario, implement data security techniques for securing enterprise architecture.**

- **Data loss prevention**
    - Blocking use of external media
    - Print blocking
    - Remote Desktop Protocol (RDP) blocking
    - Clipboard privacy controls
    - Restricted virtual desktop infrastructure (VDI) implementation
    - Data classification blocking
- **Data loss detection**
    - Watermarking
    - Digital rights management (DRM)
    - Network traffic decryption/deep packet inspection
    - Network traffic analysis
- **Data classification, labeling, and tagging**
    - Metadata/attributes
- **Obfuscation**
    - Tokenization
    - Scrubbing
    - Masking
- **Anonymization**
- **Encrypted vs. unencrypted**
- **Data life cycle**
    - Create
    - Use
    - Share
    - Store
    - Archive
    - Destroy

- **Data inventory and mapping**
- **Data integrity management**
- **Data storage, backup, and recovery**
  - Redundant array of inexpensive disks (RAID)

✓ **1.5 Given a scenario, analyze the security requirements and objectives to provide the appropriate authentication and authorization controls.**

- **Credential management**
  - Password repository application
    - End-user password storage
    - On premises vs. cloud repository
  - Hardware key manager
  - Privileged access management
- **Password policies**
  - Complexity
  - Length
  - Character classes
  - History
  - Maximum/minimum age
  - Auditing
  - Reversable encryption
- **Federation**
  - Transitive trust
  - OpenID
  - Security Assertion Markup Language (SAML)
  - Shibboleth
- **Access control**
  - Mandatory access control (MAC)
  - Discretionary access control (DAC)
  - Role-based access control

- Rule-based access control
- Attribute-based access control
- **Protocols**
    - Remote Authentication Dial-in User Service (RADIUS)
    - Terminal Access Controller Access Control System (TACACS)
    - Diameter
    - Lightweight Directory Access Protocol (LDAP)
    - Kerberos
    - OAuth
    - 802.1X
    - Extensible Authentication Protocol (EAP)
- **Multifactor authentication (MFA)**
    - Two-factor authentication (2FA)
    - 2-Step Verification
    - In-band
    - Out-of-band
- **One-time password (OTP)**
    - HMAC-based one-time password (HOTP)
    - Time-based one-time password (TOTP)
- **Hardware root of trust**
- **Single sign-on (SSO)**
- **JavaScript Object Notation (JSON) web token (JWT)**
- **Attestation and identity proofing**

This chapter discusses enterprise security and architecture, a critical component of defense in depth. Years ago, perimeter security and simply having antivirus software on a computer may have been enough. This is not true anymore. Today, every time a user turns on a computer, clicks a link, or opens an email, there is the potential that an attack could occur. This is why host-based solutions such as anti-malware, antivirus, and anti-spyware are important to the defense-in-depth strategy, but these items are part of the solution. Good logical security is just like good physical security, and it requires hardening. Logical security doesn't require you to build a 10-foot concrete wall around your computer, but it does require you to harden the enterprise in such a way as to make an attacker's job more difficult. That job starts by removing unwanted services. It also includes implementing security policies and controls. Finally, it's about building in the principle of least privilege: provide only what the user needs to do the task at hand—and nothing more—while maintaining a secure baseline.

The term *enterprise security* refers to a holistic view of security. Our view of IT security has changed over the years in that items such as data security, IT security, and physical security are now seen as just components of a total security solution. Enterprise security is a framework for applying comprehensive controls designed to protect a company while mapping key services to needed information systems. The goals of enterprise security are as follows:

- To add value to the company
- To align the goals of IT with the goals of the company
- To establish accountability
- To verify that a pyramid of responsibility has been established that starts with the lowest level of employees and builds up to top management

Enterprise security has become much more important over the last decade. It's easy to see why, when you consider the number of security breaches and reports of poor security management.

In this chapter, we'll look at enterprise security architecting and hardening. We will examine topics such as asset management and the role that intrusion detection and intrusion prevention play. CompTIA expects you to know these topics for the exam. You may be presented with scenario questions, simulations, or even drag-and-drop situations in which you must properly position required controls and countermeasures.

Security Requirements and Objectives for a Secure Network Architecture

"Without a solid foundation, you'll have trouble creating anything of value," according to Erika Fromm, a German psychologist. This quote is true of personal relationships, startup businesses, and cybersecurity architecture. Building a strong foundation and architecture is a means to reduce the risk of compromise and protect your assets using security principles, methods, frameworks, and modeling. Basically, security architecture translates the enterprise requirements to executable security requirements.

Services

The TCP/IP suite was not built for enterprise security. Its primary design consideration was usability, and although that was acceptable for the early Internet, today secure data flows, protocols, procedures, and services are needed to meet ever-changing business needs. Some weaknesses are due to unnecessary services running and protocol weaknesses, whereas others are defects in the software that implements the protocols and runs those services. It is important to know that many transmission protocols do not provide encryption.

The best way to build cyber resilience is through redundancy, having more than one of a system, service, device, or other components. Power, environmental controls, hardware and software, network connectivity, and any other factor that can fail or be disrupted needs to be assessed. Single points of failure—places where a single device or other element failing could disrupt or stop the system from functioning—must be identified, assessed, and either compensated for or documented in the design. Unneeded and extraneous open ports, applications, and services provide additional avenues for attackers. Default accounts are a huge attack vector if they aren't removed or changed. These apps and services can also leave other open ports, providing another vector for reconnaissance and attack. Secured root (Linux) and Administrator (Windows) accounts represent strong configurations. An unsecured root or administrator account could have a serious impact on the entire system and anything it's connected to.

After assessment work has been finished, a strategy is created that balances need, requirements, options, and the cost to build and operate the environment. Designs regularly have concessions made in them to meet complexity, staffing, or other limitations based on the overall risk and likelihood of occurrence for the dangers that were identified in the review and design phases.

 While most disasters won't impact something 90 miles away, hurricanes are a major example of a type of disaster that can have very broad impacts on multiple locations along their path. Security architects who build facilities in hurricane-prone regions tend to plan for resilience by placing backup facilities outside of those hurricane-prone regions, typically by moving them further inland. They will also make more investments into hurricane-proofing their critical infrastructure, including network services, for example.

Load Balancers

Load balancers make multiple systems or services appear like a single resource, allowing both redundancy and increased ability to handle the load by distributing it to more than one system. Load balancers are also commonly used to allow system upgrades by redirecting traffic away from systems that will be upgraded and then returning that traffic after the systems are patched or upgraded. Load balancers are also used to provide a centralized defense.

A proxy load balancer is a device that acts as a reverse proxy and distributes network or application traffic across a number of servers. Proxy load balancers are used to increase the capacity of concurrent users and the reliability of applications. Proxy load balancers improve the overall performance of applications by decreasing the overall burden on servers associated with managing and maintaining applications and network sessions, as well as by performing application-specific tasks. Proxy load balancers are normally grouped into two categories: layer 4 and layer 7. Layer 4 proxy load balancers act upon data found in Network and Transport layer protocols (IP, TCP, FTP, and UDP). Layer 7 proxy load balancers distribute requests based on data found in application layer protocols such as HTTP. Proxy load balancers ensure reliability and availability by monitoring the health of applications and sending requests only to servers and applications that can respond in a timely manner.

Because of advances in IDS and IPS, NIST now refers to these technologies as IDPS. CompTIA refers to these as IDS and IPS separately on the exam. A good place to learn more about IDPS is NIST 800-94, which is located at csrc.nist.gov/publications/detail/sp/800-94/final.

Intrusion Detection Systems and Intrusion Prevention Systems

Another element of protection in security architecture is the introduction of an *intrusion detection system (IDS)*. An IDS gathers and analyzes information from the computer or a network it is monitoring. An IDS can be considered a type of network management and monitoring tool. The key to what type of activity the IDS will detect depends on where the sensor is placed. Before discussing the types of intrusion detection systems, let's first review the various ways in which an intrusion is detected.

Intrusions are detected in one of three basic ways:

Signature Recognition   Signature recognition relies on a database of known attacks, and it is also known as *misuse detection*. Each known attack is loaded into the IDS in the form of a signature. Once the signatures are loaded, the IDS can begin to guard the network. The signatures are usually given a number or name so that they are easily identified when an attack occurs. For example, these signatures may include the Ping of Death, SYN floods, or Smurf DoS. The biggest disadvantage to signature recognition is that these systems can trigger only on signatures that are known and loaded. Polymorphic attacks and encrypted traffic may not be properly assessed. Tools such as Snort are still an invaluable part of the security administrator's arsenal, and custom signatures will frequently be used depending on the organizational environment. They should, however, be combined with other measures that ensure the integrity of the system on which they are installed for the goal of defense in depth.

Anomaly Detection Anomaly detection systems detect an intrusion based on the fixed behavior of a set of characteristics. If an attacker can slowly change their activity over time, an anomaly-based system may not detect the attack and believe that the activity is actually acceptable. Anomaly detection is good at spotting behavior that is significantly different from normal activity. Normal activity is captured over days, weeks, or even months to establish a baseline. Rules can be written to compare current behavior with the baseline to find any anomalies. The CASP+ exam may also use the word *heuristics* to describe monitoring behavior.

Protocol Decoding This type of system uses models that are built on the TCP/IP stack and understands their specifications. Protocol-decoding IDS systems have the ability to reassemble packets and look at higher-layer activity. If the IDS knows the normal activity of the protocol, it can pick out abnormal activity. Protocol-decoding intrusion detection requires the IDS to maintain state information. To detect these intrusions effectively, an IDS must understand a wide variety of Application layer protocols. This can be useful in a situation where an attacker is attempting to use a custom TCP stack on a compromised machine to evade detection.

Here are some of the basic components of an IDS implementation:

- **Sensors:** Detects and sends data to the system.
- **Central monitoring system:** Processes and analyzes data sent from sensors.
- **Report analysis:** Offers information about how to counteract a specific event.
- **Database and storage components:** Perform trend analysis and then store the IP address and information about the attacker.
- **Response box:** Inputs information from the previous components and forms an appropriate response. For example, the response box might decide to block, drop, or even redirect network traffic.
- **Alert definitions:** An alert definition is basically the who, what, when, where, and why of the intrusions that occur. The first step in creating an alert definition is the rule action. These rule actions let the IDS know what to do when it finds a packet that is the same as the criteria of the rule.
    - **Alert:** Generates an alert using the selected alert method and then logs the packet
    - **Log:** Logs the packet
    - **Pass:** Ignores the packet
    - **Activate:** Alerts and then turns on another dynamic rule
    - **Dynamic:** Remains idle until activated by an activate rule and then acts as log rule

- **Drop:** Blocks the log of the packet
- **Reject:** Blocks the packet, logs it, and then sends a TCP reset if the protocol is TCP. If UDP, an ICMP port unreachable message is sent.
- **Sdrop:** Blocks the packet but does not log it

Creating Your Own Rule Types

You can also define your own rule type and associate one or more output plug-ins with it. Snort is a free open-source network intrusion detection and intrusion prevention system managed by Cisco. You can use the rule types as actions in Snort rules.

The following example will create a type that will just log to `tcpdump`:

```
ruletype suspicious
{
type log
output log_tcpdump: suspicious.log
}
```

The following example will create a rule type that will log to syslog and `tcpdump`:

```
ruletype redalert
{
type alert
output alert_syslog: LOG_AUTH LOG_ALERT
output log_tcpdump: suspicious.log
}
```

Rule options from the heart of Snort's intrusion detection engine combine ease of use with power and flexibility. All Snort rule options are separated by semicolons (`;`). Rule keywords are separated from their arguments by a colon (`:`).

There are four major categories of rule options:

- **General:** These options provide information about the rule, but they do not have any effect during detection.
- **Payload:** These options all look for data inside the packet payload and can be interrelated.
- **Nonpayload:** These options look for nonpayload data.
- **Postdetection:** These options are rule-specific triggers that happen after a rule has fired.

There are three types of thresholds that you can apply to your IDS system's alerts. Most monitoring tools should support these thresholds.

Fixed Threshold   Alert-based technology is often triggered by the use of a fixed threshold. Metrics are used and often based on a fixed calculation using various numeric values.

State-Based Threshold   Metrics are sometimes used with discrete values that involve states of the information system. State-based thresholds have alerts that occur when there is a change in the metric value. An example of a state-based threshold is when a specific program process has started.

Historical Threshold   Metrics are compared by using historical thresholds, that is, numerical values from the past and present over a set time frame. Network engineers often use historical thresholds to compare traffic spikes during the current week versus past weeks.

Alert fatigue is the overall threshold where it becomes too difficult for a security analyst to discern important alerts from the stream of all of the information being received. Security analysts have to review each and every alert to decide if it really is a threat or just another false positive, as all of the alerts may appear to be the same at first. When magnified by multiple systems delivering such alerts, it can quickly become overwhelming when there are so many alerts that it becomes difficult to distinguish the true positives from the false positives. Some of these alerts require aggregation before the combination can be confirmed as a true positive and the potential business impact can be assessed. This is why many security operation centers have tiered responders with different levels of expertise evaluating the alerts.

Placement of such an IDS system is another important concern. Placement requires consideration because a sensor in the demilitarized zone (DMZ) will work well at detecting misuse but will prove useless against attackers who have already compromised a system and are inside the network. Once placement of sensors has been determined, they still require specific tuning and baselining to learn normal traffic patterns.

As technology evolves, so does the vernacular. CompTIA has replaced the term *DMZ* with *screened subnet*. A screened subnet's main purpose is isolation, adding security to high-traffic areas. The classic DMZ is the middle ground network between an organization's trusted internal network and an untrusted, external network. The screened subnet is the method of using one or more logical routers to define the perimeter network.

IDS sensors can be placed externally in the DMZ or inside the network. Sensors may also be placed on specific systems that are mission critical. Sensor placement will in part drive the decision as to what type of intrusion system is deployed. Sensors may also be placed inline where one IDS performs signature-based scanning and permits valid traffic to the second IDS, which then performs heuristic or another scan type. This helps guarantee that a bottleneck is not created by placing too much demand on a single IDS. Intrusion detection systems are divided into two broad categories: network intrusion detection system and host intrusion detection system.

Network Intrusion Detection System

Much like a network sniffer, a *network intrusion detection system (NIDS)* is designed to capture and analyze network traffic. A NIDS inspects each packet as it passes by. Upon detection of suspect traffic, the action taken depends on the particular NIDS and its current configuration. It might be configured to reset a session, trigger an alarm, or even disallow specific traffic. NIDSs have the ability to monitor a portion of the network and provide an extra layer of defense between the firewall and host. Their disadvantages include the fact that attackers can perform insertion attacks, session splicing, and even fragmentation to prevent a NIDS from detecting an attack. Also, if an inline network encryption (INE) is used, the IDS would see only encrypted traffic.

An insertion attack occurs when an attacker sends the IDS packets that have been crafted with a time to live (TTL) that will reach the IDS but not the targeted computer. The result is that the IDS and targeted computer rebuild two different streams of traffic. This allows the attacker's malicious activity to go undetected.

Host Intrusion Detection System

A *host intrusion detection system (HIDS)* is designed to monitor a computer system and not the network. HIDSs examine host activity and compare it to a baseline of acceptable activities. These activities are determined by using a database of system objects that the HIDS should monitor. HIDSs reside on the host computer and quietly monitor traffic and attempt to detect suspect activity. Suspect activity can range from attempted system file modification to unsafe activation of commands. Things to remember about HIDSs include the fact that they consume some of the host's resources, but they also have the potential to analyze encrypted traffic and trigger an alert when unusual events are discovered after it is decrypted at the endpoint.

In high-security environments, devices such as an inline network encryptor (INE) and an inline media encryptor (IME) may also be used. An INE is a device that sits along the path of a public or unsecured network when its users need to maintain communications security using that network. The network might be packet switched or ATM (allowing for higher capacity), but the INE permits strong, Type 1 encryption. (Type 1 is NSA-speak for products that ensure encryption while still allowing network addressing.) This is different from a VPN in that an INE is not point-to-point. An INE could be placed for use by a group of users.

An IME is similar to an INE, except that it sits in line between the computer processor and hard drive to secure data in transit.

Although both NIDS and HIDS provide an additional tool for the security professional, they are generally considered passive devices. An active IDS can respond to events in simple ways such as modifying firewall rules. These devices are known as *intrusion prevention systems (IPSs)*. Just as with IDS, an IPS can be either host- or network-based.

Network Intrusion Prevention System

A *network intrusion prevention system (NIPS)* builds on the foundation of IDS and attempts to take the technology a step further. A NIPS can react automatically and prevent a security occurrence from happening, preferably without user intervention. This ability to intervene and stop known attacks is the greatest benefit of the NIPS; however, it suffers from the same type of issues as the NIDS, such as the inability to examine encrypted traffic and difficulties with handling high network loads.

Host Intrusion Prevention System

A *host intrusion prevention system (HIPS)* is generally regarded as being capable of recognizing and halting anomalies. The HIPS is considered the next generation of IDS, and it can block attacks in real time. This process monitoring is similar to antivirus. The HIPS has the ability to monitor system calls. HIPSs have disadvantages in that they require resources and must process identified anomalies at the application level and while sending alerts, they do not prevent attacks.

Wireless Intrusion Detection System and Wireless Prevention System

Wireless intrusion detection systems (WIDSs) and *wireless intrusion prevention systems (WIPSs)* use devices that are built on the same philosophy as NIDS/NIPS; however, they focus on reacting to rogue wireless devices rather than singular security events. WIDS will alert when an unidentified wireless device is detected. Depending on configuration, a WIPS can do the same, as well as prevent the use of the wireless device. A best practice is to review alerts from a WIDS manually rather than shut a system down immediately. You may knock out another legitimate business's wireless access point by accident.

Web Application Firewalls

Web application firewalls (WAFs) are a technology that helps address the concerns of web application security. The WAF is not a replacement for a traditional firewall, but it adds another layer of protection. Whereas traditional firewalls block or allow traffic, WAFs can protect against cross-site scripting (XSS), hidden field tampering, cookie poisoning, and even SQL injection attacks. WAFs operate by inspecting the higher levels of the TCP/IP OSI layers and also tie in more closely with specific web apps.

Think of it in this way: a conventional firewall may deny inbound traffic at the perimeter. A WAF is a firewall sitting between a web client and a web server, analyzing OSI layer 7 traffic. These devices have the ability to perform deep packet inspection and look at requests and responses within the HTTP/HTTPS/SOAP/XML-RPC/Web Service layers. As with any security technology, WAFs are not 100 percent effective; there are various methods and tools used to detect and bypass these firewalls.

Two examples of automated detection tools are w3af and wafw00f. There are many more. Also available are various methods of exploiting inherent vulnerabilities in WAFs, which differ according to the WAF technology. One of the most prominent is cross-site scripting (XSS), which is one of the very things WAFs are designed to prevent. Some WAFs can detect attack signatures and try to identify a specific attack, whereas others look for abnormal behavior that doesn't fit the website's normal traffic patterns.

It may not be a viable option for a company or organization to cease communications across the Internet. This is where the WAF comes into the picture. A WAF can be monumental in protecting these organizations from emerging threats inherent in social networking and other web applications that the conventional firewall was not designed to defend against. One open-source example of a WAF is ModSecurity. Commercial options are offered through Barracuda Networks, Fortinet, and Cisco Systems.

EXERCISE 8.1

Configuring iptables

The CASP+ certification exam tests hands-on security skills. With this in mind, it's a good idea to review host firewall configuration techniques. For this exercise, you will download, install, and configure iptables. This tool is built into Knoppix as well as other Linux distributions. This example provides one way to download and install it.

1. Go to www.knopper.net/knoppix/index-en.html and download Knoppix.

2. Click the Download icon to view available download sites.

3. Burn the ISO file and create a bootable CD or DVD or USB.

4. Configure your computer to boot from the CD or DVD or USB.

5. Start Knoppix and open iptables.

6. Create a basic forwarding chain to allow FTP, SSH, SMTP, DNS, HTTP, and HTTPS. Drop all other traffic. An example forwarding chain that matches this requirement is shown here:

```
###### FORWARD chain ######
echo "[+] Setting up FORWARD chain..."
### state tracking rules
$IPTABLES -A FORWARD -m state --state INVALID -j LOG --log-prefix "DROP
INVALID " --log-ip-options --log-tcp-options
$IPTABLES -A FORWARD -m state --state INVALID -j DROP
$IPTABLES -A FORWARD -m state --state ESTABLISHED,RELATED -j ACCEPT

### anti-spoofing rules
$IPTABLES -A FORWARD -i eth1 -s ! $INT_NET -j LOG --log-prefix
"SPOOFED PKT "
$IPTABLES -A FORWARD -i eth1 -s ! $INT_NET -j DROP
```

```
### ACCEPT rules
8 $IPTABLES -A FORWARD -p tcp -i eth1 -s $INT_NET --dport 21 --syn -m state
--state NEW -j ACCEPT
$IPTABLES -A FORWARD -p udp --dport 53 -m state --state NEW -j ACCEPT
$IPTABLES -A FORWARD -p tcp -i eth1 -s $INT_NET --dport 22 --syn -m state
--state NEW -j ACCEPT
$IPTABLES -A FORWARD -p tcp -i eth1 -s $INT_NET --dport 25 --syn -m state
--state NEW -j ACCEPT
$IPTABLES -A FORWARD -p tcp --dport 80 --syn -m state --state NEW -j ACCEPT
$IPTABLES -A FORWARD -p tcp --dport 443 --syn -m state --state NEW
-j ACCEPT
$IPTABLES -A FORWARD -p tcp -i eth1 -s $INT_NET --dport 4321 --syn -m state
--state NEW -j ACCEPT
### default log rule
$IPTABLES -A FORWARD -i ! lo -j LOG --log-prefix "DROP " --log-ip-options
--log-tcp-options
```

To get additional help on configuring iptables, take a moment to review www.netfilter.org/documentation. Based on your use of iptables, is this something that you would recommend to a small organization that has little funding available for quarantine/remediation of suspect traffic? Also note that iptables support is often integrated into more advanced solutions and devices.

Network Access Control

For large and small businesses alike, achieving optimal network security is a never-ending quest. A CASP+ plays a big part in securing critical systems. One potential solution to these issues is *network access control (NAC)*. NAC offers administrators a way to verify that devices meet certain health standards before they're allowed to connect to the network. Laptops, desktop computers, or any device that doesn't comply with predefined requirements can be prevented from joining the network or can be relegated to a controlled network where access is restricted until the device is brought up to the required security standards. Several types of NAC solutions are available:

- Infrastructure-based NAC requires an organization to upgrade its hardware and operating systems. If your IT organization plans to roll out Windows 11 or has budgeted an upgrade of your Cisco infrastructure, you're well positioned to take advantage of infrastructure NAC.

- Endpoint-based NAC requires the installation of software agents on each network client. These devices are then managed by a centralized management console.

- Hardware-based NAC requires the installation of a network appliance. The appliance monitors for specific behavior and can limit device connectivity should noncompliant activity be detected.

Virtual Private Networks

One item that has really changed remote access is the increased number of ways that individuals can communicate with their company and clients. Hotels, airports, restaurants, coffee shops, and so forth now routinely offer Internet access. It's a low-cost way to get connectivity, yet it's a public network. This is why virtual private networks were created.

A *virtual private network (VPN)* is a mechanism for providing secure, reliable transport over the Internet. VPNs are secure virtual networks built on top of physical networks. The value of a VPN lies in the ability to encrypt data between the endpoints that define the VPN network. Because the data is encrypted, outside observers on a public network are limited in what they can see or access. From a security standpoint, it is important to understand that a VPN is not a protocol. It's a method of using protocols to facilitate secure communications.

VPNs can be either hardware- or software-based. Both hardware and software VPNs offer real value and help protect sensitive company data.

Hardware-Based VPNs   Hardware-based VPNs offer the ability to move the computational duties from the CPU to hardware. The hardware add-on product handles computationally intensive VPN tasks and can be useful for connecting remote branch offices. These solutions work well but require the purchase of additional hardware, which adds complexity to the network.

Software-Based VPNs   Software-based VPNs are easy to build and implement. Several companies, such as `PublicVPN.com`, `Anonymizer.com`, `VyprVPN.com`, and many others, offer quick, easy-to-install software VPN solutions. These options do not require an investment in additional hardware and are extremely valuable for smaller firms with a limited IT staff because they are easier for the IT engineer to set up and maintain. However, in these situations, the company is relying on a third-party VPN provider. This approach could be problematic if companies need to control all aspects of their communications, such as partner business partner agreements (BPAs).

Companies continually work to improve protocols designed for use with VPNs. For example, in the mid-1990s, Microsoft led a consortium of networking companies to extend the Point-to-Point Protocol (PPP). The goal of the project was to build a set of protocols designed to work within the realm of VPNs. The result of this work was the Point-to-Point Tunneling Protocol (PPTP). The purpose of PPTP was to enable the secure transfer of data from a remote user to a server via a VPN. A VPN can be implemented using several different protocols, but the two that will be discussed here are IPsec and SSL. At a high level, the key distinction between the two is that IPsec VPNs operate at the Network layer, while SSL VPNs operate at the Application layer.

In the context of an SSL VPN, you'll recall that the SSL protocol is no longer regarded as secure. The VPN is actually using TLS. While this VPN implementation is still popularly referred to as an SSL VPN, as a CASP+ you must understand that SSL/TLS is in use.

A big advantage to using an SSL/TLS VPN is stricter control, governing access per application rather than to the network as a whole. In fact, restricting access per user is simpler with SSL/TLS VPNs than with an IPsec VPN. The final and arguably the most common reason why small organizations lean toward an SSL/TLS VPN is cost. IPsec VPNs require specialized end-user software, which likely includes licensing costs. Such costly client software isn't a requirement when connecting via SSL/TLS, which is a common feature in any browser today.

VPN Access and Authentication

The traditional perspective of a VPN is a tunnel. That perspective comes from IPsec VPN, because functionally an IPsec VPN connects the remote client in order to become a part of the local, trusted network. IPsec VPNs function in either tunnel or transport mode. Remote access can be defined as either centralized or decentralized. Centralized access control implies that all authorization verification is performed by a single entity within a system; two such systems are RADIUS and Diameter.

> **RADIUS Configurations**   *Remote Authentication Dial-In User Service (RADIUS)* originally used a modem pool for connecting users to an organization's network. The RADIUS server will contain usernames, passwords, and other information used to validate the user. Many systems formerly used a callback system for added security control. When used, the callback system calls the user back at a predefined number.
>
> RADIUS today carries authentication traffic from a network device to the authentication server. With IEEE 802.1X, RADIUS extends layer-2 Extensible Authentication Protocol (EAP) from the user to the server.
>
> **Diameter**   *Diameter* was designed to be an improvement over RADIUS and to handle mobile users better through IP mobility. It also provides functions for authentication, authorization, and accounting. Despite these efforts, RADIUS still remains popular today.

Decentralized access control can be described as having various entities located throughout a system performing authorization verification. Authentication is a key area of knowledge for the security professional because it serves as the first line of defense. It consists of two pieces: identification and authentication. As an example, think of identification as me saying, "Hi, I am Alice." It's great that I have provided Bob with that information, but how does Bob know that it is really Alice? What you need is to determine the veracity of the claim. That's the role of authentication. Following the previous scenario, after providing her name, authentication would then require Alice to show her license, offer a secret word, or provide fingerprints.

Examples of access authentication protocols and tools include the following:

Password Authentication Protocol   Password Authentication Protocol (PAP) is a simple protocol used to authenticate a user to a network access server that passes usernames and passwords in clear text. PAP is an older authentication system designed to be used on phone lines and with dial-up systems. PAP uses a two-way handshake to authenticate, but it is considered weak.

Challenge Handshake Authentication Protocol   Challenge Handshake Authentication Protocol (CHAP) is used to provide authentication across point-to-point links using the Point-to-Point Protocol (PPP). CHAP uses a challenge/response process and makes use of a shared secret. It's more secure than PAP and provides protection against replay attacks. CHAP provides authentication by verifying through the use of a three-way handshake. Once the client is authenticated, it is periodically requested to re-authenticate to the connected party through the use of a new challenge message.

MS-CHAP v2 is the newest standard password-based authentication protocol which is widely used as an authentication method in Point-to-Point Tunneling Protocol (PPTP)–based VPNs.

Lightweight Directory Access Protocol   *Lightweight Directory Access Protocol (LDAP)* is an application protocol used to access directory services across a TCP/IP network. LDAP was created to be a lightweight alternative protocol for accessing X.500 directory services. X.500 is a series of computer networking standards covering electronic directory services.

Active Directory   *Active Directory (AD)* is Microsoft's implementation of directory services and makes use of LDAP. AD retains information about access rights for all users and groups in the network. When a user logs on to the system, AD issues the user a globally unique identifier (GUID). Applications that support AD can use this GUID to provide access control. Although AD helps simplify sign-on and reduces overhead for administrators, there are several ways that it might be attacked.

The difficulty in attacking AD is that it is inward facing, meaning that it would be easier for an insider than an outsider to target AD. One attack methodology is escalation of privilege. In this situation, the attacker escalates an existing user's privilege up to administrator or domain administrator. Other potential attack vectors may include targeting password hashes or Kerberos pre-authentication.

The primary vulnerability associated with authentication is dependent on the method used to pass data. PAP passes usernames and passwords via clear text and provides no security. Passwords can be easily sniffed; however, all of these protocols have suffered from varying levels of exploitation in the past.

VPN Placement

VPN is technology that requires consideration as to placement. You can choose among various design options for placement of VPN devices in your network. For example, you can place the VPN device parallel to a firewall in your network. The advantage of this approach is that it is highly scalable. This is because multiple VPN devices can be deployed in parallel with the firewall. Yet with this approach, no centralized point of content inspection is implemented.

Another potential placement of the VPN device is in the screened subnet on the firewall in the network. This network design approach allows the firewall to inspect decrypted VPN traffic, and it can use the firewall to enforce security policies. One disadvantage is that this design placement option may impose bandwidth restrictions.

Your final design option is an integrated VPN and firewall device in your network. This approach may be easier to manage with the same or fewer devices to support. However, scalability can be an issue because a single device must scale to meet the performance requirements of multiple features. There is also the question of system reliability. If the VPN fails, does the firewall fail too? Having a mirrored VPN and firewall is the way to ensure reliability if you choose this model.

> You will need to understand firewall design and the placement of devices for the test. During the exam, you may be presented with a drag-and-drop simulation that asks you for the placement of various devices in a secure manner for a specific purpose.

Domain Name System Security Extensions

Before service is enabled on any DNS server, it should be secured. Some of the most popular DNS server software, such as the Internet Systems Consortium's BIND, has suffered from a high number of vulnerabilities in the past that have allowed attackers to gain access to and tamper with DNS servers. Alternatives to BIND such as Unbound are available, and you should consider them if your infrastructure permits. DNS is one of the services that you should secure, as there are many ways an attacker can target DNS. One such attack is DNS cache poisoning. This type of attack sends fake entries to a DNS server to corrupt the information stored there. DNS can also be susceptible to denial-of-service (DoS) attacks and unauthorized zone transfers. DNS uses UDP port 53 for DNS queries and TCP port 53 for zone transfers. Securing the zone transfer process is an important security control.

> A *denial-of-service (DoS)* attack is a single-source computer system initiating the attack. A *distributed denial-of-service (DDoS)* attack is a much more orchestrated attack, enlisting the help of hundreds (if not thousands) of other source computers to completely overload the system.

The integrity and availability of DNS are critical for the health of the Internet. One common approach to securing DNS is to manage two DNS servers: one internal and one external. Another approach is using *Domain Name System Security Extensions (DNSSEC)*. DNSSEC is a real consideration, since one of the big issues with running two DNS servers is that the external DNS server that provides information to external hosts remains vulnerable to attack. This is because DNS servers have no mechanism of trust. A DNS client cannot normally determine whether a DNS reply is valid.

CASP+ test candidates should be aware that although DNSSEC does offer security advantages, it does not provide confidentiality of data and does not protect against DDoS attacks or domain hijacking.

With DNSSEC, the DNS server provides a signature and digitally signs every response. For DNSSEC to function properly, authentication keys have to be distributed before use. Otherwise, DNSSEC is of little use if the client has no means to validate the authentication. DNSSEC authenticates only the DNS server and not the content. Even if the DNS server is configured for DNSSEC, situations can arise where the server may sign the results for a domain that it is impersonating. You can read more about DNSSEC at `www.dnssec.net`.

EXERCISE 8.2

Using Pingdom Full Page Test

One easy way to check for misconfigured DNS servers is to make use of the SolarWinds website Pingdom.

1. Open your web browser and go to `dnscheck.pingdom.com`.

2. Select Full Page Test under DNS analyzing tools.

3. Enter the URL of your web server and complete the required details.

4. Review the report. Were any problems found?

A particularly disruptive distributed denial-of-service (DDoS) attack against DNS occurred in February 2020. DDoS protection works best by filtering website traffic so illegitimate requests are not allowed. Amazon Web Services (AWS) was hit for three days by a massive DDoS attack. This was the most intense recent DDoS attack ever, and it targeted an unidentified AWS customer using a technique called Connectionless Lightweight Directory Access Protocol (CLDAP) reflection. This technique relies on vulnerable third-party CLDAP servers and magnifies the quantity of data sent to the victim's IP address by up to 70 times.

Firewall/Unified Threat Management/Next-Generation Firewall

Today, a range of security devices are available to help security professionals secure critical assets. These include antivirus, anti-spyware, host-based firewalls, *next-generation firewalls (NGFWs)*, intrusion detection and prevention systems, and so on. But what if you could combine much of this technology into one common device?

Actually, you can do that, as it is what *unified threat management (UTM)* is designed to accomplish. UTM is an all-in-one security product that can include multiple security functions rolled into a single appliance. UTMs can provide network firewalling, network intrusion prevention, and gateway antivirus. They also provide gateway anti-spam and offer encrypted network tunnels via VPN capability, content filtering, and log/audit reporting. The real benefit of UTM is simplicity and an all-in-one approach to data flow enforcement. For smaller organizations, a single purchase covers most common security needs, and the device can be controlled and configured from a single management console. UTM devices are typically placed at the edge of the network. They offer the convenience of an all-in-one device, but the drawback is that if the device fails, there is no remaining protection.

Network Address Translation and Internet Gateway

Although IPv6 is becoming used by more organizations today, IPv4 is still the industry standard. IPv4 worked well for many years, but as more and more devices have been added to the Internet, the number of free addresses has decreased. IPv4 provides for approximately 4.3 billion addresses, which may seem like a lot, but these addresses have been used up at an increasingly rapid rate, mostly due to all of the Class B networks already allocated.

Several methods were adopted to allow for better allocation of IPv4 addresses and to extend the use of the existing address space. One was the concept of variable-length subnet masking (VLSM). VLSM was introduced to allow flexible subdivision into varying network sizes. Another was the introduction of network address translation (NAT). NAT, which is covered in RFC 1918, set aside three ranges of addresses to be designated as private: 10.0.0.0/8, 172.16.0.0/12, and 192.168.0.0/16. NAT was designed to help with the shortage of IPv4 addresses, to provide a low level of security, and to ease network administration for small to medium businesses.

A *network address translation (NAT) gateway (NGW)* is used to enable devices in a private subnet with no public IP addresses to connect to the Internet or cloud services. It also prevents the Internet from connecting directly to those devices. An *Internet gateway (IGW)*, on the other hand, allows a logical connection between an instance with a public IP to connect to the Internet.

One of the biggest differences between IPv4 and IPv6 is the address field. IPv6 uses much larger addresses. The size of an address in IPv6 is 128 bits. This is four times longer than the 32-bit IPv4 address and provides enough addresses for the foreseeable future.

Forward/Transparent and Reverse Proxy

A popular network component that is used for protection is a proxy. Many think of a proxy as a mechanism that "stands in place of." *A transparent proxy*, also called a *forward proxy*, inline proxy, intercepting proxy, or forced proxy, is a server that intercepts the connection between an end user or device and the Internet. It is called *transparent* since it does not modify any requests and responses and can block malicious incoming traffic.

Using a transparent proxy, for example, an end user on a corporate network requests to view a page on www.cnn.com and views the same information as they would on their local connection at home. The page is delivered from a transparent proxy running on the corporate network. The user's experience is precisely the same, but the user's employer now has the ability to monitor their behavior and restrict access to specific websites. Squid Transparent Proxy Server is a popular open-source transparent proxy tool.

A *reverse proxy* server sits at the edge of the network and handles the policy management and traffic routing. It receives the connection request from the user, completes a TCP three-way handshake, connects with the origin server, and sends the original request. The reverse proxy is well suited for scrubbing incoming application traffic before it goes to a backend server. This helps an organization with DDoS protection to minimize impact, helps with web application protection to drop malicious packets, and can even reroute traffic to ensure availability.

Routers

Another critical network component is the router. Routers are considered OSI layer 3 components. A router's primary purpose is to forward packets out the correct port toward their destination through a process known as *routing*. Routers primarily work with two items: routing protocols and routable protocols. A good example of a routable protocol is IP. Routers examine IP packet headers and determine the location to where they should be forwarded. The header contains the destination address. The router is already aware which port connects to the network for which that destination is local. The path they take is determined by the routing protocol. Examples of routing protocols include Routing Information Protocol (RIP) and Open Shortest Path First (OSPF). Routers can forward IP packets to networks that have the same or different medium types. Routers can also be targeted by attackers. Some common attacks include route poisoning and Internet Control Message Protocol (ICMP) redirect attacks.

Improper router configurations are a big security risk. Although physical controls are important, software controls are needed to prevent router attacks.

> **Transport Security**   Increased network security risks and regulatory compliances have driven the need for wide area network (WAN) transport security. Examples of transport security include IPsec, TLS, and SSL. IPsec is the Internet standard for security. Designed as an add-on to IPv4, it is also integrated with IPv6. TLS and SSL perform the same service but are implemented differently. The most widely used version of TLS is v1.2, but the latest, v1.3, is already supported in the current version of most major web browsers.

Port Security   Port security contains layer 2 traffic, which is a control feature of the Cisco Catalyst Switches. Port security gives security analysts and network administrators the capability to configure individual switch ports, which allow only a specific number of source MAC addresses to ingress the port. Port security's primary function is to deter the addition by users of what are known as dumb switches that illegally extend the reach of the network. Adding unmanaged devices can complicate troubleshooting for administrators and is not recommended. Port security is enabled with default parameters by issuing a single command on an interface.

Remotely Triggered Black Hole Filtering   Remotely Triggered Black Hole (RTBH) filtering is a technique that uses routing protocol updates to manipulate route tables at the network edge, or anywhere else in the network, specifically to drop undesirable traffic before it enters the service provider network.

One major area that needs to be mitigated is distributed denial-of-service (DDoS) attacks. For DDoS protection, once an attack is detected, black holing can be used to drop all DDoS attack traffic at the edge of an Internet service provider (ISP) network, based on either the destination or source IP address. Black holing is done by forwarding this traffic to a Null0 interface. A DDoS attack is then launched from the Internet targeting the server.

In addition to service degradation of the target, the entire internal infrastructure will be affected due to high bandwidth consumption and processor utilization. Because of the distributed nature of the attack, network administrators must block all inbound traffic destined for the victim at the edge.

Trunking Security   Trunking security is an important concern when discussing virtual local area networks (VLANs). VLANs started as a security and traffic control used to separate network traffic. The VLAN model works by separating its users into workgroups, such as engineering, marketing, and sales. Today, many companies prefer campus-wide VLANs because VLANs have to span and be trunked across the entire network. A trunk is simply a link between two switches that carries more than one VLAN's data.

From a security perspective, this is a concern. If an attacker can get access to the trunked connection, they can potentially jump from one VLAN to another. This is called VLAN hopping. It is important to make sure that trunked connections are secure so that malicious activity cannot occur. Cisco has several ways to incorporate VLAN traffic for trunking. These techniques may include the IEEE's implementation of 802.1Q or Cisco's Inter-Switch Link (ISL).

Distributed denial-of-service (DDoS) attacks have been around a long time, and they're still a valid area of concern. Let's look at a few protective measures that can be taken for a router or switch.

Route Protection   Route or path protection means to ensure that controls are in place to protect the network flow end to end. That's a general definition, but the actual technique depends highly on what type of network is being protected, be it an Optical Mesh network, a Multi-Protocol Label Switching (MPLS) network, or something else.

DDoS Protection   Distributed denial-of-service (DDoS) attacks can be crippling to an organization, particularly if the traffic is so debilitating that the network engineer loses control and connectivity to devices to help stem the attack. One mitigating technique is to use remotely triggered black hole routing. As the name suggests, if network traffic is identified as unwanted, that traffic is sent to the network version of a "black hole" and dropped.

VLAN hopping is a hacking technique that allows attackers to send packets outside of their VLAN. These attacks are generally launched on networks running the Dynamic Trunking Protocol (DTP) by tagging the traffic with a VLAN ID that is outside the attacker's VLAN. By disabling DTP on user access ports, you are effectively disabling trunking on that port, which is one means of mitigating this type of attack.

Mail Security

Many individuals would agree that email is one of the greatest inventions to come out of the development of the Internet. It is the most used Internet application. Just take a look around the office and see how many people use Android phones, iPhones, laptops, tablets, and other devices that provide email services. Email provides individuals with the ability to communicate electronically through the Internet or a data communications network.

Although email has many great features and provides a level of communication previously not possible, it's not without its problems. Now, before we beat it up too much, you must keep in mind that email was designed in a different era. Decades ago, security was not as much of a driving issue as usability. By default, email sends information via clear text, so it is susceptible to eavesdropping and interception. Email can be easily spoofed so that the true identity of the sender may be masked. Email is also a major conduit for spam, phishing, and viruses. Spam is unsolicited bulk mail. Studies by Symantec and others have found that spam is much more malicious than in the past. Although a large amount of spam is used to peddle fake drugs, counterfeit software, and fake designer goods, it's more targeted to inserting malware via malicious URLs today.

As for functionality, email operates by means of several underlying services, which can include the following:

Simple Mail Transfer Protocol   Simple Mail Transfer Protocol (SMTP) is used to send mail and relay mail to other SMTP mail servers and uses port 25 by default. The secure version uses SSL/TLS on port 587 or 465.

Post Office Protocol   Post Office Protocol (POP3), the current version, is widely used to retrieve messages from a mail server. POP3 performs authentication in clear text on port 110. The secure version uses SSL/TLS on port 995.

Internet Message Access Protocol   Internet Message Access Protocol (IMAP) can be used as a replacement for POP3 and offers advantages over POP3 for mobile users. IMAP has the ability to work with mail remotely and uses port 143. The secure version uses SSL/TLS on port 993.

Basic email operation consists of the SMTP service being used to send messages to the mail server. To retrieve mail, the client application, such as Outlook, may use either POP or IMAP. Using a tool like Wireshark, it is very easy to capture clear-text email for review and reinforces the importance of protecting email with PGP, SSL/TLS, or other encryption methods.

Application Programming Interface Gateway/Extensible Markup Language Gateway

Today's systems are much more distributed than in the past and have a much greater reliance on the Internet. At the same time, there has been a move toward service-enabled delivery of services.

Have you noticed that many of the web-based attacks today no longer target web servers but are focused on web applications? Web-based applications continue to grow at a rapid pace, and securing them is a huge job. Application programming interfaces (APIs) are interfaces between clients and servers or applications and operating systems that define how the client should ask for information from the server and how the server will respond. This definition means that programs written in any language can implement the API and make requests.

APIs are tremendously useful for building interfaces between systems, but they can also be a point of vulnerability if they are not properly secured. API security relies on authentication, authorization, proper data scoping to ensure that too much data isn't released, rate limiting, input filtering, and appropriate monitoring and logging to remain secure. An *API gateway* sits between an external client and the application running on premises or in the cloud. An API gateway can validate an incoming request, send it to the right service, and deliver the correct response. An API gateway can act as an API proxy so the original API is not exposed.

Web services also make use of Extensible Markup Language (XML) messages. XML is a popular format for encoding data, and it is widely used for a variety of applications, ranging from document formats such as Microsoft Office to web formats. An *XML gateway* serves as an entry point for web traffic and an outbound proxy for internal web service consumers.

Change Is the One Constant of IT Security

Years ago, web servers were one of the most targeted systems, but today this is no longer true. As security professionals sought to harden systems, attackers moved on to look for vulnerabilities in other areas.

Currently, web applications are a big area of attack. Securing web applications requires implementing good code review, building security into the development process, performing security testing, and managing patches. As web application development improves, attackers will shift to new methods of attack.

Traffic mirroring

Traffic mirroring is used by cloud vendors to monitor network traffic. Traffic mirroring copies the inbound and outbound traffic from the network interfaces that are attached to the cloud instance or load balancer. The purpose of a traffic mirror is to take the data and share with monitoring tools for content inspection, threat monitoring, and often, troubleshooting when issues arise.

Switched Port Analyzer Ports

Some tools are limited in that they can only see the span of the network to which they are attached, like a NIDS. This brings up an important fact: by stating that the NIDS may see the span, this means that they are often placed on a mirrored port or a port to which all traffic passing through the network device is forwarded. This could be a mirrored port on a switch or even a router. In the Cisco world, these ports are referred to as *Switched Port Analyzer (SPAN)* ports for obvious reasons.

Port Mirroring

A *port mirroring* technique is used often by network engineers to analyze data and troubleshoot issues. A port mirror is used on a layer 2 network switch to send a copy of packets to a monitoring device, connection, or another switch port by reserving one port. When the switch processes the packet, it makes a copy and sends it to that port. This type of monitoring is vital for network observation because of outages and bottlenecks.

Virtual Private Cloud

A *virtual private cloud (VPC)* is a highly secured, flexible, remote private cloud located inside a public cloud. A VPC user can do anything they would normally do in a private cloud, allowing an enterprise to create its own computing environment on shared infrastructure. A VPC's logical isolation is implemented for security reasons, giving very granular control to administrators.

Network Tap

A *network tap* is a hardware device plugged into a specific spot in a network where data can be accessed for testing or troubleshooting. Network taps usually have four ports, two for the network and two for monitoring. The network ports collect information. The monitoring ports provide a copy of this traffic to a device attached for monitoring. This way, traffic can be monitored without changing the flow of data.

Sensors

Sensors are being increasingly used in cybersecurity and could be a firewall log or a network tap. A sensor collects information about the network and uses it in tools around the environment, doing data analysis to make decisions about safety measures and defense. Host-based sensors provide accurate information, and network sensors provide extensive coverage but can be vulnerable to security threat actors. Developing a secure sensor network requires redundancy to ensure adequate protection against cyberattack.

Security Information and Event Management

Another popular security solution is *security information and event management (SIEM)*. A SIEM solution helps security professionals identify, analyze, and report on threats quickly based on data in log files. SIEM solutions prevent IT security professionals from being overwhelmed with audit data and endless logs so that they can easily assess security events without drowning in security event data. This service is the combination of two separate reporting and recording areas, security information management (SIM) and security event management (SEM). SIM technologies are designed to process and handle the long-term storage of audit and event data. SEM tools are designed for real-time reporting of events. Combining these two technologies provides users with the ability to alert, capture, aggregate, review, and store event data and log information from many different systems and sources, which allows for visualization and monitoring for patterns. The primary drawback to using these systems is that they are complex to set up and require multiple databases. Vendors that offer SIEM tools include ArcSight, Splunk, Lacework, and Exabeam.

File Integrity Monitoring

File integrity monitoring (FIM) works in two modes: agent-based and agentless. With agent-based FIM, an agent sits on a host and provides real-time monitoring of files. The FIM agent also removes the repeated scanning loads on the host and network. The biggest disadvantage of a FIM agent is that it eats up host resources. With a FIM agent installed, a local baseline gets established. Thereafter, only qualifying changes require the FIM agent to engage, given some host resources. FIM agents must possess all of the capabilities for detecting unauthorized changes, be platform independent, and be capable of reporting what has been changed and who has made the changes.

Agentless FIM scanners are effective only on their scheduled time. There is no real-time detection or reporting capability. Agentless FIM scanners need to be re-baselined and hashed for every single file on the system each time that they scan. One advantage of agentless FIM scanners is that they are easy to operate without the hassle of maintaining the endpoint agents.

Simple Network Management Protocol Traps

Simple Network Management Protocol (SNMP) is a UDP service that operates on ports 161 and 162, and it is used for network management. SNMP allows agents to gather such information as network statistics and report back to their management stations. Most large corporations have implemented some type of SNMP management. Some of the security problems that plague SNMP are caused by the fact that v1 and v2 community strings can be passed as clear text and that the default community strings (public/private) are well known. SNMP version 3 is the most current; it offers encryption for more robust security. SNMPv3 uses the same ports as v1 and v2.

SNMP messages are categorized into five basic types: TRAP, GET, GET-NEXT, GET-RESPONSE, and SET. The SNMP manager and SNMP agent use these messages to communicate with each other. *SNMP traps* are very popular mechanisms to manage and monitor activity. They are used to alert messages from an enabled device (agent) to a collector (manager). For example, an SNMP trap might instantly report an event like an overheating server, which would help with reliability and possible data loss. Properly configured, it can help identify latency and congestion.

NetFlow

Before you take the CASP+ exam, you should be familiar with the tool Wireshark, an example of a network sniffer and analysis tool. The topic of this section is not network sniffers; however, if you were to use a network sniffer to look at the traffic on your local network, you might be surprised by what you would see. That is because most of the network data that is flowing or traversing a typical network is very easy to inspect. This in turn is because most of the protocols, such as FTP, HTTP, SMTP, NTP, Telnet, and others, are sending data across the network via clear text. This simply means that the traffic is not encrypted and is easy to view. The early designers of TCP/IP and what has become the modern Internet were not concerned about encryption; they were simply trying to get everything to work. This is a concern for the security professional because attackers can easily intercept and view this network traffic. The concept of protection of data and secure protocols such as SSH and SSL/TLS came much later.

Even when data is protected with technologies such as SSL/TLS and IPsec, an intruder may still be able to break your network. One way to detect current threats and multiple sources of internal and external information is to analyze network data flow. This is known as network flow analysis. The concept involves using existing network infrastructure. Flow analysis provides a different perspective on traffic movement in networks. It allows you to look at how often an event occurred in a given time period. As an example, how often was traffic containing encrypted zip files leaving your network between midnight and 2 a.m. headed to Russia on weekends? With flow analysis tools, security professionals can view this type of user activity in near real time.

Distilling the massive amount of data that flows through modern networks requires tools that allow for the aggregation and correlation of data. Cisco Systems was one of the first to market this technology with the development of NetFlow. Initially, the captured network flow data answered only the most basic questions. Today, *NetFlow* and similar tools help identify data exfiltration (as mentioned), possible misconfigured devices, systems misbehaving at odd times and, of course, unexpected or unaccountable network traffic. NetFlow is still popular but arguably designed for Cisco environments. Alternatively, IPFIX is an Internet Engineering Task Force (IETF) standard-based technology for other layer 3 network devices to collect and analyze network flows.

Data Loss Prevention

Developing a secure network infrastructure requires building management controls for growth. Companies will grow and change over time. Acquisitions, buyouts, adoption of new technologies, and the retirement of obsolete technologies all mean the infrastructure will change. *Data loss prevention (DLP)* requires the analysis of egress network traffic for anomalies and the use of better outbound firewall controls that perform deep packet inspection. Deep packet inspection normally occurs by a device at a network boundary, for example by a web application firewall at the trusted network's perimeter. To select where such a device should be placed in any organization, it's important to have a data flow diagram, depicting where and how data flows throughout the network.

Companies must have the ability to integrate storage devices such as storage area networks (SANs) as needed. A periodic review of the security and privacy considerations of storage integration needs is required to keep track of storage requirements, as companies have a never-ending need for increased data storage and data backups.

Antivirus

Antivirus companies have developed much more effective ways of detecting viruses. Yet the race continues as virus writers have fought back by developing viruses that are harder to detect. Antivirus programs typically use one of several techniques to identify and eradicate viruses. These methods include the following:

Signature-Based   This technique uses a signature file to identify viruses and other malware. It requires frequent updates.

Heuristic-Based   This detection technique looks for deviation from the normal behavior of an application or service. This method is useful against unknown and polymorphic viruses and uses AI to look for patterns of malicious code.

The best defense against a virus attack is having up-to-date antivirus software installed and running. The software should be on all workstations as well as the server.

Years ago, antivirus may have been considered an optional protection mechanism, but that is no longer true. Antivirus software is the best defense against basic types of malware. Most detection software contains a library of signatures used to detect viruses. Viruses can use different techniques to infect and replicate. The following techniques are common:

Boot Record Infectors   Reside in the boot sector of the computer

Macro Viruses   Target Microsoft Office programs such as Word documents and Excel spreadsheets

Program Infectors   Target executable programs

Multipartite Infectors   Target both boot records and programs

EXERCISE 8.3

Testing Your Antivirus Program

This exercise shows you how to test the basic operation of antivirus software and verify its functionality.

1. Create a text file with the following contents:

   `X50!P%@AP[4\PZX54(P^)7CC)7$EICAR-STANDARD-ANTIVIRUS-TEST-FILE!$H+H*`

2. Rename the text file **malware.exe.**

3. Run antivirus against the file and see if it is detected.

The file should be detected, if not immediately quarantined and removed. It's an example of a European Institute for Computer Anti-Virus Research (EICAR) test. This file has the signature identified as virus code, and it is actually harmless. This particular sequence was developed as a means of testing the functionality of antivirus software. What are your results?

Once your computer is infected, the computer virus can do any number of things. Some are known as fast infectors. Fast infection viruses infect any file that they are capable of infecting. Other viruses use sparse infection techniques. Sparse infection means that the virus takes its time in infecting other files or spreading its damage. This technique is used to try to avoid detection. Still other types of malware can live exclusively in files and load themselves into RAM. These viruses are known as RAM-resident viruses. One final technique used by malware creators is to design the virus to be polymorphic. Polymorphic viruses can change their signature every time they replicate and infect a new file. This technique makes it much harder for the antivirus program to detect the virus.

 One approach to dealing with malware is to configure the network into security zones so that there are layers of protection. This approach can start at the edge of the network, extending into the screened subnet and then into the internetwork by using VLANs. This separates traffic and provides multiple layers of defense.

Preventing viruses and worms begins with end-user awareness. Users should be trained to practice care when opening attachments or running unknown programs. User awareness is a good first step, but antivirus software is essential. There are a number of antivirus products on the market, among them the following programs:

- Bitdefender
- Trend Micro
- Norton Antivirus
- McAfee Antivirus

Don't think you can afford antivirus? Many free and low-cost options are available today. Even the free solutions are much better than having no antivirus at all. Antivirus should be seen as a required first level of defense, not only on servers and PCs but mobile devices as well.

Some well-known examples of malware include the following:

- **WannaCry:** Massive ransomware attack of 2017, copied in several subsequent attacks

- **Petya:** Family of various ransomware types spread through phishing emails

- **CryptoLocker:** Malware/Trojan horse/ransomware that gained access to and encrypted files on more than 200,000 Windows-based systems

- **Mirai:** The first major malware to spread through Internet of Things devices

- **Melissa:** First widespread macro virus

- **ILoveYou:** First widespread mass-mailing worm, seducing people to click due to its name

- **Code red:** Well-known worm that targeted Windows servers running IIS

- **Nimda:** An old one, but still one of the worst worms to infect several different mechanisms

- **Zeus:** Ransomware

- **Conficker:** Widespread worm that could propagate via email, thumb drives, and network attachments

Segmentation

Segmentation is used to place systems with different functions or data security levels in different zones or segments of a network. Segmentation is also used in virtual and cloud environments. In principle, segmentation is the process of using security, network, or physical machine boundaries to build separation between environments, systems, networks, and other components.

Incident responders may choose to use segmentation techniques as part of a response process to move groups of systems or services so that they can focus on specific areas. You might choose to segment infected systems away from the rest of your network or to move crucial systems to a more protected segment to help protect them during an active incident.

Microsegmentation

Microsegmentation is a method that is used in network security that allows a datacenter to be cut up into small and distinct security segments. After the segmentation, a security architect can define security controls and deliver services for each unique segment. This allows for extremely flexible security policies and application-level security controls, increasing resistance to a cyberattack.

Local Area Network/Virtual Local Area Network

A *local area network (LAN)* is a computer network that connects computers within a local area such as a home, school, or office. A *virtual LAN (VLAN)* is used to segment network traffic. VLANs offer many benefits to an organization because they allow the segmentation of network users and resources that are connected administratively to defined ports on a switch. VLANs reduce network congestion and increase bandwidth. VLANs result in smaller broadcast domains. VLANs can also be used to separate portions of the network that have lower levels of security. This defense-in-depth technique can use specific VLANs to include additional protection against sniffing, password attacks, and hijacking attempts. Although VLAN separation can be defeated, this will add a layer of defense that will keep out most casual attackers.

To increase security, network partitioning will segment systems into independent subnets. Network partitioning requires a review of potential network access points. Once these access points have been defined, a number of different technologies can be used to segment the network. Common and upcoming technologies include the use of packet filters, stateful inspection, application proxy firewalls, web application firewalls, multilayer switching, dispersive routing, and virtual LANs (VLANs)/virtual extensible LANs (VXLANs).

Jump Box

A *jump box*, oftentimes called a jump host or jump server, is a hardened device used to manage assets in different security zones. A jump box is used by administrators logging in as an origin point to then connect, or jump, to another server or untrusted environment. This is a way to keep threat actors from stealing credentials. Jump boxes are slowly evolving into a technology called a *secure admin workstation* (SAW). Neither a jump box nor a SAW should ever be used for a nonadministrative task like surfing the Internet, opening email, or using office applications. It is strictly used by administrators for administrator tasks.

Screened Subnet

A screened host firewall adds a router and screened host. The router is typically configured to see only one host computer on the intranet network. Users on the intranet have to connect to the Internet through this host computer, and external users cannot directly access other computers on the intranet.

A *screened subnet* sets up a type of demilitarized zone (DMZ). A screened subnet is a solution that organizations can implement to offer external-facing resources while keeping the internal network protected. Servers that host websites or provide public services are often placed within the DMZ.

DMZs are typically set up to give external users access to services within the DMZ. Basically, shared services such as an external-facing web server, email, and DNS can be placed within a DMZ; the DMZ provides no other access to services located within the internal network. Of course, what traffic is allowed or denied depends on the rules put into effect on either side of the screened subnet. Screened subnets and DMZs are the basis for most modern network designs.

Organizations implement a screened subnet by configuring a firewall with two sets of rules, segmenting a network between the Internet and two firewalls. This allows the organization to offer services to the public by letting Internet traffic go through a firewall less restrictive than the firewall protecting the internal network. A screened subnet is the middle segment, which also provides an extra layer of protection by adding a perimeter network that further isolates the internal network from the Internet. The screened subnet option is not an expensive one for an organization when using a triple-homed firewall, or a firewall with three network ports.

Data Zones

Examine security in your network from endpoint to endpoint and consider building security and *data zones* of protection to limit the reach of an attacker. This extends from where traffic enters the network to where users initially connect to the network and its resources. This requires defense in depth and availability controls. One of several approaches can be used to build different zones. These approaches include the following:

Vector-Oriented   This approach focuses on common vectors used to launch an attack. Examples include disabling autorun on USB thumb drives, disabling USB ports, and removing CD/DVD burners.

Information-Centric   This approach focuses on layering controls on top of the data. Examples include information controls, application controls, host controls, and network controls.

Protected Enclaves   This approach specifies that some areas are of greater importance than others. Controls may include VPNs, strategic placement of firewalls, deployment of VLANs, and restricted access to critical segments of the network.

When considering endpoint security and data zones, who is the bigger threat: insiders or outsiders? Although the numbers vary depending on what report you consult, a large number of attacks are launched by insiders. A trusted insider who decides to act maliciously may bypass controls to access, view, alter, destroy, or remove data in ways that the employer disallows.

Outsiders may seek to access, view, alter, destroy, or remove data or information. Incidentally, you must consider the occasional external breach, such as malware, which provides an outsider with access to the inside network. Currently, there are reports of conventional attacks having high rates of success. This includes simple attack mechanisms such as various types of malware, spear phishing, other social engineering attacks, and so on. Once inside, the sophistication level of these attacks increases dramatically as attackers employ advanced privilege escalation- and configuration-specific exploits in order to provide future access, exfiltrate data, and evade security mechanisms. The configuration of a data zone will help regulation of inbound and outbound traffic through the policies created.

Staging Environments

A *staging environment* is another layer of defense in depth where an enterprise can model their production environment in order to test upgraded, patched, or new software to ensure that when the new code or software is deployed it doesn't break existing infrastructure or create new vulnerabilities. When an organization has a staging environment, it needs to match the existing environment as closely as possible so that analysis is accurate.

A best practice in a staging environment is to allow the software to run for a set period of time. In the past, it has been up to seven days before deployment in a live environment. However, the SolarWinds breach of 2021 taught the cyber community just how crafty an attacker could be. They are aware of our best practices, and the malware that was used was set up to execute after 14 days in order to bypass a staging environment. As mentioned, it is another layer in defense in depth, and bad actors know how it is used.

Guest Environments

Any large organization will occasionally have scenarios where there are visitors to the organization who need access to a guest sharing environment. These individuals are not employees of the organization and could be bringing unmanaged devices with them. For obvious security reasons, these assets should not be joined to a protected domain. For that reason alone, anyone who is coming to an organization to take a class or visit the campus should sign a terms of use agreement and have web access only for those unmanaged devices. If they are allowed to work on sensitive or classified materials, the following should be put in place:

- Configure a timeout policy so authentication happens daily.

- Create an automatically assigned classification type for any sensitive materials guests are touching.

- Set up multifactor authentication (MFA) for guests.

- Conduct reviews to validate permissions to corporate sites and information.

VPC/Virtual Network

A *virtual private cloud (VPC)* is an on-demand highly secured cloud environment hosted inside a public cloud. Many VPC customers will use this type of setting for testing code, storing information, or hosting a website. Many cloud providers offer a VPC type of ecosystem and require a more secure connection.

A *virtual network (VNET)* is exactly what it sounds like. A VNET is where all devices, virtual machines, and datacenters are created and maintained with software. Most cloud providers offering VNET capabilities give customers a lot of control over their instances with IP addressing, subnets, routing tables, and firewall rules. This allows for scalability and efficiency.

Availability Zone

Another element of defense in depth is the creation of availability zones. The purpose of an *availability zone* is to have highly available independent locations within regions for failover and redundancy. For major cloud providers, a single zone has multiple physical datacenters.

Policies/Security Groups

Policies are high-level documents, developed by management, to transmit the overall strategy and philosophy of management to all employees. Senior management and process owners are responsible for the organization. Policies are a template in the sense that they apply guidance to the wishes of management. Policies detail, define, and specify what is expected from employees and how management intends to meet the needs of customers, employees, and stakeholders.

There are two basic ways in which policies can be developed. In some organizations, policy development starts at the top of the organization. This approach, known as top-down policy development, means that policies are pushed down from senior management to the lower layers of the company. The big advantage of top-down policy development is that it ensures that policy is aligned with the strategy and vision of senior management. A downside of such a process is that it requires a substantial amount of time to implement and may not fully address the operational concerns of average employees. An alternative approach would be to develop policy from the bottom up. The bottom-up approach to policy development addresses the concerns of average employees. The process starts with their input and concerns and builds on known risks that employees and managers of organizational groups have identified. The big downside is that the process may not always map well to senior management's strategy.

For modern cloud infrastructures, you can use tools such as AWS Firewall Manager security group policies to manage Amazon Virtual Private Cloud security groups for your organization in AWS Organizations. You can apply centrally controlled security group policies to your entire organization or to a select subset of your accounts and resources. You can monitor and manage the security group policies that are in use in your organization, with auditing and usage security group policies.

You should be able to identify specific types of policies before attempting the CASP+ exam. Some basic policy types include the following:

Regulatory A regulatory policy makes certain that the organization's standards are in accordance with local, state, and federal laws. Industries that make frequent use of these documents include healthcare, public utilities, refining, education, and federal agencies.

Informative An informative policy is not for enforcement; it is created to teach or help employees and others understand specific rules. The goal of informative policies is to inform employees or customers. An example of an informative policy for a retail store is that it has a 90-day cash return policy on items bought at the store if you keep your receipt.

Advisory   An advisory policy is designed to ensure that all employees know the consequences of certain behavior and actions. An example of an advisory policy is an acceptable use policy (AUP). This policy may advise how the Internet can be used by employees and may disallow employees from visiting social networking or pornographic websites. The policy might state that employees found to be in violation of the policy could face disciplinary action, up to and including dismissal.

Does your company have clearly defined policies? Policies should be reviewed with employees at least annually by either an electronic or a paper-based manual review process so that employees are kept aware of what is and what is not allowed and what proper procedures are.

One specific type of policy in which a CASP+ should be interested is a company's security policy. The security policy is the document that dictates management's commitment to the use, operation, and security of information systems. You may think of this policy as only addressing logical security, but most security policies also look at physical controls. Physical security is an essential part of building a secure environment and a holistic security plan. The security policy specifies the role that security plays within a company. The security policy should be driven by business objectives. It must also meet all applicable laws and regulations. For example, you may want to monitor employees, but that doesn't mean placing CCTV in bathrooms or dressing rooms.

The security policy should be used as a basis to integrate security into all business functions and must be balanced in the sense that all organizations are looking for ways to implement adequate security without hindering productivity or violating laws. It's also important not to create an adversarial relationship with employees. Cost is an issue in that you cannot spend more on a security control than the value of the asset. Your job as a security professional is to play a key role in the implementation of security policies based on organizational requirements.

If you find yourself being asked to develop policies and need a framework with which to begin, you may want to visit the SANS Policy project (www.sans.org/security-resources/policies). This resource has many commonly used policy templates to help you get started.

In your role as a security professional, look closely at the security policies that apply to you and your employees. As a CASP+, you should be able to compare and contrast security, privacy policies, and procedures based on organizational requirements. If you are tasked with reviewing security policies, consider how well policy maps to activity. Also, have you addressed all new technology?

A CASP+ must be able to see the need for policy development and updates in light of new business, technology, risks, and environmental changes. Trends such as bring your own technology (BYOT) and cloud computing will develop into emerging risks that then require the CASP+ to create new or revised policies.

As business goals and strategies change, IT security policies will need to adapt to meet those changes. But factors external to the business, such as technological innovation and changing social expectations, will also force that adaptation of policies. For example, as smartphones became inexpensive and commonplace, this emerging risk called for new policies to address it. Finally, it's important to remember that policies don't last forever. For instance, a policy from 1992 that addressed the use of and restrictions on modems would need to be revisited. Older technologies, such as modems, become obsolete as new technologies become affordable; therefore, business processes have to change. It's sometimes easy to see that low-level procedures need to be updated, but this kind of change applies to high-level policies as well. Policies are just one level of procedural control. Next, our discussion will focus on procedures.

Procedures are documents that fall under policies. Consider procedures as more detailed documents that are built from the parent policy. Procedures provide step-by-step instructions. For example, your company may migrate from a Cisco to a Check Point firewall. In this situation, the policy would not change in that the policy dictates what type of traffic can enter or exit the network. What would change, however, is the procedure, because the setup and configuration of a Cisco device and a Check Point device are different.

Procedures are detailed documents; they are tied to specific technologies and devices. Procedure documents require more frequent changes than policy documents to stay relevant to business processes and procedures. Procedures change when equipment changes, when software changes, when policy changes, and even when the sales season changes. Any change will require a review of the procedure. This review process should be built into change management.

We have seen procedures that look great on paper but that cannot be carried out in real life. When policies are developed, they must be mapped back to real-life activities and validated. Although problems may be caught during an audit, that's after the fact and may mean that poor practices have been ongoing for some time. Misalignment can mean that the procedure doesn't map or is outdated, or that employees have not had the proper training on the procedure you asked to see in operation.

Regions

Geographic segmentation occurs in marketing because not all products are sold everywhere. Regional preferences are considered. A global cybersecurity organization may choose to segment networks and applications based on where the workforce resides. This helps create layers of defense in depth as well as improve performance and make for less congestion. It can also reduce compliance requirements related to auditing.

Access Control Lists and Network Access Control

Firewalls can be hardware, software, or a combination of both. They are usually located at the demarcation line between trusted and untrusted network elements. Firewalls play a critical role in the separation of important assets. Firewall rules determine what type of traffic is inspected, what is allowed to pass, and what is blocked. The most basic way to configure firewall rules to create network access control (NAC) is by means of an access control list (ACL). A network access control list is a layer of security that controls traffic coming in or out of specific subnets.

There are two types of ACLs, filesystem and networking. Filesystem ACLs work as a filter with rules allowing or denying access to directories or files. This ACL gives the operating system directions about what level of privilege the user has. A networking ACL provides information to switches and routers through rules about who is allowed to interface with the network and what devices can do once inside the network. When NAC is used but an agent is not installed on a device, it is referred to as an agentless configuration. When using agentless NAC, the policy enforcement component is integrated into an authentication system like Microsoft Active Directory. The enforcement of policies is performed when the device logs on or off the network.

An ACL is used for packet filtering and for selecting the types of traffic to be analyzed, forwarded, or influenced in some way by the firewall or device. ACLs are a basic example of data flow enforcement. Simple firewalls, and more specifically ACL configuration, may block traffic based on the source and destination addresses. However, more advanced configurations may deny traffic based on interface, port, protocol, thresholds, and various other criteria. Before implementing ACLs, be sure to perform secure configuration and baselining of networking and security components. Rules placed in an ACL can be used for more than just allowing or blocking traffic. For example, rules may also log activity for later inspection or to record an alarm. Table 8.1 shows the basic rule set.

TABLE 8.1   Basic rule set

Rule number	Action	Protocol	Port	Direction	Comment
Rule 20	Allow	DNS	53 UDP	Outbound	None
Rule 50	Allow	HTTP, HTTPS	80, 443	Outbound	None
Rule 100	Allow	SMTP	25	Inbound	To mail server
Rule 101	Allow	SMTP	25	Outbound	From mail server
Rule 255	Deny	ALL	—	Bidirectional	None

ACLs work from the top down, and by default there is an implicit deny all clause at the end of every ACL. Anything that is not explicitly permitted is denied. It is important to note that this implicit deny is there even if it is not present when you're viewing the ACL.

For the CASP+ exam, you will need to have a basic understanding of ACLs and their format. The command syntax format of a standard ACL in a Cisco IOS environment is as follows:

```
access-list access-list-number {permit|deny}
{host|source source-wildcard|any}
```

There are also extended ACLs. These rules have the ability to look more closely at the traffic and inspect for more items, such as the following:

- Protocol
- Port numbers
- Differentiated Services Code Point (DSCP) value
- Precedence value
- State of the synchronize sequence number (SYN) bit

The command syntax formats of extended IP, ICMP, TCP, and UDP ACLs are shown here:

IP Traffic

```
access-list access-list-number
 [dynamic dynamic-name [timeout minutes]]
 {deny|permit} protocol source source-wildcard
 destination destination-wildcard [precedence precedence]
 [tos tos] [log|log-input] [time-range time-range-name]
```

ICMP Traffic

```
access-list access-list-number
 [dynamic dynamic-name [timeout minutes]]
 { deny|permit } icmp source source-wildcard
 destination destination-wildcard
 [icmp-type [icmp-code] |icmp-message]
 [precedence precedence] [tos tos] [log|log-input]
 [time-range time-range-name]
```

TCP Traffic

```
access-list access-list-number
 [dynamic dynamic-name [timeout minutes]]
 { deny|permit } tcp source source-wildcard [operator [port]]
 destination destination-wildcard [operator [port]]
```

```
[established] [precedence precedence] [tos tos]
[log|log-input] [time-range time-range-name]
```

UDP Traffic

```
access-list access-list-number
 [dynamic dynamic-name [timeout minutes]]
 { deny|permit } udp source source-wildcard [operator [port]]
 destination destination-wildcard [operator [port]]
 [precedence precedence] [tos tos] [log|log-input]
 [time-range time-range-name]
```

If it has been a while since you have configured or analyzed ACLs, you may want to consider downloading one of the many router simulators that are available. These are great practice tools, and they may be helpful if you're asked an ACL question on the exam. Although the examples provided here are very straightforward, those on the exam may not be. Incidentally, access control is definitely a topic that every CASP+ should know well.

EXERCISE 8.4

Reviewing and Assessing ACLs

You have been asked to examine an ACL that was developed to allow permissible traffic that is part of a valid session to communicate with a web server. Upon reviewing the ACL, can you spot any problems with the newly created extended IP access list 101?

```
permit tcp host 4.2.2.2 eq telnet host 192.168.123.1 eq 11006
deny tcp any host WebServer eq http
deny ip any any
```

Can you identify any problems with this configuration? Notice that the second line should be an allow and not a deny. As written, the deny statement would block HTTP traffic and not allow it.

Here is another ACL whose functionality you've been asked to comment on:

```
interface ethernet0
deny ip any any
deny tcp 10.10.10.128 0.0.0.63 any eq smtp
deny tcp any eq 23 int ethernet 0
permit tcp any any
access-group 110 out
```

EXERCISE 8.4 *(continued)*

Can you see any issues with this ACL? The primary problem here is that the deny `ip any` any line will prevent the additional lines below it from processing, so the `permit tcp` any any line is irrelevant in this case. Remove the initial deny statement and the ACL will function as expected. Once the ACL reaches a matching rule, such as deny `all IP`, the two entries below it will not be acted upon.

Peer-to-Peer

As far as segmentation goes, *peer-to-peer (P2P)* networks are used for equality. In a P2P, all computers and devices share and exchange workloads, and there is no privilege and no administrator. P2P networks are perfect for file sharing because devices connected can receive and send files at the same time. A P2P network is hard to bring down and very scalable. Large files are often shared on this type of architecture; however, P2P can also be used for illegitimate activities such as piracy of copyrighted materials, which is punishable by law.

Air Gap

Air gap refers to systems that are not connected in any way to the Internet. An air-gapped system has no risk of being compromised from the outside but can still be vulnerable to an attack from the inside.

The 2010 Stuxnet attack is generally recognized as the first implementation of a worm as a cyber weapon. The worm was aimed at the Iranian nuclear program and copied itself to thumb drives to bypass air-gapped computers (physically separated systems without a network connection). Stuxnet took advantage of a number of techniques advanced for its time, including using a trusted digital certificate, searching for specific industrial control systems (ICSs) that were known to be used by the Iranian nuclear program, and specific programming to attack and damage centrifuges while providing false monitoring data to controllers to ensure that the damage would not be noticed until it was too late. For more information about Stuxnet, see this *Wired* article:

www.wired.com/2014/11/countdown-to-zero-day-stuxnet

Deperimeterization/Zero Trust

"Trust but verify" is an old Russian proverb. The phrase became popular during the late 1980s when U.S. President Ronald Reagan was negotiating nuclear disarmament with the Soviet Union's General Secretary, Mikhail Gorbachev. It fits the mindset of a cybersecurity professional. When an outcome matters more than a relationship, you have to trust but verify. In IT, safety and security are of utmost importance with outcome-critical parameters. If a relationship matters more than an outcome, then this philosophy doesn't fit as well.

The *zero trust* security model, also known as *deperimeterization* or *perimeter-less security*, describes a philosophy of design and implementation. This means never trust by default.

Key principles in zero trust include strong access and authorization policies, user and machine authentication, and a single source of truth for user identity.

Cloud

Cloud computing offers users the ability to increase capacity or add services as needed without investing in new datacenters, training new personnel, or maybe even licensing new software. This on-demand, or *elastic*, service can be added, upgraded, and provided at any time. With cloud computing, an organization is being forced to place their trust in the cloud provider. The cloud provider must develop sufficient controls to provide the same or a greater level of security than the organization would have if the cloud were not used. Defense in depth is built on the concept that every security control is vulnerable. Cloud computing places much of the control in someone else's hands. One big area that is handed over to the cloud provider is access. Authentication and authorization are real concerns. Because the information or service now resides in the cloud, there is a much greater opportunity for access by outsiders. Insiders might pose an additional risk.

Insiders, or those with access, have the means and opportunity to launch an attack and lack only a motive. Anyone considering using the cloud needs to look at who is managing their data and what types of controls are applied to individuals who may have logical or physical access. Chapter 9, "Secure Cloud and Virtualization," is dedicated to everything cloud.

Remote Work

The huge exodus from the corporate office to the home office precipitated by the recent pandemic created massive cyber-related security challenges. The biggest challenge is the mindset of the end user. Many remote workers in a recent poll said they would ignore or circumvent corporate security policies if they got in the way of work, and that includes connecting to a coffee shop Wi-Fi without a VPN. Leaders still get complaints about restrictive policies, and many work-from-home employees feel that these measures waste their time.

Most organizations have had to rework their security policies to adapt to the increased remote work while IT teams still deal with ransomware, vulnerabilities, and data exfiltration. The only way past this is to foster a more cohesive and collaborative security culture in the organization and balance ease-of-use security measures with productive operations.

Mobile

Enterprise security is already a challenge, but with the advent of mobile devices it has gotten a whole lot harder. It is enough of a challenge to secure the environment within the four walls of the corporate building. Now wireless connectivity has pushed the network boundary well past the four walls. With mobile devices, employees expect simple and easy connectivity to both the enterprise and the world around them. Thankfully, there are several technologies and techniques available to integrate security controls to support mobile and small form factor devices.

Application, Content, and Data Management   To ensure that the mobile device's integrity stays within acceptable limits, the IT team will want to maintain oversight and management of the applications, content, and data on the device.

Application Wrapping   If enterprise users rely on a third-party application but the mobile device management team desires more control or wants to implement policy on that application, then one option is to use a process called *application wrapping*. Application wrapping involves adding a management layer around an app without making any changes to the app itself.

Remote Assistance Access   Maybe those managing the mobile devices need to assist users while they're away or can't let go of their phones. The team could use an application such as virtual network computing (VNC), available on several platforms, to access the user's mobile device remotely. Another option is screen mirroring or duplicating your phone's screen display on an authorized desktop, where an administrator can take control or transfer files as needed.

Configuration Profiles and Payloads   How can an IT department manage to keep track of every user's mobile device configuration? Now increase that challenge due to the variety of available mobile devices. What makes it possible for IT departments to manage this situation is the use of configuration profiles. By establishing and remotely installing a group of configuration settings and implementing standard configuration profiles, managing a large number of mobile devices is effectively like managing a single device.

A subset of configuration settings within a configuration profile is called a *payload*. You might have a "mail" payload that configures the users' devices for all settings related to email, such as server, port, and address. Security restrictions can also be a part of the configuration profile payload.

Application Permissions   For each application, your mobile operating system will allow the user effectively to control what that application can do, access, or execute on the user's behalf. Application permissions are accessible within the configuration settings of the mobile OS. Typical objects that an application may seek access to include the camera, microphone, phone application, and address book, among others. Obviously, access to any of these objects should be granted only if the application is deemed trusted and the decision to bypass an added user action is warranted.

VPN   How mobile users connect to the enterprise environment impacts the risk that they place on the perimeter and network. If an organization allows users to connect over Wi-Fi at a coffee shop, this is unacceptable, and it is all but guaranteed to cause the CASP+ headaches in the near future. Instead, establishing and using a virtual private network (VPN) is a far safer way for users to connect to the internal, trusted network. The caveat regarding mobile devices is how much faster they consume resources. The trick is to find a VPN solution with some intelligence to it and train it (and users) to establish a VPN only when it is truly needed.

Over-the-Air Updates   In addition to managing configuration settings remotely, the team responsible for installing updates can do this remotely. This delivery, known as *over-the-air (OTA) updates*, avoids waiting for a user to come in or dock their device for the update. Software or the device's firmware can be updated in this way.

Remote Wiping   Another process that a CASP+ might need to do without relying on the user being "in the building" is remotely wiping the device. For example, as part of the process of a termination, also known as *offboarding*, an employee's device could be remotely wiped, mitigating the risk of unauthorized device usage or abuse.

In the context of mobile devices, here are some concerns of which the CASP+ should be aware:

SCEP   The *Simple Certificate Enrollment Protocol (SCEP)* is a popular method of certificate enrollment, which is the process of a user or device requesting and receiving a digital certificate. SCEP is highly scalable and widely implemented. However, its original designers went on hiatus for several years, and SCEP received little attention to address concerns about its cryptographic strength. According to CERT vulnerability note VU#971035, the authentication methods for SCEP to validate certificate requests are ill suited for any environment other than a closed one. So, any mobility device management (MDM) involving BYOD opens itself up to risks of unauthorized certificate requests.

Unsigned Apps/System Apps   The concept of code signing is designed to ensure that an application developed by a third party has not been altered or corrupted since it was signed as valid. Of course, this matters when the original developer is assumed to be a trusted source. However, what about apps that are not signed? If a user is able to download and install unsigned applications and unsigned system apps, the mobile device is no longer assured to be trustworthy.

Sideloading   Normally, when loading or installing an application, a user would use the device's application-distribution channel. For most devices, this would mean using Google Play or the Apple App Store. But if a user seeks an alternate, back-channel method to load an application that may not be accessible otherwise, that method is called sideloading. Naturally, the security concern for a CASP+ is why such an application requires sideloading and is not available through the normally vetted channel. *Sideloading*, or loading applications outside a controlled channel, means that the established process of inspecting an application for malicious code is likely being bypassed.

Context-Aware Management   Security restrictions on mobile devices can be placed in keeping with a user's behavior or their local location. Just as straightforward as the position of a mobile device, time-based restrictions can be placed on a user's access and/or authorization. If the user is attempting to access a sensitive share directory after restricted hours, employing time-based restrictions means limiting access until the permissible time period.

Outsourcing and Contracting

Organizations should go through a source strategy to determine what tasks should be completed by employees, contractors, or third parties. Outsourcing is one common approach. *Outsourcing* can be defined as an arrangement in which one company provides services for another company that may or may not have been provided in house. Outsourcing has become a much bigger issue in the emerging global economy, and it is something security professionals need to review closely. There will always be concerns when ensuring that third-party providers have the requisite levels of information security.

Outsourcing has become much more common in the IT field throughout the course of the last decade or so. In some cases, the entire information management function of a company is outsourced, including planning and business analysis as well as the installation, management, and servicing of the network and workstations. The following services are commonly outsourced:

- Application/web hosting
- Check processing
- Computer help desk
- Credit card processing
- Data entry
- Payroll and check processing

Crucial to the outsourcing decision is determining whether a task is part of the organization's core competency or proficiency that defines the organization. Security should play a large role in making the decision to outsource because some tasks take on a much greater risk if performed by someone outside the organization.

During any technical deployment, IT security professionals should have a chance to review outsourcing, insourcing, managed services, and security controls and practices of a partnered company. If irregularities are found, they should be reported to management so that expenses and concerns can be properly identified. Before combining or separating systems, a CASP+ should ask these basic questions:

- Who has access to resources?
- What types of access will be provided?
- How will users request access?
- Who will grant users access?
- What type of access logs will be used, what will be recorded, and when will it be reviewed?
- What procedures will be taken for inappropriate use of resources?
- How will security incidents be reported and recorded, and who will handle them?
- Who will be responsible for investigating suspicious activity?

The CASP+ should also be concerned with developing a course of action that is based on informed business decisions with the goal to provide for long-term security. Here are some of the technical deployment models with which a CASP+ should be familiar:

Outsourcing   Outsourcing can be defined as obtaining a resource or item from an outside provider. As an example, consider Dell. Dell might be based in Round Rock, Texas, yet its distribution hub is in Memphis, Tennessee. Further, Dell assembles PCs in Malaysia and has customer support in India. Many parts come from the far corners of the globe.

Insourcing   Insourcing can be defined as using a company's own personnel to build an item or resource or to perform an activity.

Managed Services   Some organizations use managed services. One common approach is to use managed cloud services. Managed cloud hosting delivers services over long periods of time, such as months or even years. The secure use of cloud computing is contingent upon your organization reviewing the cloud provider's policies. In such situations you may be purchasing services in time slices or as a service on a virtual server. This means that data aggregation and data isolation can occur.

The security concern with data aggregation is that your data may be combined with others or may even be reused. For example, some nonprofit donor databases offer their databases for free yet combine your donor database with others and resell it. Data isolation should be used to address how your data is stored. Is your data stored on an isolated hard drive, or does it share virtual space with many other companies?

Finally, it is important to discuss the issues of data ownership and data sovereignty with the managed service provider. Make sure that your data remains solely yours while in the custody of the managed service provider. As the volume of data grows, also ensure that the managed service provider maintains the same level of assurance.

Resource provisioning and deprovisioning should be examined before a technical deployment in order to understand how resources are handled. For example, is the hard drive holding your data destroyed, or is it simply reused for another client? How about users? Are their records destroyed and accounts suspended after they are terminated?

In addition to users, resource provisioning and deprovisioning can also include the following:

- Servers
- Virtual devices
- Applications
- Data remnants

When outsourcing is to occur, issues related to IT will be an area of real concern. As in the case of the outsourced MRI diagnosis, sensitive and personal data is often involved with outsourced services. This creates regulatory concerns, most commonly involving the

Health Insurance Portability and Accountability Act (HIPAA) or the Sarbanes-Oxley (SOX) Act. Many IT departments have mission statements in which they publicly identify the level of service they agree to provide to their customers. This may be uptime for network services, availability of email, response to help-desk calls, or even server uptime. When you are sharing resources with an outsourced partner, you may not have a good idea of their security practices and techniques. Outsourcing partners face the same risks, threats, and vulnerabilities as the client; the only difference is they might not be as apparent. One approach that companies typically use when dealing with outsourcing, insourcing, managed services, or partnerships is the use of service level agreements (SLAs).

The SLA is a contract that describes the minimum performance criteria a provider promises to meet while delivering a service. The SLA will also define remedial action and any penalties that will take effect if the performance or service falls below the promised standard. You may also consider an operating level agreement (OLA), which is formed between operations and application groups. These are just a few of the items about which a CASP+ should be knowledgeable; however, the CASP+ is required to know only the basics. During these situations, legal and HR will play a big role and should be consulted regarding laws related to IT security.

SLAs define performance targets for hardware and software. There are many types of SLAs, among them the following:

Help Desk and Caller Services   The help desk is a commonly outsourced service. One way an outsourcing partner may measure the service being provided is by tracking the abandon rate (AR). The AR is simply the number of callers who hang up while waiting for a service representative to answer. Most of us have experienced this when we hear something like, "Your call is extremely important to us; your hold time will be 1 hour and 46 minutes."

Another help-desk measurement is the first call resolution (FCR). FCR is the number of positive solutions that are made on the first call to the help desk before making any additional calls or requiring the user to call back to seek additional help.

Finally, there is the time-to-service factor (TSF). The TSF is the percentage of help desk or response calls answered within a given time. So, if Kenneth calls in at 8 a.m., is the problem fixed by 9:30 a.m.?

Uptime and Availability Agreements   Another common SLA measurement is an uptime agreement (UA). UAs specify a required amount of uptime for a given service. As an example, a web hosting provider may guarantee 99.999 percent uptime. UAs are commonly found in the area of network services, datacenters, and cloud computing.

Wireless/Radio Frequency Networks

The Institute of Electrical and Electronics Engineers Standards Association (IEEE) is an organization that develops standards for wireless communication gathering information from subject-matter experts (SMEs). IEEE is not an institution formed by a specific government but is a community of recognized leaders who follow the principle of "one country, one vote."

The IEEE 802.11 is a set of specifications on implementing wireless over several frequencies. As technology has evolved, so has the need for more revisions. If you were to go shopping for wireless equipment, you would see the array of choices you have based on those revisions of 802.11. Most consumer and enterprise wireless devices conform to 802.11a, 802.11b/g/n/ac/ax standards. These standards are better known as Wi-Fi. Bluetooth and wireless personal area networks (WPANs) are specialized wireless technologies.

Information is sent from one component called a transmitter and picked up by another called a receiver. The transmitter sends electrical signals through an antenna to create waves that spread outward. The receiver with another antenna in the path of those waves picks up the signal and amplifies it so it can be processed. A wireless router is simply a router that uses radio waves instead of cables. It contains a low-power radio transmitter and receiver, with a range of about 90 meters or 300 feet, depending on what your walls are made of. The router can send and receive Internet data to any computer in your environment that is also equipped with wireless access. Each computer on the wireless network has to have a transmitter and receiver in it as well.

There are advantages and disadvantages to communicating wirelessly. Networks are pretty easy to set up and rather inexpensive, with several choices of frequencies to communicate over. Disadvantages can include keeping this communication secure, the range of the wireless devices, reliability, and, of course, speed. The transmitter and the receiver need to be on the same frequency, and each 802.11 standard has its own set of pros and cons. The latest Wi-Fi technology is called 802.11ax or Wi-Fi 6/6E. 802.11ax is anywhere from four to ten times faster than existing Wi-Fi with wider channels available, and offers less congestion and improved battery life on mobile devices, since data is transmitted faster.

As with any technology, as it evolves, you will start making decisions on what scenario is best for you and your organization. There may be trade-offs on frequency used, speed, or the range of a device from a Wi-Fi hotspot. A hotspot is merely an area with an accessible network.

When building a typical wireless small office or home office (SOHO) environment, after you identify what technology and design is best for your situation, you configure the settings of your router using a web interface. You can select the name of the network you want to use, known as the service set identifier (SSID). You can choose the channel. By default, most routers use channel 6 or 11. You will also choose security options, such as setting up your own username and password as well as encryption.

As a best practice, when you configure security settings on your router, choose WPA3, the latest and recommended standard. Similar to WPA2, WPA3 includes both a Personal and an Enterprise version. WPA3 maintains equivalent cryptographic strength through the required use of 192-bit AES for the Enterprise version, and optional 192-bit AES for the Personal version. WPA3 helps prevent offline password attacks by using Simultaneous Authentication of Equals (SAE).

Another best practice is configuring MAC filtering on your router. This doesn't use a password to authenticate. It uses the MAC address of the device itself. Each device that connects to a router has its own MAC address. You can specify which MAC addresses are allowed on your network as well as set limitations on how many devices can join your network. If you set up your router to use MAC filtering, one drawback is every time you need to add a device, you have to grant network permission. You sacrifice convenience for better protection. After reading this book, the more advanced user will know how to capture packets, examine the data, and possibly identify the MAC address of a device in the list of permitted devices. MAC filtering with WPA3 encryption is the best way to protect your data.

Merging Networks from Various Organizations

Organizations with different cultures, objectives, security practices and policies, topologies, and tools occasionally need to be blended together to work cohesively. Both sides of the newly integrated network will have their own issues from communication to workflows. Configuration options differ from organization to organization, so knowledge and preparation are incredibly important when integrating two companies' networks.

Peering

Peering on a network is a technique that allows one network to connect directly to another for exchange of information. Benefits of peering include lower cost, greater control, improved performance, and redundancy. There are several types of peering including the following:

- **Public:** Using a single port on an Ethernet switch, this has less capacity than a private peer but can connect many networks.

- **Private:** This connects two networks with layer 3 hardware with a point-to-point cable. Private peering makes up most traffic on the Internet.

- **Partial:** Network traffic is regional.

- **Paid:** One party pays the other to participate in the peering network.

Cloud to On-Premises

Cloud computing does away with the typical network boundary. This type of deperimeterization and the constantly changing network boundary create a huge impact, as historically this demarcation line was at the edge of the physical network, a point at which the firewall is typically found.

The concept of cloud computing represents a shift in thought in that end users need not know the details of a specific technology. The service is fully managed by the provider. Users can consume the service at a rate that is set by their particular needs so on-demand service can be provided at any time.

Data Sensitivity Levels

Data classification is the process of organizing data into *data sensitivity levels* based on information characteristics such as degree of sensitivity, risk, and compliance regulations. To merge various organizations' data, sensitive data must be inventoried and classified.

For CASP+ study, data sensitivity labels/types are most often categorized into public, internal-only, confidential, and restricted/highly confidential. Other level name variations you may encounter include Restricted, Unrestricted, and Consumer Protected.

NIST recommends using three categories based on the impact of data disclosure:

- **Low impact:** Limited adverse effect such as a job posting

- **Moderate impact:** Serious adverse effect such as financial budgets

- **High impact:** Severe adverse effect such as account numbers or PHI

For more information about best data classification practices, NIST has published a guide for mapping levels of data to security categories: `nvlpubs.nist.gov/nistpubs/legacy/sp/nistspecialpublication800-60v1r1.pdf`.

Mergers and Acquisitions

Companies are constantly looking for advantages in business. For some companies, mergers and acquisitions offer a path to increased business opportunities. For example, the merger of Oracle and Cerner was a $28.3 billion ($95.00 per share) merger. These two companies are combining cloud and on-premises datacenters, medical records, distribution, subscriber networks, customer service, and all of the other pieces of their organizations into a single entity. Even though the two companies operate in somewhat similar markets, the amount of work involved with such mergers is staggering.

Businesses that have similar cultures and overlapping target audiences but individually reach those audiences differently may work better as a merged entity. To lean on a business buzzword, the merger creates a synergy that potentially benefits both companies. Take the example when Amazon, the online shopping giant, merged with Whole Foods, the brick-and-mortar chain of organic grocery stores. Between Amazon's reach and delivery and Whole Food's mass appeal to those wanting to buy organic foods, the merger has been an overwhelming success for both parties. While the merger initially stoked fears that grocery prices would rise dramatically, a report one year later noted that actual pricing experienced "downward pressure" and had dropped a few percentage points.

From the standpoint of risk, there are many things that can go wrong. Businesses typically look for synergy, but some businesses just don't fit together. For example, in 2008 Blockbuster moved aggressively to merge with Circuit City. Blockbuster saw the merger as a way to grow, but many outside analysts questioned how two companies with totally different business models, which were both failing, could be combined into one winning business. Because of these questions, the merger never occurred. Within months, Circuit City filed for Chapter 11 protection (bankruptcy), whereas Blockbuster failed and closed outright. Circuit City re-emerged from the ashes some 10 years after the failed merger. In early 2018, Circuit City relaunched online after having been acquired by TigerDirect.

Often, the different businesses cannot coexist as one entity. In other cases, companies enter the merger/acquisition phase without an adequate plan of action. Finally, people don't like change. Once a company's culture is established and people become set in their ways, attitudes are hard to change. Mergers are all about change, and that goes against the grain of what employees expect.

For the security professional, it's common to be asked to quickly establish connectivity with the proposed business partner. Although there is a need for connectivity, security should remain a driving concern. You need to understand the proposed merger partner's security policies and what controls they are enforcing. The last thing that you would want is to allow the ability for an attacker to enter your network through the merging company's network.

Security concerns will always exist when it comes to merging diverse industries. The previous example illustrates just a few of the problems that companies face when they integrate and become one single entity. There will always be security concerns when integrating diverse industries. A CASP+ should also be concerned with items such as the following:

Rules   What is or is not allowed by each individual company. Rules affect all aspects of how a business operates, ranging from the required visibility of an ID badge to how easily groups may share information.

Policies   These are high-level documents that outline the security goals and objectives of the company.

Regulations   Diverse entities may very well be governed by different regulatory entities or regulations such as PCI DSS or HIPAA. Other regulatory factors include export controls, such as use of encryption software. Companies dealing with controlled data types must meet the regulatory-imposed legal requirements, often related to storing, safeguarding, and reporting on that data.

Geography   It is all about location. A company that is located in Paris, France, will be operating on different standards than one that is based in Denver, Colorado.

Demerger/Divestiture   Anytime businesses break apart, you must confront many of the same types of issues. As an example, each organization must now have its own, separate IT security group, and it must implement its own firewalls and other defenses.

Whether the situation involves an acquisition or a company breaks into two or more entities, the leadership must revisit the data and its classification. Data ownership is affected by the change in company ownership. Similarly, a change in company structure will likely affect how data is classified or categorized, so a data reclassification will be required as well.

The CASP+ should understand technical deployment models and design considerations such as outsourcing, insourcing, partnerships, mergers, acquisitions, and demergers. The CASP+ and others responsible for the IT security of an organization should play a role during mergers and acquisitions. Generally, a merger can be described as the combining of two companies of equal size, whereas an acquisition is where a larger company acquires a smaller one. In both situations, it's important that proper security control be maintained throughout the process. This can be done through the application of due care and due diligence.

    Many companies ask employees involved in mergers and acquisitions to sign noncompete agreements and nondisclosure agreements because they may have acquired insider information during the transition.

Somewhat akin to outsourcing in terms of the security risks that they present are partnerships. A partnership can be best defined as a type of business model in which two or more entities share potential profit and risk with each other, whereas with outsourcing, the customer assigns the work to the contractor. Once the project or service has been provided, the customer pays the contractor, and the relationship ends.

Partnerships are different; they are much more like a marriage. With marriage, for example, you might want to execute a prenuptial agreement; likewise, in partnerships, you need to be prepared should things go wrong and the partnership ends. There are a number of potential risks when companies decide to acquire, merge, or form partnerships:

Loss of Competency   Once a new entity begins providing a service, the other may lose the in-house ability to provide the same service. Should the partnership end, the company is forced to deal with the fact that this service can no longer be supported. Even worse, the partner may now become a competitor.

Real World Scenario

Partnerships Don't Always Last

Ancient history: Microsoft and IBM developed a partnership in 1988 to deliver a new operating system known as OS/2 (Operating/System/2). The partnership between these two tech giants was designed to replace the existing DOS operating system with the new OS/2 operating system that could run new software as well as being backward-compatible.

What IBM did not know was that Microsoft was also designing Windows NT on its own, and it would eventually pull away from IBM and abandon the OS/2 platform to move forward with its own operating system. Microsoft introduced Windows NT in July 1993 and went on to become the dominant player in operating systems and office application software. OS/2 was not successful for IBM, and by 2004 IBM had also abandoned the PC market and sold those assets to Lenovo.

Broken Agreements   Partnerships don't always work out. In situations where things go wrong, there are costs associated with switching services back in house.

Service Deterioration   Although the partner may promise great things, can they actually deliver? Over time, do they deliver the same level of service, or does it deteriorate? Metrics must be in place to monitor overall quality. Depending on the task, the level of complexity, or even issues such as a growing customer base, the partner may not be able to deliver the product or service promised.

Poor Cultural Fit   Some partners may be in other regions of the country or another part of the world. Cultural differences can play a big part in the success of a partnership. Once a partnership is formed, it may be discovered that incentives to provide services and products don't align or that top-level management of the two companies differs.

Hidden Costs   Sometimes all of the costs of a partnership are not initially seen. Costs can escalate due to complexity, inexperience, and other problems. Partnerships that are focused on tangible production are typically less vulnerable to these interruptions than those that deal in intangible services.

This doesn't mean that partnerships are all bad. Your company may be in a situation where in-house technical expertise has been lacking or hard to acquire. Maybe you need someone to build a specific web application or code firmware for a new device. Just consider how strategic multinational partnerships are sometimes motivated by protectionist laws in other countries or marketing know-how or expertise in another country or region. In these situations, the business partner may have the expertise and skills to provide this service.

From an IT security perspective, a major risk of such partnerships is knowledge and technology transfer, both intentional/transparent and unintentional/covert. You should always keep in mind what resources are being provided to business partners, whether they are needed, what controls are being used, and what audit controls are in place.

Cross-Domain

Cross domains are integrated hardware and software solutions that make it secure to access data across multiple networks. Cross-domain solutions are extremely helpful when there are different levels of security classifications or domains. A cross-domain policy is the set of rules that grants permission to disparate data.

Federation

Federation allows you to link your digital identity to multiple sites and use those credentials to log into multiple accounts and systems that are controlled by different entities. Federation is a collection of domains that have established trust. The level of trust may vary but typically includes authentication and almost always includes authorization. In early 2022, the United States White House announced the Office of Management and Budget (OMG) released the federal zero-trust strategy in support of "Improving the Nation's Cybersecurity" calling for strict monitoring controls, identification of priorities, and baseline policies for limiting and verifying federation across network services regardless of where they are located. For more information, you can read about zero-trust architecture (ZTA) here: `zerotrust.cyber.gov/federal-zero-trust-strategy`.

A typical federation might include a number of organizations that have established trust for shared access to a set of resources. Federation with Azure AD or O365 enables users to authenticate using on-premises credentials and access all resources in the cloud. As a result, it becomes important to have a highly available AD FS infrastructure to ensure access to resources both on-premises and in the cloud.

Directory Services

Directory services are used in networks to provide information about systems, users, and other information about an organization. Directory services like the Lightweight Directory Access Protocol (LDAP) are often deployed as part of an identity management infrastructure. They are frequently used to make available an organizational directory for email. LDAP uses the same object data format as X.500, where each object is made up of attributes that are indexed and referenced by a distinguished name. Each object has a unique name designed to fit into a global namespace that helps determine the relationship of the object and allows for the object to be referenced uniquely. Each entry would also have additional information including a distinguished name, an email address, phone numbers, and office location.

Security issues with LDAP include the fact that no data encryption method was available in LDAP versions 1 and 2. Security is negotiated during the connection phase when the client and server begin communications. Options include no authentication or basic authentication. This is the same mechanism that is used in other protocols, such as HTTP. The LDAP v3 (RFC 2251) is designed to address some of the limitations of previous versions of LDAP in the areas of internationalization, authentication, referral, and deployment. It allows new features to be added to the protocol without also requiring changes to the protocol using extensions and controls.

Since directories contain significant amounts of organizational data and may be used to support a range of services, including directory-based authentication, they must be well protected. The same set of needs often means that directory servers need to be publicly exposed to provide services to systems or business partners who need to access the directory information. In those cases, additional security, tighter access controls, or even an entirely separate public directory service may be needed.

Regardless of what protocols and standards are being used to authenticate, there is a real need for strong cryptographic controls. This is the reason for the creation of secure directory services. This solution makes use of Secure Sockets Layer (SSL). LDAP over SSL (LDAPS) provides for secure communications between the LDAP servers and client systems by means of encrypted SSL connections. To use this service, SSL has to be present on both the client and server and be able to be configured to make use of certificates. LDAP supports two methods for the encryption of communications using SSL/TLS: traditional LDAPS and STARTTLS. LDAPS communication commonly occurs over a special port 636. However, STARTTLS begins as a plaintext connection over the standard LDAP port (389), and that connection is then upgraded to SSL/TLS.

Software-Defined Networking

Software-defined networking (SDN) is a technology that allows network professionals to virtualize the network so that control is decoupled from hardware and given to a software application called a *controller*.

In a typical network environment, hardware devices such as switches make forwarding decisions so that when a frame enters the switch, the switch's logic, built into the content addressable memory (CAM) table, determines the port to which the data frame is forwarded.

All packets with the same address will be forwarded to the same destination. SDN is a step in the evolution toward programmable and active networking in that it gives network managers the flexibility to configure, manage, and optimize network resources dynamically by centralizing the network state in the control layer.

Software-defined networking overcomes this roadblock because it allows networking professionals to respond to the dynamic needs of modern networks. With SDN, a network administrator can shape traffic from a centralized control console without having to touch individual switches.

Based on demand and network needs, the network switch's rules can be changed dynamically as needed, permitting the blocking, allowing, or prioritizing of specific types of data frames with a very granular level of control. This enables the network to be treated as a logical or virtual entity. SDN is defined as three layers: application, control, and the infrastructure or data plane layer.

When a network administrator is ready to move to an a SDN topology, they will have to evaluate the model to implement.

- *Open SDN*: Enables open protocols to control assets that route packets

- *Hybrid SDN*: Merges traditional protocols with SDN, allowing the choice of best protocols from each model

- *SDN overlay*: Places a virtual network over existing network hardware topology

Often the hybrid SDN is a first step into implementing SDN.

Organizational Requirements for Infrastructure Security Design

An organization must focus on defense in depth in the creation of a secure infrastructure. Defense in depth is a strategic technique for information security where many requirements are thoughtfully layered throughout the enterprise ecosystem to protect the integrity, confidentiality, and availability of the network, the data, and the people.

Scalability

Scalability and fault tolerance are vital to large networking environments measured by the number of requests they can handle at the same time. If you have a website where customers are placing orders, the transaction volume can vary. If those servers became inoperable, money can be lost, so scaling both vertically and horizontally is one of the best options. Scaling up or scaling vertically means that you are adding more machine resources, including CPU, storage, and RAM to your current ecosystem. Scaling horizontally or scaling out means you are adding more machines to the pool of resources.

Building scalability also means building flexibility into the organization. Research shows most on-premises organizations moving toward a horizontally scaled architecture because of a need for reliability through redundancy. However, moving to the elasticity of the cloud and using SaaS environments will also improve utilization as well as redundancy depending on the architecture.

Resiliency

Building a resilient, secure infrastructure requires an understanding of the risks that your organization faces. Natural and human-created disasters or physical and digital attacks can all have a significant effect on your organization's ability to function. Resilience is part of the foundation of the availability leg of the CIA triad, and this chapter explores resilience as a key part of availability.

Common elements of resilient design, such as geographic and network path diversity and high availability design elements like RAID arrays and backups, are important to the resiliency of an organization. Different methods to guarantee that records aren't missing and that services remain online despite failures should be deployed including the following:

- **High availability:** Characteristic of a system with an agreed level of uptime and performance
- **Diversity/heterogeneity:** A collective entity that interactively integrates different entities, whereas diversity implies divergence, not integration
- **Course of action orchestration:** Automatic configuration and management of computer systems
- **Distributed allocation:** Methodical approach to the design and implementation to share resources
- **Redundancy:** Building multiple assets that provide a similar role and could replace each other if disaster occurs
- **Replication:** Sharing data to ensure stability between hardware or software mechanisms
- **Clustering:** Dividing information into smaller groups based on patterns in the data

Automation

Automation describes many technologies that reduce human intervention. With workflows, relationships, and decisions made in the creation of an automation technology, ideally the efficiency and reliability of many tasks or functions that used to be done by human staffers is now done by machines. Examples of automation range from self-driving cars to smart homes to continuous delivery of software with manifests and modules.

Autoscaling

One of the distinct advantages in cloud computing is the ability to dynamically scale up or down quickly and automatically to the number of resources needed based on traffic or utilization. Benefits of autoscaling include better fault tolerance, availability, and cost management.

Security Orchestration, Automation, and Response

SOAR, or security orchestration, automation, and response, tools are devised to automate security responses, allow centralized control of security settings and controls, and provide robust incident response capabilities. Managing multiple security technologies can be challenging. Using information from SOAR platforms and systems can help design your organization's security posture. Managing security operations and remediating issues you have identified is also an important part of security work that SOAR platforms attempt to solve. As a mitigation and recovery tool, SOAR platforms allow you to quickly assess the attack surface of an organization, the state of systems, and where issues may exist. They also allow automation of remediation and restoration workflows.

Bootstrapping

Bootstrapping can mean several things in cyber, including the program that initializes during the operating system startup. Bootstrapping in infrastructure is the sequence of events that need to happen when creating a virtual machine. The term came from the expression "pulling yourself up by your own bootstraps."

In security or data science, it means extrapolating findings for a larger group based on results from a smaller collection of data. Bootstrapping can be used in machine learning by inferring results from a statistical average. Bootstrapping is a technique that data scientists can use to improve the quality of a learning model that some SOAR tools could use.

    Keep in mind the five Ps of security and performance: Proper Planning Prevents Poor Performance and security issues.

Containerization

Technologies related to virtual systems continue to evolve. In some cases, you may not need an entire virtual system to complete a specific task. In such situations, a container can now be used. *Containerization* allows for the isolation of applications running on a server. Containers offer a lower-cost alternative to using virtualization to run isolated applications on a single host. When a container is used, the OS kernel provides process isolation and performs resource management. Determining when to use containers instead of virtualizing the OS mostly breaks down to the type of workload you have to complete.

Picture the large cargo ships that sail products across the oceans. So long as the cargo can fit in a container, that's all that matters. No matter what the cargo is, whatever it's for, or who uses it, it fits in a reliable, standardized container. Thus, containerization ensures the efficient and cost-effective use of the ship on which the cargo is placed.

The same approach is used for a Linux technology that is similar to virtualization, commonly using the open-source Docker program, where each container runs the host's kernel. The container has its own network stack and incremental file system, but it is not a fully virtualized system or a Type 1 (bare-metal) hypervisor. It's more about isolating the running container, not virtualizing an entire operating system.

Virtualization

Virtualization is a technology that system administrators have been using in datacenters for many years, and it is at the heart of cloud computing infrastructure. It is a technology that allows the physical resources of a computer (CPU, RAM, hard disk, graphics card, etc.) to be shared by virtual machines (VMs). Consider the old days when a single physical hardware platform—the server—was dedicated to a single-server application like being a web server. It turns out that a typical web server application didn't utilize many of the underlying hardware resources available. If you assume that a web application running on a physical server utilizes 30 percent of the hardware resources, that means that 70 percent of the physical resources are going unused, and the server is being wasted.

With virtualization, if three web servers are running via VMs with each utilizing 30 percent of the physical hardware resources of the server, 90 percent of the physical hardware resources of the server are being utilized. This is a much better return on hardware investment. By installing virtualization software on your computer, you can create VMs that can be used to work in many situations with many different applications.

Modern computer systems have come a long way in how they process, store, and access information. One such advancement is virtualization, a method used to create a virtual version of a device or a resource such as a server, storage, or even operating system. Chapter 9 goes into cloud, containerization, and virtualization in much more detail about how to deploy virtual infrastructure securely.

Content Delivery Network

A *content delivery network (CDN)* is a regionally diverse distributed network of servers and datacenters with the ultimate goal of high availability to their end users. Many interactions on the Internet involve a CDN, from reading a news article to streaming a video on social media. CDNs are built to improve any latency between the consumer and the content. Delays can occur due to physical distance from a hosting server, and CDNs work to shorten the physical distance, increasing speed and performance by caching content on a server located in multiple geographic locations so that someone in the Asia Pacific accessing a site hosted in the United Kingdom will experience minimal, if any, lag time loading the information requested. Caching speeds up future requests for that specific data because it will store the data locally. For example, a web browser can avoid making duplicate trips to a server, saving time and resources.

Integrating Applications Securely into an Enterprise Architecture

Not only do applications themselves need to be developed securely using software, hardware, techniques, and best practices, but incorporating those applications into an enterprise architecture securely is of critical concern for organizations. One of most important tools an organization can build is an application security checklist to avoid pitfalls and create a high level of security in application integration.

Baseline and Templates

A baseline is a minimum level of security to which a system, network, or device must adhere. They are usually mapped to industry standards. Baselines may be established by comparing the security activities and events of other organizations. Baselines can be used as an initial point of fact and then used for comparison for future reviews.

A benchmark is a simulated evaluation conducted before purchasing or contracting equipment/services to determine how these items will perform once purchased. A baseline is a minimum level of security to which a system, network, or device must adhere or maintain.

Another area of benchmarking that is evolving is related to best practices, controls, or benchmark requirements against which organizations can be measured. The concept of compliance is sometimes compared to benchmarking because you may need to specify a level of requirements or provide a grade when measured against the predefined requirements.

One example of this is the Federal Information Security Management Act of 2002 (FISMA). This requirement mandates that U.S. government agencies implement and measure the effectiveness of their cybersecurity programs. Another is ISO 27001. In this document, Section 15 addresses compliance with external and internal requirements.

When you are benchmarking or baselining, keep in mind that all products under consideration must be tested and evaluated with identical methodologies.

To validate is to check or prove the value or truth of a statement. Think about watching a car commercial and noting that the automobile is rated at 32 mpg for highway driving. Has the statement been validated? Actually, it has through a process governed by the Environmental Protection Agency (EPA). This same process of validation may occur when you purchase computer network gear, equipment, or applications. Here are some government standards for this:

- NIST Special Publication 800-37 Rev. 2, Risk Management Framework for Information Systems and Organizations

- NIST Special Publication 800-53A Revision 5, According to the NIST website, this pub is called Security and Privacy Controls for Information Systems and Organizations
- FIPS Publication 199, Standards for Security Categorization of Federal Information and Information Systems

After all, automakers and computer vendors both make claims about the ratings of their products and what they can do. As sellers, they need to be able to measure these claims just as we, the buyers, need to be able to prove the veracity of them to ourselves.

One example of an early IT standard designed for this purpose is the U.S. DoD Trusted Computer System Evaluation Criteria (TCSEC). This document, also known as the Orange Book, provides a basis for specifying security requirements and a metric with which to evaluate the degree of trust that can be placed in a computer system.

A more current standard is Common Criteria (CC). CC is an international standard (ISO/IEC 15408) and is used for validation and computer security certification. CC makes use of protection profiles and security targets, and it provides assurance that the process of specification, implementation, and evaluation of a computer security product has been conducted in a rigorous and standard manner. The protection profiles maintain security requirements, which should include evaluation assurance levels (EALs).

The levels are as follows:

- EAL1: Functionally Tested
- EAL2: Structurally Tested
- EAL3: Methodically Tested and Checked
- EAL4: Methodically Designed, Tested, and Reviewed
- EAL5: Semi-Formally Designed and Tested
- EAL6: Semi-Formally Verified Design and Tested
- EAL7: Formally Verified Design and Tested

 Even when a product is certified via Common Criteria, that does not mean it is 100 percent secure. Systems certified at EAL 4 will still require security patches as vulnerabilities are discovered.

Secure Design Patterns/Types of Web Technologies

Security by design means that the security measures are built in and that security code reviews must be carried out to uncover potential security problems during the early stages of the development process. The longer the delay in this process, the greater the cost to fix the problem. Security by default means that security is set to a secure or restrictive setting by default. As an example, OpenBSD is installed at the most secure setting; that is, security by default. See www.openbsd.org/security.html for more information. Security by deployment means that security is added in when the product or application is deployed. Research has shown that every bug removed during a review saves nine hours in testing, debugging, and fixing of the code. As a result, it is much cheaper to add in early on than later. Reviews make the application more robust and more resistant to malicious attackers. A security code review helps new programmers identify common security problems and best practices.

Another issue is secure functionality. Users constantly ask for software that has greater functionality. Macros are an example of this. A macro is just a set of instructions designed to make some tasks easier. This same functionality is used, however, by the macro virus. The macro virus takes advantage of the power offered by word processors, spreadsheets, or other applications. This exploitation is inherent in the product, and all users are susceptible to it unless they choose to disable all macros and do without the functionality. Feature requests drive software development and hinder security because complexity is the enemy of security.

An application security framework is a great framework for system development that can make the development process easier to manage for the security manager. It is designed to build in security controls as needed. There are many different models and approaches. Some have more steps than others, yet the overall goal is the same: to control the process and add security to build defense in depth. One industry-accepted approach is a standardized System Development Life Cycle (SDLC) process. NIST defines SDLC in NIST SP 800-34 as "The scope of activities associated with a system, encompassing the system's initiation, development and acquisition, implementation, operation and maintenance, and ultimately its disposal that instigates another system initiation."

Some development use cases and programming languages used are as follows:

- **Front-end web development:** JavaScript

- **Back-end web development:** JavaScript, Java, Python, PHP, Ruby

- **Mobile development:** Swift, Java, C#

- **Game development:** C++, C#

- **Desktop applications:** Java, C++, Python

- **Systems programming:** C, Rust

Storage Design Patterns

To become more efficient, reduce complexity, and increase performance working with large forms of information, using plans and design patterns for repeatability becomes a way to simplify big data applications. Storage design patterns have various components including data sources as well as ingestion, storage, and access layers.

The ingestion layer takes information directly from the source itself and with that comes a great deal of noise, as well as important data. Filtering the noise from the important data can be difficult when you have multiple sources, data compression, and validation. After the separation, architects have to decide which pattern to use. Some of these patterns include the following:

- **Multidestination:** Great for multiple data streams
- **Protocol converter:** Best for data coming in from different types of systems
- **Real-time streaming:** Used for continuous processing of unstructured data

The data storage layer is important to convert any data into a format that can be readily analyzed. Once the data has been normalized, then data access patterns focus on two primary ways to consume the data, through a developer API or an end-to-end user API. There are many ways to structure data at each layer and use those to efficiently pattern the way data will be consumed in an enterprise.

Container APIs

You may not need an entire virtual system to complete a specific task; a container can be used. Containers allow for the isolation of applications running on a server. Containers offer a lower-cost alternative to using virtualization to run isolated applications on a single host. When a container is used, the OS kernel provides process isolation and performs resource management. When exchanging information between the container and other resources, one of the best ways to do that is through an application programming interface (API). A container API allows for building complex functionality between containers, systems, and other services.

Secure Coding Standards

A standard library for a programming language is the library that is made available in every implementation of that language. Depending on the constructs made available by the host language, a standard library may include items such as subroutines, macro definitions, global variables, and templates. The C++ Standard Library can be divided into the following categories:

- A standard template library
- Inputs and outputs
- Standard C headers

The C++ Standard Library provides several generic containers, functions to use and manipulate these containers, function objects, generic strings and streams (including interactive and file I/O), support for some language features, and functions for everyday tasks. The problem is that some C standard library functions can be used inappropriately or in ways that may cause security problems when programmers don't follow industry-accepted approaches to developing robust, secure applications.

> The CASP+ exam will not require you to be an expert programmer, but you may be asked to identify C functions that can lead to improper bounds checking.

Code quality is the term relating to the utility and longevity of a particular piece of code. Code that will be useful for a specific, short-lived function is deemed "low code quality." A code module that will be useful for several years to come, possibly appropriate for multiple applications, possesses "high code quality."

> The CASP+ exam may quiz the test candidate on items related to SDLC practices such as what activities occur at what point in the process.

API Management

Application programming interfaces (APIs) are the connection between a consumer and a provider. This could be a client and server or an application and operating system. An API defines how the client should ask for information from the server and how the server will respond. This definition means that programs written in any language can implement an API and make requests.

APIs are useful for building interfaces, but they can also be a point of vulnerability if they are not properly secured and managed. API security relies on authentication, authorization, proper data scoping to ensure that too much data isn't exposed, and appropriate monitoring and logging to remain secure. There are four major types of APIs that need to be managed:

- **Open or Public API:** Publicly available to developers, focuses on external users accessing a service or data

- **Internal or Private API:** Hidden from external users and used only by internal systems

- **Partner API:** Shared with business partners with a specific workflow to get access

- **Composite API:** Built with API tooling, allowing access to multiple endpoints in one call

Managing APIs is the process and procedure of creating, publishing, documenting, and validating all the APIs used within an organization to ensure security. Benefits of implementing API management also include the ability to change quickly and automation.

Middleware

Middleware is the software that works between an application and the operating system and is the enabler for communication, authentication, APIs, and data management. Some common examples are database, application server, web, and transaction processing. Each of these applications needs to be able to communicate with the others, and middleware will perform the communication functions depending on what service is being used and what information needs to be sent. Middleware can use messaging frameworks like SOAP, REST, and JSON to provide messaging services for different applications.

Software Assurance

When development is complete, software is expected to behave in a certain way. The software is not expected to have vulnerabilities, to have issues handling unexpected or large volumes of input, or to be weakened by being overworked. The term that describes the level of confidence that the software will behave as expected is known as *software assurance*.

There is a long list of controls, testing, and practices, all for the purpose of raising this confidence level. In the following sections, we cover some of these controls and practices, as well as several ways in which software can be tested.

By employing industry-accepted approaches to raise software assurance, two outcomes happen:

- Software developers can be confident that their time and effort will be spent on translating the requirements definition into workable, secure code.

- Users can trust that the software development process was executed with a high level of care and due diligence.

Sandboxing/Development Environment

Application sandboxing is the process of writing files to a sandbox or temporary storage area instead of their normal location. Sandboxing is used to limit the ability of code to execute malicious actions on a user's computer. If you launch an application in the sandbox, it won't be able to edit the Registry or even make changes to other files on the user's hard drive.

One application area where sandboxing is used is with mobile code. Mobile code is software that will be downloaded from a remote system and run on the computer performing the download. The security issue with mobile code is that it is executed locally. Many times, the user might not even know that the code is executing. Java is mobile code, and it operates within a sandbox environment to provide additional security. Data can be processed as either client-side processing or server-side processing. Server-side processing is where the code is processed on the server, whereas with client-side processing the code will run on the client. PHP is an example of a server-side processing language, whereas JavaScript is processed on the client side and can be executed by the browser.

    A virtual server can act as a type of sandbox to execute suspect programs or potential malware.

Malware is software. Malware sandboxing is a technique used to isolate malicious code so that it can run in an isolated environment. You can think of a malware sandbox as a stand-alone environment that lets you view or execute the program safely while keeping it contained. Microsoft has several good articles on how to build a Windows Sandbox here: docs.microsoft.com/en-us/windows/security/threat-protection/windows-sandbox/windows-sandbox-overview.

When using a sandbox, you should not expect the malware creators to make analysis an easy process. As an example, malware creators build in checks to try to prevent their malware from running in a sandbox environment. The malware may look at the MAC address to try to determine if the NIC is identified as a virtual one, or it may not run if it does not have an active network connection. In such cases you may need additional tools such as FakeNet-NG, which simulates a network connection to fool the malware so that the analyst can observe the malware's network activity from within a sandboxed environment.

Validating Third-Party Libraries

An application issue that plagues a surprisingly large number of companies is the use of third-party libraries. The attraction of using something already created is clear: money and time saved! However, there is a big security risk as well.

When developers at a company can find code that fits their needs and is already working, then why would they reinvent the wheel? They can plug in a third-party library to accomplish the required tasks. The problem is that the third-party library is an unknown, untested product when compared with the policies and safe coding practices of the in-house developers.

Code reuse is, as the name implies, the use of a single piece of code several times, whether it's within an application or reused as an application evolves from one version to the next.

Similar to using a third-party library, reusing code saves time and money. The developer doesn't have to rewrite the same block of code (and possibly introduce errors) and instead can direct the application to a single block of code to be used repeatedly when needed.

When practiced with security in mind, code reuse is certainly a positive practice—for example, when a subroutine is required for several aspects of an application. The subroutine was developed securely, so there is little or no added risk. However, if one application's code, however modular it is, were repurposed for the next version or for another application, then this practice might skip the evaluation steps required and introduce new risks.

Defined DevOps Pipeline

Software today is created much faster than in the past, so it becomes important to software companies to remain competitive and create a defined DevOps pipeline to keep track of customers' demands and requirements. A DevOps pipeline also helps an organization stay organized and focused.

 NOTE   The term *DevOps pipeline* is misleading because it is not a linear process. The DevOps pipeline is actually shaped like an infinity symbol because it is cyclic. The shape has the following components that repeat: plan, code, build, test, release, deploy, operate, and monitor.

This DevOps pipeline is a set of tools and automated processes used to write, compile, and deploy code. If effective, this enables a software company to rapidly test new code on an ongoing automated basis. Moving from a manual process to an automated one results in fewer errors and pushes out higher-quality code that is signed and distributed to customers.

Code signing is the process of digitally signing a piece of software guaranteeing the integrity of the code from the time of signature. If the software has been tampered with, the signature will appear untrusted and invalid.

Application Security Testing and Application Vetting Processes

Application testing is an important part of IT security. Applications are not like any other item. Should you purchase a car that has a defective accelerator or tire, the vendor will typically repair or replace the items. Software, however, is very different. If software is defective, the vendor may no longer support it, may offer a patch, or may even offer an upgrade for a fee. These are just a few of the reasons why testing applications for security issues is so important.

Application security testing is the process of using software, hardware, and procedural methods to prevent security flaws in applications and protect them from exploit. As a CASP+, you are not expected to be an expert programmer or understand the inner workings of a Python program. What the CASP+ must understand, however, is the importance of application security, how to work with programmers during the development of code, and the role of testing code for proper security controls. As a CASP+, you need to understand various testing methodologies. For example, when the code is available, a full code review may be possible. In situations where you do not have access to the code, you may choose no knowledge application assessment techniques.

Regardless of the type of software test performed, your task is to help ensure that adequate controls are developed and implemented and that testing an application meets an organization's security requirements. What security controls are used in part depends on the type of project. A small in-house project will not have the funding of a major product release. The time and money spent on testing commercial applications is typically much greater than for IT projects. IT projects result in software tools and applications that a company uses internally, that a consultant installs in a client's environment, or that the company installs on an internal or external website. Commercial software applications are developed by software manufacturers for sale to external customers. These may be further classified into stand-alone applications (installed on the user's machine), client-server applications, and web applications, all with their own systems development life cycle (SDLC) considerations.

A code analyzer is a Java application compatible with C, C++, Java, assembly, HTML, and user-defined software source metrics. Code analyzers calculate metrics across multiple source trees as one project. Code analyzers have a nice tree view of the project and offer flexible reporting capabilities.

Analyzing code can be done one of several ways. The first method, using a fuzzer, involves intentionally injecting a variety of input into the code in order to produce an unexpected or unwanted result, such as a crash. The input will come fast and furious, in large volumes of data (dubbed "fuzz"), with the goal that the application will reveal its weaknesses.

Another approach is to use *static application security testing (SAST)*. With this method, the software is neither run nor executed; rather, it is reviewed statically. As you can imagine, if an application has millions of lines of code, a static code review is impossible. Therefore, you must rely on static code analysis tools. The code to be reviewed is fed input into the static code analysis tool.

There is also *dynamic application security testing (DAST)*. The difference between dynamic and static code analysis is that while a static review does not execute the application, during dynamic code analysis, the application is run, and you can observe how the code behaves.

Finally, when you combine SAST and DAST, you end up with *interactive application security testing (IAST)*. According to the research firm Gartner, "Next generation modern web and mobile applications require a combination of SAST and DAST." With IAST, an agent performs all the analysis in real time from inside the application. It can be run during development, integration, or production. The agent has access to all the code, runtime control, configuration, and libraries. With all the access to all the things at the same time, IAST tools can cover more code with more security rules and give better results.

Considerations of Integrating Enterprise Applications

When integrating products and services into the environment, the CASP+ will need to determine what type of interoperability issues exist. One useful tool to help is computer-aided software engineering (CASE). CASE can be used not only for software process activities but also for reengineering, development, and testing. Testing can help find interoperability issues that have not been discovered during the development process.

 It is always cheaper to find interoperability issues early in the development process. However, a good security design process will look for problems at each step of the development process.

CASE tools are generally classified into different areas, such as the following:

- Reverse engineering
- Requirement management
- Process management
- Software design

Interoperability issues that are not found during development may be discovered during deployment. That is one reason a deployment strategy is so important. Deployment techniques include the following:

Hard Changeover   A hard changeover deploys the new product or service at a specific date. At this point in time, all users are forced to change to the new product or service. The advantage of the hard changeover is that it gets the change over with and completed. We would compare it to removing a Band-Aid quickly, though there is the possibility of some initial pain or discomfort.

Parallel Operation   With a parallel operation, both the existing system and the new system are operational at the same time. This offers the advantage of being able to compare the results of the two systems. As users begin working with the new system or product, the old system can be shut down. The primary disadvantage of this method is that both systems must be maintained for a period of time, so there will be additional costs.

Phased Changeover   If a phased changeover is chosen, the new systems are upgraded one piece at a time. So, for example, it may be rolled out first to marketing, then to sales, and finally to production. This method also offers the advantage of reduced upheaval, but it requires additional cost expenditures and a longer overall period for the change to take effect.

Ideally, the users of new products and services have been trained. Training strategies can vary, but they typically include classroom training, online training, practice sessions, and user manuals. After the integration of products and services is complete and employees have been trained, you may be asked to assess return on investment (ROI) or to look at the true payback analysis.

 At the end of this process, ask some basic questions, such as whether the new system is adequate, what is its true ROI, whether the chosen standards were followed, and whether all security standards were observed and implemented.

With the rise of the global economy, enterprises have increasingly been faced with the fundamental decision of where to acquire materials, goods, and services. Such resources often extend far beyond the location where products are made and can be found at diverse areas around the globe. Some potential solutions include the following:

Customer Relationship Management   *Customer relationship management (CRM)* consists of the tools, techniques, and software used by companies to manage their relationships with customers. CRM solutions are designed to track and record everything you need to know about your customers. This includes items such as buying history, budget, timeline, areas of interest, and their future planned purchases. Products designed as CRM solutions range from simple off-the-shelf contact management applications to high-end interactive systems that combine marketing, sales, and executive information. CRM typically involves three areas: sales automation, customer service, and enterprise marketing.

Enterprise Resource Planning   Another process improvement method is *enterprise resource planning (ERP)*. The goal of this method is to integrate all of an organization's processes into a single integrated system. There are many advantages to building a unified system that can service the needs of people in finance, human resources, manufacturing, and the warehouse. Traditionally, each of those departments would have its own computer system. These unique systems would be optimized for the specific ways that each department operates. ERP combines them all together into one single, integrated software program that runs off a unified database. This allows each department to share information and communicate more easily with the others. ERP is seen as a replacement for business process reengineering.

Configuration Management Database A *configuration management database (CMDB)* is a database that contains the details of configuration items and the relationships between them. Once created and mapped to all known assets, the CMDB becomes a means of understanding what assets are critical, how they are connected to other items, and their dependencies.

Configuration Management System A *configuration management system (CMS)* is used to provide detailed recording and updating of information that describes an enterprise's hardware and software. CMS records typically include information such as the version of the software, what patches have been applied, and where resources are located. Location data might include a logical and physical location.

Integration Enablers

To complement the enterprise integration methods and systems mentioned in the preceding sections, there are other services that serve to mend or unite dissimilar parts of the enterprise. The following are additional integration enablers:

Directory Services *Directory services* are the means by which network services are identified and mapped. Directory services perform services similar to those of a phone book, as they correlate addresses to names.

Enterprise Service Bus The *enterprise service bus (ESB)* is a high-level concept to describe the middleware between two unlike services. It is used in service-oriented architectures as a technique of moving messages between services. You can describe an ESB as middleware because it acts as a service broker. ESB is a framework in that different ESB products have different capabilities. What they share in common is an abstraction layer. Not all ESBs offer encryption. It depends on the particular vendor's product. ESB is fast becoming the backbone of many service-oriented enterprises' services.

Service-Oriented Architecture *Service-oriented architecture (SOA)* specifies the overall multilayered and multitier distributed infrastructure for supporting services such as ESB. Although using web services allows you to achieve interoperability across applications built on different platforms using different languages, applying service-oriented concepts and principles when building applications based on using web services can help you create robust, standards-based, interoperable SOA solutions.

Domain Name System *Domain Name System (DNS)* is the service that lets people find what they're looking for on the Internet. DNS operates behind every address translation, working to resolve fully qualified domain names (FQDNs) and human-readable addressing into numeric IP addresses. DNS serves a critical function for people. If DNS as a service were to cease, the Internet would continue, but users would need to know the IP address of every site they wanted to visit. DNS is a request-response protocol. When a DNS server sends a response for a request, the reply message contains the transaction ID and questions from the original request as well as any answers that it was able to find.

Integrating Security into the Development Life Cycle

Depending on the company, product or service, and situation, different methodologies may be used to develop an end-to-end solution. The first challenge is to select which methodology to use. Choosing a formal development methodology is not simple, because no one methodology always works best. Some popular software models include the spiral model or prototyping. These models share a common element in that they all have a predictive life cycle. This means that at the time the project is laid out, costs are calculated, and a schedule is defined. A second approach, end-to-end development, can be categorized as agile software development. With the agile software development model, teams of programmers and business experts work closely together. Project requirements are developed using an iterative approach because the project is mission-driven and component-based. The project manager becomes much more of a facilitator in these situations. Popular agile development models include extreme programming and scrum programming.

One good source of information on the systems development life cycle (SDLC) is NIST 800-64. Although there are many models for SDLC, NIST 800-64, NIST website calls this Security Considerations in the System Development Life Cycle, breaks the model into five phases. These phases are described here:

Phase 1: Initiation/Requirements   The purpose of the initiation phase is to express the need and purpose of the system. System planning and feasibility studies are performed.

Phase 2: Development/Acquisition   During this phase, the system is designed, requirements are determined, resources are purchased, and software is programmed or otherwise created. This phase often consists of other defined steps, such as the system development life cycle or the acquisition cycle.

Phase 3: Fielding   After validation and acceptance testing, the system is installed or released. This phase is also called deployment or implementation.

Phase 4: Operation/Maintenance   During this phase, the system performs its stated and designed work. The system is almost always modified by the addition of hardware and software and by numerous other events, such as patching. While operational, there may also be insertions or upgrades, or new versions made of the software.

Phase 5: Disposal and Reuse   The computer system is disposed of or decommissioned once the transition to a new system is completed.

One important part of operation and maintenance is certification and accreditation. Certification is a formal testing of the security safeguards implemented in the computer system to determine whether they meet applicable requirements. Accreditation is the formal authorization by the accrediting official for system operation and an explicit acceptance of risk.

Planning is the key to success. You may not have a crystal ball, but once solutions are proposed, you can start to plan for activities that will be required should the proposal become reality. It's much the same as thinking about buying a car. You come up with a car payment each month but will also need to perform operational activities such as buying fuel and keeping insurance current. And there is also maintenance to consider. Should you decide that you no longer want your car, you may decide to sell it or donate it to a charity, but regardless of your choice, it will need to be decommissioned.

Although the purpose of NIST 800-64 is to assist in integrating essential information technology security steps into their established SDLC process, the security systems development life cycle (SecSDLC) is designed to identify security requirements early in the development process and incorporate them throughout the process.

The idea of SecSDLC is to build security into all SDLC activities. The goal is to have them incorporated into each step of the SDLC.

Microsoft developed the security development life cycle (SDL) to increase the security of software and to reduce the impact severity of problems in software and code. The SDL is designed to minimize the security-related design and coding bugs in software. An organization that employs the Microsoft SDL is expected to have a central security entity or team that performs security functions. Some objectives of SDL are as follows:

- The team must create security best practices.

- The team must consist of security experts and be able to act as a source of security expertise to the organization.

- The team is responsible for completing a final review of the software before its release.

- The team must interact with developers and others as needed throughout the development process.

Security Requirements Traceability Matrix

The security requirements traceability matrix (SRTM) is another grid that allows easy viewing of requirements and documentation supporting specific activities. The SRTM is a spreadsheet document that typically contains items such as the following:

- Requirement number

- Description

- Source

- Objective

- Verification

Operational Activities

You should understand the threats and vulnerabilities associated with computer operations and know how to implement security controls for critical activities through the operational period of the product or software. Some key operational activities are as follows:

- Vulnerability assessment
- Security policy management
- Security audits and reviews
- Security impact analysis, privacy impact analysis, configuration management, and patch management
- Security awareness and training; guidance documents

Monitoring

A routine and significant portion of operational activity is the monitoring of systems. Not limited to just servers, monitoring includes staying aware about software licensing issues and remaining receptive to potential incidents or abuses of privilege.

Maintenance

When you are responsible for the security of a network or IT infrastructure, periodic maintenance of hardware and software is required. Maintenance can include verifying that antivirus software is installed and current; ensuring that backups are completed, rotated, and encrypted; and performing patch management. Maintenance should be driven by policy. Policy should specify when activities are performed and the frequency with which these events occur. Policy should align as closely as possible to vendor-provided recommendations. The maintenance program should document the following:

- Maintenance schedule
- The cost of the maintenance
- Maintenance history, including planned versus unplanned and executed versus exceptional

Responsibility for the security of the network includes times of incident response. Maintenance of devices or workstations includes those systems that have been recovered from an incident. The digital forensics of collected data is then passed on to the forensics team responsible for investigating the incident.

Test and Evaluation

An important phase of the systems development life cycle is the testing and evaluation of systems. Before a system can be accepted or deemed to reach a milestone in its development, that system must be evaluated against the expected criteria for that phase or project. If the system is tested against its specification requirements and passes, then its owners and users gain the assurance that the system will function as needed.

Testing spans hardware and software development, but the goal is to raise the assurance that the system will operate as expected. Further, testing may seek to verify that undesired aspects do not exist. For example, during the course of software development, an application might be evaluated for forbidden coding techniques.

General Change Management

As far as possible, compliance with standards should be automated in order to ensure that interorganizational change does not reduce the overall level of security. Unless strong controls have been put in place, the result of change will usually be that the level of security is reduced and that system configurations fall to a lower level of security. This is why it is so important to tie security process to change management.

ISO 20000 defines change management as a needed process to "ensure all changes are assessed, approved, implemented and reviewed in a controlled manner." NIST 800-64 describes change management as a method to ensure that changes are approved, tested, reviewed, and implemented in a controlled way. Regardless of what guidelines or standards you follow, the change management process can be used to control change and to help ensure that security does not fall to a lower state. A typical change management process includes the following:

1. Change request

2. Change request approval

3. Planned review

4. A test of the change

5. Scheduled rollout of the change

6. Communication to those affected by the planned change

7. Implementation of the change

8. Documentation of all changes that occurred

9. Post-change review

10. Method to roll back the change if needed

One important issue is to have a plan to roll back a change if needed, because some changes can have unexpected results. An example of this can be seen in the Windows Updates in an out-of-band (OOB) update in January 2022 that broke VPNs, caused Windows Server 2012 to get stuck in a boot loop, and not only rebooted servers but caused hard drives to appear as RAW formats and be unusable. This required users to remove or roll back the update, leaving many servers vulnerable with no security patches.

Regardless of what change control process is used, it should be documented in the change control policy. Also, what is and is not covered by the policy should be specified. For example, some small changes, like an update to antivirus programs, may not be covered in the change control process, whereas larger institutional changes that have lasting effects on the company are included. The change control policy should also list how emergency changes are to occur, because a situation could arise in which changes must take place quickly without the normal reviews being completed before implementation. In such a situation, all of the steps should still be completed, but they may not be completed before implementation of the emergency change. Change management must be able to address any of the potential changes that can occur, including the following:

- Changes to policies, procedures, and standards
- Updates to requirements and new regulations
- Modified network, altered system settings, or fixes implemented
- Alterations to network configurations
- New networking devices or equipment
- Changes in company structure caused by acquisition, merger, or spinoff
- New computers, laptops, smartphones, or tablets installed
- New or updated applications
- Patches and updates installed
- New technologies integrated

 Maintaining good security practices in the midst of change is important for many reasons. One is regulatory. For example, the Securities and Exchange Act of 1934 (amended in 1977) requires "all publicly held companies to keep accurate records and maintain internal control systems to safeguard assets." Failure to do so can result in criminal and financial penalties of up to $10,000 and five years of imprisonment.

Disposal and Reuse

Some products can have a long, useful life. For example, Windows XP was released in 2005 and was updated and maintained until 2014. Regardless of the product, at some point you will have to consider asset object reuse. Asset object reuse is important because of the remaining information that may reside on a hard disk or any other type of media. Even when data has been sanitized, there may be some remaining information. This is known as data remanence. Data remanence is the residual data that remains after data has been erased. Any asset object that may be reused will have some remaining amount of information left on media after it has been erased. Best practice is to wipe the drive with a minimum of seven passes or random ones and zeros. For situations where that is not sufficient, physical destruction of the media may be required.

When such information is deemed too sensitive, the decision may be made not to reuse the objects but to dispose of the assets instead. Asset disposal must be handled in an approved manner. As an example, media that has been used to store sensitive or secret information should be physically destroyed. Before decommissioning or disposing of any systems or data, you must understand any existing legal requirements pertaining to records retention. When archiving information, consider the method for retrieving the information.

Common methods of destruction of physical media include crushing, drilling, shredding, and acid baths. As more computers start to use solid-state drives, dealing with data remanence will become even more complicated.

Testing

Before products are released, they must typically go through some type of unit, integration, regression, validation, and acceptance testing. The idea is to conduct tests to verify that the product or application meets the requirements laid out in the specification documents.

For some entities, validation is also performed. The U.S. federal government specifies this process as certification and accreditation. Federal agencies are required by law to have their IT systems and infrastructures certified and accredited. Certification is the process of validating that implemented systems are configured and operating as expected. If management agrees with the findings of the certification, the report is formally approved. When comparing products, all products must be validated with identical tests. The formal approval of the certification is the accreditation process and authorization to operate in a given environment.

Testing is discussed in more detail later in the "Best Practices" section of this chapter.

Development Approaches

Carrying out security activities across the system or software life cycle requires that specific controls be put in place. These controls and security checkpoints start at design and development and do not end until decommissioning. Software development models provide the framework needed to plan and execute milestones and delivery cycles. Some of the most popular development approaches include agile, waterfall, and spiral methodologies.

SecDevOps

DevOps as a word is the shortened combination of two words, two groups of IT workers: development and operations. Traditionally, in the old school of thought, development and operations were teams who met at the point where an application completed development and was being rolled out to production. However, in today's world, applications change more rapidly, with new services being required from developers more often than in the past. This need called for more collaboration between the people who make the software and the people who administer the software as well as security.

In the past, development (Dev) and operations (Ops) were siloed disciplines, but now, as the term implies, there is a new, blended discipline that has added security best practices to the buzz word and is now called SecDevOps. For the collaboration between developers and operations staff to work well, SecDevOps relies on the agile software development model, which follows a continual flow of interaction between coders and users across phases of planning, building, testing, and feedback and adds the process of integrating security right into the development and deployment workflows. It gets developers to think about best practices as well as security standards very early in the processes to keep up with a rapid DevOps approach.

Agile

Agile software development allows teams of programmers and business experts to work closely together. According to the Agile Manifesto at `agilemanifesto.org`, this model builds on the following:

- Individuals and interactions over processes and tools
- Working software over comprehensive documentation
- Customer collaboration over contract negotiation
- Responding to change over following a plan

Agile project requirements are developed using an iterative approach, and the project is mission-driven and component-based.

Waterfall

The waterfall model was developed by Winston Royce in 1970 and operates as the name suggests. The original model prevented developers from returning to stages once they were complete; therefore, the process flowed logically from one stage to the next. Modified versions of the model add a feedback loop so that the process can move in both directions. An advantage of the waterfall method is that it provides a sense of order and is easily documented. The primary disadvantage is that it does not work for large and complex projects because it does not allow for much revision.

Spiral

The spiral design model was developed in 1988 by Barry Boehm. Each phase of the spiral model starts with a design goal and ends with the client review. The client can be either internal or external and is responsible for reviewing the progress. Analysis and engineering efforts are applied at each phase of the project. Each phase of the project contains its own risk assessment. Each time a risk assessment is performed, the schedules and estimated cost to complete are reviewed, and a decision is made to continue or cancel the project. The spiral design model works well for large projects. The disadvantage of this method is that it is much slower and takes longer to complete.

Versioning

Version control, also known as versioning, is a form of source control. Everyone, not just software developers, is familiar with the idea of app version 1.0 versus app version 2.0. The concept of how minor revisions and updates compare with major version upgrades can also be considered fairly common knowledge. We all understand that version 1.1 from version 1.0 likely includes a small set of changes or fixes, while going from version 1.0 to version

2.0 might include a completely different interface in addition to revisions and updates. This concept carries not just through the software but through the documentation as well.

Continuous Integration/Continuous Delivery Pipelines

Continuous integration/continuous delivery (CI/CD) pipelines allow for the speedy incorporation of new code. Continuous integration (CI) is the process in which the source code updates from all developers working on the same project are continually monitored and merged from a central repository. Continuous delivery (CD) automates code changes and testing, and provides the preparation for the code to be delivered or deployed into test or production after the build stage.

CI allows for the rapid integration of small chunks of new code from various developers into a shared repository. CI also allows you to repeatedly test the code for errors to detect bugs early on, making them simpler to fix. CD is an extension of CI, enabling software developers to execute additional tests such as UI tests, which helps ensure clean deployment. CD also helps the DevOps team improve the regularity of new feature releases and automate the entire software release. These features reduce the overall expense of a project.

Best Practices

Programmers must also assume that attempts will be made to subvert the behavior of the program directly, indirectly, or through manipulation of the software. The following are some programming best practices:

- Do not rely on any parameters that are not self-generated.
- Avoid complex code, keeping code simple and small when possible.
- Don't add unnecessary functionality. Programmers should only implement functions defined in the software specification.
- Minimize entry points and have as few exit points as possible.
- Verify all input values. Input must be the correct length, range, format, and data type.

 Examples of input values include dollar amounts, transaction counts, and error detection and correction. Testing the controls used to validate the correctness of these values is an important part of secure coding.

- Interdependencies should be kept to a minimum so that any process modules or components can be disabled when not needed.
- Modules should be developed that have high cohesion and low coupling.

 Cohesion addresses the fact that a module can perform a single task with little input from other modules. Coupling is the measurement of the interconnection between modules.

Testing Best Practices

Once the secure code has been written, it will need to be tested. Tests are classified into the following categories:

Unit Testing   Examines an individual program or module

Interface Testing   Examines hardware or software to evaluate how well data can be passed from one entity to another

System Testing   A series of tests that may include recovery testing and security testing

Final Acceptance Testing   Usually performed at the implementation phase after the team leads are satisfied with all other tests and the application is ready to be deployed

No matter the size of the job, any developer will attest to how important documentation is to software development. It does not matter if there is a team of developers collaborating across the world or one coder doing it all. Documentation answers the same questions for all people: what does this software need to do? Documentation exists to assist and chronicle all phases of development. Documents should detail the various requirements and plans.

Some documents might include a list, such as the requirements definition, which specifies the overall requirements of the software. The software requirements definition document will detail all functional and nonfunctional requirements. While this definition document is non-technical and high level, it is rarely a small list or simple document. The purpose of the document is to state in clear terms the objectives of that piece of software. From this document, other more technical specifications can be made.

Regression testing is used after a change is made to verify that the inputs and outputs are still correct. This is very important from a security standpoint, as poor input validation is one of the most common security flaws exploited during an application attack.

User acceptance testing is the stage in software development where users interact with and test the application. The big questions on the developers' minds consist of the following:

- Does the application meet users' needs?
- Do users operate the application as expected?
- Can users break the software, either inadvertently or maliciously?

Unit testing is a piecemeal approach to testing software. Depending on the cohesion of individual modules, it may be possible to test a particular unit in development. By examining an individual program or module, developers can ensure that each module behaves as expected. The security questions on their minds might include the following:

- Is the module accepting input correctly?
- Does the module provide output properly to the next module?

Integration testing checks the interface between modules of the software application. The different modules are tested first individually and then in combination as a system. Testing the interface between the small units or modules is part of integration testing. It is usually conducted by a software integration tester and performed in conjunction with the development process.

Integration testing is done to do the following:

▪ To verify whether, when combined, the individual modules comply with the necessary standards and yield the expected results.

▪ To locate the defects or bugs in all of the interfaces. For example, when modules are combined, sometimes the data that is passed among the modules contains errors and may not produce the expected results.

▪ To validate the integration among any third-party tools in use.

A *peer review* is a walk-through of each module or software unit. That walk-through is a technical, line-by-line review of the program, diving deep into each subroutine, object, method, and so forth. A peer review, also known as a code review, is meant to inspect code to identify possible improvements and to ensure that business needs are met and security concerns are addressed.

A disadvantage of peer reviews, as viewed by most programmers, is they take too much time. The investment in time and effort often results in delays that outweigh the benefits, such as fewer bugs, less rework, greater satisfaction with the end product, and better team communication and cohesiveness.

Prototyping is the process of building a proof-of-concept model that can be used to test various aspects of a design and verify its marketability. Prototyping is widely used during the development process and may be used as a first or preliminary model to test how something works. Virtual computing is a great tool to test multiple application solutions. Years ago, you would have had to build a physical system to test multiple solutions. With virtual computers and tools such as VMware, users are provided with a sophisticated and highly customizable platform that can be used to test complex customer client-server applications. Elastic cloud computing can also be used to prototype and test multiple solutions. This pay-as-you-go model of prototyping allows designers to speed solutions and significantly reduce the prototype phase.

ISO 27002

An ISO document worth reviewing is ISO 27002. This standard is considered a code of best practice for information security management. It grew out of ISO 17799 and British Standard 7799. ISO 27002 is considered a management guideline, not a technical document. You can learn more at `www.27000.org/iso-27002.htm`. ISO 27002 provides best practice recommendations on information security management for use by those responsible for leading, planning, implementing, or maintaining security. The ISO 27002 standard latest 2022 release notes can be found here: `www.iso.org/obp/ui/#iso:std:iso-iec:27002:ed-3:v2:en`.

Open Web Application Security Project (OWASP)

"The Open Web Application Security Project® (OWASP) is a nonprofit foundation that works to improve the security of software. Through community-led open-source software projects, hundreds of local chapters worldwide, tens of thousands of members, and leading educational and training conferences, the OWASP Foundation is the source for developers and technologists to secure the web," according to `owasp.org`. Standards and guidelines may be sourced from government or the open-source community, including the CMU Software Engineering Institute (SEI), NIST, and OWASP. The OWASP project provides resources and tools for web developers. OWASP maintains a collection of tools and documents that are organized into the following categories:

Protect   Tools and documents that can be used to guard against security-related design and implementation flaws

Detect   Tools and documents that can be used to find security-related design and implementation flaws

Life Cycle   Tools and documents that can be used to add security-related activities into the SDLC

Application exploits are a broad category of attack vectors that computer criminals use to target applications. There are many ways in which an attacker can target applications. Regardless of the path taken, if successful, the attacker can do harm to your business or organization. The resulting damage may range from minor impact to putting your company out of business. Depending on how the application has been designed, an application exploit may be easy to find or extremely difficult to pinpoint. With so much to consider, there needs to be a starting point. As such, OWASP lists the top 10 application security risks in 2021 as follows:

1. Broken access control
2. Cryptographic failure
3. Injection
4. Insecure design
5. Security misconfiguration
6. Vulnerable and outdated components
7. Identification and authentication failure
8. Software and data integrity failure
9. Security logging and monitoring failure
10. Server-side request forgery (SSRF)

Proper Hypertext Transfer Protocol Headers

Hypertext Transfer Protocol (HTTP) is one of the best-known applications. HTTP makes use of TCP port 80. Even though HTTP uses TCP, it makes use of a stateless connection. HTTP uses a request-response protocol in which a client sends a request, and a server sends a response.

HTTP headers are an important part of HTTP requests and responses. They are mainly intended for the communication between the server and client. More specifically, they are the name or value pairs that are in the request and response messages separated by a single colon. There are four types of HTTP headers:

- **Request Header:** To the server and includes OS used by client and page requested
- **Response Header:** To the client and includes type, date, and size of file
- **General Header:** For both client and server and includes date, caching information, warnings, and protocol upgrade data if necessary
- **Entity Header:** Information for encoding, language, location, and MD5 hashing for integrity of message upon receipt

Attacks that exploit HTTP can target the server, browser, or scripts that run on the browser. Cross-site scripting (XSS) and cross-site request forgery (XSRF or CSRF) attacks are two such examples. Basically, hackers craft special packets in a way that exploits vulnerable code on the web server.

Again, there are automated tools that can do this, and a good place to start researching this technology is the Open Web Application Security Project (OWASP) website at www .owasp.org/index.php/Main_Page. Consider instead using HTTPS over port 443.

Data Security Techniques for Securing Enterprise Architecture

There are daily headlines of breaches where data is stolen and leaked. No enterprise is immune to data breaches, but with layers of defense in depth, you can make your organization more difficult to attack than others. By taking measures that have been proven to ensure data security, you promote trust in corporate stakeholders, consumers, and auditors.

Data Loss Prevention

Detecting and blocking data exfiltration requires the use of security event management solutions that can closely monitor outbound data transmissions. Data loss prevention (DLP) requires the analysis of egress network traffic for anomalies and the use of better outbound firewall controls that perform deep packet inspection. Deep packet inspection normally is done by a device at a network boundary, for example by a web application firewall at the trusted network's perimeter. To select where such a device should be placed in any organization, it's important to have a data flow diagram, depicting where and how data flows throughout the network.

Blocking Use of External Media

Enterprise organizations rely on controlling which services and device capabilities can be used, and even where they can be used. Limiting or prohibiting the use of cameras and cell phones can help prevent data leakage from secure areas. Limiting the use of external media and USB functionality that allows devices to act as hosts for USB external devices like cameras or storage can also help to limit the potential for misuse of devices. This can be a useful privacy control or may be required by the organization as part of documentation processes.

Some organizations, like contractors for the United States Department of Defense, ban cell phones with cameras from their facilities. While it used to be easy to buy a phone without a camera, finding one now is very difficult. That's where mobile device management features that can block camera use can be handy. While there may be workarounds, having a software package with the ability to block features like this may be an acceptable and very handy control for some organizations.

Some organizations go so far as to block printers from accessing the Internet. *Print blocking* means if you work around many Wi-Fi locations or you have many computers or printers in one area, you can prevent others from being able to print on your printer or intercept files being sent to that printer.

Remote Desktop Protocol Blocking

Desktop sharing programs are extremely useful, but there are potential risks. One issue is that anyone who can connect to and use your desktop can execute or run programs on your computer. A search on the Web for Microsoft Remote Desktop Services returns a list of hundreds of systems to which you can potentially connect if you can guess the username and password.

At a minimum, these ports and applications should be blocked or restricted to those individuals who have a need for this service. Advertising this service on the Web is also not a good idea. If this is a public link, it should not be indexed by search engines. There should also be a warning banner on the page that states that the service is for authorized users only and that all activity is logged.

Another issue with desktop sharing is the potential risk from the user's point of view. If the user shares the desktop during a videoconference, then others in the conference can see what is on the presenter's desktop. Should there be a folder titled "divorce papers" or "why I hate my boss," everyone will see it.

Application sharing is fraught with risks as well. If the desktop sharing user then opens an application such as email or a web browser before the session is truly terminated, anybody still in the meeting can read and/or see what's been opened. Any such incident looks highly unprofessional and can sink a business deal.

Clipboard Privacy Controls

When working on any type of application on any type of device, sometimes it is much easier to cut, copy, and paste that address information into a text or the URL into a browser. However, security professionals should know that some systems, including Androids, have incredibly insecure clipboards. Any application on an Android phone can read it without your permission. Any application that is installed that declares the permission *android.permission.READ_CLIPBOARD* in their `AndroidManifest.xml` file is automatically granted this permission when it is installed, meaning they can read the Android clipboard. In Windows, information is copied into Clipboard History in clear text and synced across different devices and accounts. It is convenient but not very secure. It is generally recommended that you never copy any sensitive data.

Restricted Virtual Desktop Infrastructure Implementation

Remember dumb terminals and the thin client concept? This has evolved into what is known as the virtual desktop infrastructure (VDI). This centralized desktop solution uses servers to serve up a desktop operating system to a host system. Each hosted desktop virtual machine is running an operating system such as Windows 11 or Windows Server 2019. The remote desktop is delivered to the user's endpoint device via Remote Desktop Protocol (RDP), Citrix, or other architecture. Technologies such as RDP are great for remote connectivity, but they can also allow remote access by an attacker. Questions about these technologies are likely to appear on the CASP+ exam.

This system has lots of benefits, such as reduced onsite support and greater centralized management. However, a disadvantage of this solution is that there is a significant investment in hardware and software to build the backend infrastructure, as well as security issues. To create a more restrictive interface, best practices include disabling local USB, segregating networks, restricting access, and doing a thorough job building the master image. An administrator should avoid bundling all applications in the base image. The best way to manage this is to create a clean base image and then manage applications with profiles and groups.

Data Classification Blocking

Not all data is created equal. A data classification policy describes the classification structure used by the organization and the process used to properly assign classifications to data. Data classification informs us of what kind of data we have, where it is, and how well we need to protect it. Combining data classification with a data loss prevention (DLP) policy results in your most sensitive data being the most protected. Security policies around the protection of data should be implemented with realistic and easy-to-understand procedures that are automated and audited periodically. Security policy should also outline how employees are using data and downloading files and how they are protecting them. A rule of not allowing certain data classes to be removed from protected enclaves is one way of blocking sensitive data from leaving the environment.

Data Loss Detection

The Information Age, also known as the computer age, is a period that began in the mid-20th century as the world shifted from the Industrial Revolution to a digital one. Data became instantly accessible to anyone with an Internet connection, as well as a monetized commodity. Data in use, data in motion/transit, and data at rest must be strategically protected to prevent any unauthorized access.

Watermarking

Although the term *steganography* is typically used to describe illicit activities, *watermarking* is used for legal purposes. It is typically used to identify ownership or the copyright of material such as videos or images. If any of these items are copies, the digital copy would be the same as the original; therefore, watermarking is a passive protection tool. It flags the data's ownership but does not degrade it in any way. It is an example of digital rights management.

Digital Rights Management

Digital rights management (DRM) is an entire suite of technologies designed to protect digital content. As an example, you may be reading a copy of this book on your tablet, yet that does not mean the publisher wants to provide free copies to 100 of your closest friends! That is the situation for which DRM is designed: it helps prevent copyright infringement online and thus helps the copyright holder maintain control of the information.

Network Traffic Analysis

Network traffic analysis (NTA) is important for networks because sophisticated attackers frequently go undetected in a victim's network for an extended period. Attackers can blend their traffic with legitimate traffic that only skilled network analysts know how to detect. A skilled cybersecurity professional should know how to identify malicious network activity as well as network protocols, network architecture, intrusion detection systems, network traffic capture, and traffic analysis. Network tools commonly used to analyze captured network traffic include Wireshark and the command-line versions Tshark or TCPdump.

Network Traffic Decryption/Deep Packet Inspection

Wireshark can also be used for some packet inspection, but there are tools that go deeper. Deep packet inspection (DPI) is a form of packet filtering that is able to inspect the information as well as the contents of the packet itself. Wireshark can tell that HTTP is being used but cannot view the contents of an encrypted packet. DPI has the ability to do something about traffic that fits a profile, such as dropping the whole packet or limiting bandwidth. Tools like nDPI are open-source tools, while Cisco's Network Based Application Recognition (NBAR) is on many Cisco devices.

Data Classification, Labeling, and Tagging

Information classification strengthens the organization in many ways. Labeling information *secret* or *strictly confidential* helps employees see the value of the information and give it a higher standard of care. Information classification also specifies how employees are to handle specific information. For example, a company policy might state, "All sensitive documents must be removed from the employee's desk when leaving work. We support a clean desk policy." Tagging and marking a piece of data based on its category helps make it searchable, trackable, and protected in the most efficient way.

There are two widely used information classification systems that have been adopted. Each is focused on a different portion of the CIA security triad. These two approaches are as follows:

> **Government Classification System**   This system focuses on confidentiality.
>
> **Commercial Classification System**   This system focuses on integrity.

The governmental information classification system is divided into the following categories:

- **Top Secret:** Its disclosure would cause grave damage to national security. This information requires the highest level of control.

- **Secret:** Its disclosure would be expected to cause serious damage to national security and may divulge significant scientific, technological, operational, and logistical secrets, as well as many other developments.

- **Confidential:** Its disclosure could cause damage to national security and should be safeguarded against disclosure.

- **Unclassified:** Information is not sensitive and need not be protected unless For Official Use Only (FOUO) is appended to the classification. Unclassified information would not normally cause damage, but over time Unclassified FOUO information could be compiled to deduce information of a higher classification.

The commercial information classification system is focused not just on confidentiality but also on the integrity of information; therefore, it is divided into the following categories:

- **Confidential:** This is the most sensitive rating. This is the information that keeps a company competitive. Not only is this information for internal use only, but its release or alteration could seriously affect or damage a corporation.

- **Private:** This category of restricted information is considered personal in nature and might include medical records or human resource information.

- **Sensitive:** This information requires controls to prevent its release to unauthorized parties. Damage could result from its loss of confidentiality or its loss of integrity.

- **Public:** This is similar to unclassified information in that its disclosure or release would cause no damage to the corporation.

Depending on the industry in which the business operates and its specific needs, one of these options will typically fit better than the other. Regardless of the classification system chosen, security professionals play a key role in categorizing information and helping to determine classification guidelines. Once an organization starts the classification process, it's forced to ask what would happen if specific information was released and how its release would damage or affect the organization.

Metadata/Attributes

Metadata generated as a regular part of operations, communications, and other activities can also be used for incident response. Metadata is information about other data. In the case of systems and services, metadata is created as part of files and embedded documents, is used to define structured data, and is included in transactions and network communications amongst many other places you can find it. Metadata attributes express qualifications on content and can be used to modify how the content is processed or filtered. Another use is to flag content based on values or status. Metadata attributes can provide a list of one or more qualifications such as `administrator programmer`. This means the content applies to both administrators and programmers.

The following are common types of metadata to understand:

- **Email:** This includes headers and other information found in an email. Email headers provide specifics about the sender, the recipient, the date, and time the message was sent, and if the email had an attachment.

- **Mobile:** Data is collected by phones and other mobile devices including call logs, SMS and other message data, data usage, GPS location tracking, and cellular tower information. Mobile metadata is incredibly powerful because of the amount of geospatial information that is recorded about where the phone has traveled.

- **Web:** This is embedded into a website as part of the code of the website but is invisible to average users and includes meta tags, headers, cookies, and other information that may help with search engine optimization, website functionality, advertising, and tracking.

- **File:** This is a powerful tool when reviewing when a file was created, how it was created, if and when it was modified, and who modified it. Metadata is commonly used for forensics and other investigations, and most forensic tools have built-in metadata viewing capabilities.

Another key consideration is metadata embedded into documents or PDFs, or even EXIF data in photos. This has become a serious risk, and tools like Fingerprinting Organizations with Collected Archives (FOCA) can show hidden metadata with sensitive information like internal shares, usernames, software versions, and so on. Take a moment to review the article at www.darkreading.com/risk/-foca-and-the-power-of-metadata-analysis.

Obfuscation

Obfuscation means being evasive, unclear, or confusing. Encryption is a way to obfuscate data, rendering it extremely difficult to use. Other ways to obfuscate data in an enterprise are to use the following techniques:

- **Tokenization:** Replace sensitive data with a unique nonsensitive identification element, called a token, that has no exploitable value
- **Scrubbing:** Sometimes called cleansing; fixing incorrect or duplicate data in a data set
- **Masking:** Hiding or filtering data so only the data you want is shown

Tokenization, scrubbing, and masking are important terms to understand on the exam. Some exam questions may have obfuscated data, and the exam taker must distinguish how the information has been made difficult to use.

Anonymization

Anonymization of data is removing anything in a data set that could identify an individual. By removing sensitive or private information such as names, Social Security numbers, or phone numbers, the data itself remains, but it cannot be attributed to a single individual, preserving a data subject's privacy. When data becomes anonymized, it can be used for the greater good while ensuring the rights of the individual.

Encrypted vs. Unencrypted

Cryptography can be defined as the art of protecting information by transforming it into an unreadable format using a form of encryption. Everywhere you turn you see cryptography. It is used to protect sensitive information, prove the identity of a claimant, and verify the integrity of an application or program. As a security professional for your company, which of the following would you consider more critical if you could choose only one?

- Provide a locking cable for every laptop user in the organization.
- Enforce full disk encryption for every mobile device.

Our choice would be full disk encryption. Typically, the data will be worth more than the cost of a replacement laptop. If the data is lost or exposed, you'll incur additional costs such as client notification and reputation loss.

Encryption is not a new concept. The desire to keep secrets is as old as civilization. There are two basic ways in which encryption is used: for data at rest and for data in motion/transit. Data at rest might be information on a laptop hard drive or in cloud storage. Data in motion/transit might be data being processed by SQL, a URL requested via HTTP, or information traveling over a VPN at the local coffee shop bound for the corporate network. In each of these cases, protection must be sufficient.

Data classification should play a large role in the strategy of data being encrypted vs unencrypted. If data is available to the public, then unencrypted makes perfect sense. If the data is sensitive, then encryption is important to keep that information secure.

Data Life Cycle

The data life cycle, sometimes called the information framework, is the process of tracking data through its evolution, start to finish. As shown in Figure 8.1, the data life cycle is called a cycle but is more of a linear process.

FIGURE 8.1   The data life cycle

Data is first generated or captured. After the raw data is captured, it is processed or used in analysis or integrations. At this stage, often it is ingested, reformatted, or summarized into another workflow. Data gets shared when analysis turns into a decision and more information is gained. The storage of data after it has been gathered and analyzed can be kept in a location where it can be easily accessed for even more evaluation. Once the information has served its current purpose and before it's destroyed permanently, it is archived for any possible future value it might have.

Data Inventory and Mapping

Data inventory records basic information about a data asset including name, contents, privacy, compliance requirements, use license, data owner, and data source. To create a data inventory, a project manager or committee needs to form, since data will be gathered from multiple areas of the business. After business needs are collected, then a definition of the inventory scope is formalized, and a catalog of data assets can be built. With data coming from multiple areas of the business and possibly from disparate databases, data must be mapped by matching fields from one database to another, very much like creating a primary key in a table. For the best decisions to be made, the information must be digested and analyzed in a way that makes logical sense.

Data Integrity Management

Improper storage of sensitive data is a big problem. Sensitive data is not always protected by the appropriate controls or cryptographic solutions. As mentioned previously, during the requirements phase of the SDLC process, security controls for sensitive data must be defined. At this point, these questions must be asked:

▪ Does the data require encryption?

▪ Is personal information such as credit card numbers, health records, or other sensitive data being stored?

▪ Is a strong encryption standard being used?

If you answered yes to any of these questions, controls should be implemented to protect the data. A CASP+ must be concerned with not just the storage of sensitive data but also how the data is accessed.

 Sensitive data exposure is one of the Top 10 application security risks as judged by OWASP. According to OWASP, a common flaw in this area is using no encryption on sensitive data.

A CASP+ must also be concerned about what happens to the data at its end of life. This is when data remanence becomes a big concern. Data remanence refers to any residual data left on storage media. Depending on the sensitivity of the information, wiping a drive may be sufficient, or you may need to oversee the destruction of the media. Services are available that offer secure hard drive destruction that shreds or crushes drives before disposing of the pieces that remain. Data remanence is also a major concern when using the cloud.

Data Storage, Backup, and Recovery

Think of how much data is required for most modern enterprises. There is a huge dependence on information for the business world to survive. Although the amount of storage needed continues to climb, there is also the issue of terminology used in the enterprise storage market.

As a CASP+ candidate, you will be expected to understand the basics of enterprise storage and also grasp the security implications of secure storage management. Before any enterprise storage solution is implemented, a full assessment and classification of the data should occur. This would include an analysis of all threats, vulnerabilities, existing controls, and the potential impact of loss, disclosure, modification, interruption, or destruction of the data.

From a security standpoint, one of the first tasks in improving the overall security posture of an organization is to identify where data resides. The advances in technology make this much more difficult than it was in the past. Years ago, *Redundant Array of Inexpensive/ Independent Disks (RAID)* was the standard for data storage and redundancy.

The use of redundant arrays of inexpensive disks, or RAID, is a common solution that uses multiple disks with data either striped (spread across disks) or mirrored (completely copied), and technology to ensure that data is not corrupted or lost (parity) to ensure that one or more disk failures can be handled by an array without losing data.

RAID can be deployed several ways, depending on the need of the system for either speed or redundancy. RAID 0 is all about optimizing the speed of your hard drives. If you have at least two drives, using RAID 0 will combine them and write data on both of them simultaneously or sequentially, creating data striping. This will help with read and write speeds. If one drive fails, you will lose all of your data. RAID 1 requires a two-drive minimum and is called *data mirroring* because the same information is written on both drives. RAID 3 and RAID 5 each have a three-drive minimum. RAID 10 (also called 1+0) requires four drives at a minimum. It combines RAID 1 and RAID 0. A variant exists, called 0+1. Both provide fault tolerance and increased performance.

Today, companies have moved to *dynamic disk pools (DDPs)* and cloud storage. DDP shuffles data, parity information, and spare capacity across a pool of drives so that the data is better protected and downtime is reduced. DDPs can be rebuilt up to eight times faster than traditional RAID.

Enterprise storage infrastructures may not have adequate protection mechanisms. The following basic security controls should be implemented:

Know your assets.   Perform an inventory to know what data you have and where it is stored.

Build a security policy.   A corporate security policy is essential. Enterprise storage is just one item that should be addressed.

Implement controls.   The network should be designed with a series of technical controls, such as the following:

- Intrusion detection system (IDS)/intrusion prevention system (IPS)
- Firewalls
- Network access control (NAC)

Harden your systems.   Remove unnecessary services and applications.

Perform proper updates.   Use patch management systems to roll out and deploy patches as needed.

Segment the infrastructure.   Segment areas of the network where enterprise storage mechanisms are used.

Use encryption.   Evaluate protection for data at rest and for data in transit.

Implement logging and auditing.   Enterprise storage should have sufficient controls so that you can know who attempts to gain access, what requests fail, when changes to access are made, or when other suspicious activities occur.

Use change control.   Use change control and IT change management to control all changes. Changes should occur in an ordered process.

Implement trunking security.   Trunking security is typically used with VLANs. The concept is to block access to layer 2 devices based on their MAC address. Blocking the device by its MAC address effectively prevents the device from communicating through any network switch. This stops the device from propagating malicious traffic to any other network-connected devices.

Port Security   When addressing the control of traffic at layer 2 on a switch, the term used today is port security. Port security specifically speaks to limiting what traffic is allowed in and out of particular switch ports. This traffic is controlled per layer 2 address or MAC address. One example of typical port security is when a network administrator knows that a fixed set of MAC addresses are expected to send traffic through a switch port. The administrator can employ port security to ensure that traffic from no other MAC address will be allowed into that port and traverse the switch.

Now that we've explored some of the security controls of enterprise storage, let's look at some of the storage technology used in enterprise storage.

Virtual Storage   Over the last 20 years, virtual storage options have grown, evolved, and matured. These online entities typically focus either on storage or on sharing. The storage services are designed for storage of large files. Many companies are entering this market and giving away storage, such as Microsoft's OneDrive, Amazon Drive, and Google Drive.

Virtual file sharing services are a second type of virtual storage. These services are not meant for long-term use. They allow users to transfer large files. These virtual services work well if you are trying to share very large files or move information that is too big to fit as an attachment.

On the positive side, there are many great uses for these services, such as keeping a synchronized copy of your documents in an online collaboration environment, sharing documents, and synchronizing documents between desktops, laptops, tablets, and smartphones.

Security Requirements and Objectives for Authentication and Authorization Controls

The major objective for authentication and authorization is to confirm the identity of who is accessing your data, applications, and websites. Authentication confirms someone is who they say they are, and authorization gives them access to use a certain resource. It is one of the major tenets of cybersecurity.

Credential Management

Credential management policies describe the account life cycle from provisioning through active use and decommissioning using a set of tools to manage local, network, or internet credentials. This policy should include specific requirements for personnel who are employees of the organization, as well as third-party contractors. It should also include requirements for credentials used by devices, service accounts, and administrator/root accounts.

Password Repository Application

A password repository is a password vault to keep all your passwords safe. Just about every website that you visit today, from banking and social media accounts to shopping applications, require a user account and password. It is very difficult for a human being to remember different passwords for all of those accounts, so many end users create simple passwords like "123456789" or "Password123!" if complexity is required. Several examples of these include LastPass, Dashlane, and Keychain.

End-User Password Storage

A password repository will store passwords for you securely and assist in the generation of new ones. A password manager is essentially an encrypted vault for storing passwords that is itself protected by a master password. To obtain access to the passwords stored in the manager, a user has to know the master password; in many cases, a second authentication factor is required as well.

Password vaults can be used to simply store passwords for easy recall, but one of the best features of most password managers is their ability to generate passwords. A lengthier password is more protected and harder to crack, and the passwords generated by password managers are combinations of random numbers and letters that are very secure.

Another significant feature of most password managers is the ability to automatically fill in passwords to stored sites. By using that feature you won't have to type anything but the master password, and it's also a good way to avoid having passwords stolen by keylogging malware.

Most organizations have somewhat limited visibility into what passwords their employees are using, which can increase their risk both on premises and in the cloud. Another risk factor for passwords is that many of those employees reuse those passwords for multiple accounts, both personal and professional. With the adoption of cloud infrastructure, many organizations still struggle with enforcing password policies on all systems. With so many applications in the SaaS model, a business should look to using a next-generation password management system using multifactor authentication (MFA) and single sign-on (SSO) for security and compliance.

Another option for enterprise organization is a physical *hardware key manager* to combat the challenge of memorizing complex passphrases and keep employees from reusing passwords across multiple applications. Using a hardware key manager is a really good way of creating and maintaining passwords for all account logins.

Privileged Access Management

Privileged users have accounts that give them complete access to your IT ecosystem. These accounts can belong to internal administrators or external contractors, allowing them to manage network devices, operating systems, and applications. Because of their level of access, admin credentials are the number-one target of most bad actors. Admins can create other admins.

With an ever-changing landscape and staffing, managing these privileged accounts becomes difficult. Access management tooling allows insight into who is doing what in the environment. This allows secure access from a central location and adapts to security solutions already deployed in the environment.

Password Policies

As a security administrator, you've no doubt heard many stories about how some people do very little to protect their passwords. Sometimes people write their passwords down on sticky notes, place them under their keyboards, or even leave them on a scrap of paper taped to the monitor. As a security professional, you should not only help formulate good password policy but also help users understand why and how to protect passwords. One solution might be to offer password manager programs that can be used to secure passwords. Another approach is migration to biometric or token-based authentication systems.

Testing Password Strength

For this scenario, you'll need to put yourself in the position of an attacker wanting to examine the strength of your password. From this perspective, you will test passwords at www.security.org/how-secure-is-my-password with the following attributes:

- Create a password that is seven lowercase characters.

- Create a password that is seven uppercase and lowercase characters.

- Create a password that is 14 uppercase and lowercase characters and that includes at least one special character.

Some best practices include the following:

- Configure passwords to be a minimum certain length as well as using special characters to increase complexity.

- Set options to enforce password history to 24. This helps mitigate any vulnerabilities caused by password reuse.

- Set maximum password age to expire between 60 and 90 days.

- Configure password age so that passwords can be changed only once within a specific time frame such as 24 hours.

One of my favorite penetration tester stories is of a targeted phishing campaign launched against a specific department where six people clicked the link in the email, and two of the six were logged in to their administrators' accounts when they clicked and were compromised in 22 seconds. Within hours, the entire network belonged to the pen tester. You have to control who has administrative privileges and even how those administrators use their credentials. When you are logged in as an admin, you should not be opening your email under any circumstances. That is what your standard user account is for.

Two very common attacks rely on privilege to execute. That is one reason the Common Vulnerability Scoring System (CVSS) actually measures if privilege is necessary for exploitability. The first type of an attack is like the one I described previously where a user with elevated credentials opens a malicious attachment. The other is the elevation of privilege when cracking a password for an administrator. If the password policy is weak or not enforced, the danger increases exponentially.

Educate leadership and help create a robust security posture where you restrict admin privilege. Have IT admins make a list of the tasks that they do on an average day. Check the tasks that require administrative credentials. Create an account for normal tasks that all users can use, and use the admin account for only those tasks where it's necessary. If you have executives insisting that they need admin privileges, remind them that they are the ones that hackers are targeting.

Microsoft has guidance on implementing least privilege. For Linux, each sysadmin should have a separate account and enforce the use of sudo by disabling su. You should also change all default passwords on all assets in your environment as well as making sure that each password is as robust as possible. Use multifactor authentication and configure systems to issue an alert if an admin mistypes their password.

Password hygiene is a fiercely debated topic in IT. If a user thinks they are compromised, immediately change any passwords that might have been revealed. If the same passwords are used on multiple sites for different accounts, change those as well, and don't ever use that password again. Some sites require the password to be a certain length with uppercase, lowercase, and special characters. Some people swear by using password managers like Last-Pass, Keeper, and Dashlane. A password manager is a tool that does the work of creating and remembering all the passwords for your accounts. It sounds great in theory but is a single point of failure.

To make accounts safer, you should make sure your passwords are:

- Long and complex. Ideally, your password should be totally randomized with uppercase and lowercase letters, making it very difficult to remember. Try to create a long passphrase out of one of your favorite books—for example, Wh0i$J0hnG@1t!.

- Do not write them down or use birthdays.

- Do not reuse passwords.

- Change passwords when instructed according to policy.

- Always use multifactor authentication, whenever possible.

- Don't be too terribly social on social media. Nearly 90 million Facebook accounts had their profile information shared by researchers using a third-party quiz app. If you aren't paying for it, you are the product. Nothing is ever truly private on social media.

A single weak password can expose your entire network to a bad actor. A password audit is using an application that allows an internal team to verify that the passwords used in the environment are not easy for a dictionary attack or brute-force attack to reverse engineer. Storing encrypted passwords in a way that is reversible means that an experienced attacker could decrypt those passwords and then log into network assets using that compromised account.

Password auditing tools run on and verify passwords on different operating systems. Applications like RainbowCrack use a brute-force hash to generate all possible plaintexts and compute the hashes. Once a match is found, the plaintext is found. This can be time consuming but is very important to the security of a large enterprise.

Federation

Wouldn't it be nice if you could log into one site such as outlook.live.com/owa and not have to repeat the login process as you visit other third-party sites? Well, you can do just that with services such as federation. Federation is similar to single sign-on (SSO). SSO allows someone to log in once and have access to any network resource, whereas federation allows you to link your digital identity to multiple sites and use those credentials to log into multiple accounts and systems that are controlled by different entities.

Federated ID is the means of linking a person's electronic identity and attributes, stored across multiple distinct identity management systems. Of course, these kinds of systems are often just as vulnerable as any other. One example is in RSA Federated Identity Manager under CVE-2010-2337. This specific example could potentially allow a remote attacker to redirect a user to an arbitrary website and perform phishing attacks, as referenced in the NIST National Vulnerability Database at nvd.nist.gov/vuln/detail/CVE-2010-2337.

Transitive Trust

Transitive trust theory means that if A trusts B and B trusts C, then logically A should be able to trust C. In Microsoft Active Director, transitive trust is a two-way relationship between domains. When a new domain is created, it automatically shares resources with its parent by default. This allows a user to access resources in both the child and the parent.

OpenID

OpenID is an open standard that is used as an authentication scheme. OpenID allows users to log on to many different websites using the same identity on each of the sites. As an example, you may log in to a news site with your Facebook username and password. OpenID was developed by the OpenID Foundation. OpenID works as a set of standards that includes OpenID Authentication, Attribute Exchange, Simple Registration Extension, and Provider Authentication Policy Exchange.

OpenID Connect (OIDC) is an authentication protocol built on OAuth 2.0 that you can use to sign in a user to an application securely. When you use the Microsoft identity platform's implementation of OpenID Connect, you can add sign-in and API access to your apps.

Security Assertion Markup Language

Security Assertion Markup Language (SAML) is one example of a protocol designed for cross-web service authentication and authorization. SAML is an XML-based standard that provides a mechanism to exchange authentication and authorization data between different entities.

Over time, SAML promises to improve new generations of web service. The protocol was created by the Organization for the Advancement of Structured Information Standards (OASIS), a nonprofit consortium that develops and adopts open standards for the global information society. One outcome of its work is SAML, which allows business entities to make assertions regarding the identity, attributes, and entitlements of a subject. This means that SAML allows users to authenticate once and then be able to access services offered by different companies. At the core of SAML is the XML schema that defines the representation of security data; this can be used to pass the security context between applications.

For SAML to be effective on a large scale, trust relationships need to be established between remote web services. The SAML specification makes use of pairwise circles of trust, brokered trust, and community trust. Extending these solutions beyond the Internet has been problematic and has led to the proliferation of noninteroperable proprietary technologies. In terms of protocol sequences, SAML is similar to OpenID.

SAML assertions are communicated by a web browser through cookies or URL strings. These include the following:

MIME   SAML assertions are packaged into a single Multipurpose Internet Mail Extensions (MIME) security package.

SOAP   SAML assertions are attached to the Simple Object Access Protocol (SOAP) document's envelope header to secure the payload.

 Topics such as SAML, XML, and SOAP are all likely to be seen on the CASP+ exam.

Shibboleth

Shibboleth can be described as a distributed web resource access control system. Shibboleth enhances federation by allowing the sharing of web-based resources. When you use Shibboleth, the target website trusts the source site to authenticate its users and manage their attributes correctly. The disadvantage of this model is that there is no differentiation between authentication authorities and attribute authorities.

Access Control

Authentication is the process of proving the veracity, or truth, of a claim, or to put it differently, proving that a user is who they claim to be. Various network authentication methods have been developed over the years. These are divided into four basic categories known as authentication factors:

- Something you know

- Something you have

- Something you are

- Somewhere you are

These four authentication factors are discussed again later in the "Multifactor Authentication" section of this chapter.

If authentication is controlled by virtue of a person's location, time, or even behavior, this is an example of context-based authentication. For example, if a user doesn't ever normally sign in on a weekend, or past 7 p.m. on weeknights, you can set a deny rule for that user if they attempt to authenticate after 7 p.m. Monday through Friday or anytime on weekends. Alternatively, the rule could prompt the user for a second form of authentication, such as using a key fob.

Another form of authentication is when a user opens an application on a mobile device, for example. The user approves the sign-in request, and then they are signed into the system. That process is called *out-of-band push-based authentication*.

Discretionary Access Control

Discretionary access control (DAC) gives users the capability to access organizational files and directories. DAC is based on the decision of the owner of the file or directory. DAC uses access control lists (ACLs) along with the Unix permission file system.

Mandatory Access Control

Mandatory access control (MAC) has been used by the government for many years. All files controlled by the MAC policies are based on different security levels. MAC allows for the system to run at the same or lower levels. Overriding MAC requires authorization from senior management.

Role-Based Access Control

Role-based access control (RBAC) systems rely on roles that are then matched with privileges that are allocated to those roles. This makes RBAC a popular option for enterprises that can quickly categorize personnel with roles like "cashier" or "database administrator" and provide users with the appropriate access to systems and data based on those roles. RBAC systems have some fundamental criteria to follow:

- Role assignment, which states that subjects can only use permissions that match a role they have been assigned.

- Role authorization, which states that the subject's active role must be authorized for the subject. This prevents subjects from taking on roles they shouldn't be able to.

- Permission authorization, which states that subjects can only use permissions that their active role is allowed to use.

These rules together describe how permissions can be applied in an RBAC system and hierarchies can be built that allow specific permissions to be accessible at the right stages based on roles in any particular ecosystem.

Rule-Based Access Control

Rule-based access control, sometimes called RBAC (and sometimes RuBAC to help differentiate it from role-based access control) is an applied set of rules or ACLs that apply to various objects or resources. When an attempt is made to access an object, the rule is checked to see if the access is allowed. A popular model of rule-based access control is a firewall rule set.

Attribute-Based Access Control

Attribute-based access control (ABAC) schemes are suitable for application security, where they are often used for enterprise systems that have complicated user roles and rights that vary depending on the roles that users have and the way they relate with a system. They're also used with databases and content management systems, microservices, and APIs for similar purposes.

Protocols

Secure protocols are another component of secure network infrastructure design. Routers and other network infrastructure devices should be capable of management by multiple secure access protocols. Insecure protocols such as Telnet and FTP should not be used.

Remote Authentication Dial-in User Service

In the Microsoft world, the component designed for remote access is Remote Access Services (RAS). RAS is designed to facilitate the management of remote access connections through dial-up modems. Unix systems also have built-in methods to enable remote access. Historically, these systems worked well with Remote Authentication Dial-In User Service (RADIUS), a protocol developed to be a centralized sign-on solution that could support authentication, authorization, and accountability. This method of remote access has been around for a while.

When other devices want to access the server, it sends a request message for matching the credentials. In response to this request, the server will give an access-accept message to the client if the credentials are correct and access-reject if the credentials are not. RADIUS is an open standard and can be utilized on other devices. RADIUS encrypts only passwords, not the username.

Terminal Access Controller Access Control System

Cisco has implemented a variety of remote access methods through its networking hardware and software. Originally, this was *Terminal Access Controller Access Control System (TACACS)*. TACACS has been enhanced by Cisco and expanded twice. The original version of TACACS provided a combination process of authentication and authorization. This was extended to Extended Terminal Access Controller Access Control System (XTACACS). XTACACS is proprietary to Cisco and provides separate authentication, authorization, and accounting processes. The most current version is TACACS+. It has added functionality and extended attribute control and accounting processes. TACACS+ also separates the authentication and authorization process into three separate areas: authentication, authorization, and accounting. While these processes could even be hosted on separate servers, it's not necessary.

Diameter

The *Diameter* protocol was designed to be an improvement over RADIUS and have better handling of mobile users (IP mobility). Diameter provides the functions of authentication, authorization, and accounting. However, RADIUS remains very popular.

Lightweight Directory Access Protocol

Lightweight Directory Access Protocol (LDAP) is an application protocol that is used for accessing directory services across a TCP/IP network. Active Directory (AD) is Microsoft's implementation of directory services and makes use of LDAP.

Kerberos

Kerberos has three parts: a client, a server, and a trusted third-party key distribution center (KDC) to mediate between them. Clients obtain tickets from the KDC, and they present these tickets to servers when connections are established. Kerberos tickets represent the client's credentials. Kerberos relies on symmetric key cryptography. Kerberos has been the default authentication mechanism used by Windows for both the desktop and server OS since Windows 2000 going forward. Kerberos offers Windows users faster connections, mutual authentication, delegated authentication, simplified trust management, and interoperability. Kerberos V5 [RFC4120] implementation may upgrade communication between clients and Key Distribution Centers (KDCs) to use the Transport Layer Security (TLS) [RFC5246] protocol. The TLS protocol offers integrity and privacy protected exchanges that can be authenticated using X.509 certificates, OpenPGP keys [RFC5081], and usernames and passwords via SRP [RFC5054].

Kerberos does have some areas that can be targeted by criminals. One of these is the fact that Kerberos, like all authentication protocols, has a defined life span. As such, any network using the Kerberos protocol for authentication will need to ensure that the clocks on all systems are synchronized through the use of a protocol such as Network Time Protocol (NTP). Also note that it is important to secure NTP. How to do so depends on your particular configuration; however, if for instance your network was receiving NTP information from pool.ntp.org, then the IP addresses associated with those particular NTP servers should be the only IP addresses permitted into your network over UDP port 123, the default NTP port. More advanced configurations are available. Kerberos is discussed further in the "Single Sign-On" section later in this chapter.

OAuth

Open Authorization (OAuth) is an authorization standard used by many websites. Its purpose is to allow a user or a service to access resources. It allows a user to authorize access to a third-party resource without providing them with the user's credentials. As an example, you might allow a Facebook app to access your Facebook account. In this situation, OAuth would allow an access token to be generated and issued to the third-party application by an authorization server with the approval of the Facebook account holder. As a side note, the process of using a small piece of data in place of data to be kept more secure is called tokenization.

802.1X

IEEE 802.1X is an IEEE standard for port-based Network Access Control (NAC). 802.1X is widely used in wireless environments, and it relies on EAP. 802.1X acts as an application proxy. It's much like a middleman in the authentication process.

For wireless authentication, 802.1X allows you to accept or reject a user who wants to be authenticated. There are three basic parts to 802.1X:

- The user
- An authentication server
- An authenticator acting as the go-between, typically the access point or wireless switch

It starts with a user initiating a "start" message to authenticate. The message goes to the authenticator, usually the access point. The AP requests the user's identity. The user responds with a packet containing the identity, and the AP forwards this packet to the authentication server. If the authentication server validates the user and accepts the packet, the AP is notified. The AP then places the user in an authorized state, allowing their traffic to go forward.

Extensible Authentication Protocol

Extensible Authentication Protocol (EAP) is an authentication framework that is used in wireless networks. EAP defines message formats and then leaves it up to the protocol to define a way to encapsulate EAP messages within that protocol's message. There are many different EAP formats in use, including EAP-TLS, EAP-TTLS, EAP-PSK, and EAP-MD5. Two common implementations of EAP are PEAP and LEAP.

Multifactor Authentication

Another important area of control is multifactor authentication. Authentication has moved far beyond simple usernames and passwords. Single sign-on (SSO), multifactor authentication, biometrics, and federated identity management are good examples of how this area is evolving. *Multifactor authentication (MFA)* is a method where a user is granted access after presenting two or more pieces of evidence. This evidence is usually broken down into the four types that were introduced earlier in the "Access Control" section.

- Type 1: Something you know (a PIN or password)
- Type 2: Something you have (a badge or token)
- Type 3: Something you are (a fingerprint or retina scan)
- Type 4: Where you are (geography)

Two-factor authentication (2FA) means you present two different types of authentication to a verification source. They cannot be two of the same type, like a handprint and a voice print. They have to be two different types for acceptance. The username and password, for example, is the knowledge factor of Type 1. The token or code that is generated is the Type 2. The user must know and have both to gain access.

In May 2021, Google announced that it was automatically enrolling its users into two-step verification. *Two-step verification* means you present one type and after verification, you are asked to present another, usually a verification code that was sent to your phone via text or voice call. To log in, users must enter that in addition to their usual password.

If that verification code is generated internally and it is sent via SMS to the mobile phone you just logged into the mobile application from, that is considered *in-band authentication*.

In-band authentication factors are not considered to be as secure as *out-of-band (OOB)* authentication. OOB factors in proofs of identity that do not arrive on or depend on the same system that is requesting the authentication. It is often used by organizations that require high security, such as healthcare and banking, where high security is needed to prevent unauthorized access.

One-Time Passwords

A *one-time password (OTP)* is exactly what it sounds like. It is a unique password that can be used only once and sometimes has a time expiration on it. Password resets will sometimes generate an OTP that must be used within 15 minutes or it expires. It is valid for a single login session or transaction. It can also be used in conjunction with a regular password for added security.

An HMAC-based one-time password (HOTP) is a hash-based message authentication code where the password algorithm will generate and be validated based on a counter. The code is usually valid until you request a new one that is, again, validated by the authentication server. YubiKey programmable tokens are an example of an HOTP.

A time-based one-time password is similar to the HOTP, but instead of a counter, it's based on a clock. The amount of time in each password is called a timestep. As a rule, a timestep is 30 to 60 seconds. If you don't use your password in that window, you will have to ask for a new one.

Hardware Root of Trust

According to NIST SP 800-172, *hardware root of trust* is defined as a "highly reliable component that performs specific, critical and security functions. Because roots of trust are inherently trusted, they must be secure by design." A hardware root of trust is a set of functions that is always trusted by an OS. It serves as a separate engine controlling the cryptographic processor on the PC or mobile device it is embedded in. The most popular example is the TPM or trusted platform module, which is a cryptoprocessor chip on the motherboard that is designed for security-related cryptographic procedures.

Single Sign-On

Another approach to managing a multitude of passwords is *single sign-on (SSO)*. SSO is designed to address this problem by permitting users to authenticate once to a single authentication authority and then access all other protected resources without reauthenticating. One of the most widely used SSO systems is Kerberos.

SSO allows a user to authenticate once and then access all of the resources that the user is authorized to use. Authentication to the individual resources is handled by SSO in a manner that is transparent to the user. There are several variations of SSO, including Kerberos and Sesame. Kerberos is the most widely used. Kerberos, which was previously discussed in the "Kerberos" section earlier in the chapter, is composed of three parts: client, server, and a trusted third party, the key distribution center (KDC), which mediates between them.

The authentication service issues ticket-granting tickets (TGTs) that are good for admission to the ticket-granting service (TGS). Before network clients are able to obtain tickets for services, they must first obtain a TGT from the authentication service. The ticket-granting service issues the client tickets to specific target services.

A common approach to using Kerberos is to use it for authentication and use Lightweight Directory Access Protocol (LDAP) as the directory service to store authentication information. SSO enables users to sign in only once without IT having to manage several different usernames and passwords. By making use of one or more centralized servers, a security professional can allow or block access to resources should changes be needed. The disadvantage of SSO is that the service may become a single point of failure for authentication to many resources, so the availability of the server affects the availability of all of the resources that rely on the server for authentication services. Also, any compromise of the server means that an attacker has access to many resources.

Another concern is mutual authentication; if SSO is not used to authenticate both the client and the server, it can be vulnerable to on-path (formerly known as man-in-the-middle) attacks. Even when SSO is implemented, only the authentication process is secured. If after authentication an insecure protocol is used, such as FTP, passwords and other information can be sniffed, or captured, by keylogging or other means.

JavaScript Object Notation Web Token

JavaScript Object Notation (JSON) is a lightweight, human-readable programming format that is a natural fit with JavaScript applications. It's an alternative to XML, and it is primarily used to transmit data between a server and a web application. One potential security issue is that JSON can be used to execute JavaScript. Representational State Transfer (REST) is used in mobile applications and mashup tools as a type of simple stateless architecture that generally runs over HTTP. It is considered easier to use than other technologies, such as SOAP. Its advantages include ease of use and modification and that it helps organize complex datasets.

JavaScript Object Notation (JSON) Web Token (JWT) is a way to securely send information between entities as a JSON object because it is digitally signed. It can be signed with a secret or public/private keys using RSA. This creates a signed token that verifies the integrity of the information. When using a private/public key pair, it also gives the data non-repudiation. JSON JWT is used quite a bit with SSO because of its ability to be used across different domains.

Attestation and Identity Proofing

Attestation is the act of proving something is true and correct. Attestation is a critical component for trusted computing environments, providing an essential proof of trust. Attestation is used in the authentication process, and it is also part of services such as TPM.

Identify proofing, also called identity verification, is as simple as it sounds: verifying the user's identity as being legitimate. For example, let's say that a certification candidate is ready to take a proctored exam. Being proctored means that a trusted authority will oversee the exam and verify that each person coming in to take the exam is indeed the same registered person who paid for it and who will receive the credential upon passing. The authority will greet the candidate at the entrance and ask for an ID. The next step is identity proofing or verifying that the person is who they say they are.

Summary

This chapter focused on the duties and responsibilities of a CASP+ with regard to appropriate security controls for an enterprise. This chapter examined the following subjects:

- Secure network architecture
- Requirements for proper infrastructure security design
- Integrating software apps securely
- Implementing data security techniques
- Providing authentication and authorization controls

The subjects fit into the broader concepts of network protocols and applications and services.

Modern networks are built on the TCP/IP protocol stack. As a CASP+, you should have a good understanding of how TCP/IP works. You should also have a grasp of network flow analysis. You must also understand the importance of securing routing protocols and be familiar with controls put in place to improve transport security, trunking security, and route protection.

Applications and services are also of importance to a CASP+. You must know how to secure DNS, understand the importance of securing zone transfers, and know how to configure LDAP.

There are authentication along with authentication protocols. This critical component is used as a first line of defense to keep hackers off your network. Systems such as federated ID, AD, and single sign-on can be used to manage this process more securely.

Communication is the lifeblood of most modern organizations, and a failure of these systems can be disastrous. However, these systems must also be controlled. Email is one example of a modern communication system that most organizations rely on. Email is clear text and can easily be sniffed and, as such, requires adequate security controls. With email, there is also the issue of content. A CASP+ must understand threats to the business, potential risks, and ways to mitigate risks. Risk is something that we must deal with every day on a personal and business level. Policy is one way to deal with risk. On the people side of the business, policy should dictate what employees can and cannot do. Even when risk is identified and has been associated with a vulnerability, a potential cost must still be determined. You must also understand aspects of the business that go beyond basic IT security. These items include partnerships, mergers, and acquisitions.

Exam Essentials

Be able to describe IDSs and IPSs.   An intrusion detection system (IDS) gathers and analyzes information from a computer or a network that it is monitoring. There are three basic ways in which intrusions are detected: signature recognition, anomaly detection, and protocol decoding. NIDSs are designed to capture and analyze network traffic. HIDSs are designed to monitor a computer system and not the network. A network IPS system can react automatically and actually prevent a security occurrence from happening, preferably without user intervention. Host-based intrusion prevention is generally considered capable of recognizing and halting anomalies.

Be able to describe advanced network design concepts.   Advanced network design requires an understanding of remote access and firewall deployment and placement. Firewall placement designs include packet filtering, dual-homed gateway, screened host, and screened subnet.

Be familiar with the process of remote access.   Cisco has implemented a variety of remote access methods through its networking hardware and software. Originally, this was Terminal Access Controller Access Control System (TACACS). The most current version is TACACS+. Another, newer standard is Diameter. Although both operate in a similar manner, Diameter improves upon RADIUS by resolving discovered weaknesses.

Be able to describe switches, routers, and wireless devices.   A security professional must understand the various types of network equipment and the attacks that can be performed against them. Both switches and routers can be used to increase network security, but techniques such as MAC flooding and route poisoning can be used to overcome their security features.

Be able to describe IPv6.   Internet Protocol version 6 (IPv6) is the newest version of the IP and is the designated replacement for IPv4. IPv6 brings many improvements to modern networks. IPv6 increases the address space from 32 bits to 128 bits and has IPsec built in. Security concerns include the fact that older devices may not be compatible or able to provide adequate protection.

Know how DNSSEC works. DNSSEC is designed to provide a layer of security to DNS. DNSSEC allows hosts to validate that domain names are correct and have not been spoofed or poisoned.

Know the importance of securing zone transfers. Securing zone transfers begins by making sure that your DNS servers are not set to allow zone transfers. If your host has external DNS servers and internal DNS servers, the security administrator should also close TCP port 53. Internal DNS servers should be configured to talk only to the root servers.

Know how LDAP operates. LDAP was created to be a lightweight alternative protocol for accessing X.500 directory services. With LDAP, each object is made up of attributes that are indexed and referenced by a distinguished name. Each object has a unique name designed to fit into a global namespace that helps determine the relationship of the object and allows for the object to be referenced uniquely.

Be able to describe the importance of transport security. Increased network security risks and regulatory compliances have driven the need for transport security. Examples of transport security include IPsec, TLS, and SSL. IPsec is the Internet standard for security.

Know the concerns and best practices related to remote access. Remote access is the ability to get access to a computer, laptop, tablet, or other device from a network or remote host. One concern with remote access is how the remote connection is made. Is a VPN used or the information passed without cryptographic controls? Some authentication methods pass usernames and passwords via clear text and provide no security.

Understand SSO. Single sign-on (SSO) allows a user to authenticate once and then access all the resources the user is authorized to use. Authentication to the individual resources is handled by SSO in a manner that is transparent to the user.

Understand the SDLC process. The security/systems/software development life cycle (SDLC) is designed to identify security requirements early in the development process and incorporate them throughout the process.

Understand the advantages and disadvantages of virtualizing servers. Virtualized servers have many advantages. One of the biggest is server consolidation. Virtualization allows you to host many virtual machines on one physical server. Virtualization also helps with research and development. It allows rapid deployment of new systems and offers the ability to test applications in a controlled environment.

Be able to describe virtual desktop infrastructure (VDI). Virtual desktop infrastructure is a centralized desktop solution that uses servers to serve up a desktop operating system to a host system.

Be able to define the purpose of a VLAN. VLANs are used to segment the network into smaller broadcast domains or segments. They offer many benefits to an organization because they allow the segmentation of network users and resources that are connected administratively to defined ports on a switch. VLANs reduce network congestion and increase bandwidth, and they result in smaller broadcast domains. From a security standpoint, VLANs restrict the attacker's ability to see as much network traffic as they would without VLANs in place. VLANs are susceptible to VLAN hopping. This attack technique allows the attacker to move from one VLAN to another.

Know how to secure enterprise storage.   Securing enterprise storage requires a defense-in-depth approach that includes security policies, encryption, hardening, patch management, and logging and auditing. These are just a few of the needed controls.

Be able to describe antivirus.   Antivirus typically uses one of several techniques to identify and eradicate viruses. These methods include signature-based detection, which uses a signature file to identify viruses and other malware, and heuristic-based detection, which looks for deviation from normal behavior of an application or service. This detection method is useful against unknown and polymorphic viruses.

Know how and when to apply security controls.   Controls may or may not be applied. All companies have only limited funds to implement controls, and the cost of the control should not exceed the value of the asset. Performing a quantitative or qualitative risk assessment can help make the case for whether a control should be applied.

Review Questions

You can find the answers in Appendix.

1. Nicole is the security administrator for a large governmental agency. She has implemented port security, restricted network traffic, and installed NIDS, firewalls, and spam filters. She thinks the network is secure. Now she wants to focus on endpoint security. What is the most comprehensive plan for her to follow?

   A. Anti-malware/virus/spyware, host-based firewall, and MFA

   B. Antivirus/spam, host-based IDS, and 2FA

   C. Anti-malware/virus, host-based IDS, and biometrics

   D. Antivirus/spam, host-based IDS, and SSO

2. Sally's CISO asked her to recommend an intrusion system to recognize intrusions traversing the network and send email alerts to the IT staff when one is detected. What type of intrusion system does the CISO want?

   A. HIDS

   B. NIDS

   C. HIPS

   D. NIPS

3. Troy must decide about his organization's File Integrity Monitoring (FIM). Stand-alone FIM generally means file analysis only. Another option is to integrate it with the host so that Troy can detect threats in other areas, such as system memory or an I/O. For the integration, which of the following does Troy need to use?

   A. HIDS

   B. ADVFIM

   C. NIDS

   D. Change management

4. The IT department decided to implement a security appliance in front of their web servers to inspect HTTP/HTTPS/SOAP traffic for malicious activity. Which of the following is the BEST solution to use?

   A. Screened host firewall

   B. Packet filter firewall

   C. DMZ

   D. WAF

5. Your employees need internal access while traveling to remote locations. You need a service that enables them to securely connect back to a private corporate network from a public network to log into a centralized portal. You want the traffic to be encrypted. Which of the following is the BEST tool?

   A. Wi-Fi

   B. VPN

   C. RDP

   D. NIC

6. The IT security department was tasked with recommending a single security device that can perform various security functions. The security functions include antivirus protection, antispyware, a firewall, and an intrusion detection and prevention system. What device should the IT security department recommend?

   A. Next-generation firewall

   B. Unified threat management system

   C. Quantum proxy

   D. Next-generation intrusion detection and prevention system

7. The IT group within your organization wants to filter requests between clients and their servers. They want to place a device in front of the servers that acts as a middleman between the clients and the servers. This device receives the request from the clients and forwards the request to the servers. The server will reply to the request by sending the reply to the device; then the device will forward the reply onward to the clients. What device best meets this description?

   A. Firewall

   B. NIDS

   C. Reverse proxy

   D. Proxy

8. Your network administrator, George, reaches out to you to investigate why your ecommerce site went down twice in the past three days. Everything looks good on your network, so you reach out to your ISP. You suspect an attacker set up botnets that flooded your DNS server with invalid requests. You find this out by examining your external logging service. What is this type of attack called?

   A. DDoS

   B. Spamming

   C. IP spoofing

   D. Containerization

9. The Cisco switch port you are using for traffic analysis and troubleshooting and has a dedicated SPAN port is in an "error-disabled state." What is the procedure to reenable it after you enter privilege exec mode?

    A. Issue the `no shutdown` command on the error-disabled interface.

    B. Issue the `shutdown` and then the `no shutdown` command on the error-disabled interface.

    C. Issue the `no error` command on the error-disabled interface.

    D. Issue the `no error-disable` command on the error-disabled interface.

10. Your news organization is dealing with a recent defacement of your website and secure web server. The server was compromised around a three-day holiday weekend while most of the IT staff was not at work. The network diagram, in the order from the outside in, consists of the Internet, firewall, IDS, SSL accelerator, web server farm, internal firewall, and internal network. You attempt a forensic analysis, but all the web server logs have been deleted, and the internal firewall logs show no activity. As the security administrator, what do you do?

    A. Review sensor placement and examine the external firewall logs to find the attack.

    B. Review the IDS logs to determine the source of the attack.

    C. Correlate all the logs from all the devices to find where the organization was compromised.

    D. Reconfigure the network and put the IDS between the SSL accelerator and server farm to better determine the cause of future attacks.

11. After merging with a newly acquired company, Gavin comes to work Monday morning to find a metamorphic worm from the newly acquired network spreading through the parent organization. The security administrator isolated the worm using a network tap mirroring all the new network traffic and found it spreading on TCP port 445. What should Gavin advise the administrator to do to immediately to minimize the attack?

    A. Run Wireshark to watch for traffic on TCP port 445.

    B. Update antivirus software and scan the entire enterprise.

    C. Check your SIEM for alerts for any asset with TCP port 445 open.

    D. Deploy an ACL to all HIPS: DENY-TCP-ANY-ANY-445.

12. Jonathan is a senior architect who has submitted budget requests to the CISO to upgrade their security landscape. One item to purchase in the new year is a security information and event management (SIEM). What is the primary function of a SIEM tool?

    A. Blocking malicious users and traffic

    B. Administers access control

    C. Automating DNS servers

    D. Monitoring servers

13. Your security team implemented NAC lists for authentication as well as corporate policy enforcement. Originally, the team installed software on the devices to perform these tasks. However, the security team decided this method is no longer desirable. They want to implement a solution that performs the same function but doesn't require that software be installed on the devices. In the context of NAC, what is this configuration called?

A. Agent

B. Agentless

C. Volatile

D. Persistent

14. You had your internal team do an analysis on compiled binaries to find errors in mobile and desktop applications. You would like an external agency to test them as well. Which of these tests BEST suits this need?

A. DAST

B. VAST

C. IAST

D. SAST

15. Your company is looking at a new CRM model to reach customers that includes social media. The marketing director, Tucker, would like to share news, updates, and promotions on all social websites. What are the major security risks?

A. Malware, phishing, and social engineering

B. DDoS, brute force, and SQLi

C. Mergers and data ownership

D. Regulatory requirements and environmental changes

16. Michael is selected to manage a system development and implementation project. His manager suggests that you follow the phases in the SDLC. In which of these phases do you determine the controls needed to ensure that the system complies with standards?

A. Testing

B. Initiation

C. Accreditation

D. Acceptance

17. Your IT group is modernizing and adopting a DevSecOps approach, making everyone responsible for security. Traditionally, storage and security were separate disciplines inside IT as a whole. As a security analyst, what is your primary concern of data at rest?

A. Encryption

B. Authentication

C. Infrastructure

D. Authorization

18. Jackie is a software engineer and inherently prefers to use a flexible framework that enables software development to evolve with teamwork and feedback. What type of software development model would this be called?

   A. Prototyping

   B. Ceremony

   C. Agile

   D. Radical

19. You are working on a high-risk software development project that is large, the releases are to be frequent, and the requirements are complex. The waterfall and agile models are too simple. What software development model would you opt for?

   A. Functional

   B. Cost estimation

   C. Continuous delivery

   D. Spiral

20. Many of your corporate users are using laptop computers to perform their work remotely. Security is concerned that confidential data residing on these laptops may be disclosed and leaked to the public. What methodology BEST helps prevent the loss of such data?

   A. DLP

   B. HIPS

   C. NIDS

   D. NIPS

Chapter

9

Secure Cloud and Virtualization

THE CASP+ EXAM TOPICS COVERED IN THIS CHAPTER INCLUDE:

✓ **1.6 Given a set of requirements, implement secure cloud and virtualization solutions.**

- Virtualization strategies
    - Type 1 vs. Type 2 hypervisors
    - Containers
    - Emulation
    - Application virtualization
    - VDI
- Provisioning and deprovisioning
- Middleware
- Metadata and tags
- Deployment models and considerations
    - Business directives
        - Cost
        - Scalability
        - Resources
        - Location
        - Data protection
    - Cloud deployment models
        - Private
        - Public
        - Hybrid
        - Community

- Hosting models
    - Multitenant
    - Single-tenant
- Service models
    - Software as a service (SaaS)
    - Platform as a service (PaaS)
    - Infrastructure as a service (IaaS)
- Cloud provider limitations
    - Internet Protocol (IP) address scheme
    - VPC peering
- Extending appropriate on-premises controls
- Storage models
    - Object storage/file-based storage
    - Database storage
    - Block storage
    - Blob storage
    - Key-value pairs

✓ **3.4 Explain how cloud technology adoption impacts organization security.**

- Automation and orchestration
- Encryption configuration
- Logs
    - Availability
    - Collection
    - Monitoring
    - Configuration
    - Alerting
- Monitoring configurations
- Key ownership and location

- Key life-cycle management
- Backup and recovery methods
  - Cloud as business continuity and disaster recovery (BCDR)
  - Primary provider BCDR
  - Alternative provider BCDR
- Infrastructure vs. serverless computing
- Application virtualization
- Software-defined networking
- Misconfigurations
- Collaboration tools
- Storage configurations
  - Bit splitting
  - Data dispersion
- Cloud access security broker (CASB)

This chapter discusses securing virtualized, distributed, and shared computing. Virtualized computing has come a long way in the last 20 years, and it can be found everywhere today, from major businesses to small office, home office (SOHO) computing environments. Advances in computing have brought about more changes than just virtualization, including network storage and cloud computing. Cloud computing changed the concept of traditional network boundaries by placing assets outside the organization's perimeter.

In this chapter, we'll look at both the advantages and the disadvantages of virtualization and cloud computing as well as the concerns that they raise for enterprise security.

Implement Secure Cloud and Virtualization Solutions

A question that increasingly concerns security professionals is who has the data. With the rise of cloud computing, network boundaries are much harder to define. A network boundary is the point at which your control ends, and cloud computing does away with the typical network boundary. This fluid elasticity and scalability of a network boundary creates a huge impact because historically this demarcation line was at the edge of the physical network, a point at which the firewall is typically found.

The concept of cloud computing represents a shift in thought in that end users do not know the details of a specific technology. The service can be fully managed by the provider, and cloud consumers can use the service at a rate that is set by their particular needs. Cost and ease of use are two great benefits of cloud computing, but you must consider significant security concerns when contemplating moving critical applications and sensitive data to public and shared cloud environments. To address these concerns, the cloud provider must develop sufficient controls to provide the same or a greater level of security than the organization would have if the cloud was not used.

Cloud computing is not the only way in which network boundaries are changing. Telecommunicating and outsourcing have altered network boundaries. Telecommunicating allows employees to work from home and avoid the drive to the office. The work-from-home (WFH) model adopted during the COVID-19 pandemic affected healthcare, IT, education, nonprofit, sales, and marketing sectors, and those are just some of the industries to allow telecommuting.

Cloud computing can include virtual servers, services, applications, or anything you consume over the Internet. Cloud computing gets its name from the drawings typically used to describe the Internet. It is a modern concept that seeks to redefine consumption and delivery models for IT services. In a cloud computing environment, the end user may not know the location or details of a specific technology; it can be fully managed by the cloud service. Cloud computing offers users the ability to increase capacity or add services as needed without investing in new datacenters, training new personnel, or maybe even licensing new software. This on-demand, or elastic, service can be added, upgraded, and provided at any time.

 Although cloud computing offers many benefits, a security professional must keep in mind that if policy dictates, all in-house security requirements must be present in any elastic cloud-based solution.

Virtualization Strategies

Virtualization is a technology that system administrators have been using in datacenters for many years, and it is at the heart of cloud computing infrastructure. It is a technology that allows the physical resources of a computer (CPU, RAM, hard disk, graphics card, etc.) to be shared by virtual machines (VMs). Consider the old days when a single physical hardware platform—the server—was dedicated to a single-server application like being a web server. It turns out that a typical web server application didn't utilize many of the underlying hardware resources available. If you assume that a web application running on a physical server utilizes 30 percent of the hardware resources, that means that 70 percent of the physical resources are going unused, and the server is being wasted.

With virtualization, if three web servers are running via VMs with each utilizing 30 percent of the physical hardware resources of the server, 90 percent of the physical hardware resources of the server are being utilized. This is a much better return on hardware investment. By installing virtualization software on your computer, you can create VMs that can be used to work in many situations with many different applications.

A *hypervisor* is the software that is installed on a computer that supports virtualization. It can be implemented as *firmware*, which is specialized hardware that has permanent software programmed into it. It could also be hardware with installed software. It is within the hypervisor that the VMs will be created. The hypervisor allocates the underlying hardware resources to the VMs. Examples of hypervisor software are VMware's Workstation and Oracle's VM VirtualBox. There are free versions of each of these hypervisors that you can download and use. A VM is a virtualized computer that executes programs as a physical machine would.

A virtual server enables the user to run two, three, four, or more operating systems on one physical computer. For example, a virtual machine will let you run a Windows, Linux, or virtually any other operating system. They can be used for development, system administration, or production to reduce the number of physical devices needed. Exercise 9.1 shows how to convert a physical computer into a virtual image.

EXERCISE 9.1

Creating a Virtual Machine

One of the easiest ways to create a virtual machine is to convert an existing physical computer to a virtual image. A tool for doing this is VMware vCenter Converter Standalone. You can download it from `customerconnect.vmware.com/downloads/info/slug/infrastructure_operations_management/vmware_vcenter_converter_standalone/6_2_0`.

The following steps will walk you through the process of using VMware to convert a physical image into a virtual machine:

1. Download and start the converter program.

2. Enter the IP address or hostname of the system that you would like to convert.

3. Click Next once a connection is made.

4. A screen will open, prompting you to install the Converter Client Agent.

5. Choose the destination where you would like to store the newly created VMware image.

6. Allow the process to finish. This will require some time if the image is large.

Once the process is completed, you have successfully created a VMware image.

Virtualization sprawl is a common issue enterprise organizations have. Virtualization or VM sprawl happens when the number of machines on a network exceeds the point where system administrators can handle or manage them correctly or efficiently. To keep this from happening, strict policies should be developed and adhered to as well as using automation to stay on top of resources being used. Creating a VM library is helpful as long as you have a VM librarian to go with it.

Type 1 vs. Type 2 Hypervisors

Virtual servers can reside on a virtual emulation of the hardware layer. Using this virtualization technique, the guest has no knowledge of the host's operating system. Virtualized servers make use of a hypervisor too.

Hypervisors are classified as either Type 1 (I) or Type 2 (II). Type 1 hypervisor systems do not need an underlying OS, while Type 2 hypervisor systems do. A *Type 1 hypervisor* runs directly on the bare metal of a system. A *Type 2 hypervisor* runs on a host operating system that provides virtualization services. It will have its own operating system and be allocated physical hardware resources such as CPU, RAM, and hard disk, as well as network resources.

The *host operating system* is the operating system of the computer the hypervisor is being installed on. The *guest operating system* is the operating system of the VM that resides within the hypervisor.

The hypervisor validates all of the guest-issued CPU instructions and manages any executed code that requires additional privileges. VMware and Microsoft Hyper-V both use the hypervisor, which is also known as a *virtual machine monitor (VMM)*. The hypervisor is the foundation of this type of virtualization; it accomplishes the following:

- Interfaces with hardware
- Intercepts system calls
- Operates with the operating system
- Offers hardware isolation
- Enables multi-environment protection

Let's Get Physical

There may be times when you need to convert an existing virtual machine to a physical machine. Tools are available for you to do this. One use for this technology is to reproduce support issues on physical hardware. To learn more about this process, take a moment to review V2P. The V2P process is generic, and virtual machines can be imaged onto any physical server if the process is followed correctly. More information can be found at www.vmware.com/support/v2p.

Just like any environment, each hypervisor has its pros and cons. Some of the pros of running a VM are that you can run more than one OS at a time; you can install, reinstall, snapshot, roll back, or back up any time you want quite easily; and you manage the allocation of resources. The cons would be that performance may not be as robust as if you were on bare metal. USB and external hard drives can cause major issues, and some of us would rather roll back an image rather than take the time to troubleshoot an issue.

Modern computer systems have come a long way in how they process, store, and access information. *Virtual memory* is the combination of the computer's primary memory (RAM) and secondary storage. When these two technologies are combined, the OS lets application programs function as if they have access to more physical memory than what is actually available to them. Virtualization types can include the following:

Mainframe Virtual Machines   This technology allows any number of users to share computer resources and prevents concurrent users from interfering with each other. Systems like the hardware-emulated IBM Mainframe z/OS built on AWS with IBM ZD&T falls into that category.

Parallel Virtual Machines   The concept here is to allow one computing environment to be running on many different physical machines. Parallel virtual machines allow a user to break complex tasks into small chunks that are processed independently.

Operating System Virtual Machines This category of virtual systems creates an environment in which a guest operating system can function. This is made possible by the ability of the software to virtualize the computer hardware and needed services. VMware, XEN, and Oracle VM all fall into this category of virtualization.

Technologies related to virtual systems continue to evolve. In some cases, you may not need an entire virtual system to complete a specific task. In such situations, a container can now be used. *Containers* allow for the isolation of applications running on a server. Containers offer a lower-cost alternative to using virtualization to run isolated applications on a single host. When a container is used, the OS kernel provides process isolation and performs resource management. Determining when to use containers instead of virtualizing the OS mostly breaks down to the type of workload you have to complete. Containers allow for applications to be deployed faster and support accelerated development. Modern container technology was popularized by Docker in 2013. Since then, Google introduced the container organization platform Kubernetes. Other vendors include VMware Tanzu, Microsoft Azure Kubernetes Service, and Amazon Elastic Container Service.

Virtual machines and containers have many layers of implementation. Another method of creating an environment that takes the properties of one system into another is *emulation*. Emulators allow you to turn your PC into a Mac and play games designed for hardware that was built decades ago. Most emulators tend to run slower than the machine they are simulating. Dolphin Emulator is a free and open-source video game console that allows Nintendo GameCube or Wii games to be played on a PC or Android. Parallels is an emulator program that allows you to run Windows on a Mac computer. *Application virtualization* permits a user to access applications that are not installed on their devices, encapsulating the program from the OS they are executed on. The application experience is the same as if it were present on the end user's computer. The software allows applications to run on a variety of operating systems and web browsers.

Security Advantages of Virtualizing Servers

Virtualized servers have many advantages. One of the biggest is server consolidation. Virtualization lets you host many virtual machines on one physical server. This reduces deployment time and makes better use of existing resources. Virtualization also helps with research and development. Virtualization allows rapid deployment of new systems and offers the ability to test applications in a controlled environment. Virtual machine snapshots allow for easy image backup before changes are made and thus provide a means to revert to the previous good image quickly. From a security standpoint, you physically have to protect only one physical server where you may have had to protect many servers in the past. This is useful for all types of development testing and production scenarios.

Physical servers may malfunction or experience a hardware failure during important times or when most needed. In these situations, virtualization can be a huge advantage. Virtual systems can be imaged or replicated and moved to another physical computer very quickly. This aids the business continuity process and reduces outage time. Virtualization minimizes physical space requirements and permits the replacement of physical servers with fewer machines.

Security Disadvantages of Virtualizing Servers

With every advantage there is usually a drawback, and virtualization is no different. Virtualization adds another layer of complexity. Many books are available that explain how to manage a Microsoft server, but virtualization may result in your having a Microsoft server as a host machine with several Linux and Unix virtual servers or multiple Microsoft systems on a single Linux machine. This new layer of complexity can cause problems that may be difficult to troubleshoot. Vulnerabilities associated with a single physical server hosting multiple companies' virtual machines include the comingling of data. If this happens and a data breach occurs, your data may be affected. There can also be security issues when a single platform is hosting multiple companies' virtual machines. These can include the following:

Physical Access   Anyone who has direct access to the physical server can most likely access the virtual systems.

Separation of Duties   Are the employees who perform networking duties the same individuals who handle security of the virtual systems? If separation of duties is not handled correctly, a security breach may occur.

Misconfigured Platforms   If the platform is misconfigured, it can have devastating consequences for all of the virtual systems residing on the single platform.

Virtualization also requires additional skills. Virtualization software and the tools used to work within a virtual environment add an extra burden on administrators because they will need to learn something new. Security disadvantages of virtualizing servers can also be seen in Type 1, Type 2, and container-based systems.

With Type 1 VMs, you manage guests directly from the hypervisor. Any vulnerabilities of the VMs must be patched. With Type 2 VMs, you also have the issue of the underlying OS and any vulnerabilities that it may have. A missed patch or an unsecured base OS could expose the OS, hypervisor, and all VMs to attack. Another real issue with Type 2 VMs is that such systems typically allow shared folders and the migration of information between the host and guest OSs. Sharing data increases the risk of malicious code migrating from one VM to the base system.

   Privilege escalation, sometimes simply called escalation, is a problem on both physical and virtual machines. A privilege escalation attack takes advantage of programming errors or design flaws to grant an attacker elevated access on a system.

Some basic items to review for securing virtual systems include those in Table 9.1.

TABLE 9.1   Common security controls for virtual systems

Item	Comments
Antivirus	Antivirus must be present on the host and all VMs.
Hardening	All VMs should be hardened so that nonessential services are removed.
Physical controls	Controls that limit who has access to the datacenter.
Authentication	Strong access control.
Resource access	Only administrative accounts as needed.
Encryption	Use encryption for sensitive data in storage or transit.
Remote Desktop Services	Restrict when not needed. When it is required, use only 256-bit or higher encryption.

 You can use a VPN through a virtual machine using IPSec. IP Security (IPSec) is a suite of protocols used across an IP network providing authentication, integrity, and confidentiality. This includes Authentication Header (AH), Encapsulating Security Payloads (ESP), and Security Associations (SA), which provide the different configurations and keys used for those connections. Internet Security Association and Key Management Protocol (ISAKMP) is a component of SA and how the keys are managed and exchanged between the devices. An IPSec VPN will protect traffic being forwarded from client to server or from server to server.

VDI

Remember dumb terminals and the thin client concept? This has evolved into what is known as the *virtual desktop infrastructure (VDI)*. This centralized desktop solution uses servers to serve up a desktop operating system to a host system. Each hosted desktop virtual machine is running an operating system such as Windows 11 or Windows Server 2022. The remote desktop is delivered to the user's endpoint device via *Remote Desktop Protocol (RDP)*, Citrix, or other architecture. Technologies such as RDP are great for remote connectivity, but they can also allow remote access by an attacker.

This system has lots of benefits, such as reduced onsite support and greater centralized management. However, a disadvantage of this solution is that there is a significant investment in hardware and software to build the backend infrastructure.

Although it is easy to see the benefits of a service, it's important not to overlook the costs. A CASP+ should be aware that most services require a startup fee. This is known as *provisioning*, which is nothing more than preparing and equipping a cloud service for new users. Some providers may also require minimum service length and even *de-provisioning* fees.

Tools that can be used for structural planning and construction of enterprise cloud instances for speed and ease of use include middleware and metadata.

Between the operating system and an application, *middleware* gives some communication functionality to the user, making a connection between any two clients, servers, or databases. Advantages of using middleware include faster deployment of applications in the cloud as well as in containerized environments.

Metadata in the cloud helps organize assets, data, and virtual instances so that it is easier to find, understand, and manage information. Many different metadata *tags* can be used from a template or created uniquely. Most tags have a field and a type for classification, and the type can be a string, a Boolean, or a date/time. Tags are usually optional unless they are explicitly required. The most important question to ask about metadata and tags is what information your organization wants to keep track of and how that metadata will be used. Metadata can be used for compliance and governance as well as grouping for cost analysis. Fields such as **data_owner** could be important to one department, while **data_confidentiality** or **storage_location** could be important to another department.

Deployment Models and Considerations

Cloud computing architecture can include various cloud deployment models and layers. *Public use services* are provided by an external provider. *Private use services* are implemented internally in a cloud design. A *hybrid architecture* offers a combination of public and private cloud services to accomplish an organization's goals. A *community cloud service model* is a shared and cooperative infrastructure where several organizations with common concerns share data and resources.

The following is a partial list of the top cloud provider companies:

- Amazon Web Services (AWS)
- Azure
- GoogleCloud
- AlibabaCloud
- Salesforce
- Adobe Creative Cloud
- Dropbox
- Digital Ocean
- IBM Cloud
- Dell

These providers offer a range of services including the following:

Public Clouds   Available to the general public. An example would be Google Drive.

Private Clouds   Operated for a single company or entity. An example would be a company's private cloud storage of travel expenses.

Hybrid Clouds   A combination of a public and private cloud. An example would be a company's cloud storage of projects with varied access for internal employees and vendors.

Community Clouds   Shared between several organizations. An example would be cloud storage for a group of schools or government offices.

Multitenancy   Used to host a single software application that hosts multiple customers through a multitenant hosting model. An example would be a collaborative workspace for several project contributors.

Single Tenancy   Hosts a single software application designed to support one customer through a single-tenant hosting model. An example would be a specialized HR application for one organization. Although single tenancy is more secure due to isolation and you control access, backups, and cost with scaling, it also requires more maintenance because single-tenant environments need more updates and upgrades that are managed by the customer.

Highly regulated industries such as banking, healthcare, and government have been slow to adopt cloud technologies. The market is always evolving, and these organizations are evaluating the approach to the cloud. Customers have high expectations when interacting with businesses today. Some notable announcements have been made, such as partnerships between AWS and Goldman Sachs to create a Financial Cloud for data, and Microsoft has announced availability of the Microsoft Cloud for Financial Services.

Business Directives

On-demand, or elastic, cloud computing changes the way information and services are consumed and provided. Users can consume services at a rate that is set by their particular needs. Cloud computing offers several benefits, including the following:

Reduces Cost   Cloud technology negates the need for procurement and maintenance of a company's own infrastructure and/or applications. Additionally, a cloud service is paid for as needed and can grow and shrink as business demands. This allows for scalability, which results in cost savings.

Increases Storage and Scalability Cloud providers have more storage capability that is elastic and has lower costs. These storage locations, for some global cloud providers, are regional in nature and redundant, with layers of security and data backups built in, so if one storage location goes down, the resources, applications, data, and access are still available.

Provides High Degree of Automation Fewer employees are needed because local systems have been replaced with cloud-based solutions. The user does not need IT personnel to patch and update servers that have been outsourced to the cloud.

Offers Flexibility and Data Protection Cloud computing offers much more flexibility than local-based solutions. Cloud data protection is practiced wherever the data is located, no matter if it is at rest or in motion. Being so flexible, security can be managed internally by the enterprise organization or externally by a third party or providers themselves.

Provides More Mobility with Variety of Locations One of the big marketing plugs is that users can access their data anywhere rather than having to remain at their desks. There are ways of deploying applications and data in the cloud to make it accessible from anywhere.

Allows the Company's IT Department to Shift Focus No hardware updates are required by the company—the cloud provider is now responsible. Companies are free to concentrate on innovation.

 **Real World Scenario**

The Cloud Is Not a Bulletproof Solution

Not all cloud computing is the same, and most certainly not all cloud providers can give the service levels that they purport to offer—even if they believe that they can do so. Amazon Web Services, which allegedly runs about 33 percent of all cloud infrastructure worldwide, crashed on December 7, 2021, and took about a third of the worldwide cloud services with it. According to the AWS team, the internal network for monitoring, internal DNS, and authorization services were overwhelmed, and it caused traffic delays and shutdowns for more than seven hours. Amazon could not make deliveries, Alexa and Ring cameras did not work, and third-party apps like Disney+ and Venmo all broke down.

According to the International Data Corporation (IDC):

"The proliferation of devices, compliance, improved system performance, online commerce, and increased replication to secondary or backup sites is contributing to an annual doubling of the amount of information transmitted over the Internet."

What this means is that we are now dealing with much more data than in the past. Servers sometimes strain under the load of stored and accessed data. The cost of dealing with large amounts of data is something that all companies must address.

There are also increased economic pressures to stay competitive. Companies are looking at cost-saving measures. Cloud computing provides much greater flexibility than previous computing models, but the danger is that the customer must perform due diligence.

 Anyone considering cloud-based services should make sure that they get a "try it, then buy it" clause. It's much the same as taking a new car for a test-drive before buying. You should never commit to a cloud-based service until you are sure that it functions the way you want it to. Some items to consider include an SLA, uptime guarantees, CPU, memory levels, bandwidth, cloud provider support time, and response time.

The benefits of cloud computing are many. One of the real advantages of cloud computing is the ability to use someone else's storage. Another advantage is that when new resources are needed, the cloud can be leveraged, and the new resources may be implemented faster than if they were hosted locally at your company. With cloud computing, you pay as you go. Another benefit is the portability of the application. Users can access data from work, from home, or at client locations. There is also the ability of cloud computing to free up IT workers who may have been tied up performing updates, installing patches, or providing application support. The bottom line is that all of these reasons lead to reduced capital expense, which is what all companies are seeking. In Exercise 9.2 you will examine the benefits of cloud computing.

EXERCISE 9.2

Identifying What Services Should Be Moved to the Cloud

One of the first steps after identifying the benefits of cloud computing is to determine what services should or should not be moved to the cloud. Identify the parts of your organization's datacenter or application set that are not appropriate to move into the cloud. Answer these questions:

1. What process would benefit most from the move?

2. Is the move cost effective?

3. What is the cost to provision the cloud service?

4. Does the cloud provider offer a trial period in which to evaluate the cloud services?

5. Is the cloud provider's business model suitable for this system?

6. Is the solution proprietary or open source?

7. Will the move offer the company a competitive advantage?

8. How does the company roll back if the cloud move doesn't go well?

9. What kind of disaster recovery can take place with the cloud configuration?

10. Can my company data be encrypted and isolated?

Based on your findings, what facts can you provide management about cloud sourcing the data or application?

 Real World Scenario

The Chain of Custody Evaporates in the Cloud

One concern with cloud computing is how one company's data is separated from another company's data in the cloud. If the virtual slice next to yours is an illegal site or loaded with malware, what happens when the FBI seizes the data? More likely than not, they will seize the entire rack of servers. If they do so, your server would then be offline. When a company needs to figure out what happened in the event of a hack or compromise, cloud computing has the potential to be complicated and a tangled mess from a forensics perspective. That is because the traditional methods and techniques don't apply. How will chain of custody be assured?

Service Models

Cloud models can be broken into several basic designs that include infrastructure as a service, monitoring as a service, software as a service, and platform as a service. Each design is described here:

Infrastructure as a Service　*Infrastructure as a service (IaaS)* describes a cloud solution where you are buying infrastructure. You purchase virtual power to execute your software as needed. This is much like running a virtual server on your own equipment, except that you are now running a virtual server on a virtual disk. This model is similar to a utility company model, as you pay for what you use. An example of this model is Amazon Web Services, aws.amazon.com.

Monitoring as a Service　*Monitoring as a service (MaaS)* offers a cloud-based monitoring solution. This includes monitoring for networks, application servers, applications, and remote systems. An example of this model is AppDynamics, a division of Cisco at www.appdynamics.com. It provides a Java-based MaaS solution.

Software as a Service　*Software as a service (SaaS)* is designed to provide a complete packaged solution. The software is rented out to the user. The service is usually provided through some type of front end or web portal. While the end user is free to use the service from anywhere, the company pays a per-use fee. As an example, Salesforce is a customer relationship management service providing customer service, marketing automation, analytics, and application development; it offers this type of service at www.salesforce.com.

Platform as a Service *Platform as a service (PaaS)* provides a platform for your use. Services provided by this model include all phases of the software development life cycle (SDLC) and can use application programming interfaces (APIs), website portals, or gateway software. These solutions tend to be proprietary, which can cause problems if the customer moves away from the provider's platform. An example of PaaS is Google Workspace, `workspace.google.com`.

With so many different cloud-based services available, it was only a matter of time before security moved to the cloud. Such solutions are known as *security as a service (SECaaS)*. SECaaS is a cloud-based solution that delivers security as a service from the cloud. SECaaS functions without requiring onsite hardware, and as such it avoids substantial capital expenses. The following are some examples of the type of security services that can be performed from the cloud:

Antispam Cloud-based *antispam* services can be used to detect spam email. Providers include SpamTitan, MailWasher, and MX Guarddog.

Antivirus Cloud-based *antivirus* applications offer a number of benefits, and they can be useful for quickly scanning a PC for malware. Two examples of such services are Webroot and Avast.

Anti-malware Cloud-based *anti-malware* monitors and reacts to more than viruses. Anti-malware stops a broader set of malicious software. A good example of such a tool is Malwarebytes.

Content Filtering This cloud service allows companies to outsource the *content filtering* service so that the cloud-based provider can manage and monitor all outbound and inbound traffic, so tools like FortiGuard and Cisco Umbrella would help.

Cloud Security Broker A *cloud security broker* will act as a gateway or go-between, being placed between an organization's infrastructure and the cloud service provider (CSP). The cloud security broker is becoming more commonly known as the *cloud access security broker (CASB)*. There is no hard boundary on how a CASB functions or what benefits the organization can expect from a cloud security broker. The cloud security broker may react to threats, performing like an IDS/IPS, or the cloud security broker may send alerts on learned activity or inspect logs, performing more like SIEM. Realistically, most CASBs will function in both ways. According to Gartner's 2020 Magic Quadrant for CASB, the leading vendors are McAfee, Microsoft, Netskope, and Bitglass.

Hash Matching This service allows the user to search for known malicious files quickly or to identify known good files by searching online repositories for hash matches. One great example can be found at `www.hashsets.com`. This hash set is maintained by the National Software Reference Library (NSRL). These hashes can be used by law enforcement, government, and industry organizations to review files on a computer by matching file profiles in the database.

Sandboxing   A cloud-based *sandbox* is a stand-alone environment that allows you to view or execute a program safely while keeping it contained. Good examples of sandbox services include Zscaler and FortiSandbox.

> Sandboxing is widely used for analysis of malware. The idea is to allow the malware to run in an isolated environment. One great example of a sandbox is Cuckoo. Cuckoo Sandbox is the leading open-source automated malware analysis system. You can download a copy of Cuckoo for Windows, macOS, Linux, and Android here: cuckoosandbox.org.

Managed Security Service Providers   *Managed security service providers (MSSPs)* provide outsourced monitoring and management of security devices and systems. Common services include managed firewall, intrusion detection, virtual private network, vulnerability scanning, and antiviral services. MSSPs use high-availability security operations centers at their own facilities or from other datacenter providers to provide $365 \times 24 \times 7$ services designed to help reduce the number of operational security personnel an enterprise needs to hire, train, and retain in order to maintain an acceptable security posture.

Vulnerability Scanning   Many companies don't have the expertise or capability to perform all of the security services they need. One such service that can be outsourced is *vulnerability scanning*. Cloud-based solutions offload this activity to a third-party provider.

 **Real World Scenario**

Read the Fine Print

For any cloud-based service that you are considering using, you will always want to read the fine print carefully. For example, Apple prohibits using iTunes services for the manufacture of biological weapons, and AWS/Amazon permits cloud computing services to be deployed to combat a zombie apocalypse. These clauses are funny but real and highlight how most people do not take the time to understand the rights they sign away when clicking the I Agree button. The potential for abuse and restricting speech will certainly lead to new legislation.

You should always pay close attention to what you are agreeing to for yourself or your company. Terms of service are a moving target!

To explain more about how terms of service can change over time, the following white-paper from the Cloud Standards Customer Council offers a practical guide to service agreements:

www.omg.org/cloud/deliverables/CSCC-Practical-Guide-to-Cloud-Service-Agreements.pdf

From a security standpoint, one of the first questions that must be answered in improving the overall security posture of an organization is where data resides. The advances in technology make this much more difficult than in the past. Years ago, Redundant Array of Inexpensive/Independent Disks (RAID) was the standard for data storage and redundancy. Today, companies have moved to *dynamic disk pools (DDPs)* and cloud storage. DDP shuffles data, parity information, and spare capacity across a pool of drives so that the data is better protected and downtime is reduced. DDPs can be rebuilt up to eight times faster than traditional RAID.

Enterprise storage infrastructures may not have adequate protection mechanisms. The following basic security controls should be implemented:

Know your assets.   Perform an inventory to know what data you have and where it is stored.

Build a security policy.   A corporate security policy is essential. Enterprise storage is just one item that should be addressed.

Implement controls.   The network should be designed with a series of technical controls, such as the following:

- Intrusion detection system (IDS)/intrusion prevention system (IPS)
- Firewalls
- Network access control (NAC)

Harden your systems.   Remove unnecessary services and applications.

Perform proper updates.   Use patch management systems to roll out and deploy patches as needed.

Segment the infrastructure.   Segment areas of the network where enterprise storage mechanisms are used.

Use encryption.   Evaluate protection for data at rest and for data in transit.

Implement logging and auditing.   Enterprise storage should have sufficient controls so that you can know who attempts to gain access, what requests fail, when changes to access are made, or when other suspicious activities occur.

Use change control.   Use change control and IT change management to control all changes. Changes should occur in an ordered process, documented with a plan to roll back if systems crash.

Implement trunking security.   *Trunking security* is typically used with VLANs. The concept is to block access to layer 2 devices based on their MAC addresses. Blocking a device by its MAC address effectively prevents the device from communicating through any network switch. This stops the device from propagating malicious traffic to any other network-connected devices.

Employ port security.   When addressing the control of traffic at layer 2 on a switch, the term used today is *port security*. Port security specifically speaks to limiting what traffic is allowed in and out of particular switch ports. This traffic is controlled per layer 2 address or MAC address. One example of typical port security is when a network administrator knows that a fixed set of MAC addresses are expected to send traffic through a switch port. The administrator can employ port security to ensure that traffic from no other MAC address will be allowed to use that port and traverse the switch.

Cloud Provider Limitations

Cloud computing has many benefits, but there are disadvantages as well, especially with smaller organizations.

Downtime   Loss of access is one of the biggest disadvantages and can occur for any reason.

Privacy   Cloud service providers are expected to manage and safeguard the underlying hardware infrastructure, but with recent credit card breaches and login credentials stolen, you have to be aware of best practices.

Limited control   To different degrees, cloud users find they have less control over cloud-hosted infrastructure, and switching between cloud services can be difficult.

Limited Internet Protocol (IP) address scheme   Cloud providers can limit IP address ranges and availability so what is used in the cloud is different than on premises. It is also usually dynamic, so users cannot force an on-premises IP address to route properly to a cloud provider.

VPC Peering Limits   A virtual private cloud (VPC) can experience networking connectivity issues because of incorrect or missing route tables. Only one connection can exist between two VPCs at the same time and they must be able to communicate as if they are on the same network using private IP addressing. A virtual private cloud (VPC) customer has exclusive access to a segment of a public cloud. This deployment is a compromise between a private and a public model in terms of price and features. Access can also be restricted by the user's physical location by employing firewalls and IP address whitelisting. Using the cloud is a trade-off—you gain speed, performance, and cost, but you lose control over the security processes.

Extending Appropriate On-Premises Controls

Although cost and ease of use are two great benefits of cloud computing, there are significant security concerns when considering on-demand/elastic cloud computing.

Cloud computing is a big change from the way IT services have been delivered and managed in the past. One of the advantages is the elasticity of the cloud, which provides the online illusion of an infinite supply of computing power. Cloud computing places assets outside the owner's security boundary. Historically, items inside the security perimeter were trusted, whereas items outside were not. With cloud computing, an organization is being forced to place their trust in the cloud provider. The cloud provider must develop sufficient controls to provide the same or a greater level of security than the organization would have if the cloud were not used.

As a CASP+, you must be aware of the security concerns of moving to a cloud-based service. The pressures are great to make these changes, but there is always a trade-off between security and usability. Here are some basic questions that a security professional should ask when considering cloud-based solutions and the controls that must be put in place.

Does the data fall under regulatory requirements?   Different countries have different requirements and controls placed on access. For example, organizations operating in the United States, Canada, or the European Union have many regulatory requirements. Examples of these include ISO 27002, Safe Harbor, Information Technology Infrastructure Library (ITIL), and Control Objectives for Information and Related Technology (COBIT). The CASP+ is responsible for ensuring that the cloud provider can meet these requirements and is willing to undergo certification, accreditation, and review as needed.

Who can access the data?   Defense in depth is built on the concept that every security control is vulnerable. Cloud computing places much of the control in someone else's hands. One big area that is handed over to the cloud provider is access. Authentication and authorization are real concerns. Because the information or service now resides in the cloud, there is a much greater opportunity for access by outsiders. Insiders might pose an additional risk.

Insiders, or those with access, have the means and opportunity to launch an attack and only lack a motive. Anyone considering using the cloud needs to look at who is managing their data and what types of controls are applied to individuals who may have logical or physical access.

Does the cloud provider use a data classification system?   A CASP+ should know how the cloud provider classifies data. Classification of data can run the gamut from a fully deployed classification system with multiple levels to a simple system that separates sensitive and unclassified data. Consumers of cloud services should ask whether encryption is used and how one customer's data is separated from another customer's data. Is encryption being used for data in transit or just for data at rest? Consumers of cloud services will also want to know what kind of encryption is being used. For instance, is the provider using Advanced Encryption Standard (AES) 128 or 256? How are the keys stored? Is the encryption mechanism being used considered a strong one? One strong control is virtual private storage, which provides encryption that is transparent to the user. Virtual private storage is placed in your screened subnet and configured to encrypt and decrypt everything that is coming and going from your network up to the cloud.

Even Cloud-Based Email Needs Adequate Controls

Even basic services such as email require a thorough review before being moved to the cloud. Organizations are starting to move their email to cloud services hosted by Gmail, Yahoo, and others, but there are issues to consider.

In November 2021, the FBI and the Cybersecurity and Infrastructure Security Agency told NBC News in a statement that one of its email servers had been hacked, resulting in more than 100,000 spam emails being sent to the public that appeared to come from the Department of Homeland Security. The FBI said it was not able to provide any other information on the case; however, companies such as Microsoft have issued recent warnings on potential cyberattacks. In December 2021, Microsoft warned that the Russian hacking group NOBELIUM, which was behind the SolarWinds cyberattack, was targeting U.S. cloud service providers. Cloud services have many controls built in, but it is not impossible for them to be compromised.

What training does the cloud provider offer its employees?   This is a rather important item in that people will always be the weakest link in security. Knowing how your provider trains their employees is an important item to review. Training helps employees know what the proper actions are and understand the security practices of the organization.

What are the service level agreement (SLA) terms?   The SLA serves as a contracted level of guaranteed service between the cloud provider and the customer. An SLA is a contract that provides a certain level of protection. For a fee, the vendor agrees to repair, replace, or provide service within a contracted period of time. An SLA is usually based on what the customer specifies as the minimum level of services that will be provided.

Is there a right to audit?   This particular item is no small matter in that the cloud provider should agree in writing to the terms of audit. Where and how is your data stored? What controls are used? Do you have the right to perform a site visit or review records related to access control or storage?

Does the cloud provider have long-term viability?   Regardless of what service or application is being migrated to a cloud provider, you need to have confidence in the provider's long-term viability. There are costs not only to provision services but also for de-provisioning should the service no longer be available. If they were to go out of business, what would happen to your data? How long has the cloud provider been in business, and what is their track record? Will your data be returned if the company fails and, if so, in what format?

🌐 **Real World Scenario**

What Happens if the Clouds Disappear?

In November 2021, Samsung Cloud gave users less than two months to prepare for the end of online cloud service functionality, specifically the Gallery Sync, My Files, and Premium Storage. The failed service line left behind unhappy users who were unaware of the deprecation and focused concerns about the reliability and sustainability of cloud computing.

How will the cloud provider respond if there is a security breach?   Cloud-based services are an attractive target for computer criminals. If a security incident occurs, what support will you receive from the cloud provider? To reduce the amount of damage that these criminals can cause, cloud providers need to have incident response and handling policies in place. These policies should dictate how the organization handles various types of incidents. Cloud providers must have a computer security incident response team (CSIRT) that is tied into customer notification policies for law enforcement involvement.

What is the business continuity and disaster recovery plan (BCDR)?   Although you may not know the physical location of your services, they are physically located somewhere. All physical locations face threats, such as fire, storms, natural disasters, and loss of power. In case of any of these events, the CASP+ will need to know how the cloud provider responds and what guarantee of continued services they are promising. There is also the issue of retired, replaced, or damaged equipment. Items such as hard drives need to be decommissioned properly. Should sensitive data be held on discarded hard drives, *data remanence* is a real issue. Data remanence is the remaining data, or remnants, that remain on the media after formatting or drive wiping. The only way to ensure there are no data remnants is to physically destroy the media.

In Exercise 9.3, you will examine some common risks and issues associated with cloud computing as they would affect your organization.

EXERCISE 9.3

Identifying Risks and Issues with Cloud Computing

Before moving to any cloud-based service, a company needs to ensure that due diligence has been carried out. To help clarify some of the issues related to cloud computing, here is a list of questions regarding common risks and issues associated with cloud computing. What additional risks and issues may affect your organization specifically?

1. Is the data sensitive? Would loss or exposure of the data result in financial loss, fines, or penalties?

2. What regulatory compliance requirements are met by storing information on the cloud-based service and transmitting such data between your company and the cloud?

3. How well can the company adjust to the loss of control of the data or application? If the solution is proprietary, how easy would it be to move to another provider?

4. What backup plan does the cloud provider have to protect customers in case of disasters?

5. What SLA does the cloud provider offer?

Based on your findings, what facts can you provide management about cloud-sourcing the data or application? Would you recommend the service?

Data Sovereignty and the Cloud

Data sovereignty refers to a country's laws and the control that country has over the data that resides within its jurisdiction. A country's data laws could restrict the cross-border transfer of data, imposing legal requirements that may conflict with those of the country in which the user currently resides. Data laws can impose jurisdiction over data that may change as the data is transferred across borders. Legal obligations are different from privacy, data security, and transfer obligations that may apply if the data is hosted within different countries or is controlled by different cloud providers.

There is no known uniform, worldwide regulation that governs the protection of a user's data, but the *General Data Protection Regulation (GDPR)* comes as close as any standard to meeting this objective so far. Laws of various countries are often different in terms of where the data is stored and where the third-party storage provider is based. For example, a U.S.-based company may opt to store financial data in Ireland or protected health information (PHI) in Germany. As mentioned, the GDPR is an example of a more recent regulation that affects any online organization that collects or processes the personal data of people in the European Union (EU) countries. GDPR is a regulation, very specific to the area of data privacy, and applies externally—outside of Germany, as opposed to, say, a German law. As of May 25, 2018, any such organization must ensure compliance with the GDPR or face substantial penalties. The GDPR is the strongest case of data sovereignty through regulation to date.

To complicate matters further, some countries have laws against overly strong encryption. This can result in complex compliance issues.

When addressing potential data sovereignty issues, corporations can begin the process by analyzing the different technical, legal, and business issues. Corporations should also conduct a detailed analysis of the following:

-   Legal issues to include licenses, industry regulation, labor laws, intellectual property, and digital assets within the corporations

-   Applications of particular provisions of applicable laws on data sovereignty, which are relevant within jurisdictions

Cloud Computing Vulnerabilities

Computer criminals always follow the money, and as more companies migrate to cloud-based services, look for the criminals to follow. Here are some examples of attacks to which cloud services are vulnerable:

Authentication Attacks   Authentication systems may not adequately protect your data. Authentication is a weak point in many systems, and cloud-based services are no exception. There are many types of *authentication attacks*, including cross-site scripting (XSS) and cross-site request forgery (CSRF). The mechanisms and methods used to secure the authentication process are a frequent target of attackers.

Denial of Service   A *denial-of-service (DoS) attack* seeks to disrupt availability or access to a service, application, infrastructure, or some other resource that is normally available. The attack begins by sending a massive wave of illegitimate requests over the network. The massive amount of traffic can overwhelm nearby network devices or a targeted system, thus preventing authorized users from having access. In some cases, this traffic originates not from one source, but from many. When the attack is a shared effort by several sources, it is called a *distributed denial-of-service (DDoS) attack*. In recent years, DDoS attacks have increased significantly, often for financial gain. DDoS attacks can be launched for extortion, so-called *hacktivism*, or other reasons to disrupt normal operations. Tools such as Low Orbit Ion Cannon (LOIC) are easily accessible for these activities. Cybercriminals often use botnets to launch the attacks.

Data Aggregation and Data Isolation   Sometimes too much or too little of something can be a bad thing. For example, can a cloud provider use the data for its own purposes? Can the provider aggregate your data along with that of other clients and then resell this information? Also, is your data on a stand-alone server or is it on a virtual system that is shared with others? In such cases, your data may be stored along with data from other companies. This raises concerns about the comingling of data.

Data Remanence   Your data will most likely not be needed forever. This means that data disposal and destruction are real concerns. An attacker could attempt to access retired hard drives and look for remaining data. Even in situations where the drives have been formatted or wiped, there may be some remaining data. The remaining data (data remanence) could be scavenged for sensitive information. Other data exfiltration techniques include hacking backups or using backdoors and covert channels to send data back to the attacker. To achieve this end, social engineering techniques are used, such as going after cloud employees with access and targeting the cloud employees at their homes, since so many engineers maintain less secured paths back to their work networks.

Security professionals must understand the importance of sanitization of media. Techniques such as formatting are not adequate. Drive wiping or physical destruction of the media is preferred. One great tool for drive wiping is Darik's Boot and Nuke (DBAN). You can find out more about this tool at www.dban.org.

Other kinds of attacks include keyloggers, custom malware sent via phishing (such as malicious PDFs), and trojaned USB keys dropped in the cloud provider employee parking lot. A dedicated attacker who is targeting a big enough cloud provider might even apply for a job at the facility, simply to gain some level of physical access.

All systems have an inherent amount of risk. The goal of the security professional is to evaluate the risk and aid management in deciding on a suitably secure solution. Cloud computing offers real benefits to companies seeking a competitive edge in today's economy. Many more providers are moving into this area, and the competition is driving prices even lower.

Attractive pricing, the ability to free up staff for other duties, and the ability to pay for services as needed will continue to drive more businesses to consider cloud computing. Before any services are moved to the cloud, the organization's senior management should assess the potential risk and understand any threats that may arise from such a decision. One concern is that cloud computing blurs the natural perimeter between the protected inside and the hostile outside. Security of any cloud-based services must be closely reviewed to understand what protections exist for your information. There is also the issue of availability. This availability could be jeopardized by a DoS attack or by the service provider suffering a failure or going out of business. Also, what if the cloud provider goes through a merger? What kind of policy changes occur? What kind of notice is provided in advance of the merger? All of these issues should be covered in the contract.

Unfortunately, one of the largest vulnerabilities in the cloud is simple customer error or misconfiguration. Cloud misconfiguration can be any errors or gaps that leave risk exposure. This risk could be exploited by an attacker or malicious insider, and it doesn't take much technical knowledge to extract data or compromise cloud assets. Security researchers disclosed that a nonprofit organization in Los Angeles exposed more than 3.5 million records including PII because an AWS S3 storage bucket leaked databases of information because they were programmed to be "public and anonymously accessible." Misconfigured cloud services pose a high security risk, so make sure the people administering your cloud are well trained.

Storage Models

Even though your data is in the cloud, it must physically be located somewhere. Is your data on a separate server, is it co-located with the data of other organizations, or is it sliced and diced so many times that it's hard to know where it resides? Your cloud storage provider should agree in writing to provide the level of security required for your customers.

Tape was the medium of choice for backup and archiving for most businesses for many years. This was in part due to the high cost of moving backup and archival data to a data warehouse. Such activities required hundreds of thousands of dollars in infrastructure investment. Today that has started to change as cloud service providers are beginning to sell attractively priced services for cloud storage. Such technologies allow companies to do away with traditional in-house technologies. Cloud-based archiving and warehousing have several key advantages.

Content Management   The cloud warehousing provider manages the content for you.

Geographical Redundancy   Data is held at more than one offsite location.

Advance Search   Data is indexed so that retrieval of specific datasets is much easier.

How much storage is enough? How big a hard drive should I buy? These are good questions—there never seems to be enough storage space for home or enterprise users. Businesses are no different and depend on fast, reliable access to information critical to their success. This makes enterprise storage an important component of most modern companies. *Enterprise storage* can be defined as computer storage designed for large-scale, high-technology environments.

Think of how much data is required for most modern enterprises. There is a huge dependence on information for the business world to survive. Organizations that thrive on large amounts of data include government agencies, credit card companies, airlines, telephone billing systems, global capital markets, e-commerce, and even email archive systems. Although the amount of storage needed continues to climb, there is also the issue of terminology used in the enterprise storage market. Terms such as *heterogeneous*, *SAN*, *NAS*, *virtualization*, and *cloud storage* are frequently used.

Before any enterprise storage solution is implemented, a full assessment and classification of the data should occur. This would include an analysis of all threats, vulnerabilities, existing controls, and the potential impact if loss, disclosure, modification, interruption, or destruction of the data should occur.

Now that we've explored some of the security issues of enterprise storage, let's look at some of the technologies used in enterprise storage.

Virtual Storage   Virtual storage options have grown, evolved, and matured. These online entities typically focus either on storage or on sharing. The storage services are designed for storing large files. Many companies are entering this market and now giving away storage, such as Microsoft's OneDrive, Amazon Drive, and Google Drive.

Virtual file sharing services are a second type of virtual storage. These services are not meant for long-term use. They allow users to transfer large files. Examples of these services include Dropbox, DropSend, and MediaFire. These virtual services work well if you are trying to share very large files or move information that is too big to be sent as an attachment.

On the positive side, there are many great uses for these services, such as keeping a synchronized copy of your documents in an online collaboration environment, sharing documents, and synchronizing documents between desktops, laptops, tablets, and smartphones.

The disadvantages of these services include the fact that you are now placing assets outside the perimeter of the organization. There is also the issue of loss of control. If these providers go out of business, what happens to your data? Although these services do fill a gap, they can be used by individuals to move data illicitly. Another concern is the kind of controls placed on your data. Some of these services allow anyone to search sent files.

In Exercise 9.4, you'll look at security issues involved in online storage.

EXERCISE 9.4

Understanding Online Storage

A small advertising firm has been routinely running out of storage. The employees use a variety of systems and network connections and must share large files. The business's survival requires that this information be exchanged to meet the needs of clients. Network storage has been upgraded in the past, but it has not been able to keep up.

You've been appointed to the IT department at this company and asked to solve this problem. Although one solution would be to buy additional storage, cost is an issue—the company is hesitant about making capital improvements under current economic conditions. Another solution would be to use a free online storage solution. You are considering recommending OneDrive. OneDrive is a file storage and sharing service from Microsoft that allows users to upload files to the cloud and then access them from a web browser. This solution would provide additional storage space at no cost. The biggest downside to this approach is that each user is in charge of their own account, and this method lacks centralized control. You would also be depending on a service over which you would have little or no control. Using this service would require users to do the following:

- Create a Microsoft account. Whether you use Windows 10 or macOS or have an iPhone or Android phone, you will need a Microsoft account to use OneDrive. If you have a @outlook.com, @live.com, or @hotmail.com email address, or Xbox network account, you already have a Microsoft account, and you can use it to access the cloud storage service.

- Configure OneDrive for sharing.

- Provide others with the ability to read shared OneDrive files.

What would you recommend the company do? Can you accept the fact that such a service lacks a centralized control? Is it acceptable that security of the OneDrive is placed in the hands of the end user?

Network-Attached Storage   *Network-attached storage (NAS)* is a technology that contains or has slots for one or more hard drives using a hierarchical storage methodology. These hard drives are used for network storage. NAS is similar to direct access storage (DAS), but DAS is simply an extension of one system and has no networking capability.

Many NAS devices make use of the Linux OS and provide connectivity via network file sharing protocols. One of the most common protocols used is Network File System (NFS). NFS is a standard designed to share files and applications over a network. NFS was developed by Sun Microsystems (now part of Oracle) back in the mid-1980s. The Windows-based counterpart used for file and application sharing is Common Internet File System (CIFS); it is an open version of Microsoft's Server Message Block (SMB) protocol.

For the CASP+ exam, this is often referred to as *object storage* or *file-based storage*. This type of cloud solution is seen in Amazon Simple Storage Services (S3).

 An important consideration with cloud services is encryption. Ask yourself what the result would be if unauthorized individuals accessed the data you placed on the cloud. The 2021 Thales Global Cloud Security Study, commissioned by Thales and conducted by 451 Research, reported that 40 percent of organizations have experienced a cloud-based data breach in the past 12 months.

SAN   The Storage Network Industry Association (SNIA) defines a *storage area network (SAN)* as "a data storage system consisting of various storage elements, storage devices, computer systems, and/or appliances, plus all the control software, all communicating in efficient harmony over a network." SANs are similar to NAS. One of the big differences is that NAS appears to the client as a file server or stand-alone system. A SAN appears to the client OS as a local disk or volume that is available to be formatted and used locally as needed.

For the CASP+, this is referred to in the objectives as *block storage*. Block cloud storage solutions include Amazon Elastic Block Store (EBS) and are provisioned with ultra-low latency for high performance.

Virtual SAN   A *virtual SAN (VSAN)* is a SAN that offers isolation among devices that are physically connected to the same SAN fabric. A VSAN is sometimes called *fabric virtualization*. (*Fabric* can be defined as the structure of the SAN.) VSANs were developed to support independent virtual networking capability on a single switch. VSANs improve consolidation and simplify management by allowing for more efficient SAN utilization. A resource on any individual VSAN can be shared by other users on a different VSAN without merging the SAN's fabrics.

Redundancy (Location)   *Location redundancy* is the idea that content should be accessible from more than one location. An extra measure of redundancy can be provided by means of a replication service so that data is available even if the main storage backup system fails. This further enhances a company's resiliency and redundancy. *Database storage* using shadowing, remote journaling, and electronic vaulting are all common methods used for redundancy. Electronic vaulting describes the transfer of data by electronic means rather than a physical shipment of backup tapes. Some organizations use these techniques by themselves, whereas others combine these techniques with other backup methods.

Secure Storage Management and Replication   *Secure storage management and replication* systems are designed to enable a company to manage and handle all corporate data in a secure manner with a focus on the confidentiality, integrity, and availability of the information. The replication service allows for the data to be duplicated in real time so that additional fault tolerance is achieved.

Multipath Solutions   Enterprise storage multipath solutions reduce the risk of data loss or lack of availability by setting up multiple routes between a server and its drives. The multipathing software maintains a list of all requests, passes them through the best possible path, and reroutes communication if one of the paths dies. One of its major advantages is its speed of access.

SAN Snapshots   *SAN snapshot software* is typically sold with SAN solutions and offers the user a way to bypass typical backup operations. The snapshot software has the ability to stop writing to a physical disk temporarily and then make a point-in-time backup copy. Think of these as being similar to Windows System Restore points in that they allow you to take a snapshot in time. Snapshot software is typically fast and makes a copy quickly, regardless of the drive size.

Data De-duplication (DDP)   *Data de-duplication* is the process of removing redundant data to improve enterprise storage utilization. Redundant data is not copied. It is replaced with a pointer to the one unique copy of the data. Only one instance of redundant data is retained on the enterprise storage media, such as disk or tape.

Storage Configurations

Data dispersion consists of information being distributed and stored in multiple cloud pods, which is a key component of cloud storage architecture. The ability to have data replicated throughout a distributed storage infrastructure is critical. This allows a cloud service provider to offer storage services based on the level of the user's subscription or the popularity of the item. *Bit splitting* is another technique for securing data over a computer network that involves encrypting data, splitting the encrypted data into smaller data units, distributing those smaller units to different storage locations, and then further encrypting the data at its new location. Data is protected from security breaches, because even if an attacker is able to retrieve and decrypt one data unit, the information is useless unless it can be combined with decrypted data units from the other locations.

Security Implications with Storage

Whether you are storing objects, files, databases, blocks of data, or *binary large objects* (BLOBs) in the cloud, there are several best practices that help accomplish the safety of your information.

- Apply data protection policies.
- Limit access and implement classification.
- Prevent data exfiltration to unmanaged devices.
- Audit configuration for critical settings.

Encryption of sensitive data in the cloud is a vital security step. There are many ways to implement key design with a data store. A data store is a repository for storing and managing a collection of data.

A key/value store associates each data value to a specific and unique key. To modify a value, the key is overwritten using an application that replaces the entire value. While a single key/value is extremely scalable, it can also distribute that key across multiple instances. Amazon DynamoDB is probably the most well-known key/value store. A *key-value pair* consists of two related pieces of data. The key is a constant, such as color, and a value, such as an article of clothing, which belongs to that set of data. A fully formed key-value pair could be the "color=green, clothing=shirt" pair. In addition to cloud-based storage sites, other storage types pose security and privacy concerns. The actual risks depend largely on whether storage is nonremovable or removable. *USB On-The-Go (USB OTG)* is the solution to the problem of not being able to connect a standard USB flash drive directly to a mobile device. USB OTG is flash drive storage with a physical interface capable of attaching to almost every smartphone or small form-factor device. The risk of misplacing this portable storage is based on how private or critical the information stored on it is.

Other removable storage, such a swappable drive from a larger device, also carries the risk of being easily misplaced. Most likely, the removable storage would be maliciously stolen from its bay. The malicious person may transfer or send backup data to removable or uncontrolled storage.

In Exercise 9.5, you will use the cloud to store and transfer a large file.

EXERCISE 9.5

Turning to the Cloud for Storage and Large File Transfer

One area of cloud computing that most Internet users can appreciate is large file transfer services. These services allow users to transfer files that are larger than those that can be sent by email or other conventional means. Such services allow large files to be sent easily to other users via elastic cloud-based providers.

1. Go to www.dropsend.com. Start your free trial.

2. You can create a unique email account for just this purpose if necessary. Choose someone to receive a large file.

3. Select the file that you want to send. A large image file or video will work well to demonstrate this process.

4. Enter your address as the return address.

5. Click Send File.

Now, ask the recipient to check their email for the link to the downloadable file.

How Cloud Technology Adoption Impacts Organization Security

Years ago, many organizations resisted cloud technology adoption because of the lack of control and understanding. There are risks, threats, and vulnerabilities no matter where the data is stored. Moving to the cloud is a big decision, and modern cloud computing has many benefits including increased security, flexibility, and cost savings.

Automation and Orchestration

Cloud automation is technology that does not require human intervention in processes and procedures. By having decisions made based on relationships and the actions that should be taken, human-made mistakes can be avoided, and processes that required involvement of IT staff can happen automatically. By using automation of a single task or orchestration of many automated tasks, enterprise organizations improve standard operating procedures for specific use cases as well as increasing efficiency and consistency. There are several cloud orchestration tools including software like Puppet, Ansible, and Chef. These three tools are fairly simple to use and have robust capabilities. Puppet works best with automated provisioning of assets, configuration automation with great visualization, and reporting. Chef is used more for compliance and security management, while Ansible is the easiest of all three to implement; Ansible is good with simple orchestration but does not scale in large environments as well as the other two.

Encryption Configuration

Sensitive information is being moved to the cloud now more than ever. According to the Ponemon Institute, the average cost of a breach is now more than $3.8 million USD. One of the most essential elements of preventing the loss of data being moved to the cloud is having robust encryption for the data while at rest as well as in transit.

Encryption makes data unreadable to anyone without access to the encryption keys. Kerckhoffs's principle states that a cryptosystem should be secure, even if everything about the system, except the key, is public knowledge. Only 1 percent of cloud providers support tenant managed encryption keys. With the right tools and configuration, you can protect data with standards-based AES encryption for data at rest, ensuring compliance with PCI, HIPAA, and other federal or industry requirements.

Cloud encryption solutions can encrypt information as it moves in and out of applications and into storage with strong key-based encryption. Most reputable cloud service providers offer cloud encryption options. The most used type of cloud data in transit encryption is the HTTPS protocol. When using the more modern and secure version of Secure Sockets Layer (SSL) called Transport Layer Security (TLS), all traffic is encoded so only authorized users can access the data. If an unauthorized third party sees the data, it remains unreadable because the digital keys to lock and unlock it are at the user and destination layers. Keys should be generated and issued using an asymmetrical algorithm between trusted entities, while certificates are certified during the original connection.

Logs

Every device on a modern cloud network generates logs. Some logs are human readable, and some logs look like gibberish. Some logs are more useful than others, and we should understand which cloud logs need to be preserved for future analysis and for how long. You don't need to log everything, but what you do log should be purposely collected and managed because the logs can show you who did what activity and how the systems they touched responded.

The Center for Internet Security (CIS) Critical Security Controls Version 8 focuses on the collection, maintenance, monitoring, and analysis of audit logs. Our organizations are evolving quickly, and we have to learn to deal with log data in the big data cloud era. Analyzing audit logs is a vital part of security, not just for system security but for processes and compliance. Part of the process of log analysis is reconciling logs from different sources and correlation even if those devices are in different time zones. Network Time Protocol (NTP) will help synchronize devices using the cloud. Google Cloud has its own NTP protocol called Google Public NTP.

In a basic network topology, you will have many types of devices, including routers, switches, firewalls, servers, and workstations. Each of these devices that helps connect you to the rest of the world will generate logs based on its operating system, configuration, and software. Examining logs is one of the most effective ways of looking for issues and investigating problems happening on a system or in an application.

Synchronization and the ability to correlate the data between these devices are vital to a healthy environment. Attackers can hide their activities on assets if logging is not done correctly; therefore, you need a strategic method of consolidating and auditing all your logs. Without solid audit log analysis, an attack can go unnoticed for a long time. According to the 2021 Verizon Data Breach Investigations Report, The Verizon Threat Research Advisory Center intelligence collections in both 2019 and 2020 began with cyber espionage targeting cloud environments by the Chinese menuPass threat actor. Among the ongoing threats were attacks on remote access. The full report was based on detailed analysis of more than 79,600 security incidents, including 5,258 data breaches. You can download the full details at www .verizon.com/business/resources/reports/dbir/2021/year-in-review-2021.

Logging involves collecting data from a large number of data sources, which has its own challenges including collection, storage, encryption, and parsing. Key considerations when configuring logs for collection include normalization, alerting, security, correlation. availability, monitoring, and analysis.

Normalization or parsing logs enables analysis of the data. Parsing the logs into specific fields allows for easier reading, correlation, and analysis. Correlation means that you are able to connect the dots to identify a sequence of events that have the potential to be a breach. Monitoring and alerting for specific events, or after analysis has been done on several scenarios that are being monitored for security incidents, is important because it is a more proactive approach. To be able to go back into storage requires availability. The logging solution chosen must make sure that the logs are not only secure but provide data compression and other procedures to address the high volume.

Without logging, a threat actor can be in an environment and fly completely under the radar. There are many solutions for logging for audit and centralization, including Elasticsearch, Logstash, and Kibana (ELK), which is the most common open-source solution used. There are some security information and event management (SIEM) tools that are customizable for security analytics. SIEM tools centralize information gathering and analysis and provide detailed dashboards and reporting that allow critical information to be seen through visualization, and they offer manual analysis as well as automated analysis capabilities. They work with logging infrastructures using tools such as syslog, syslog-ng, or others that gather and centralize logs, building logging infrastructures that capture evidence used for incident analysis and creating an audit trail. At the same time, additional information captured such as network flows and traffic information, file and system metadata, and other artifacts are used by responders who need to analyze what occurred on a system or network.

Gartner's Magic Quadrant report for 2021 includes Splunk, Rapid7 InsightIDR, LogRhythm, and Exabeam. These SIEM tools work by taking a baseline of two to four weeks of log ingestion to learn the normal state of an organization and then can start monitoring and alerting for anomalies.

Monitoring Configurations

The cloud is not a single object. There are many moving parts that affect performance and availability, with each part needing to work well with other parts. When looking at monitoring a cloud environment, you have to watch the network, the individual VMs, the databases, the websites, and storage. With the network, cloud administrators have to watch for connectivity to make sure they are not overwhelmed with traffic. The VMs will have to be monitored for access and status to make sure they are operating as intended. Database monitoring is incredibly important because of what is in the database, usually sensitive organizational data. Databases will need to be monitored for queries, access requests, integrity, and backups. Proactively monitoring websites will allow for optimal uptime, and storage is costly, so making sure performance and analytics are kept within proper ranges will keep expenses down.

Some cloud monitoring best practices may include the following:

- Decide the most important metrics and events
- Choose the right cloud monitoring software
- Monitor all your cloud infrastructure from one platform
- Automate monitoring tasks
- Track end-user experience
- Test for cloud failure
- Monitor services and costs

It is difficult to keep up with shifting policies and compliance, but with automation open-source software like Puppet or other tooling such as SolarWinds, the organization must be able to monitor the cloud ecosystem for changes and revert as needed. It can be time-consuming and tedious to manually do audit inspections to prepare for an auditor. Puppet is mostly used on Linux and Windows, but it's capable of managing infrastructure through continuous monitoring using policy as code. For more information, visit `puppet.com/ use-cases/continuous-compliance`.

Key Ownership and Location

Chapter 6, "Cryptography and PKI," covered public key infrastructure, which allows two parties to communicate securely even if they were previously unknown to one another. This chapter covers the certificate authority (CA), registration authority (RA), certificate revocation lists (CRLs), digital certificates, and how they are distributed. The question this chapter covers is how this process can be different in a cloud-based ecosystem.

Most cloud service providers offer some type of encryption for customer data. As mentioned earlier in this chapter, protecting data in transit using HTTPS in the cloud between servers or user devices is reliable and straightforward. Encryption protection becomes more complicated for data at rest on a cloud server. Cloud providers can encrypt the data and maintain control over the keys. This can be a security risk because now a company is dealing with malicious insiders and nefarious outsiders who target the cloud provider. Many organizations are not willing to use cloud-based storage for their most sensitive data.

The other two options for key ownership and location are *bring your own key (BYOK)* and *hold your own key (HYOK)*. With BYOK, the customer can generate and manage encryption keys, but the cloud provider has access to them. With HYOK, customers generate, manage, and store them, and the cloud provider is not able to see the contents of the encrypted files.

Key Life-Cycle Management

With the use of keys in securing cloud environments comes the need for a key management system. National Institute of Standards and Technology (NIST) special publication 800-57 Part 2, Revision 1, gives recommendations for key management and best practices and introduces a set of key management concepts such as key life cycle, practice statements, policies, and planning documents.

Key life-cycle management refers to everything from the creation of to the retirement of cryptographic keys. There are several key life-cycle management models that can be used such as NIST or Microsoft. The six states a key goes through in the Microsoft Key Life-Cycle Model are as follows:

Creation   The key object is created on a domain controller.

Initialization   The key object has attributes set.

Full Distribution   The initialized key is available to all domain controllers.

Active   The initialized key is available for cryptographic operations.

Inactive   The initialized key is unavailable for some cryptographic operations.

Terminated   The initialized key is permanently deleted from all domain controllers.

Defining and enforcing key management policies will influence each state of the life cycle and needs to be governed by a key usage policy that defines the cloud assets and applications and what operations those asset and applications can perform.

Details on this publication can be found here: nvlpubs.nist.gov/nistpubs/ SpecialPublications/NIST.SP.800-57pt2r1.pdf.

Backup and Recovery Methods

As our cybersecurity industry moves to a software-defined infrastructure using virtualization, cloud infrastructure, and containers, this translates to systems that would have once been backed up not being backed up in a traditional way. Instead, the code that defines them is backed up, as well as the key data that they are intended to provide or to access. This changes the policies and procedures for server and backup administrators, and it means that habits around how backup storage is accomplished and maintained are changing for backup and recovery. Reviewing organizational backup habits to see if they match new frameworks or if current procedures are failing disaster recovery tests is an important element in planning.

For on-premise systems, some organizations choose to utilize physical storage either at a site they own and operate or via a third-party service that specializes in storing secure backups in environmentally controlled facilities, or they choose cloud-based offsite storage for their backup media. Offsite storage is a form of geographic diversity and helps to ensure that a single disaster cannot destroy an organization's data entirely. This is done both physically and in the cloud for BCDR. For geographic diversity, distance considerations are important to ensure that a single regional disaster is unlikely to harm the offsite storage. BCDR plans define the processes and procedures that an organization will take when a disaster occurs, which is equally important when those assets are in the cloud.

In a BCDR plan, processes describe all of the documented, procedural "how-tos" of the organization's way of conducting operations. Some processes are so routine and so ingrained in the minds of those performing them that they hardly seem necessary to document. On the other end of the spectrum, some processes must be documented because they are performed only under extraordinary circumstances, perhaps even in times of crisis, such as, for example, during disaster recovery.

Preparation for an incident or disaster includes building a team, putting policies and procedures in place, conducting exercises, and building the technical and information-gathering infrastructure that will support incident response needs. These plans cannot exist in a vacuum.

Instead, they are accompanied by communications and stakeholder management plans, as well as other detailed response processes unique to each organization.

Infrastructure vs. Serverless Computing

As mentioned earlier in this chapter, infrastructure as a service (IaaS) is a type of cloud computing model that offers essential computation, storage, and networking on demand. Migrating an organization to an IaaS model helps an enterprise reduce the number of physical datacenters needed and gives an organization a great deal of flexibility to spin resources up and down as needed. Serverless computing is a type of infrastructure as a service with a slightly different strategy.

In serverless computing, you don't worry about the infrastructure and configuration; everything is managed by the cloud provider. This means that cloud customers are paying for the quantity of times their code runs on a serverless service. This enables developers to build applications faster while the cloud service automatically handles all tasks required to run the code. Some serverless offerings are workflows, Kubernetes, and application environments where the back and front ends are fully hosted.

Software that is written for application virtual machines allows the developer to create one version of the application so that it can be run on any virtual machine and won't have to be rewritten for every different computer hardware platform. Java Virtual Machine (JVM) is an example of such application virtualization.

Software-Defined Networking

Software-defined networking (SDN) is a technology that allows network professionals to virtualize the network so that control is decoupled from hardware and given to a software application called a *controller*.

In a typical network environment, hardware devices such as *switches* make forwarding decisions so that when a frame enters the switch, the switch's logic, built into the content addressable memory (CAM) table, determines the port to which the data frame is forwarded. All packets with the same address will be forwarded to the same destination. SDN is a step in the evolution toward programmable and active networking in that it gives network managers the flexibility to configure, manage, and optimize network resources dynamically by centralizing the network state in the control layer.

Software-defined networking allows networking professionals to respond to the dynamic needs of modern networks. With SDN, a network administrator can shape traffic from a centralized control console without having to touch individual switches. Based on demand and network needs, the network switch's rules can be changed dynamically as needed, permitting the blocking, allowing, or prioritizing of specific types of data frames with a very granular level of control. This enables the network to be treated as a logical or virtual entity.

SDN is defined as three layers: application, control, and the infrastructure or data plane layer. At the core of SDN is the OpenFlow standard. *OpenFlow* is defined by the Open Networking Foundation (ONF). OpenFlow provides an interface between the controller and the physical network infrastructure layers of SDN architecture. This design helps SDN achieve the following, all of which are limitations of standard networking:

- Ability to manage the forwarding of frames/packets and applying policy
- Ability to perform this at scale in a dynamic fashion
- Ability to be programmed
- Visibility and manageability through centralized control

   Infrastructure as a service is one example of the application of SDN.

Misconfigurations

The definition of misconfiguration is to configure a system incorrectly. Cloud misconfiguration seems avoidable, but according to the IBM Security Cost of a Data Breach Report in 2021, the cost of a breach is $4.24 million, and two-thirds of cloud breaches can be traced to misconfiguration, specifically cloud application programming interfaces.

The cloud has many settings, assets, services, resources, and policies, and that makes it an environment that is difficult to set up correctly. It is even more true for organizations that have had to migrate quickly to the cloud for remote work with an IT department that does not fully understand the details of configuration. Misconfiguration is one of the leading causes of financial damage done to enterprise as well as governmental organizations.

Cloud providers like AWS have a service called Cloud Conformity Checks. These are rules run against the customer's configuration or infrastructure. These scans will take a rule, run it against a system, and determine whether it was successful. According to AWS, the top service scanned in 2021 for misconfiguration was Amazon Elastic Compute Cloud, better known as EC2. The rule most broken in 2021 was AWS CloudTrail Configuration Changes. CloudTrail is a service that enables governance, compliance, and auditing and keeps an organization in compliance with APRA, MAS, and NIST4.

With this tool, you can log, continuously monitor, and retain account activity related to actions across the AWS infrastructure, providing event history of AWS account activity, including actions taken through the Management Console, command-line interface (CLI), AWS SDKs, and APIs. This event history feature simplifies security auditing, resource change tracking, and troubleshooting. You can identify who or what took which action, what resources were acted upon, when an event occurred, and other details that can help you analyze and respond to any activity within your account.

Collaboration Tools

According to the International Engineering Consortium, *unified communications and collaboration* is an industry term "used to describe all forms of call and multimedia/cross-media message-management functions controlled by an individual user for both business and social purposes." This topic is of concern to the CASP+ because communication systems form the backbone of any company. Communication systems can include any enterprise process that allows people to communicate.

Web Conferencing

Web conferencing is a low-cost method that allows people in different locations to communicate over the Internet. While useful, web conferencing can potentially be sniffed and intercepted by an attacker. Attackers inject themselves into the stream between the web conferencing clients. This could be accomplished with tools such as Ettercap or Cain & Abel, and then an attacker starts to capture the video traffic with a tool such as UCSniff or VideoSnarf. These tools allow the attacker to eavesdrop on video traffic. Most of these tools are surprisingly easy to use in that you capture and load the web conferencing libpcap-based file (with the .pcap extension) and then watch and listen to the playback. Exercise 9.6 shows you how to perform a basic web conference capture.

EXERCISE 9.6

Eavesdropping on Web Conferences

To better appreciate the risks of web conferencing, this exercise will highlight the threat of eavesdropping.

1. Open your browser and go to sourceforge.net/projects/vipervast/files.

2. Download the latest Viper_Vast.iso.

3. Burn the image to a DVD drive or load it to a bootable USB thumb drive using the imaging tool of choice.

4. Reboot the system and choose to boot from the appropriate drive.

5. Log in with a username of **viper** and a password of **password**.

6. Start VideoSnarf.

7. Load a sample capture file. These can be found in the directory called pcap.

8. If you decide to perform a live capture, make sure that you have signed, written permission from the network owner.

Disclaimer: Capturing or eavesdropping on real-world web conference conversations could be breaking state or federal wiretapping statutes.

Videoconferencing

Today, many businesses make use of videoconferencing systems. *Videoconferencing* is a great way for businesses to conduct meetings with customers, employees, and potential clients.

If videoconferencing systems are not properly secured, there is the possibility that sensitive information could be leaked, and considering how much of the global workforce is working and schooling from home, this could be a big risk. Most laptops and even some desktop systems come with webcams, and there are a host of programs available that will allow an attacker to turn on a camera to spy on an individual. Some of the programs are legitimate, while others are types of malware and Trojan horses designed specifically to spy on users. One example is gh0st Rat. This Trojan was designed to turn on the webcam, record audio, and enable built-in internal microphones to spy on people. You can read more about this malware here: `attack.mitre.org/software/S0032`.

To prevent these types of problems, you should instruct users to take care when opening attachments from unknown recipients or installing unknown software and emphasize the importance of having up-to-date antivirus. Also, all conference calls should require strong passcodes to join a meeting, and the passcodes for periodic meetings should be changed for each meeting.

Audio Conferencing

When videoconferencing, a user often has the obvious indication that conferencing is still ongoing; that is, they see the screen of their conferenced co-workers. Such is not the case with audio conferencing. When sharing an open line, for example on a telephone, an employee can easily forget that all ambient noise will be heard by all of the conference attendees.

Instant Messaging

Instant messaging (IM) has been around a long time and evolved into modern corporate landscapes in tools like Microsoft Teams, Slack, and Discord Server. It is widely used and available in many home and corporate settings. What has made IM so popular is that it differs from email in that it allows two-way communication in near real time. It also lets business users collaborate, hold informal chat meetings, and share files and information. Although some IM platforms have added encryption, central logging, and user access controls for corporate clients, others operate without such controls.

From the perspective of the CASP+, IM is a concern due to its potential to be a carrier for malware. IM products are all highly vulnerable to malware, such as worm viruses, backdoor Trojan horses, hijacking and impersonation, and denial of service. IM can also be used to send sensitive information. Most of this is because of the file transfer and peer-to-peer file sharing capabilities available to users of these applications. Should you decide to use IM in your organization, there are some basic questions that you need to address:

- Is the IM solution a critical business requirement?
- What IM product will be used? Is it just one or will multiple applications be permitted?
- Will encryption be used?
- Is IM just for internal use?
- Will IM be used for external clients?
- Is the company subject to regulatory compliance requirements for IM? If so, how will data be logged and recorded?

- Will users be allowed to transfer files and applications?

- Will virus scanning, file scanning, and content-filtering applications be used?

- How many employees will use the system over the next 24 to 36 months?

- Will the IM application be available to everyone or only to specific users?

- Will the IM solutions use filters on specific words to flag for profanity or inappropriate content?

- Will there be user training for secure use of IM?

Spam has found its way into other forms of unwanted messaging beyond email, giving birth to acronyms such as SPIM (spam over instant messaging).

Desktop and Application Sharing

Desktop sharing software is nothing new. Some early examples of desktop sharing programs were actually classified as malware. One such program is Back Orifice (BO), released in 1998. Although many other remote Trojan programs have been created, such as NetBus and Poison Ivy, BO was one of the first to have the ability to function as a remote system administration tool. It enables a user to control a computer running the Windows operating system from a remote location. Although some may have found this functionality useful, there are other functions built into BO that made it much more malicious. BO has the ability to hide itself from users of the system, flip the images on their screens upside down, capture their keystrokes, and even turn on their webcams. BO can also be installed without user interaction and distributed as a Trojan horse.

Desktop sharing programs are extremely useful, but there are potential risks. One issue is that anyone who can connect and use your desktop to execute or run programs on your computer. A search on the Web for Microsoft Remote Desktop Services returns a list of hundreds of systems to which you can potentially connect if you can guess the username and password.

At a minimum, these ports and applications and related ports should be blocked and restricted to those individuals who have a need for this service. Advertising this service on the Web is also not a good idea. If this is a public link, it should not be indexed by search engines. There should also be a warning banner on the page that states that the service is for authorized users only and that all activity is logged.

Another issue with desktop sharing is the potential risk from the user's point of view. If the user shares the desktop during a videoconference, then others in the conference can see what is on the presenter's desktop. Should there be a folder titled "why I hate my boss," everyone will see it.

Application sharing is fraught with risks as well. If the desktop sharing user then opens an application such as email or a web browser before the session is truly terminated, anybody still in the meeting can read and/or see what's been opened. Any such incident looks highly unprofessional and can sink a business deal.

Table 9.2 lists some programs and default port numbers to be aware of.

TABLE 9.2 Legitimate and malicious desktop sharing programs

Name	Protocol	Default Port
Back Orifice	UDP	31337
Back Orifice 2000	TCP/UDP	54320/54321
Beast	TCP	6666
Citrix ICA	TCP/UDP	1494
Loki	ICMP	NA
Masters Paradise	TCP	40421/40422/40426
Remote Desktop Control	TCP/UDP	49608/49609
NetBus	TCP	12345
Netcat	TCP/UDP	Any
Reachout	TCP	43188
Remotely Anywhere	TCP	2000/2001
Remote	TCP/UDP	135-139
Timbuktu	TCP/UDP	407
VNC	TCP/UDP	5800/5801

Remote Assistance

Remote assistance programs can be used to provide temporary control of a remote computer over a network or the Internet to resolve issues or for troubleshooting purposes. These tools are useful because they allow problems to be addressed remotely and can cut down on the site visits that a technician performs.

Why Use Crack When You Can Pass the Hash?

Although the title may have caught your attention, we are referring to two security-related tools. Crack is a Unix password-cracking program, and Pass the Hash is used to grab NTLM credentials.

> Pass the Hash is a toolkit that contains several software utilities that can be used to manipulate the Windows Logon Sessions maintained by the Local Security Authority (LSA) component. For example, suppose an attacker phones the help desk and asks if someone can remote-desktop in and fix a problem. When the remote connection is made, the attacker uses Pass the Hash to capture the administrative credentials and then change the runtime, current username, domain name, and NTLM hashes. Thus, the attacker is now operating as an administrative user. Learn more about this tool here:
>
> `attack.mitre.org/techniques/T1550/002`

Presence

Presence is an Apple software product that is somewhat similar to Windows Remote Desktop. Presence gives users access to their Mac's files wherever they are. It also allows users to share files and data between a Mac, iPhone, and iPad.

Domain Bridging

Nominally, a device operates in one network, viewing traffic intended for that network domain. However, when the device is connected via remote assistance software or a virtual private network connection to a corporate network, it is conceivable that device can bridge two network domains. Unauthorized domain bridging is a security concern with which the CASP+ needs to be familiar.

Email

Many individuals would agree that email is one of the greatest inventions to come out of the development of the Internet. It is the most used Internet application. Just take a look around the office and see how many people use Android phones, iPhones/iPads, tablets, and other devices that provide email services. Email provides individuals with the ability to communicate electronically through the Internet or a data communications network.

Although email has many great features and provides a level of communication previously not possible, it's not without its problems. Now, before we beat it up too much, you must keep in mind that email was designed in a different era. Decades ago, security was not as much of a driving issue as usability. By default, email sends information via clear text, so it is susceptible to eavesdropping and interception. Email can be easily spoofed so that the true identity of the sender may be masked. Email is also a major conduit for spam, phishing, and viruses. Spam is unsolicited bulk mail. Studies by Symantec and others have found that spam is much more malicious than in the past. Although a large amount of spam is used to peddle fake drugs, counterfeit software, and fake designer goods, it's more targeted to inserting malware via malicious URLs today.

As for functionality, email operates by means of several underlying services, which can include the following:

Simple Mail Transfer Protocol *Simple Mail Transfer Protocol (SMTP)* is used to send mail and relay mail to other SMTP mail servers and uses port 25 by default.

Post Office Protocol   *Post Office Protocol (POP3)*, the current version, is widely used to retrieve messages from a mail server. POP3 performs authentication in clear text on port 110.

Internet Message Access Protocol   *Internet Message Access Protocol (IMAP)* can be used as a replacement for POP3 and offers advantages over POP3 for mobile users. IMAP has the ability to work with mail remotely and uses port 143.

Basic email operation consists of the SMTP service being used to send messages to the mail server. To retrieve mail, the client application, such as Outlook, may use either POP or IMAP. Exercise 9.7 shows how to capture clear-text email for review and reinforces the importance of protecting email with PGP, SSL/TLS, or other encryption methods.

EXERCISE 9.7

Sniffing Email with Wireshark

One easy way to demonstrate the vulnerabilities of email is to perform a clear-text capture of an insecure email service.

1. Open your browser, go to `mail.yahoo.com`, and open a free burner email account.

2. Download Wireshark and install it on your computer. You can download it from `www.wireshark.org/download.html`.

3. Start Wireshark and begin a capture.

4. Go to the `mail.yahoo.com` website and log into your account.

5. Stop Wireshark.

6. Search through the Wireshark capture for the frame containing the word *username*.

The CASP+ should work to secure email and make users aware of the risks. Users should be prohibited by policy and trained not to send sensitive information by clear-text email. If an organization has policies that allow email to be used for sensitive information, encryption should be mandatory.

Several solutions exist to meet this need. One is Pretty Good Privacy (PGP). Other options include link encryption or secure email standards such as Secure Multipurpose Internet Mail Extensions (S/MIME) or Privacy Enhanced Mail (PEM).

Telephony

Businesses with legacy PBX and traditional telephony systems are especially vulnerable to attack and misuse. One of the primary telephony threats has to do with systems with default passwords. If PBX systems are not secured, an attacker can attempt to call into the system and connect using the default password. Default passwords may be numbers such as 1, 2, 3, 4, or 0, 0, 0, 0. An attacker who can access the system via the default password can change the prompt on the voice mailbox account to "Yes, I will accept the charges." The phone hacker then places a collect call to the number that has been hacked. When the operator asks about accepting charges, the "Yes" is heard and the call completes. These types of attacks are typically not detected until the phone bill arrives or the phone company calls to report unusual activity. Targets of this attack tend to be toll-free customer service lines or other companies that may not notice this activity during holidays or weekends.

A CASP+ should understand that the best defense against this type of attack is to change the phone system's default passwords. Employees should also be prompted to change their voicemail passwords periodically. When employees leave (are laid off, resign, retire, or are fired), their phones should be forwarded to another user, and their voicemail accounts should be immediately deleted.

Slamming and Cramming

Slamming and *cramming* are terms associated with telephony. *Slamming* refers to switching a user's long-distance phone carrier without their knowledge. *Cramming* involves unauthorized phone charges. Sometimes these charges can be quite small and seem incidental, yet multiplied by hundreds of users, they can make a criminal millions! While slamming and cramming have been a recognized problem for decades, it took until summer 2018 for the FCC to officially ban the practice. You can read more about the ban here:

www.androidauthority.com/fcc-slamming-cramming-874289

VoIP

Once upon a time, a network engineer was asked to run data over existing voice lines. Years later, another company asked him what he thought about running voice over existing data lines. This is the basis of VoIP. *VoIP* adds functionality and reduces costs for businesses, as it allows the sharing of existing data lines. This approach is typically referred to as *convergence*—or as triple play when video is included.

Before VoIP, voice was usually sent over the circuit-switched public switched telephone network (PSTN). These calls were then bundled by the phone carrier and sent over a dedicated communications path. As long as the conversation continued, no one else could use the same fixed path.

VoIP changes this because VoIP networks are basically packet-switched networks that utilize shared communications paths easily accessible by multiple users. Since this network is accessible by multiple users, an attacker can attempt to launch an on-path attack. An on-path attack allows an attacker to sit between the caller and the receiver and sniff the voice data, modify it, and record it for later review. Sniffing is the act of capturing VoIP traffic and replaying it to eavesdrop on a conversation. Sophisticated tools are not required for this activity. Easily available tools such as Cain & Abel (www.oxid.it) make this possible. Expensive, specialized equipment is not needed to intercept unsecured VoIP traffic.

Exercise 9.8 demonstrates how Cain & Abel can be used to sniff VoIP traffic. It's also worth mentioning that if network equipment is accessible, an attacker can use Switched Port Analyzer (SPAN) to replicate a port on a switch and gain access to trunked VoIP traffic. It's important that the CASP+ understand the importance of placing physical controls so that attackers cannot get access to network equipment.

EXERCISE 9.8

Sniffing VoIP with Cain & Abel

An easy way to demonstrate the vulnerabilities of VoIP is to perform a VoIP phone capture.

1. Open your browser, go to www.oxid.it, and download a copy of Cain & Abel (also known as Cain).

2. Install Cain on your computer.

3. Start Cain.

4. Select the Sniffing tab and choose VoIP.

5. Click the NIC icon in the top-left corner to start the sniff.

6. Start an unencrypted VoIP conversation on your computer and capture the traffic.

7. When you're done, right-click the captured VoIP traffic and choose Playback.

Although VoIP uses TCP in some cases for caller setup and signaling, denial of service (DoS) is a risk. VoIP relies on some UDP ports for communication. UDP can be more susceptible to DoS than TCP-based services. An attacker might attempt to flood communication pathways with unnecessary data, thus preventing any data from moving on the network. Using a traditional PSTN voice communication model would mean that even if the data network is disabled, the company could still communicate via voice. With convergence, a DoS attack has the potential to disrupt both the IP phones and the computer network.

Yet another more recent inclusion into VoIP vulnerabilities was demonstrated at DEF CON when the presenters demonstrated that VoIP could be used as a command-and-control (C&C) mechanism for botnets. Basically, infected systems can host or dial into a conference call in order to perform a wide range of tasks, such as specifying what systems will participate in a distributed DoS (DDoS) attack, downloading new malware, or using the botnet for the exfiltration of data. This poses data loss prevention questions, to say the least. Here are some basic best practices that can be used for VoIP security:

- Enforce strong authentication.
- Implement restrictive access controls.
- Disable any and all unnecessary services and ports.
- Encrypt all VoIP traffic so that attackers can't easily listen in on conversations.

- Deploy firewalls and IDSs.
- Keep systems and devices patched and updated.

 Although encryption is a great control, the network used for VoIP must be fast enough to overcome the overhead that results from encryption. If this aspect is not factored into the equation, voice quality will deteriorate.

Problems with SPIT

Spam over Internet Telephony (SPIT) is similar to spam. SPIT offers spammers a low-cost alternative to unsolicited marketing. Just imagine dozens of prerecorded voice messages for Cialis and Viagra in your voice mail! SPIT has yet to become a major problem, but security experts agree that the potential exists. Some companies, among them Qovia, have filed patents for applications to stop SPIT. There are tools designed for SPIT, such as SPITTER. This software solution can be used to block SPAM over VoIP lines.

VoIP Implementation

VoIP is a replacement for the PSTN of the past. PSTN is composed of companies such as AT&T, Verizon, and smaller, localized companies still managing the lines and other public circuit-switched telephone networks. These traditional phone networks consisted of telephone lines, fiber-optic cables, microwave transmission links, and so forth that were interconnected and allowed any telephone in the world to communicate with any other.

The equipment involved was highly specialized and may have been proprietary to the telecommunications carrier, which made it much harder to attack. After all, traditional telephones were only designed to make and receive calls.

VoIP Softphones

VoIP softphones can be a single application on a computer, laptop, tablet computer, or smartphone. A VoIP softphone resides on a system that has many different uses. A softphone opens another potential hole in the computer network or host that an attacker can exploit as an entry point. Hardware devices have advantages over software (softphones).

Hardware-Based VoIP

Hardware-based VoIP phones look like typical phones but are connected to the data network instead of PSTN. These devices should be viewed as embedded computers that can be used for other purposes.

A well-designed VoIP implementation requires the CASP+ to consider the design of the network and to segregate services. Using technologies like a virtual local area network (VLAN), the CASP+ can segregate data traffic from voice traffic; however, convergence is making this task much harder. Implementing VLANs correctly can drastically reduce and often eliminate the potential for sniffing attacks that utilize automated tools such as those referenced earlier, as well as many other tools that focus on this type of attack exclusively, regardless of hardware- or software-based phones. One such tool is Voice Over Misconfigured Internet Telephones (VOMIT), which deciphers any voice traffic on the same VLAN or any VLANs that it can access.

Another implementation concern is quality of service (QoS). Although no one may notice if email arrives a few seconds later, voice does not have that luxury. Fortunately, segmentation via VLANs can assist with remedying this kind of issue as well. Here are some QoS examples:

- *Jitter* is the variation in transmission latency that can cause packet loss and degraded VoIP call quality.
- *Latency* is a delay in the transmission of a data packet.

Before VoIP systems are implemented, a CASP+ must explore techniques to mitigate risk by limiting exposures of data networks from spreading to voice networks. VoIP equipment, gateways, and servers tend to use open standards based on RFCs and open protocols. This also allows an attacker to have a better understanding of the equipment and technology. If that is not enough, most of the vendors place large amounts of product information on their websites. This aids the attackers in ramping up their knowledge very quickly.

Bit Splitting

Mentioned earlier in the chapter, *bit splitting* is another technique for securing data over a computer network that involves encrypting data, splitting the encrypted data into smaller data units, distributing those smaller units to different storage locations, and then further encrypting the data at its new location. Data is protected from security breaches, because even if an attacker is able to retrieve and decrypt one data unit, the information would be useless unless it can be combined with decrypted data units from the other locations.

Data Dispersion

Data dispersion consists of information being distributed and stored in multiple cloud pods, which is a key component of cloud storage architecture. The ability to have data replicated throughout a distributed storage infrastructure is critical. This allows a cloud service provider to offer storage services based on the level of the user's subscription or the popularity of the item.

Summary

In this chapter, we examined the advantages and disadvantages of virtualization and cloud computing as well as the issues that they bring to enterprise security.

Cloud and virtualized computing has become the way of the future. So many advances in computing have brought about more changes than just virtualization, including network storage and cloud computing. Cloud computing changed the concept of traditional network boundaries by placing assets outside the organization's perimeter and control.

The idea of cloud computing represents a shift in thought as well as trust. The cloud service can be fully managed by the cloud provider. Consumers use the service at a rate that is set by their particular needs. Cost and ease of use are two great benefits of cloud computing, but you must consider significant security concerns when contemplating moving critical applications and sensitive data to public and shared cloud environments. To address these concerns, the cloud provider must develop sufficient controls to provide the same or greater level of security than the organization would have if the cloud was not used, and organizations will continue to evolve as new technologies become available.

Exam Essentials

Be able to explain virtualization strategies.   After this chapter, you should be able to explain the difference between hypervisor types, containers, and emulation, choosing the best model for different situations.

Understand the different cloud models.   The CASP+ professional should be able to explain the difference between the different cloud service models, hosting models, and the considerations of deployment including resources, protection, location, and cost.

Be able to explain cloud technology adoption and security.   Understand how adoption of cloud technologies affects the entire organization from automation to encryption to logging and monitoring.

Be able to choose the correct backup and recovery methods.   After this chapter, you should be able to understand the repercussions of the cloud as business continuity and disaster recovery as well as primary and alternative providers of backups.

Review Questions

You can find the answers in Appendix.

1. You are setting up a new virtual machine. What type of virtualization should you use to coordinate instructions directly to the CPU?

   A. Type B.

   B. Type 1.

   C. Type 2.

   D. No VM directly sends instructions to the CPU.

2. Your DevOps team decided to use containers because they allow running applications on any hardware. What is the first thing your team should do to have a secure container environment?

   A. Install IPS.

   B. Lock down Kubernetes and monitor registries.

   C. Configure antimalware and traffic filtering.

   D. Disable services that are not required and install monitoring tools.

3. You work in information security for a stock trading organization. You have been tasked with reducing cost and managing employee workstations. One of the biggest concerns is how to prevent employees from copying data to any external storage. Which of the following *best* manages this situation?

   A. Move all operations to the cloud and disable VPN.

   B. Implement server virtualization and move critical applications to the server.

   C. Use VDI and disable hardware and storage mapping from a thin client.

   D. Encrypt all sensitive data at rest and in transit.

4. You are exploring the best option for your team to read data that was written onto storage material by a device you do not have access to, and the backup device has been broken. Which of the following is the *best* option for this?

   A. Type 1 hypervisor

   B. Type 2 hypervisor

   C. Emulation

   D. PaaS

5. You are a security architect building out a new hardware-based VM. Which of the following would *least* likely threaten your new virtualized environment?

   A. Patching and maintenance

   B. VM sprawl

   C. Oversight and responsibility

   D. Faster provisioning and disaster recovery

6. Management of your hosted application environment requires end-to-end visibility and a high-end performance connection while monitoring for security issues. What should you consider for the most control and visibility?

    A. You should consider a provider with connections from your location directly into the applications cloud resources.

    B. You should have a private T1 line installed for this access.

    C. You should secure a VPN concentrator for this task.

    D. You should use HTTPS.

7. As the IT director of a nonprofit agency, you have been challenged at a local conference to provide technical cloud infrastructure that will be shared between several organizations like yours. Which is the *best* cloud partnership to form?

    A. Private cloud

    B. Public cloud

    C. Hybrid cloud

    D. Community cloud

8. Your objectives and key results (OKRs) being measured for this quarter include realizing the benefits of a single-tenancy cloud architecture. Which one of these results is a benefit of a single-tenancy cloud service?

    A. Security and cost

    B. Reliability and scaling

    C. Ease of restoration

    D. Maintenance

9. With 80 percent of your enterprise in a VPC model, which of the following is *not* a key enabling technology?

    A. Fast WAN and automatic IP addressing

    B. High-performance hardware

    C. Inexpensive servers

    D. Complete control over process

10. You have a new security policy that requires backing up a database offsite specifically for redundancy. This data must be backed up every 24 hours. Cost is important. What method are you most likely to deploy?

    A. File storage

    B. Electronic vaulting

    C. Block storage

    D. Object storage

11. A software startup hired Pamela to provide expertise on data security. Clients are concerned about confidentiality. If confidentiality is stressed more than availability and integrity, which of the following scenarios is BEST suited for the client?

  A. Virtual servers in highly available environment. Clients will use redundant virtual storage and remote desktop services to access software.

  B. Virtual servers in highly available environment. Clients will use single virtual storage and remote desktop services to access software.

  C. Clients are assigned virtual hosts running on shared hardware. Physical storage is partitioned with block cipher encryption.

  D. Clients are assigned virtual hosts running shared hardware. Virtual storage is partitioned with streaming cipher encryption.

12. Your company decided to outsource certain computing jobs that need a large amount of processing power in a short duration of time. You suggest the solution of using a cloud provider that enables the company to avoid a large purchase of computing equipment. Which of the following is your biggest concern with on-demand provisioning?

  A. Excessive charges if deprovisioning fails

  B. Exposure of intellectual property

  C. Data remanence from previous customers in the cloud

  D. Data remanence of your proprietary data that could be exposed

13. Pedro has responsibility for the cloud infrastructure in the large construction company he works for. He recorded data that includes security logs, object access, FIM, and other activities that your SIEM often uses to detect unwanted activity. Which of the following BEST describes this collection of data?

  A. Due diligence

  B. Syslog

  C. IDR

  D. Audit trail

14. Marcus is a remote employee needing to access data in cloud storage. You need to configure his Windows 10 client for a remote access VPN using IPSec/L2TP. Why is a VPN so important for remote employees?

  A. VPN traffic is accessible.

  B. VPN traffic is encrypted.

  C. A VPN allows you remote access.

  D. A VPN is an option if you are on your home network.

15. Dana has a three-layer line of defense working to protect remote access to his network and cloud applications, including a firewall, antivirus software, and VPN. What action should your network security team take after standing up this defense?

  A. Log all security transactions.

  B. Monitor alerts from these assets.

    C. Check the firewall configuration monthly and antivirus weekly.

    D. Run tests for VPN connectivity once every 24 hours.

16. Your CIO approached the CISO with the idea to configure IPSec VPNs for data authentication, integrity, and confidentiality for cloud assets. Which of the following reasons would help support the CIO's goals?

    A. IPSec only supports site-to-site VPN configurations.

    B. IPSec can only be deployed with IPv6.

    C. IPSec authenticates clients against a Windows server.

    D. IPSec uses secure key exchange and key management.

17. Frederick's company is migrating key systems from on-premise systems to a virtual data center in the cloud managed by a third party. Remote access must be available at all times. Access controls must be auditable. Which of these controls BEST suits these needs?

    A. Access is captured in event logs.

    B. Access is limited to single sign-on.

    C. Access is configured using SSH.

    D. Access is restricted using port security.

18. Your business cannot overlook the need for allowing employees to have remote access and collaboration tools. You never know when an employee will need to connect to the corporate intranet from a remote location. The first thing to do is create a comprehensive network security policy. Which one of these will not fit into that policy?

    A. Definition of the classes of users and their levels of access

    B. Identification of what devices are allowed to connect through a VPN

    C. The maximum idle time before automatic termination

    D. Allow list ports and protocols necessary to everyday tasks

19. You work for the power company that supplies electricity to three states. You rely heavily on the data you collect and that is replicated in the cloud. Data is split into numerous arrays, and a mapper processes them to certain cloud storage options. What is this process called?

    A. Encryption

    B. Data dispersion

    C. Bit splitting

    D. Perimeter security

20. Jonathan is a cloud security sales consultant working for a cloud access security broker (CASB) company. His organization is advocating applying the highest level of protection across all your cloud assets. You suggest this is not what the priority should be. What would be a more strategic priority?

    A. Determining what to protect through data discovery and classification

    B. Running anti-malware software on all cloud instances

    C. Using vulnerability scanning software on mission-critical servers

    D. Implementing threat mitigation strategies

Chapter

10

Mobility and Emerging Technologies

THE CASP+ EXAM TOPICS COVERED IN THIS CHAPTER INCLUDE:

✓ **1.8 Explain the impact of emerging technologies on enterprise security and privacy.**

- Artificial intelligence
- Machine learning
- Quantum computing
- Blockchain
- Homomorphic encryption
    - Private information retrieval
    - Secure function evaluation
    - Private function evaluation
- Secure multiparty computation
- Distributed consensus
- Big Data
- Virtual/augmented reality
- 3D printing
- Passwordless authentication
- Nano technology
- Deep learning
    - Natural language processing
    - Deep fakes
- Biometric impersonation

✓ **3.1 Given a scenario, apply secure configurations to enterprise mobility.**

- Managed configurations
    - Application control
    - Password
    - MFA requirements
    - Token-based access
    - Patch repository
    - Firmware Over-the-Air
    - Remote wipe
    - WiFi
        - WiFi Protected Access (WPA2/3)
        - Device certificates
    - Profiles
    - Bluetooth
    - Near-field communication (NFC)
    - Peripherals
    - Geofencing
    - VPN settings
    - Geotagging
    - Certificate management
    - Full device encryption
    - Tethering
    - Airplane mode
    - Location services
    - DNS over HTTPS (DoH)
    - Custom DNS
- Deployment scenarios
    - Bring your own device (BYOD)
    - Corporate-owned

- Corporate owned, personally enabled (COPE)
- Choose your own device (CYOD)
- Security considerations
  - Unauthorized remote activation/deactivation of devices or features
  - Encrypted and unencrypted communication concerns
  - Physical reconnaissance
  - Personal data theft
  - Health privacy
  - Implications of wearable devices
  - Digital forensics of collected data
  - Unauthorized application stores
  - Jailbreaking/rooting
  - Side loading
  - Containerization
  - Original equipment manufacturer (OEM) and carrier differences
  - Supply chain issues
  - eFuse

✓ **3.3 Explain security considerations impacting specific sectors and operational technologies**

- Embedded
  - Internet of Things (IoT)
  - System on a chip (SoC)
  - Application-specific integrated circuit (ASIC)
  - Field-programmable gate array (FPGA)
- ICS/supervisory control and data acquisition (SCADA)
  - Programmable logic controller (PLC)
  - Historian

- Ladder logic
- Safety instrumented system
- Heating, ventilation, and air conditioning (HVAC)

- Protocols
  - Controller Area Network (CAN) bus
  - Modbus
  - Distributed Network Protocol 3 (DNP3)
  - Zigbee
  - Common Industrial Protocol (CIP)
  - Data distribution service

- Sectors
  - Energy
  - Manufacturing
  - Healthcare
  - Public utilities
  - Public services
  - Facility services

This chapter discusses trends that can potentially impact a company. We live in a much different technological environment than we did just 10 to 15 years ago. Technology is advancing at a much faster pace, and attackers are learning to adapt quickly. There have also been big changes in that so many more of today's systems are connected to and rely on the Internet. This includes systems such as databases; artificial intelligence; supervisory control and data acquisition (SCADA) systems; water distribution systems; and other critical infrastructure.

For the CASP+ candidate, all of this points to the need for being much more aware of what is going on, what is connected to the network, and how critical the system is. It's not unusual in this business to see changes occur weekly if not daily. Part of being prepared for this change is doing ongoing research and situational analysis. This chapter covers things you need to know and provides websites and resources that can help you keep abreast of current trends, emerging threats, and new exploits that have been released.

This chapter is all about analysis and impact. Before you implement security controls, you must determine if they are the correct solution for your environment. You might be asked to do a cost-benefit analysis or even evaluate the proposed solution as to its performance, latency, scalability, capability, usability, and maintainability while taking availability metrics into account.

Emerging Technologies and Their Impact on Enterprise Security and Privacy

New and revolutionary technology impacts enterprise security and privacy in many ways. With new technology come new threats, governance, and challenges for defenders as well as opportunities for bad actors. New technology can be transformative and disruptive and can bring about major change in the way a society functions, but there are always concerns that if technologies are easy to access and adopt, they can serve malicious purposes. Much of technology advances so quickly that it becomes difficult for governments to keep up with the impact on the national landscape or societal contest. Today, governance structures and frameworks must work to be agile to give guidance on policy and regulation.

Artificial Intelligence

Artificial intelligence (AI) points to increasingly "smarter" systems when such systems are developed to engage in problem solving and learning. AI is being used when systems or machines accept input, either from their surroundings or from other systems, and then analyze and interpret that data in a way to understand (analyze) future data better. In other words, the system comes to learn and "understand" from past experience and simulate human intelligence.

Deloitte, for example, has launched CortexAI, a platform that assists customers in running many different aspects of an enterprise including finance, procurement, and supply chain autonomously. In 2021, AI was used with vaccine development. Vaccines usually take years to create, but the speed to production of a vaccine for the most recent pandemic was partly due to AI models used for research. Hardware including microchips and AI processors continue to be developed for optimized performance, which will lead to reduction in cost for companies.

Machine Learning

AI and machine learning systems are increasingly common throughout the security tools space. Machine learning is a component of AI. *Machine learning (ML)* leverages large amounts of data to make predictions based on a learning model that could find ways to identify malware that may include heuristic, signature, and other detection capabilities. Machine learning works with an algorithm using specific domains. For example, if you create a machine learning model for recommendations, then a search engine can anticipate what you might type in as you type it and automatically self-correct with each keystroke you make as you finish typing your search query.

Deep Learning

AI is copying the intelligence or behavior patterns of a human using a set of rules, and machine learning is the technique where a computer can learn from data without a set of rules but with a model. Deep learning is the ability to perform machine learning based on the human brain's neurological network. Deep learning helps solve extremely complex problems that might have a secret pattern or need profound understanding of a complicated relationship. Deep learning is used when a high level of accuracy is necessary from large amounts of tagged data.

Natural language processing (NLP) is a type of deep learning mixed with linguistics. Natural language processing is the ability of a computer system to understand human language both spoken and written. NLP machines work hard to respond with text or speech of their own such as GPS systems, digital assistants, or customer service chatbots. Google Translate is an example of NLP; however, it is not perfect. Not too long ago, translating "The spirit is willing, but the flesh is weak" from English to Russian and back yielded "The vodka is good, but the meat is rotten."

Deep fakes are another example of deep learning and intentionally fake results. This is where a person's likeness in an image or video is replaced with another. Many social media platforms allow the physical enhancement of photographs, but it becomes dangerous when the imitation is of another real person, especially if that person is a world leader spreading disinformation or a college professor endorsing an investment fund. To learn more about deep fakes, visit this site:

www.wsj.com/articles/deepfake-technology-is-now-a-threat-to-everyone-what-do-we-do-11638887121

Quantum Computing

Quantum computing is an evolving field that attempts to use quantum mechanics to execute computing and communication tasks. If it advances to the point where theory becomes practical to implement, quantum cryptography may be able to defeat cryptographic algorithms that depend upon factoring large prime numbers.

Quantum computing made significant progress recently in 2020, including the Jiuzhang computer's achievement of quantum supremacy. Quantum computing can be utilized to move a generative machine learning model through a larger dataset than a classical computer can handle, making the model extra precise and effective in real-world problem solving. Other advanced technologies such as the previously mentioned deep learning algorithms are performing an increasingly crucial role in the advancement of quantum computing research.

Blockchain

Blockchain is a digitized, decentralized, publicly used ledger of all cryptocurrency transactions. Blockchains are always growing as completed blocks, which is the most recent transaction. They are then recorded and added to the block in chronological order, allowing the market participants to keep track of all digital currency transactions without centralized recordkeeping. Each node gets a copy of the blockchain, and these copies are downloaded automatically.

Blockchain was originally developed as the revolutionary accounting method for the well-known virtual currency Bitcoin. Blockchain is a form of *distributed ledger technology (DLT)*. Think of a DLT as one database spread across multiple locations, and blockchain is one implementation of a DLT. DLTs appear in a variety of commercial sectors at Oracle along with applications within today's market. The technology is primarily used to verify transactions within digital currencies. It is possible to digitize, code, and insert any document into the blockchain. This allows for an indelible record that cannot be altered. The record's authenticity can also be verified by the entire community using the blockchain instead of a single centralized authority. Blockchain offers enhanced security, transparency, improved speed and traceability, and reduced costs of doing business internationally.

Blockchain is the main technological innovation of Bitcoin. Bitcoin is not regulated by a specific central authority. Users of blockchain can validate transactions when one person pays another for goods or services. This helps eliminate the need for a third party to process or store payments. The newly completed transaction is then publicly recorded within blocks and eventually into the blockchain. Then it is verified and relayed by the other Bitcoin users. On average, a new block is appended to the blockchain every 10 minutes through a process called *mining*.

Homomorphic Encryption

Privacy concerns introduce some focused application uses for encryption. We oftentimes have applications where we want to defend the privacy of individuals but still want to analyze the data. Homomorphic encryption technology allows this, encrypting data in a way that preserves the ability to perform computation on the data. When you encrypt data with a homomorphic algorithm and then analyze that data, you get a result that, when decrypted, matches the result you would have received if you had performed the computation on the plaintext data in the first place, while lacking attribution to the individual.

There are several ways to deploy homomorphic encryption. In *private information retrieval (PIR)*, an item can be retrieved from a database without revealing to anyone what was actually taken or used. The premise of PIR is that one party owns the database and the other wants to query information but subscribes to privacy restrictions or compliance regulations.

In *secure function evaluation (SFE)*, the protocol aims for secure comparison. The most well-known example of SFE is the millionaire case. Alice and Bob are both millionaires and want to know who is wealthier without revealing their wealth. SFE allows for the two entities to evaluate a function without having to reveal the inputs.

With *private function evaluation (PFE)*, the problem is evaluating one entity's private data using a private function of another party. For example, an organization owning a proprietary piece of software needs to offer a service using that software to someone else who has confidential data that needs analyzation but cannot share the data. Using PFE, the software-owning organization can run the algorithms necessary without revealing consumers' data, even to the company receiving the result.

Strong private information retrieval (SPIR) is private information retrieval with the additional requirement that someone only learns the elements they are querying for, and nothing else, which answers the need for privacy of a database owner.

Another subfield of encryption that is less traditional is *secure multiparty computation (MPC)*. The goal of MPC is for the entities to compute a function while keeping all the inputs being used for calculations private. This protects all the data from being shared with the other organizations with the assumption that the parties are being cooperative. In some cases, an adversary could deviate from the protocol to cheat the system and try to get the information. With MPC, the only thing to do should someone attempt to be dishonest is to "abort" the process if cheating is detected.

Distributed Consensus

Consensus means to reach an agreement of opinion in a group. In computing, a distributed consensus means that processes must agree on specific data needed during calculation or computation. Application of *distributed consensus* in computer systems would be the synchronization of time or load balancing. If one of several processes fails or is wrong, consensus becomes important. These processes communicate directly with each other and agree on a single value. For example, an aircraft has many different units working together to make a flight successful from point A to point B. Algorithms running in the background work toward reaching consensus or agreement. If an agreement is not reached, then the process is terminated until a value is agreed on.

Big Data

Simple and concise, the term *big data* refers to very large sets of data coming from transactions on the Internet, customer databases, mobile devices reporting locations, medical records, streaming movies, social networks, emails, the Internet of Things, and so much more. Our organizations are evolving so quickly, and we have to learn to deal with yottabytes of data in the big data cloud mobile device streaming era. Given access to a great number of sources, companies encounter massive volumes of available data, which often requires special tools and databases when it's time to analyze.

Splunk (`www.splunk.com`) originated as a log collector or aggregation tool, but it has evolved into a quasi "big data" analysis tool. When placed in a heterogenous environment, Splunk is often used to aggregate and normalize data from many diverse sources. Splunk is not a beginner-level tool for home use. However, it would be useful for a CASP+ candidate to become familiar with the tool. For advanced users, Splunk offers its Search Processing Language (SPL) to create more advanced data correlations among devices and events.

Virtual/Augmented Reality

Virtual reality (VR) or *augmented reality (AR)* started out primarily as a gaming experience where the gamer would wear a headset that simulated an event. Samsung Gear and Oculus are some of the most popular headsets because they can connect to a video game console or smart device to give the wearer an experience that imitates real-world scenarios with little to no risk.

Some industries have used VR more recently for the benefits of that real-world experience. For example, in healthcare, VR is helping to teach specialty surgical techniques. It is also used by mental health professionals in cognitive behavior therapy to help people work through anxiety and phobias. VR has been used in the military to help with simulations by placing someone in a specific situation, such as flight or combat on the battlefield. In the auto industry, BMW has been using VR for many years to conduct design and engineering reviews before any money is spent on the fabrication of a vehicle, saving millions of dollars on prototypes.

With the development and adoption of any new technology, there are always risks and concerns. In VR, there are potential security and privacy concerns involving the rush to market of gear that could be vulnerable to a breach where the gear and applications are part of payment or registration processes. In healthcare, VR could help a real surgical procedure, but if the live stream is hacked, it could be dangerous for the patient, and if the information is leaked, it could be devastating. There have been issues with malware in VR applications as well as in cloud environments hosting VR platforms.

Augmented reality is a type of virtual reality where designers create digital content that lies on top of the real world, very much like Pokémon GO. Pokémon GO is an augmented reality game where you find characters on a map and can see them with your camera/application. Innovative businesses have started adopting augmented reality in their advertising, giving customers a different experience on their mobile devices.

3D Printing

Three-dimensional or *3D printing* is a technology that increases the capabilities of the production of parts and products in different materials on a machine that builds layer by layer. 3D printing can use a variety of materials including polyamide plastics, nylon, and metals, such as stainless steel and titanium, as well as ceramics and paper. More recently, there have been experiments to 3D print food, specifically chocolate.

There are many benefits to 3D printing, including in the medical and dental, automotive, and aerospace industries, but there are concerns as well. There are challenges with regulations, quality control, and safety. There are specific cyber threats that include IP theft and sabotage. 3D IP can be stolen from the cloud, or 3D printed parts can be reverse engineered. With sabotage, the risk is the modification of parts, which would increase failure rates.

Passwordless Authentication

Authentication is a key area of knowledge for the security professional because it serves as the first line of defense. It consists of two pieces: identification and authentication. Identification is saying, "Hi, I am Bob." It's great that I have provided you with that information, but how do you know that it is the truth? What you need is to determine the claim. That's the role of authentication.

Authentication types usually include *something you know (a password)*, *something you are (a fingerprint)*, *something you have (a badge)*, and *somewhere you are (GPS)*. Passwordless authentication is a way that a user can forget about remembering complex or random passwords to log into a system, application, or account. Passwordless authentication is based on either something the user has, like a phone or hardware token, or something the user is, like a fingerprint or iris scan. Many organizations find passwordless authentication to be expensive, and most end users are dubious of the effectiveness. Disney World has used fingerprints to prevent ticket fraud, with park visitors authenticating with biometrics, for many years. However, it suspended the practice during the global pandemic.

Nano Technology

Nano comes from the Greek word for "dwarf." Nanotechnology is the science of objects that are one billionth of a meter, or 0.000000001 meter. In terms of technology, there are many applications for tiny bits, from crop fertilization to medical treatments to energy production. Nanoparticles can enter the body through the skin, lungs, and digestive system, which means anything you touch, breath, or eat. There are industry concerns that nanoparticles could damage the DNA of humans, give an incorrect "doctor on a chip" diagnosis, or, because they are so miniscule, cross the blood-brain barrier. With new technology come new questions to ask about safety and security.

Biometric Impersonation

It is a good thing that new security systems and services are developed and modernized. Just consider one area, such as authentication. Although the security offered by passwords may have seemed great back in the 1990s, think of the current state of passwords. Today, for example, you may use a password when you log in to Gmail, another password when you log into your website to upload a new web page, another password for Amazon's Author portal, and even another for all banking, social media, and online applications! The convenience of passwords seems to evaporate when you start to consider how many passwords you must keep up with today. Luckily, new techniques are available that you can use to perform authentication.

Biometrics is one such solution. *Biometric systems* have advanced in the last decade. Today in some airports, you don't need a physical ID. Facial recognition is used to allow you through airport security lines. There are many different types of biometric systems, including iris scan, voice recognition, fingerprint, and signature dynamics; however, they all basically work the same way.

1. The user enrolls in the system. The user allows the system to take one or more samples for later comparison.

2. The user requests to be authenticated. A sample is compared to the user's authentication request.

3. A decision is reached. A match allows access, and a discrepancy denies access.

The accuracy of a biometric device is measured by the percentage of Type 1 and Type 2 errors it produces. Type 1 errors (false rejection rate [FRR]) measure the percentage of individuals who should have received access but were denied. Type 2 errors (false acceptance rate [FAR]) measure the percentage of individuals who gained access who shouldn't have. When these two values are combined, the accuracy of the system is established. The point at which the FRR and FAR meet is known as the crossover error rate (CER). The CER is a key accuracy factor: The lower the CER, the more accurate the system. Another attribute of biometric systems is that fingerprints, retinas, or hands cannot be loaned to anyone. Some common biometric systems include the following:

- *Fingerprint scan systems*: These systems are widely used and are installed in many new laptops.

- *Hand geometry systems*: These systems are accepted by most users; they function by measuring the unique geometry of a user's fingers and hand to identify that user.

- *Palm scan systems*: Palm scan systems are much like hand geometry systems except that they measure the creases and ridges of a palm for identification.

- *Retina pattern systems*: Retina pattern systems are very accurate; they examine the user's retina pattern.

- *Iris recognition*: Iris recognition matches the user's blood vessels on the back of the eye.

- *Voice recognition*: A voice recognition system determines who you are using voice analysis.

- *Keyboard dynamics*: Keyboard dynamics analyze the user's speed and pattern of typing.

The final consideration for any biometric system is user acceptance and usability. The acceptability of a system depends on how the user perceives it. For instance, iris scanning is considered more accurate than retina scanning. This is because the retina can change over time due to conditions such as diabetes and pregnancy. Retina scanning is also more intrusive for the user and is therefore used less frequently. User education is helpful, because many individuals worry that retina or iris systems can damage their eyes or that their information is not adequately protected.

To ensure that a biometric system is usable, you must examine the processing time and environment and guarantee that the "what you are" authentication protocol is not impersonated. No one can change their iris pattern or their hand geometry. There are threat actors that social engineer a victim into saying certain words on the phone to use in the future for impersonating voice recognition.

An aspect of biometrics that is not frequently discussed is biometric data management and decommissioning. Biometric data needs to go into a system database, and there is additional risk in having people's biometric data stored in a database, even one with a proprietary format. This risk will increase in the future as more biometric systems are rolled out. Biometric systems need to be securely decommissioned as well so that individuals' biometric information is never leaked.

Secure Enterprise Mobility Configurations

Enterprise security is already a challenge, but with the advent of mobile devices it has gotten a whole lot harder. It is enough of a challenge to secure the environment within the four walls of the corporate building. Now wireless connectivity has pushed the network boundary well past the four walls. With mobile devices, employees expect simple and easy connectivity to both the enterprise and the world around them. Thankfully, there are several technologies and techniques available to integrate security controls to support mobile and small form-factor devices.

Managed Configurations

As a cybersecurity professional, you play an important role in the security of your organization, but you must also work with other areas in your organization in order to meet the needed security requirements. You must work to provide guidance and recommendations to staff and senior management on security processes, configurations, and controls as well. Secure data flow requires a structured approach to security and a review of a variety of elements.

Application Control

To ensure that the mobile device's integrity stays within acceptable limits, the IT team will want to maintain oversight and management of the applications, content, and the data on the device. If enterprise users rely on a third-party application but the mobile device management team desires more control or wants to implement policy on that application, then one option is to use a process called *application wrapping*.

Application wrapping involves adding a management layer around an app without making any changes to the app itself. For each application, your mobile operating system will allow the user effectively to control what that application can do, access, or execute on the user's behalf. Application permissions are accessible within the configuration settings of the mobile OS. Typical objects that an application may seek access to include the camera, microphone, phone application, and address book, among others. Obviously, access to any of these objects would be granted only if the application is deemed trusted and the decision to bypass an added user action is warranted.

Mobile application management (MAM) is a piece of software that secures and enables IT control over enterprise applications on end users' corporate and personal smartphones and tablets. MAM software allows IT administrators to apply and enforce corporate policies on mobile apps and limit the sharing of corporate data among apps. MAM can also separate personal and corporate data on these devices, schedule updates, and improve security. As an administrator or consumer of this type of software, policies and procedures should be clearly communicated so it is documented how the device is treated when the employee leaves the company or is terminated. There have been cases where an employer has remotely wiped a phone and the contents of the device are lost.

Password

As a security administrator, you've no doubt heard many stories about how some people do very little to protect their passwords. Sometimes, people write their passwords down on sticky notes, place them under their keyboards, or even leave them on a scrap of paper taped to the monitor. As a security professional, you should not only help formulate good password policy but also help users understand why and how to protect passwords.

Mobile devices include cell phones, tablets, and other portable units. On these systems, a complex passcode should be at least six characters and avoid using words in the dictionary, repeating digits, or characters. One solution might be to offer password manager programs that can be used to secure passwords. Another approach is migration to authentication systems that use multifactor authentication (MFA) or token-based access with limitations on the number of failed logon attempts before the device locks.

Multifactor authentication requires more than one factor for access. For example, if you are using a PIN of four numbers and a password to authenticate, that represents two of the same factor, which is something you know. Multifactor would require a PIN as well as a fingerprint, for example, which is something you are.

Patch Repository

When you are responsible for the security of a network or IT infrastructure, periodic maintenance of hardware and software is required. Maintenance can include verifying that antivirus software is installed and current; ensuring that backups are completed, rotated, and encrypted; and performing patch management. You can use the patch repository for various tasks such as managing patches, viewing details, viewing baselines where the patch is included, and seeing recalled patches. Patch management policy should align as closely as possible to vendor-provided recommendations for mobile devices.

Firmware Over-the-Air

In addition to managing configuration settings remotely, the team responsible for installing updates can do this remotely. This delivery, known as *over-the-air updates (OTA updates)*, avoids waiting for a user to come in or dock their device for the update. Software or the device's firmware can be updated in this way. Factory and OTA update images are encrypted using a device-specific key and stored in a secure file system. This process prevents attackers from analyzing or running the image on another device to clone or to load an older image with known security vulnerabilities.

Remote Wipe

Another process that a CASP+ might need to do without relying on the user being "in the building" is remote wiping the device. For example, as part of the process of a termination or offboarding, an employee's device could be remotely wiped, mitigating the risk of unauthorized device usage or abuse.

WiFi

Wireless security is important when considering network segmentation. Wireless networks extend the network beyond the boundaries of the physical site. Although cabled connections require an attacker to plug in to gain access, wireless access points offer an attacker the ability to connect remotely. With the correct antenna, the attack may be a quarter mile away or more. *Wi-Fi Protected Access version 3 (WPA3)* was released in June 2018 and still uses 128-bit AES encryption but requires protected management frames (PMFs). WPA3 should be used because Wired Equivalent Privacy (WEP) is easily broken and WPA2 is increasingly recognized as insecure. As a best practice, when you configure security settings on your router, choose WPA3.

WPA3 can also be used with 192-bit mode for enhanced security by offering cryptographic tools for protection of sensitive data.

- *Authentication*: Extensible Authentication Protocol – Transport Layer Security (EAP-TLS) using Elliptic Curve Diffie-Hellman (ECDH) exchange and Elliptic Curve Digital Signature Algorithm (ECDSA) using a 384-bit elliptic curve

- *Authenticated encryption*: 256-bit Galois/Counter Mode Protocol (GCMP-256)

- *Key derivation and confirmation*: 384-bit Hashed Message Authentication Mode (HMAC) with Secure Hash Algorithm (HMAC-SHA384)

- *Robust management frame protection*: 256-bit Broadcast/Multicast Integrity Protocol Galois Message Authentication Code (BIP-GMAC-256)

Other controls include wireless intrusion detection systems (WIDSs) and wireless intrusion prevention systems (WIPSs). WIDSs can monitor the radio spectrum for the presence of unauthorized access points, whereas WIPSs can automatically take countermeasures against those misusing the radio spectrum.

Device Certificates and Management

Managing trust for mobile ecosystems is the same in theory as an IT department will manage corporate machines. Policies are put in place to prevent employees from downloading any software on their company machines so only authenticated devices should be allowed to access a corporate network. Mobile digital certificates are used for secure email access, encryption, and authentication as well as securing Wi-Fi and VPN access.

Using a Mobile Device Management (MDM) or Enterprise Mobility Management (EMM) can enhance the deployment of digital certificates, streamlining the process to devices by provisioning digital identities without the end user having to set it up.

The Simple Certificate Enrollment Protocol (SCEP) is a popular method of certificate enrollment, which is the process of a user or device requesting and receiving a digital certificate. SCEP is highly scalable and widely implemented. However, its original designers went on hiatus for several years, and SCEP received little attention to address concerns about its cryptographic strength. According to CERT vulnerability note VU#971035, the authentication methods for SCEP to validate certificate requests are ill suited for any environment other than a closed one. So, any MDM involving BYOD opens itself up to risks of unauthorized certificate requests.

Profile Configuration

How can an IT department manage to keep track of every user's mobile device configuration? Now increase that challenge due to the variety of available mobile devices. What makes it possible for IT departments to manage this situation is the use of configuration profiles. By establishing and remotely installing a group of configuration settings and implementing standard configuration profiles, managing a large number of mobile devices is effectively like managing a single device.

A subset of configuration settings within a configuration profile is called a *payload*. You might have a "mail" payload that configures the users' devices for all settings related to email, such as server, port, and address. Security restrictions can also be a part of the configuration profile payload.

Bluetooth

Wireless isn't just Wi-Fi and 802.11b/g/n/ac/ax. Wireless can include Bluetooth or even more esoteric protocols like Zigbee, such as in wireless HVAC systems. There is also radio frequency identification (RFID), which is used in everything from tags in clothing at big-box chain stores to employee badges for building access control.

Bluetooth technology is designed for short-range wireless communication to mobile and handheld devices. Bluetooth started to grow in popularity in the mid-to-late 1990s. Bluetooth technology has facilitated the growth of a variety of personal and handheld electronic devices. Although Bluetooth does have some built-in security features, it has been shown to be vulnerable to attack.

Leveraging a cellular data plan is not the only way to connect another device via tethering. Other forms of tethering include wireless technologies, such as Bluetooth, or a wired connection such as using a USB port. USB tethering is of course restrictive in the sense that you have to use a wire to connect the two devices. Bluetooth, which is wireless, can be quite slow as compared to Wi-Fi tethering. Bluetooth 5.0 offers data transfer of up to 2 Mbps, double the rate of Bluetooth 4.2. The newest advances in Bluetooth feature LE Power Control and LE Audio for faster pairing and increased battery life.

Many organizations place controls or restrictions on peripheral devices to deal with the problem of data exfiltration. These include controls on USB, wireless technologies like Bluetooth and NFC, as well as ports and other technologies. Setting up external I/O restrictions ahead of time can mitigate the risk of data exfiltration and help limit the possible damage.

Near-Field Communication

There are a variety of technologies using radio frequency (RF) waves to transmit data wirelessly. While devices communicating using Bluetooth can be up to 100 meters apart, one specialized, high-frequency technology called *near-field communication (NFC)* requires the two devices to be within 4 cm of each other. The data rate is considerably lower than Bluetooth, only in the range of 106 to 424 Kbps. NFC is commonly used for small amounts of data exchanged between two phones, such as a picture, or for completing a credit card transaction, like "tapping" your phone or NFC-enabled credit card to a point of sale. It's less likely an attacker could attack using NFC without being obvious at close distance, but the best mitigating control is to not enable the technology except when it's needed.

Mobile device owners can use their devices to conduct payment transactions. In this section, we will focus on the methods and technologies unique to mobile devices regarding mobile payments. The CASP+ should understand some of the key concepts and security implications regarding mobile payments.

NFC Enabled   Near-field communication allows enabled devices to communicate and pass information between them so long as the devices are within 4 cm of each other. Mobile devices capable of NFC communication can also make NFC-enabled payments. Of course, when money is involved, the difficulty of hacking or interfering with that transaction is often overcome for the sake of profit.

Inductance Enabled   NFC works by way of inductance. This feature of NFC-enabled payments is simply another name for inductance-enabled payments. Unlike Bluetooth, which is the actual transmission of radio waves by way of an antenna, NFC-enabled devices contain a coil or inductor that acts as an NFC "antenna." When in very close proximity to another inductor coil, devices with this NFC antenna can utilize the electromagnetic field between them to permit the transmission of data.

Mobile Wallets   Making mobile payments, whether by NFC or some other transmission technique, is a service. An app designed for the service of making mobile payments is called a mobile wallet.

Peripheral-Enabled Payments (Credit Card Reader)   Picture yourself being ready to pay at a department store or restaurant. You tell the employee that you intend to use a credit card. Many years ago, perhaps before many of you were born, that employee would pull out a heavy, flatbed device called a *credit card imprinter*. An imprint would be taken of the card on a receipt with multiple copies for manually completing the transaction at a later time. This was before magnetic strips were in wide use and long before EMV (Europay, Mastercard, and Visa) chips were imagined. There are no more credit card imprinters today. Now, given the EMV chip, you can slide your credit card into a device enabled for mobile payments.

Peripherals

Mobile phone peripherals like cell phones, wearable computing devices, and tablets are able to be plugged in and connected to a computer system. The key indicator that makes them peripherals is that they can also function independently of the computer system. These peripherals are a business multiplier. Instant and constant access to people with smartphones make the world more productive than ever before, and organizations have been quick to capitalize on this. What should not be forgotten is work-life balance, so the adage of just because you can doesn't mean you should be on call 24/7. Disconnecting from these mobile devices can be important to corporate culture as well as an employee's mental health.

VPN Settings

How mobile users connect to the enterprise environment impacts the risk that they place on the perimeter and network. If an organization allows users to connect over Wi-Fi at a coffee shop, this is unacceptable, and it is all but guaranteed to cause the CASP+ headaches in the near future. Instead, establishing and using a virtual private network (VPN) is a far safer way for users to connect to the internal, trusted network. The caveat regarding mobile devices is how much faster they consume resources. The trick is to find a VPN solution with some intelligence to it and train it (and users) to establish a VPN only when it is truly needed.

Some of the technologies used with VPNs include Layer 2 Forwarding, Point-to-Point Tunneling Protocol, Layer 2 Tunneling Protocol, and IPSec. This example refers to a remote access VPN, but other types exist, such as site-to-site, leased line, and ISP-managed VPNs such as the multiprotocol label switching (MPLS) VPN. In some cases, these VPN types can be subcategorized. For example, the site-to-site VPN could be further broken down as an intranet-based VPN or an extranet-based VPN.

Geotagging

It's all but guaranteed that any mobile device today contains a GPS module or is equipped to be GPS aware. That makes it possible and practical for a security team to implement controls based on location. Network access could be controlled if, for example, the user is at a certain location.

Instead of tracking a person's exact location, *geofencing* refers to determining whether the device falls within a boundary or established perimeter. If the device moves beyond the perimeter, such as when a pet breaches the edge of a fence, then a restriction may be triggered, or a function denied.

Geolocation and location-based services are a definite concern for the CASP+. This technology includes the ability to geotag the location of photographs. Most smartphone and tablet users turn this feature on when they activate a device, yet they never realize that this information is used in every photograph they take. Most people don't realize that geotagging is active on their smartphones, either because it is enabled by default and not exposed to the user as an option, or they were asked to enable it and then promptly forgot about it. As a result, individuals often share too much information, right down to their exact location. In the recent conflict in the Ukraine and Russia, threat actors have used geolocation in social media to find those resisting.

The security concern is that hackers or others may have the ability to track the location of specific individuals. If you think this sounds a little creepy, it is! There is an application known as Creepy (`www.geocreepy.com`) that allows users to track individuals using the photos they have posted online. Creepy gathers geolocation-related information from social networking sites and presents the results using Google Maps.

Many applications also make use of this technology to identify a user's exact location. The idea is that that you can identify a user by their location for service or revenue. Examples include coupons from nearby coffee shops and restaurants.

Full Device Encryption

Your company may set a standard that makes it mandatory that all company laptops use full device encryption (FDE). This standard will most likely not specify how encryption is done but will specify that regardless of the technology (EFS, BitLocker, or an equivalent), encryption is a required activity. Full device disk encryption is a useful tool for the security professional. Full device encryption offers an easy way to protect information should equipment be lost, stolen, or accessed by unauthorized individuals. The real benefit of these programs is that everything on the device is encrypted, including files and directories.

Tethering

There are times when you need to connect a device to the network, often the Internet, by leveraging another device's present connection. Readers who are parents can empathize with the scenario of being in a waiting room and your child's device absolutely must connect to the Internet temporarily to download a game, for example. In this case, perhaps the parent might create a mobile hotspot using their phone and tether their child's device to their phone's cellular connection. Regardless of why you need to tether a device to your connection, doing so requires only a quick visit to the device's operating system configuration settings. Under Network settings, you will find tethering and/or hotspot options.

The ability to tether, and thus share connectivity, across multiple devices results in a greater total data consumption. This does not sit well with cellular data providers who promote *limitless* data plans. The benefits of a limitless data plan are assumed to be for a single device covered by that plan. Thus, potential abuse of that device's connection by tethered devices can become acrimonious. Therefore, you will find that some carriers place restrictions on "limitless" data plans by way of a "fair use" policy.

Analysis of the traffic can reveal what device is using bandwidth—whether it is the connected device or a secondary device tethered from the connected device. Due to this ability, data providers can detect (and possible react to) tethering. For example, a provider may charge a onetime fee.

How exactly tethering is enabled depends on the operating system and the particular configuration settings therein. Android OS devices can complicate matters because with each update, the OEM or carrier may customize the device further. One security concern that is key to this discussion is the unauthorized remote activation/deactivation of devices or features. Given how easily tethering can be used to connect an unmanaged device to the network, you should remain vigilant and monitor tethering from unauthorized activations.

Airplane Mode

If you have flown recently, you know that on every flight you are reminded to place any cellular device in airplane mode before the plane taxis down the runway. FCC regulations ban the use of cell phones in order to protect instrumentation in the cockpit. At 20,000 feet in the air, active cell phones could pick up service from cell towers on the ground, as well as stop scanning for nearby Wi-Fi networks and attempt to join them. Years ago, some models of the Boeing 737 were found to be sensitive to radio interference from phones. This is the same reason you are not supposed to use cell phones in some parts of hospitals.

Airplane mode also disables Bluetooth and GPS. Airplane mode can block your device from attacks and protect privacy. Turning airplane mode on keeps applications from reporting the location of the device.

Location Services

Mobile devices store and sometimes share geolocation data. Location services make life easier by guiding us to the nearest Starbucks, but how are vendors using this information and how might they monetize it? Accumulating all this information over time lets a company create a detailed profile of your behavior and preferences. If this information is accessed by someone with nefarious intentions, it could become a security threat. Criminals have used this information to steal identities, and law enforcement has used location data to track innocent people such as those who happened to be in the vicinity of a crime.

DNS over HTTPS

Domain Name System (DNS) is the service that lets people find what they're looking for on the Internet. DNS operates behind every address translation, working to resolve fully qualified domain names (FQDNs) and human-readable addressing into numeric IP addresses. DNS serves a critical function for people. If DNS as a service were to cease, the Internet would continue, but users would need to know the IP address of every site they wanted to visit. DNS is a request-response protocol. When a DNS server sends a response to a request, the reply message contains the transaction ID and questions from the original request as well as any answers that it was able to find.

   DNS over HTTPS (DoH) is a protocol for performing remote DNS via HTTPS to increase privacy and security. Some organizations also use DNS over TLS (DoT) for encrypting DNS queries. *Custom DNS* allows people to specify the IP address of the faster or more reliable DNS server they want to use by using special settings that allow them to specify what DNS resolvers to use. It is very useful when you want to block specific types of ads or trackers, as well as filtering websites.

Deployment Scenarios

Given how affordable it is to own a mobile device, or several devices, organizations have been forced to decide how to regulate employees' selection of mobile devices at work. The principal decision is clear: can an employee use their own device or not? The pros and cons are not quite as clear, but what follows are the popular choices and consequences with which every CASP+ should be familiar.

COBO

Corporate-owned, business only (COBO) devices were the norm before nearly everyone had their own mobile device. COBO means a company not only dictates your choice of mobile device but also enforces its content and use. While not a Draconian policy, it certainly seems rigid when compared to companies supporting users to install their choice of applications or even bring their own device. The COBO policy is rigid but secure, offering no flexibility or latitude to users, and mobile devices can be managed more closely than with any of the other options.

COPE

Corporate-owned, personally enabled (COPE) is one step removed from COBO. It appeases users greatly by offering more freedom in mobile device usage, perhaps allowing independence in application, installation, and browsing. Exactly how much independence is allowed can be controlled to varying degrees, but in the end security is of greater concern than with COBO.

CYOD

With *choose your own device (CYOD)*, an organization offers its users a choice among a small number of approved mobile devices. CYOD is a compromise for employees who are loyal to a particular mobile operating system. It's understandable that people can become accustomed to one type of device or another, so CYOD is a solution that offers a couple of models that use one of the popular mobile OSs.

CYOD doesn't necessarily mean that users have the freedom to install any application they like. It is more about giving the choice of which platform, and perhaps which set of features, appeals to employees.

BYOD

If you ask most employees, they will choose the option to bring their own device to work. An organization with a *bring your own device (BYOD)* policy in place offers its employees the greatest degree of flexibility and variety in what mobile device they want to use. Based on recent statistics, it seems that between 60 and 70 percent of organizations have a BYOD policy in place. More details on these different approaches, including their popularity, can be found here: `www.techtarget.com/searchmobilecomputing/feature/ BYOD-vs-COPE-Why-corporate-device-ownership-could-make-a-comeback`.

By being a CASP+ candidate, you already know that allowing users to bring their own devices to work poses the greatest risks and security concerns to the organization. BYOD risks are not mitigated by using standard configuration profiles or standardized device management, but more through management of access control and network and resource connections.

Mobile Device Security Considerations

If one thing is constant, it's that attackers continually look for new methods of attack. Emergent threats are those that are becoming more prominent and were not seen in the past. These threats include the following:

Smartphone Attacks   Smartphones are much more powerful than they were just a few years ago, and today they are just very small, powerful computers. They are an appealing target for attackers. Although some have sounded the alarm for smartphone viruses, worms, and bots for a number of years, these threats have yet to reveal themselves in a major way. Several factors have contributed to the slower than expected advancement of this category of malware. These factors include lack of bandwidth, a fragmented market, and a much shorter life cycle for smartphones than for a computer.

Nevertheless, the factors that worked against the spread of these types of malware are changing. More smartphone providers are moving from just supporting voice communications to providing an increasing number of data management features. Devices such as the iPhone and Android phones have captured a large portion of the smartphone market. It is important to remember that many threats evolve in an incremental manner. Yesterday's proof of concept may become tomorrow's mainstream attack. There have even been examples of bad applications found in the Apple App Store and on Google Play as well as unauthorized application stores. Some of these applications were used to track users and steal personal data, while others were designed to record user activity and perform physical reconnaissance. There have been applications that remotely activate features on a device without permission. For those who decide to go outside the security perimeter of the vendor, such as those who jailbreak their iOS-based devices, other risks are present. (Jailbreaking is the process of removing the limitations imposed by Apple to control the operating system and what programs can be loaded.)

Botnets   Botnets are collections of zombies that are controlled by a hacker. Since the beginning of the Internet, these bots or zombies may be used to send spam, install Trojans, mine Bitcoins, attempt pump-and-dump stock manipulation, or even launch DDoS attacks. An end user can become infected by visiting a malicious site, clicking the wrong email attachment, or even following a link in a social networking site. What most botnets have in common is that they are designed to make money. Very rare is the scenario where a botnet is designed to remove money-making zombie networks, but it does happen. More can be read of that last case here:

toshitimes.com/new-vigilante-botnet-tracks-down-and-destroys-crypto-mining-malware

Scareware   These are several classes of software, often with limited or no benefit, that are sold to consumers through certain unethical marketing practices. Scareware has been growing for a few years, and it has spread to macOS. Scareware is designed to frighten you into buying fake or malicious software.

Most financially based criminal attacks make use of a money mule. A *money mule* is nothing more than a person who transfers stolen money or merchandise from one country to another or one person to another. Most plead ignorance when caught and claim that they did not know they were doing anything wrong. In one example, U.S. prosecutors charged 37 suspected money mules for participating in the illegal activities related to the Zeus botnet. You can read more about money mules at www.fbi .gov/scams-and-safety/common-scams-and-crimes/money-mules.

Smishing   This is a form of criminal activity that uses a smartphone's Short Message Service (SMS) and social engineering techniques to send fake SMS messages designed to trick users into clicking bogus links.

Search Engine Poisoning   Search engine poisoning or black hat search engine optimization is a technique by which attackers ensure that their sites appear high in the results lists of queries so that users are redirected to infected sites.

Crimeware Kits   Crimeware kits are complete attack toolkits that have everything needed for the wannabe criminal who lacks the technical expertise to launch phishing and malicious attacks. These kits consist of a builder that enables a user to create malware capable of web injections. It's not uncommon for a basic kit to cost about $1,000 or more. You can think of the basic kit in much the same way as if you purchased Windows 11 Home; if you would like more features, you can move up to Windows 11 Pro.

Clickjacking   This online threat is increasing and works by hiding the true purpose of a link or button. If a hacker can trick you into clicking an innocent-looking link, the victim actually executes something completely different, often resulting in the remote execution of arbitrary code.

Security considerations aren't limited to just threats of attack. The CASP+ professional needs to be aware of many significant security considerations. A few notable ones include the following:

Unauthorized remote activation/deactivation of devices or features   Remote disabling enables you to lock or erase data stored on a mobile device if it is lost or stolen. However, it could be catastrophic to an end user for a device to be wiped of all content accidentally or maliciously. One of the best ways to secure a mobile device is never download apps from an unknown source and keep the OS up-to-date. Don't ignore the latest update or security patch.

Encrypted and unencrypted communication concerns   Most mobile devices come with some type of built-in encryption. Encryption makes data unreadable to anyone attempting to intercept communication from mobile devices. To encrypt a mobile device, find this feature, which is usually located under settings, and enter your password. The process of encrypting a mobile device can take a long time depending on the size of the data. The more data, the longer it takes. Do not forget your encryption password. With some devices it is required every time you want to use your mobile device, and with some, it is required only when you restart or reboot.

Physical reconnaissance   Mobile digital surveillance is dangerous and can be used to track a person's physical location. SMS messages can be recorded in an online account that is compromised even if the messages are deleted from the mobile device. Call logs can be viewed if the mobile provider account is hacked, providing the caller as well as time of call. GPS locations can be used to provide location at any time and recorded to an online account. Using any of Google's applications on a mobile device means you are likely being physically tracked, even if you have location history turned off. Turning off location history removes only where you have been at a specific time. Google tracking can be helpful for an organization managing a fleet of cars, deliveries, or shipments but can be invasive for most people. Google consumers should periodically log into Manage your Google Account and review data privacy settings.

Personal data theft   Spying on mobile devices is important to understand. SMS messages can be recorded from the target phone. These messages can be recorded in an online account even if they are deleted from the device. Call logs can be stolen, providing the caller and time of call. Photos, videos, contact lists, and voicemail, as well as websites visited on the mobile device, can be stolen, and your privacy is no longer secure.

The following sections will examine many additional security considerations that relate to mobile and emerging technologies.

Health Privacy

When you picture medical sensors or medical diagnostic devices, you imagine a scene where these devices are connected to a patient only and include a display screen for healthcare professionals in the room. However, today these devices are also connected to a wireless network, visible to professionals far from the patient. As so often happens with Internet of Things (IoT) devices, there is increased connectivity without a corresponding increase in security controls. The need for controls like authentication and input validation were not anticipated, so these devices are left "wide open" for potential exploitation.

Of course, the greatest concern with medical sensors is health privacy. Privacy of your health data is taken seriously, protected by federal regulations such as the Health Insurance Portability and Accountability Act (HIPAA) of 1996, which protects sensitive patient information.

Implications of Wearable Devices

These days, we have an ever-increasing range of wearable devices, and they all come with potential security considerations.

Fitness Devices   People buy Fitbits and other fitness devices to track their heartbeat, calculate calories spent, and so on. Add in GPS and people can monitor running distance and elevation. When people are proud of keeping active, they're willing to broadcast it to the world using social media and the vendor's own applications.

But blending connectivity, social media, and GPS tracking can easily lead to unexpected disclosure and physical reconnaissance. That's why the U.S. military was embarrassed about the disclosure of sensitive base locations through their soldiers' use of fitness devices.

Watches   Watches now have almost every feature offered by a typical smartphone. And for any features they lack, their connectivity to your smartphone bridges that gap. If a smartwatch is compromised, not only could it disclose your location, contacts, and email, it would also be able to make phone calls and send texts on your behalf.

The main concern surrounding a smartwatch vulnerable to compromise is personal data theft. The watch either contains an abundance of personal data locally or possesses a direct connection to the phone that contains the personal data. Of course, device loss/theft is a concern, but more so with devices that are often set down or out of pocket.

Cameras and Glasses   Like other wearable devices, cameras and glasses also present security and privacy concerns. When they're connected to social media, or with any automatic uploading of media capability, the privacy concerns escalate. Location data could be accessible from the embedded EXIF data, which includes camera-related specifications, date and time stamp information, and location. There is little assurance that such a device isn't still receiving and transmitting data even without the user explicitly turning it on.

There are two types of "smart" glasses. The first type is functionally the same as a camera, streaming or recording the physical world around the user. These glasses carry the same security and privacy concerns as a camera. The second type includes those that alter or augment the physical world to the user. Readers might remember Google Glass when it seemed poised to revolutionize how people walk around with a heads-up display. The devices hardly made any impact when they were first introduced but do continue to survive with occasional upgrades and updates. Google Glass offers an augmented reality view and has some unique security issues, including physical safety. The uninitiated user could be easily distracted by the display of virtual promotions and not appreciate the real threat of road traffic.

Headsets   Headsets include a microphone that can be compromised. Headsets paired with a smartphone using Bluetooth are particularly vulnerable.

The primary security problem with Bluetooth headsets is centered around encrypted and unencrypted communication concerns. Though the connection is likely encrypted, Bluetooth communication is vulnerable to attack, whether by bypassing and undermining the encryption or by jamming the communication.

Digital Forensics of Collected Data

The term *digital forensics* describes a structured, step-by-step process and analysis of data stored, processed, or retrieved on a computer system in a legal, approved way so that any evidence can be used in court as needed. The forensic process typically addresses the following items:

- Identification
- Preservation
- Collection
- Examination
- Analysis

- Presentation

- Decision

Although law enforcement has been practicing criminal forensics for many years, private companies are just starting to see the value of digital forensics. Digital forensics can be broken down into three broad categories:

Computer Forensics   The examination of physical media to obtain information for evidence

Software Analysis   The review of malware, viruses, and other dangerous software for analysis and potential identification of the author

Network Analysis   The analysis of network traffic and logs to identify the source and effect of the event

Security professionals should look carefully at the policies and procedures that define how forensic activities are to be carried out. Forensic analysis of compromised systems, smartphones, tablets, digital cameras, and USB thumb drives must be addressed. Any existing policy must specify how evidence is to be handled. The chain of custody helps protect the integrity and reliability of the evidence by providing an evidence log that shows every access to evidence, from collection to appearance in court.

Forensic specialists must know how to record evidence at the scene by taking photographs, documenting their activities in an investigator's notebook, interviewing suspects and witnesses, and knowing the proper procedures for collecting or seizing suspected systems or media. Doing the right thing is required to protect the chain of custody and legality of the evidence. Forensic procedures must document the complete journey of the evidence (from its beginning to the end) and be able to answer these questions:

- Who collected the evidence?

- How and where was it collected?

- Who took possession of the evidence?

- How was it stored, and was it secured while in storage?

- Who took it out of storage, and why was it removed?

This process, also known as electronic discovery, or e-discovery, deals with the review of electronic information for the purpose of recovery of evidence. The e-discovery process is all about how you find and extract documents and data stored in electronic format. The trend toward its use will only intensify in the future. Although most investigations may not go to court, computer forensic specialists must collect, review, and preserve structured data that may come from electronic records, contracts, and forms as well as a large amount of unstructured data like emails, chat sessions, and even electronic file fragments. During an investigation, formal records make up an essential part of the discovery process, but this is only half of the picture in today's electronic world. It is becoming increasingly common to ask for copies of selected emails and other electronic communications for court cases and legal hearings. The data retention policy should specify how long information is stored.

Unauthorized Application Store

With hundreds of mobile app stores with millions of apps being marketed, policing and protecting assets is difficult. Threat actors are using mobile applications as an attack vector, especially the Android platform. The app stores are a huge revenue driver for iOS and Android, so unauthorized application stores have been around since July 2009, when Apple first launched its app store. Independent developers creating legitimate as well as malicious applications want access to users. Apple and Google try hard to maintain quality and user security in their app stores, and while most users stick with the legitimate app stores, some rogue users will still want the applications that are not available.

Jailbreaking/Rooting

As previously mentioned, *jailbreaking* (iOS), also called *rooting* (Android), means to unlock a phone so that it works on any carrier. Depending on local law, this act can carry consequences such as voiding the device's warranty or even prohibiting continued coverage. However, jailbreaking or rooting a phone also provides freedom from restrictions placed on the device by the original carrier. Jailbreaking enables you to do things like change the default browser and mail client. It also enables you to use software of which the manufacturer does not approve. Not only should your company have an inventory of mobile devices, but a security policy and a scanning process should be required as well. Some companies have an annual "eyes on inventory," where mobile devices are scanned physically by IT.

Side Loading

Normally, when loading or installing an application, a user would use the device's application-distribution channel. For most devices, this would mean using Google Play or the Apple App Store. But if a user seeks an alternate, back-channel method to load an application that may not be accessible otherwise, that method is called *sideloading*. Naturally, the security concern for a CASP+ is why such an application requires sideloading and is not available through the normally vetted channels. Sideloading, or loading applications outside a controlled channel, means that the established process of inspecting an application for malicious code is likely being bypassed.

Containerization

Picture the large cargo ships that sail products across the oceans. So long as the cargo can fit in a container, that's all that matters. No matter what the cargo is, what it's for, or who uses it, it fits in a reliable, standardized container. Containerization ensures the efficient and cost-effective use of the ship on which the cargo is placed. *Containerization* is a type of virtualization where applications run in an isolated space, while using the same shared operating system (OS). A container is a fully packaged and portable computing environment.

The same approach is used for a Linux technology that is similar to virtualization, commonly using the open-source Docker program, where each container runs the host's kernel. The container has its own network stack and incremental file system, but it is not a fully virtualized system or a Type 1 (bare-metal) hypervisor. It's more about isolating the running container, not virtualizing an entire operating system.

Original Equipment Manufacturer and Carrier Differences

In the smartphone industry, the biggest fight of all between Apple iPhone and Android will never have a winner. It is all about personal preference.

The *original equipment manufacturer (OEM)* is the company that makes and sells their own phones in their own factories. The companies making Android OEMs include LG and Samsung. One of the reasons for Android's success is the ability to have many carriers, device manufacturers, and customized software. However, this is also one of its biggest headaches. Most Androids come with bloatware that cannot be removed and features that cannot be disabled, but they are usually more cost effective, and sometimes storage can be expanded.

Apple makes many different tech products, and if you own any device, it makes sense to stay with the same ecosystem. Generally speaking, the third-party apps on iOS are better, and there is a better selection of accessories for Apple products. Apple also introduced app tracking notifications.

Both Android and iProducts track tons of data about you, but it is nice to be able to deny information to a third-party app. Both platforms have pros and cons, as do the carriers that provide service. Choice will depend on what is appreciated most.

Supply Chain Issues

During the past decade, enterprise resilience has become a hot topic. The meaning of enterprise resilience has grown from its original business continuity and disaster recovery objectives associated with IT data crashes. Today, the enterprise is viewed as an organism facing a myriad of risks, including both physical and logical, manmade and natural, external and internal. The scope of planning may be as local as the home office or as far-reaching as the global supply chain.

eFuse

An older technology known as eFuse has recently been highlighted as another method of anti-tampering. *eFuse* was developed by IBM back in the early 2000s as an innovative way to alter a hardware chip in real time. A chip designed with eFuse allows a company to reprogram its purpose and features on the fly, in real time, and alter the pathways of its hardware. However, in 2010, Microsoft and Motorola had to defend their use of eFuse technology to enforce that only authorized software would be in use on devices such as the Xbox or smartphones. In other words, the companies could, on detecting a jailbroken phone or altered Xbox, disable the device in real time.

Security Considerations for Technologies, Protocols, and Sectors

Enterprise companies are impacting and technologically innovating every industry, from healthcare and travel to manufacturing to banking. The very nature of technology makes it particularly vulnerable to many of the advanced threats that exist in the modern landscape. Threats originate from inside and outside the organization and result from unpatched vulnerabilities, third-party applications, and employee negligence. A security professional must consider not only the technology being used but the sectors it is being used in.

Embedded Technologies

Embedded technologies, like the Internet of Things (IoT), system on a chip (SoC), and other technologies, are a combination of hardware and software designed for a very specific purpose. Embedded systems can be inside other technologies as well. IoT describes the development of everyday objects that have network connectivity, allowing them to send and receive data. One example would be your Nest thermostat talking to your Maytag dishwasher or your Samsung refrigerator. Although such technology offers great advantages, such as allowing your thermostat to adjust your heating and cooling based on when you are at home, or maybe having your refrigerator send an email to you when it's low on Refrigerant 410A, there is a security concern with such devices. If you don't think so, consider the fact that a refrigerator was discovered among a botnet of more than 100,000 Internet-connected devices that sent upward of 750,000 malicious emails. It may seem far-fetched that someone could build a botnet out of a refrigerator or a microwave oven, but it is entirely possible. As so often happens with IoT devices, there is increased connectivity without a corresponding increase in security controls. The need for controls like authentication and input validation were not anticipated, so these devices are left "wide open" for potential exploitation. Some of the other consumer network-enabled devices about which a CASP+ should be aware are the following:

Building Automation Systems   Designed to monitor and control the mechanical, security, fire alarms, lighting, and HVAC of a building

IP Video   A digital video camera that can send and receive data via a network or the Internet

How often do you update firmware? If you are like most users, that answer is probably not very often, if it is even technically possible. One example of how that might be a problem is that a vulnerability discovered in the firmware that powers a broad array of webcams IP surveillance cameras, and baby monitors made by Foscam allows anyone with access to the device's Internet address to view live and recorded video footage. This happened to one family, and the hackers taunted the family via the IP video camera. Read more about this problem here: `www.securityweek`
`.com/serious-vulnerabilities-found-firmware-used-many-ip-`
`camera-vendors`.

HVAC Controllers   Systems designed to control a home or business HVAC system over the Internet

Sensors   A variety of components that can be used to activate light switches, open gates and doors, and provide other home automation over the Internet. Medical equipment, pacemakers, implantable devices, and auto/truck computers/sensors/locks are just some of the devices with sensors.

Physical Access Control Systems   Items used for the control of access, such as Bluetooth and RFID locks

A/V Systems   Technology designed for the automation of audiovisual (AV) systems. These systems can include in-home TVs, home AV networks (PC controlled), and also corporate AV with projectors and videoconferencing.

Scientific/Industrial Equipment   This includes power generation equipment, SCADA, industrial motors, and even power generation.

System on a Chip   A *system on a chip (SOC)* is a microchip that has all of the components required to power a computer. An example of a system on a chip is the Raspberry Pi. The Broadcom chip contains a 700 MHz ARM processor and a VideoCore 4 GPU. A system on a chip also pairs a field programmable gate array (FPGA) and a processor on a single chip. In digital electronics, a FPGA is a circuit designed to be configured by the customer, hence the name "field programmable."

Application-specific integrated circuit   An *application-specific integrated circuit (ASIC)* is an integrated circuit chip tailored for a specific use, rather than general-purpose. ASIC chips can include those designed to run in a digital voice recorder, satellites, or cell phones.

ICS/supervisory Control and Data Acquisition

It wasn't that long ago that the most exotic item you may have placed on your network was a networked printer. Modern networks have moved far beyond simple printers and may now include VoIP systems or even critical infrastructure or SCADA components. The need for proper controls is more critical when critical infrastructure is involved. Industrial control systems (ICSs) include Supervisory Control and Data Acquisition (SCADA), such as a system for managing a water or gas pipeline. When malware affects industrial control systems, it's conceivable that it could have disastrous consequences. If not causing imminent danger or widespread interruption to a community, ICS outages could at least produce costly results. Recall that the ICS malware Stuxnet targeted Iranian nuclear centrifuges. Their outage included permanent self-destruction of the industrial machinery.

A large portion of emerging threats are driven by people out for financial gain, hacktivists, and nation-state hackers. Some believe that out of these three categories, the nation-state hackers are the most serious threat to both corporations and governments. To deal with emerging threats, companies should be prepared with a plan that lays out the key steps and resources to deploy immediately when a breach is detected.

Yesterday's analog controls have become today's digital systems. From a security standpoint, these systems are an important consideration, since they are typically used by the utilities industry to monitor critical infrastructure systems and control power distribution, as well as many other forms of automation. SCADA systems have evolved into a networked architecture. They are also used for more mundane deployments such as heating, ventilation, and air conditioning systems (HVAC) in buildings, elevator controls, and so forth. To learn more, visit `nvlpubs.nist.gov/nistpubs/SpecialPublications/NIST.SP.800-82r2.pdf`.

SCADA systems and networks used to be stand-alone, but today they are integrated directly within an organization's business systems. If the integration is not handled correctly, a security risk could arise. SCADA system best practices include the following:

- Create and enforce a network protection strategy.

- Conduct site surveys and physical reviews. Assess all remote sites connected to SCADA systems.

- Enforce strong logical and physical controls over access points into the SCADA network.

- Harden, patch, and secure SCADA networks. Remove and disable unnecessary services.

- Review the network topology and identify all connections to SCADA networks.

- Unplug all unnecessary connections to the SCADA network.

Conduct periodic penetration testing and vulnerability assessments of all remaining connections to the SCADA network to evaluate the security controls associated with these access points.

The *programmable logic controller (PLC)*, which automates and monitors processes, needs securing as well. For physical security around the PLC, monitoring who has access, limiting access with USB, and changing default passwords go a long way to ensuring that the environment remains secure. You also have to control how this network is linked to the Internet and other systems. IT departments often lack expertise with PLC and SCADA equipment, and knowledge of industrial standards might be limited.

Many years ago, the nuclear plant in Athens, Alabama, crashed when an IP address was pinged. A couple of years later, the same nuclear plant shut down when an engineer applied a software update to a single system that was used to collect diagnostic information from the PLC. Plant operators did not understand the dependencies between devices on the network. SCADA operators must understand the *Historian*, which is responsible for storing and logging all data that the SCADA system aggregates. The Historian allows operators to look at past data for the plant and create reports.

Documentation can also be created for SCADA using *ladder logic*. This logic is used to develop software for PLCs and is based on the diagram resembling a ladder. Each rung of the ladder begins with an entry and ends with an exit. A device can appear in multiple rungs of a ladder, while the inputs and outputs should be identified precisely.

Hardening and patching SCADA is a real challenge because of the uptime requirements as well as the complexity and testing. This is a huge point of contention in the security community with SCADA operators. In some situations, such as those using unsupported OSs like Windows XP, there may be no support available; in other situations, you may be able to contact the vendor to learn more about how to harden the SCADA infrastructure.

One of the most notorious examples of a SCADA system attack was Stuxnet. This malware was discovered in July 2010, and it was intended to target specific systems with military precision. Stuxnet was designed to target Siemens systems with specific settings as would be found in a nuclear facility. Once installed on the PLC hardware device, the malware injects its own code into the system. The result was to cause the system to damage the targeted device slowly while sending fake "all is okay" responses to a monitoring station called the *safety instrumented system (SIS)*. These systems are responsible for operation and safety. The SIS makes sure that the emergency stop is within the parameters of a safe stop. In August 2020, SafeBreach Labs revealed at a Black Hat conference that new zero-day vulnerabilities demonstrated that the threat of Stuxnet is still alive and well.

Protocols

Computer protocols are sets of rules for transmitting data between devices so that information can be exchanged. These protocols agree on the syntax and semantics of how data is sent. For industrial microcontrollers, these protocols are often utilized:

- *Controller Area Network (CAN) bus*: Used for engine controllers, instrument panels, power windows. The CAN protocol uses a shared broadcast network without a built-in encryption mechanism. This allows an adversary to eavesdrop all the nodes and understand the communication. Use encryption so eavesdropping is not allowed.

- *Modbus*: Used serially between electronic devices such as PLCs. Using TLS sessions will help with secure communications. SCADA MODBUS is the most widely used SCADA protocol. Modbus is restricted to addressing 24/7 devices on one data link, which limits the number of field devices that may be connected to a master station.

- *Distributed Network Protocol 3 (DNP3)*: Often used in automation in electric and water companies, DNP3 supports authentication and encryption. DNP3 consists of Application and Data Link Layers. Both protocols are used over many different types of transport, such as RS-232, RS-485, and TCP/IP. When it comes to TCP/IP, Modbus has a separate variant called Modbus TCP/IP, but the DNP3 is wrapped within TCP/IP.

- *Zigbee*: Used in IoT wireless sensors and is based on symmetric key cryptography. The main security risk for a Zigbee wireless network is theft of sensitive data from a node. This may be user data that can be used for criminal purposes but is more likely to be network security data, such as encryption keys, that will allow access to the node and network.

- *Common Industrial Protocol (CIP)*: Used for data organization and messaging. A CIP device deployed correctly will reject messages sent by untrusted devices.

- *Data distribution service (DDS)*: A middleware protocol and API standard used in air traffic control and autonomous vehicles. DDS includes authentication, access control, confidentiality, and integrity using a peer-to-peer architecture.

Sectors

Threat intelligence tells us that some threats are global in nature, but many industries face targeting from organizations that are concentrating on their specific vertical. Customers must shape their cybersecurity programs based on their most pressing cyber threats and challenges.

- *Energy*: Energy and utility companies have complex environments with many systems, sensors, and controls. This specific sector has to protect against broad attacks from state-sponsored threat actors.

- *Manufacturing*: Cyber attacks have huge implications including financial and reputational damage.

- *Healthcare*: Attacks against hospitals and healthcare organizations don't just affect operations but put lives at risk. The healthcare ecosystem is increasingly exposed to risk of attacks if externally facing systems are not properly protected. Healthcare also has to safeguard patient and employee data while facing many regulatory compliance requirements.

- *Public utilities and public services*: Maintaining a strong security posture can be difficult, and attack surfaces grow as legacy systems age. Threat groups refine attack methodologies and attack critical infrastructure. Public utilities and service providers must become proactive rather than reactive in their cybersecurity programs.

- *Financial services*: Protecting financial records and adhering to government regulations in the midst of being heavily targeted by advanced threats is essential to the well-being of a financially oriented organization.

Summary

This chapter focused on enterprise security integration. For many security professionals, the words *enterprise security* might immediately bring to mind thoughts of firewalls, intrusion detection, and other hardware devices; however true, security requires more than the purchase of hardware. Hardware must be deployed, and that is not easy without the cooperation of others. This means that you are going to have to work with teams of individuals throughout the organization in order to achieve your security goals.

The CASP+ will even need to know how to deploy security solutions so that security is not decreased and the overall protection of the organization is maintained.

Exam Essentials

Understand the need to integrate enterprise disciplines to achieve secure solutions. Effective security requires the CASP+ to work with others throughout the organization to integrate the needs of the company into holistic security solutions. A comprehensive security solution is essential to enterprise continuity of business operations and maintaining the confidentiality and integrity of data.

Demonstrate familiarity with emerging issues in cryptography. The blockchain is an immutable distributed public ledger made possible through the use of cryptography. Homomorphic encryption allows the protection of sensitive data while still facilitating computation on that data in a manner that preserves privacy. Quantum computing challenges modern approaches to cryptography and may be a disruptive force in the future.

Be able to describe the security impact of interorganizational change and using new technology. Many times, the result of change will be that the level of security is reduced and that system configurations fall to a lower level of security. Control processes are needed to make sure that change occurs in an orderly fashion and that no unintended consequences occur because of organizational change.

Be able to describe the security concerns of interconnecting multiple industries. When companies or networks are interconnected, there is a heightened risk that a security breach may allow an attacker to migrate to the "other company/system."

Know the impact that products and services can have on security in specific sectors. When integrating products and services into the environment, the CASP+ will need to determine what method will be used to control the deployment.

Review Questions

You can find the answers in Appendix.

1. You are a network defender and are finding it difficult to keep up with the volume of network attacks. What can you leverage to help with early detection and response to these threats, especially new ones?

   A. Machine learning

   B. SIEM

   C. DevSecOps

   D. Security as Code

2. Your company wants to begin using biometrics for authentication. Which of the following are not biometrics that can be verified by a system to give an individual access?

   A. Facial recognition

   B. Iris recognition

   C. Retina recognition

   D. PIN recognition

3. The rise of the Internet of Things (IoT) has presented challenges for your organization's security team while trying to secure your corporate network. Attacks on IoT have been steadily trending upward as attackers enlist devices to launch attacks. What is the BEST method to combat this threat?

   A. Adding network intrusion devices

   B. Performing inventory management

   C. Adding more security tools

   D. Reducing the attack surface

4. Terry is heading a project to implement a chatbot on the home page of your insurance company to move away from live agents. What technology will he most likely employ?

   A. Natural language processing

   B. Biometrics

   C. Virtual reality

   D. Deep fake

5. Felipe wants to use a protocol that allows a client to retrieve an element of a database without the owner of that database knowing which element was selected. If implemented securely, the client will only learn about the element they are querying for and nothing else, preserving privacy. Which of the following provides the BEST solution?

   A. Strong private information retrieval

   B. Secure function evaluation

   C. Private function evaluation

   D. Big data

6. Augmented reality (AR) advances are exciting, and cybersecurity is now dealing with a vast amount of complexity. The adoption of AR brings an expanding landscape of new cybersecurity vulnerabilities. Consumers and businesses are grappling with big data breaches, and implementing effective cybersecurity measures is essential for modern businesses. Which of these is not an urgent or relevant cybersecurity issue involving AR?

    A. Cloud structure

    B. Innovation outpacing secure development

    C. Wearable exposure

    D. Micro/nano technology

7. 3D printers include computers and run software that could be vulnerable to security issues that bad actors can take advantage of. To mitigate this issue, 3D printing vendors need to make secure coding and design a core part of their development process. Printer owners should also consider doing which of these first?

    A. Securely downloading plans for 3D printers

    B. Hardening their devices when possible and considering the security of the 3D production

    C. Encrypting SD cards used to hold all printing plans

    D. Cleaning the laser that melts the powdered material into objects layer by layer

8. Naomi wants to use passwordless authentication in her corporate network. Which of the following statements is not true?

    A. Linux supports passwordless SSH logins.

    B. Microsoft supports passwordless sign-in on Windows products and networks running Microsoft Active Directory.

    C. Passwordless can be used only on mobile devices.

    D. Microsoft LDAP supports passwordless authentication through FIDO2 keys.

9. You want your organization to benefit from artificial intelligence, but some in the application development department are confused about what AI actually is. Which statement is true?

    A. Artificial intelligence and machine learning are the same.

    B. Machine learning and deep learning are the same.

    C. Machine learning leads to deep learning, which leads to artificial intelligence.

    D. Artificial intelligence parses big data to make decisions.

10. Your new CISO wants to implement a mobile device strategy. All staff have mobile devices, and you need something quickly implemented that is not very expensive. Which of the following strategies is the BEST one for your organization?

    A. BYOD

    B. CYOD

    C. COPE

    D. IDEA

11. Your organization is revisiting its mobile device strategies due to security's need to have vetted hardware on corporate networks. You want to give employees a choice, but you need to keep costs down. What is the BEST strategy to deploy?

    A. BYOD

    B. CYOD

    C. COPE

    D. TPM

12. Your global banking organization wants to use mobile devices in their main offices as well as remote branches. Employees handle sensitive financial documents, including bank statements, loan applications, and mortgage documents. Given that your organization is very risk averse, what type of mobile strategy would work BEST for them?

    A. BYOD

    B. CYOD

    C. COPE

    D. OSPF

13. Your employees need internal access while traveling to remote locations. You need a service that enables them to securely connect to a private corporate network from a public network to log into a centralized portal. You want the traffic to be encrypted. Which of the following is the BEST tool?

    A. Wi-Fi

    B. VPN

    C. RDP

    D. NIC

14. Your marketing team wants to share files between local devices without using the network or a physical memory card at the next conference. Which of these terms is BEST suited for the preceding situation?

    A. Uploading

    B. Downloading

    C. Sideloading

    D. P2TP

15. An audit for your mobile device policies found that your COPE devices are allowing unsigned applications. The default value on these assets is set to $true. After developing an app, the developer must sign it in or make it traceable and publish it to the Play store. Is there a valid business need for installing unsigned applications on a company device?

    A. If a developer wants to test and troubleshoot an app.

    B. To validate the keystore: debug and release.

    C. To remove the app's digitally signed certificates.

    D. No, there is never a reason to use unsigned apps.

16. You are traveling for work, and no Wi-Fi is available. You are in a public space and need to use your laptop to go online. If supported, you could tether through a mobile device to the Internet. What are the drawbacks of tethering?

    A. Your mobile connection will be slow, and the battery will draw down quickly on your mobile device.

    B. You must have an app to tether your phone to your laptop.

    C. Your phone calls will go straight to voicemail.

    D. Security will be an issue.

17. You want to evaluate the most secure authentication method on a mobile device, primarily your phone. Authentication includes many options and could possibly use multiple methods for secure access. Which of the following is not something you know?

    A. Password

    B. Pattern lock

    C. Fingerprint

    D. PIN

18. Mobile apps in your environment are causing concern because of the unintentional data leakage. "Riskware" applications pose the biggest problem for mobile users who give all permissions asked for without checking the need or security. These apps are usually the free fun apps and can be found in official app stores. What should you advise mobile device users about data leakage?

    A. Make sure that your network is fast.

    B. Instruct users to check for upgrades often.

    C. Only give apps permissions they must have, and delete any app that asks for more than is necessary.

    D. Give apps all the permissions they ask for.

19. To facilitate ease of access for mobile device users, many apps use tokens. These tokens enable users to perform multiple actions without requiring them to reauthenticate their identities. Which of the following is a best practice in using this methodology?

    A. Generating new tokens with each access attempt.

    B. Keeping old tokens for a specific amount of time.

    C. Using a token until the app or page is closed.

    D. Tokens should never expire.

20. Your terminated IT network administrator surrendered his company iPhone. You found that he was able to remove the limitations put in place by the device's manufacturer. Third-party unauthorized software is installed on the device. What did the IT network administrator do?

    A. Locking

    B. Rooting

    C. Jailbreaking

    D. Recompiling

Appendix

Answers to Review Questions

Chapter 1: Risk Management

1. C. Subjective opinions are not an advantage of quantitative risk assessment but rather an advantage of qualitative risk assessment.

2. A. What helps demystify these formulas is recalling what each value represents. Recall that SLE is the single loss expectancy of an asset, EF is the exposure factor, and a higher EF means a higher exposure (higher vulnerability of that asset). So, it's reasonable to understand that expectancy of a loss goes higher when the exposure is higher. Single loss expectancy is a product of both the asset's value and how vulnerable that asset is to a loss.

3. B. Although a qualitative assessment generally requires much less time than a quantitative one, a qualitative assessment does not provide cost values.

4. B. Recall that ALE represents the annual loss expectancy of an asset while SLE is the single loss. Once you understand that ALE is simply a year's value of the SLE, then you understand that the number of occurrences per year is what's needed to calculate ALE. The Annual Rate of Occurrence (ARO) represents that number of occurrences. Just remember that ARO can be less than once per year, which means the loss is expected to happen once over multiple years. And if ARO is less than one, then ALE will be less than SLE.

5. D. To transfer the risk is to deflect it to a third party. The most common third party is an insurance company. Instead of managing the risk directly, the organization incurs an ongoing cost from that third party.

6. C. To mitigate the risk means that a control is used to reduce the risk. For example, installing a firewall is one method by which risk can be mitigated.

7. A. Once you have the asset's value (AV) and the exposure factor (EF), the product of those two values is the single loss expectancy (SLE).

8. A. This is where you make a step-by-step list of the possibilities for testing. Test each possibility to see if it corrects the problem. Be careful to change one thing at a time to avoid creating any new problems. If the step-by-step procedure fails to fix the problem, then return to the beginning of the process and start over.

9. C. Employees are often the target of cybercrime, and one simple mistake can have catastrophic consequences. Security awareness training educates employees about the cyber landscape and how to remain secure in the corporate ecosystem.

10. A. A *vulnerability* can be described as a weakness in hardware, software, or components that may be exploited in order for a threat to destroy, damage, or compromise an asset.

11. C. A threat is any agent, condition, or circumstance that could cause harm, loss, damage, or compromise to an IT asset or data asset. The likelihood of the threat is the probability of occurrence or the odds that the event will actually occur.

12. D. OpenVAS is a vulnerability assessment tool, not an audit standard.

13. D. The gap analysis examines an area or environment and is designed to report the difference between "where we are" and "where we want to be." The analysis of that gap provides an objective viewpoint that helps form the steps necessary to close that gap.

14. D. Vulnerability assessment tools and scanners provide information on vulnerabilities within a targeted application or system or an entire network. Vulnerability assessment tools usually provide advice on how to fix or manage the security risks that they have discovered.

15. B. *Uptime agreements (UAs)* are one of the most well-known types of SLAs. UAs detail the agreed-on amount of uptime.

16. D. The principle of least privilege is a best practice that ensures a person has only enough access to perform their duties.

17. C. Personnel will manually perform recovery steps without causing any actual disruption.

18. B. Equipment is effectively only available, but not yet set up. At least partial setup and configuration are assumed not yet done. A *cold site* is the cheapest and will require the most time to have running.

19. A. The mean time to recovery (MTTR) describes the length of time between an interruption and the recovery from that interruption.

20. A. Dual control requires employees to work together to complete critical actions. A common example is that of a combination or code for a safe. Two employees are required to open it successfully. Separation of duties limits what one employee can do, likely requiring a more senior employee to validate the employee's action.

Chapter 2: Configure and Implement Endpoint Security Controls

1. C. Yes, there are synonyms for hardening, but the term hardening is the right word to recognize on the exam.

2. D. The TCB is the sum of all protection mechanisms within a computer, and it is responsible for enforcing the security policy. This includes hardware, software, controls, and processes.

3. A. The Hardware Security Module (HSM) and the Trusted Platform Module (TPM) do provide the option to encrypt hard drives and fixed storage, but not portable storage devices like USB drives. HSM and TPM authenticate the system, not the user.

4. B. Security-Enhanced Linux is a Linux kernel security module that provides a mechanism for supporting access control security policies, including mandatory access controls. SELinux is a set of kernel modifications and user-space tools that have been added to various Linux distributions; it was started by a collaboration between the NSA and Red Hat.

5. C. HSM and TPM provide the option to encrypt hard drives and fixed storage, not portable drives such as a USB drive.

6. D. Examples of trusted OSs include SELinux, SEAndroid, and Trusted Solaris. Security-Enhanced Linux (SELinux), available now for just over 20 years, started as a collaborative effort between the NSA and Red Hat, and it continues to be improved. SELinux brings MAC to the Linux kernel, allowing for much stricter access control.

7. B. The Hardware Security Module (HSM) is a type of secure crypto processor used to manage cryptographic keys. TPMs use endorsement key and storage root key, and SEDs use random Data Encryption Key (DEK), which the drive uses to both encrypt and decrypt the data.

8. C. Attestation services can be designed as hardware-based, software-based, or hybrid. The Trusted Platform Module (TPM) is a specialized form of hardware security module, which might contain an asymmetric key or some other secret.

9. D. Basic attributes of a trusted OS include long-term protected storage, separation of user processes from supervisor processes, isolation, and hardware protection.

10. A. The total cost of ownership (TCO) is lower when using a standard operating system throughout the organization.

11. C. A data interface is used with databases to generate process templates. Process templates are reusable collections of activity types. They allow system integrators and others who work with different clients to manipulate similar types of data.

12. D. One of the original trusted OS testing standards was the Trusted Computer System Evaluation Criteria (TCSEC). TCSEC, also known as the Orange Book, was developed to evaluate stand-alone systems but was replaced by the Common Criteria.

13. D. If a hardware system is particularly critical and cannot be easily replaced, a way to reduce downtime is to employ high availability (HA) with redundant hardware.

14. C. Common Criteria categorizes assurance into one of seven increasingly strict levels of assurance, called the evaluation assurance levels (EALs). EALs provide a specific level of confidence in the security functions of the system being analyzed.

15. C. A SED is a hard disk drive (HDD) or solid-state drive (SSD) designed to automatically encrypt and decrypt drive data without the need for user input or disk encryption software. When the SED is powered on in the host system, data being written to and read from the drive is being encrypted and decrypted instantly, and no other steps or software are needed to encrypt and decrypt the drive's data.

16. A. Computers rely on system firmware, commonly known as the system Basic Input/Output System (BIOS), to facilitate the hardware initialization process and transition control to the operating system. Unauthorized modification of BIOS firmware by malicious software is a significant threat because of its unique and privileged position within the PC architecture. The move from BIOS to implementations based on the Unified Extensible Firmware Interface (UEFI) may make it easier for malware to target the BIOS.

17. C. The NX (No-eXecute) bit segregates memory areas used for processor instruction and data storage.

18. C. User and entity behavior analytics (UEBA) can possibly detect an unauthorized user or a Trojaned device.

19. C. ASLR protects against buffer overflow attacks by randomizing the location of different portions of the code. Therefore, even if an attacker managed to make a buffer overflow work once, it may never work again on the same code.

20. C. SEAndroid uses the concept of application sandboxing, or isolating and restricting its applications in their own respective memory and drive spaces.

Chapter 3: Security Operations Scenarios

1. A. Threat hunting is to search for and identify security threats and problems that have yet to be discovered in the environment. The prize to be sought would be the capable insider threat or shadow IT, which, until discovered, had been "flying under the radar." Other potential discoveries can be bad configurations or outdated processes.

2. B. Originating from Russia or former Soviet states have been some of the most notorious malware that has targeted global consumers, banks, and retailers over the past few years: LoJax, BadRabbit, and NotPetya, to name just a few.

3. D. Indicators of compromise (IoCs) are evidence that a security incident occurred, and more investigation is needed to reveal the consequences. IoCs can be subtle or blatantly obvious and can range from log entries, alerts, and notifications to detecting activity or traffic that seems out of the ordinary.

4. A. Insider threat is especially dangerous since the insider is already trusted within the organization. The insider knows internal policies, is familiar with the organizational structure, has awareness of business processes, and most of all, has network access as a trusted employee.

5. B. Cisco created the network monitoring protocol NetFlow to assist in collecting statistics on IP traffic as it traverses the network. There are a variety of tools to gather and report on what NetFlow monitors. Those NetFlow logs are a gold mine to answer questions around network traffic.

6. C. DLP alerts warn the security analyst or administrator of the likelihood of data being exfiltrated out of the network.

7. B. In earlier years, intrusion detection and antivirus systems used regular expressions (regex) and scripts to identify a match between a known signature and what was seen on the wire. Regex or regular expression matching was the default approach, but regex matching does take considerable overhead in memory.

8. D. An ACL is used for packet filtering and for selecting the types of traffic to be analyzed, forwarded, or influenced in some way by the firewall or device. ACL configuration can block traffic based on the source and destination address.

9. B. In this access control list (ACL), all TCP traffic bound for port 23 is blocked. The ACL group number is 102.

10. C. File integrity monitoring (FIM) will monitor for changes in files. FIM alerts can notify you practically in real time, permitting you to immediately investigate.

11. B. Diamond Model of Intrusion Analysis has two axes, with the first axis labeled Victim – Adversary, while the second axis is Infrastructure – Capability.

12. C. OSINT sources include commercial, scientific, and technical databases; symposium proceedings; published strategies and doctrine; think-tank publications; patent information; and other open-source documents available to the general public.

13. D. This might be a challenging question only because it's tempting to choose an indicator of compromise. In the scenario, we are past suspecting an IoC. Advanced persistent threats (APTs) are definitely evidence of a compromised system. APTs can be near impossible to remove, with the best approach being to rebuild from scratch. The APT serves to maintain accessibility to the "pwned" machine. Given that APT malware can be advanced, the threat may stay even if the system administrators attempt to contain and eradicate the malware.

14. C. Human intelligence (HUMINT) is the personal side of spying or collecting intelligence. While OSINT might involve dumpster diving and scouring social media, HUMINT involves building a genuine rapport and leveraging it for information or access.

15. D. If an attacker wants to learn more about the organization's technical contact or registration information about their domain, the site that provides both is WHOIS.

16. A. Reconnaissance is the first step, common to both Cyber Kill Chain and the ATT&CK framework. Exfiltration and discovery are unique to the ATT&CK framework.

17. C. Discovery happens last and is the 9th of the 13 labeled tactics. Discovery happens after credential access and before lateral movement.

18. A. Human intelligence (HUMINT) is the personal side of spying or collecting intelligence. HUMINT involves building a genuine rapport and leveraging it for information or access.

19. D. Nation-state hackers and cyberterrorists are individuals or groups of individuals seeking to engage in recruitment, attacks, or, worse, compromise critical infrastructures in the target countries such as nuclear power plants, power generation stations, and water treatment plants.

20. D. Supply chain attack is the correct answer. When a hacker focuses on a weaker service or organization with the goal to disrupt the target organization, this type of attack is called a supply chain attack. Hackers opt to cripple or disrupt a different organization on which the target relies.

Chapter 4: Security Ops: Vulnerability Assessments and Operational Risk

1. A. The BEST definition of a risk in IT is a vulnerability in your ecosystem and the high probability of compromise with a known active threat actor.

2. D. A list of root passwords is not a requirement. A vulnerability assessment is the testing of systems and access controls for weaknesses.

3. C. Ethical Hackers will perform a no knowledge penetration test. They will use the same methods as the bad guys but get permission first. Yes, there are blue-hat hackers. A blue-hat hacker is someone who typically tests systems before they launch and looks for bugs.

4. A. Cross-site scripting (XSS) is an attack that can be mitigated by using input validation and sanitization. Like a CSRF attack, an XSS attack is attempting to steal information from a user. If a web application is not able to properly sanitize input from a user, the attacker can use form input to inject malicious code.

5. D. Social engineering is malicious activity where data is disclosed by accident. It is typically performed by an attacker outside of the organization. The goal is to get the victim to disclose confidential or sensitive information. Fraud, espionage, and embezzlement are all malicious actions where the attacker is internal and commits these crimes on purpose.

6. D. This one is all about strategy! You need to test for resilience and reliability of the rebuilt site before you restore any mission-critical functions. Financial and communication assets should be restored only after you know the foundation is good.

7. A. A denial-of-service (DoS) or distributed denial-of-service (DDoS) attack makes legitimate users unable to use devices or network resources. It affects availability.

8. C. The golden rule of forensics is never touch, change, or alter anything until it has been documented, identified, measured, and photographed. An image is a complete image of all the contents of a storage device. A bitstream copy of an image copies all areas of a storage device. When documenting for an incident, you need to list the software/hardware used, source and destination name, start/end timestamp, and hashed values.

9. C. Virtualization creates an abstract computing platform. Many servers can be replaced by one larger physical server to decrease the need for hardware. Many hosts allow the execution of complete operating systems, and access can be restricted for security depending on the hardware access policy created by the host. In this scenario, the most secure option with a focus on confidentiality would be to assign virtual hosts to the client and physically partition storage. If confidentiality is in the question, look for encryption in the answer.

10. D. A keylogger, by its very nature, is meant to steal the keystrokes the victim makes on their keyboard and violate the security tenet of confidentiality. From this information, the attacker can replay websites/usernames/passwords typed in by the victim.

11. B. When the decision is made to outsource any IT function, process, or system, there is a risk to operations and process flows, confidentiality, continuity, and compliance. You cannot use the excuse, "It wasn't me." Regulators and compliance auditors will still hold your organization responsible for performing the correct level of due diligence to confirm that a third-party service has the right people, processes, and technology in place to support your business need.

12. C. The threat in this scenario is the hacker/hacktivist or nation-state hacker who wants to use this third-party vendor as a gateway into your organization. Vetting a third-party organization is mission critical if that vendor is going to be working with any type of sensitive data or project.

13. B. If Adriana encrypts her database, she is using an algorithm to transform readable data into unreadable data. Without knowing the key or algorithm used, you cannot reverse engineer the data. The purpose of this is to protect data from theft, malicious intent, or misuse.

14. C. Threat and risk assessments are the best ways to identify the risks this company is facing. Pentesting will come after controls are in place.

15. C. The best way to control dumpster diving is to control what leaves the facility by way of disposal and what form that takes. Larger enterprise organizations will hire third-party organizations for their shredding, whereas some organizations create a policy based on what type of document has been manufactured. Either way, this needs to be in your policies and procedures and communicated to staff and periodically audited.

16. A. The vulnerability time is the time between when the vulnerability is discovered and when it is patched. The vulnerability window is when an IT asset is most vulnerable. This window has become increasingly important because it can be much larger than it was in the past. The cycle of creating malware based on known vulnerabilities keeps getting shorter.

17. D. The third-party organization should be contractually obliged to perform security activities noted in the business documents signed by the parties. Evidence of those contracts should be negotiated, investigated, and confirmed prior to beginning the project.

18. B. A buffer overflow occurs when a program writes more data to a buffer than is expected. An attacker can take advantage of this situation by injecting their own malicious code or variables into the buffer. Because these commands don't check buffer size, they make a program susceptible to buffer overflow attacks.

19. D. A patch management system can automate the process of installing patches on systems. Using automation, it is more likely that all systems will be patched and none mistakenly missed. A security assessment identifies the current security posture of an organization. Vulnerability management is the continual process of identifying, evaluating, treating, and reporting on security vulnerabilities. A vulnerability scanner scans a network looking for known vulnerabilities and reporting on them.

20. A. A cross-site request forgery (CSRF) is an attack that takes advantage of a software vulnerability and will redirect static content from a trusted site. An example might be stealing online banking credentials and account information from a user that logs into a legitimate banking site. CAPTCHA forms require solving some type of puzzle to validate the user is human, confirming the authenticity of the user.

Chapter 5: Compliance and Vendor Risk

1. B. An external audit must have an independent certified authority and be performed against a recognized auditable standard. This is why an external audit can hold so much value for a company.

2. D. The business impact analysis (BIA) is a systematic process to determine the potential effects of the failure of processes and systems that are critical to business operations, whether the interruption is a natural disaster, an accident, or an upgrade.

3. A. A master service agreement (MSA) provides a strong foundation for future business. It typically specifies payment terms, warranties, geographic location, and intellectual property ownership.

4. A. The major question that you should ask the vendor is what level of encryption they offer, and if the tools encryption is comprehensive. If your organization is not compliant with PCI-DSS, it could be open to major regulatory compliance risk.

5. A. In no event should access of any kind be granted to any data that is classified as sensitive without the express permission of the data owner.

6. C. Data retention is the amount of time that specific data is maintained in storage. Data stored for more time than is needed becomes a security risk to an organization. If you have a vendor managing your data archives, they need to know what type of compliance your organization falls under so they know how long to keep the data.

7. B. The definition of attestation according to Merriam-Webster's dictionary is "an act or instance of proving the existence of something through evidence." The Payment Card Industry (PCI) is governed by the PCI Security Standards Council, which will certify an organization has completed and passed or failed an audit with an attestation of compliance.

8. A. A global organization that collects data from customers must be concerned with data sovereignty. A learning management system (LMS) and a content management system (CMS) collect information on global students taking classes, viewing videos, and accessing files. This data is subject to the laws of the country where the data was collected. Many countries have passed various laws around the control and storage of data.

9. C. A data owner has administrative control over a specific dataset. Some examples of a data owner are a treasurer who has administrative control and is accountable for financial data or a human resources director who has responsibility for employee data. In most enterprise organizations, the owner is not the custodian.

10. D. Many local, state, federal, and international laws, as well as industry restrictions, require that data be kept for specific periods of time.

11. C. Due diligence means "required carefulness." Due diligence is exercising informed care that is expected of reasonable people. Performing this kind of process ensures that the proper information is systematically and deliberately protected.

12. A. A cloud-based deployment solution will probably be entirely operated and maintained by a third-party vendor. You are able to pay a usage fee for access to that solution but lose some control over hardware and software.

13. C. Infrastructure as a services (IaaS) enables a company to use hardware resources provided by a third party, including processing and networking to host varied multiple hosts.

14. C. One of the biggest benefits of moving virtual hosts to the cloud is elasticity. Businesses adopting this cloud computing solution can enjoy the dynamic allocation of resources to projects and workflows. It makes using the cloud efficient and cost effective.

15. D. PaaS allows you to avoid the expense and complexity of having to buy and manage software licenses, application infrastructure, development tools, and other resources. You manage the applications and services that you have developed, and the cloud provider does everything else.

16. A. A public cloud is the cloud computing model where IT services are delivered across the Internet. The defining features of public cloud solutions are elasticity and scalability for IT services at low cost. Public cloud offers many solutions for all types of computing requirements.

17. D. Easy deployment and lower cost for less IT expertise can be good things.

18. C. While the multitenancy cloud services would be less expensive since usage and resources are shared, they operate at maximum usage, making for best efficiency. They are easier to set up because there is a high volume of customers that should have a good experience onboarding. The limitation of multitenancy is multiple access points and less control, and if one tenant is affected, all tenants are affected. With multiple access points and all cloud tenants affected, this is not an OKR to be measured by an organization in a shared responsibility cloud model.

19. A. The first priority should be to understand what data this organization has and classify it through a data classification engine. Look for a comprehensive solution that locates and protects sensitive content on the assets uploaded to the cloud.

20. D. Negotiating an SLA is an administrative contract guaranteeing service, and it is created, not deployed, to a cloud environment. You should absolutely have one that will protect the business and processes.

Chapter 6: Cryptography and PKI

1. B. Encryption provides confidentiality since the data is scrambled by cryptographic algorithm. Symmetric encryption offers that privacy through the use of a unique, shared key.

2. D. Rivest Cipher 5 (RC5) is a fast-block cipher. As a symmetric algorithm, it supports a variable block size, a variable key size, and a variable number of rounds. Allowable choices for the block size are 32, 64, and 128 bits.

3. D. Asymmetric encryption provides confidentiality, integrity, authentication, and nonrepudiation. By comparison, symmetric encryption offers only confidentiality.

4. C. The CRL is maintained by the CA, which signs the list to maintain its accuracy. Whenever problems are reported with digital certificates, the digital certificates are considered invalid, and the CA has the serial number added to the CRL.

5. D. Like passports, digital certificates do not stay valid for a lifetime. Certificates become invalid for many reasons, such as someone leaving the company, information changing, or a private key being compromised. For these reasons, the certificate revocation list (CRL) must be maintained.

6. D. There is no one type of certificate to secure all subdomains and domains. A wildcard certificate allows the purchaser to secure an unlimited number of subdomain certificates on a domain name. While the wildcard secures multiple subdomains, the multidomain certificate will secure multiple top-level website domains, such as `example.net`, `example.com`, and `example.org`.

7. D. Symmetric encryption does offer speed, but if you're looking for a cryptographic system that provides easy key exchange, you will have to consider asymmetric encryption.

8. A. Public key cryptography (asymmetric encryption) is made possible by the use of one-way functions. A one-way function, or trapdoor, is a math operation that is easy to compute in one direction, yet is almost impossible to compute in the other direction.

9. C. MD5 is the only option that is a hash. The others are encryption algorithms. A hash is a one-way calculation of input data, such as a file. Comparing the hashes for two files can indicate that the files either are identical or have the slightest difference. Thus, a hash acts to prove the integrity of a file.

10. B. Symmetric encryption does offer speed, but if you're looking for a cryptographic system that provides easy key exchange, you will have to consider asymmetric encryption.

11. D. SSL/TLS uses both asymmetric and symmetric encryption. Almost all modern cryptographic systems make use of hybrid encryption. This method works well because it uses the strength of symmetric encryption and the key exchange capabilities of asymmetric encryption. Some good examples of hybrid cryptographic systems are IPsec, Secure Shell, Secure Electronic Transaction, Secure Sockets Layer (SSL), PGP, and Transport Layer Security (TLS).

12. A. A wildcard certificate allows the purchaser to secure an unlimited number of subdomain certificates on a domain name. For example, a wildcard certificate could secure `sub1.example.org`, `sub2.example.org`, and `sub3.example.org`.

13. D. The International Data Encryption Algorithm (IDEA) is a 64-bit block cipher that uses a 128-bit key. Although IDEA is patented by a Swiss company, it is freely available for non-commercial use. It is considered a secure encryption standard, and there have been no known attacks against it.

14. B. Disk encryption can use either hardware or software to encrypt an entire hard drive or volume. Such technology is incredibly important today. Mobile security is especially enhanced by encryption, considering how much sensitive information individuals have stored on mobile devices and tablets. Such items are easily lost or stolen. Common disk encryption products include BitLocker and AxCrypt.

15. A. Hashing refers to a broad category of algorithms that are useful for their ability to provide integrity and authentication. Integrity ensures that the information remains unchanged and is in its true original form.

16. D. Hashing algorithms operate by taking a variable amount of data and compressing it into a fixed-length value referred to as a hash value. Hashing provides a fingerprint or message digest of the data. A well-designed hashing algorithm will not typically produce the same hash value or output for two different inputs. When this does occur, it is referred to as a collision.

17. D. A web of trust model is the least complex, is the lowest trust of the options, and is most suited for small groups. The single authority model is simple, though not well suited for large organizations; a hierarchical model is typically provided by a commercial entity, requiring a more robust model.

18. B. Symmetric encryption is fast, but key distribution is a problem. Asymmetric encryption offers easy key distribution, but it's not suited for large amounts of data. Combining the two into hybrid encryption uses the advantages of each and results in a truly powerful system.

19. B. Block encryption secures data in fixed-size groups of bits. An example of a block cipher is 3DES ECB, which encrypts data in 64-bit blocks.

20. A. Many organizations use hardware security modules (HSMs) to store and retrieve escrowed keys securely. Escrowed keys allow another trusted party to hold a copy of a key. They need to be managed at the same security level as the original key.

Chapter 7: Incident Response and Forensics

1. C. A false positive alert is an alert that is generated but that is not associated with a true attack. Having tumbleweeds hitting your fence, triggering alerts, is an example of a false positive alert. A true positive is an alert triggered from an attack. A true negative is no alert triggered because no attack occurred. A false negative is an attack happening with no alert triggered.

2. D. During lessons learned, one step to include in the process is to evaluate the effectiveness of the playbooks involved. Any changes to those documents should be documented in procedure controls and implemented as soon as an incident occurs.

3. D. In digital or cyber forensics, no matter what action has been taken and what the implied burden of proof is, you must treat the incident as if a crime had been committed. If the process is broken, the risk of challenging or diminishing the value of the evidence could make it inadmissible and reduce its value to the company. The IRT should have well-documented policies and procedures in place and have chain-of-custody rules. According to the National Institute of Standards and Technology (NIST), there are four steps: 1) preparation, 2) detection and analysis, 3) containment and eradication and recovery, and, lastly, 4) post-incident activity, better known as lessons learned.

4. A. After an incident, managers can evaluate the effectiveness of their response and then identify areas that need improvement—specifically assessment, detection, notification, and evaluation. The lessons learned document details how your emergency response process can be improved.

5. D. In an after-action report (AAR), it is time for reflection and to record what was done well and the areas that need improvement. Capturing and regularly updating the lessons learned can keep the incident response on track. In the long run, it can also help continually improve how organizations execute incident response. The network topology diagrams should be created and updated often and are not part of an AAR.

6. B. You should have this documented in an IR response manual. Disconnecting the intruder is the best response if confidentiality is of utmost importance. Allowing any more time to the intruder might enable them to pivot deeper into the network. Delaying, auditing, or monitoring the intruder is the correct response if you are going to prosecute the intruder. This is the type of scenario that has already been discussed so that you know exactly what the response should be in an incident/event.

7. C. This actually happened. A casino in North America detected a ransomware attack that used the network-attached fish tank as a point of entry. The attack was spotted due to a security orchestration, automation, and response (SOAR) solution that detected the intrusion, and no damage was done.

8. D. According to Gartner, social engineering is the single greatest security risk faced in cybersecurity. Social engineering is the art of manipulating, influencing, or deceiving to gain information or control of a system, process, or finances.

9. C. When a situation arises, such as a service interruption or some other significant incident, the security operations center (SOC) receives word via its monitoring system. Once it has identified an issue, you must manually initiate an incident response, which will in turn notify the appropriate parties, providing the necessary information so they can begin working to resolve the problem. Critical issues must be addressed quickly, as any downtime can have a tremendous negative impact on the organization, from lower revenue to lost customers. This puts a lot of pressure on SOC managers to handle any and all incidents with the utmost attention given to quality and turnaround time. The problem comes into play when businesses are still relying on antiquated systems to manage their incident response processes. The result is a huge margin for human error and unnecessary delay.

10. C. Due care is acting responsibly. Due diligence is verifying those actions are sufficient. An organization that shows due care means it took every reasonable precaution to protect its assets and environment. A runbook is created before an incident happens, documenting policies, procedures, and due care taken by an organization. An AAR is created after an incident occurs. A statement of work (SOW) is a document used in project management. It is the narrative description of a project's work requirement. It defines project-specific activities, deliverables, and timelines for a vendor providing services to the client. A nondisclosure agreement (NDA), also known as a confidentiality agreement, confidential disclosure agreement, or secrecy agreement, is a legal contract or part of a contract. Runbooks are often confused with playbooks, and some IT professionals use the terms synonymously. While runbooks define individual processes, playbooks deal with overarching responses to larger issues or events and may incorporate multiple runbooks and personnel within them—think of a runbook as a chapter within a playbook.

11. B. Security orchestration and automation response (SOAR) helps teams improve their security posture and create efficiency—without sacrificing control of important security and IT processes. SOAR technology helps coordinate, execute, and automate tasks between various people and tools, allowing companies to respond quickly to cybersecurity attacks and improve their overall security posture. SOAR tools use security "playbooks" to automate and coordinate workflows that may include any number of disparate security tools as well as human tasks.

12. D. Because time is important, as a project manager you need to estimate how long the merge will take and then look at ROI—how much to sustain and how much to change. Involve the stakeholders and present them with a communication plan clarifying who is involved in the decision-making process.

13. C. The golden rule of forensics is to never touch, change, or alter anything until it is documented, identified, measured, and photographed. An image is a complete image of all the contents of a storage device. A bitstream copy of an image copies all areas of a storage device. When documenting for an incident, you need to list the software/hardware used, its source and destination name, the start/end timestamps, and hashed values.

14. D. If the logs are evidence, then as evidence they cannot be altered. If the timestamps are from years before the crime occurred, they may not be allowed in court.

15. A. Understand what can be contained in volatile memory before you power down a machine that you believe is compromised. Use a tool that is able to quickly analyze RAM and add that data to digital evidence.

16. A. The Internet Engineering Task Force (IETF) released guidelines for evidence collection known as RFC 3227. This document explains the order of volatility, which is least volatile to most—archives, physical, logging, disk, temporary files, routing and ARP tables, registers, and cache.

17. B. Once you determine which machines were compromised, make sure that nothing was left behind that will do more damage or allow the attackers access again. Collect all evidence and logs that are appropriate; then ensure that other assets are protected against the method the attackers used to get into your organization.

18. A. In criminal cases, a defendant can petition the court to exclude evidence that the prosecution obtained if someone breaks the chain of custody for any reason.

19. D. The U.S. NSA recently outsourced Ghidra, a reverse engineering tool used to forensically analyze malware. Hydra is a network login cracker, Immunity Debugger is not open source, and AngryIP is open source but used for network scanning.

20. B. A well-organized attack by skilled individuals is extremely difficult to solve with a technical investigation, but your data will be extremely helpful for detectives (i.e., authorities). They may have parts of a puzzle that you do not have access to or have established a modus operandi of hacking groups in your specific industry.

Chapter 8: Security Architecture

1. A. You want to protect your endpoints from malware, viruses, and spyware. A host-based firewall will prevent malicious traffic, whereas the IDS will only report there is an intrusion. All 2FA is MFA, but not all MFA is 2FA. Multifactor authentication grants a user access after presenting several separate pieces of evidence that belong to different categories (including something you are, something you know, or something you have). 2FA is two pieces of evidence.

2. B. A network-based intrusion detection system (NIDS) is an intrusion detection system used to detect intrusions traversing the network and alert on those intrusions. The alerts can come in various forms, including email and text messages. HIDS is host-based intrusion detection, and HIPSs/NIPSs are intrusion prevention systems.

3. A. Some more advanced FIM solutions are a part of a host-based intrusion detection system (HIDS). As a general rule, they can detect threats in other areas, not just files. NIDS is network intrusion detection and change management is an administrative control. ADVFIM is made up.

4. D. A Web Application Firewall (WAF) is used to inspect OSI Layer 7 data for malicious activity. HTTP/HTTPS/SOAP are all web application protocols that operate at OSI Layer 7. Screened host firewalls and packet filter firewalls don't inspect OSI Layer 7 data. A DMZ is a type of screened subnet that permits external users' access to a part of a private network.

5. B. A virtual private network (VPN) enables employees to access sensitive data and systems on mobile devices while away from the secure corporate network. A VPN's traditional role is to enable employees to authenticate from anywhere in the world and seamlessly access the company's network. Wi-Fi is wireless networking technology that allows equipment to connect to the Internet. RDP is remote desktop protocol and is a Microsoft technology that gives end users a graphical user interface to connect to another computer. A NIC is a network interface card, that is, hardware that connects a computer to a network.

6. B. A unified threat management (UTM) system is a single device that provides multiple security functions including antivirus protection, antispyware, a firewall, and an intrusion detection and prevention system. A concern with using a UTM is that it could become a single point of failure. A next-generation firewall or NGFW combines a traditional firewall with other network device filtering functions such as deep packet inspection or IPS. A quantum proxy is a signature scheme that makes a proxy signer generate a signature on behalf of the original signer. There is no security model for quantum proxy, and it is susceptible to forgery attacks. There is no such thing as a next-generation intrusion detection and prevention system.

7. C. A reverse proxy performs the function mentioned in the question. Because traffic intended for the servers goes through the reverse proxy, it can provide filtering of malicious traffic destined for the servers. A proxy sits in front of clients, receiving their requests and forwarding them on to the destination. Replies associated with these requests are also forwarded through the proxy to the clients. A basic firewall filters traffic based on packet header information. A network-based intrusion detection system (NIDS) examines traffic, looking for malicious content.

8. A. A DoS attack is a single-source computer system initiating the attack. A DDoS is a much more orchestrated attack, enlisting the help of hundreds (if not thousands) of other source computers to completely overload the system. Spamming is the use of messaging systems to send an unsolicited message to multiple addresses. IP spoofing is the creating of IP packets with a false source IP address to impersonate another computer system. Containerization is an alternative or companion to virtualization involving encapsulating software code and all dependencies so it can run consistently on any infrastructure.

9. B. A Switched Port Analyzer or SPAN port is a dedicated port on a switch. It takes a mirrored copy of network from within the switch and sends it to the proper destination. That destination is typically a monitoring device. The proper way to bring a switch port out of the error-disabled state is to go to the interface and issue the shutdown and then no shutdown commands.

10. A. If you place an IDS sensor somewhere in your network for intrusion detection, your end goal is important. If you want to see what threats are being aimed at your organization from the Internet, you place the IDS outside the firewall. If you want to see potentially malicious internal traffic that you have inside the perimeter of your network, you place the monitor between the firewall and internal LAN. Considering what traffic is most important, find the relevant point in the network that traffic MUST pass through to get there.

11. D. A network TAP is an external network device that creates a copy of the traffic for use by various monitoring devices. It allows traffic mirroring and is an intricate part of an organization's network stack. The network TAP device is introduced at a point in the path of the network that it is felt should be observed so that it can copy data packets and send them to a monitoring device. By deploying the correct ACL rule, it will immediately prevent data coming or going anywhere on port 445. The others could be options, but they would take more time than you have to stop the spread immediately.

12. D. A SIEM monitors servers on your network, ideally providing a real-time analysis of security incidents and events. SIEM (pronounced "SIM") can be performed with hardware or software by examining and correlating logs the servers produce. A SIEM can be used to monitor alerts from an IDS and to perform trend analysis. If an anomaly is detected, rules are then written to inform security administrators.

13. B. When network access control or NAC is used but an agent is not installed on the devices, we refer to it as an agentless configuration. When using agentless NAC, the policy enforcement component is integrated into an authentication system like Microsoft Active Directory. The enforcement of policies is performed when the device logs on or off the network.

14. C. Interactive Application Security Testing (IAST) combines the best of a SAST and a DAST. IAST security tools provide the advantages of a static view because they can see the source code and also the advantages of a web scanner viewing the execution flow of the application during runtime. Static analysis security testing (SAST) tools can scan binaries in software to find errors, vulnerabilities, and flaws in web and desktop applications. SAST is often called known-environment testing or white-box testing. Dynamic analysis (DAST) tools are used for unknown environment testing (black-box testing), employing injection techniques like SQLi and CSS. Interactive analysis (IASP) is a combination of both SAST and

DAST testing, applying analysis to all code, runtime controls, and data flow. Vendor application security testing (VAST) is a third-party risk assessment.

15. A. Customer relationship management (CRM) is the process of managing interactions with existing as well as past and potential customers. It is one of many different approaches that allow a company to analyze interactions with its past, current, and potential customers. The first phase of any future attack will be active and passive reconnaissance. Using social media capriciously will open your organization to knowledge that can be used against you. Even job descriptions can be used to find out what technology your organization is using to craft social engineering attacks, such as when HR advertises a need for a CCNP and an attacker knows you are probably using Cisco devices in your network.

16. A. When the exam uses the acronym SDLC, reread the question to clarify if it is the software development life cycle or the system development life cycle. They have different stages but use the same acronym. The SDLC this question refers to is focused on systems. There are six stages beginning with (1) requirement analysis, (2) planning, (3) design, (4) development, (5) testing, and finally (6) deployment.

17. A. Encryption for data at rest is a key protection against a data breach. Data at rest is stored and usually protected by a firewall or antivirus software. Defense in depth is important to data at rest and begins with encryption.

18. C. Agile software development has been in use since 2001 when the waterfall methodology was too strict and rigid. Agile emphasizes teamwork and feedback, which changes the direction of the software. There are two major types of agile methods, including Scrum and Kanban. Scrum defines roles and events, whereas Kanban is simple and has a lot of flexibility.

19. D. A spiral software development process is beneficial because of risk management; development is fast, and there is always room for feedback. It is not advisable if it is a small project because it is known to be expensive. There is more documentation with the spiral model because it has intermediate phases that require it. To be effective, the model has to be followed precisely.

20. A. Data loss prevention (DLP) is a technology term that can refer to a methodology or a tool that monitors the system, the user, and data events on an endpoint, looking for and blocking suspicious activity. You can use DLP solutions to classify and prioritize data security. You can also use these solutions to ensure access policies meet regulatory compliance, including HIPAA, GDPR, and PCI-DSS. DLP solutions can also go beyond simple detection, providing alerts, enforcing encryption, and isolating data. NIDS and NIPS are for network intrusion detection and prevention. HIPS could have been the answer if DLP was not an option. HIPS tools can take a variety of actions, including sending an alarm to the computer user, logging the malicious activity for future investigation, resetting the connection, dropping malicious packets, and blocking subsequent traffic from a suspect IP address. Most host intrusion prevention systems use known attack patterns, called signatures, to identify malicious activity. Signature-based detection is effective, but it can protect the host device only against known attacks. It cannot protect against zero-day attacks or other signatures that are not in the software provider's database.

Chapter 9: Secure Cloud and Virtualization

1. B. The main difference between Type 1 and Type 2 hypervisors is that Type 1 runs on bare metal and Type 2 runs in an operating system.

2. D. When using containers, host them in a container-focused OS and reduce the initial attack surface by disabling unnecessary services. Add monitoring tools for additional visibility, and then develop a strong set of security controls to preserve the integrity of the systems.

3. C. Virtual desktop infrastructure (VDI) is the hosting of desktop environments on a central server. This has been called providing desktop as a service (DaaS). Thin clients are protected from unauthorized software, and data is saved in another location than the server. It uses centralized processing for better management and monitoring.

4. C. Emulation is important in fighting obsolescence and keeping data available. Emulation lets you model older hardware and software and re-create them using current technology. With emulation, you can use a current platform to access an older application, operating system, or data while the older software still thinks it is running in its original environment. Type 1 hypervisor is a hypervisor installed on a bare-metal server, meaning that the hypervisor is its own operating system. Type 1 hypervisors usually perform better due to the direct access to physical hardware. Type 2 hypervisors run inside an operating system of a physical machine. Platform as a service (PaaS) is a kind of cloud computer service that enables a customer to develop and manage applications without a need to build and maintain the usual infrastructure.

5. D. The only answer that is a benefit to virtualization is faster provisioning and disaster recovery. Risks to virtual environments include patching, maintenance, and oversight, but the biggest is probably sprawl. It is easy to create VMs, push them out, duplicate machines, and forget about them. Once you bring them up, they could be up for weeks or months and get behind in patching, which creates a vulnerability.

6. A. The management of your application requires end-to-end monitoring, so a connection from your location to the cloud environment is the best way to have great control over and visibility into attacks that threaten your environment.

7. D. A community cloud is defined by National Institute of Standards and Technology (NIST) as a collaborative effort in which infrastructure is shared between several organizations from a specific community with shared concerns. It can be managed and controlled by a group of organizations with shared interests so that costs are spread over several users. The public cloud model is the most widely used cloud service. This cloud type is a popular option for web applications, file sharing, and nonsensitive data storage. A public cloud model is available to anyone, but a private cloud belongs to a specific organization. That organization controls the system and manages it in a centralized fashion. A hybrid cloud environment is a combination of public, private, or community.

8. D. While single tenancy is more secure due to isolation and you control access and backups and cost with scaling, it requires more maintenance because single-tenant environments need more updates and upgrades that are managed by the customer.

9. D. A virtual private cloud (VPC) customer has exclusive access to a segment of a public cloud. This deployment is a compromise between a private and a public model in terms of price and features. Access can also be restricted by the user's physical location by employing firewalls and IP address whitelisting. Using the cloud is a trade-off—you gain speed, performance, and cost, but you still lose control over the security processes.

10. B. Electronic vaulting will enable you to transmit bulk data to an offsite data backup storage facility. You can choose to back up hourly, daily, or weekly. If a server fails, you can restore data quickly, but because the information is sent over the Internet, it should be encrypted. File storage organizes and represents data as a hierarchy of files in folders; block storage chunks data into arbitrarily organized, evenly sized volumes; and object storage manages data and links it to associated metadata.

11. C. Virtualization creates an abstract computing platform. Many servers can be replaced by one larger physical server to decrease the need for hardware. Many hosts enable the execution of complete operating systems, and access can be restricted for security depending on the hardware access policy created by the host. In this scenario, the most secure option with a focus on confidentiality would be to assign virtual hosts to the client and physically partition storage. If confidentiality is in the question, look for encryption in the answer.

12. D. When you drag a file into the trash and empty the trash, it doesn't actually erase the file. It simply indicates to the file system that the file is deleted, but the data in the file remains on the hard drive until the file system eventually overwrites the file. We call this problem data remanence. Cloud computing complicates the data remanence issue. You have little or no visibility into the physical location of your data in the cloud, so overwriting the physical media is virtually impossible. The cloud infrastructure may distribute your storage or virtual machine instance across multiple physical drives. Deprovisioning that instance is similar to dragging it to the trash. The data that is written to various drives remains until the cloud provider reallocates the sectors you were using to other customers.

13. D. Creating an audit trail is vital. Security policy often specifies which data should be collected, how it should be stored, and how long it will be kept. An audit trail is often used to find unauthorized activity on a network.

14. B. A virtual private network (VPN) is a tool to protect privacy and security on the Internet. VPN securely connects two computers with an encrypted tunnel to transfer data between a remote user and a corporate network. Employees should use VPNs when accessing cloud storage services. If you connect to the cloud over an unsecured Internet connection, there is a risk of exposing data to attackers.

15. B. An alert from any one of these assets should trigger the security organization to take a closer look at the cause of the alert. Monitoring and alerting are interrelated and have the ability to provide visibility into the health of your systems and help you understand trends in usage or behavior and the impact of changes you make. If the metrics fall outside of your expected ranges, these systems can send notifications to prompt someone to take a look and can assist in surfacing information to help identify the possible causes.

16. D. IP Security (IPSec) is a suite of protocols used across an IP network providing authentication, integrity, and confidentiality. This includes Authentication Header (AH), Encapsulating Security Payloads (ESP), and Security Associations (SA), which provide the different configurations and keys used for those connections. Internet Security Association and Key Management Protocol (ISAKMP) is a component of SA and how the keys are managed and exchanged between the devices. An IPSec VPN will protect traffic being forwarded from client to server or from server to server.

17. A. For these specific requirements, the ability to audit event logs that include source address and timestamps is most critical. If the systems are on premises, you have more physical control. Assets in the cloud require more technical controls.

18. D. Defining user access as well as devices and idle time are especially important to a network security policy. You should also decide what authentication methods are used, how authentication will be implemented, and what the standard operating procedures (SOPs) are, should your organization be compromised.

19. B. Data dispersed and stored in multiple cloud pods is a key component of cloud storage architecture. The ability to have data replicated throughout a distributed storage infrastructure is critical. This allows a cloud service provider to offer storage services based on the level of the user's subscription or the popularity of the item. Bit splitting is another technique for securing data over a computer network that involves encrypting data, splitting the encrypted data into smaller data units, distributing those smaller units to different storage locations, and then further encrypting the data at its new location. Data is protected from security breaches, because even if an attacker is able to retrieve and decrypt one data unit, the information would be useless unless it can be combined with decrypted data units from the other locations.

20. A. The first priority should be to understand what data your organization has and to classify it through a data classification engine. Look for a comprehensive solution that locates and protects sensitive content on the assets uploaded to the cloud.

Chapter 10: Mobility and Emerging Technologies

1. A. Leveraging machine learning and innovating artificial intelligence will help find and respond to threats. Unfortunately, as with every tool, attackers are using this technology as well. In the future, we will see new machine learning malware and AI spear fishing that increases the length and breadth of cyberattacks. SIEM comes later in the attack life cycle. DevSecOps and security as code are proactive pre-attack rather than post-attack.

2. D. A PIN is something you create and memorize. The others are something you physically are.

3. D. Organizations today must reduce their IoT attack surfaces, increase the attack surfaces they monitor, and attempt to reduce false positive alerts that often affect IoT devices.

4. A. Chatbots are evolving, and advancements in natural language processing (NLP) have increased their usefulness to the point that live agents no longer need to be the first point of communication for some customers. Some features of chatbots include being able to help users navigate support articles and knowledge bases, order products or services, and manage accounts. NLP describes the interaction between human language and computers. It is a technology that many people use daily and has been around for years, from spell check to Siri, Alexa, or Google Assistant. Biometrics are body measurements related to human characteristics such as fingerprints or retina scans. Virtual reality is a simulated experience that is created by computer technology, placing the user in that reality. Deep fake refers to a manipulated image or video produced by artificial intelligence (AI) that makes someone appear to do or say something they did not.

5. A. Private Information Retrieval (PIR) is a protocol that allows someone to retrieve an element of a database without the database owner knowing which element was selected. Strong Private Information Retrieval (SPIR) is private information retrieval with the additional requirement that someone only learns the elements they are querying for, and nothing else, which answers the need for the privacy of a database owner. Secure function evaluation (SFE) and private function evaluation (PFE) are special protocols used in cryptography, based on secretly or privately sharing all the inputs to search for potentially malicious computations that benefit an attacker. They are primarily used in digital currency, blockchain, and multiparty computations. A National Institute of Standards and Technology (NIST) report defines big data as "extensive datasets, primarily in the characteristics of volume, velocity, and/or variability that require a scalable architecture for efficient storage, manipulation, and analysis." Some have defined big data as an amount of data that exceeds a petabyte—one million gigabytes.

6. D. A cloud-related challenge is structural. Once committed to a cloud service, companies become dependent on that service provider, often with no easy way to change providers. IT departments need to build up the skill set to work in the cloud safely and reliably. The business proposition of AR is causing it to be adopted before the risks have been vetted or having tech developed by companies without significant IT experience, leading to technologies that are vulnerable. Wearable devices can host malware, enabling cameras, collecting data, corrupting work instructions, or disrupting operation. It is fairly easy to steal network credentials off wearable devices using Android and exposing networks. The only one that does not make sense here is micro/nano technology. Micro and nano technologies include a wide range of advanced techniques used to fabricate and study artificial systems with dimensions ranging from several micrometers (one micrometer is one millionth of a meter) to a few nanometers (one nanometer is one billionth of a meter; a human hair is about 60,000 nanometers wide).

7. B. The one thing all 3-D printers share, whether proprietary or open source, is that they are computer-controlled. Those computers run software that may be prone to development errors that result in security vulnerabilities. The rest of these options are important, but hardening existing systems first should be the priority.

8. C. The use of passwordless authentication methods like biometric and facial recognition has become a norm on mobile devices, but that's not the only place it's used. Windows and Linux support passwordless authentication. In a 2018 update to Active Directory LDAP service, Microsoft added native support for passwordless authentication through FIDO2 keys. This means that with the proper server-level configurations, AD users can walk up to any domain-connected workstation and insert their key to log in to their accounts without making changes at the machine level. Linux also has native support for software keys, which can replace passwords. When passwordless authentication is implemented on a Linux server, users can remotely log in to their SSH consoles by presenting their software keys instead of typing in their passwords.

9. C. Machine learning uses algorithms to parse data, learn from that data, and make informed decisions based on what it has learned. Deep learning structures algorithms in layers to create an "artificial neural network" that can learn and make intelligent decisions on its own. Deep learning has enabled many practical applications of machine learning and by extension the overall field of AI. Deep learning breaks down tasks in ways that make all kinds of machine assists seem possible—like driverless cars, better preventive healthcare, and even better movie recommendations on Netflix.

10. A. There is no one-size-fits-all solution, and each mobile device strategy has its own pros and cons. With bring your own device (BYOD), no wireless carrier needs to be engaged, and fast deployment is available and has a lower cost because the employee owns the device.

11. B. A mobile strategy that works well for some organizations is choose your own device (CYOD), and there are a few select models from which to choose (for example, an organization may ask if you want a Mac laptop or a PC tablet when starting a job).

12. C. When you are in a situation where security and data protection are of the utmost importance, corporate-owned, personally enabled (COPE) is the best mobile device strategy to use. COPE has strict specific procurement standards and has the highest hardware costs of the three options.

13. B. A virtual private network (VPN) enables employees to access sensitive data and systems on mobile devices while they are away from the secure corporate network. A VPN's traditional role is to enable employees to authenticate from anywhere in the world and seamlessly access the company's network.

14. C. Sideloading is a term that applies to transferring a file from one local device to another using either a USB, a lightning cable, or Bluetooth. The process involves establishing a connection between two devices and moving files to the right location.

15. A. Android requires that all apps be digitally signed with a certificate before they can be installed. This certificate proves authorship and that the app came from you and not a suspicious entity.

16. A. The benefits of tethering include getting Internet access to upload and download files and check your account balances securely through your personal area network (PAN). The downsides are that there is a possible cost with your carrier, the mobile connection will be slow, and the battery on your phone or tablet can die quickly.

17. C. Your fingerprint is a biometric. It is something you are, not something you know.

18. C. Only give apps permissions they must have and delete any app that asks for more than is necessary. For example, there is no need for your flashlight app to record your voice and have access to all your pictures/video.

19. A. New tokens must be generated with each access attempt. Improper session handling occurs when apps accidentally share session tokens with malicious attackers, enabling them to impersonate legitimate users.

20. C. Some people have the perception that jailbreaking is used only to do nefarious things or piracy. Jailbreaking enables you to do things like change the default browser and mail client. It also enables you to use software of which the manufacturer does not approve. Your company should have both an inventory of mobile devices and a security policy, and a scanning process should be required as well. Some companies have an annual "eyes on inventory," where mobile devices are scanned physically by IT.

Index

D

J

K

Online Test Bank

To help you study for your CASP+ certification exam, register to gain one year of FREE access after activation to the online interactive test bank—included with your purchase of this book! All of the chapter review and practice questions in this book are included in the online test bank so you can study in a timed and graded setting.

Register and Access the Online Test Bank

To register your book and get access to the online test bank, follow these steps:

1. Go to www.wiley.com/go/sybextestprep. You'll see the "**How to Register Your Book for Online Access**" instructions.
2. Click "here to register" and then select your book from the list.
3. Complete the required registration information, including answering the security verification to prove book ownership. You will be emailed a pin code.
4. Follow the directions in the email or go to www.wiley.com/go/sybextestprep.
5. Find your book on that page and click the "Register or Login" link with it. Then enter the pin code you received and click the "Activate PIN" button.
6. On the Create an Account or Login page, enter your username and password, and click Login or, if you don't have an account already, create a new account.
7. At this point, you should be in the test bank site with your new test bank listed at the top of the page. If you do not see it there, please refresh the page or log out and log back in.

SYBEX®
A Wiley Brand